THE LEGAL HISTORY

The Legal History of Wales

By

THOMAS GLYN WATKIN

UNIVERSITY OF WALES PRESS
CARDIFF

© Thomas Glyn Watkin, 2007
Second edition 2012

British Library Cataloguing-in-Publication Data.
A catalogue record for this book is available from the British Library.

ISBN   978-0-7083-2517-9
eISBN   978-0-7083-2545-2

Typeset in Wales by Eira Fenn Gaunt, Pentyrch, Cardiff
Printed by CPI Antony Rowe, Chippenham, Wiltshire

For Hannah,
in memory of her grandparents

Contents

Preface to the Second Edition

It was ten years ago, in 2002, that the first edition of this work was written. The idea of writing it followed the devolution settlement created for Wales by the Government of Wales Act 1998. Publication was then deliberately postponed to take account of the recommendations of the Richard Commission, which was followed by the UK Government's white paper on the future governance of Wales. By then, it had become clear that it was pointless to postpone publication further in the hope that a 'final version' of the Welsh devolution settlement would appear. The first edition therefore went to press as the Government of Wales Act 2006 was making its passage through Parliament and had actually been published before the Act came into effect. It seemed likely that further change would occur. The pace of such change can truly be said to have defied all expectations.

Ten years on from the preparation of the first edition and five years on from its publication, Wales is experiencing the third version of its devolution settlement, with the nation enjoying its own distinct legislature and executive, each respectively making primary and secondary legislation for Wales in relation to numerous devolved subjects. The new chapter in the history of law in Wales which devolution opened in 1999 is proving to be as fascinating legally as it is exciting socially and politically, and the story has not ended.

The author wishes to thank the University of Wales Press, and in particular Sarah Lewis, its commissioning editor, for recognizing and suggesting that a second edition was now needed, tracing events up to, and beyond, the 2011 referendum on increased legislative powers for the National Assembly for Wales. As well as rewriting the last chapter on the devolution settlement, the opportunity has also been taken to revise the bibliography and notes to take account of recent scholarship, as well as to make a small number of corrections to the text. The author thanks reviewers and others for drawing the need for some of these to his attention, and also the very many people who have welcomed the appearance of this work and have been so generous in their encouragement of it. As always, the author alone is responsible for any errors or infelicities of style which remain.

Thomas Glyn Watkin
Gŵyl Ddewi 2012

Preface to the First Edition

'Fe sgrifennais y llyfr hwn am fod arnaf eisiau ei ddarllen' – 'I wrote this book because I wanted to read it'. So wrote Professor Dafydd Jenkins in the foreword to *Cyfraith Hywel*, his introduction to the native laws of Wales, which was first published in 1970. Much the same could be said by the author of the present volume. Whereas the twentieth century saw the production of a wealth of scholarship regarding the native legal tradition of Wales, there has not been an introduction to Welsh legal history as a whole, a history which has seen the people of Wales emerge from what once would have been called the Celtic twilight to come into contact with the classical law of ancient Rome, the legal content of the Christian Scriptures, the canon law of the Western Church, the common law of England and finally, as part of the United Kingdom, the legal regime of the European Union.

For a thousand years after the departure of the Romans, the people of Wales – in whole or in part – lived according to their own laws, while those laws responded to the various influences circumstances forced upon them. Then, for almost three hundred years after union with England under the Tudor dynasty, Wales had a distinct legal identity within which English law was dispensed by Wales's own discrete law courts, the Great Sessions. In less than two centuries after the abolition of those courts, arguments that Wales deserved that distinct legal identity have matured into the devolution settlement which is, though as yet in its infancy, one more chapter in the remarkable story of how the Welsh people have retained their national identity despite, or perhaps because of, the variety of external pressures they have faced. In each age, some have readily embraced the influences from outside, while others have despaired of the consequences of doing so. The tensions between the two approaches have succeeded in producing a legal culture which combines a readiness to assimilate what is good in other traditions with a jealous determination to preserve the best of one's own.

The devolution settlement is the context within which a fresh interest in the legal past of Wales has arisen. It therefore seems timely to reflect upon the whole history of law in Wales so that what is being shaped for the future is not formed in a vacuum, but in full awareness of the achievements of past generations. The legal history of Wales is a remarkable one, because the people of Wales have been touched by so many of the great legal systems not only of Europe but also, by virtue of European hegemony, the world. A knowledge of the legal history of Wales requires an appreciation of that wider legal context.

Much of my own career as a university teacher has been spent teaching firstly English legal history and Roman law, and later the legal history of the European mainland. It was against that background that I came to the study of Welsh legal history and to the clear view that the legal history of Wales could only be understood against that broader backdrop. I am grateful to those who spurred me on to undertake that study, and in particular to those who founded the Welsh Legal History Society in the year 2000 – Lord Hooson QC, Sir John Thomas, Professor Dafydd Jenkins, Dr Peter Roberts and Mr Richard Ireland. This work is an initial effort to set the scene for much more detailed work, which it is hoped the Society will succeed in accomplishing.

I am very grateful to the University of Wales, Cardiff Law School for a semester's study leave early in 2002 to undertake research for this volume and without which it would have been much more difficult to accomplish. I am also grateful to the University of Wales Press for its support from the initial proposal of the work to its final publication. I am grateful to the staff of the university libraries at Cardiff and Bangor, and to the staff of the National Library of Wales, Aberystwyth, for their ready assistance at all times. I have benefited greatly from participating in the seminars organized by the Board of Celtic Studies' Seminar *Cyfraith Hywel*, the London Legal History Seminars and the Welsh Legal History Society.

I owe two particular debts of gratitude. First, to Miss Rebecca Mansell LLB, who in the Spring of 2004 compiled the bibliography, and to Cardiff Law School for funding her to do this. As well as carrying out this task with exemplary efficiency and accuracy, she crowned her achievement by obtaining a first-class honours degree only a few weeks later. Secondly, I must thank Mr Siôn Hudson, an undergraduate student at Robinson College, Cambridge, who also worked with great efficiency, patience and accuracy to produce the first draft of the index during the summer of 2005, and to the University of Wales, Bangor Law School, for funding his endeavours.

The author alone is responsible for any shortcomings which remain.

Thomas Glyn Watkin

Abbreviations

AAST	*Anglesey Antiquarian Society Transactions*
BBCS	*Bulletin of the Board of Celtic Studies*
Bleg.	The text of *Llyfr Blegywryd* in S. J. Williams and J. E. Powell (eds), *Llyfr Blegywryd* (Cardiff, 1961), pp. 1–131
CHST	*Caernarvonshire Historical Society Transactions*
Col.	The text of *Llyfr Colan* in D. Jenkins (ed.), *Llyfr Colan* (Cardiff, 1963), pp. 1–41 (cited by sentence number)
Cyfn.	The text and translation of *Llyfr Cyfnerth* in A. W. Wade-Evans, *Welsh Medieval Law* (Oxford, 1909; Aalen, 1979), pp. 1–143 (Welsh text); 145–204 (English translation)
DHST	*Denbighshire Historical Society Transactions*
Ellis	T. P. Ellis, *Welsh Tribal Law and Custom in the Middle Ages* (Oxford, 1926; Aalen, 1982)
FHSJ	*Flintshire Historical Society Journal*
FHSP	*Flintshire Historical Society Papers*
Ior.	The text of *Llyfr Iorwerth* in A. R. Wiliam (ed.), *Llyfr Iorwerth* (Cardiff, 1960), pp. 1–103 (cited by section)
JHSCW	*Journal of the Historical Society of the Church in Wales*
JMHRS	*Journal of the Merionethshire Historical and Record Society*
Latin A *Latin B* *Latin C* *Latin D* *Latin E*	Latin texts *A, B, C, D,* and *E* in H. D. Emanuel (ed.), *The Latin Texts of the Welsh Laws* (Cardiff, 1967), pp. 105–58 (*A*), 176–259 (*B*), 273–90 (*C*), 300–97 (*D*), 419–509 (*E*)

NLWJ   *National Library of Wales Journal*

RHST   *Radnorshire Historical Society Transactions*

THSC   *Transactions of the Honourable Society of the Cymmrodorion*

TPTHS   *Transactions of the Port Talbot Historical Society*

Triads   The text of the legal triads in S. E. Roberts (ed.), *The Legal Triads of Medieval Wales* (Cardiff, 2007; repr., 2011)

WHR   *Welsh History Review*

1

Pre-Roman Britain

Modern Wales has both a natural and a man-made boundary. Its natural boundary is its coastline, which bounds it to the north, west and south, while its man-made boundary separates it from, or joins it to (according to one's point of view), England to the east. This eastern boundary was not defined until the sixteenth-century Act of Union, which united the two countries politically and legally. For a thousand years previously, the demarcation of Wales and England had been a zone rather than a boundary line, a zone known to this day as the March, an area encompassing most of the modern border counties created by the Act of Union – the shires of Glamorgan and Monmouth, of Hereford and Brecon, Montgomeryshire and Shropshire, of Denbigh and Flint. The distinction of Wales from England was not merely geographical, but rather the geographical expression of a division between two peoples, the English having invaded most of the island following the departure of the Romans, the Welsh in the west being descendants of the natives who had lived throughout the island during and indeed before the Romans came. Before that invasion, what is now Wales was not a distinct entity from what is now England, both being parts of Roman Britain.[1]

The island which the Romans were to call Britain was inhabited before they arrived, but their arrival, under the leadership of Julius Caesar in 55 and 54 BC, marks the first defined date in British history. Caesar's forces did not occupy or settle Britain. Their invasion was short-term, but did institute links between the south-east of the island and the European mainland across the narrow sea. This link was to inaugurate trade between the mainland and Britain, a link which was destined to change the main trade route between Britain and the continent. Before the Roman incursion, the main trade routes between Britain and Europe had tended to follow the western seaboard. From Caesar's time onwards, overland links to the Channel ports began to dominate the native economy.

The inhabitants of Britain at the time of Caesar's invasion did not possess a literary culture. Writing was not an art at their disposal. This is why Caesar's invasion is the first known date in British history, for it was recorded in the annals of a literate people, the Romans. The Romans and the Greeks, however, were exceptional in ancient Europe in having a literary culture. Such cultures were otherwise confined to the Middle and Near East, but Greek and Roman influence would leave writing and a literary education as a legacy in many lands. Like many peoples who lacked a written culture, the native British compensated with a highly developed and sophisticated oral tradition. By feats of memory which astonish those accustomed to commit what they wish to recall to writing, they were able to communicate from one generation to the next vast quantities of information and guidance concerning their religion, their customs, their practices and their history. It is known from the Roman record that they achieved this in part by their famed eloquence and highly developed arts in speech and poetry. The structures and devices of their poetic composition made for ease in their commission to memory, guaranteeing their ready recollection.[2]

The lack of written evidence concerning Britain and therefore Wales before the coming of the Romans means that virtually nothing can be known about the laws and customs by which the early inhabitants of this island lived. The first firm evidence which has survived of law and its enforcement within Britain relates to the Roman period. The earliest written evidence which has survived of specifically Welsh laws comes arguably from the tenth century, but has survived in manuscripts which were compiled later in the twelfth and thirteenth centuries of the Christian era, leaving open the possibility that there had been interpolation in the intervening period if not whole-scale re-composition. Even if these laws are accepted as being those of the tenth-century ruler, Hywel Dda, and it is also accepted that they contain the material relating to the customs of the Welsh in earlier times, one must still face the fact that they are separated from the pre-Roman age by a thousand years. It would clearly be foolish to take them as representative of the customs of native Britain before Roman times. It must also be remembered that, for much of the Roman period, Britain was not a militarily occupied territory; it was a part of the Roman empire in the full sense, meaning that all of its free inhabitants were Roman citizens and therefore entitled to utilize and live by Roman law. Even after the Roman legions left, there is widespread evidence from other neighbouring parts of the abandoned empire that the native citizens continued to live by, indeed clung to, Roman law as part of their Roman heritage.[3] As it is known that the native people of Wales retained much of their Roman heritage, from the dragon flag of the legions to the Christian faith, the possibility that they continued to use Roman rules and not just Roman roads requires serious contemplation. The influence of Roman law, the law of the Christian Church and the law of the Bible needs to be taken into account when assessing the extent to which the medieval laws of Wales are based on native British custom. Immigration from Ireland, Scotland and the Isle of Man in the post-Roman period may also have led to imports of legal practice, and these sources of legal influence must be taken into account, together with that of Anglo-Saxon England from the time of Alfred onwards.

In other words, if one is to find anything of pre-Roman native British custom in the laws of medieval Wales, one must first strip away all elements which are or may be derived from Roman, canon, biblical or Irish law. Anything which is similar or identical to the laws to be found in such sources is suspect as far as attribution to the native British is concerned. What is left at the end of such an exercise is likely to be very little, and even then one has to contemplate that it may be left because of the incomplete nature of modern knowledge of, in particular, Irish law. Nevertheless, some things may remain, and these will be persuasive if they correspond to the little of what is known about life in pre-Roman Britain from archaeological and later literary sources, such as what the Romans recorded about the natives or elements in the later literary record of the British themselves.[4] Although little may have survived, all may not be lost.

One very interesting instance of this relates to the use of triads within the later legal texts. This is the device of grouping things in threes, with the probable intention of thereby rendering the subject matter more readily memorable. Such a mnemonic device suggests that these triads, which are very common in medieval law texts, were originally composed with a view to oral rather than written transmission. In other words, the triadic presentation of legal rules may be a technique which survived from the time before the Romans brought a written culture to these shores. While such triadic devices also exist in the Irish literature, the significance of threes in native British art confirms that triads were not exclusively an Irish phenomenon.[5]

Among those educated in the oral tradition of the native peoples, there were certainly the druids. Caesar described the druids of Gaul as judges and advisers to the rulers, a description which has been doubted, although it is important to remember that Caesar was writing for a Roman audience and sought to express himself in terms which his readership would understand.[6] In medieval Ireland, druids (*druíd*) were differentiated from the poets-cum-seers (*filid*), the legal scholars (*brithemin*) and those entrusted with the traditional genealogies and history (*Senchaid*). All however formed part of the protected intellectual class, who learnt their crafts in darkened rooms by memorizing the oral traditions in the form of songs. The chief druid was regarded as the equal of a king in status.[7] While there is no evidence that druids in Britain ever played a political role, they are recorded as having exercised religious functions, for instance cursing the advancing Roman army of Suetonius Paulinus on the shores of the Menai Straits in AD 60.[8] In medieval Wales, many of the functions attributed to the Irish *filid*, *brithemin* and *Senchaid* were the concern of the *bardd teulu*, the court poet, who not only sang and recited for his patrons, but also preserved their genealogy and family history in poetic and later written form as well as acting as tutor to their children.[9] The structure of the Welsh princely court as recorded in the law texts emphasizes the place of the poet, the priest and jurist alongside the ruler, and it is tempting to speculate that perhaps all these roles were once occupied by the same person, much as in regal Rome the king had once performed the functions of not only the religious *rex sacrorum*, but also the political and judicial functions later to be performed by the republican magistrates.[10] At Rome also, legal advice in the republic was initially given by a priestly caste, the College of Pontiffs headed by the Pontifex Maximus, until this function was taken over by professional jurists, leaving the pontiffs with their ritual role alone.[11] This is however pure speculation; there is insufficient evidence for any certain conclusions to be drawn.

Tacitus reports that, after Suetonius Paulinus had stiffened his men's resolve to confront and defeat the somewhat weird British array which challenged and cursed them on the Anglesey shore, he proceeded to destroy the sacred groves of the druids upon the island. The groves were almost certainly of oak, a tree which was valued above all others in the medieval law texts, although this was for its use in building castles and fortifications, albeit a churchyard yew was allotted the same value due to its religious dedication.[12] Pliny the Elder has a story concerning what is thought by some to be an oak apple, a rare fruit which was believed in druidic lore to grant the possessor powers of victory in litigation.[13] The Romans certainly believed in the power of the curse,[14] and in the Lives of the later Welsh saints, there is a strong emphasis upon the power to cause miraculous damage by cursing, which may be an Irish influence or the re-emergence of a native druidic tradition.[15]

The druids were also however implicated in human sacrifice, believed to have been performed in the sacred groves. Caesar, Tacitus and Strabo all affirm this practice. The blood of captives taken in war was, according to Tacitus, poured over the altars in the sacred groves, and the entrails of sacrificed humans examined for divine portents. The practice of killing enemies captured in time of war was commonplace in the ancient world, but was significantly abhorrent to the Romans. Roman law provided for the enslavement of enemies taken in time of war, a rule ascribed to the *ius gentium*, the law of all nations, but in truth only the Romans themselves and the Greeks stopped short of killing their captives. The *ius gentium* ascribed the condition of slavery to two possible sources, hostile capture and birth to a slave woman, the former of which must be logically prior to the latter. In Latin, the word for a slave, *servus*, derives from the verb *servare* meaning to save. The Roman slave was therefore one who had been saved, that is spared from execution after capture in time of war, and thereafter was destined to serve, *servire*, his captors. A slave was one saved to serve. Nevertheless, the fate of an enemy captured by the Romans was markedly different from that of one taken by the native British.[16]

The British also dedicated to their gods the spoils of war generally, sacrificing all living things to their deities and hoarding their other spoils in consecrated places as gifts to the gods, sometimes giving them to the gods by casting them into sacred lakes or rivers.[17] The archaeological record bears witness to such lacustrine deposits. Again, there is a marked difference with the laws of the incoming Romans. Roman law allowed the spoils of war to be taken into the ownership of the captor in the same manner as captives were taken as slaves.[18] The British viewpoint was that all spoils were reserved for the gods, probably on the basis that victory had been given by them and therefore to them belonged the profit. To retain goods taken in war or to spare a captive would probably have been deemed sacrilege.[19] An interesting parallel is the account of Saul's failure to sacrifice all he had taken in battle from the Philistines.[20] As a consequence, he lost divine favour and the kingship became destined to pass to others than his heirs. This is no more than a parallel, but one which highlights the methodological difficulties in discovering the legal practice of pre-Roman Britain, for in the absence of the archaeological and Roman literary evidence one would have to disclaim any later mention as possibly the product of biblical influence.

Among the items known to have been cast into sacred lakes were cauldrons, particularly famous examples coming from Llyn Mawr in Glamorganshire and Llyn Cerrig Bach on Anglesey.[21] Cauldrons are known from the medieval law texts to have been among the most important possessions of Welsh men. The harp, the *brycan* and the cauldron were the three indispensables of the goodman, and a husband when separating from his wife was always allowed to keep his *brycan* and the cauldron.[22] The cauldron on a man's death passed with his homestead to his youngest son.[23] Again, therefore what might otherwise be ascribed to Irish influence can on the evidence of archaeology be confirmed as being a native British element in the Welsh laws. The importance of the cauldron, whatever it might be, was a survival of pre-Roman times.[24]

An interesting hypothesis can however be developed as to why such precious objects which were clearly meant to remain with the family were cast into sacred lakes. As has already been established, booty taken in time of war was always consecrated to the gods and sometimes thrown into lakes. Lakes and rivers were generally regarded as places under the special protection of the gods, so that vows or agreements made in their vicinity were thought to achieve divine protection.[25] Gildas, writing after the departure of the Romans, remained aware of the ancient belief in the numinous of such watery locations.[26] In the medieval laws, the ruler was described as being the recipient of certain forms of bounty, which were described as his packhorses. These were eight in number, the *wyth pynuarch*.[27] Among them were things carried to land by the sea, which were the ruler's provided he took them within three ebbs and three flows. If water is thought of as sacred, then such items were regarded in effect as divine gifts to the king, the converse of things being cast into water by humans. Likewise, the property of aliens passing through the realm was seen in the medieval laws as being the ruler's, arguably a later reflection of the idea that all aliens were originally enemies and their goods and lives forfeit to the gods, whereas now not all aliens were enemies and those who were not hostile enjoyed the protection of the ruler for their lives and their possessions.[28] A thief was also numbered among the king's packhorses, in that his goods were forfeit to the king, and so was the man who died without heirs, because the king again inherited his goods, including in both cases, one assumes, the deceased's cauldron. It is tempting to speculate that what was now given to the king, as a divine gift, was originally sacrificed to the gods, so that the property of a thief or *bona vacantia* of a deceased person without heirs, including their precious cauldrons, might have been cast into sacred lakes or rivers.[29]

It seems likely that the bodies recovered from Lindow Moss in Cheshire of human beings killed in the first and second centuries AD are those of sacrificial victims.[30] Remarkably preserved owing to the conditions within the bog, they would appear to have been dispatched from this life as they entered it, naked. This may also be a sign that they had been passed into the protection of the divinity, because there is evidence that across Europe, the pre-Roman peoples regarded nakedness as an outward and visible sign of divine protection. The Celtic warriors termed *gaesatae* fought naked apart from a *torch* around their necks.[31] Almost certainly, this practice preserved one which is witnessed in other ways in other cultures. For instance, in republican Rome, the owner of stolen property might call upon the occupier of premises in which he believed the property to be hidden to allow him in to search for it. If the occupier refused, the owner could remove all his clothes and claim the right to search carrying only a platter and halter. If the occupier refused the naked man the right to search, he became liable to the fourfold penalty exactable from a thief caught in the act. The nakedness of the searcher is sometimes ascribed to the need to guarantee that he was not secreting goods onto the premises, but a ritual dimension based on a religious origin is likely. By the second century AD, the Roman jurist Gaius thought the whole proceeding ridiculous, but it had nevertheless occupied a role in the law relating to one of the most serious crimes.[32] Other parallels would include the manifestation of the original sin of Adam and Eve in the Garden of Eden by clothing themselves in unconscious recognition of having forfeited divine protection,[33] and the reversal of this in the Christian rite of baptism in the early Church when the candidates entered and emerged from the waters of baptism naked in symbolic recognition of the divine protection they had again achieved by being purged from original sin through the power of the sacrament.[34]

The preceding examples demonstrate that, despite the difficulties of identifying pre-Roman remnants of the customs of the ancient British among the later laws of the Welsh people, the task is not hopeless. Although one has to remove all material which is compromised by similarity to other legal orders with which the Welsh had been in contact in the thousand years separating the coming of the Romans from the first surviving law texts, nevertheless it is occasionally the case that the general historical record as gleaned from Roman and other literary remains and archaeological finds confirms that elements in the later laws correspond to much earlier British practice. Some slight awareness of the customs of the ancient British can therefore be achieved, although this is unlikely to be extended other than by further significant archaeological discoveries. Nevertheless, the existing evidence is sufficient to demonstrate that some knowledge of the ancient customs can be achieved. This is not surprising. There is clear evidence that ancient British settlements continued to be occupied throughout the Roman period and into the medieval age. Llandough near Cardiff was a settlement in the Iron Age, remained one in the Roman period and became an important Christian community in the wake of the Romans' departure.[35] Likewise, it is clear that pre-Roman tribal identity often survived even within the romanized administration of a *civitas* such as Caerwent.[36] The remains of Iron Age enclosed settlements in south-west Wales suggest that the partible inheritance called *cyfran* by which all the sons of a deceased ancestor benefited equally was a feature of pre-Roman and not just post-Roman arrangements.[37] Post-Roman artwork and early Welsh literature both seem to make use of pre-Roman motifs and themes respectively. It is likely therefore that there would also have been legal survivals, but great caution is required in attempting to identify them.[38]

2

Wales in the Roman Empire

THE ROMANS AND THEIR LAW

A century after Julius Caesar's initial sorties into Britain, the emperor Claudius (AD 41–54) undertook a full-scale conquest of the island. The invasion was under the command of Vespasian, a general who himself was to become emperor (69–79), although Claudius himself arrived to lead the victorious armies into Colchester and to receive the acclaim of his troops. He may also have played a significant role in determining how the new province was to be governed. The process of conquest and assimilation was a lengthy one, the Romans reaching the modern border counties between Wales and England by the end of the 40s, but as has been noted only reaching Anglesey under Suetonius Paulinus in 60–1 and only finally placing the whole of modern Wales under their control during the 70s. Thereafter, their path of conquest was pursued northwards into modern Scotland, but in effect the northern limits of the Roman empire were set by the walls built by Hadrian (117–38) and to a less permanent extent by his successor, Antoninus Pius (138–61). Wales however was to remain a part of the empire from the 70s AD until the withdrawal of the legions at the turn of the fourth and fifth centuries.

The Roman conquests within the island were at first known as the province of Britannia, a province of the emperor, having nominally been conquered by Claudius. In Claudius' time, Colchester, the Roman Camulodunum, was the provincial capital, but was eventually replaced by London. As an imperial, as opposed to a senatorial, province, Britain was governed by a governor who was in effect the emperor's delegate, or legate, answerable to the emperor rather than to the senate at Rome. This distinction between imperial and senatorial provinces was more apparent than real, for in effect the senate at Rome had already become and was destined to remain under the emperor's control. Technically, senatorial provinces were governed by proconsuls, men who had held the highest magistracy of the Roman republic, the consulship, and were then sent away from the city to govern a province or group of provinces and thereby win their fortunes. It was as a proconsul in Gaul that Julius Caesar had invaded Britain in 55 and 54 BC.[1]

The Romans were to remain in Britain until the start of the fifth century of the Christian era, the traditional date for their abandonment of the island being 410 when the emperor Honorius issued a rescript indicating that Roman government of the island had ceased. The withdrawal of Roman administration and of the legions had in fact been more gradual and what is now Wales had been vacated almost two decades earlier in 393. The Romans were therefore a presence in Britain and in Wales for over three hundred years, that is, a period as long, for instance, as that which separates the sixteenth-century Act of Union from the nineteenth-century abolition of the Courts of Great Sessions which the Tudor union established, and longer than that which separates Edward I's conquest of Wales from the Tudor union. It would be foolish therefore to discount the possibility, indeed the probability, of Roman influence upon the customs and social practices of the British people during the Roman period. Moreover, there are sound reasons for not doing so.

First, it is clear virtually from the outset that the Roman government intended in Britain as elsewhere that the native population should be romanized. Julius Agricola, who conquered the tribe of the Ordovices in northern Wales and whose career is recorded in the writings of Tacitus, strongly supported a policy of conciliating the conquered tribes and of encouraging them to adopt Roman institutions and the Latin language. Agricola himself was by birth a provincial who had proved the willingness of Rome to further the careers of those who were not geographically or racially Roman by birth. His tour of duty from 78–85 or 86 coincided with the reigns of the three Flavian emperors, Vespasian (69–79), Titus (79–81) and Domitian (81–96), under whom native Romans and Italians came to form for the first time less than half of the membership of the Roman senate.[2]

Secondly, as will be discussed in the following chapter, it is clear that the native British had been prepared to embrace Roman culture. Not only did they acquire the Latin tongue, which they continued to use after the legions had left and even referred to as *nostra lingua*,[3] but in many areas, including south Wales, they willingly inhabited Roman settlements, such settlements sometimes occupying, as at Llandough, the site of British Iron Age forts. While they may initially have been forced rather than encouraged to contribute to the imperial cult and to support the building of temples to the Roman gods,[4] they would appear to have enthusiastically embraced the Christian religion which was first permitted at the start of the fourth century by the emperor Constantine and was later that century to become the official state religion of the empire.[5] It is even possible that a rebellion against imperial rule at the close of the Roman period was actuated in consequence of the emperor Julian's attempt to re-establish paganism as the imperial religion.[6] Christian churches may have first all been founded in the houses of those of senatorial rank, and such establishments continued to exist and impress later in the fifth century when St Germanus of Auxerre visited Wales to combat the Pelagian heresy. He found well-to-do landowners, confident enough of their *romanitas* to display their wealth and sumptuous clothing, still clearly leading native society.[7] Pelagius himself was a Briton who had studied Roman law at Rome before turning his attention to theology and taking holy orders, thus indicating that people from Britain were not only travelling the empire but also active in acquiring a knowledge of Roman law.[8] An up-to-date knowledge of Roman law shortly after the end of the Roman period is also indicated by the use in a curse tablet found in Britain of the word *commonitorium*, a technical legal term known otherwise only from its occurrence in the *codex Theodosianus* of 438, twenty years after the formal Roman withdrawal.[9]

The high degree of British involvement in imperial affairs is witnessed by the fact that four bishops from Britain are recorded as having attended the Council of Arles in 314 only a year after the emperor Constantine's Edict of Milan granted official toleration to the Christian faith. It is worth noting that these four probably represented the four provinces which at that time constituted the civil dioceses of Britain, and one of them, perhaps based at Cirencester, would almost certainly have been responsible for the province of Britannia Prima which was composed of Wales and the border country together with the south-west of England. It is even likely that this bishop had a residence in a senatorial house at Caerwent, *Venta Silurum*, for a house there appears to have had not merely a place of worship but a baptistery incorporated within it, and baptism at that time was an episcopally administered sacrament.[10]

Thirdly, the high level of romanization achieved in Britain during the Roman period was by no means exceptional. Across Europe, as the western empire contracted during the fifth century, those who had formerly lived under Roman rule are known to have been jealous of their Roman heritage and to have continued to live according to Roman habits and to have regulated their affairs by reference to what they remembered of the Roman legal order. This relic of Roman jurisprudence retained in the memory and practice of the former imperial citizenry and their descendants was what came to be known as Vulgar Roman law. It was sometimes recorded for their benefit in texts drawn up by their new rulers, the Goths and the Lombards, texts to which they gave the force of enacted law and which have survived as a memorial to the tenacity of Roman culture among the former citizenship and of the legal policy of the Gothic rulers. As will become apparent, the policy of romanization of hostile people was not new when the Romans conquered Britain and did not begin with Agricola.

Before embarking upon an account of the law and legal order which the Romans brought with them to Britain, certain points concerning the general history of the Roman empire need to be noted. It is important to recognize that Roman government and society was not static during the three and a half centuries of Roman rule which Britain enjoyed. The Romans arrived in Britain at a time when their system of government was experiencing what was probably its greatest change. The republic established when Rome was a small city state at the start of the fifth century BC had fallen victim to stresses which had resulted from the city's acquisition of an empire first in Italy, then around the Mediterranean and finally in northern Europe. The institutions of government which had been developed for the city state were no longer suitable and indeed could not cope with the governance of the largest empire which the world had at that time seen. When, after the Social War of 91–88 BC, Rome was forced to concede citizenship to all free Italians south of the River Po, the nature of the popular legislative assemblies, the *comitiae*, within the city was bound to change as the non-Roman citizens were not going to be able to attend the assemblies on a regular basis if at all. This meant that the *comitiae* were no longer representative of the Roman people and ceased to meet on a regular basis. It was also the case that the republican magistrates, who shared their office with colleagues and held office for only a year, were no longer sufficiently powerful to control the ambitions of towering political figures, such as Sulla, Julius Caesar or Pompey, who had held the office of consul, enjoyed proconsular rank in the provinces and returned with vast fortunes and the support of large numbers of loyal veterans to exert unprecedented influence in the political life of the city. The upshot was civil war between the factions and the *de facto* ending of republican government with Julius Caesar's nephew, Octavian, later known as Augustus, assuming a combination of magisterial offices in his person which in effect gave him total control of the institutions of government. Henceforth, legislation would no longer be passed by the people on the advice of the senate, but would be made by the first citizen, the *princeps* as Augustus was styled, initially by proposing such legislation to the senate, but eventually by simply indicating that the legislation was supported by the imperial will. No longer were laws (*leges*) made by the people in their assemblies; they were now initially made by the senate, in the form of *senatusconsulta* which followed obediently the text of the speech of support by the *princeps*, his *oratio*, and were ultimately regarded as being made simply by wish of the *princeps*, in accordance with the maxim, *quod principi placuit legis habet vigorem*, what is pleasing to the *princeps* has the force of a law enacted by the people. The rule of the *princeps* in tandem with the senate, the so-called Dyarchy, continued until the second century AD, but thereafter legal changes were made in imperial constitutions, made either as general statements of the law (*edicta*), or as responses to individual problems in actual litigation where the emperor was the final court of appeal (*decreta*), or replies (*rescripta*), directions given to officials (*mandata*), or magistrates (*epistolae*), or written at the foot of petitions from individual citizens (*subscriptiones*).

In truth, the change from republican to imperial government had been fully achieved by the end of the second century, but it was another hundred years before it was formally admitted. That occurred under the rule of the emperor Diocletian (284–305), who ended the fiction of first citizenship and established a full-blown imperial system of government with all the trappings of oriental despotism. Diocletian, who retired from the imperial office, instigated the practice of having two emperors, called *Augusti*, who were to become the rulers respectively of the eastern and western portions of the empire,[11] each with an already appointed heir apparent with the title of Caesar. Diocletian also established new imperial capitals, one in the east, later to be at Constantinople, the city founded by Constantine, and one in the west, which eventually came to be sited at Milan. The provincial structure of the empire was also changed at this time, with the old division between senatorial and imperial provinces, which had long ceased to have any significance, being replaced by a new structure in which provinces, each under the control of a *praeses* or governor, were grouped into dioceses or vicariates, under the tutelage of an imperial vicar or *vicarius*, who were in turn answerable to one of the two praetorian prefects who held office directly under one or other of the *Augusti* or *Caesares*. In Britain this meant that the old province of Britannia created by Claudius, which had already been divided into two, *Britannia Superior* and *Britannia Inferior* under Caracalla early in the third century with capitals respectively at London, *Londinium*, and York, *Eboracum*, was again restructured, this time into a civil diocese with its capital at London, consisting of four provinces, *Maxima Caesariensis* with London as its capital, *Flavia Caesariensis* centred on York, *Britannia Prima* with Cirencester, *Corinium*, as its capital, and *Britannia Secunda* based in Lincoln. At the end of the fourth century, Theodosius I (378–95) renamed York's province *Valentia*, and transferred the name *Flavia Caesariensis* to a smaller fifth province based on Carlisle. Wales was part of *Britannia Prima*, having previously been part of *Britannia Superior*.

Diocletian's reforms occurred within two decades of the momentous change wrought by Constantine, when in 313 in the Edict of Milan, an item of direct imperial legislation, he declared Christianity to be a tolerated religion within the empire. As has been seen, within a year, British bishops, probably one from each of Diocletian's new British provinces, were attending an ecclesiastical council at Arles in southern France. The process of change whereby Christianity replaced the pantheon of Roman gods as the official religion of the Roman state was completed by Theodosius I when he became emperor in 378.

Caracalla's division of *Britannia* into two, *Britannia Superior* and *Britannia Inferior*, in 212,[12] is attributable to another major change which he wrought in that year. By the *constitutio Antoniniana*, an imperial edict, Caracalla made every free inhabitant of the empire a Roman citizen.[13] This meant that every free person in Britain automatically achieved the citizenship. While some attribute what appears an act of imperial largesse to a cynical motive, to increase the number of citizens who were liable to taxation, it is nevertheless the case that all those who achieved the citizenship by virtue of the edict enjoyed all the benefits that flowed therefrom, including the right to live by Roman law, one of the most sophisticated and practical systems of jurisprudence which the world has so far produced, and one the merits of which allowed it to re-emerge in medieval and modern Europe as the basis of the family of legal systems known as the civil law which includes for instance the legal systems of most of modern continental Europe, Central and South America, Quebec, the American state of Louisiana, Japan, the Philippines, and aspects of the modern law of Scotland, South Africa and Sri Lanka. That the free population of Britain lived by Roman law within the Roman empire for almost two hundred years following Caracalla's grant cannot but have been significant for the legal development of the native people, particularly when one recalls that the Christian religion which they embraced and so faithfully maintained even after the Roman departure was institutionalized in a Church whose legal order was itself grounded and remained grounded in principles derived from Roman law. As later ages were to say *ecclesia vivit lege Romana*, the Church lives by Roman law.

The grant of Roman citizenship to persons who were not Roman by birth or descent was far from novel. Indeed, it had been a feature of Roman law since the republic and was the context for Agricola's policy of romanization within Britain.[14] In the previous chapter, it was recorded that Roman law provided for the enslavement of captives taken in war rather than their execution. These slaves, *servi*, were saved to serve, but they and their descendants were not condemned to serve for ever. By loyal service and the acquisition of Roman habits, culture and the Latin language, they could aspire to freedom, and not only freedom but to full Roman citizenship. The Romans were unique in the ancient world in granting those slaves who had been formally freed not only freedom but Roman citizenship as well. To the Greeks this was folly, but to the Romans it was the due reward for having achieved *romanitas*. The same was the case for free foreigners, *peregrini*, who provided worthwhile service to the state over a long period. They also could receive grants of citizenship status in return for their acquisition of *romanitas*. During the republic, such grants were usually made to individuals, so-called viritane grants, but under the Principate it became common for grants to be made to the whole population of a town or city in return for their loyalty, service and acquisition of Roman culture. It was usual for such grants to be made in two stages. Initially, the grant would be of Latin status, which gave some but not all of the rights of a citizen.[15] A generation later, a grant of full citizenship might follow. A similar halfway house was introduced for slaves who had been granted their freedom informally, the status called Junian Latinity. Such Junian Latins could thereafter earn full citizenship by further service to the state, for example by serving for a set period in the watch or *vigiles*, a sort of combined police force and fire brigade. The need for merit to justify manumission, as the process of granting freedom and citizenship was called, is also evidenced by the legislative checks that were placed upon indiscriminate freeing of slaves.[16] The native British were therefore from the first made aware that the Roman social ladder was there for them to climb, and even after 212 and the enfranchising of all free inhabitants, the route to equestrian and senatorial status was still there to be pursued.

Roman citizenship is generally described as an amalgam of three private law and two public law rights. In private law, the citizen was able to trade using Roman law contracts, the right of *commercium*, had the capacity to contract a Roman law marriage, *conubium*, and was able to make, witness and benefit under a Roman law will, *testamenti factio*. These private law rights remained important, but the two public law rights waned into insignificance. They were *suffragium*, the right to vote in the legislative assemblies, which long before 212 had ceased to meet, and the *ius honorum*, the right to stand for the republican magisterial offices at Rome, which offices had become purely honorific. In effect, enfranchisement did not confer the franchise, other than in terms of local government, which was probably significant enough for most inhabitants of the empire. Law making, as has been seen, was by 212 purely a matter for the emperor. His will now made law.

One other source of law continued to thrive, the source known as *responsa prudentium*. The responses of those learned in the law had been a source of law from republican times. The jurists of republican Rome had taught law to students, written commentaries on the texts of civil law, mainly the Law of the XII Tables, and had provided legal opinions to litigants, judges and magistrates. They were an important professional class who practised their skills independently of those who argued cases before the law courts, who practised the art of rhetoric not jurisprudence. Jurisprudence was to be defined by the jurist Ulpian, who was active at the time of the *constitutio Antoniniana*, as the knowledge of things human and divine, the science of what was just and unjust.[17] Ulpian's definition emphasized that law was not merely the arbitrary will of a ruler, but required some conformity with higher, god-given standards of justice. He also defined justice as the constant and perpetual wish to give to every one their due,[18] a definition which underlies the Roman practice of allowing slaves and peregrines to earn freedom and citizenship by good works. It is a definition which also recognizes human free will and choice. Both definitions were to remain influential and be repeated in the great compilations of Roman law made by the Byzantine emperor, Justinian, in the sixth century.

During the imperial period, both under the Principate and later, after Diocletian's reforms, during the period known as the Dominate, the jurists continued to be active, the most eminent now working as imperial civil servants, sometimes holding very senior posts.[19] They continued to write treatises on the civil law and also on the *ius honorarium*, the body of supplementary rules which had been developed by the magistrates, in particular the urban praetor, during the republic, which had eventually been codified in AD 120 by the jurist Julian on the instructions of the emperor Hadrian, so that henceforth that body of law, known as the *edictum perpetuum*, could only be amended by imperial instruction.[20] The writings of the jurists were however a source of law in their own right and were to be collected in the sixth century to form the massive work known as Justinian's Digest, which is one and a half times as long as the Bible and contains the cream of Roman legal writing, mainly drawn from the first and second centuries AD, the period acknowledged to have been the classical age of Roman jurisprudence. It is significant that this source of law, quite foreign to the later common law of England, was to have its counterpart in the high respect accorded to jurists in the native Welsh laws.

It was not only the processes of law making which changed during the Roman period of British history. The manner in which justice was administered also altered, although the change would have been less dramatic in the provinces than at Rome. Under the republic and early empire, justice among citizens was administered in accordance with what is called the formulary system, taking its name from the *formula* which was drafted by the magistrate responsible for the administration of justice in the city, the urban praetor, which set out the issues in dispute and the solutions which were possible, and which was then sent to a judge chosen by the parties to settle the issues. The system appears to modern eyes more a form of arbitration than a trial in court, for the judge chosen by the parties need not be, and usually was not, legally qualified and his decision was binding by virtue of the parties' agreement to accept it and not by virtue of the judge's own authority. His authority came from the parties and not from the state, but if he failed to act properly, he would be liable in a separate action to the party adversely affected.[21]

With the growth of empire, a different system emerged in the provinces, originally as an exception to the formulary system, but which eventually came to replace the older process even at Rome. This procedure was known as *cognitio*, and involved litigation being heard and decided by the provincial governor or his nominee, the *iudex pedaneus*. The most famous trials in the Roman provinces, those of Christ before Pilate and St Paul before Felix and Festus, were according to this method. Here, the parties were tried by state authority, and the decision of the governor or the *iudex* was binding by virtue of that authority and was not founded on the parties' agreement. This left the way open for a jurisdiction by way of appeal, the ultimate appeal as in St Paul's case lying to the emperor himself. After Diocletian's reform of the structure of the empire, it was open for litigants to commence their legal actions at any level. If they commenced in the province, their case would be tried by the governor or his deputy judge, from whom an appeal lay to the governor; from the province, an appeal lay to the imperial vicar of the civil diocese in which the province lay – in Britain this would be to London – and thence to the praetorian prefect and finally to one of the Augusti. Two appeals were to be allowed in every case, a principle which is still followed in civil law countries to this day and has even influenced the structure of appeals in the United Kingdom in recent centuries.[22]

In both the formulary system and the later procedure by *cognitio*, the judge was a judge of law as well as of fact, although in deciding questions of law he could call upon the advice of the jurists. Juristic opinion could also be cited to the judge as legal authority. A judge was bound to follow the opinion of the jurists where they were agreed on a point of law, but if there was disagreement, he was free to decide the point as he saw fit.[23] The growing body of legislation flowing from the emperors would also be cited, and attempts were made to reduce this source of law to manageable size and form. Two compilations of legislation appeared during the reign of Diocletian, both named after their juristic authors. The *codex Gregorianus* was published in 291 and *codex Hermogenianus* in 297. Although neither was promulgated as legislation, both enjoyed great authority, the former being a collection of the laws of earlier emperors which were still in force and the latter being a supplement containing Diocletian's own vast outpouring of enactments, which was subsequently updated until the latter half of the fourth century. It may therefore be assumed that both would have been known in Britain. The officially promulgated *codex Theodosianus* of 438 was issued after the legions withdrew from these parts, but, as has been seen, there is evidence for knowledge of its contents in fifth-century Britain.

ROMAN LAW IN BRITAIN

The population of Britain prior to 212 would not in the main have been Roman citizens. Initially, only the legionaries and the administrators, together with their families and freemen in their entourage, would have been Romans. After 212, of course, all free persons inhabiting Britain would have been citizens. For the period before 212, it is therefore of importance to discover the attitude of Roman law to foreigners within the empire. Certain evidence is available in the writings of the jurists, most notably from the *Institutes* of Gaius, written sometime in the second century, and from the extracts from the works of the classical jurists which have survived through being excerpted in Justinian's Digest.[24] The jurists distinguish between three kinds of law: the civil law, *ius civile*, which applied to citizens; the law of nations, *ius gentium*, which was originally the laws which the Romans observed appeared to be common to all societies and included such things as prohibitions on theft and murder; and the law of nature, *ius naturale*, which appeared to apply to all animals, and included such things as the union of male and female and manner in which parents reared their young. During the late republic, the meaning of the *ius gentium* had undergone a change. As increasing numbers of non-citizens, *peregrini*, came to Rome to trade, a system of law was needed to regulate relations between citizens and non-citizens, and between non-citizens who needed to litigate while at Rome. As the *ius civile* was only available to citizens,

its institutions and procedures were not applicable to peregrines, and therefore a body of rules was developed by a magistrate called the peregrine
praetor who was given jurisdiction over such cases with a foreign element
from 242 BC. These rules were set out in the edict of the peregrine praetor, the
text of which has not survived. The name *ius gentium* was however applied to
this body of law, which continued to be important until AD 212, when, by
virtue of the grant of citizenship to all the free inhabitants of the empire, cases
with a foreign element to all intents and purposes ceased to exist. Thereafter
the phrase *ius gentium* gradually reverted to its earlier theoretical meaning.

The free inhabitants of Britain were therefore until 212 officially peregrines,
and their legal relationships would have been regulated by the Roman authorities according to the *ius gentium*, that is, the law contained in the edict of the
peregrine praetor. It is likely from what is known of other parts of the empire,
particularly southern France and eastern Spain, that the native population
would have been permitted to continue to live according to their own
customs, which might have been enforceable for them by the Roman *cognitio*
procedure. In 212, however, the free inhabitants of Britain would have all
ceased to be peregrines and become citizens, and therefore able to utilize the
ius civile. While this was their right as citizens, they were not obligated to do
so, and again, on the evidence from other parts of the empire, it is likely that
they would have been permitted to continue to live by their own customs
where these did not conflict with Roman law and even to have those customs
enforced by the Roman tribunals. In areas such as public law, the law relating to
public property and crime, the law of the state would obviously have prevailed,
but in relation to family organization and succession to property, it is more
likely that native customs may have continued. Trade is likely to have early
become subject to the *ius gentium*, and it is widely believed that by the time of
Caracalla's constitution, the *ius civile* itself had been substantially influenced
by the rules of the *ius gentium*. It must also be remembered that the Roman
authorities, virtually from the first, were encouraging the native population to
adopt Roman ways.

Although it was open for native populations to continue to live by their
own family customs, it is clear from evidence from the sub-Roman period in
many parts of the former western empire that the pattern of Roman family life
proved attractive, possibly through the influence of the Church once the empire
had become Christian. This may have been especially so given that it was
open to baptized Christians to take their disputes to the courts of the Church,
particularly that of the bishop, for resolution rather than to those of the state.
The Roman family centred on the father, the *paterfamilias*, as head of the household or *familia*. Within his power were all the children born to him of a lawful
Roman marriage, *iustum matrimonium* or *iustae nuptiae*. Such marriages were
usually contracted informally, without any ceremony, the mutual intention of
the couple to live together as man and wife being sufficient. Such a marriage

was intended to last for life, but would in fact be terminated if either party repudiated the other, *repudium*, or both agreed that the marriage was at an end, *divortium*. The Christian emperors attempted to limit repudiation other than for good cause, but their efforts enjoyed but mixed success.

Women married by the informal method described, which was general, remained independent of their husbands, particularly with regard to the ownership of their own property. Only if they were married with *manus*, and such marriages were very few in number, did they pass into the power of their husbands. Their children were in the power, *patriapotestas*, of the father, and remained such normally until the father's death. Only then did children become independent in the sense of being in control of their own property and business affairs. In legal terminology, they were in the power of another, *alieni iuris*, while the father lived, becoming *sui iuris* on his death. Within the father's *potestas* also were the children born to sons whose marriages were *iustum matrimonium*, but not of daughters for their children would be in their own father's or grandfather's *potestas*. Kinship which is traceable in this manner through males is called agnatic, whereas where kinship is traced through both the male and female lines it is termed cognatic. When a *paterfamilias* died, his own children became *sui iuris*, and his sons' children passed from his power into those of their fathers who now each became a *paterfamilas* in his own right. Children would only become *sui iuris* in the lifetime of their *pater* if they were emancipated by him during his lifetime.

Technically, a *paterfamilias* had the power of life and death over his children, the *ius vitae necisque*. This was hardly ever exercised, but the Christian emperors found it very hard to eradicate the practice of exposing unwanted children at birth. This method of disposing of children suffering from defects at birth or even of healthy offspring if the family were thought to be already large enough was defended in much the same manner and with some of the same arguments as are used in attempts to justify abortion in the contemporary world. Fathers who had no children to become their heirs could adopt the adult children of others to provide for the continuation of the family, and Roman law made no distinction as far as inheritance was concerned between biological and adopted children.

While he lived, the *paterfamilias* had complete control of the family property, his sons and daughters were incapable of owning anything. While they might be allowed to manage fractions of the family property, their so-called *peculium*, in law this was still the property of their father. He was liable for their wrongs and could sue for wrongs committed against them. Contracts made with them benefited or burdened him. While they reached marriageable age at 14 in the case of males and 12 in the case of females, ages which were to be continued by the Church in its canon law, the father's consent had to be obtained for their marriage, although they could seek that of a magistrate if it were shown that consent was unreasonably withheld.

Kinship was reckoned agnatically for some purposes and cognatically for others. In the early republic, it would appear that marriage was prohibited in the direct line of ancestors and descendants and within the sixth or seventh degree of collateral relationship. Kinship was reckoned by degrees, the Roman method being to count each generation as one degree and to count upwards to the common ancestor and then downwards to the relative. Thus, parent and child were related in the first degree, brothers and sisters in the second degree, first cousins in the fourth degree and second cousins in the sixth degree. A boundary of relationship set at the sixth or seventh degree would therefore in effect have prohibited the marriage of the children of the same great-grandparents, in all probability preventing intermarriage of any who had ever been within the same household. In later law, the prohibition was set at marrying anyone related within one degree of a common ancestor, so that while marriage of uncle and niece and of aunt and nephew were outlawed, that of first cousins was not. Adopted children might not marry within that limit in either their original or adoptive family.

If a *paterfamilias* died before his children had reached mature years, again defined as 14 for boys and 12 for girls, a tutor looked after the child's property interests until the relevant age was reached. Such a tutor was originally the child's nearest male agnatic relative, usually an elder brother or an uncle, but later could be chosen by the father in his will or appointed by a magistrate. The tutor had to administer the property of children under 7 and interpose his judgement in the dealings of children above that age. By the time that Britain was conquered, curators were required to ratify the dealings of young people under 25 on pain of any burden being voidable at the young person's choice, thus ensuring that in effect no one would deal with a young person without the ratification of a curator. Women had originally required the services of a tutor throughout their lives, but this had become a formality by the time Britain was romanized and not even the formal requirement was imposed if the woman had given birth to three children within a civil law marriage.[25]

A curator would also be appointed to manage the family property if it were shown that the *paterfamilias* was unfit to do so through insanity or, very interestingly, if he proved prodigal of the family's resources. This last feature emphasizes that the *paterfamilias* was in effect in sole charge of the family property for the family's benefit not his own. This is also apparent from the fact that he was not free to dispose of it as he wished upon his death, a feature which to this day differentiates the civil law systems of continental Europe from the law of England. Most Romans died testate, that is having made a will, *testamentum*. If a Roman died intestate, his property passed to all of his surviving children, that is, all those who became *sui iuris* upon his death. They took in equal and undivided shares. No preference was given to males over females, nor to the eldest over the younger issue. Moreover, they took the property as a group, not as individuals, and if they wished to split the property among themselves, the initiative lay with them in that they had to commence a legal proceeding called the *actio familiae erciscundae*, the action for dividing the family or the household. If they chose not to split the proceeds, but to continue to manage the property as an integral whole, the arrangement was termed a *consortium*, which was the earliest joint business arrangement known to Roman law. It formed the model for later partnerships of unrelated persons and for the pooling of property by those who wished to live a common life together, such as in the formation of a religious community. If a will had been made, provision had in the normal run of things to be made for all of the children. Failure to do this rendered the will void at the suit of a disappointed child, the will being said to be unduteous, *inofficiosi*. While marriage did not automatically revoke a will, the birth of any child did, for the testator would not have been able to take account of the interests of the child when it was made. While it was open for the father to appoint someone from outside the household as his heir, provision had to be made for the children, and an extraneous heir was also entitled to a fraction of the estate, eventually settled at a quarter by the *lex Falcidia* from which the Falcidian quarter took its name. Each child was entitled to his or her legitimate share, *legitima portio*, which gave rise to the modern civil law's legitim. This was also fixed at one-quarter of what the child would have received had the father died intestate. The ownership of property was far from being individualistic in Roman law.

In earlier Roman law, the most important items of agricultural property – beasts of draught and burden, slaves, land and certain rights over land called servitudes – required formal transfer before witnesses, who were usually seven in number. Alternatively, transfer could occur before a magistrate, but by the time that Britain became part of the empire informal methods had also been established. The sort of land which had required formal transfer was land in Italy only, Italic land, for land in the provinces was not technically available for private ownership. Provincial land had originally been either the property of the senate and people of Rome, in the senatorial provinces, or, in the imperial provinces, the property of the emperor. In other words, land in Britain was never technically privately owned during the Roman period. Those who held it, and who were to all intents and purposes its owners, technically held it of the state. On the death of the tenant without heirs, the land reverted to Caesar.

Certain other forms of property were also not susceptible to private ownership according to Roman law. Some things – the air, the sea and the sea shore – were said to be common to all mankind. Rivers, ports, harbours and roads were the property of the state, while streets, market places and stadia belonged to the communities in which they were situated. As well as these things, temples and shrines were thought to belong to the gods and therefore not open to human ownership. Graves and tombs belonged to the spirits of the dead, and certain boundary areas such as city walls and gates were also not ownable by private persons as they were deemed to be under the special protection of the gods. Indeed, owners were forbidden to build or cultivate within a certain distance of the property of their neighbours, so important were clear boundaries deemed to be. All these things which were not open to private acquisition were called *res extra commercium* while those which could be owned were called *res in commercio*.

Things which could be owned could be acquired by a number of methods, listed by the jurists, some of which were the artificial creation of Roman law, such as the means of formal transfer, and some of which were deemed to be part of the natural order and common to all legal systems. Among these was *occupatio*, the taking of something which was not currently owned either because it had never been owned, such as a wild animal, or because it had been abandoned by its former owner. Hunting and fishing were therefore ways of acquiring ownership, and both were free in Roman law, the proprietor of an estate having no rights to the game on his land or the fish in the rivers. Special rules protected the interests of an owner in wild creatures which had the habit of flying away and returning while they were out of his immediate possession, pigeons for instance and bees. Property could also be acquired by transfer, simply by handing over in the case of most things, and also by long possession in good faith. Land in the provinces had to be occupied for at least ten years to be acquired in this fashion, and sometimes for twenty or even thirty.[26] Chattels on the other hand were originally acquirable in this way by a single year's possession, although in the sixth century this was extended to three.[27]

With the arguable exception of provincial land, Roman law did not admit of the idea of a hierarchy of owners, each with a full right to the land, as was the case for example in feudal systems of landholding. Roman law insisted that there could only be one person or group of persons constituted as owner; persons with other rights to the land could only have rights less than ownership. Thus, if another was allowed to use the land and take its profit by means of an usufruct, that usufructuary enjoyed a personal servitude over the property, as might a person with a right of use without the right to take the profits, a person with a right to inhabit a house or to enjoy the services of slaves or animals.

The jurist Gaius writing in the second century states that obligations arise from one of two sources – agreement, contract, or wrongdoing, delict. Justinian in the sixth century added a further two, quasi-contract and quasi-delict, but it is thought he increased the number to four because the number is used as a sort of mnemonic device throughout the discussion of obligations. Thus, for instance, there are four main delicts – theft (*furtum*), robbery (*rapina*), insult (*iniuria*) and the wrongful causing of damage to property (*damnum iniuria datum*). Theft was regarded as a very serious wrong; Gaius states that the penalties were sometimes so severe because they were motivated by the hatred of thieves.[28] It was divided into manifest theft, where the thief was caught in the act or while being pursued with the stolen property still about him, and non-manifest theft, where the wrong had to be proved by evidence. The former resulted in a fourfold penalty; the latter only twofold. Moreover, a person who refused to allow his premises to be searched in an attempt to find stolen goods was liable to a fourfold penalty, while the person who permitted a successful search was liable to only threefold and was able to recoup that three-fold penalty from a person whom he could prove had concealed the stolen property there. Robbery was a violent taking, and exacted a fourfold penalty.

Iniuria, insult, at the time of the XII Tables in the fifth century BC, was as its name suggests, an unjust act which resulted in loss. Fixed sums of money were payable according to the gravity of the injury.[29] However, after the *lex Aquilia*, traditionally dated to 287 BC, had introduced more efficient means of compensating for losses to property deliberately or negligently caused, *iniuria* was reduced to being a remedy for deliberate and contumacious insult, including damages not just for injury to reputation but also to the victim's feelings. The Aquilian action was extended in time by the praetor to cover not just direct injuries to property, but also physical injuries to the person, wrongs which had also initially been remedied as species of *iniuria*.

Contractual obligations were subdivided also into four categories, depending upon whether the contract was enforceable because some thing had been transferred between the parties in furtherance of the agreement – a real contract; whether the promise had been made using a solemn form of question and answer – verbal contract; whether there was a written record of the trans-action – literal contract, or whether it was based solely on the meeting of the minds of the parties in relation to certain key features of the agreement – a consensual contract. The real contracts were also four in number, being loans for consumption (*mutuum*), use (*commodatum*), safe-keeping (*depositum*) or as security, that is a pledge, for money lent (*pignus*). The most important of the verbal contracts was *stipulatio*, where a promise was made in the form of a question and answer, the answer having to correspond exactly in classical law to the question – *spondes-ne? spondeo; promittis-ne? promitto*. The original literal contract was extinct long before Britain became subject to Roman rule, but the four consensual contracts were of undoubted importance at that time and some believe that they had made their way into Roman civil law from the *ius gentium* administered by the peregrine praetor on the basis of the now lost text of his edict. The four consensual contracts were sale (*emptio/venditio*), hire (*locatio/conductio*), partnership (*societas*) and mandate (*mandatum*).

Of these, sale was both the most important and the most developed in legal terms. The contract basically required that the parties had reached agreement on the nature of the agreement, the thing to be sold and the price. There was a dispute between the two schools of jurists, known as the Sabinians and the Proculians, as to whether the price had to be in money or whether it could be some other thing. Eventually, it was resolved that it had to be in money, the contract being one of exchange (*permutatio*) if what was being given in order to acquire one thing was another thing. Exchange was classified as one of Roman law's innominate contracts, that is contracts falling outside of the four-fold dichotomy of real, verbal, literal and consensual, of which more is said below. The contract of sale however developed elaborate rules guaranteeing the quality of goods, particularly animals and slaves sold in the open market, and also the title of the seller. A vendor without sound title could not give the purchaser a better title than he himself had, and Roman law never allowed stolen goods to become the property of a new owner by long possession even in good faith.

The contract of hire did not receive the same level of attention and development from the jurists, but it did provide, as the jurists of medieval Europe were to recognize, for the hire of goods, specialist skills and labour.[30] *Societas*, the contract of partnership, as has been mentioned, had its roots in the undivided equal ownership of Roman heirs to the family property. It was to be developed to permit the creation of business associations, banking and tax-gathering operations and even provide a mechanism for the joint ownership of single items of property such as boundary walls and hedges. It is known that craftsmen in Roman Wales formed such associations to carry on their businesses.[31] In Roman law, however, such associations were always contractual agreements between individuals; the association itself never achieved legal personality in the manner of modern limited companies and partnerships. This meant that a third party dealt with the individual partner alone, and had no claims or liabilities with regard to the other partners, the contract of *societas* only regulating their relationship within the association or partnership. The contract was moreover entirely dependent upon the continued consent of the parties to the arrangement. The withdrawal or death of any one partner ended the contract, and if the others wished to continue, a new *societas* would need to be established, the same being true if a new member was to be introduced. In the same manner that Roman law lacked a concept of the juristic personality of a non-human person, it also wanted any idea of agency, whereby one person had the authority to bind another by entering into legal relationships on that other's behalf. The closest the Roman law came to the modern concept of agency was the contract of mandate, whereby one person agreed to undertake commissions on behalf of another including as a rule entering into legal relationships which were ultimately meant to benefit that other. However, the other was not bound to third parties with whom the mandatory contracted, only to the mandatory himself. The contract nevertheless did permit of important uses whereby business and agricultural affairs, as well as single commissions, could be entrusted to another.

The jurists were aware that not all contractual arrangements fitted neatly into the above fourfold categorization. Mention has already been made of the difficulty and dispute over whether exchange was a species of sale. Ultimately,

the jurists admitted that some agreements fell outside of the traditional com-
partments and, somewhat misleadingly, these contracts came to be termed
innominate, although some like exchange (*permutatio*) clearly had acquired
names. Into the same category of innominate contracts fell that of sale or
return (*aestimatum*), the agreement to compromise a legal action (*transactio* –
suitably named as it cut across, *trans*, an action, *actio*), and the gratuitous
agreement to allow another use of land or goods revocable at will (*precarium*).
These contracts however were not enforceable merely upon agreement with
regard to their essentials, as was the case with the four consensual contracts,
but required that one party should have performed his side of the bargain.
This principle eventually became the hallmark of innominate contracts, so
that any agreement which did not otherwise fall under one of the traditional
contractual headings might be enforced by the party who had already performed.

According to the sophisticated analysis of Roman law achieved by the
second-century jurist Gaius in his *Institutes*, the whole of private law could be
described under three broad headings – persons, things and actions. This
institutional scheme, as it has become known, is one of the greatest achievements in the history of jurisprudence, although the full extent of its persuasive
power was not perhaps fully appreciated until it was utilized by the civil law
jurists of France in the seventeenth century, from where it has come to
influence and shape the modern codifications of civil law. The law of persons
dealt with those who had rights and duties; the law of things with the objects
of those rights – things owned, the law of property, and things owed, the law
of obligations. The law of actions was concerned with how persons enforced
their rights and the duties of others. Roman law provided actions whereby
persons could assert their ownership of land and other things, claim rights
over land, claim that they were owed money or the return or delivery of goods
or even the performance of promises or services. Very importantly, Roman law
had also developed protection for the possession of property, so that those in
possession could not be dispossessed by persons claiming a better right and
who were prepared to resort to direct action rather than legal processes. These
possessory remedies, which became known as interdicts, were to prove massively influential in framing similar protective devices in the legal systems of
later ages, particularly those of the Church and of secular societies in the
Middle Ages.

The foregoing brief outline of Roman law during the imperial period should
be sufficient to indicate that the legal order with which Britain and other parts
of the Roman empire in western Europe came into contact during the early
Christian centuries was one of great sophistication. It was indeed one of the
greatest systems of jurisprudence that the world has ever known, the greatness of which has led to its influence lasting to the present time and beyond.
Its greatness however did not lie primarily in its sophistication but in its
practicality. The Roman genius, unlike that of the Greeks, did not lie in their

capacity to theorize, but rather in their capacity to provide practical solutions to the problems and difficulties which confronted them. The great feats of engineering in road, canal and aqueduct building which are visible features of the Roman legacy to the medieval and modern world are complemented by the utility of their approach to law as a form of social regulation. The immense influence which the legal achievement therefore had upon the initially conquered but later romanized and assimilated peoples of the western empire, including the British, must not be underestimated let alone discounted. When one connects this experience with the pride that was felt in many quarters at participating in the membership of this great society by sharing in the privileges of its citizenship, it is not difficult to appreciate why, as the Roman government was forced to abandon its territories across the western empire, the people of that empire clung tenaciously to their Roman way of life, their Christian faith and their Roman legal customs. It is important to remember as the discussion moves to the post-Roman period that, although the history of the different parts of the western empire was now about to diverge, the once Roman peoples of the former empire, including the British, had that Roman inheritance in common. This may provide an important comparative clue in attempting any worthwhile reconstruction of what occurred in the legal history of the native British and subsequently the Welsh of the succeeding centuries.

3

The Sub-Roman Period

Over half a millennium separates the withdrawal of Roman government from Britain and the supposed date of promulgation of the laws of Hywel Dda. It is tempting therefore to assume that nothing can be known of the legal customs of the British during this period. Yet, despite the lack of direct evidence, such a negative conclusion is unnecessarily pessimistic.

Although this period is sometimes described as the Dark Ages, it does not entirely lack illumination. What Britain suffered, with the withdrawal of Roman administration at the start of the fifth century, was not unique, indeed it was part of the common experience of western Europe. Honorius, the emperor whose rescript in 410 signalled Rome's decision that Britain was a lost cause, was also forced from fear of invasion by other tribes to remove the capital of the western empire from Milan to Ravenna. Despite this retreat, the influx of the Goths – Visigoths in south-west France and Spain, Ostrogoths in south-eastern France and Italy – continued unabated. At first, the Gothic tribal leaders were content to exercise their political and military power as nominal under-kings of the western emperors. This was however a fiction; they were the real rulers and the western emperor the puppet. In 476, Odoacer ended the charade; Romulus Augustulus was deposed as western emperor and the rule of Rome in western Europe was officially drawn to a close.[1]

The free inhabitants of all those areas which had once formed the western empire and were now under Gothic control found themselves in exactly the same situation as the former Roman British. All had been, in their own eyes still were, Roman citizens. Confronted with a people for whom law was a matter of tribal membership rather than geographical location, they presented their conquerors with Roman law as their personal legal system. Roman law was not, like the customs of the incoming Goths, a customary law recorded in the memories of the people subject to it and declared at annual or other regular intervals at assemblies of the people. Instead, it was a written law, to be found in codes and the treatises of learned jurists. Although the full sophistication of the classical Roman law was not able to survive the loss of imperial government in the western empire, the memory of the inhabitants was sufficient to ensure that some semblance of the Roman legal order was to survive into Dark Age Europe. It was this survival which was subsequently to become known as Vulgar Roman law, as it was not Roman law in its classical guise but as remembered by the common people.[2]

It would appear that the texts which remained available in the former western empire were primarily the Gregorian, Hermogenian and Theodosian codes, knowledge of the last of which had clearly reached Britain even though it was not promulgated until 438. That these continued to be known in the West is apparent from the inclusion of much material from them in law codes compiled by the barbarian rulers either for the sole use of their Roman subjects or for the joint use of all the peoples whom they governed. The earliest of these compilations is the Edict of Theodoric, promulgated *c*.460, when the Visigothic rulers were still notionally dependent upon the western emperors. It is possible that it was the example of Roman written law which inspired such rulers to have their customs set down in writing and may indeed have led to the title of 'edict', with its distinguished Roman pedigree, being used for such compilations. Theodoric's Edict was basically a considerable simplification of the Gregorian, Hermogenian and Theodosian codes, dwelling much upon procedure and penal provisions and very lacking in sophistication when compared with the Roman originals.[3] It was in the Visigothic kingdom of southern France and Spain that in 506 one of the most famous of these barbarian codes was produced. This was the *Lex Romana Visigothorum*, more generally known as the *Breviary of Alaric*. Alaric II ruled the western Goths from 484 until he was defeated and killed in 507 at the battle of Vouillé by Clovis, the Merovingian king of the Franks. Alaric's predecessor, Euric (466–84), had also produced a law code for his people, parts of which have survived in the form finally given to it by Leovigild (569–86). Euric's code however is thought to have been intended solely for the use of the king's Visigothic as opposed to Roman subjects, and it may be significant that his reign overlaps the deposition of the last western emperor. Alaric was therefore the first Visigothic king to rule former Romans directly, and may therefore have felt it incumbent upon him to provide them with a similar legal text. His *Breviary*, drawing mainly upon the Theodosian Code and a much simplified version of the jurist Gaius' second-century *Institutes*, was intended for the use of his Roman subjects only. Important examples had however been set.

With the defeat of Alaric, the Visigothic kingdom became confined to Spain, but its rulers continued to issue laws for their subjects, adding to the text originally produced by Euric. At the end of the sixth century, documents began to be drafted to govern legal transactions between the two peoples, and these documents for the first time show an intermingling of the Germanic customs and the vulgar Roman law. Early in the seventh century, these documents were collected into the *Fórmulas Visigóticas*, a text which evidences the growth of a new communal identity among the two peoples. Kindasvinth (642–53) abrogated the *Breviary* in favour of a new code to apply to all his subjects, a text which has become known as the *Liber Iudiciorum*, revised by later rulers and in its final form, the *Forum Iudicium* or *Fuero Juzgo*, was to become a key element in the emergence of the Hispanic legal tradition. It is a fusion of Germanic and Roman legal material, with marriage, family law and family property exhibiting Germanic emphasis, while succession, prescription and contractual obligations have a more pronounced Roman flavour. The Church played a key role in encouraging the emergence of a communal identity between the two peoples once the Visigoths had been converted from the Arian heresy to Catholic Christianity, and many of the laws were issued at councils held in the Visigothic capital, Toledo.

Clovis, the Frankish king who defeated Alaric II, also published a law text, the *Pactum legis Salicae* or Salic law. The word *pactum* probably reflects not only the binding nature of the law but also the fact that the people in the assembly had agreed the text. Clovis' example was in turn followed by other Frankish peoples, including the *lex Ripuaria* for those Franks living in the Rhineland, an area known to have had trading contacts with Wales, as had south-west France and northern Spain. The Frankish laws were however far less sophisticated than the Visigothic compilations. Despite evidence of Church influence in some places, there is still considerable emphasis upon compensation tariffs for wrongs suffered.

The rule of the Ostrogoths in Italy was relatively short-lived, for the great Byzantine eastern emperor Justinian, through whose legal compilations in the sixth century the full sophistication of classical Roman law was to survive into the medieval and modern world,[4] launched military attacks to recover the western empire. In 540, his generals succeeded in recapturing Ravenna itself, and most of northern Italy by 561. As a result, Justinian's revived Roman law was introduced into the reconquered territories. Although the territory around Ravenna and parts of southern Italy remained under Byzantine control, the greater part of their conquests were lost to the invading Lombards in 568. These remained in control of most of northern and central Italy until defeated by the Franks under Charlemagne in 773–4. In the meantime, codifications of Lombard law had appeared. The first was the Edict of Rothari (636–52) in 643. The Roman influence on this work extended beyond its title, for it attempted some degree of systematization, definition and description in imitation of Roman models. Its content was nevertheless strikingly Germanic, and although it was to apply to all Rothari's subjects, they were free to follow their personal law in relation to any matters not dealt with in the Edict. Moreover, provision was made for the Edict's amendment by the king's successors and such occurred, most notably under Liutprand (712–44), where considerable Roman and ecclesiastical influence can be discerned.

Thus, across the territories of the former western empire, one is confronted with a series of legal developments each of which has its distinct features but among which are also to be found similarities. The former citizens of the western empire were loath to relinquish their Roman status, and particularly so as long as their new rulers were heretics rather than Catholic Christians. They maintained their Roman customs, in the form of Vulgar Roman law, and their new governors often accommodated them by producing written compilations of their customs for use alongside the Germanic practices of their own people. Gradually, as the Arian heresy was overtaken by orthodox belief, the two sets of customs were assimilated, often with Germanic rules regulating family affairs, but Roman practice governing succession, trade and acquisition of property. At the same time, the influence of the Church increased and began to shape the laws of Dark Age Europe. Much Romanism was retained through the people's own conservatism, a retention which the Roman Church encouraged and sustained for its own purposes. The question is whether the former Roman citizens of Britain, who were to be forced westwards into Wales, exhibited the same tendencies and shared some of the same development.

One thing is abundantly clear from the evidence. The Church within Britain after the Romans left definitely maintained what can only be described as a cultural Romanism. In this respect, post-Roman Britain was similar to the rest of the abandoned western empire. South Wales in particular in the centuries following the departure of the Romans was most certainly in terms of its cultural development very much part of the wider European picture. It has been noted that the affinities of southern Wales, particularly the south-east, at this time are with Spain, non-Frankish Gaul and parts of Italy, that is, with those parts of the former western empire where extensive traces of Romanism were to be found, traces which included not only retention of the Christian faith but also loyalty to Roman law as the proper law of the former Roman citizens. The British at this time thought of themselves as being civilized and Christian, and both qualities were referable to their former status as citizens of the western empire.[5] Centuries later, the medieval rulers of Wales, the successors to the ruling class of post-Roman Britain, would be portrayed as looking back to the Roman world as the golden age of their origins. Several factors contributed to this initial identification and the outlook which it eventually produced.

Chief among these factors must be accounted the Christian faith, which it was claimed had come to these islands when in the second century missionaries were requested by Lucius from Pope Eleutherius.[6] This aspect of continued Romanism, like the continuity itself, was at its strongest in south-east Wales. Archaeological and numismatic evidence from this area confirms that the Christian Roman influence persisted in these parts throughout the fifth century.[7] At one time, it was thought that the continued Romanism of the south-east was attributable to immigration from and contact with the Gallo-Roman world, but it is now acknowledged that there is also considerable evidence for British Roman survivals which probably acted as a magnet to the continued Roman populations of the continent.[8] The sub-Roman period in this area was marked by the emergence of a territorial bishopric, centred in the district which is described in Welsh as Erging, in English as Archenfield, and was based on the Roman Ariconium. The bishop whose name is associated with this diocese is Dyfrig, in Latin Dubricius, who is sometimes claimed as the first bishop of Llandaff on the somewhat misleading basis that the historical see of the south-east is the nearest subsequent diocese to the saint's jurisdiction. As well as Dyfrig, the saints in this part of Wales at this time include Cadog, for whom a Roman descent was claimed,[9] and Illtud, for whom a classical education is postulated. Monastic schools emerged both at Llanilltud Fawr and at Llancarfan in the Vale of Glamorgan, where Christian and classical learning continued to be combined right through to the coming of the Normans to south Wales.[10] At Llanilltud Fawr, the English Llantwit Major,[11] the Roman element in the curriculum included poetry, grammar, rhetoric and arithmetic.[12] Such knowledge, clearly derived from the Roman past, was thought appropriate to the Christian young. It is also significant, as will be seen, that the monasteries in the south were situated near the old Roman roads and also near the coast.

This combination of Christian and classical learning was also to be found at monastic centres dedicated to Padarn in mid and west Wales, most notably the great monastery at Llanbadarn Fawr near modern Aberystwyth. Interestingly, however, the same was not the case at houses dedicated to Teilo, not even at the principal monastery dedicated to him at Llandeilo Fawr in modern Carmarthenshire.[13] The reason for this comparative absence of a Roman emphasis in the south-west will become apparent later.

North Wales had not experienced the same degree of romanization as the south. It is notable that no Roman villas have been found north of the Severn and that no scholastic monasteries were to be found at this time in the north. Nevertheless, while it was once thought that the north had only experienced a military occupation as opposed to the civil settlement of the south, this view is now tempered by the knowledge that in the north-west, around the fortress town of Segontium, the modern Caernarfon, Roman influence continued to be felt in the centuries following the withdrawal of the empire.[14] Again, this has been connected with immigration into the area, this time from the subsequently conquered British kingdoms of northern Britain, a movement connected with the settlement of the north-west by the Votadini, a British tribe governed by a leader called Cunedda and thereafter by his sons.[15] The Christian faith played a full part here also in preserving a Roman identity, with the cult of Beuno to be found along the Roman roads and at Roman sites.[16]

The church dedicated to Beuno at Clynnog Fawr near the Llŷn peninsula was built over the saint's tomb, a practice which became regular in Wales as it was in Rome itself. Churches were as a matter of course named after the holy men or women who had founded them, again as at Rome. Thus, there are numerous dedications to the major saints, which take the form of the place name *Llan* followed by the name of the saintly founder: *Llandeilo* – the church of Teilo; *Llangadog* – the church of Cadog; and so on. The fifth-century practice in

Wales was broadly in line with what might be termed conservative continental custom,[17] for in the south too, in Glamorgan, grave shrines were the sites upon which churches were built.[18] From the sixth century onwards, especial veneration was accorded the tombs of martyrs.[19]

The larger churches, termed *clas* churches with a college of priests, were situated near the Roman roads, which assisted the clergy in the itinerant aspect of their ministry. The presence of religious sites, in particular those in the south dedicated to St Cadog, near Roman roads and forts has at times been attributed simply to the fact that such locations were central. However, it is also the case that many *clas* churches were closely connected with the territorial divisions called *cantrefi* or with the subdivisions thereof – when these were especially large – the *cymydau*. While the *clas* church was to be found associated with the *cantref* or *cwmwd*, smaller dependent churches, served by clergy from the *clas*, would be found in the smaller territorial subdivisions such as the *trefi*. Llanilltud Fawr is representative of this phenomenon, with the mother church being built on the site of a Roman villa, situated in close proximity to the *llys*, the court, of the *cantref* of Gorfynydd.[20]

It is noteworthy that the territorial divisions and subdivisions which were to be characteristic of Wales were already making their appearance while the *clas* system was developing. All in all, however, what is most noteworthy is that the official religion of the later Roman empire clearly continued as a central feature of Welsh life throughout the fifth and sixth centuries. One can hardly improve upon Jocelyn Toynbee's oft quoted conclusion that Christianity in Wales in the wake of the Roman period was 'thoroughly Roman in creed and origin; Roman, too, initially, in its organization and practice'.[21]

A second feature of continued Romanism was the use of Roman roads. It has already been mentioned that these now connected religious sites, and that dedications to particular saints, most notably Dyfrig, Illtud, Cadog and Padarn, followed these routes.[22] It is also known that Gallo-Roman immigrants, possibly fleeing from those parts of France which were falling under Frankish rather than Visigothic rule, utilized the Roman routes as well, seeing them like the native British as part of their Roman heritage. These Gallo-Romans brought with them the monastic culture which was emerging in France and the Mediterranean world, introducing monasticism to Wales where it vied with the earlier territorial concept of ecclesial jurisdiction. Travellers from Wales to the continent continued to use these roads through the lands by that time occupied by the Anglo-Saxon invaders, as did Irish pilgrims passing through Britain on their way to Rome.[23] It is tempting to speculate that they still felt the assurance of Roman protection as they passed along *their* highways. The Welsh settlements of the post-Roman period also favoured the former Roman sites on lower ground in preference to the former British hill forts occupying higher terrain.[24] Parish churches were sometimes built on the actual site of Roman forts, as at Caergybi (Holyhead) in the north and at

Caerleon and Caerwent in the south-east. Some settlements were located where Roman and earlier British sites coincided, thus continuing the tradition of human occupation. Llandough in Glamorgan and Llandegai in Caernarfonshire are both examples.[25] Three large monasteries in Glamorgan alone occupied former Roman sites.[26] The diet of the people at these settlements even exhibited Roman tastes. Pig-keeping was clearly important at Dinas Powys in the Vale of Glamorgan, pork being by far the most generally eaten meat amongst the Romans.[27]

A third feature of the continued *romanitas* of the British in Wales was their effort to provide for their leaders, secular and spiritual, a distinguished Roman ancestry. In later ages, the Welsh would be famed for their fascination with their descent and their ability to recount their pedigree over several generations. It is interesting therefore to reflect upon whether this trait was one which had its roots in establishing a family's Roman credentials or whether it was something which antedated the Roman period and was associated with the oral traditions of the ancient British. The holy men of sub-Roman Wales were routinely supplied with a noble Roman lineage.[28] Cadog, for instance, was said to have descended from a line of Roman emperors, able to trace their pedigree back to Augustus, as well as claiming the cultural credentials of being a great admirer of Virgil.[29] The connection of holy men with ruling families is a further theme. Brychan, the ruler from whom the territory of Brycheiniog took its name, was accredited with a quiverful of saintly descendants,[30] and it is abundantly clear that many of the *clas* churches were family institutions, sons succeeding fathers as priests within them.[31]

If saints were able to trace their descent from rulers, the rulers themselves traced their descent from prestigious figures in their Roman past as an expression of pride in their Roman inheritance. Many claimed descent from Macsen Wledig, Magnus Maximus, who was proclaimed emperor in Gaul and Spain as well as Britain during the 380s.[32] Probably of Spanish descent, Macsen assumed imperial control of parts of Gaul and Spain from 383 to 388, having been stationed in Britain from where he made his bid for the imperial purple taking with him the bulk of the soldiery. He was eventually defeated and killed by Theodosius in 388, but his wife, Helena, was said to have returned to Britain, indeed to Wales, where she led a religious life, several churches apparently being dedicated in her memory.[33] Macsen clearly became a popular hero among the Roman Britons, and his status in their minds was reflected in the number of later rulers who traced their pedigree from him.[34] Distinguished descent was also claimed by reference to the sons of Cunedda, the northern British leader of the Votadini who was said to have moved to north Wales following the loss of the northern British kingdom of Gododdin to the English. Cunedda and his eight surviving sons were attributed with the founding of many of the Welsh kingdoms, for instance his son Ceredig was associated with Ceredigion and his grandson Meirion with Merioneth. A believed Goidelic ruler of parts of Wales, Dyfnwal Moelmud, whose name is connected with the establishment of the territorial divisions of the *cantref* and the *cwmwd*, was said by some to have been a grandson of the British king Coel Hen, the historical figure lurking behind the legend of Old King Cole, whose daughter was said to have married Cunedda.[35]

The tracing of dynastic pedigrees back to Roman times was but one facet of how patterns of government retained a discernible vestige of Romanism. According to a different tradition, Cunedda was said to have married into the family of Macsen Wledig,[36] the title *Gwledig* indicating a sort of overkingship by which a ruler so recognized was something more than *primus inter pares* among his fellow rulers.[37] The title is not dissimilar therefore to the Anglo-Saxon *Bretwalda*, and both concepts may ultimately have derived from the presence of the imperial *vicarius* at London during the Roman period, an official with jurisdiction over the whole of the civil diocese composed of the four or five provinces making up Britain after Diocletian's reforms.[38] Cunedda's own pedigree was traced through several generations with Roman names, his grandfather having been apparently some kind of Roman official, for he is accorded the sobriquet of *Peisrudd*, red tunic, suggesting an official garb.[39] One of the early rulers of the south-eastern kingdom of Glywysing, later to be divided into Morgannwg, Gwynlliw and Gwent, was Emrys Wledig or Ambrosius Aurelianus.[40] Emrys was a contemporary of Vortigern, or Gwrtheyrn, the eponymous founder of the mid-Wales kingdom of Gwrtheyrnion. Vortigern, who was also credited with Roman ancestors,[41] became despised by his neighbouring rulers, particularly those in the north-west, for having invited the Saxons into his lands in 428, during the consulship of Felix and Taurus. Emrys may well have won the title of *Gwledig* out of respect for his defence of what remained of *Britannia* from the incursions of the pagan Saxons with whom Vortigern had allied his kingdom. In all of this, there is a distinct foreshadowing of two attitudes at large among the surviving British. One view was that their superior culture, Christian and ultimately Roman, would not be compromised by confusion with that of the incoming pagan barbarians. This view may have been buttressed by the immigration of Gallo-Roman refugees from other parts of the western empire who had left their homeland rather than suffer the rule of less civilized peoples. The opposite view, which Vortigern situated on the borders rather than in the comparative security of land farther west, let alone that in the fastnesses of the north-west, was that peaceful co-existence required some accommodation between the two peoples. Those of the former view detested the latter.[42]

Long after the Romans had left, Rome was still viewed in Wales as what has been described as 'the fount of all legitimate authority'.[43] The surviving Romano-British thought of their land as having been founded by, indeed having taken its name from, Brutus, a refugee from the fall of Troy and a descendant of Aeneas, the founder after the fall of Troy of Alba Longa, the city that would one day be Rome. The notion of an eponymous founder connects the legend with those regarding the founding of the Welsh kingdoms after Roman rule ceased. The rule of the upper classes, bearing Roman names, survived the abandonment of Britain, but having no longer to acknowledge the authority of an imperial *vicarius* in London. The new kingdoms over which they ruled were nevertheless rooted in the last days of Roman government. It is thought that the early Welsh kingdoms may well have emerged from reorganized Roman territories, established if not by Roman then at least by romanized authority. The early post-Roman rulers traced the root of their title to govern to Macsen Wledig, and it may well have been the would-be emperor who appointed administrators loyal to him at home before setting off with his forces on his ill-fated imperial adventure.[44] Those administrators may then have become hereditary rulers in the wake of Roman governmental withdrawal. It is noticeable that the early Welsh kingdoms accord with the tribal divisions known to have existed within the Roman province: Gwynedd being associated with the lands of the Ordovices, Powys with those of the Cornovii, Gwent and Glywysing with the Silures, and Dyfed and Deheubarth with the Demetae. It has even been suggested that the settlement of Cunedda and his sons in Gwynedd was a resettlement from north Britain in late Roman times, possibly by Macsen himself, to prevent Irish incursions into the area and to preserve its *romanitas*.

It may well be therefore that the tribal divisions of Roman Wales were to form the basis of the subsequent Welsh kingdoms as the result of a deliberate act of policy towards the close of the fourth century or at the beginning of the fifth. Whether this was the case or not, there can be no doubting the survival of a Roman style of government. In north Wales, Roman terms such as *magistratus* and *civis* can still be found in inscriptions long after the Roman departure. At Penmachno, a consular date is used to identify the year as late as 540, when mention is made of the consulship of Justinus, the very last consul to be mentioned by name in the west, that final mention coming from the Lyons area of south-central France.[45] The kingdom/bishopric would appear to have been the usual unit of ecclesiastical government in the aftermath of the Romans, in Wales as in England and other parts of the former western empire. Dyfrig's episcopal base in Erging is the best known and earliest example of this.[46] Church synods, later to be sanctioned in the native laws, were held in Wales certainly from the sixth century onwards.[47] Continuity was also shown as the agricultural organization of the land reflected the pattern of Roman estates, so that both the large and the small divisions of later medieval Wales were remarkably well-settled, perhaps themselves being a legacy of late Roman rule.[48]

The political and territorial organization that bore this Roman imprint has itself been ascribed to the time of the settlement of Cunedda and his sons, and to be their handiwork. However, it is perhaps more likely that the ordering was ascribed to Cunedda by a later generation which sought to justify the assertion of Gwynedd's hegemony over other parts of Wales. A story to the effect that those other parts were territories given by Cunedda to his descendants and which indeed took their names from them would have had a valuable propaganda value. It is possible that it was during the reign of Maelgwn Gwynedd that such propaganda took shape. Maelgwn, who died *c*.547, was referred to as Dragon, harking back to the symbol of the Roman legions, and was known by the Roman title of *dux*, leader, the Welsh *tywysog*. His grandson, Cadwallon, who was to be defeated and killed by Oswald of Northumbria in 634 or 635, also bore the title *dux*, and is so-called by the English ecclesiastical historian Bede. Cadwallon's defeat ended the attempts of the native British kings to regain control over the north of Britain, and the kings of Northumbria were not slow to assert their new-found control by adopting one of the emblems of Romano-British rule, the carrying of a tuft of feathers before their ruler in the manner of a later Roman emperor.[49]

According to later sources, the land divisions within the *cwmwd* had been settled by Dyfnwal Moelmud. Although these divisions were never standard throughout Wales, they do seem to have embodied a system of division, and it is not impossible that the variations in later centuries were deviations from a once common approach. The most important units were those of the *cantref* and the *cwmwd*, each of the former consisting of two of the latter. Each *cwmwd* consisted of fifty *trefi*, so that there would as the name suggests be one hundred *trefi* in a *cantref*. Forty-eight of the fifty *trefi* would in addition have been grouped into fours, each group of four being termed a *maenol*. The *trefi* would have been the village or hamlet settlements served by the smaller daughter churches of each *clas*, the *clas* being associated with the court, the *llys*, of the *cantref* or *cwmwd*.[50]

Dyfnwal Moelmud is believed to have been Goidelic, that is Irish, by descent. One version of the Cunedda story has the leader and his sons expelling the Irish from north-west Wales, some say from all of Wales. That there was Irish immigration is beyond doubt, and it would appear that it was in the south-west, the tribal area which was to become Dyfed, that this was of most importance, although Irish incursions would appear to have extended as far inland as Brycheiniog. What is fascinating is that even the Irish rulers of the south-west accommodated, or even adopted, an element of Romanism. Thus their memorials are engraved not only with the Ogam characters of their own language, but also with the traditional Latin inscriptions of the Romano-British. MEMORIA VOTEPORISIS PROTICTORIS one famously reads, adopting the Roman concept of the ruler as protector, the earlier concept of procurator.[51]

Latin was and remained the language of the Church at this time, and language was another feature of Roman identity. Whereas a ruler of Irish descent, like Vortepor, had bilingual monuments, the tombstones of the native kings have Latin inscriptions only. Cadfan, the son of Maelgwn Gwynedd and father of Cadwallon, had a Latin epitaph in the seventh century.[52] Gildas, the British writer of the previous century, wrote in Latin and bemoaned the decline of *nostra lingua*, our language, by which he meant Latin, in those parts of southern England which were gradually falling under Saxon control.[53] There is no doubting that both spoken and written Latin continued through the fifth and sixth centuries and that the native British of that period were bilingual in Latin and the emerging Welsh language, just as the Irish settlers of Dyfed were bilingual in Latin and Irish.[54] Indeed, the Welsh were to continue to refer to themselves as *Brytaniaid* until the late twelfth century, and until that century also they referred to the land in which they lived as the Romans had done, *Britannia*.[55] As Welsh developed a distinct linguistic identity, so the former Roman names for tribal regions provided the root for the Welsh name of the kingdom: *Venta* became Gwent; *Ariconium* supplied Erging.[56]

Place names also were often based upon Latin terms for features or associations with the area. The continued use of, and pride in, Roman roads is illustrated by the number of places in Wales which bear the name *Sarn* meaning a metalled road. A direct borrowing from Latin is the Welsh *Merthyr*, martyr, which also features in place names and connects with the veneration accorded to martyrs in post-Roman Wales. Other ecclesiastical elements in place names include *eglwys*, a church, from the Latin *ecclesia*, and *capel*, a chapel, from the Latin *capella*.[57] The Welsh word for a parish, *plwyf*, is derived from the Roman *plebs*; a Breton charter of 837 refers to Pleucadeuc as being *in plebe Cadocis*.[58]

One very interesting use of a Latin term merits mention. When itinerant Irish holy men came to Wales and wandered about the countryside with small bands of followers, they were referred to as *peregrini*. The word would come to be interpreted as pilgrims, indeed it would produce the Welsh word *pererin* and the French *pélérin*. However, the original Latin meaning, the meaning in Roman law, is not absent here. A peregrine was a foreigner, who was crossing the fields, *per agros*; in other words he was not a Roman citizen. The incoming Irish had not been Roman citizens for Ireland had never formed part of the empire. The incomers were therefore *peregrini* in both the past and future senses of the word.[59]

There was also continuity in trade and industry between Roman and sub-Roman Britain. Maritime routes had been of importance to Britain before the Romans arrived; their importance continued throughout the Roman period and survived beyond it. South Wales in particular was part of the Roman empire's trade network, the Severn Sea – what is now called the Bristol Channel – being an especially important artery of trade. Evidence of the survival of trade links with the Romano-Christian continent is the widespread Roman influence upon fifth- and sixth-century Christian pottery in Britain.[60]

Industries also continued from Roman times. The mining of iron, lead and gold remained important, and ironworking may have continued practices that dated from before the Roman period. The production of wool and textiles also continued.[61]

Against this background of continued Romanism in relation to religion, transport, ancestry, government, language, trade and industry, the question must be asked as to whether there is evidence that in Wales as in other parts of the former western empire this loyalty to the Roman heritage also manifested itself in some retention of Roman law, or at least what was remembered of it. The lack of any firm legal evidence for several more centuries makes any definite answer impossible. However, given that it is known that in other parts of the former western empire where the Roman inheritance remained valued, there were also legal survivals, even relatively minor indications of legal survivals in Wales are of significance. There are some significant indicators which point to certain Roman attitudes to law as having survived.

One of the most important of these indicators is that, despite the fragmentation of Wales into kingdoms based upon earlier tribal units, there was nevertheless an abiding concept of the legal unity of the British people. This in part was no doubt fostered by stories which emphasized a common inheritance from a particular ruler, be it Cunedda at the start of the fifth century, Maelgwn later or Hywel Dda in the tenth. By that latter date, there is clear evidence that that sense of legal unity had been and was being cultivated by a class of quasi-professional jurists,[62] a circumstance highly reminiscent of the work of the jurists in the Roman empire. Moreover, the Welsh legal tradition was to be a written legal tradition, based upon juristic texts not remembered customs. On the continent, it was the example of Roman law which led to the production of written legal texts, and the southern third of France was to become known as the land of written law, *pays du droit écrit*, in contrast to the northern two-thirds which was the land of customs, *pays des coutumes*. Wales was also a land of written law and, in the light of the other evidence for surviving Romanism, the possibility of Roman legal survivals cannot be readily discounted.[63] When the law texts appear in later centuries, they refer to the jurists as wise men, *doethion*, in the same manner as the Roman jurists were called *prudentes*, and the Welsh law texts like the Roman were a living source of law, being adapted to changing circumstances in every generation through the activity of the jurists, very unlike the static quality of the written laws of neighbouring Ireland where the writ of Roman law had not run.[64]

Whereas a fuller response to the question of the extent of Roman influence upon the Welsh laws must await the examination of those laws in the next chapter, some factors relating to the sub-Roman period need to be mentioned here as they form the slender evidence for a legal bridge between the two epochs. Thus, Gildas, writing in the sixth century, comments that public weddings were unusual among the British, just as Roman marriages were very much private affairs depending upon the consent of the parties rather than any public form.[65] It would appear that from as early a time as the post-Roman period, land in Wales was treated as belonging to the family rather than an individual proprietor and was therefore inalienable and not disposable by will. While land as other property was controlled by the *paterfamilas*, it has been shown that he had but limited powers of testation and that alienation had to be responsible upon pain of being declared prodigal and losing control of the family property. Land may have been a very special case in the provinces, given that officially it was not susceptible of private ownership in the full Roman sense of *dominium*, but was held from the state.[66]

There are also stray expressions used in the law texts which manifest continued Romanism. The *Cyfnerth* tradition, particularly connected with the heavily Romanized south-east, uses Roman terms to measure dates. Speaking of the time in the life cycle of bees when 'every swarm assumed the status of a mother hive', this is stated to occur nine days before the start of August, a very Roman method of reckoning the date – nine days before the Kalends of August.[67] It is also noteworthy that trial by ordeal, common across northern Europe in Frankish lands but absent from Roman law, is also absent from the Welsh laws. Significantly perhaps, a story attaches to this fact, for it is said that the ordeal was indeed introduced into Wales by the Goidelic Dyfnwal Moelmud, but was subsequently abolished by Hywel Dda.[68] If there is any substance to this tale, it confirms the absence of the ordeal from Romano-British society, its import from Ireland by a ruler of foreign descent and its subsequent abolition by a Welsh ruler bent upon unifying the Welsh laws, therefore suggesting that Dyfnwal's introduction of the ordeal had not been general, but confined to the territories under Irish influence and that it had not spread to other parts of Wales.

It is also known that the incoming abbots of Welsh monasteries, often literally inheriting their position from a deceased ancestor, were required to pay the death duty known as the *ebidew* to the local ruler.[69] It was once believed that the name of this death duty was derived from the Latin, *obitum*, although some now doubt this and emphasize its connection with giving an animal, here a colt, the Welsh *ebol*, as a render. It is also interesting that Roman jurisprudential ideas appear to feature in the works of the Welsh poets of the period. Aneurin, for instance, mourning the loss of Gododdin in his lament of that name, speaks in a well-known passage of a warrior having 'got his dues', a reflection possibly of the Roman jurists' concept of justice as giving each his due, *suum cuique tribuens*.[70]

There is a danger however that, in seeking to establish the influence continued Romanism might have exercised on Welsh law, one loses sight of other possible influences. Among those must still be counted survivals from the pre-Roman age, for if there is evidence of continued Romanism, there is also evidence of native British ideas and concepts having survived. One obvious element here is the fact that some settlement sites had continued to be used from pre-Roman times, through the Roman period and into the post-Roman centuries. Thus, Llandough in south Wales and Llandegai in the north had existed since the Iron Age, and the same is true of Lesser Garth, north of Cardiff in the Vale of Taff.[71] Professor Glanville Jones considered that the courts, *llysoedd*, of some Welsh freemen were located in a 'reconditioned hill fort or in the ruins of a Roman villa', emphasizing the two strands of continuity reaching the sub-Roman period. However, Professor Leslie Alcock, while accepting the Roman continuance, has doubted whether there is any real evidence to support Glanville Jones's views concerning the reconditioning of hill forts.[72]

On a larger scale, it is noticeable that the Welsh kingdoms that emerge almost contemporaneously with the Roman departure correspond to the tribal territories existing before the Roman conquest.[73] Even in the heavily romanized south-east, native influences continued to operate. In Gwent, for instance, one discovers a native ruler bearing the name of Caradog, that is, the name of the British hero called in Latin *Caractacus*, who had distinguished himself by hostile opposition to the incoming Roman forces.[74] It is difficult therefore not to conclude that the native British would appear to have been capable of preserving what they regarded as best in their own traditions while adopting worthwhile practices from other sources. This in itself, of course, may be attributable to Roman influence, as the Romans were masters of imbuing the worthy ideas of other nations into their own forms and agendas. From the *ius gentium* to the Christian faith, Roman syncretism was manifested. So, in the Britain of the sub-Roman period, one finds native, supposedly Celtic, designs emerging to decorate the stone crosses and illuminated manuscripts of the early Christian period.[75] Brooches which have survived from the fifth century exhibit a curious blend of Roman artistic skill and Celtic design.[76] In literature as well as art, ancient Celtic myths appear at this time to have been reworked so as to carry a Christian rather than a pagan message.[77]

This last example furnishes another problem, namely how had the Celtic tales survived. It would appear that they were preserved in the memory of the people, possibly of the learned classes, for Gildas in the sixth century speaks of pagan practices which he is unlikely to have encountered but which people of his generation were obviously aware had existed and had remembered.[78] One particularly intriguing Christianization of an earlier tradition relates to the native British fascination with the number three, as manifested in triads for instance. With the coming of Christianity and the definition of the doctrine of the Trinity, this fascination with the number three developed a whole new significance for the British. Praise of the Trinity abounded, so that it became a distinguishing feature of British Christianity, where the Christian faith itself could be described as the faith of the Holy Trinity, with dedications to the Trinity abounding from the seventh century onwards.[79]

One source for these Celtic survivals may have been Ireland, but it is no more acceptable to discount native British survivals in favour of Irish imports than it was to reject internal Roman continuity and emphasize Gallo-Roman immigration. In each case, both strands played important parts. It must however be remembered that initially it was Britain which influenced Ireland, particularly with regard to the Christian faith. Later, that influence was reversed, but one cannot maintain that the influence was ever all one way.[80] Throughout the period of native rule, links to Ireland were important, in terms of politics, trade and the arts, including literature. Highly significant commercial connections existed between Ireland and both north and south Wales, extending as far as Chester and Bristol respectively.[81] In south-west Wales, as has been noted, Irish influence was particularly strong with the two cultures being assimilated rather than one predominating. Thus, memorials were inscribed in Ogam and Latin in Dyfed and Brycheiniog, whereas in Ireland itself they were in Ogam only.[82] In Ireland, as in Wales, bishops were regarded as the heirs of the founders of their sees, a distinctly Roman perspective.[83]

In the specifically legal sphere, the character of Dyfnwal Moelmud stands out, being by tradition of Goidelic stock and having introduced both land measurements and possibly the ordeal into Wales.[84] Equally interesting is the fact that, in the native Irish laws, land as in Wales belonged to the family and could not be disposed of by individuals.[85] This common feature of Irish and Welsh native law, and less similar to Roman law despite certain points of comparison, raises the question of whether on this issue the native Welsh had imported their rules of landholding from Ireland or whether both nations were utilizing an approach drawn from their own ancient traditions, customs which in Britain had been unaltered despite the Roman occupation, a far from unlikely scenario given that provincial land was not regarded as open to private ownership according to Roman law.

Modern knowledge of the Irish legal tradition begins with a sixth-century law book called the *Senchas Mór*, a work of uncertain date but claimed by some to be as early as the fifth century. It purports to be a collection of customs drawn from poetic and other sources and preserved when not in opposition to the teachings of the Church. It is claimed that it is was approved by St Patrick himself at an assembly and that the laws are in the main based on those of Moses, but tempered by the law of nature. This description calls to mind the fourth-century Roman work, the *Collatio legum Mosaicarum et Romanarum*, in which someone who was fairly obviously not a jurist attempted to harmonize biblical and Roman law. Likewise, *Senchas Mór* attempts a harmonization of Irish customs with Christian precepts.[86]

Whether the *Collatio*, as it is generally known, may have inspired the *Senchas Mór* or not, the existence of native survivals, Irish influence and Roman continuity within Wales must not blind one to the importance of the continued contact that the native British had with the continent after the Romans left, particularly with those parts of the mainland which had also been under Roman governance and continued Roman in culture and Christian in faith. Christianity, by virtue of its having come to western Europe and Britain in particular during the Roman period, necessarily implied a degree of *romanitas*.[87] In itself, it suggested links with a wider world, as extensive as the

Roman empire had been. With Christianity becoming the official religion of the Roman empire, the Church as an institution partook of an experience which was Europe-wide and exhibited in its mission and activities a similar European approach. Bishops from Britain attended councils on the continent throughout the fifth and sixth centuries: at Tours in 461, Vannes in 465, Orléans in 511 and Paris in 555.[88] These came from the Christian British areas, for the English had yet to be converted to Christianity as a result of St Augustine of Canterbury's mission beginning in 597.

Developments such as the veneration for the tombs of martyrs and saints occurred across Europe and not just in Wales, but their occurrence in Wales testified to the region being part of the greater whole that had once been the empire.[89] The liturgy of the Church in the Celtic parts was Gallican, reflecting continued links with those parts of the continent, and it was Gallic monasticism which made headway in Wales during the fifth and sixth centuries, partly through these links and partly through the immigration of Gallo-Romans into the north and south along the Roman roads. Contacts with southern Gaul, in particular the areas around Lyons and Vienne are testified by the style and content of inscriptions found on memorials in north Wales.[90] Inscriptions bearing the formula HIC IACET are to be found, a form which had its origins in fourth-century Italy and early fifth-century Gaul. Notably, it was to be found in Trèves, an area connected with the campaigns of Macsen Wledig at the end of the fourth century and from which his widow Helena is said to have returned to Wales. Inscriptions of the form IN HOC TUMULO and IN PACE are also to be found, having a similar provenance and attesting to the extent of the cultural links with other areas of the former empire.[91] These inscriptions only became current in Gaul after the Romans had withdrawn from Britain.[92] In the sixth century, Italianate half-uncial script makes an appearance.[93]

Likewise, it is known that when Celtic emigrants settled in Brittany in north-west France, they lived alongside their fellow Romano-Gaulish Christians. There, as in Wales, the holy men claimed kinship with the rulers, and it is also known that the monastery of St Budoc was founded in the ruins of a fourth-century Roman villa, mirroring foundations in Wales. It is even possible that the emigration of people from Wales into Brittany was a deliberate act of late Roman policy as with the supposed settlement of the Votadini in north-west Wales, the migrants in Brittany being *foederati* drawn from the Cornovii of eastern mid Wales.[94]

Roman liturgical usage, that is, liturgy based on the usage of the contemporary Church at Rome, only spread into Wales at a later date, reaching Bangor in 768 and St David's by 928.[95] By this time, the important links with southern Gaul had been severed as a result of the Moorish invasions, the Moors having overrun most of Spain in the course of six weeks in 711, before proceeding to an invasion of France that was only reversed by Charles Martel at Poitiers in 732.[96] This disaster for western Christendom nevertheless led to increasing links between Wales and the non-Celtic world. There is evidence that south-east Wales had links as far afield as Byzantium, probably through the activities of merchants.[97] Ninth-century coins found on the Gower peninsula include a *denier* from Pavia in northern Italy, minted in the reign of Lothar (823–55). Links with this city may have considerable legal significance, for it was here according to some scholars that the revival of legal learning which was to occur in later centuries had its roots.[98] Another ninth-century coin found on the Gower was minted at Melle in Poitou for another Carolingian Frankish ruler, Charles the Bald (843–77), who had his court at Liège. It is known that rulers of Gwynedd in the ninth century, including Merfyn Frych and Rhodri Mawr, had links with Charles's court.[99] Both Lothar and Charles the Bald were descendants of Charlemagne, the first Holy Roman Emperor, who was crowned by Pope Leo III at Rome on Christmas Day, 800. This same pope, Leo III, had in 789 written of all the inhabitants of Britain as Christian, but accepted that the jurisdiction of Canterbury extended to the English only. Although Wales had no metropolitan of its own, its Church was therefore recognized and treated as independent of England by the Papacy.[100] These links with the Frankish court and with Rome may be significant for the subsequent development of law in Wales, and testify to the influence of continental connections.

One final source of possible influence needs to be recognized: the Bible. It is sometimes overlooked that the Romano-Christian population of Wales would have been able to turn to the Bible as a source of law, in much the same manner that agreement with biblical law was regarded as important to the compilers of both the Roman *Collatio* and the Irish *Senchas Mór*. Gildas, writing in the sixth century, is thought to have imported into his accounts biblical notions of kingship,[101] but it needs to be borne in mind that such a perspective need not have been confined to Gildas alone. The Irish *Book of Aicill* as well as the *Senchas Mór* state that kings had to be without blemish, recalling the emphasis that is placed in the laws of the Old Testament upon things and people dedicated to God being so free.[102] The manner in which the sons of Cunedda become the eponymous rulers of the tribal kingdoms of Wales recalls the division of the promised land among the tribes of Israel descended from the sons of Jacob. In both cases, it is possible to read the history as an attempt to justify and underpin the federation by explaining it in terms of common descent.[103]

There is therefore a great deal of indirect evidence to suggest the general direction in which law in Wales was developing in the sub-Roman period. Comparison with other parts of the former western empire, with which Wales remained in regular close contact suggests that the native Romano-Christian population would have been assiduous in maintaining their Romanism, and this is borne out by the evidence regarding the Christian faith, transport, attitude to ancestry, the structure of government, language, trade and industry.

Although the legal evidence is more sparse, it is fair to conclude that the Roman element would have been preserved in some measure. It is however also the case that there is evidence too which points to the natives having retained some knowledge of their pre-Roman customs, some of which may have remained in use during the Roman period. These may have been buttressed as a result of Irish immigration and influence in the succeeding centuries, and an Irish element may even have been imported into the law. Nevertheless, continental influences continued to operate as well during this time in north and south Wales. Further, the Christian communities of the Romano-British would also have had the Bible to draw on for some of their legal inspiration.[104]

There is also evidence at this time of two attitudes developing among the Welsh as their country became defined geographically as a result of the English invasion. While some, such as Vortigern, were prepared to come to terms with their new neighbours, others were not and were sharply critical of those who were. There is widespread evidence that the Romano-British remnant were loath to interact with the Anglo-Saxons, placing emphasis upon preserving their own culture and language – that is, Roman culture and the Latin language. Where Irish immigration occurred, Latin was preserved alongside Ogam. Central to this culture was the Christian faith, which the British appear to have made little if any attempt to proclaim to the pagan invaders. Bede, looking back at this period from the vantage point of newly converted Christian England, deplored the native British for this failure, particularly as St Augustine's mission had not encountered immense difficulty.[105] It is even possible that the emerging Welsh were here too emulating the biblical precedent of the children of Israel refusing to compromise their religious purity by mingling with other nations. Instead, the emerging Welsh were prone to look back to the Roman empire as a golden age and to look forward longingly for some form of restoration. It is tempting to speculate that in this, their Christian faith, with its expectation of a second coming, may have encouraged them, or it may be that their native attitude of mind made them particularly receptive of a faith which contained such elements.

4

The Age of the Native Princes

In 825, the direct male line of the ruling house of Gwynedd was extinguished with the death of Hywel ap Rhodri, who had succeeded his brother Cynan in 816. Political control of Gwynedd passed to one Merfyn Frych, who may have been the brother-in-law or more likely the nephew of the deceased rulers.[1] Merfyn may have been the son of Gwriad, a ruler of the Isle of Man, *Ynys Manaw*, and he continued as king of Gwynedd until his death in 844, when he was succeeded by his son, Rhodri, who was to become known as Rhodri Mawr. Rhodri left several sons, four of whom would appear to have been politically active, namely Anarawd, Cadell, Meurig and Gwriad. These four would appear not to have divided their father's kingdom upon his death, but to have exercised some form of joint sovereignty.[2] In due course, the northern kingdom of Gwynedd would appear to have become Anarawd's sphere of influence, while Cadell concentrated his attention on Dyfed in the south-west. He established himself as king of Dyfed early in the tenth century when the local ruler, Llywarch ap Hyfaidd, died in 904 and his brother Rhydderch was executed in the following year. Cadell became ruler not only of Dyfed, but also of Ystrad Tywi, the enlarged kingdom which was to be known as Deheubarth, the southern part of the territory ruled by the line of Rhodri Mawr.

The line's grip upon the south-western kingdom was cemented by the marriage of Cadell's son, Hywel, to Elen, the daughter of Llywarch ap Hyfaidd. Hywel succeeded to his father's lands on the latter's death in 910.[3] Hywel ap Cadell has become better known by the epithet which was attached to his name from the twelfth century onwards, Hywel Dda. It is during his reign and on his initiative that the extant native laws of Wales are traditionally said to have been reduced to writing. Under Hywel, the focus of Welsh foreign policy shifted from Ireland in the west to England in the east. Hywel recognized Aethelstan as king in England in 927 and was known to admire the work and policy of Alfred the Great (877–99). The traditional anti-English stance of Welsh foreign policy, which had endured at least in north Wales from the time of Cadwallon to that of Rhodri Mawr, began to change under his sons, with the south in particular becoming much more open to English influences. All the rulers of Wales did homage to Alfred, although Anarawd of Gwynedd was the last to do so.[4] Hywel Dda however was a frequent visitor to the English court. He signed official documents as a *sub-regulus* of the English king from 929 through to his death in 949, and was always the first in order of any Welsh princes present to do so.[5] It is possible that his acceptance of the position of *sub-regulus* of the English king reflected a continued notion among the Welsh of the superior position of the king in London as a successor of the imperial vicar of the diocese of Britannia who had been the superior of the governors in the other provinces of Britain. Hywel is also credited with having gone on pilgrimage to Rome and to have met the Pope in 929, testifying to his willingness to admit influence from the European mainland as well as from England, although such influences already existed during the ninth century.[6]

In 942, Hywel invaded Gwynedd following an unsuccessful rebellion by his cousin, Idwal Foel, against the English. The northern kingdom had separated from Deheubarth following Anarawd's death in 916, but had extended its sphere of influence into Powys and Ceredigion. By extending his rule into Gwynedd therefore, Hywel became the ruler of a very substantial portion of the land of Wales, particularly when after 944 he also acquired Brycheiniog by invasion. It may well have been the need to provide some focus of unity among the disparate parts of his domains that led him to convene the assembly at Hendygwyn-ar-Daf, Whitland, which tradition states met to promulgate laws for Hywel's kingdoms.

According to the surviving texts of these laws, the manuscript sources for which have not survived from before the twelfth century, Hywel summoned six men from every *cantref* within his kingdoms to the assembly at Whitland. There, they met to examine the old laws, to continue some, to amend others and to abolish the remainder, occasionally agreeing on the introduction of new laws.[7] The laws as established were not thereafter to be changed other than by an enactment of a similar constituted assembly.[8] In particular, it was claimed that the laws enacted were not to contain anything which was contrary to either the law of the Church or that of the emperor.[9]

Accounts of the work of Hywel's assembly are to be found in the law texts themselves and in the work of other writers, such as Caradog of Llancarfan.[10] It is possible that Hywel's initiative was influenced by the Church, which itself was moving towards the compilation of written laws and encouraging secular rulers to do likewise. Hywel's admiration for Alfred of Wessex may also have led him to follow that ruler's example with regard to law-making and the assembly may have been based upon the English *witan*.[11] *Llyfr Blegywryd*, the Welsh manuscript tradition which is particularly associated with Dyfed, records that within the assembly twelve commissioners were appointed to assist Blegywryd, who was to act as secretary to the assembly in its work of framing the laws.[12] The concept of commissioners performing this task parallels other such legislative ventures, including that of Justinian in sixth-century Byzantium, when he appointed a commission of six to extract the best laws from the writings of the classical Roman jurists and to collect them in the work which has become known as the Digest. Hywel's assembly may have been consciously emulating an English or continental example as it met and set about its work, probably around the year 945.

Blegywryd, who is said to have been the assembly's scribe and is believed by some to have been the archdeacon of Llandaff, was certainly an ecclesiastic and his activity emphasizes the influence of the Church upon Hywel's endeavours. When Alfred had had laws composed for Wessex in the previous century, his work began with the Ten Commandments and continued with the laws contained in chapters 21 and 23 of Exodus. His law-making was a serious attempt to bring into harmony the customs of his people and the precepts of the Christian faith. The same was probably true of Hywel's laws.[13] The influence of the Christian Church in Wales as elsewhere is evidenced by such factors as stressing the importance of intention in the punishment of wrongs, the encouragement of testamentary gifts to the Church, the use of writing in legal transactions and emphasis upon the particular sanctity surrounding the person of the king.[14] This last factor is peculiarly significant with regard to the Welsh laws, for they depart radically from the model of the law books of Ireland in giving considerable space to the laws of the king's court, in which the status and duties of a whole host of royal officers are set out in some detail. This inclusion of *Cyfreithiau Llys* is markedly similar to, for instance, book 6 of the late Roman Theodosian Code, and also mirrors the discussion of the royal entourage given by Hincmar, archbishop of Rheims, in the thirteenth chapter of his *De Ordine Palatii*, written in 882 and reflecting the structure of the imperial court under Charlemagne and Louis the Pious.[15]

The example of Charlemagne deserves to be pondered. The links between his grandson, Charles the Bald, and the court of Gwynedd have already been mentioned. After Charlemagne extended his rule in 800 by becoming Holy Roman Emperor, he tackled the problems posed by the legal diversity within his empire by requiring in 802 that the laws of its various domains be set out in writing to enable his legislative and governmental work to proceed more efficiently. Hywel may have felt the same in the 940s as his rule extended from Deheubarth into Gwynedd, Powys, Ceredigion and Brycheiniog.

Moreover, it is clear that this Carolingian influence did not stem entirely from the court of Aethelstan, and while the idea of reducing the native customs to writing may have come from outside, by and large the substance of the laws consists of the native Welsh customs with relatively few outside influences.[16]

The influence of Wessex can be discerned in the manner in which the laws were framed and in some of the terminology used.[17] One of the clearest examples of the latter is the use of the Anglo-Saxon *edling* to describe the royal heir apparent. During Alfred's reign, Asser, the Welshman who was to record his achievements, spent half of each year with his royal master in Wessex and the other half in his native Dyfed, where doubtless his information and advice proved useful and possibly influential.[18] The idea of the English king as a *regulus*, little king, beneath the emperor on the larger stage, with the Welsh kings as *sub-reguli*, reflects an assumption that perhaps an older European hierarchy was being restored, an idea which the Church would have been keen to foster. Under Hywel, the sovereign tribute due to the king of London from Wales was defined as £63; whether it was paid is another matter.[19]

All in all, given Hywel's supremacy within Wales and the example and influence of the English court under Alfred to which it is known Hywel was susceptible, some legal activity within Wales must be regarded as likely. That some took place during Hywel's reign is supported not only by the law texts' accounts but also by contemporaneous increase in literary activity.[20] Some however would argue that, given the fact that extant versions of the laws come from the twelfth and thirteenth century, there may have been at least substantial interpolation of the texts and that their whole attribution to Hywel may be no more than a propaganda ploy to give the customs of a later time a more distinguished pedigree by appealing to an age when Wales knew an unprecedented degree of political unification under a ruler whose reputation was manifested in the designation *Da*, good. There can be no doubting that the laws of Hywel were regarded in later centuries as a major focus of unity for the Welsh people.[21]

There is extrinsic evidence to connect the laws as they appear in the manuscripts with earlier centuries. Marginalia to the Lichfield Gospels, written between the eighth and the tenth centuries, include a description of a lawsuit in the so-called *Surrexit* memorandum. Terms used in this description accord with those employed in Hywel's laws.[22] Likewise, the tales contained in the *Mabinogion* affirm the legal customs of the law texts and in particular those of the laws of court.[23]

Equally, there are items which suggest a later provenance. *Llyfr Blegywryd* as it has survived, with its strong ecclesiastical influence, belongs to the twelfth century, the age of the Lord Rhys, Henry II's justiciar in south Wales. A case can perhaps be made for this text being compiled under the Lord Rhys's patronage to facilitate his work and enhance the reputation of his native Deheubarth through magnifying the reputation of its royal house at a previous moment when cooperation with England was at a zenith.[24] To this age also belongs some of the learning of Roman law which features in the Latin texts of the native laws. There, various syntactical elements, such as the introduction of examples with the words *si quis*, and references to Roman law concepts which may have been communicated through the medium of canon law – such as the need for the evidence of two witnesses – point to some knowledge of the revived Roman-law learning of the eleventh, twelfth and thirteenth centuries.[25] Some of these flourishes can however be attributed to the knowledge of earlier generations, when for instance parallels to the *Proemium* to Hywel's laws can be found not only in twelfth and thirteenth century texts but also in the introductions to the laws of Alfred and the *Breviary of Alaric*.[26] The capacity for the survival of such notions from post-Roman times should not be discounted.

The truth would appear to lie not with maintaining that the laws are an unadulterated distillation of native Welsh custom in the tenth century nor with suggesting that they are a twelfth-century attempt to pass off contemporary customs as belonging to an earlier age. The reality is more likely to be that Hywel, seeking to harmonize the laws of his disparate territories, had the diverse customs recorded in writing and sought, on the example of illustrious predecessors across Europe, to modernize and systematize the laws of his kingdoms. After his time, when the divisions within Wales resumed, the laws remained a focus of unity, albeit that they were adapted in the several jurisdictions as occasion demanded, so that the legal and intellectual influences of those later times can be discerned in the surviving texts. By the twelfth and thirteenth centuries, the lawyers of north Wales were sufficiently well-versed in the contemporary legal culture of western Europe to speak of there being three systems of law, by which they almost undoubtedly meant their native law (the law of Hywel), the law of the emperor (Roman law) and canon law (the law of the Church).[27] Between the age of Hywel and that of the Lord Rhys, other figures had played their part. Bleddyn ap Cynfyn, for instance, the king of Powys who died in 1075, is credited with his share of legal reform.[28]

Welsh law was in other words not static. In this, as with its emphasis upon the laws of court, it was markedly dissimilar to its Irish neighbour. There were however Irish influences present within the Welsh customs. Most notably these concerned the organization of the family and the rules of family law.[29] However, the whole idea of kingly enactment as witnessed by the Hywelian tradition and the activities of a Bleddyn ap Cynfyn are foreign to the Irish perspective.[30] There are accounts of quite substantial innovations, such as Benlli's decree that his subjects should be at work by sunrise upon pain of death,[31] the truth of which is secondary to the presence of the idea of royal law-making authority.

The native laws were essentially the customs of the people, but required royal authority from Hywel's time to be valid. Customs could supplement the law provided they were not at odds with it, but only precede the law if confirmed by royal authority. If not approved, they were of doubtful authority.[32] While the law could be changed, the law books appear to have been slow to discard their contents, so that they preserve much that by the twelfth century must have been anachronistic.[33] The law books as they have survived are not authoritative legal enactments in the manner of the Lombard Edicts or Justinian's Digest. They are works from which legal rules could be cited, in the manner in which the works of the Roman jurists could be cited within the courts of the empire prior to the Law of Citations of the emperors Theodosius II and Valentinian III in 426.[34] Moreover, the texts emphasize that it was possible to enter into agreements which were to be regulated outside of the law, thus creating a custom particular to a transaction or occasion.[35] The Welsh king's role was to enforce the customs of his country; he was not in himself a source of law.[36] The Roman imperial maxim *quod principi placuit, legis habet vigorem* had no place in the native jurisprudence of Wales, and this may be due to the fact that the Welsh kings saw themselves not as successors to the emperors, nor to their imperial vicars in London, but to the provincial governors who would have enforced the law and not made it. The restoration of the western empire under Charlemagne may have accentuated their perception of themselves as *sub-reguli* in a larger Christian empire, and the activities of Hywel in 945 may have been thought part of a pan-European response to what Charlemagne had commenced in 802.

THE CONTENT OF THE NATIVE LAWS

Certainly, the laws of Hywel commence with a lengthy treatise on the laws of the Welsh king's court, a section which is very similar to the texts from the Carolingian empire. The laws of court contain discussion of the status of the king, the members of the royal family, the members of the royal household with their respective status and the succession to the office of king. It is noteworthy at the outset that the queen is allotted one-third of the king's income for her personal use and that she is accorded a status greater than that of any of the court officers.[37] This reflects, as will be seen, the higher status enjoyed by women under the laws of Hywel than in most contemporary legal systems.

The heir to the throne is described in the law texts as the *edling*, a term borrowed from the Anglo-Saxon kingdom of Wessex. There was a Welsh term, *gwrthrychiad*, and it would appear that the change in terminology marked a change in the institution reflecting English influence.[38] The king was entitled to nominate his successor from amongst his family, but in Hywel's time it appears that the range of relatives from amongst whom he could choose became more limited. His choice was confined to his sons, nephews and first cousins.[39] The choice of a successor would suggest that only one person, always male, should succeed to the kingly office, contradicting what had occurred on the death of Rhodri Mawr and upon the death of Hywel's own father, Cadell. The succession in those cases passed to the sons as a group, in the same manner as land was inherited under the Welsh laws. If the introduction of the *edling* was an idea of Hywel's, it was a clear break with native tradition. While the laws might state that the successor was to be chosen by the king during his lifetime, the historical record indicates that from Hywel's own century partibility was not uncommon and military might also played its part in choosing the successor when the moment actually came.[40]

The problems of partibility with regard to kingship may also have stemmed from observation of the difficulties experienced by the Carolingians following the death of Charlemagne. The virtual disintegration of the empire which resulted was an issue which would almost certainly have been widely discussed in contemporary Europe and have provided the backdrop for the attempts of legislators to discover a more serviceable mode of succession. The idea of the current ruler choosing his successor during his reign may have been adopted from the practice of the late Roman empire following the reforms of Diocletian, who attempted to overcome the difficulties experienced during the third century when military might predominated in determining succession to the emperorship and resulted in chaos and regular assassinations. His solution was also to allow the ruling emperor, the Augustus, to choose his successor, his Caesar, during his lifetime. The Welsh model preserved the concept of a royal caste by limiting choice to within the royal family, always excluding those who were unsuitable by reason of some blemish, such as physical disability, insanity and the like. Such exclusions mirrored the position in Irish law. The *edling* moreover did not receive any land while he was heir,[41] as this would preclude him from inheriting from the king, a rule which reflected both the general Welsh practice with regard to youngest sons and a similar practice which was widespread among Germanic legal systems.

The royal household consisted of the captain of the household, the priest, the steward, the chief falconer, the court judge, the chief groom, the chamberlain, the bard, the usher, the chief huntsman, the mead brewer, the physician, the butler, the doorkeeper, the cook, the candleman, the queen's steward, the queen's priest, the queen's chief groom, the queen's chamberlain, the queen's handmaid, the queen's doorkeeper, the queen's cook, the queen's candleman and some further figures who were regularly to be found at court – the groom of the rein, the footholder, the dung maer, the serjeant, the porter, the watchman, the fueller, the bakeress, the court smith, the pencerdd and the laundress. It is noted that amongst the duties of the court priest was to act as a scribe so as to report cases decided within the royal court.[42] This is noted in *Llyfr Blegywryd*, where the influence of the Church is most pronounced, and offers an useful vignette upon how ecclesiastical influence may have been exerted upon the activities of the Welsh courts.[43]

The king's court was supported by food renders offered by the subdivisions of the kingdom. The principal subdivisions as has been shown were the *cantref* and the *cwmwd*.[44] According to the standard pattern maintained in some of the north Walian texts, each *cantref* consisted, as its name suggests, of one hundred *trefi*, and was formed of two *cymydau*, each of fifty *trefi*. Within the *cwmwd*, the *trefi* were grouped in fours into twelve *maenolau*,[45] with two *trefi* outside of the *maenol* groupings. One of these was the *maerdref* and the other consisted of the king's waste and summer pasture. The *maerdref* was farmed by the *maer* for the king's benefit, as was the use of the waste and summer pasture.[46] The *trefi* were composed of four *gafaelion*, the *gafael* of four *rhandiroedd*, each *rhandir* of four *tyddynnod* and each *tyddyn* of four *erwau*, *erw* being the Welsh for *acre*.[47] It is doubtful whether these standard divisions reflected actual conditions on the ground even in north Wales, but they are useful in that they give a rough idea of the units involved. Even in south Wales, there is evidence from Glamorgan that the arrangement of the *cwmwd* into *trefi* with a *maerdref*, waste and summer pasture was followed. Place names bear this out.[48]

Each *cwmwd* would have had its lord, its *arglwydd*. He would have been responsible for the administration of justice within its bounds and his *llys* or court would probably have imitated the structure of the king's court. Within each *cwmwd* there would also have been a *maer* and a *canghellor*, to supervise the *maerdref*, the king's waste and the summer pasture. Professor Glanville Jones believes there would have been a *llys* and a *llan* (church) in each *maenol*, ready to receive and entertain the *arglwydd* as he progressed around his lordship and also originally to receive the king as he progressed around his kingdom. Each free *maenol* would be expected to provide the king's court with hospitality, *gwestfa*, for a certain number of nights each year, but gradually the practice of actually touring the kingdom was replaced by the giving of *gwestfa* in the form of supplies to be consumed at the principal royal residence. Servile *maenolau* gave a food render, *dawnbwyd*, twice a year in summer and winter, which renders were defined. Professor Glanville Jones has also suggested that the arrangement of the *maenol* may go back to Roman organization within Wales.[49] Traditionally, however, the land divisions were ascribed to Dyfnal Moelmud. The existence of *arglwyddi* points to the introduction of feudalism, which almost certainly replaced an earlier tribal arrangement based on the *cenedl* rather than lordship, the *cenedl* being an agnatic descent group of wider relationship than the *teulu*, the family as an extended household group.

The *cenedl* has been called one of the principal features of the ancient pan-Celtic way of life.[50] It postulated agnatic descent, that is descent through the male line, from a common ancestor. Within each *cenedl*, there would be many *teuluoedd*, family units headed by the oldest surviving male ancestor, the *penteulu*. There would also be a head of the *cenedl*, the *pencenedl*, whose role as a sort of chieftain may have gradually been replaced by that of the *arglwydd* as the feudal principle gained ground.[51] The relationship of the *cenedl* to the *teulu* is similar to that which existed in Roman society between the *gens* and the *familia*, the latter being an extended household family under the power of the eldest surviving male ancestor while the former was a wider grouping, in theory based on common descent. The Welsh *cenedl* and the Latin *gens* are derived from a common linguistic root meaning birth. They postulate the common descent of *plant*, children, to form a *clan*. *Plant* and *clan* are also derived from a common linguistic root.[52] A biblical parallel exists in the notion of the twelve tribes of Israel being descendants of the twelve sons of Jacob from which they took their names. Each Roman's name identified both the *gens* and the *familia* to which he or she belonged: Julius Caesar, for example, being a member of the *gens Julia* and of the family *Caesar*, his personal name or *praenomen* being Gaius. Interestingly, it was the name of the *gens* that was called *nomen*, the name.

Status within the native laws was generally dependent upon birth, although it could be determined by office or the tenure of land.[53] The highest class was that pertaining to royalty, to which members of the king's *cenedl* belonged. Among the royal houses, claims were made for the primacy of the royal house of Gwynedd, although these claims are believed to have been advanced by texts which are associated with that kingdom, namely *Llyfr Iorwerth* and *Llyfr Colan* among the Welsh traditions and Latin Redactions B, C and E. Thereafter, social divisions depended upon whether a person was Welsh or a foreigner, and whether he was free or unfree.

Free-born Welshmen fell into one of two classes. The former consisted of the nobility or gentry, the *gwŷr bonheddig* or *uchelwyr*. These were the people who were of gentle birth, gentlemen and women, the gentry – all terms connected with *geni* to be born and therefore with the Latin *gens*. To this class, there attached certain privileges. The *uchelwyr* could hunt freely, and only they were entitled to enter certain professions, such as that of advocate, judge, bard, priest or smith. Those of lower status needed permission to become judges, bards, priests or smiths and would acquire the higher rank upon admission to the profession, although the higher status would then be personal to them and would not pass to their children, unless the child followed the father in the profession.[54] A grant of higher status would also attach to residence within a *tref* where a church was consecrated, as the Church disliked variations of status amongst its tenants and frequently had its lands granted and regranted specifically to achieve this end.[55] Gentle status also followed from the grant of one of the twenty-four privileged offices attached to the royal court.[56]

The *aillt* or *taeog* class were also free in the sense that they were not slaves, but their freedom was subject to restriction when compared with that of the *uchelwyr*. It has been suggested that this class was originally formed of the Goidelic peoples who inhabited Wales before the British or Brythonic tribes occupied the land forcing the Goidels into a position of social inferiority.[57] It has also been claimed that these people originally traced their descent and pedigree through the female rather than the male line, a custom which the Romans thought to be common to most of mankind other than themselves.[58] The Welsh customs traced descent patrilineally in much the same way as the Romans had. The *aillt* or *taeog* while free was tied to the land which he worked in *trefi* which operated different systems of land tenure from those enjoyed by the nobility. While a *taeog* got his status by birth, it was possible to purchase the higher status by payment of a fine to the king and thereafter receive a royal grant,[59] in a manner not dissimilar to that in which Roman citizenship had sometimes been purchased.[60]

While the *taeog* class were not unlike the bondmen or villeins of neighbouring medieval England, they were not slaves. Medieval Wales did admit of slavery, the group classified as *caeth*. As in Roman law, slavery followed from hostile capture, that is, capture in time of war. Slaves were spared the sword at the cost of their freedom. Thereafter, they were classified as property and not as persons; they were the human spoils of war. Slavery could also be the fate of native Welshmen and of foreigners enslaved other than in wartime. Thus, enslavement followed upon purchase as a slave or upon a free person deliberately selling himself or herself into slavery, again a possibility that existed in Roman law. Slavery was also a possible punishment for theft, and interestingly, it was only for theft that a Welsh owner was liable for the wrongdoing of his slave.[61] Slaves could be freed, and a record of such a manumission survives in the marginalia to the Lichfield Gospels, describing a grant of freedom from Llandeilo Fawr.

A foreigner or *alltud* upon Welsh soil enjoyed certain privileges. The custom of the Welsh was that such a visitor was not to be refused food and hospitality. If an *alltud* became embroiled in litigation, he was to enjoy the services of an advocate free of charge and if commended to a lord was answerable at law through his superior. This somewhat generous treatment of foreigners was markedly dissimilar to that which obtained in Anglo-Saxon customs and amongst the Germanic laws generally, although it bears similarity with both the Irish approach and that of the Burgundian laws of Gundobad.[62] A foreign family who stayed in Wales under the commendation of a lord and remained on the same land under the patronage of the same lordly family for four generations would become free Welsh of the *taeog* class, so-called *alltud cenedlauc*, as they had established a kindred group for themselves.[63] If they intermarried with Welsh families, two customs are recorded. One, the older and derived from the triadic literature, asserts that they became Welsh in the fourth generation only if they intermarried with free Welsh people in every intervening generation. The evidence for this custom is virtually nil and it is much at odds with the custom of *mamwys* described in the native law books which permitted the sons of a free-born *Cymraes* who had been given in marriage by her family (known as marriage by *rhodd cenedl*) to a foreigner, to succeed with their uncles to the lands of their maternal grandfather.[64] The method of succession described here relates to *uchelwyr* and such intermarriage therefore not only quickened the process of naturalization and provided a better result for the children, but would have had to contend with any reluctance on the part of gentry families to allow their daughters to marry foreigners. The older rule accords with the other methods of acquiring Welsh *taeog* status by four generations under one lord but links the grant with intermarriage rather than feudal loyalty, and may be evidence of the move from tribal to feudal principles in Welsh society.

Status was reflected in the payment which had to be made to a person for deliberate insult, *sarhad*. This, like *cenedl*, was another of the concepts which

Professor Norah Chadwick identified as a principal feature of an ancient pan-Celtic way of life.[65] *Sarhad* however also has many features in common with the Roman law concept of *iniuria*, which by the time of Roman settlement in Britain had also become a payment for deliberate insult. The essence of *sarhad* was not harm or damage suffered by an individual, but the hurt to the person's honour and the possible shame, *gwaradwydd*, attached thereto. Such an affront could only be requited by the taking of vengeance, *dial*, the payment of compensation or the reconciliation of the parties. This approach to insult is evident from the literature of the period, for instance the *Mabinogion*.[66] Whether the literature reflects an ancient Celtic notion or the result of the successive impacts of Roman and Christian culture upon the initial Celtic idea is debatable, but there are clear resemblances with the Roman delict of *iniuria*. Both required intention, so that an unintentional blow, while compensatable, could not amount to *sarhad*. Likewise, the need for intention ruled out the possibility of a person lacking the capacity to commit an intentional act – such as a child or a deranged person – being liable for *sarhad*. In Welsh law, unlike Roman law, this meant that none could be liable for the acts of another in this regard; only the actual offender was liable. The law texts set out the compensation that must be payable to persons according to their status and worth, from the king down through his courtiers to the *uchelwyr*, and those of lower status. The *sarhad* payable to the *uchelwr* was the mean, all other payments being multiples or fractions thereof. There is however evidence that the honour-prices, as they are sometimes called, within the codes were maxima which could be reduced if such was the custom of the locality, in which case the amount to be paid was to be decided by arbitrators.[67] In *iniuria* also the magistrate would fix the maximum amount payable and the judge would then have the discretion to make an award up to, but not exceeding, that amount. One interesting feature of the Welsh laws is that they allotted an honour-price to unborn children, being fractions of what would be payable according to their status had they actually been born. In north Wales, one-third was payable during the first three months of pregnancy, two-thirds during the second period of three months, and the full price thereafter. In the south, the rule was different, four shillings being payable in the first three months (or sixty pence according to one source), one-third during the second three months and one-half thereafter.[68] Such protection for the unborn suggests ecclesiastical influence, as indeed does the heavy emphasis upon the need for intention, although this was also present in Roman law but not to the extent of precluding vicarious liability for the insults of those for whom one was generally answerable at law.

Status for the purpose of compensation for *sarhad* was in part dependent upon whether one was married. Marriage according to the native customs was a secular arrangement rather than a spiritual one and therefore, as in Roman law, it was dissoluble.[69] This was very much at odds with the teachings of the Christian Church and was to result in tensions between the Church and the

Welsh traditionalists. Nor did the Welsh laws find any difficulty in allowing the marriage of clergy and the inheritance of their ecclesiastical offices by their children, even in monastic settings.[70] Married women held property in their own right, and their standing within the *cenedl* of their birth was not affected by their marriage.[71] On marriage, women came under the protection, *nawdd*, of their husbands, but continued to enjoy rights in their original family.[72]

Being a secular arrangement, marriage was dependent upon the consent of the immediate parties and of the wife's *cenedl*. Such a marriage was normative and was described as being by *rhodd cenedl*. The contract was entered into verbally in the presence of witnesses, with the wife's family granting her a dowry, called her *gwaddol*, and her husband also giving her a share of property as her own, namely her *agweddi*. She also took with her into marriage her personal paraphernalia or *argyfreu*, and would receive from her husband after consummation of the union a gift called the *cowyll*. The husband was also bound to pay to the wife's lord an *amobr*, a payment for the taking of her virginity.[73] By and large, these features of marriage are present in most other legal systems, including Roman law, but are more especially similar here to the Germanic customs.[74] No ceremony was required, although the customs associated with south-west Wales in *Llyfr Blegywryd* and the Latin Redaction D use the modern term *priodas* for ecclesiastical wedding exclusively.[75]

Much has been written concerning the law relating to prohibited degrees and the Welsh customs, largely due to the strictures of twelfth- and thirteenth-century ecclesiastics concerning the regularity of 'incest' among the Welsh. This allegation is totally misunderstood if thought to apply to carnal knowledge with close relatives in the sense used to define the modern crime. The western Church considerably extended the prohibited degrees of marriage with the inevitable result that a substantially greater number of unions became classified as 'incestuous'. The Church prohibited unions within six degrees of a common ancestor. This resulted from an amalgamation of the Roman number of degrees and the Germanic method of calculating them. In Roman law, degrees of relationship were counted up to the common ancestor and then back down to the relative. Six degrees therefore extended no further than second cousins. The Germanic system however calculated degrees of relationship by counting down from the common ancestor, so that second cousins were related in the third degree. The 'incest' of the Welsh therefore lay in their countenancing of intermarriage with third, fourth and fifth cousins. In fact, classical Roman law allowed intermarriage provided the parties were each more than one degree distant from a common ancestor and the medieval Church was prepared to grant dispensations for persons within the third and fourth degree of relationship to marry. The Welsh evil on this count certainly lay in the novel perspective of the beholder.[76]

In Roman law, marriage was based upon the consent of the parties and the termination of consent on the part of either brought the relationship to an end. If the wish to terminate was shared, it was called divorce; if it was on one side only, it was repudiation. Welsh law knew of both, and was therefore closer to Roman law in its approach to the termination of marriage than either English law or the Germanic customs, let alone the law of the Church. It was permissible for the couple to separate at any time by mutual agreement or repudiation of one spouse by the other. If the marriage was dissolved within the first seven years of its existence by agreement of the parties, the wife was entitled to take with her, her *agweddi*, the *gwaddol* she had brought with her, her *cowyll* and her *argyfreu*. If the parties separated after seven years, each was entitled to one-half of the matrimonial property which would be split according to elaborate rules contained in the law books. The same division of property was to be effected upon the death of either spouse. If the parties separated within seven years as a result of one repudiating the other, then their respective rights depended upon whether the repudiation was with or without cause. The husband was entitled to repudiate his wife for her immorality after marriage, loss of virginity before marriage or underpayment of her *gwaddol* by her family. She was entitled to repudiate him for three adulteries, impotency, fetid breath or leprosy, or if he introduced a concubine into the matrimonial home. Such an intruder is referred to by the biblical expression 'strange woman'. A wife repudiated with cause had no rights whatsoever; a wife repudiating without cause had to forfeit her *agweddi* and her *gwaddol*, and return home with only her *cowyll* and any compensation payment, *gowyn*, her husband had had to pay her for a first or second adultery. According to some north Walian sources, she was not even allowed to keep her *argyfreu*.[77]

Marriage could be contracted according to the Welsh customs by boys who had reached the age of 14 and by girls who had attained the age of 12. These are the same ages as were employed in Roman law and which the Church's canon law adopted from that source. Although girls were of marriageable age at 12, the Welsh laws state firmly that they should not bear children until they were 14 and that the period for childbearing should extend from that time until they were 40.[78] The age of 14 for boys was the age of majority. At that age, a youth would originally have been commended to his *pencenedl*, but in later times, with the advancement of the feudal over the tribal principle, such commendation was to the lord. From the lord, the young man would eventually, on reaching the age of 21, receive cattle and possibly land, but would have to perform military service.[79] Such fostering of the children of warriors in the houses of the nobility was a long-standing tradition among the Welsh.[80]

A child's father did not have the extensive powers of a Roman *paterfamilias*. Instead, the father was seen as the child's proper guardian, the laws stating that 'a son should have a guardian over him until he is fourteen years old', the father being the proper guardian if living, the lord appointing one otherwise.[81] Again, it would appear that the lord had been substituted for the *pencenedl* with regard to this function. A father who physically disciplined a child who had reached majority was liable for having committed a wrong.

As in Rome, the life of a young person progressed in seven-year segments. From birth to age 7, a child was incapable of wrongdoing and entering into legal relationships. From 7 to 14 (12 in the case of girls), some guidance in the accomplishment of legal undertakings was given in preparation for reaching majority, together with spiritual direction from a priest and any other appropriate education. From 14 to 21, a young man was receiving military training from his lord.[82] Young women would have started childbearing. Significantly perhaps, marriages undertaken at an early age would have been dissoluble without substantial property loss during these early years.

Children born to a married woman were presumed to be the children of her husband, but Welsh law also regarded children born out of wedlock as the responsibility of their natural father and as equal to those of his children born within marriage. In effect, unlike most legal systems, the Welsh customs did not categorize persons as legitimate or illegitimate. A child born outside of marriage could be affiliated by admission of the father and would therefore be a full child of the father in every way. Problems arose when the father did not freely accept his responsibility or denied the allegation of paternity. Allegations of paternity could be made by the mother to her parish priest immediately prior to the child's birth, that is, when her life was in some danger, or when the child reached the age of 14 by going to a church and swearing that the child was the alleged father's by taking an oath with one hand on the child and one hand on the altar or the relics. If the mother were dead, her *pencenedl* could swear that the child was the alleged father's, provided his oath was supported by that of seven kinsmen, a number reminiscent of the required number of participants in the Roman ceremony of *mancipatio*.[83] In the absence of the *pencenedl*, the oaths of fifty kinsmen were required. It was then for the putative father to admit paternity or rebut the oaths. If he chose to admit or if he failed to rebut the oaths, the child became his, as would be the case if more than a year and a day elapsed and he had done nothing. Moreover, during this period, his family were liable for the child as though it were indeed his, while they had no rights respecting the child which could benefit them, thus ensuring that it was in their interest to bring about a speedy conclusion to the issue. If the father chose to deny, this he would have to do by taking an oath in church with one hand on the child and one on the altar or the relics, or if the putative father were dead, his *pencenedl* with seven kinsmen had to deny his paternity or, in the absence of the *pencenedl*, fifty of the deceased's kinsmen. The oath, of whatever kind, if achieved, was conclusive of the issue. If the required number failed to swear, the paternity was proven and the child was affiliated to the family.[84]

Affiliation was important in that it defined those whose obligation it was to claim and pay *galanas* if a person suffered or committed homicide. It was also important in that issue had rights to succeed to family property and in the case of male issue to land. According to the native tradition, the family land was vested in the head of the family unit, the oldest surviving male ancestor, the *penteulu*.[85] *Gwŷr bonheddig*, the gentry class, enjoyed land as a family group, the *gwely*, which extended across four generations. On the death of a *penteulu*, the family land, the *tir gwelyawc*, passed to the deceased's sons, who succeeded to it jointly.[86] In other words, they were joint owners of the whole rather than owners of equal portions, in the same manner as had been the case under the Roman *consortium*. This method of inheriting land was also very similar to that which operated in medieval Ireland. In Wales it was known as sharing, *cyfran*, and there is some evidence that its roots within Wales extend back to the practice of the Iron Age,[87] so that it was a native tradition of long-standing rather than a borrowing from either Roman or Irish law. Attention has also been drawn to the fact that evidence of such peaceful homestead settlements continuing from the Iron Age through the Roman period down to the later Christian epoch exists for the Isle of Man, where as in Ireland and Wales each was known as a *rhath*.[88] This is particularly interesting given the possible connection between Man and Merfyn Frych's ascent to the rulership of Gwynedd in 825.

The practice of *cyfran* extended beyond one generation. On the death of an *uchelwr*, his family land passed to his sons in equal but undivided shares. If a son had predeceased his father, that son's share went to his sons. Daughters had no part in this succession, although a land charter from Llancarfan in the Vale of Glamorgan records two brothers and a sister inheriting the family land in that part of south-east Wales, which is interesting given that lingering Roman influences were strongest in that region and that Roman law allowed sons and daughters to participate in the succession to the family property on equal terms.[89] When the last of the sons had died, a further sharing or *cyfran* took place, whereby the grandsons of the first owner took in equal and undivided shares. This was repeated on one further occasion upon the death of the last of the grandsons to die, when the great-grandsons inherited. Thereafter, the next generation would trace their entitlement only as far back as their respective great-grandfather, who would be one of the sons of the first owner. The *gwely* endured for four generations only.

Although each generation took in equal and undivided shares, to manage the land it was necessary for them to distribute the land amongst themselves as a group. This duty fell to the youngest son in the first generation, and thereafter to the youngest son of the youngest son or grandson. The youngest divided the land into the requisite number of portions, and then each son, beginning with the eldest, chose which portion was to be his. The youngest got whatever was left over, thus ensuring that, when he made the initial divisions, he would strive to achieve a sharing which was equal in quality and quantity for his own sake. The youngest son was however entitled to the homestead, the *rhath*, and eight *erwau* of land, and if he was intending to keep the homestead, partition was carried out by the next youngest so as to achieve equality. The youngest son was therefore expected to remain resident in his father's house until the father died,[90] in the same manner as was widespread among the Germanic tribes. The father was not able to devise the youngest son's share to any other of his children, each of whom was notionally entitled to a *rhath* and eight *erwau*.

The system of *cyfran* was to survive in Wales throughout the medieval period. It is sometimes assumed that it inevitably led to landholdings becoming smaller and smaller in each generation. This would have been the case if fertility rates were high and every son produced several male offspring. The reality would appear to have been different. There is no evidence of any land shortage in Wales prior to the invasion of the Normans, so that *cyfran* cannot be taken to be a contributing factor to any such shortage in later times, and such evidence as exists suggests that fertility rates were not high, with two, three or four surviving male children being the norm in families of the highest status,[91] with possibly fewer children surviving lower down the social ladder. Nor should one discount the possibility that, in order to reduce the level of partition in families, some brothers would deliberately choose not to marry so that the land would continue in one line of descent. Such practices are known to have occurred even in recent generations,[92] and would give an interesting context from which to assess the importance of affiliation in the case of the issue of unmarried males who wished to remain childless for reasons of the family wealth.

While the land and the homesteads would be distributed amongst the sons, some forms of property would not, continuing in undivided joint ownership. These included mills, fisheries and an enclosure (*llan*) of any sort.[93] There was no obligation to mill at the lord's mill in Wales unlike England, and mills apparently remained family rather than feudal enterprises.[94]

One of the consequences of the system of *cyfran* operating in relation to *tir gwelyawc* was that the interests of successive generations overrode those of the present owners, making alienation difficult if not quite impossible. A wrongful alienation could be rectified by the heirs in the next generation recovering the land alienated by means of the action called the *gofyniad*,[95] provided they were prepared to return the consideration for the transfer, the *wrth prid*, to the disappointed purchaser. Possible disputes about the amount due, if any, led in later law to any such transfers by sale having to be recorded in the record of the appropriate court, in much the same manner as the English fine and the manner in which authenticated court records came to be used to prove transactions in Lombard and later other continental systems of law. While total alienation was therefore very difficult, it was perfectly possible for a participant in the *gwely* to let his land on a yearly basis either gratuitously (*benffyc*) or for payment (*llog*), a distinction which reflects exactly that between the *commodatum* (loan for use) and *locatio/conductio* (lease or hire of land) in Roman law.[96] Land could be alienated to make up a shortfall of other wealth when a family had to compensate for a homicide with a payment of *galanas*. Such land was known as *waed tir*, blood land.[97]

The longest period for which an individual was able to alienate land with any security for the transferee was the period of the transferor's life, in itself of uncertain length. To accomplish a permanent alienation, the consent of everyone in the *gwely* was required, together with that of the lord of the land.[98] From the perspective of the law books, all land must have a lord, an inherently feudal view. One suspects that originally it would have been the head of the tribe, the *pencenedl*, whose consent would have been needed and for the same reason, namely that if the family line, the *gwely*, died out, the land would revert to the wider kin.[99] With feudalism, it would pass into the lord's waste and be available for redistribution at a later time. The lord's consent was therefore needed to ensure that his interest was not affected if and when the family line was extinguished.

The law books record that kings controlled gifts of land and allotments from their waste to foreigners.[100] The lord's consent was also needed for any alienation to a church prior to consecration,[101] and such grants were required to be confirmed by the king each time a new king came to rule.[102] Thus, all Church land was held of the king within Wales, that is it had been taken out of the system of *tir gwelyawc*,[103] but the practice also indicates that the Church was not independent of the king in Wales but definitely subordinate to him. This was also indicated by the fact that no right of sanctuary was admissible within Wales without royal grant. Kings had much greater control over the Church in Welsh law than in either English law or the Germanic customs.[104] This may be token of a survival of the relative positions of the secular and spiritual authorities in the later Roman empire. Priests however enjoyed their lands as *tir gwelyawc* with their families.[105]

Another similarity with Roman practice emerges with regard to the demarcation of separate land units. The Romans had insisted on boundaries being evidenced by clear liminal zones of fixed width. The Welsh laws also employ this practice, requiring two furrows between each *erw*, three or four feet between each *rhandir*, five feet or one-and-a-half fathoms between *trefi*, seven feet between each *cwmwd* and nine feet between neighbouring *cantrefi*.[106]

The arrangements described above related to the landholding of the gentry. Those of *taeog* status held their lands not by *cyfran* but by *cyfrif*. *Tir cyfrif*, which was also the system of landholding in *trefgefery*, required that all the land in the *tref* was held in common by the male inhabitants. In the *maerdref*, control of the holdings was in the hands of the *maer*, the king's officer. He allocated land to each male every year to produce crops of his choosing for the king. Each *tref* in *tir cyfrif* was bound to supply the king with a fixed quantity of produce. This did not vary with the number of inhabitants; if the population declined, the obligations did not decrease. This distinguished *tir cyfrif* and *trefgefery* on the one hand from *treweloghe* on the other, for in the latter the obligation was distributed among the holdings within the *tref* so that no inhabitant's obligation increased if other holdings fell vacant. As sons came of age within *tir cyfrif*, they received allocations of their own, separate from that of their father to which they had no rights of succession, having been provided for already within the *tref* – that is apart from the youngest son, who was required to remain with his father for as long as the latter lived, and thereafter succeeded to his father's holding.[107]

Succession to land, *tir*, was confined to males, who were required to pay to the lord, possibly originally to the *pencenedl*, an *ebidew* when they inherited the property. This was not unlike the relief or *heriot* payable in English law, and the amount of the *ebidew* varied with the status of the deceased.[108] Other forms of property were referred to as *da*, goods, and were inheritable by all of the deceased's children. When a person died, the moveable family property was divided into two halves, one-half of which went to the surviving spouse. There was therefore no dower[109] or curtesy required under Welsh law once a couple had been married seven years and the right to *agweddi* had ended. The deceased's half was then divided amongst the children, daughters getting one-half of a son's share, the sons taking equally. In south Wales, however, it would appear that daughters took equally with the sons, perhaps once more a reflection of the continuation of Roman influence in those parts.[110] Daughters were given their share as *gwaddol* in readiness for their marriage upon their twelfth birthday, and did not thereafter receive a second tranche. Deceased sons were represented by their issue, as were those who were not permitted to inherit by reason of some blemish, such as insanity, leprosy or crippled limbs, the same disabilities as precluded succession to the king.[111] Those who inherited land were liable for the debts of their deceased ancestor.[112]

It would appear that testamentary disposition was originally limited to making provision for the payment of debts. Under ecclesiastical influence, gifts upon death to the Church, *daered*, also came to be deemed lawful, and it was provided that a son who failed to pay his deceased parent's debts or to comply with the deceased's wishes regarding *daered* was to be excommunicated.[113] Any other bequest, *cymyn*, did not obligate the heirs, albeit a son who failed to honour such gifts was deemed 'uncourteous'.[114] The power to make testamentary gifts of moveable property in Wales as in other parts of Europe was probably developed by the Church, and the excommunication of a son who refused to pay the Church the *daered* given may reflect a reluctance on the part of Welsh families to accept that such testamentary gifts were any different from others which could be avoided.[115]

As in the works of the Roman jurists, the Welsh law books address the question of how property was acquired. Water, air and land were open to all, so that unoccupied land was available to be possessed. If it were possessed, the first possessor was regarded as one who had come to the land, *gŵr dyfod*. Unlike the situation in Roman law, his occupation of unowned land did not make him an owner, *priodawr*. What he obtained was *gwarchadw*, just possession, which would ripen into *priodolder* right, ownership, after the land had been in the just possession of the family for four generations. In other words, he, his sons and grandsons had *gwarchadw*, but the great-grandsons would be *priodorion*. *Gwarchadw* was a method of acquisitive prescription; it gave the occupier title by lapse of time, but the occupation had to be uninterrupted or else it had to restart. *Gwarchadw* could not commence against the will, without the knowledge of or by agreement with a previous owner, rules which mirror the Roman rule that just possession could not be achieved by force, stealth or agreement (*nec vi, nec clam, nec precario*). Various signs of occupation were recognized, including building and tilling of the land, together with the presence of little children, dogs and cockerels which were deemed the three signs of inhabitation.[116] Some property, such as forests, quarries, mills and fishing weirs, was not capable of being appropriated, but surprisingly this did not apply to land owned by the Church, a further indication of the subordinate position of the Church with regard to landholding under the laws of Wales.[117]

A period of four generations for land to be acquired might appear very long compared with the two years only demanded for *usucapio* of immoveable property in classical Roman law. However, it must be remembered that *usucapio* only applied to land in Italy. In the provinces, *longi temporis praescriptio* required up to twenty years' continuous possession.[118] Claims by previous owners were barred after the passage of three lifetimes. *Llyfr Cyfnerth* from the south-east gives sixty years as equivalent to a lifetime, so that allowing for over-lapping generations three lifetimes might be taken to be roughly a century.[119] It is significant that Welsh law had such limitation periods, unlike Germanic custom which had none and Irish law which knew little of them.[120]

The law books also discuss the acquisition of other forms of property in a manner which is very reminiscent of the works of the Roman jurists. From these discussions, it is learnt that fishing in rivers, fish being a very important product in the Wales of that time,[121] was freely open to lords and free tenants, permission only being necessary to build traps or weirs. If fish were caught by such devices when no permission for their use had been given, then the fish caught had to be divided between the lord and the captor, the latter still getting two-thirds.[122] This looks like a compromise solution between the Roman rule that the captor took all and the feudal notion that fishing was the lord's preserve, and many such compromises are evidenced in the law books.[123]

The discussion of the pursuit of wild animals is remarkably similar to that contained in the Roman texts, with many of the same problems considered, although compromise solutions feature. Thus, it is provided that one who shoots at a hart in the king's forest from the highway is entitled to pursue the creature if he hits it, but only until the beast escapes from his sight, from which moment he must leave it alone. If he caught it, the beast was his. If such a hart was shot and pursued on the land of another and taken, the landowner received a quarter of the beast and the hunter three-quarters, again a compromise between the landowner's claims and those of the captor. Hunting, like fishing, was free, with only certain birds and animals being reserved to the king – ravens, buzzards, cranes, beavers, martens and ermines.[124]

The Roman writers also devoted space to problems associated with bee-keeping, and it is known that bees were kept in early medieval Wales and that honey was a very important product, both in its own right and for use in the production of beer and mead.[125] Again, compromise solutions feature and they vary from one part of Wales to another, a clear indication that the solutions are of later date than the original law texts, suggesting they may reflect the influence of the Normans. In the north, a person who found a swarm of bees on the land of another had to surrender the swarm to the landowner and was only entitled to a penny or the wax for his trouble. In Gwent, the same solution is presented with a slightly different emphasis, in that ownership is given to the finder unless the landowner chooses to purchase the swarm for either a penny or the wax, while in Dyfed, the landowner has to pay four pence for the privilege.[126]

Although the tensions between the rights of the finder and those of the land-owner may be ascribed to a clash between the native customs and incoming feudal principles, it should also be borne in mind that such tensions had also been present in Roman law, where, for instance, there was a long-running conflict as to who should have title to treasure trove, with various compromises being attempted from time to time between the interests of the landowner, the finder and the state.[127] In Welsh law, everything a *priodawr* found concealed on his land belonged to him, apart from gold and silver which went to the king.[128] Likewise, the spoils of war were, with the exception of gold, silver, precious stones, buffalo horns, gold-embroidered clothing, goats, furs, arms and prisoners, to be divided amongst the soldiers who captured them. Goods recovered after warfare were to be divided between the recoverer and the previous owner.[129]

A ship which was wrecked before port dues had been paid belonged to the king if he claimed it, but otherwise went to the first taker. If the wreck grounded on bishop land, the property was shared half-and-half between the bishop and the king, an interesting and unusual compromise with the ecclesiastical authorities. Once port dues had been paid, the owner of the vessel could claim the property as his own.[130] Likewise, dead fish washed up on the shore were available to the king for three tides, but then available to the first taker. These rules were justified on the basis that the sea was the king's packhorse, a principle which may hark back to ancient native ideas of what came from the water being a divine gift.[131] The same might be true of living things found upon land, for an animal which was found did not become the property of the finder. Instead, it had to be taken to the lord and proclaimed as lost property. If claimed, it went back to its owner; if not, it became part of the lord's waste, a term which clearly included any property which was left without an owner or lawful possessor.[132]

Timber could be cut freely from the king's forest to furnish repairs to a church roof or to fashion a spear or a funeral bier. Likewise, timber could be cut from private woods without any payment to the owner if the purpose was to employ it for roofing.[133] If the timber was used, however, to build a house on another's land without the permission of that other, *camlwrw* had to be paid to the king for the offence and the house belonged to the owner of the land unless the timber had come from elsewhere and could be removed without damage to the site, in which case it was to be removed within nine days and if not removed passed into the ownership of the landowner.[134] This discussion in the law books of the south-east bears some resemblance to that of *inaedificatio* in the works of the Roman jurists, together with the rule about reclaiming the materials, but much of the Roman sophistication is absent.

Such sophistication is however notably present in the law books' discussion of contractual obligations, where many of the distinctions made echo those of the Roman jurists. The laws differentiate clearly between loans for consumption (*echwyn*), use (*benffyg*), safe-keeping (*adneu*) and the pledge of moveables (*gwystl*), distinctions which mirror exactly those between *mutuum*, *commodatum*, *depositum* and *pignus* in Roman law.[135] Moreover, *benffyg*, loan for use, is distinguished from *llog*, hire, in the same manner as *commodatum* differed from *locatio/conductio*, namely the presence of a reciprocal payment.[136] It is likely that the word *llog* is derived from the Latin *locatio* or at least the root verb, *locare*. Like *locatio/conductio*, the contract of *llog* in Welsh law was consensual, that is, it was based upon the agreement or meeting of minds of the parties rather than the transfer of the property or the payment, no formalities being required. In one respect, however, the Welsh law relating to *llog* appears more sophisticated than the Roman *locatio/conductio*. The hirer of an animal was not liable, as in Roman law, for any accidental loss arising out of use within the terms of the agreement, but if he exceeded those terms he became liable.[137] Whereas Roman law regarded such excessive use as a form of theft, *furtum usus*, Welsh custom went further and, as well as imposing a fine for unlawful taking, required the hirer to hand over to the owner a third of any profit he had acquired by virtue of his unlawful conduct.[138] In effect, this was a remedy for unjust enrichment.

One major difference between the Welsh laws and Roman law was their refusal to differentiate between sale and exchange, both of which were termed *cyfnewid*. In effect, Welsh law treated sale as a form of exchange. The reason for this may have been connected with the absence of any minting of money in Wales prior to the Norman invasion.[139] Although a coin bearing Hywel Dda's imprint remains, it was minted at Chester. *Cyfnewid* was, like *llog* and the Roman contract of sale *emptio/venditio*, a consensual contract, but required the formality of a hand clasp and the presence of witnesses to be valid. What is particularly interesting is that there had been a juristic dispute between the Sabinian and Proculian schools of jurisprudence at Rome as to whether the price in a contract of sale had to be in money or could be in the form of some other property, essentially confounding the concepts of sale and exchange. The Sabinians were prepared to allow the price to be in money's worth rather than money, but ultimately the Proculian view prevailed. It is interesting that the Welsh laws favour the opposite conclusion. Another similarity with the Roman rules on sale concerns the warranties that were inherent in the contract with regard to the soundness of animals exchanged. Such *teithi* were very detailed in the Welsh laws,[140] more detailed than what has survived of the warranties required under the edict of the curule aediles who controlled sales in the markets of ancient Rome. One wonders whether modern knowledge of the terms of the aedilician edict is confined to a fraction as the result of the selective nature of the extracts chosen by Justinian's compilers or whether the Welsh customs expanded upon the basis of the original Roman rules, if indeed the Welsh laws were derived from that source.

Contractual agreements could be entered into according to the law books in one of three ways. The simplest was possibly the *briduw*, a formal oath to do or not do some thing, calling upon God to be a witness to the obligation. Such a promise, reminiscent in some ways of the Roman verbal contracts but with clearer religious elements, could be enforced either before the king or by the Church.[141] It is likely that the Church claimed jurisdiction over such promises because of the religious dimension but that the contractual form predated that ecclesiastical jurisdiction. Contractual obligations could also be entered into by means of a hand clasp before witnesses, a distinctly Germanic formality, in which the contract was termed an *amod deddfol*, and the taking of sureties was sometimes added to this making the contract one of *mechnïaeth*. A surety replaced the party to the agreement as regards liability in case of default and was entitled to take a pledge, *gwystl*, from the contracting party to coerce performance.[142] The laws prohibited the taking of a person's only overgarment as a pledge, in a manner reminiscent of biblical law.[143] A surety's liability passed to his descendants if they received assets from him upon his death.[144] Fraud or coercion nullified agreement, *amod*, in a manner similar to the effects of *dolus* and *metus* in Roman law.[145]

Obligations could also arise from wrongdoing, and the Welsh laws were particularly concerned with liability for homicide, theft and arson, the so-called three columns of the law.[145a] Punishment and compensation went hand in hand under the native customs, in the same manner as in the English appeal of felony. While a killing had to be intentional for the killer to be punished, it was not necessary for any intention to be present for the death to require compensation.[146] Therefore, if the wrongdoer were suffering from some incapacity, such as being below the age of 7, mentally unsound, deaf or dumb, intoxicated, or acting under duress or some other form of compulsion, no punishment would be due but reparation would have to be made. In the case of a child between the ages of 7 and 14, punishment would be confined to the father having to pay a *dirwy*, that is, a heavy fine.[147]

This victim-based approach to wrongdoing required that compensation be paid if the victim had not deserved to suffer. Thus, no compensation was payable if the victim had deserved to die. In such circumstances, the killing was said to be justifiable. This was so not only with lawful execution but where revenge was taken against a killer when his family failed to pay the appropriate compensation, where a wife killed her husband's concubine, where outlaws or traitors were captured and put to death, when thieves were taken in the king's chamber at night and when ferocious men were dispatched.[148] Compensation was however due in the case of an accidental killing, because the victim was undeserving of his fate, but not if the act causing death was justifiable, so that killing an innocent bystander while attempting a justifiable killing was excused, as was causing the death of a person one was attempting to rescue.[149] A physician, however, was liable for the death of a wounded man to whom he gave treatment and was advised therefore to take assurances against his liability.[150] This would appear to be an application of the maxim *imperitia culpae adnumeratur*, that skill increases blameworthiness, so that higher standards are required of professionals. Certain kinds of homicide were regarded as particularly heinous, so that compensation was doubled. These included killing by ambush, in secret, upon premeditation, concealing the deed, killing privily by night, killing with savage violence or through the use of poison.[151] Certain persons were privileged in being able to escape punishment even for killing, namely the king, a priest – who would be answerable before the Church courts – and a bard,[152] the last two or all possibly being interesting survivals of the privileges attaching to Druidic status.

Generally, there was no liability in homicide without some act on the part of another; an omission would not suffice. However, if the owner of a spear left it in circumstances which rendered it a danger to others and someone died as a result of what was in effect the owner's negligence, the owner became liable to pay one-third of the compensation that would have ordinarily been due for the undeserved death of the victim.[153] This extension of the normal rule is reminiscent of the manner in which the Roman law regarding the wrongful causing of harm, *damnum iniuria datum*, which was originally confined to directly caused harms by the body to the body, *corpori corpore*, was extended to cover harm caused as a consequence of wrongful conduct, such as that of the negligent owner of the spear, which was *corpori non corpore*, to the body but not by the body.

The compensation payable, indeed the wrong of unlawful killing, was termed *galanas*. It was payable by the family of the slayer to that of the slain, and there were elaborate rules relating to the distribution of the liability and benefit among the two groups respectively. The payment was meant to buy off the vengeance of the other group and prevent a blood feud arising. Failure to pay therefore meant that vengeance could still be wrought, but significantly only against the actual slayer and not against his kin.[154] This reflects both the refusal in Roman law to allow liability for wrongdoing to pass to the heirs of the delinquent and the Bible's injunctions against visiting the sins of the father upon the children.[155] The payment of *galanas* was divided into thirds. One-third was due from the killer, his father and mother, and his brothers and sisters. Amongst these, the killer himself was responsible for the payment of one-third, and the other members of the group for the remaining two-thirds, each male being responsible for double that paid by each female. The killer also had to pay *sarhad* to the father, mother, brothers, sisters and any surviving spouse of the slain, one-third going to any surviving spouse. The remaining two-thirds of the *galanas* had to be paid by the remoter relatives of the killer, extending back as far as the great-grandparents and collaterally as far as fifth cousins; in all, nine degrees of relationship. The paternal kin were responsible for two-thirds of this payment, the maternal kin for one-third, and within each kin group, the nearer relatives paid double that of the next remote degree. The payment was then shared among the deceased's family in the same manner and to the same extent. Descendants of the killer were not liable to pay.[156] If the family of the homicide did not have sufficient moveable property to meet their liability to the family of the victim, they were entitled to alienate their *gwely* land to meet their obligation, such land being known as *waed tir*, and such alienations being a major exception to the rule that *tir gwelyawc* was not alienable. The alternative of course would have been vengeance and the possibility of a blood feud.

The second of the three columns of the law was theft. Thieves, say the law books echoing the words of the Roman jurist Gaius, were hated, Welsh law stating they were hated by their own *cenedl*.[157] This hatred was manifested and justified by the particularly stringent rule that any house in which stolen goods were hidden was to be forfeited, with obviously dire results to the thief's family.[158] One can readily imagine, therefore, that there would be some resistance to a suggestion that premises should be searched, but such resistance in itself was sufficient to ground a charge of theft.[159] If someone had lost property, he was entitled to search for it and to detain it if he found it.[160] Confiscation of the family's property was only avoided if the thief had been put to death.[161] In the public domain, a thief ceased to be eligible to be a witness, a compurgator or a judge.[162]

As with homicide, proceedings for theft involved both compensation and punishment. Theft, *lladrad*, was a wrongful taking of property in the owner's absence which was subsequently denied. A secret taking which was subsequently admitted was not *lladrad* but *anghyfarch*, sometimes rendered into English as 'surreption'. This meant that, although the taking was wrongful, without consent, there was no intention to retain the thing.[163] An open taking of another's property against their will was *trais*, while the wilful destruction of another's property which rendered it useless was termed *fyrnygrwydd dywuynau*. Taking by mistake was called *anoddeu*.[164]

Only *da* could be stolen, and for the purposes of reclaiming lost or stolen property, *da* was divided into two kinds, animate and inanimate. A claim that a thing belonged to one was asserted by *arddelw*, and in relation to both kinds of *da* could be made on the basis of possession before loss or of the warranty of a third person. In the case of animals, a claim could also be based upon birth and rearing.[165]

Lladrad was either *cynharchawl* or *angynharchawl*, a distinction which is akin to the Roman manifest and non-manifest theft. *Lladrad cynharchawl* was punishable in the case of property worth more than four pence with death, while for property worth less than that amount, the culprit became a saleable thief, that is, could be sold into slavery.[166] A saleable thief could redeem himself by paying his value, £7, or else face banishment. These penalties for *lladrad cynharchawl* applied to *gwŷr bonheddig*. Thieves of the *taeog* class faced a monetary penalty of ten shillings for a first offence, £1 for a second, while for a third they were proclaimed to be a *lleidr cyhoeddog*, and sentenced to lose a limb, a sentence which was never literally executed but instead required the value of a limb to be paid in redemption.[167]

For the *lladrad angynharchawl*, there was no death penalty and trial was by compurgation.[168] The convicted *uchelwr* would have to pay a *dirwy* of £3, while for theft of less than a pennyworth a *taeog* would pay only £1 at most. For either kind of theft, priests could not be punished before the secular courts, and children who had not reached the age of majority were also unpunishable. The most curious rule however is that which absolves the so-called necessitous thief, that is one who had stolen comestibles to the value of no more than five shillings, having wandered through three *trefi* and having been unable to obtain anything to eat. This is a signal example of the Welsh duty to provide aliment to those in need being worked out in the context of its criminal provisions. The *Vita Cadoci* records slaves being punished for theft,[169] but the later law exceptionally makes their owners vicariously liable for their stealing.[170] During the eleventh century, it is known that Bleddyn ap Cynfyn considerably moderated the penalties for theft.[171]

If Welsh law's distinction between *lladrad cynharchawl* and *lladrad angynharchawl*, its provision for punishing those with stolen goods on their premises and its insistence on the right to search, all recall Roman law, there is also a fascinating echo of the older system's ritual search for stolen goods, *lance licioque*. According to the Roman jurist Gaius, who found the whole matter quite ridiculous,[172] an owner searching for his stolen property, if denied entry to another's premises would then remove all his clothes, apart possibly for a loin cloth, and then request entry bearing only a halter and a platter. If refused entry so accoutred, he was immediately entitled to recover four-fold the value of his interest in the thing stolen from the occupier, exactly the same penalty as attended discovery as a manifest thief. Refusal of the search with *lanx* and *licium* has been seen by some as sacrilegious in that the searcher appears in the attire of *Jupiter Dialis* to call upon the god to vindicate his claim. Welsh law knew what appears to be a Christianized ritual of a similar kind. The owner would confront the suspected thief with a cross in his hands and thrust it into the ground in front of the suspect. This challenged the suspect either to admit the taking and return the property, in which case the matter was at an end, or else to take an oath, the *llw gweilydd*, denying liability, which was also conclusive of the suspect's innocence. If the challenge were refused however, the suspect had to make compensation to the owner. The procedure was also used to recover debts.[173] One suspects that this ceremony reflects the Church's civilizing of a pagan original, in which a spear would have featured rather than a cross, which weapon would have been put to use if satisfaction was not forthcoming. If the suspect took the oath and the oath proved false, the charge against him would then be one of perjury, and the Church punished this as a sin, the secular courts having no jurisdiction in the matter.[174]

The three columns of the law – homicide, theft and arson – were each attended by nine abetments, three concerned with conspiring to commit the wrong, three with assistance given to the wrongdoer before its perpetration and three concerned with assistance in its commission. The influence of the Church upon this area of the law is suggested by the need for intention to be proved for there to be liability for any abetment.[175] The ninth abetment was a failure to render assistance to prevent the wrong, thus rendering a bystander who failed to intervene liable as an abettor unless he was able to establish his innocence by the oath of one hundred compurgators. If this tall order could not be met, the bad Samaritan was liable to a *camlwrw*, a less serious form of fine.[176] Those in the company of one who killed another and failed to intervene to prevent a second or third blow being struck were liable to the heavier fine, the *dirwy*. The *dirwy*, the usual penalty for serious wrongs such as theft, violence and fighting, was a mulct of twelve kine and £3, while the *camlwrw* was a fine of three kine and fifteen shillings (expressed as nine score pence).

Liability for the wrongdoing of one's human companions was to some extent more severe than for that of one's animal friends. While it was obligatory upon everyone to keep their animal from doing wrong,[177] and the purchaser of livestock was expected to get them home without harm to others,[178] liability for damage caused by dogs was limited to those known by their owners to have a dangerous proclivity,[179] while there was no liability for wild animals which had been tamed, such as a fox or a fawn.[180]

Injury to the person required compensation according to an elaborate system of tariffs based upon the worth of the individual as a whole. According to this system, the value of the tongue was one-half that of the whole body, for it was said that the tongue was the member which defended the other limbs.[181] This is an interesting perspective, as it regards eloquence rather than physical strength as being of greatest value in defending, and connects also with the reputation of the Welsh for fine speaking as recounted later by Giraldus. The testicles were valued as one-quarter of the body, and the remaining eleven limbs – the two hands, feet, eyes, ears, lips and the nose – added up to the other quarter, the whole adding up to the value of the entire body, £88.[182] Further valuations were given for smaller body parts, and twenty-four pence was payable for the shedding of blood, which *Llyfr Cyfnerth* explains as being so fixed to be less than the value placed upon Christ's blood by those who betrayed him.[183] Special rates of compensation were allotted to serious scars, the nature of which varied as between north and south Wales, and upon the three serious wounds, a wound to the head exposing the brain, a wound to the body exposing the intestines and the breaking of an arm or a leg, each of which required the payment of £3 as well as any further medical expenses.[184]

If trespasses to the person were taken very seriously, somewhat less attention was paid to incursions upon land. In Welsh law, a wrong to land required that use be made of it which impugned the owner's title. Such an incursion would involve building, ploughing, making a kiln or squatting upon the land.[185] Merely walking across it would not be enough, nor apparently driving cattle or a vehicle. Somewhat unsurprisingly therefore, the Welsh customs have nothing to say of praedial servitudes.

A *camlwrw* would however be due for the use of insulting language, so-called *gweli dafod*. The wrong was particularly connected with protecting the administration of justice but, probably under ecclesiastical influence, was extended to prevent bad language in the precincts of a church.[186] Those who falsely accused another of wrongdoing were also liable to a fine.[187] The land and life of a traitor were forfeit.[188]

Roman law knew of a wrong which seems alien to most modern legal systems but which had a parallel in the native laws of Wales, the wrong done by a judge who made the cause his own – *iudex qui litem suam fecit*. The wrong was concerned with a judge who gave wrong judgement, and there being no method of appeal under the classical formulary system, the avenue of redress for the disappointed litigant was to sue the judge. Welsh law also allowed of this possibility. The technique employed was known as mutual pledging. It involved the disappointed litigant challenging the correctness of the judge's judgement before he left the judgement seat having concluded the litigation. The challenge was to the correctness of the law which the judge had applied. The challenge would then be heard at a specially constituted court.[189]

Such a challenge to the judge's competence was a serious matter. If it was established that he had indeed erred, the judge would be deprived of his office and suffered a financial penalty. The texts say he lost his tongue, but this in fact meant that he had to redeem his tongue by the payment of its value, £44. A judge who failed to reach a decision or who refused to was also fined and dismissed, and loss of office also awaited a judge who had failed to act impartially or who had taken fees illegally.[190] As a consequence, a judge whose judgement was wrongly impugned was entitled to a special compensation payment for loss of face, the *wynebwerth*.[191] A challenge to the correctness of a judgement had to be based on written authority: the laws of Hywel or a proof book or some other juristic work.[192] When the royal court considered a case of mutual pledging involving a judge, its judgement had to be based on legal texts, and if the law books conflicted, expert canonical assessors would be called to assist.[193] The problem is similar to that which Roman law experienced when juristic opinion conflicted; the Roman solution ultimately was the Law of Citations of Theodosius II and Valentinian III which only allowed certain jurists' works to be cited and provided a formula for reconciling conflicts among the select few.[194] The solution set out in the Welsh texts looks like a late innovation, for it suggests a society in which ecclesiastics were skilled in at least canon law and probably the revived learning of Roman law as well. It smacks of the twelfth and thirteenth centuries.[195] Only if the law texts themselves were in conflict was the judge free to decide an issue of law for himself, and he had to be consistent with previous decisions which were recorded in writing and with those which he had previously given himself.[196]

THE ADMINISTRATION OF JUSTICE

Law was being administered within courts in Wales during the sub-Roman period and thereafter; Gildas provides evidence of courts for the sixth century and the marginalia to the Lichfield Gospels bear witness to the *meliores* of Gwent and Erging participating in quasi-judicial activities in the eighth and ninth centuries.[197] This was one of the differences between the legal processes of north and south Wales. In the south-east, the nobility had been present at local meetings where transactions were performed and disputes settled from the eighth century onwards, and throughout south Wales, the *uchelwyr* were the judges in the courts of the *cwmwd* where they lived and held land. Only in the courts of the Church were professional judges to be found in the south, and no less a personage than the eponymous Blegywryd is to be found acting in that capacity in a record of a case in the Llandaff charters.[198]

In north Wales, on the other hand, use was made of professional judges in the courts. Such judges had professional training and were learned in the law. The jurists who wrote the law books acted as advisers in the south, but decided cases themselves in the north. They were referred to as 'wise men', *doethion*, a term which mirrors the use of *prudentes* in the Roman tradition.[199] Much that is contained in the law books is reminiscent of the juristic texts of the Roman world, but it is difficult to determine whether this was a survival of the Roman period or a reflection of Wales sharing the influence felt in other parts of Europe when there was a renaissance of Roman legal learning from the tenth century onwards. Either way, it speaks of a land which had a share in a much wider legal culture, that of western Christendom. Juristic disputes are reported as in the Roman authorities: *rey a dyweyt . . . ereyll a dyweyt* – 'some say . . . others say', and reference to the laws (*cyfreithion*) in *Llyfr Iorwerth* appear to mean the two learned laws – the civil law of Rome and the canon law of the Church. This is probably evidence of later interpolation, but the law books were from an earlier period as in Rome the work of jurists who were conservative in outlook like their Roman predecessors and slow to discard material.[200] They also use formulae, even in Welsh, which reflect Roman influence: 'O derfydd', 'If it happens . . .'.[201]

Litigants were represented before the courts by two types of lawyer: the *cynghaws* or pleader and the *canllaw* or guide.[202] This distinction is again one which is common in civilian systems of law and is not the same as the modern distinction between a barrister and a solicitor in England and Wales. The pleaders were advocates, skilled in the art of speaking and also renowned for their knowledge of genealogy which was of great import in settling claims to land and compensation for homicide in Welsh law. Giraldus in the twelfth century praises the Welsh for their eloquence, and this art and that of genealogy hark back to skills which may have been valued and preserved from pre-Roman times.[203] The *canllaw* on the other hand was not an advocate but a procurator or attorney who did not argue his client's case before the court but was entitled to perform acts in the client's name, thus representing him, which the client could adopt or disavow.

The Welsh law books are exceptional in the detail they supply with regard to the judicial processes of the country. There were well-defined legal terms, constructed around the agricultural calendar, the courts being open from 9 November to 9 February and from 9 May to 9 August, apart from closure each Sunday and Monday and on other holy days.[204] Crimes were to be tried in the king's courts, unless the accused was a clerk, and sins were cognizable in the courts of the Church, there having been apparently none of the jurisdictional conflict between the secular and spiritual tribunals which was such a feature in England and elsewhere.[205] The one serious jurisdictional problem, which was to endure right up to the union of Wales and England in the sixteenth century, was that offenders could only be extradited from one *cwmwd* to another to stand trial if both *cymydau* were within the same lordship.[206]

Litigation was always directed at achieving either possession of property, compensation for a wrong or punishment for a crime. Pleadings were admitted in the week leading up to the commencement of the law term and were meant to expose the points of difference between the parties. This was often achieved by being set out in a written *rhwym dadl*, reminiscent of the classical Roman *formula*, and four items were required to be set forth: the names of the parties; the 'cause of action'; the remedy sought and time and place when the cause arose together with a statement of the law alleged to be applicable.[207] The process was a party process inasmuch as judgement could only be given for what a party had claimed.[208] According to the law of Hywel, the plaintiff bore the costs of the proceedings, but this was changed under Bleddyn ap Cynfyn so that costs followed the outcome.[209]

Welsh law also resembled Roman law and differed from the English and Germanic systems in that it appears to have known nothing of the ordeal. It has been claimed that Dyfnwal Moelmud introduced the ordeal of the hot iron, hot water and combat into Wales for the trial of theft, *galanas* and treason, only for Hywel to abolish the practice, substituting proof by compurgation, *rhaith*, or evidence. There is however no evidence for the claim, and the mention of trial by combat, which only came to England with the Normans and the inclusion of treason rather than arson in the list of three serious crimes, both suggest that the claim was a post-Norman interpolation. Compurgation and evidence would appear to have been the traditional Welsh methods of proof.[210]

Whether proof was to be made by compurgation or other evidence depended upon the nature of the claim. Compurgation, *rhaith*, was used when the statement of one of the parties was to be conclusive and the oath of that party had to be supported by that of a number of other persons, usually drawn from amongst the kindred. The number also varied with the cause. In south Wales, *rhaith* of kin had given way to *rhaith* of country, neighbours rather than relatives being the oath-helpers, possibly a further indication of the move from a tribal to a feudal society. The *rhaith* of country gradually merged with the bench of landowning judges.[211] Seven was the number of compurgators needed to support a claim of suretyship (*machni*), contract (*amod*) and *briduw*, consisting of the claimant himself and six kinsmen, four from the paternal and two from the maternal kin.[212] Again, it is interesting that seven was the number of people required to be present in the Roman formal *mancipatio*.[213] Also as in the *mancipatio*, if property was being claimed it had to held in the hand to be the subject of the swearing.[214] The oath, called the *damdwng*, was sworn on relics, and the claimant asserted that no one was owner of the thing save him, his lord and his wife.[215]

Where the outcome of a case depended not upon the justice of a claim but the proof of some question of fact, evidence of that fact could be adduced in a number of ways. Documentary evidence eventually became admissible, probably under ecclesiastical influence, but the classic Welsh method was by the quantity and quality of witnesses. A litigant would claim that he could produce a sufficient number of witnesses to establish the facts upon which his claim or defence rested. In certain limited circumstances, the word of one person alone might serve to establish a fact, but such *tafodiog* evidence was rare, being limited to situations such as that of a fellow thief confessing immediately before execution and implicating an accomplice and possibly, although there was some dispute about its conclusiveness, the statement of a maiden with regard to who had raped her. Such *tafodiog* evidence was one form of supporting fact, evidence which in the absence of any other was sufficient to establish an issue. Other supporting facts were the obstruction of an owner's search so as to establish liability for theft, or the refusal to take a conclusive oath.[216] One very interesting instance is the *dognfanag*, whereby an owner who was not prepared to accuse another of theft by virtue of that other's rank or wealth, could go to his lord and privately inform him of the facts. The lord would then send the informant with a priest to a church, where the informant would swear to the accusation three times – at the door, on the chancel step and before the altar – after which the priest's affirmation to the swearing having been accomplished was proof of the wrong. The informant would have been solemnly admonished of the severity of perjury prior to being sworn.[217]

Other witnesses were classed as *ceidwad*, *gwybyddiad* or *tystion*. In each case, the law books are clear that the romano-canonical, indeed biblical, requirement that there be at least two such witnesses, applied.[218] *Tystion* testified as to facts which they had witnessed in court, while *gwybyddiaid* testified to words, acts or deeds which they had actually witnessed. A *ceidwad* however was a special form of witness. The word means 'protector' and they were especially used in defending possession in claims to property. It was always, as in the later English Grand Assize, the person in possession who called for *ceidwad* evidence, and such evidence was used for instance in the avouchment of birth and rearing (*geni a meithrin*), when the possessor asserted that an animal had not been separated from him for three nights by sale or gift, three nights being the time limit within which its loss would have had to be reported to the lord.[219] Such swearing was also used to establish custody before loss in a charge of theft, warranty being required no further than the third hand to defend a person from such a charge.[220] Under the law of Hywel according to *Llyfr Blegywryd*, sworn appraisals were also used to fix the value of things the value of which were not fixed by law, a procedure which was extended in the south to all valuations, regardless of whether the native laws gave them a value, a change attributed to Henry II's justiciar in south Wales, the Lord Rhys.[221]

The detail the law books supply with regard to the judicial processes of the Welsh laws go far to revealing their sophistication. Several other features demarcate them significantly from the law of neighbouring England, both before and after the Norman conquest of that land: the structure of *cenedl* and the *teulu*; the succession to land within the *gwely*; the requirement that the whole kindred pay and receive *galanas* in the wake of a homicide; the strong juristic tradition of the law itself. Some of these factors can be compared with Roman law, some with English and Germanic custom; some may have been imported from Ireland or even survived from pre-Roman times in Wales. All provided the Welsh customs with a clear identity, an identity which was associated with the name of Hywel Dda and his law-making assembly in the tenth century. It was that identity which made them a focus of unity for the people of Wales as a whole, a focus which was to prove significant as the Norman invaders of England extended their sphere of influence and their own legal culture into Wales from the eleventh century onwards. The laws of Hywel once more supplied a golden age to which the people could look back amid the uncertainties of the Norman and Plantagenet present.

5

The Norman Invasion and Edward I

LEGAL INFLUENCES IN THE LATER ELEVENTH AND TWELFTH CENTURIES

When William, duke of Normandy, defeated Harold Godwinson on the battle-field of Hastings in 1066, he had by invasion successfully pursued his claim to the throne of England. It was England alone that he claimed, and his ascent to the English throne did not directly affect the government of either Wales or Scotland. While as king of England, he would continue to be in the eyes of the Welsh rulers their royal superior as the successor of the king in London, this was understood to be bare overlordship and not any form of feudal dependence. The barons and knights who accompanied him on his English expedition were, of their very nature, adventurers, and they were unlikely to pass by the chance of further gains within Britain beyond the boundaries of England. Thus it was that Norman invaders had by the end of the eleventh century found their way into Wales and were thereafter to reach Ireland, leaving a profound mark upon the political, economic, social and legal structures of both countries.[1]

The England which Duke William acquired by conquest in 1066 was already a well-governed country.[2] For well over a century, it had been divided into the shires which were to remain its principal internal boundaries until the second half of the twentieth century. Each shire had its own monthly assembly or meeting, called the shire moot, at which the local earl, or his deputy or reeve in the shire, the shire reeve or sheriff, presided. This meeting transacted all manner of business, administrative as well as judicial, making regulations for the good government of the shire as occasion demanded, but by and large administering the county and settling disputes within it according to the customs of the area. The shires were in turn divided into hundreds, areas defined by size or population. These also had their three-weekly meetings or moots at which the general business of the hundred was transacted under the presidency of a bailiff. The hundreds sent representatives to the monthly meetings of the shire court, but all free men were expected to attend the court at its three plenary sessions each year, at Michaelmas, Easter and Whitsun. The king's court was a meeting for the nobility of the realm, following the king as he progressed around his kingdom, but generally meeting at fixed locations at the major festivals: Gloucester at Christmas, Winchester at Easter and Westminster at Whitsun. It dealt with the general business of the kingdom. Most litigation of a serious nature would be dealt with before the shire moots, lesser matters before the hundred. The king's court was intended solely for the nobility, the king's peers, and the prelates of the Church. The law administered at every level was the custom of the locality as recalled by the inhabitants who owed suit to that court. Questions of fact were generally resolved by compurgation, oath helping, or failing that by testing the oath of a litigant in the ordeal, generally by cold water, hot water or the hot iron, a method of proof of pagan origin which was probably foreign to the customs of Wales. The court selected which of the parties to put to the test.

William the Conqueror found most of these institutions serviceable, but he did make some innovations. The most significant change to the legal customs of the English which followed the Norman invasion was the introduction of a thoroughly feudal form of landholding. The king rewarded his chief followers by granting to them parcels of land, in the main scattered across the kingdom to prevent them developing localized power bases which could threaten his authority. These lands were given them in return for services, the hallmark of feudal tenure. Some services were honorific and personal to the king, the so-called tenures in grand serjeanty, but the most usual requirement from a baron was that he should supply a fixed number of knights to fight for the king in defence of his newly gotten kingdom for forty days each year. This obligation the barons, who held their lands directly from the king as tenants-in-chief, discharged by recruiting knights to perform the military service in return for grants of land, knights' fees, from the baron. The king was lord to the tenants-in-chief; they were the lords of their knights, who performed the military service in return for their tenures. The knights in turn would sublet their lands to those who by farming it would produce the agricultural goods needed to support the knight and his family. Where the amount of such agricultural service was fixed, the tenure was a socage freehold. Where the tenant had to work at the discretion of the lord, yielding all of the produce to him and retaining only a smallholding from which to eke out a living for himself and his family, the tenure was in villeinage. At home, the knight was the lord of his holding, the manor, and held a court for his tenants. Holding a court and doing justice for one's tenants was one of the obligations of good lordship; land was given in return for services, and loyalty was exacted in return for justice in the lord's court.[3]

At the top end of the feudal pyramid, land was given in return for military service, and the estate granted was intended to support the knight and his family. The grant is best viewed as a capital sum given to the military employee so that he could live off the income. It followed that it was not intended to be divided up among the knight's descendants upon his death; indeed, some

doubt that the land was initially meant to be heritable at all, but would only
remain the knight's as long as he lived or indeed for as long as he was fit
enough to perform the services.[4] As the defence of a kingdom newly acquired
by conquest ceased to be the prime concern of the Normans, and times of peace
became more common, so tenants appear to have driven harder bargains with
their lords with regard to their tenures, supplying the monetary wherewithal
to acquire the services of soldiers rather than performing the military services
themselves and securing themselves grants of land that would endure for
their lifetime or which could even descend to their children. However, as lords
did not wish the feudal obligations arising from the land to become fragmented, only one person was to be responsible for the services arising from each
tenure, with the result that on a tenant's death his land passed to his eldest
son, the rule of primogeniture, very different from the partibility practised in
Wales.[5] Disputes relating to the tenure of land were decided in the court of the
lord from whom the land was held, and such disputes, as with the trial of
serious wrongs involving Normans, were tried by a new procedure introduced
by the invaders, trial by battle. The disputants took oaths as to the justice of
their respective causes and then fought the issue out to a decision by combat.
The land went to the victor, might triumphed rather than right, but the procedure is not as maverick as might at first sight appear if one recalls that
originally the lord was seeking to recruit the best fighting men who were to be
paid with grants of land. Such disputes would therefore initially have been
about who ought to be employed as a fighter, and to resolve the matter by
battle was far from irrational.[6]

   Within the local courts of the shire and the hundred, the Normans made
minor but significant innovations. The sheriff ceased to be the reeve of the
local lord and became that of the king. Thereafter, there was in effect royal
supervision if not control of the proceedings in the shire court, and twice every
year the sheriff would render account for the administration of justice within
his shire at the king's exchequer, which settled permanently at Westminster.
The sheriff also undertook a twice-yearly tour of his shire, visiting each of the
hundreds in turn. Within the hundred, every free man had now to be placed
in a tithing, a group of ten who were responsible for the good behaviour of
one another in that, if one transgressed, the other nine were responsible for
presenting him for punishment before the court or else were answerable for
his wrong. The sheriff visited the hundred to ensure that everyone was placed
within a tithing, so that as men died and others came of age, the system did
not fail to provide accountability. The sheriff supervised the hundreds and the
hundreds sent representatives to the shire court. Likewise, the sheriff went to
the king's court at the exchequer and from the start of the twelfth century, the
exchequer began occasionally to send out members of the royal court to hold
special sessions of the shire court to supervise its business. Their visitation of
the shire was known as an eyre,[7] and the royal servants who conducted the

visitation were known as justices in eyre, although they were not lawyers or professional judges, but trusted servants of the king, often drawn from the nobility or the ranks of the higher clergy, but by the end of the twelfth century more in the nature of professional civil servants. The structure of government was therefore at each level one of upward accountability and of downward supervision, but each tier in the governmental pyramid concerned itself solely with the next tier above and below; there was no greater range of supervision or accountability.

At roughly the same time as the government of England was being re-organized in the wake of the Norman invasion, the Catholic Church was developing new structures for itself across western Christendom, possibly for fear that further splits might occur of the sort which had recently separated the Catholic West from the Orthodox East in the middle years of the eleventh century.[8] Pyramidal structures played their part in these changes too, as arch-bishops were called to go to the Pope in Rome to receive the *pallium*, the insignium of their office, while bishops were expected to swear canonical obedience to the archbishop of the province within which their diocese was situated before assuming responsibility for it. Indeed, dioceses and provinces were in the process of becoming more territorial in nature, and subdivision of the diocese into archdeaconries, rural deaneries and parishes was becoming standard practice. Clergy discipline was also being tightened, with the require-ment of celibacy starting to be enforced and Church courts being established at each territorial level to impose discipline upon the clergy and upon the laity alike. Many of these reforms are associated with the lawyer pope, Hildebrand, who as Gregory VII implemented during his papacy (1073–85) the reforms which continue to be known by his name. These reforms came to England with the appointment of the first Norman archbishop of Canterbury, Lanfranc, in 1072, who introduced the requirement that all bishops in his province of Canterbury should swear canonical obedience to him before assuming their sees, and introduced the Hildebrandine reforms in a series of councils which he called during his archiepiscopate. Lanfranc came to England from Normandy, where he had been a monk at the abbey of Bec before becoming the first abbot of Duke William's abbey foundation of St Etienne in Caen. Before becoming a monk, however, he had been a famous teacher of the law, probably beginning his career in the Italian city of Pavia prior to moving north of the Alps to found a cathedral school in the Norman city of Avranches. Lanfranc personifies the connections between the renaissance of legal learning taking place in the cities and emerging universities of northern Italy and the Catholic Church in northern France and England. His successor as archbishop of Canterbury, St Anselm, was also from south of the Alps, from Aosta, had also studied in the uni-versities of the Italian north, and also progressed to England via Normandy and the office of abbot at Bec. Later in the twelfth century, a third archbishop would come to Canterbury from the same abbey, Theobald of Bec. These were the very years in which the learning of Roman civil law was being revived in the universities of Bologna and Pavia and in which the scientific study of canon law was beginning in the same academies. The intellectual impact of men such as Lanfranc, Anselm and Theobald cannot be underestimated; they were the living link with central currents of the intellectual life of Christendom, and they brought their learning with them to Norman England.

Like the Romans before them, the Normans established themselves on the borders of Wales, creating important fortified settlements at Chester in the north, Shrewsbury in the middle and Chepstow in the south. From the borders, Norman adventurers went out conquering lands along the border and along the fertile coastal plains of the south.[9] As territory fell under their control, so feudal landholding was introduced into Gwent, the Usk valley, the lowlands of Glamorgan and Gower, the Llyfni valley and the area around Carmarthen. The coastline of south Wales through Pembrokeshire and on into Ceredigion became settled by Norman lords who in part adopted the customs of the Welsh rulers whom they replaced, in part treated the lands as their private domains by conquest and in part introduced the sort of laws which the Norman kings were establishing in neighbouring England.[10] Pembrokeshire in particular became organized along the lines of an English shire with a sheriff and visits from justices in eyre.[11] This occurred from the early twelfth century onwards after the constable of Pembroke castle, Gerald of Windsor, married Nest, sometime mistress of Henry I of England, and the daughter of Rhys ap Tewdwr, the ruler of Deheubarth.[12] Rhys, and possibly Gerald, must have realized the advantages of such a match. Nest was given in marriage by her *cenedl*, and thus their children by the custom of *mamwys* would be treated as co-heirs of Rhys along with his own offspring. They would unite the native and the Norman houses, just as the dynastic marriages of Hywel Dda's time had united the sons of Gwynedd to the royal houses of Dyfed and Deheubarth.

As the Normans advanced into Wales, so the native tribal systems of government began to be overtaken by the thorough version of feudalism practised by the Normans. While it was probably the case that feudal elements had for some time been finding a place amid the Welsh customs, the Norman incursion accelerated the process. Lands began to be given in return for military service, whether in the lord's retinue or on duty at the local castle – so-called service by castle guard.[13] Attendance at the lord's court emerges as an obligation of tenure.[14] Tenants, other than those within the *maerdref*, acquired an obligation to maintain and repair the Norman castles, a duty which was in later centuries, after the Edwardian conquest, to become both onerous and odious.[15] Tolls on sales were introduced by the Norman lords within their lands, and the Church authorities are known to have done the same within the diocese of St David's.[16] The Black Book of St David's bears witness to Norman attempts to describe the ancient Welsh tenures in the language of Norman custom, *cyfran* not inaptly being equated with coparcenary.[17] Statements in the Welsh law texts that, for instance, no one could properly become the owner of land other than by the judgement of a court or investiture by the lord bear distinctly Norman influence.[18] The gradual replacement of *rhaith* of *cenedl* by *rhaith* of country in south Wales may also have been a consequence of Norman practice.[19]

The arrival of the Normans led to the segregation of legal customs along the borders and the coasts. Areas under the jurisdiction of the Norman lords were often divided into Englishries, where the Norman customs obtained, and Welshries, where the population continued to live according to their native laws at least insofar as private law rights and duties, such as those relating to landholding, succession and family matters, were concerned. The lands occupied by the Normans became known as the March, an area which in the eyes of the Norman lords belonged to them by right of conquest, giving them the right to introduce their customs and legal procedures into those parts. Although these Normans owed personal allegiance to the Norman kings of England, they did not hold their lands by grant of the king. Their position was therefore not dissimilar to that of the Welsh rulers whom they replaced, recognizing the overlordship of the English king, but not owing their positions in Wales to his grace. The Norman lords were there by right of conquest and therefore exercised quasi-regal rights and privileges within their domains. Only if they had to require the king of England's help to recover or retain their lands would they become his tenants rather than his vassals. Questions of whether the full quasi-regal status had been retained in a particular Marcher lordship would bedevil the law and politics of some parts of Wales, for instance Gower, for centuries.

The Marches were, and were to remain, a mix of English and Welsh cultures and customs. Welsh territorial arrangements, including the *cwmwd* and the traditional native dues and obligations, coexisted with institutions modelled on the practice of neighbouring England, particularly at the level of the lord and his tenants-in-chief. Within lordships such as Glamorgan, Gower, Pembroke, Brecon and Clun, it was the lord who had jurisdiction, in his courts that his justice was administered, and these courts often operated with the full panoply of writs and common-law procedures modelled on those of the English kingdom.[20] Those who lived in these lordships lived under the lord's protection, within his peace, and wrongs began to be treated not only as injuries to the persons concerned and their families but also as crimes in that they violated the lord's peace. Criminal and civil justice began to be differentiated and on the civil side the influence of the common law began to shape some developments within even the native customs.

The proximity of two different legal traditions in Norman Wales led writers to emphasize the differences where they felt this was necessary. *Llyfr Blegywryd* gratuitously points out that rape was not punished by castration under Welsh law, a comment which takes its context from the presence of that penalty under Norman law.[21] However, the adoption of Norman practices by the Welsh was

a cause of friction, particularly regarding the regalian rights which many
Marcher lords assumed in imitation of rulers across Europe. Whereas Roman
law had provided that rivers, roads, bridges, the sea, its shore, ports and
harbours were not susceptible to private ownership but were rather in the
public domain, the feudal perspective lacked the same sharp division of private
from public law and emphasized that any property which was not owned by
a private individual was under the protection of the lord. From here it was but
a short step to lords believing that such property under their protection was
in truth their own, so that they could raise tolls from the use of roads, rivers,
bridges, harbours and ports. Likewise, as wild animals were not owned by
anyone, they were claimed as the lord's privilege, so that hunting and fishing
came to be seen as aristocratic pursuits to the exclusion of other classes. The
numerous references in the Welsh laws to the sharing of fish captured in nets
between the owner of the river and the captor, the sharing of rights in the
swarms of bees and in animals taken in the chase all indicate the compromises
achieved to solve the problem of the clash of legal cultures.[22] It is not impossible
that feudal claims were already forcing the adoption of such compromise
solutions before the Normans came, but it is certain that their presence exacerbated the problems and therefore these rules may well date from the years
following the advent of the Normans.[23] The assumption of such regalian rights
was much disliked by the native population, as for instance when the lords
of Brecon gave the tithe of hunting and honey to the abbey of St Peter at
Gloucester.[24] The Norman lords may have assumed with some degree of innocence that such perquisites were theirs as of right, for the assertion of such
regalian rights was occurring across Europe, where it also met with some
resistance. The communes of Italy, for instance, forced a partial climbdown on
these issues from the Holy Roman Emperor in the Peace of Constance in 1183,
and in Wales the competing claims were to be regularly settled by compromise
agreements as for instance in the lordship of Clun in 1292, in Maelienydd in
1297 and in Gower in 1306.[25] They also feature in charters given to burgesses
at an earlier date.[26] Welsh lords who attempted to assume regalian rights were
targets for criticism: Meirchion it was said had been admonished by an angel
having refused to accept the saintly Illtud's strictures concerning the retention
of his waste, land without an owner, for hunting rather than granting it out
for cultivation.[27] Norman lords sometimes adopted Welsh customs, when it
suited them and it was to their advantage, on occasions not fully understanding
the principles or wilfully extending them. Thus, Norman lords claimed the
payment of *amobr* not only when a maid married but sometimes when a widow
remarried.[28]

One of the features of the Norman incursion was the creation of boroughs
as trading centres situated in close proximity to the castles. Often these
boroughs adopted legal customs directly from a settlement in Normandy or
indirectly through a previously established borough in England. Brecon for

instance obtained its customs from Breteuil. The borough customs differed markedly from the traditional Welsh rules relating to trade. For example, under Norman influence, the concept of *caveat emptor* replaced suretyship as the general approach to sales in the markets of south Wales, and, in marked contrast to the Welsh custom, a man was allowed to stand surety for himself by giving a pledge or *wadium*.[29] The need for a third party under Welsh law in such situations was the essential difference between the Welsh *gwystl* and the civilian *pignus*.

The arrival of the Normans also brought the Welsh Church into closer contact with, indeed under the control of, Canterbury.[30] There would appear to have been a general assumption within Wales from the sixth century onwards that there should be royal control over the appointment of prelates, and these men were often related to the ruling families.[31] Priests retained their place within their respective families, taking their share of, and living off the income from, their *gwely* lands. Clerical marriage was the norm with the sons of clergy often inheriting their fathers' ecclesiastical positions. In the very years of the Hildebrandine reforms, the diocese of St David's had as its bishop the famous Sulien (1073–8; 1080–5), who was married and virtually founded an ecclesiastical dynasty. In the eyes of the reformed Church, Welsh secular rulers had too much power over matters which to the ecclesiastical eye should not be under secular control. These included jurisdiction over testaments, the goods of deceased bishops, sanctuary, the punishment of criminous clerks, the property of intestates, and rights over Church lands and the Church's tenants.[32]

The reform of the western Church initiated by Hildebrand took place in the very years that Norman control, ecclesiastical as well as secular, was being extended in Wales. Territorial dioceses were created: Llandaff in 1107, St David's in 1115, Bangor in 1120.[33] The dioceses themselves were subdivided into archdeaconries, rural deaneries and parishes.[34] It is interesting that the century from 1150 to 1250 saw increased definition of territorial divisions in secular life as well, possibly in imitation of what the Church was accomplishing,[35] and it is possible that the standardized territorial descriptions of the Welsh law texts reflect the spirit of this age. From the appointment of Urban as bishop of Llandaff in 1107, Welsh bishops were required to take an oath of canonical obedience to the archbishop of Canterbury prior to their consecration,[36] an innovation imposed upon their English brethren in 1070. The Welsh dioceses were thereby incorporated into the province of Canterbury where they were to remain until 1920. Herewald, bishop of Llandaff (1056–1104), introduced pan-European concepts of episcopal organization into his see, appointing two archdeacons, and in St David's diocese, the three archdeaconries created were based on the three ancient Welsh kingdoms of Ceredigion, Brycheiniog and Deheubarth, with the rural deaneries based upon the *cymydau*.[37] This shows an admirable, indeed skilful, sensitivity to local feeling when innovating; even as stern a critic of Welsh resistance to ecclesiastical reform as Archbishop

Pecham in the thirteenth century was sufficiently sensitive to argue that the bishop of the English diocese of Coventry and Lichfield should have a Welsh-speaking suffragan to assist him in the Welsh-speaking areas of his diocese.[38]

Long before Pecham, prelates were finding fault with Welsh customs when viewed from the perspective of the Gregorian reforms. The dissolubility of marriages and the refusal to classify children as legitimate and illegitimate produced strictures in the twelfth century from both Archbishop Theobald and Giraldus Cambrensis, the grandson of Gerald of Windsor and Nest.[39] Giraldus was a prime protagonist in the cause of St David's diocese to become the metropolitical see at the head of a distinctly Welsh province of the Church, independent of Canterbury.[40] This was first proposed by Bernard, bishop of St David's (1115–48), in the years when various dioceses in France and Ireland, and also Winchester in England, attempted to achieve metropolitical status.[41] Bernard died in 1148 just as the issue was due to be heard and perhaps determined at Rheims. His successor in the see of St David's was David Fitzgerald (1148–76), a son of Gerald of Windsor and Nest, upon whose appointment and that of his successor Peter de Leia, the archbishop of Canterbury demanded as a condition of consecration a promise that the matter would not be raised anew. Giraldus sought the appointment for himself in 1176 and again on Peter de Leia's death in 1198. On the latter occasion, he skilfully took the matter to Rome for a hearing in order to sidestep the objection of the archbishop of Canterbury, Hubert Walter. He succeeded in pressing the issue to a final determination before the papal judges delegate at Worcester in 1202–3, but the decision went against him and the aspirations of his native diocese.[42] Giraldus's campaign however manifests a great knowledge of the canon law and canonical procedure of his day. He was prepared to take on as powerful a person as Hubert Walter, himself a considerable legal scholar, the nephew of Henry II's great justiciar Ranulf de Glanvill, and some believe the true author of the first systematic text on the English common law which bears his uncle's name. Giraldus himself, for all his contemporary views and learning, was in some respects a typical Welsh ecclesiastic, the descendant of a Welsh royal house of which he remained a member by virtue of the custom of *mamwys*.[43]

Giraldus's knowledge and wide perspective was not atypical for a cleric of his time. Welsh churchmen travelled extensively across Europe in the twelfth century, and this was particularly true of the scholars in their number.[44] Welsh men were involved in the great twelfth-century revival of learning, visiting the principal centres in Britain and northern Europe to get their education, for example, at Paris, Oxford and Lincoln.[45] Interestingly, it is at Lincoln that the Bolognese scholar, Vacarius, is now thought to have been the first in England to teach the revived study of Roman law in the 1140s.[46] In Italy, one John of Wales is credited with having been the author of the second addition to Gratian's great concordance of canon law, the *Decretum*, which also appeared in the same decade. John of Wales's addition, the *Secunda*, appeared in 1215.[47] Wales sent causes to be adjudicated before the papal curia, and trained canon lawyers brought the basic texts of the canon law, the decretals of successive popes, back to Wales where they were collected at ecclesiastical centres, for example, St Dogmael's.[48] It is noteworthy that the Welsh native laws state that, where the native customs contained in the law books were in conflict, trained canonists should resolve the impasse.[49] Whereas under the Welsh laws, the *brawdwyr* were arbitrators as much as judges, seeking to reconcile the parties as much as to decide between them, jurists found their position elevated during the twelfth and the thirteenth centuries so that they took over the role of judge in the courts of north Wales, much as across the continent of Europe, those learned in the law began to adjudicate and not merely advise on legal custom, as witness the *Schöffen* in Germany and the *scabini* in Italy. The canons of general, legatine, English and provincial councils of the Church, being sources of its written law, circulated throughout Wales and especially in the south, as consistory courts emerged in each diocese to deal with sin, matrimonial causes, contractual issues and succession by testament.[50] These courts began the process of inculcating the international standards of the Church with regard to marriage, divorce, legitimacy and clerical celibacy.[51] It may have been as a result of witnessing their legal expertise in these tribunals that canonists were called upon to participate and bring their learning into secular courts, where churchmen began to act as mediators and to regulate the taking of oaths and the conduct of compurgation,[52] much as they officiated at ordeals in England. Principles of canon law began to be accepted into the native customs as well as the Norman jurisdictions. The trial of criminous clerks was claimed for the Church,[53] with the *Damweiniau* recording that clergy were not to suffer double jeopardy by being tried twice – once before the secular courts and again before the spiritual forum – for the same crime.[54] The marriage or concubinage of clergy was disapproved of by the Church authorities through to the time of Archbishop Pecham,[55] and priests' sons were barred from inheriting from their fathers if they were born after he had been ordained.[56] Neither rule made much headway in Wales. There can however be no doubt that ecclesiastical influence was felt in some areas of Welsh law, and that this influence was increasing throughout the Norman period.[57] The Welsh law texts show an awareness of a phraseology and legal style which links them with the European legal renaissance,[58] and it is clear that the compilers were fully conversant with the technical legal vocabulary of their day, as even the most cursory comparison of the Latin texts with the common law *Glanvill* will illustrate.[59] Like the thirteenth-century English treatise attributed to Bracton, the Welsh compilers can quote the classical poets,[60] and *Llyfr Iorwerth* in north Wales refers in its opening *proemium*, itself an import from the civilian tradition, to *cyfreithiau* in the plural, a possible reference to the learning of the civil and canon law, the *utriusque iuris* of the European mainland.[61] *Llyfr Colan*, also from the north, presents itself as an attempt to harmonize discordances within the laws in true imitation of the techniques of the Glossators of the civil and canon law at Bologna.[62]

Although the influence of the Church was considerable and the Norman example pervasive – for even in the north, courts based upon the authority of the prince and of the lord made headway – the Welsh customs nevertheless held their ground. As early as William the Conqueror's great survey of his new kingdom recorded in *Domesday Book*, the Hereford Domesday records the survival of Welsh customs in the Erging area, and in particular the three columns of the law dealing with homicide, theft and arson.[63] The Normans do not appear to have interfered with such customary survivals in any way. Indeed, they appear to have respected the survival of the native laws in many areas which came under their control. In the fertile Vale of Glamorgan, despite considerable Norman influence upon such things as church architecture, the local customs of Morgannwg would appear to have survived for instance in a variety of tenancy called the Custom of Glamorgan, which is quite distinct from other native Welsh arrangements.[64] Upland Glamorgan remained an area of Welsh custom,[65] and in upland areas generally, Norman control was nominal, Welsh customs surviving in these Welshries while the lowland areas were reorganized as manors.[66] Throughout the March, this amalgam of the native and the Norman persisted, and the law of the March, that of an area with its own liberties where the writ of the king of England did not run, was specifically recognized as a third method of legal organization in Magna Carta in 1215. Each Marcher lordship was an entity in itself, so that delinquents were not ordinarily extraditable from one lordship to another, each lordship being sovereign in itself. Inter-lordship *parlements* and love-days had to be held to deal with problems of extraditing criminals, retrieving stolen property and resolving boundary disputes. Conventions about such matters came to be agreed between the several lordships.[67] If the biggest divisions between the native Welsh customs and the canon law were concerned with marriage, legitimacy and clerical celibacy, the greatest distinction between the native and Norman jurisprudence was that between the Welsh partibility of inheritance and the English rule of primogeniture.

The differences between the native laws on the one hand and those of the incoming Normans and the Church on the other may have been one motivating force behind the compilation of the legal texts in Latin and Welsh which have survived from these centuries. Despite their attribution to Hywel Dda two centuries earlier, the earliest extant evidence for the native Welsh customs comes from the law books composed during the later twelfth and thirteenth centuries. The law books are written in either Welsh or Latin, and the principal texts have been attributed to certain parts of Wales. The earliest of the five Latin texts, Latin A, is believed to reflect the native customs of the south-east of Wales, possibly those of Gwent and Morgannwg or even extending northwards as far as Maelienydd. Latin A is thought to be part of the legal tradition of the south-east of Wales which is also reflected in the loose assemblage of sources termed *Llyfr Cyfnerth*. Latin B, C and E are all thought to have a northern provenance, linking them to the kingdom of Gwynedd, where the native laws are also recorded in the Welsh traditions which are referred to as *Llyfr Iorwerth* and *Llyfr Colan*, the second being a later but abbreviated version of the former. Finally, Latin D and *Llyfr Blegywryd*, which are very similar indeed in structure and content, are connected with the south-western kingdom of Deheubarth.[68] Within these texts, there are elements which are of clear feudal provenance, and therefore it must be postulated that either the native customs had already begun to develop in the direction of feudalism before the coming of the Normans, or otherwise that the texts embody innovations which had taken place since the Norman incursions. That the texts were a living, juristic source of law which was dynamic and not static has already been noted,[69] and the clear ecclesiastical influence to be found, particularly in the *Blegywryd* tradition, confirms that some incorporation of later eleventh and twelfth century material had occurred; likewise with regard to the influence of the European legal renaissance upon the terminology and style of the texts even in the north. Equally clearly, the texts retain many rules and expressions which are of native provenance and which on occasion are clearly at odds not only with the approach of the Norman and ecclesiastical authorities but also with their known wishes and pursued policies.

The law books may have been compiled for the benefit of the incoming rulers, so that they and their stewards would be fully cognizant of the customs which were followed in the Welshries of their newly acquired lands, particularly when the Welsh tenants sought to have their disputes resolved by their Norman lords according to Welsh custom but in the lord's court and sometimes according to the lord's procedures. It is known for instance that the men of Morgannwg requested such a privilege.[70] It is also possible that the law books were compiled for the benefit of the Church authorities at least to inform and possibly to counteract criticism of the Welsh customs by the Church. However, the clear needs of the Norman lords and the prelates of the Church should not eclipse the tradition of a native written law which existed before the Normans came, a tradition which may have merely continued in the wake of their arrival and the demand for spiritual conformity, albeit also serving the needs of the new moment. The law books may have been primarily intended, as they always had been, to serve the needs of the Welsh rulers and their subjects, although the Latin versions may well have been designed to serve the needs of the newcomers with no, or insufficient, knowledge of the native tongue.

The same phenomenon of translation of native laws into Latin also occurred in England. The native customs which had been recorded in Anglo-Saxon were in the second decade of the twelfth century gathered together and rendered into Latin in the text which is known as *Quadripartitus I*, having been intended as the first part of a four-part work. The motivation behind *Quadripartitus* may have been the same as that behind the Latin versions of the Welsh laws – to inform the new Norman ruling class regarding the customs of the native population. The Norman governors of the Church in both England and Wales may have been instrumental in seeking such information, although, as the record of Welsh customs in the Hereford Domesday indicates, the secular rulers were not unaware of the same need with regard to their jurisdictions. Nor should the contemporary impulse to reduce legal rules to writing in order to systematize their presentation and content be forgotten. This trend had begun among the legal scholars at the University of Bologna following the rediscovery of the Digest of Justinian. The scholars at Bologna looked upon this vast compendium of Roman juristic learning as the equivalent in legal study to the Bible in theology, but while the Bible was revealed truth the Digest was written reason, *ratio scripta*. Accordingly, they believed that it contained no errors and no contradictions, being entirely consistent with itself in all places. Apparent errors and inconsistencies must therefore be the consequence of the imperfect understanding of the reader not the fault of the compiler, and the scholars sought to gloss the text in order to explain and thereby remove these apparent, but inadmissible, shortcomings. The techniques they adopted of glossing the text gave their school of juristic learning the name of Glossators and during the twelfth and thirteenth centuries they succeeded in producing a lengthy gloss of the entire Digest, the so-called *Glossa ordinaria*, completed by the jurist Accursius. Following the example of the Glossators of the civil law, scholars of canon law surmised that a similar process and technique could be applied to the disparate sources of Church law in order to reduce it to a manageable whole. Whereas earlier generations had attempted to compile collections of canons and other items of ecclesiastical legislation, in the twelfth century the jurist Gratian sought to systematize those collections by applying the techniques of dialectic reasoning as practised by the philosophers and theologians of Paris and the Bolognese Glossators. The result was the *Decretum*, or more properly the Concordance of Discordant Canons, the *Concordia discordantium canonum* of 1140–2. What had been done for the Digest could also be done for a living legal system, and it is not fanciful to suppose that, as the learning of the Glossators and canonists spread outwards across western Christendom, so their techniques would have been recognized as applicable to other bodies of secular law. The first step would be to collect the sources; this *Quadripartitus* in England and the Latin texts of the native laws in Wales accomplished. That Welshmen were being educated at the centres of the new learning, that knowledge of the new learning was reaching Wales and that Welsh scholars like John of Wales were active at the centre of these developments is known. One should not therefore be surprised, let alone discount the possibility, that the production of the twelfth and thirteenth century texts was connected with these developments.

THE COMMON LAW OF ENGLAND

While this legal renaissance was taking place across western Christendom, events in England were unfolding in the manner which was destined to result in the development of the common law. William I was faced towards the end of his reign by a rebellion, led significantly by his half-brother, Odo of Bayeux. Before leaving for Normandy in 1086, he summoned a great assembly of all the landholding men of England and, on Salisbury Plain, they took an oath of allegiance to William as their sovereign lord, to whom they promised to be loyal above any other lord. The Sarum Oath may not have been intended to challenge the feudal order, but it did traverse it, for the free men of England were no longer linked to their king by a series of feudal bonds through inter-mediary, or mesne, lords; they now bore him direct allegiance. They did not hold land directly from him and therefore owed him no services, but inasmuch as they had promised him allegiance, they were, by the logic of feudalism, entitled to his protection and that of his court should they be in want of justice. The final working out of that equation may not have occurred until the reign of William's great-grandson, Henry II, but the seeds of enhanced royal juris-diction were sown on Salisbury Plain.

William's innovation in the Sarum Oath was meant to protect his kingdom from the civil strife that could arise if the military loyalty of chivalric tenants lay first and foremost to their immediate lords. These lords would then have at their disposal private armies to war with one another and even to rebel against the king. The Sarum Oath contradicted such loyalties; henceforth, the primary loyalty was to the Crown and no act which imperilled the king's peace should be countenanced by a loyal subject whatever his lord's wishes. The period of almost seventy years separating the death of William the Conqueror from the accession of Henry Plantagenet was to see the problems of civil war made manifest. Linked with this threat was the absence of any clear rule relating to the succession to the English throne.

The Conqueror's claim to the throne of England was based on the wishes of Edward the Confessor, despite the fact that the English kingship at that time was elective, lying in the hands of the Witan. On William the Conqueror's death, he appears to have assumed the right which his claim presupposed the Confessor to have enjoyed; he granted the duchy of Normandy to his eldest son, Robert Curthose, and the kingdom of England passed to a younger son, William Rufus. On Rufus's sudden death while out hunting in 1100, his younger brother Henry successfully claimed the throne, basing his claim on the fact that he was the first son of the Conqueror to have been born while William was king, *porphyrogenitus*. Henry had two legitimate children, a son, William who predeceased his father by drowning in the disaster of the *White Ship*, and a daughter Matilda who married first the Holy Roman Emperor, Henry IV, and after his death, Count Geoffrey of Anjou, the marriage which produced Henry II. Henry I wanted his daughter to succeed him, and on several occasions sought to ensure her succession by having his subjects swear that they would accept her as queen. However, on his sudden death in 1135, it was another of the Conqueror's grandchildren, Stephen of Blois, who successfully took the throne, a move which thrust England into a civil war over the rival claims which lasted intermittently throughout his reign until he recognized Henry Plantagenet and not his own son, Eustace, as his heir. Henry acceded to the throne peacefully on Stephen's death in 1154. Throughout his reign, Henry worried over the succession to his dominions, going so far as to have his eldest son, Henry, crowned king during his own lifetime in order to ensure his succession. Henry the young king, as he was called, died before his father, but Henry was succeeded by his next eldest son, Richard, in 1189. If the Welsh rules relating to partibility gave rise to problems, the birth of primogeniture in England was a painful and protracted process, which was not complete until the thirteenth century.[71]

Henry II repeated the Conqueror's request that all free tenants should swear allegiance to him before any other lord. Significantly he pursued this as a clear policy in 1176, a year which saw the regularization of legal innovations which would result in the birth of the English common law. Henry was to insist that no free man was to answer for his land without the king's written permission, a signal indication that all free men were protected by royal justice. He also introduced remedies and procedures in his courts which were open to all his subjects and not just to his tenants-in-chief. It was during his reign that kings of England began to describe themselves routinely as the lord king, emphasizing that they were the lords of their subjects as well as their rulers, and the provision of justice in a properly constituted court was a recognized feature of good lordship. In this, Henry may have deliberately imitated, and thereby sought to undermine, a similar attempt by the papacy to claim universal jurisdiction over the Christian faithful by making the papal *curia* a court of general jurisdiction with the Pope describing himself as the lord Pope.[72] Such royal lordship was very different from the bare kingship exercised by previous monarchs, the kind of bare overkingship which the rulers of Wales recognized was enjoyed by 'the king in London'. The overkingship which Hywel Dda, for instance, had acknowledged in Aethelstan and which Gruffydd ap Llywelyn had conceded to the Confessor was little more than a token submission, an overlordship expressed in the giving of hostages, visiting the overking's court, witnessing his charters, paying tribute, swearing fealty – but not homage – and promising service. This was the concept of sub-kingship, the Welsh ruler as the king in London's *subregulus*, which the Normans inherited from the Anglo-Saxons. Thus, the last native king of Deheubarth, Rhys ap Tewdwr, submitted to William I in 1081 with the promise of £40 a year payment for his lands.[73] Henry I also obtained the allegiance and submission of the rulers of Gwynedd and Powys.[74]

Henry II may well have benefited from the tradition of the king in London being the overking of the Welsh rulers, and may also have been the beneficiary in south Wales of certain similarities between his position and that of Hywel Dda. Hywel had by birth and marriage assembled the various parts of Wales into something approaching a unified if not uniform kingdom; Henry II had done much the same to construct his empire stretching from the Pennines to the Pyrenees – England and Normandy from his mother, Anjou from his father and south-west France by marriage to Eleanor of Aquitaine. It is even possible that the reputation of Hywel Dda and his connection with the pedigree of the Welsh laws was derived from a comparison with Henry, who was also unifying his kingdom by means of providing his subjects with a law common to them all – the law of his court. One man in particular was a cornerstone of Henry's influence in Wales and had the motive and the opportunity to embellish the name of Hywel Dda – Rhys ap Gruffydd, the ruler of Deheubarth, known significantly as the *lord* Rhys, possibly in imitation of Henry's adoption of the designation 'lord king'.[75]

When Henry II became king of England in 1154, the most powerful of the Welsh rulers was Owain Gwynedd, who recognized Henry's overlordship in 1157.[76] Following a rebellion against the Plantagenets by Rhys ap Gruffydd in the south, Henry returned to Wales in 1163 and, in July of that year at Woodstock, Rhys, Owain Gwynedd and other Welsh rulers did homage to Henry II and his son.[77] This taking of homage was the first indication that the former overkingship was changing into feudal overlordship, with the English king asserting some form of jurisdiction not only over the Welsh rulers but over their lands.

After Owain Gwynedd died in 1170, Rhys ap Gruffydd became the foremost of the Welsh rulers, and he established a close relationship with the English king. In 1171, Henry II visited Rhys on his way to Ireland, significantly stopping at Whitland, the Hendygwyn-ar-Daf associated with Hywel Dda's law-making assembly. There, Rhys again acknowledged Henry's overlordship. On his return from Ireland the following year, Henry appointed Rhys justiciar of south Wales, the king's representative in the area with powers over the other Welsh rulers and possibly even over the Anglo-Norman lords of the area.[78] In 1177, the year after Henry had taken steps to ensure all tenants of knights' fees in England had sworn allegiance to him, Rhys and Dafydd ap Owain Gwynedd both did him homage, a sign of their personal relationship and client-kingship.[79] Rhys was instrumental in introducing into south Wales important modifications to the native laws. Under his aegis, food renders were commuted into money payments, and whereas previously appraisement of value had only been used where the law books did not dictate a sum, *Blegywryd* records that Rhys extended the system of appraisal so that it was of general application.[80]

Under the auspices of the Lord Rhys, a literary revival commenced within Wales. In 1176, he held an eisteddfod at Cardigan, and it may well be the case that he sponsored the translation of the laws of the south-west into Latin, the version known as Latin D, for this version emphasizes his reforms.[81] Latin D, of which *Llyfr Blegywryd* is virtually a translation, has a keen awareness of the civilian legal culture, with plentiful awareness not only of technical legal vocabulary but of maxims and legal theories.[82] The influence of canon law is also heavy upon the Blegywryd tradition, where the insistence upon the laws' acceptance by the Church is emphasized, as is the role of Blegywryd, archdeacon of Llandaff, as scribe to Hywel's commission.[83] Some have taken this emphasis upon the canonical regularity of the law to mean that Latin D was composed after Archbishop Pecham's visitation and criticism of the native customs at the end of the thirteenth century,[84] but it should not be forgotten that similar criticisms had been lodged by Archbishop Theobald in the twelfth century and by Giraldus, who was a contemporary of the Lord Rhys, and that even in the twelfth century knowledge of canon law and canonical procedures was scarcely foreign to St David's diocese, which saw the careers of bishops such as Bernard and Dafydd Fitzgerald, as well as archdeacon Giraldus himself. Whatever the date of the extant text, there is no doubting that the law books as they have survived began to be compiled during the period of literary revival for which Rhys was in part responsible and that it was probably on his initiative that they were assembled into book form.[85]

Rhys's position as justiciar mirrored that of Ranulf de Glanvill in England, where the justiciar in the king's absence acted as vice-gerent of the kingdom. In other words, Rhys was virtually Henry's viceroy in south Wales. It is scarcely surprising that he would have sought to emulate the policies of his English master and accentuate Deheubarth's traditional connection with law-giving in Wales. During these years, Wales began to fall more and more under the tutelage of the English king, becoming part of the great Plantagenet empire, which might again have appealed to the native consciousness. By the end of the twelfth century, talk of *Britannia* ceased; there would appear to have been a new confidence abroad, with a preparedness to accept the overlord-ship of a ruler whose methods of achieving unity amongst his several domains did not require uniformity and thereby echoed the rule of Hywel, whom this age learned to call *Da*. Wales was drawn into the Plantagenet net. All lords and rulers in Wales met with Henry in 1177 and he demanded fealty and liege homage from them in return for gifts of land, much as he had insisted upon the oaths of English military tenants being taken the previous year.[86] The years 1176–9 saw the culmination of Henry's legal policies in England, and the example of these procedures does not appear to have been lost upon Wales.

In that all free men owed allegiance to Henry, Henry owed them justice in his court. From 1179, he introduced regular visitations of the English shires by his justices, the general eyre, to dispense justice to his subjects, and his subjects could also come to his court at Westminster to seek legal redress there when the royal justices were not in the shire where they lived. As they were only entitled to bring causes before the royal justices in the shire of their domicile, they needed special permission to present their case before the Westminster court, and this permission was given in the form of a writ, ordering that their case be heard and determined. Thus was born the writ system of the English common law.

Among the writs which provided his subjects with a remedy, Henry introduced speedy mechanisms for dealing with alleged wrongful dispossession of land, the possessory assizes, based in all likelihood upon canonical models which were ultimately derived from the Roman possessory interdicts. The earliest, which was introduced as a primarily criminal measure in 1166 but returned as a civil proceeding in 1176, was the assize of novel disseisin. By virtue of the assize, a tenant of freehold land who claimed that he had been wrongly dispossessed, disseised, of his holding, could obtain a writ from the king's chancery ordering the sheriff of the county where the land was situated to empanel an assize, a jury, of twelve persons, to answer two factual questions: had the defendant wrongly disseised the claimant without a judgement of the court, and had this occurred since the king's last crossing to Normandy. If both questions were affirmatively answered, the claimant was put back into possession, seisin, and the defendant, if he wanted to press his claim to the land, had to bring an action to argue the more complicated issues of right title. In 1176, Henry also introduced the assize of mort d'ancestor, a procedure under which the claimant asserted that he had been kept out of possession by the defendant following the death of the claimant's father, mother, brother, sister, uncle or aunt. Again, the writ ordered the sheriff to empanel an assize of twelve persons to answer whether the deceased ancestor had been possessed of an inheritable estate in the land and whether the claimant was his nearest heir. If both questions were answered affirmatively, the claimant would be put into seisin. In the thirteenth century, the procedure was extended to remoter ancestors,[87] and by that time further remedies had been introduced called writs of entry, to deal with situations where the claimant averred that the defendant's coming to the land, his entry, was in some way blemished and that accordingly the claimant should be put into possession.

The Welsh law books contain material which appears to reflect the impact of the influence of Henry's legal reforms in Wales. Thus, in the south, *Llyfr Cyfnerth*, adopting the traditional triadic mnemonic, speaks of there being three ways in which land can be lawfully obtained: by inheritance from parents, by buying from the previous owner, and by gift of the previous owner. There were also three ways in which causes of action relating to land could arise: wrongful possession, which echoes novel disseisin, *dadanhudd*, similar to mort d'ancestor, and by kin and descent, which mirrors the claim by right and inheritance in the common law writ of right, the *breve de recto*. Threefold also were the kinds of wrongful possession, namely in opposition to the owner against his will and without judgement – language which reflects very closely the terms of the assize of novel disseisin; in opposition to the previous owner's heir against his will and without a judgement – similar to mort d'ancestor, and through a guardian in opposition to the right proprietor and against his will and without a judgement – one of the situations which might give rise to a writ of entry, the means of coming to the land being tainted.[88]

Dadanhudd appears also in the texts from north Wales, the term being linked with the traditional Welsh reverence for the hearth of the family home. The fire in the hearth was never extinguished, only covered overnight, and the term *dadanhudd* related to the question of who had the right to uncover the fire. By means of the action, a son claimed land which his father or mother had possessed and of which he alleged he had been wrongfully refused possession or been dispossessed. The procedure could also be brought if the land had previously been in possession of a grandfather or great-grandfather, and the intermediate generations had predeceased the previous tenant, in other words the claimant had been the ancestor's nearest heir on the ancestor's death. If the claimant failed in his suit of *dadanhudd*, then, as with the English mort d'ancestor, he could still proceed by writ of right.[89] Very interestingly, the sections on *dadanhudd* in the texts of Latin A, from the *Cyfnerth* tradition, and Latin B, from the north, are virtually identical, suggesting that they were incorporated as innovations, probably imitating the Henrician reforms and perhaps evidencing the Lord Rhys's influence in the south but also the influence of English developments in the north, perhaps via the Church. Pressure from the ordinary people for this sort of development should not be discounted either, for this was the time when the men of Gower expressed their preference for 'the law of twelve and of inquest' in imitation of the common law jury, when the Lord Rhys introduced sworn valuations and when the men of Ceri asked for the abolition of the custom of *galanas* in cases of homicide.[90]

Henry II had also introduced into the English shires methods for trying those who were widely believed to have committed serious wrongs and who had not been accused by their victims or their victims' families. Such notorious delinquents could be presented for trial before the king's commissioners by juries of presentment in every county, the precursors of the later grand juries. Until the commissioners arrived, the suspects were to be held in county gaols. The commissioners sat on a regular basis, undertaking circuits of several shires, to hear and determine, *oyer* and *terminer*, these charges and to deliver the gaols, that is empty them by trying all those on remand. The commissioners' powers derived from the Assize of Clarendon of 1166 and the Assize of Northampton of 1176, from which they became known as assize judges and their courts as the county assizes, which courts were destined to last until 1971. Effectively, they introduced for the first time a procedure which was solely concerned with punishing a wrongdoer without providing for the compensation of his victim, whereas the older system of appeal by the victim or his family led to both punishment and compensation. The appeal was not abolished at this time, but the assize procedure had separated the civil remedy from the criminal trial. Crimes were now being tried because they were an offence to the king as well as to his injured subjects, and a distinct system of criminal justice was being born. A corollary inevitably was that some civil remedy which did not have a criminal dimension was required to complement the assize procedure and relieve the victim of the need to bring an appeal which would contravene the double jeopardy principle. The writs of trespass, writs for wrongs, would be developed to fill this gap.

During the twelfth century, wrongdoing in Wales was also coming to be seen as an offence against the prince and not just the victim, exhibiting the same underlying principle of crimes being a breach of the prince's peace or protection. The custom of *galanas* was starting to decline and in some parts of Wales it would survive on the basis of arbitrated settlements rather than fixed payments, perhaps once again showing the influence of Rhys ap Gruffydd. The procedure in such causes became markedly more English in approach and the idea was gaining ground that the prince might have the power to change the law and certainly had the right to dictate the procedure that would be used in his court, for after all the court was his. In effect, that was the principle by which Henry II had introduced both his juries of presentment and his possessory assizes.[91] All of this may manifest the influence of the civilian concept that what was pleasing to the prince had the force of law – *quod principi placuit legis habet vigorem*.

On the civil side, Henry expressed his protection of all his freehold tenants by establishing the principle of *nemo respondetur sine brevi regis*, none is to be made to answer for their freehold land without the king's writ. This meant that, even though a tenant held land of another lord, the lord could not try any issue regarding that land in his feudal court unless empowered to do so by the king's writ, the writ in question being the *breve de recto*. This issued to the lord of the tenant instructing him to maintain full right to the demandant who was claiming the land and threatening that if he did not do so the matter would be moved into the king's jurisdiction. Moreover, Henry also introduced an alternative to trial by battle in such disputes, namely trial by grand assize, that is by an empanelled jury of twelve who would consider which of the parties had the greater right to the land.[92] The choice of procedure, battle or assize, was for the tenant to decide, and if he chose the assize the matter had to be moved into the king's court for only it had the authority to empanel a jury. The grand assize provided a mechanism whereby tenancies granted in time of peace could be established as being for life or for inheritance without risk of their being forfeit as the result of a trial of strength with a younger, fitter demandant. In the Marches of Wales, however, the harsh realities of feudal needs may not have progressed so far in the direction of peacetime bargains. The presence of local danger and the absence of royal control was apparent in the continued application of strict feudal principles, so that when those who held by military tenure failed to respond to the call to defend the castles of Glamorgan in the troubles of 1183–4, their lands were confiscated. What Professor R. R. Davies has termed 'the military rationale of lordship' endured in these parts.[93]

Where, in England, the title of a tenant-in-chief of the king to his lands was challenged, the dispute by feudal principle belonged in the king's court because the king was the tenant's lord. In such cases, the king's writ ordered the tenant either to hand over the land to the demandant or appear before the king's justices to explain why he had not done so, that is, why he had not obeyed the king's command. This was the writ *praecipe* and it commenced litigation concerning tenancies held in chief of the crown. During the reigns of Henry's sons, Richard I and John, and possibly in the later years of Henry's own reign, it would appear to have been used in the case of other freeholders who were not the king's direct tenants so as to shortcircuit the need for a *breve de recto* to the tenant's lord and then a reversion to the king's court if the tenant chose the grand assize. In effect, using *praecipe* in these circumstances underlined the king's perception of himself as lord as well as king to all his free subjects, and as their lord his obligation to provide justice in his court for them. Lesser lords, however, saw in this an usurpation of their rights and in 1215, by clause 34 of Magna Carta, King John had to agree not to issue the writ called *praecipe* so as to deprive a free man of his jurisdiction over his tenants. The issue, however, illustrates very neatly the tension between the lordship of the king and that of the feudal lords. In the thirteenth century, perhaps in imitation of Henry II's policies in England, the princes of Gwynedd were to assert their lordship over the other Welsh rulers and their claims came to conflict with the lordship claimed by the kings of England. The idea of 'the king in London' having a bare overkingship was being changed into one which resembled the claims made by the English kings over their English tenants-in-chief, just at the moment when the Welsh rulers were embarking upon what appears to be a similar policy at home. The result was to be conflict and, for the Welsh rulers, catastrophe.[94]

THE THIRTEENTH CENTURY

Llywelyn ap Iorwerth, a grandson of Owain Gwynedd and also known as Llywelyn Fawr, became the sole ruler of the northern kingdom during the first four decades of the thirteenth century. As he consolidated his control over Gwynedd, so too he sought to regularize his relationship with the kings of England. In July 1201, he swore fealty and liege homage to John, who in return allowed either English or Welsh law to be utilized to resolve disputes in Llywelyn's lands, according to whether they were held of Welsh or English lords.[95] It was agreed that the nobility, the *maiores*, of Wales should also swear fealty to the English king, and that John could send commissioners into Llywelyn's lands to try causes and that Llywelyn could refer cases to the English king's court.[96] Four years later, Llywelyn married Joan, John's illegitimate daughter – her illegitimacy perhaps mattering little to a Welsh prince.[97] If Welsh law paid little regard to legitimacy, it also pointed to a closer relationship with the English ruling dynasty, for if one looked at the offspring of Llywelyn's marriage with Joan from the viewpoint of the Welsh custom of *mamwys*, John should treat any son of the marriage as his son. This alliance could bode very well for the lineage of Llywelyn in the future. Llywelyn may have been consciously seeking such an outcome given that the Welsh rule of partible inheritance had played havoc with the royal succession in Gwynedd during the thirty years following Owain Gwynedd's death in 1170. Llywelyn would appear, like Henry II in England, to have wished to find a solution to this running sore of a problem.

Llywelyn had two sons: one, Dafydd, by the princess Joan, and an earlier child, Gruffydd, to English and ecclesiastical eyes born outside of lawful wedlock.[98] Llywelyn pursued a clear policy of having Dafydd recognized as his sole heir. This he did by disinheriting Gruffydd in 1220, a step which was recognized by the English government of Henry III, the infant half-brother of Joan. In 1222, Pope Honorius III unsurprisingly accepted Dafydd as Llywelyn's lawful heir and in 1226, more surprisingly, the Welsh leaders accepted the situation which was contrary to Welsh custom. Not surprisingly, Llywelyn was to be deemed an innovator regarding inheritance practices. In 1228, Henry III accepted Dafydd's homage as heir to Gwynedd.[99]

John's attitude to his relationship with Llywelyn had however changed. Whereas in 1201, he had been content with the fealty of Llywelyn's magnates, in 1211 he demanded hostages and the allegiance of as many of Llywelyn's subjects as he, John, should wish. In addition, Dafydd at that time not having been born, he claimed the right of escheat over Llywelyn's lands in the absence of his having a direct heir by Joan.[100] For the first time, an English king was seeking to treat a Welsh ruler as a tenant-in-chief rather than an under-king. The claim to an escheat carried the clear suggestion that Gwynedd was Llywelyn's by John's grant rather than by his own right.

Not surprisingly, when John found himself in difficulty with his own barons in 1215, Llywelyn was not slow to take advantage of the changed circumstances. Under the terms of Magna Carta, the hostages were returned.[101] In 1216, the year of John's death and the accession of the infant Henry III, Llywelyn moved to unify his kingdom by requiring the homage of his subjects at Aberdyfi. Other princes were now his clients not his equals, he alone having a direct relationship with the English king. Litigation was to go to his courts and he claimed the authority to confiscate the lands of the other rulers.[102] Llywelyn was learning lessons from his dealings with the Plantagenets, and applying his knowledge at home in Wales. Llywelyn saw Wales as part of a federation under the English crown, not part of a unified English kingdom, reflecting the earlier tradition of client kingship under the king of London.

Two years later, in March 1218, Llywelyn did homage to Henry III at Worcester, and in the same year he and the lesser Welsh princes went to Woodstock to do homage to the young king, thereby acknowledging dependence upon the English crown.[103] Thereafter, as he strove to get Dafydd alone recognized as his heir, so too he sought to strengthen his position as the superior ruler within Wales. In 1230, he married Dafydd to the daughter of one of the principal Marcher lords, Isabella, the daughter of William de Braose.[104] Unfortunately, while negotiating the marriage, the bride's father made the most of his opportunities and seduced Llywelyn's wife, Joan. On 2 May 1230, Llywelyn hanged de Braose for his adultery, a penalty which savours not only of revenge but also of princely pretensions, for death was to the medieval mind the appropriate penalty for the treason of ravishing a queen consort.[105] The marriage nevertheless went ahead and could have led to its offspring having claims to the de Braose lands in due course, thus further consolidating the claims of the house of Gwynedd to suzerainty throughout Wales. In 1238, Llywelyn called the princes of Wales together to an assembly at the Cistercian abbey of Strata Florida to do homage to Dafydd, but Henry III intervened to prevent this kingly claim. Recalling that, in 1228, all the princes and magnates who had met the king at Montgomery had done him homage, Henry forbade their also doing homage to Dafydd, insisting that their fealty only should be taken.[106] If Llywelyn had succeeded in having Dafydd accepted as his heir, thus transforming the Welsh custom with regard to the inheritance of a kingdom, he had not succeeded in establishing himself as the sole link with the English crown, all other Welsh rulers holding their lands of him.

He had however adopted the trappings and the propaganda of a prince.[107] Not only did he describe himself as prince of north Wales in the manner of his predecessors, he claimed a superior status over other Welsh princes as prince of Aberffraw and lord of Snowdon.[108] It is possible that the northern legal texts, Latin B and *Llyfr Iorwerth*, have their origins in this period, for they were compiled during the period of Gwynedd's supremacy and emphasize the superior status of the prince of Aberffraw.[109] The knowledge of Roman law manifested by Latin B is very similar to that of the *De Legibus* attributed to Bracton in England, which probably dates from the late 1230s, thus further suggesting that these traditions are connected with the aspirations of Llywelyn Fawr. He died in April 1240, noted for his governmental innovations as well as his changes to the practice of inheritance.

Llywelyn had his wish in that it was Dafydd who succeeded him.[110] Only a month after his father's death, Dafydd did homage to Henry III for Gwynedd, but remarkably Henry intervened to uphold Gruffydd's rights according to Welsh law.[111] In this, Henry appears to have taken seriously his duty of maintaining right to his Welsh subject, Gruffydd, according to the laws of Wales, an interesting application of the principle of maintaining full right as illustrated by the words of the *breve de recto*.[112] The friction caused by this policy led to conflict between Dafydd and Henry, and when peace was restored in 1241, the terms included Dafydd's surrender to the English king of the homage of 'all noble Welshmen' and it was again emphasized that Gwynedd would escheat to the king if Dafydd died without direct heirs. Dafydd was only to receive oaths of fealty from the Welsh nobility on pain of forfeiting his lands.[113] Dafydd was being treated as a tenant-in-chief and not as a subking. Henry during the 1240s exacted homage from Maredudd ap Rhys Grug and claimed jurisdiction over the disputes of that family within his own courts, again undermining any claim by the ruler of Gwynedd to an intermediary jurisdiction.[114]

Dafydd did however do his best to assert his royal status during his brief reign. In 1244, he attempted to break free of Henry III's control by placing Gwynedd under the protection of the Pope. Pope Innocent IV initially appeared to be content with this arrangement, and when Dafydd began to use the title of prince of Wales, being the first prince to do so, alarm bells sounded at the English court for again the Pope appeared ready to accept Dafydd's claim. All other Welsh rulers were described as lords.[115] Dafydd's princely authority was also exhibited in his exercise of the prerogative to change the law; he is credited with the abolition of *galanas* in Gwynedd.[116]

Dafydd died in 1246 and, despite the peace terms of 1241, his nephews, the sons of his half-brother Gruffydd who had predeceased him in 1244,[117] were allowed to succeed to Gwynedd. Among these, Llywelyn ap Gruffydd was to emerge as the foremost and was to continue the practice of modernizing the laws of Wales in line with the influences from England, the Church and the March. Under Llywelyn's rule, the ancient food rents were commuted to money payments, a step which blurred the distinction in status between the nobility and the *maerdref* tenants. This led to a strong dislike of Llywelyn in certain quarters and left the way open for both his brother, Dafydd ap Gruffydd, and the bishops of Bangor and St Asaph to present their subsequent disputes with him as being attempts on their parts to uphold native traditions in the face of Llywelyn's modernizing or even betrayal of his nation's laws.[118] Under his rule, the prince's rights to wreck, treasure trove and *bona vacantia* were asserted, where previously such rights would have benefited the territorial lord or earlier the *cenedl*. He continued to collect occasional dues such as *amobr*, *ebidew*, *gobr estyn* and the profits of justice, but innovated by introducing a duty to grind corn at the lord's mill which was previously unknown to the laws of Wales.[119] In much the same way as Henry III was doing in England,[120] he claimed the right to confirm the alienations of lesser lords, summoning them to his court for the purpose, a step which met with resistance and assertion of more regional loyalties.[121] He treated the king's waste as tantamount to his own property, something which had been unpopular in Wales since the Normans had introduced this perspective, and seemingly advocated the escheat of lands for failure to perform services, an approach which may have endured in the March but was by this time virtually obsolete in England. He also emphasized that disloyalty to the prince, *brad*, was of a different order to breach of faith to a lesser lord, and perhaps under ecclesiastical influence stressed the particularly heinous nature of crimes committed by ambush or by premeditation, *cynllwyn*. He introduced the feudal incident of wardship, whereby the lands of a military tenant who died leaving an infant heir were taken by the lord until the heir came of age, the lord keeping the profits, and it is also under his rule that the short lease, or *prid*, for four years makes its appearance, the thirteenth century seeing the introduction of legal remedies for leaseholders under the English common law as well.[122]

Llywelyn's rule saw an increase in judicial activity within his territories, and he clearly regarded the administration of justice as his princely preroga-tive, so that he was entitled to adapt procedure as he saw fit. In this, he was similar to princes throughout western Europe at the time. His royal council of *gwyrda* in Gwynedd became a more formal body, and key royal servants and ecclesiastics found their way into its ranks.[123] Henry II had led the way with such developments in England, raising 'men from the dust' to be his most trusted servants, a step resented by the peers who saw themselves as the king's natural counsellors. Such resentment was also sparked in Wales, adding to criticism of Llywelyn for ignoring distinctions of status as with his policy of commuting food rents to money payments. Ednyfed Fychan, a progenitor of the Tudor dynasty, was appointed steward, *distain*, at Llywelyn's court, a post which the English understood to be that of justiciar throughout Wales.[124]

At Woodstock on 30 April 1247, Llywelyn and his brothers, the four sons of Gruffydd ap Llywelyn Fawr, did homage to Henry III for Gwynedd, ceding the four cantrefs of the Perfeddwlad to the English crown and promising military service. The terms of the grant make them look very much like tenants-in-chief, which was probably the aim of the English crown. Again, it was asserted that, if they died without direct heirs, Gwynedd was to escheat to the king of England, opening up the way for a further regrant the terms of which the king could control rather than his having to admit any collateral relatives as of right.[125]

At Woodstock, the English king claimed and obtained the homage and service of all the barons and nobles of Wales, thus giving himself jurisdiction over all disputes relating to lands and succession for these persons. Henry III was achieving in Wales what Henry II had achieved in England and by the same methods. The legal consequences of Welsh freemen having sworn homage to the king of England were worked out in the detail of the king's jurisdiction and entitlement to services in the succeeding decade. The rulers of Gwynedd were treated as holding their lands of the English crown; they were to all intents and purposes tenants-in-chief.[126] Henry also attempted to assert his policies in the March, appointing royal commissioners to settle disputes between Marcher lords and requiring that the record of proceedings in their own courts should be reviewable by the justiciar of south Wales. Throughout Wales, he ordered his officials to respect the native laws and customs, but the very fact that such reminders were necessary points to there having been problems of high-handedness in the behaviour of some officials.[127] He also appointed royal justices to hear and determine disputes between the four sons of Gruffydd ap Llywelyn Fawr relating to their inheritance of Gwynedd, ordering Llywelyn to appear before his presence and treating each brother as holding in chief of the king. Ultimately, this was the behaviour which Llywelyn could not countenance and he went to war with Henry.[128]

Between the years 1255 and 1258, Llywelyn began to draw the other rulers of Wales to do homage to him for their lands, thus making him, and not Henry III, their liege lord.[129] Basically, his technique was that of the Sarum Oath and of Henry II; he was to be the focus of feudal unity within Wales. This done, in 1258, he asserted the fullness of his achievement; he took the title prince of Wales.[130] Henry III determined upon a truce with Llywelyn at this point, for 1258 saw the English monarchy at a low ebb. It was the year of the Provisions of Oxford, when the king had to agree upon terms with his barons to secure his kingdom from civil war. He could not afford to have a war in Wales. Thus the way was clear for Llywelyn to take oaths of allegiance from the native lords and to imprison Maredudd ap Rhys Grug for treason.[131]

The north Wales law text Latin C most likely comes from this period. It is certainly later than 1238, given its insistence upon the superiority of Gwynedd, but it is most consistent with the years after 1258, when Llywelyn had taken the homage of the other Welsh rulers.[132] While Llywelyn was able to consolidate his position in Wales during the first half of the 1260s, Henry III's kingdom slipped towards civil war, the baronial party being led by Simon de Montfort, earl of Leicester. Llywelyn seized his chance when Simon had the upper hand in 1265, and agreed with the earl at Pipton-on-Wye that his title as prince of Wales should be recognized and that he should have as of right the homage of the other Welsh princes. In return, he promised Simon 30,000 marks over a period of ten years. The treaty was made in June, but never came into effect, for Simon died at the Battle of Evesham in August of that year.[133] Nevertheless, the terms of the treaty are significant; they show a hankering for a return to the situation where the English king was an overking, but not a feudal overlord. The prince of Wales was to be the only feudal overlord in Wales.

Simon's death marked the end of baronial rebellion in England. After much difficulty, the papal cardinal legate, Ottobuono Fieschi, the future Pope Adrian V, settled the terms of an agreement between Henry and Llywelyn in the space of four days. The Treaty of Montgomery of September 1267 was the high-water mark of Llywelyn's reign. He was granted the title prince of Wales with the homage and fealty of all the Welsh barons with the exception of Maredudd ap Rhys Grug, whose homage he could buy for 5,000 marks. In return, he was to pay 25,000 marks to the English crown. The disadvantage was that the treaty was couched in the terms of a royal grant and not a recognition of Llywelyn's antecedent rights. He was to hold of the king of England and he owed justice to his subjects, and in particular to his brother, Dafydd ap Gruffydd, for whom he had to make provision. Any disputes within Llywelyn's principality were to be settled by Welsh law, but English representatives were to be present in order to ensure that justice was done.[134] In other words, the king of England was the guarantor of justice within Wales, just as he guaranteed full right among the subjects of his feudal barons in England. Llywelyn, like any other vassal, could be supervised by the royal justices to ensure right was maintained. Llywelyn did homage and swore fealty and service to Henry.

If English representatives were to attend the courts of the Welsh prince to see that justice was done, they would have needed to know what the laws of Wales were. It is possible therefore that one or more of the law book traditions stems from the years following the Treaty of Montgomery. Again, Latin C fits the bill, although it is also possible that a statement of the law would have been needed in Deheubarth to accommodate the separation of Maredudd's lands, in which case an early version of Latin D is also a possibility. In either case, a Welsh text and a Latin translation might have been required.

Henry III died in 1272 after more than half a century as king. Edward I, his son and heir to the English throne, was returning from crusade and did not arrive in England until 1274. Probably because he wanted his position as prince recognized rather than regranted, Llywelyn refused to do homage to Edward after he became king. In 1273, he failed to swear fealty and insultingly failed to attend Edward's coronation in the following year. Llywelyn's third refusal to do homage to Edward having been summoned to do so left the king free to wage war against him in April 1276.[135] Edward had to deal with his insubordinate Welsh tenant-in-chief, whereas Llywelyn had to resist the pretensions of an overking who wished to be an overlord.[136]

Llywelyn was as determined to assert his feudal overlordship within Wales as he was to resist Edward's claims to such a position within his principality. Llywelyn not only demanded the homage of the other princes, but also the homage of their vassals, seeking to establish his direct lordship over all free Welshmen as Henry II had done almost a century earlier in England, and in the same manner he sought to attract their disputes into his courts at the expense of those of their immediate overlords.[137] This raised exactly the same questions within Wales regarding royal authority as the issuing of the writ *praecipe* to persons other than the king's tenants-in-chief had raised in England. Moreover, Llywelyn also attempted to assert his right to confirm the grants made by other lords within Wales by summoning them to his court to have the confirmations made.[138] This inevitably caused a backlash of local loyalty, which bridled at Llywelyn's attempts at centralization. The policy of demanding that grants of land by the king's barons should be confirmed by royal authority had been pursued in England under Henry III, but without much success. Edward I was to abandon it in England in favour of more drastic reforms, which marked the beginning of the end of feudalism in England.[139]

Within a year, Edward I had overcome Llywelyn's attempt at rebellion. By the Treaty of Aberconway in 1277, Llywelyn forfeited virtually all he had won at Montgomery ten years earlier and was reduced to the position he had enjoyed at the start of his reign by the Treaty of Woodstock.[140] As a result of his disobedience, Llywelyn had to pay Edward £50,000 to be reinstated in the king's grace and mercy. Thereafter, he had to pay 1,000 marks every year for Anglesey, although the island was later entailed to him. He was required to do homage and swear fealty to the English king, who, perhaps mockingly, allowed him to keep the title prince of Wales, but only granted him the homage of five Welsh magnates, and this was to be for his lifetime only and was not to be enjoyed by his heirs. Edward also insisted that provision be made for Dafydd and that right be done for the other sons of Gruffydd ap Llywelyn Fawr, again seemingly applying the principles behind the English writ of right to fulfil the requirements of the native Welsh laws of partibility. Territorial disputes in Wales were to be settled by Welsh law, while those in the March were to be settled by the law of the March.[141]

From 1277 onwards, it was Edward I who began to insist upon confirming the charters of Welsh rulers and overseeing their jurisdictions, asserting that it was his right to arbitrate their disputes and appointing justices to oversee law-suits in Wales on his behalf.[142] In January 1278, he appointed seven justices to hear and determine all suits and pleas both of land and of trespass in the Marches and in Wales according to Welsh law. Although Edward later reduced the number of justices to four, when Llywelyn's presence was needed before such tribunals, he was summoned like any other litigant.[143] In the March, Gruffydd ap Gwenwynwyn, the ruler of Powys Wenwynwyn, chose to be treated as a Marcher lord and was forced to accept the English common law within his territories. He succeeded however in obtaining royal approval for a change in the inheritance customs of his lordship, English primogeniture replacing Welsh partibility.[144] Powys had suffered badly from the effects of partibility during the thirteenth century, being divided among five heirs in 1236, four in 1269, and among a further six in the southern Powys Wenwynwyn in 1277.[145]

Gruffydd ap Gwenwynwyn's status as a Marcher lord was to result in a serious dispute with Llywelyn which was to contribute to the downfall of the Welsh prince.[146] The dispute concerned the *cantref* of Arwystli in the upper Severn valley, which both parties claimed to be part of their territories. This now had the additional complication that, for Llywelyn, Arwystli was in Wales, while for Gruffydd, if it was his, it was now in the March. Llywelyn sued before Edward I's justices, claiming that Welsh law was the proper law of the dispute, whereas Gruffydd countered that it should be tried by the law of the March. In 1280, Edward I set up a commission to determine how actions concerning Welsh princes and lords had been tried in the past. The commission reported in June 1281 and Edward decided that as it was a land dispute it was under royal jurisdiction and the choice of law was for him. He decided that English procedure should be used, and that it was for him to decide where and when the cause should be heard. Welsh law required land disputes to be heard on the land.[147]

The years following the Treaty of Aberconway in 1277 again saw a need for English royal justices to have some familiarity with the native Welsh laws, a need which may have led to the production of Latin texts and even of Welsh texts as a precursor to their translation into Latin. In the south, Latin D and *Llyfr Blegywryd* may belong to this period, and in the north, Latin E as well. These lack the stress of Latin B, Latin C and *Llyfr Iorwerth* upon the supremacy of Gwynedd, but exhibit considerable canonical and indeed religious influence. Latin D, of which *Blegywryd* is almost certainly a translation, contains a deal of legal sophistication, but it has been claimed that even greater emphasis upon legal principles and an even greater ecclesiastical influence can be discerned in Latin E. There, for the first time, the principle of one witness being insufficient and of two being necessary is stated in the term *vox unius, vox nullus*, and biblical episodes are quoted as illustrations of the rules of Welsh law.[148] This may have been a response to criticism of the Welsh laws by churchmen, which was not new, although Archbishop Pecham of Canterbury told Llywelyn in the wake of Aberconway that Welsh customs were only to be observed if they were reasonable.[149] This may have provided the impetus for producing texts which emphasized not only the reasonableness but also the canonical propriety of the Welsh customs, suggesting that the *proemium* with its account of Hywel Dda's assembly being attended by churchmen as well as secular representatives, being serviced by archdeacon Blegywryd and having its product approved by the Pope, most probably dates from this time. The tradition may not have been new, but its inclusion in the text may well have been. Typical of the age also is the inclusion in Latin D of the principle *de similibus simile iudicium dandum est*, that like cases should be decided alike, which finds an echo in the provisions of the Edwardian Statute of Westminster II in 1285, chapter 24 of which included the celebrated *in consimili casu* clause which carried the principle into effect with regard to the issuing of original writs to commence litigation before the English courts of common law.

From 1277, however, Edward I regarded Wales as part of his dominions and Llywelyn as a mere tenant-in-chief in those parts, whose pretensions to princely status were reduced to size by the terms of the Treaty of Aberconway, which provided for their end upon his demise. The conflict over Arwystli and a dispute with the justice of Chester over rights to wreck provoked another rising in 1282. The rising was instigated by Llywelyn's brother Dafydd, who may have moved before Llywelyn was ready. Llywelyn rose to the challenge, but lost his life in an ambush at Cilmeri in mid Wales at the end of the year. With his death ended the attempt of the Welsh princes to achieve a feudal unity within Wales of the kind achieved by Henry II in England in the wake of the Norman invasion.[150] Edward I now moved to consolidate the position of the English monarchy in Wales and to ensure that Wales should never again pose a problem for the kings of England. The Edwardian settlement ushered in a new phase in the legal history of the Welsh nation.

6

The Later Middle Ages

PRINCIPALITY AND MARCH IN THE FOURTEENTH CENTURY

Edward I conquered Wales, bringing the whole country under his direct or indirect control. The portions under his direct control were the principalities of north and south Wales, the territories of the once independent princes. The area under his indirect control was the March, where the Marcher lords still exercised quasi-regalian powers, but under the watchful eye of their royal overlord. The outward and visible signs of Edward's control were the great castles which he built along the coast of north Wales, castles which all his Welsh subjects with the exception of the *maerdref* tenants were, according to an ancient rule of Welsh law, obligated to maintain, an ancient rule given a fresh and much resented lease of life in the lands of Wales following the Edwardian Conquest.[1] Around the castles grew boroughs, drawing inhabitants from England, whose loyalty to the English crown could be taken for granted, and who in return enjoyed privileges denied the native population. The Welsh were however, from the first, attracted to the boroughs and many coveted the status of burgess.[2]

If the castles and the attraction of the boroughs were the visible signs of the Conquest, the introduction of English law was an inner manifestation of the same phenomenon. The Statute of Rhuddlan, 1284, ushered many of the common law's standard features into the Principality, and these too were to be a magnet drawing the native Welsh into the legal culture of the conquering English.[3] Edward I is sometimes hailed as the English Justinian, after the sixth-century Byzantine emperor under whose rule the great compilations of Roman law were produced, the compilations which were to preserve the legal culture of the classical world for it to be resurrected by scholars in the Middle Ages. In the same way as other imitators of Justinian presented the fruits of their labours, Edward claimed to have examined closely the native laws and customs: 'Which being diligently heard and fully understood, We have . . . abolished certain of them, some of them We have allowed, and some We have corrected: and We have likewise commanded certain others to be ordained and added thereto . . .'.[4] Among those customs abolished was the right of illegitimate offspring to inherit alongside the legitimate, an unsurprising reform given the attitude of the Church. Partibility of land among heirs was among those allowed, as was much of the native law relating to moveable property, while inheritance customs might also have been said to be among those corrected by Edward's introduction of dower for Welsh widows and a right of female inheritance to land in the absence of male heirs.[5] The native law with regard to crimes was abolished wholesale and replaced with a thoroughly English approach to criminal justice, with the concept of felonies being introduced together with that of unamendable offences, that is, those for which amends could not be made by compensation.[6]

The greatest changes involved the introduction of English structures of government and for the administration of justice in the north and south-west of Wales.[7] North Wales was for the first time divided into shires, the former land of Gwynedd being divided into the counties of Anglesey, Caernarfon and Merioneth. In the north-east, a new county of Flint was also created, but this was placed under the jurisdiction of the justice of Chester. In the south-west, shiring had already taken place since 1241, Deheubarth being divided into the counties of Cardigan and Carmarthen.[8] The shires of the north-west composed the principality of north Wales, those of the south-west, the principality of south Wales. In effect, these were provinces of the English crown,[9] where, as chapter 14 of the Statute of Rhuddlan stated, the king could whensoever and wheresoever and as often as he liked, declare, interpret, enlarge or diminish the provisions of the statute according to his 'mere will'. In other words, the laws depended upon the royal prerogative; Edward was asserting the Roman maxim *quod principi placuit, legis habet vigorem*.

Both in the north and in the south, the principal officer of royal government was the justiciar, in effect a vice-gerent or viceroy, in the manner of the justiciars who had served the English crown in the twelfth century when the kings had to be absent on a regular basis to govern their other territories. Each justiciar was assisted by a chamberlain, who ran the respective exchequers of the two principalities. Beneath the justiciar in each shire was a sheriff who presided at the shire courts, which, according to the English model, were to be held on a monthly basis. Courts were also established in every *cwmwd*, areas of Welsh governance which continued to be preferred to the *cantref* which might be thought to equate more readily to the English hundred. The *cwmwd* court was to meet every three weeks under the presidency of a bailiff, and each *cwmwd* was to have a coroner, chosen at the county court. Twice a year, at Easter and Michaelmas, the sheriff would visit each *cwmwd* to conduct his *tourn*.[10]

In the southern principality, the sheriff did not hold the *tourn* nor did he preside at the county court. The greater part of the lesser judicial work was done in the *cwmwd*, with the *cwmwd* officials accounting to the sheriff. In Carmarthenshire, there was both an English and a Welsh county court.[11] In the north and the south, however, the more serious criminal charges, accusations of homicide, arson and rape, were to be taken by the justice at his sessions in the county.[12] In cases of suspected homicide, the coroner of the *cwmwd* inquired into the circumstances and enrolled the paternal and maternal kin of the victim so that they could present an appeal for the felony.[13] This in effect meant that those who would in the past have had an interest in the payment of *galanas* or, in default, the pursuit of the blood feud were rapidly absorbed into the judicial process in order to prevent any risk of disorder through resort to the older procedures.

As well as the introduction of the English methods of prosecuting wrongs – the presentment and the appeal – the justice's sessions were also seised of the more important civil pleas, the statute introducing into the Principality the original writs which could be used to initiate civil actions, setting out within the text precedents to be followed in each case. Thus, chapter 6 of the statute introduced the writs relating to pleas of land, the assizes of novel disseisin and mort d'ancestor, together with a general writ relating to questions of right. The assize of novel disseisin, as in England, was to deal with questions of recent dispossessions achieved by unlawful means, that is, not justly and by judgement. The disseisins had to be recent, novel, but in the Principality the time limit was set from the time 'after the Proclamation of our Peace in Wales', that is, the moment when the Principality had been annexed to the English crown. The same time limit applied to mort d'ancestor. Moreover, the latter could be extended to remoter degrees of relationship than those specifically mentioned in the original English writ, ensuring that extensions of the kind which had been required in England and which had necessitated the creation of the new writs of *aiel*, *besaiel* and *cosinage* were obviated in Wales. Such extensions were to be allowed to litigants in Wales 'upon their Case', and even more significantly it was enacted that the 'Forms of the Writs shall be changed according to the Diversities of the Cases'.[14] This in effect anticipated the solution to a problem then obtaining in England, namely that the chancery was required to work within the limits set by the then existing register of writs and was not allowed of its own motion to amend the form of a writ to deal with cases which were clearly within the purview of the existing remedy though not within its verbal limits. This situation had obtained since 1258 when, in the Provisions of Oxford, the Chancellor had had to swear that he would not create any new writs, so as to stop royal justice poaching upon the jurisdictions of lesser lords. The year after the Statute of Rhuddlan, in the Statute of Westminster II 1285, power was to be given to the chancery clerks to do the same in England by virtue of the *in consimili casu* provision of chapter 24 of the statute. The Welsh provision appears to have anticipated the English solution.

This raises an important dimension of the statutory provisions for Wales. Whereas in England, the common law was already to some extent, a large extent, developing within the context of the royal and feudal politics of the previous century, in Wales the common law procedures and remedies were largely free from the restrictions of that history. Thus, the courts of the

Principality were not divided as in England into the King's Bench and the Common Pleas, the former with jurisdiction over matters of specific interest to the king while the latter dealt with litigation between ordinary subjects. In later centuries, as will be seen,[15] rivalry between these jurisdictions would develop and arguably hamper the development of the law in England. Likewise, the Welsh system did not have a separate court of Exchequer to deal with matters of financial interest to the Crown. In England, until 1285, again the year after the annexation, unless royal justices were present in the shire, all civil litigation before the royal courts had to be tried before the Common Pleas at Westminster, the administration of justice being to that extent centralized. Judicial eyres were becoming less frequent, and general eyres of the whole country would cease altogether in 1337, although at this time the Court of King's Bench continued to follow the king around his realm, returning to Westminster only when the king was there or when he was absent from the realm. The Common Pleas however, by virtue of Magna Carta, were fixed at Westminster. This was a manifest inconvenience for litigants who had to travel to Westminster with not only witnesses but also jurors from the county for their case to be heard. In the Principality, the Sessions would sit regularly in the new shires, and in 1285 England would see the introduction of a new system whereby litigation could be commenced before the Common Pleas at Westminster and then adjourned to a future date there, unless before (*nisi prius*) that date the assize judges arrived in the county from which the cause came, in which case the verdict of the jury could be taken locally prior to judgement being given back at Westminster. The date chosen would always ensure that the verdict could be taken locally and this method of trying civil litigation, the *nisi prius* system, would endure until 1971. In Wales, however, the procedure from 1284 was even simpler, with all stages of the litigation being taken locally.

The Statute of Rhuddlan followed the provisions of the earlier Statute of Gloucester of 1278 in England in reserving civil litigation of the value of forty shillings or more to the justice's sessions, while matters of less value could be proceeded for by writ or simple complaint in the courts of the shire or the *cwmwd*.[16] The statute provided precedents for actions to recover debts and moveable goods, a writ of dower to support the introduction of the concept into the Principality, and a writ of covenant, which could be varied according to the requirements of the parties and was available in the form *Justicies* to commence litigation before the sheriff if the parties preferred. This was also an interesting time in the development of covenant in England in that it was only gradually being settled by the common law courts that they would not specifically enforce such an agreement but only give damages for its breach and also that they would always require written proof under seal to allow the action.

Another clear indication that royal control was not as fettered as in England lies in the form of the general writ to claim land as of right or its possession.

The writ is given in the form *praecipe*, instructing the sheriff to command (*praecipe*) the tenant to give the land to the demandant or else to explain his refusal or contempt of the command before the royal justice. In effect, this reverses in Wales the policy of chapter 34 of Magna Carta, whereby *praecipe* was only to be used if the land was held in chief of the king (*in capite*) or the seigniorial overlord no longer held a court for his tenants (*quia dominus remisit curiam suam*), otherwise the appropriate remedy was a writ of right (*breve de recto*) commencing litigation in the lord's court. Edward may have recognized that in the Principality lords would no longer be holding courts, but equally may have determined that that should be the case and acted decisively by statute to achieve the desired result in a way not open to him in England. In England, he would commence the comparatively slower process of winding up the feudal system of landholding and accelerating its demise when in 1290 the statute *Quia emptores* would prohibit for the future subinfeudations of the fee simple in land, so that thereafter land would be transferred by substitution like any other form of property, so that the feudal ladder could no longer be extended but could only shrink.

Edward and his advisers also acted to obviate some of the procedural difficulties that affected the common law in England. For questions of right to land, as with the possessory assizes of novel disseisin and mort d'ancestor, trial was to be by jury with no need of the grand assize and no possibility of trial by battle. In personal actions, proof was to be by bond or wager of law, although in covenant a jury was to be used. In actions of debt, judgement could go by default if the defendant did not appear, an advance upon the position in England.[17] In chapter 10, treating of covenants, specific mention is made of the situation where, having promised land to one person, the promisor conveys to another, a scenario which was to form the background to much litigation and legal development in fifteenth-century England. Trespasses, where more than forty shillings was claimed, were also to be tried by a jury,[18] and in chapter 7, where those issues destined for trial by assize are differentiated from those to go to the jury, a wealth of examples of possible causes of action are given, suggesting that the statute's draftsmen were drawing upon the previous experience of the common law in England in devising the measures that were to be established in Wales, giving a fascinating insight into the techniques and methods of those framing the statutes of the age. While the trial of issues relating to land were to follow the English pattern in the Principality, Welsh methods were still to be available in trials relating to moveable goods.[19]

The provisions of the statute applied only to the Principality. In the Marches, the statute did not apply, but often the Marcher lords imitated the king's organization and structures.[20] For instance, in Bromfield and Yale, a seigniorial version of the statute was promulgated for the lordship,[21] while in the south, in what were effectively the counties palatine of Pembroke and Glamorgan, justice was administered with sheriffs, coroners and county courts following the English pattern, with what would in the Principality be the pleas of the crown, the most serious criminal cases, being reserved for the lord's personal jurisdiction.[22]

Pembroke, Glamorgan and Flint were however special cases. In other areas of the March, along the border with England from Chester to Chepstow, the law was a thorough mixture of English and Welsh customs with both constituencies from time to time borrowing freely to their advantage. Englishmen were happy to lease inalienable Welsh land by means of the *prid*, a loan of the land usually for a short term of about four years with the produce being charged to meet the sum due to the lender, what in some legal systems is called a *vifgage*.[23] Welshmen on the other hand were happy to adopt the procedures of the common law, most particularly trial by inquest or jury, in their causes. Welsh customs retained their force: in the south west, Welsh land law would survive until well after the sixteenth-century union, with even priests continuing to enjoy their share of the family's *gwely* lands in the diocese of St David's well into the fourteenth century.[24] In the lordship of Clun the payment of *galanas* was to continue into the sixteenth century. The law of the March varied from place to place, being based upon the will of the lord, the practice of his courts and the memory of the local community. Among the Welsh inhabitants, great respect was accorded the law of Hywel, another instance of the past being venerated as a lost golden age. Payments, such as *amobr*, continued to be made, *cynnwys* was claimed, *rhaith* of *cenedl* was still in use in cases of theft, despite the abolition of Welsh criminal procedure in the Principality, and there was accordingly a demand for legal advisers who were skilled in both Welsh and English law, albeit the influence of the latter system was most definitely waxing steadily.[25] English lords often adapted Welsh customs to their advantage, as for instance demanding the payment of *amobr* on a second marriage as in Bromfield and Yale,[26] although in some areas compromise solutions are once more to be found – in Monmouth a payment of one-half of the *amobr* only was required in such cases.[27] The Marches however were not entirely free from royal interference, for Edward I himself began to intervene there, claiming the right to impose taxes, to raise troops and to send his justices there.[28] Although the king's writ did now run in the Principality by virtue of the statute, it still did not run in the March, so that Wales as a whole was a land with little legal uniformity at the start of the fourteenth century,[29] a century in which even greater legal uniformity was to be achieved in England. The independence of the individual Marcher lordships was particularly evidenced by the inability to have criminals extradited from one lordship to another, extradition being only possible from one *cwmwd* to another within the same lordship.[30]

Despite their readiness to adopt some of the advantageous features of the common law, there remained sensitivity among the Welsh regarding the loss of some of their rights. Among these, the loss of native procedures for dealing with crimes, and the loss of communal rights such as those to forests and pasture land loomed large.[31] Although mills belonging to the family continued to exist, in some cases the imposition of the obligation to take one's corn to the lord's mill for grinding, so-called suit of mill, was a further grievance.[32] Suit of court, the obligation to attend the various courts introduced by the statute, was also burdensome, particularly as the timing of the sessions was often inconvenient and potentially ruinous in an agricultural community. Having to plead according to the requirements of English law was cited as a cause of his rebellion by Rhys ap Maredudd in 1287,[33] but the effect of this rebellion and more particularly that of 1294–5 was to increase the disabilities and thereby the sensitivities of the native population. Boroughs such as Denbigh increased their emphasis upon their Englishness. Welshmen were not to live there, not to trade either there or on their outskirts, were not to bear arms within their precincts and indeed were never to assemble without the king's permission and then only in the presence of royal officers.[34] The land of Wales, Principality and March, was not represented in the parliaments which from the reign of Edward I were a regular feature of the government of England; knights from the Welsh shires, burgesses from the English boroughs in Wales were not cited to attend. Only on two occasions in the reign of Edward II, in 1322 and 1327, were representatives from the Principality, but not from the March, invited to attend a parliament at Westminster. Nor did the courts at Westminster exercise any jurisdiction in error over the sessions in Wales, so as to achieve uniformity in the judicial interpretation of the law.[35]

Following Archbishop Pecham's visitation of the Welsh dioceses in the wake of the annexation, bishops followed the royal example and issued legislation for their dioceses in the form of constitutions, largely based on Pecham's views of what needed to be done.[36] The Church was to become one avenue for advancement for the Welsh during the fourteenth century, with Welshmen being appointed to the episcopal bench and playing key roles in the government of the Church.[37] The law was to be another such route. For even though the native legal system suffered somewhat inevitably following the annexation, it is clear from the continuing production of manuscripts recording Welsh legal development that the study and application of the native laws continued, so that some form of schooling in the native tradition clearly survived.[38] Welshmen however did not confine themselves to the study of their own legal culture; they willingly embraced the common law as well. Men like Sir Edward Hanmer forged legal careers for themselves, Hanmer rising to become chief justice of the English King's Bench. His daughter was to marry Owain Glyn Dŵr, perhaps having met him when he was a student at the Inns of Court in London – institutions emerging during the fourteenth century to provide legal education, and to which ambitious Welsh families were ready to send their sons for instruction in the law and as a sort of finishing school in courtly manners and behaviour.[39] Welshmen also came to hold offices occasionally, such as that of sheriff, in the Principality, for instance the descendants of Ednyfed Fychan in the north and men like Sir Rhys ap Gruffydd in the south.[40]

If Welsh law continued to develop and some Welsh families began to prosper in post-Conquest Wales, it was the English common law which experienced the greater increase during the fourteenth century and Englishmen who were uppermost among the office holders of both Principality and March. English procedures were borrowed extensively by the native Welsh, with the influence of the common law extending outwards from the Principality, the English boroughs and as a result of the influence of lawyers in the community who were acquiring an English legal training. Sometimes a Welsh term might be coined for an English legal institution, as with *cwyn newydd difeddiant* for novel disseisin,[41] although in the main legal terminology was borrowed from England. Families seeking to make their way in the world of the new order readily adopted English practices, such as granting dower to their wives and requiring that their daughters be allowed to inherit in the absence of male issue, in both cases following the statute rather than the indigenous Welsh custom. They also began to entail their lands, that is, requiring that they descend to their eldest son and then to his eldest son and so on, and thus avoiding the fragmentation caused by the custom of partibility while yet insisting that the land remain within the family, achieving primogeniture while avoiding the land becoming alienable. Entails had become inalienable in England following the Statute of Westminster II, chapter 1, *De donis conditionalibus*, in 1285. Leading Welsh families also began to convey their lands by charter, that is, by written instrument, and also by final concord, an English practice by which transferor and transferee both went before the king's court, the latter claiming that the land was his and the former compromising the action in return for a monetary consideration, what was really the purchase price. The court record, the foot of the fine, would witness that the land was the new owner's, and the final concord was therefore for the Welsh an excellent method of breaking the inalienability of *gwely* land.[42]

While the racial divide between the Welsh and the English remained significant with regard to what procedure was to be used in certain personal actions, with regard to whether property was to be inherited and with regard to whether lands were freely alienable, developments such as the entailing of estates and conveyance by final concord began to confuse the situation. The fourteenth century also saw the Welsh begin to infiltrate the English boroughs. The extent of such penetration varied from place to place, but in some places, such as Aberystwyth and Ruthin, it was considerable.[43] The disability of the Welsh to hold property in these areas led to the development of the *prid*, an institution which combined the concepts of the lease and the *vifgage*. The would-be Welsh purchaser of land in a borough or town would purchase the land by giving the previous owner a capital sum in the form of a loan, receiving in return possession of the land for a fixed number of years as security for the loan. Usually the period was fairly brief, for instance four years. While in possession of the land, the Welshman would keep the profits, in effect enjoying the land and its fruits as an owner. At the end of the period, he was theoretically entitled to repayment of his money and the land should be given back, but the reality was that the loan would be extended, so that he kept the land and its profits. In effect, he had purchased it, but the method overcame his inability to take the legal title.[44]

The *prid* offered opportunities to Welshmen on Welsh lands as well as in the English boroughs. *Gwely* land which could not be alienated could be subjected to a *prid*, enabling a purchaser to take possession and the profits for his purchase money, the family's rights in effect being transferred to the cash. Technically, the land was still theirs, but their interests had been converted into interests in the liquid capital. Lords saw a way of profiting from such transactions, and began to insist upon their permission, in the form of a licence, being obtained before land was subjected to a *prid*,[45] recalling the thirteenth-century attempts by lords in England to require their permission for alienation but perhaps more so Edward I's method of requiring licences to be granted exempting the grantors from the provisions of the Statute of Mortmain of 1279, the Statute *De viris religiosis*, before land could be given to churches or other corporations. Lords also moved towards allowing alienation of family lands provided their permission was obtained, a move which illustrates how feudal lordship had for some time been usurping the position of the *cenedl* in Welsh landholding and social life generally.[46] The lord's right to an escheat when the family died out replaced the residuary right of the larger family group beyond the household.

When land did escheat, lords were loath to regrant, and possibly tenants were loath to receive, land according to Welsh customs of partibility. Instead, escheated land was leased rather than regranted. As the racial divide between Welsh and English decreased, the importance of social divisions among the Welsh themselves, between free men and bondmen, increased, so bondmen began to be emancipated and granted copyhold tenancies on the English manorial model. The land which had formerly been held by the bondmen was again regranted by lease, often to free tenants.[47]

These changes to the social standing and the landholding practices among the Welsh began in the first half of the fourteenth century, but the social changes which affected England and Wales in the aftermath of the great visitation of the plague in 1348, the Black Death, were both to accelerate this process and to aggravate some of the resistance to it. Within the boroughs, the English burgesses began to insist once more upon their privileged trading position and argue for the exclusion of the Welsh from the boroughs, given that the fall in population meant an inevitable fall off in profits. Envy of Welsh burgesses was rife, and even before the Black Death some boroughs had sought to expel those Welshmen who had wormed their way in, for instance, Criccieth in 1337 and Beaumaris in 1345.[48] Shortage of labour after the plague led to Welsh seasonal labourers going to work in England at harvest time being exempted from the restrictive provisions of the 1351 Statute of Labourers.[49] The decline in population led to the abandonment of some previously cultivated agricultural land

and its being given over to pasture, and the demise of whole families in the pestilence inevitably increased the number of escheats and the leases of demesne lands in manors.[50] Lords who saw their incomes decline as a consequence of losing large numbers of tenants to the plague were all the more insistent upon their dues and perquisites, claiming monopoly rights in the profits of forests, timber, assarts, pannage, mills, tolls and escheats.[51] While the native Welsh welcomed the freedom from hereditary customs which the second half of the fourteenth century witnessed, a development which went hand in hand with a gradual anglicization of landholding between 1350 and 1450, with many landholders paying a fine to convert their *prid* into an English legal estate in the land, there was also widespread resentment at the manner in which lords insisted upon the collection of Welsh dues such as *amobr*, and at the loss of freedom to exploit forests and pastures in accordance with the native Welsh custom. Seigniorial interference was hated as a foreign import, and insistence upon suit of mill and suit of court continued to fuel resentment.[52]

Many fourteenth-century Marcher lords made substantial profits from their monopoly of the administration of justice within their lands. Already at the start of the fourteenth century, Edward II had by ordinance in 1315–16 sought to confine the taking of *amobr* to a limited period after the loss of maidenhood and to the occasions when it had been collected under Welsh law. He also sought to restrain the levying of taxes, the taking of bloodwyte and the intrusion of English procedures in actions for contracts and trespasses. He provided that, if an inquest had to be taken in a dispute between an Englishman and a Welshman, the jury should be composed of both races in equal proportions. The stringency of exactions by bailiffs in the taking of *gwestfa* and indeed the superabundance of bailiffs was addressed, and all of these things both in the north and the south. In the north, specific provision was added to the effect that a man with two sons should not be prevented from allowing one to proceed in religion and that interference with transfers of land should cease provided the transfers were not to a mortmain corporation.[53]

In 1354, it was emphasized that the Marches were not dependent on the Principality but depended directly on the Crown.[54] That there should have been any confusion perhaps reflects the similarity of practice which was developing between the two parts of Wales. In the administration of justice, Marcher lords in the south especially had begun to employ justices in eyre to take judicial sessions in their lordships on the model of what was done in the Principality. These Marcher sessions were to be held every three to five years, and were meant to exercise jurisdiction over the most serious wrongs, and a jurisdiction in error over the lesser tribunals in each lordship together with the power to pardon criminals and exact fines was given them. However, attendance at them was accounted a great burden by the tenants, and the practice arose before the end of the fourteenth century of allowing the sessions to be redeemed by the paying of a sum of money, somewhat euphemistically called a *donum*, gift. While very common in the south, this was not so in the north, other than in the lordships of Denbigh and Bromfield and Yale. The income derived from the redeeming of sessions was to become very important to the Marcher lords, but the cancellation of justice involved was to bedevil law and order on the March in the coming century.[55]

THE FIFTEENTH CENTURY

Resentment at English high-handedness and what was coming to be viewed as the oppression of their seigniorial demands were among the factors that led to the rebellion of Owain Glyn Dŵr in the opening decade of the fifteenth century. The revolt has a place in the legal history of Wales for three main reasons. First, it brought to the fore some able Welsh lawyers who had achieved their legal learning not in the service of the common law but in that of the canon law of the western Catholic Church. Owain was joined by Welshmen who had attained ecclesiastical preferment, among them Lewis Byford, bishop of Bangor, John Trefor, bishop of St Asaph, and Gruffydd Young, archdeacon of Meirioneth, who became Owain's chancellor. All of these men were experienced canonists.[56] John Trefor, alias Ieuan ap Llywelyn, had been a student of the Roman civil law as well as of the Church's canon law, and had served at the papal curia from 1389 to 1394.[57] Gruffydd Young was a lawyer of considerable ability, whose influence it is believed had much if not everything to do with Owain's vision of Wales being a separate province of the western Church, with its own archbishop at St David's, two universities of its own, one in north and the other in south Wales, and with a clear requirement that only those fluent in the Welsh language should be appointed to benefices within the Welsh Church.[58] Interestingly, Gruffydd Young was illegitimate by birth, and this may have been a handicap to his preferment in post-Conquest Wales whereas it would have not have mattered a jot under the native customs. He also may have been the inspiration behind Owain's summoning a parliament to Machynlleth in 1404, a move which highlighted the lack of Welsh representation in the councils and parliaments of the English king. The civilian influence upon Owain's policies may well indicate that for some Welshmen there was a feeling that Wales could still be legally as well as politically independent of England, with the legal deficit being made good by the learning of the civil and canon law, a learning which during the fourteenth century had on the European mainland moved out of the universities and into the courts of princes to shape their legal policies and the procedure within their tribunals.[59] In this, John Trefor had not merely been an eyewitness but an active participant. Interestingly, when a century later Henry Tudor became king of England and Welshmen began to make their way at court in greater numbers, a substantial number chose to practise before the civilian jurisdictions of the Church and the Admiral rather

than before the common law courts at Westminster. The civilians among Glyn
Dŵr's entourage, not to mention John of Wales at the start of the thirteenth
century, may indicate that this tradition was established well before the sixteenth
century. Owain's ideas of Wales as a separate province in Christendom with its
own archbishop and universities were presented to the Avignon pope, Benedict
XII, Owain having conveniently recognized a different pope during the Papal
Schism from that recognized by the English king. The Welsh civilians' idea of
Wales as a separate nation became manifest as the schism was healed at the
Council of Constance in 1417, a claim of separate nationhood which was strenu-
ously denied by the English representatives. The claim is evidence nonetheless
of how learned Welsh civilians utilized their legal expertise in the service of
their native land as they perceived it.[60]

The rebellion predictably resulted in an English backlash against the Welsh
and the imposition of restraints upon their rights. A series of legislative measures
at the start of Henry IV's reign prohibited Welshmen from holding lands in
England and in English boroughs within Wales, together with towns along
the Welsh border from Cheshire to Herefordshire.[61] Welshmen were not to be
burgesses in the boroughs,[62] and Englishmen were not to be convicted at the
suit of Welshmen other than by English justices.[63] Welshmen were debarred
from carrying arms in towns, markets, assemblies, church, the highway and
were not to make assemblies or *commorthas*.[64] They were not to hold castles,
fortresses or defensible houses, and the garrisons of castles within Wales had
to be entirely English.[65] No arms or other victuals were to be imported into
Wales without royal licence, and Welshmen were not to hold offices relating to
the administration of justice within either the Principality or the March.[66] Englishmen married to Welsh women were subject to the same penal restrictions.[67]
The goods of Welshmen generally were placed at the mercy of Englishmen in
England who had not been satisfied in their claims against other Welshmen,
as stark an instance of the concept of reprisal against the goods of foreigners
as can be envisaged.[68]

These provisions were to remain on the English statute book until the seventeenth century, and were to be re-enacted at intervals during the fifteenth century,
for instance in 1431, 1433, 1444 and 1447.[69] It is not clear to what extent they
were acted upon once the rebellion had run its course and the threat from Wales
had receded. But they were called into operation, it would appear vindictively,
to remove two of Owain's own relatives from office in later years, a kinsman
Robert Trefor of Trefalun in the north and Owain's son-in-law John Scudamore
in the south.[70] Not for nothing were later generations to castigate the provisions
as unchristian and unnatural.[71]

The most lasting and important legal effect of the revolt was the further
acceleration of the change to English land tenure and the terminal decline of
bond status. The rebellion resulted in further depopulation, ringing the death
knell of the *gwely* and the *gafael* as means of landholding, with a concomitant

increase in the leasing of land and of land purchase in the manner of English law.[72] The *prid* became almost the typical form of Welsh landholding during the fifteenth century as more and more land was leased rather than granted.[73] On his accession, Henry V had guaranteed inheritance of land according to the customs of Wales,[74] but less and less land was actually being held according to those customs. Two factors during the fifteenth century played an important role in producing this change. First, the civil wars of the middle years of the century, which became known as the Wars of the Roses, involved many magnates who held lands in the March. As the fortunes of the rival houses of Lancaster and York waxed and waned, so did those of their followers, many of whom found themselves condemned as traitors or met their end on the field of battle. Either way, many Marcher lordships escheated or were forfeited to the Crown, so that the Crown became the principal player in the lordships of the March. Much land therefore on the Marches was leased to tenants by the Crown itself. Another major landowner in Wales and the March was the Cistercian order, an order which, like the Church generally during the fifteenth century, benefited greatly from gifts of land upon the deaths of previous owners. Such gifts were facilitated by the development in England of the use, a device outside of the common law by which the legal title to land would be given to one or more feoffees to hold to the use of others, those others being the persons entitled to the benefit. During the fifteenth century, the king's chancellor came to enforce these uses in his own court, the court which was to become known as the court of Chancery, essentially a prerogative court dispensing justice in cases with which the common law either could not deal or could not deal adequately. One advantage which the use afforded was that it made it possible to make unofficial wills of land, wills of land not being permitted at common law until 1540. By the use, however, a landowner could transfer his land during his lifetime to feoffees and instruct them as to who was to receive it on the owner's death. If the ultimate donee was a church or some other mortmain corporation, a royal licence would be needed,[75] but such gifts were rendered comparatively straightforward and redounded much to the Church's benefit. The Cistercians in Wales during the fifteenth century cleared a lot of such land for leasing, selling the timber for use in lead smelting.[76] By the end of the century, they were also active in the leasing of mineral rights for secular exploitation.[77]

Despite the penal statutes and their periodic re-enactment during the fifteenth century, many Welshmen distinguished themselves in the service of the English crown, particularly in the French wars of Henry V. Whether in war or peace, such service often led to the favoured few receiving grants of denizen status as a mark of royal esteem, rather in the manner that Roman and Latin status had been accorded to worthy individuals in the ancient world. Such grants freed the recipients from the restrictions of the penal statutes and opened a route for them to advance in terms of wealth and social standing within Wales and at court.[78] Such persons were likely to adopt the manners and customs of their new-found status rather than cling to their native traditions, so that denizen status among leading figures was a further impetus to anglicization. Intermarriage also spread English ways, ambitious Welshmen finding the approach of English law to the inheritance and alienation of property, particularly with the development of the use, much more attractive than the native Welsh traditions.[79] The emerging class of Welsh gentry also began to occupy positions of influence in the government of both the Principality and the March.

The reason for this was that during the fifteenth century, with war first in France and then civil war at home, the Englishmen who held the principal offices in the Principality or who were lords in their own right in the March, were often absent from their responsibilities. Initially, the deputies who were appointed to carry out their duties were also English, but as the century progressed the appointment of Welshmen became more common.[80] A notable example was the appointment of William Herbert in 1463 to be chamberlain and chief justice of Meirioneth, thereby severing the county from the administration of the northern Principality.[81] These deputies had their own agenda and ambitions, not to mention the rivalries that attended the opening up of these offices to the ambitious.[82] The net result was an increase in disorder and lawlessness, with the Commons at Westminster complaining that the March was actually out of control and that the common people of England should not have to foot the bill for its recovery.[83]

The profits of being a Marcher lord had declined sharply in the wake of the Black Death and again after the Glyn Dŵr revolt. Instead of the traditional dues and renders, the lords now looked primarily to the redemption of their judicial sessions for their gains: 2,000 marks were paid at Brecon in 1418–19 to redeem the sessions, 650 at Newport in 1476 and in the whole of the period 1422–75, only twelve out of the fifty-two sessions commenced at Carmarthen completed their business.[84] Not surprisingly, lawlessness and disorder was the outcome. Amongst the catalogue of crime regularly recounted as endemic to the March were mentioned murders, cattle stealing, kidnapping, piracy on the Severn, attacks upon merchants, feuds, *commorthas* and organized raids on towns.[85] There was a steady increase in the payment of *arddel*, a fine paid to come under the protection of a Marcher lord,[86] which might well mean support in the event of being accused of wrongdoing in the manner of the granting of livery and maintenance which so bedevilled law and order in England in the second half of the century. As dissatisfaction with the situation in the March increased, treaties or *cydfodau* were entered into between lordships to assist in the extradition of criminals and the situation became so bad that from 1442 to 1448, statute extended the definition of treason to cover abduction and theft by the Welsh in the border counties. Proposals to deal with the difficulties by establishing a Council for the Principality and the March in 1437 and again in

1443 came to nothing, but eventually that was the route which was to lead to the reimposition of order in the troubled border country.[87]

It was the Yorkist king, Edward IV, who effectively established the Council of Wales and the Marches.[88] In 1471, he made his son, Edward, prince of Wales and gave him a council of fifteen to manage his estates. The prince's council was increased in size to twenty-five in 1473, when the king sent his eldest son to Ludlow with his council.[89] Technically, the prince of Wales's lands did not extend beyond the Principality, but the jurisdictional difficulties attending the March and the fact that so many Marcher lordships were now in the Crown's hands militated against a narrow view being maintained. In particular, the need to ensure that criminals could be extradited from one lordship to another necessitated the wider perspective.[90] In 1476, the Council was given a commission of oyer and terminer which was to cover the Principality, the March and adjacent counties. The prince was to have a council 'learned in the law' maintained at Westminster.[91] Edward IV also tackled the problem of lawlessness by requiring recognizances for good behaviour to be entered into by likely delinquents.[92]

Edward, prince of Wales, who became king as Edward V, was never to be crowned, being one of the princes who died in the Tower, probably at the behest of their uncle, Richard III. The defeat of Richard at Bosworth in 1485 brought Henry Tudor to the English throne, and in the eyes of the Welsh, a Welshman had become king of England. Henry VII followed Edward IV's precedent when in 1489 he created his son, Arthur, prince of Wales and re-established the prince's council. Although Arthur was to die in 1502 without ascending the throne, Henry kept the council in being after the young prince's death because of its effectiveness in dealing with the government of Wales. He extended its initial jurisdiction to Chester, Shropshire, Worcestershire, Herefordshire and Gloucestershire, at one time taking in Bristol. The Council now had its seat at Ludlow, and its powers and jurisdiction were all given it not by Act of parliament but under the royal prerogative. In 1493, John Arundel and others were appointed commissioners, and the prince, acting through his council, was given judicial power in both Wales and the March, including a commission of oyer and terminer, the power of inquiring into liberties and of investigating the flight of criminals, this last power being added in 1504. A substantial body of the Council's work was undertaken by the king's uncle, Jasper Tudor, earl of Pembroke.[93]

The Council was eventually to have a lord president, who would be the chief and supreme governor of the Principality and the Marches of Wales, and would include in its membership the chief justice of Chester, and three of the justices from Wales, with power to co-opt further persons as required. Its powers and procedures were set out in instructions, again indicating its roots in the prerogative rather than the common law. While it was to enjoy a common law jurisdiction over real and personal actions, it also had a criminal jurisdiction similar to the prerogative court of Star Chamber in England, and, like Star Chamber, its methods and procedures were inquisitorial and it could subject suspects to interrogation under torture in cases of felony. It also possessed an equitable jurisdiction, thus making good the deficit created by the fact that at the time of the Edwardian annexation, the Court of Chancery, also in reality a prerogative court, had not come into being in England and therefore had not been introduced into Wales. The Council also had a jurisdiction to assist poor suitors, in the manner of the Tudor prerogative court of requests.[94]

Chancery, Star Chamber, Requests were all courts which had grown out of the prerogative powers of the king's council, and the Council of Wales and the Marches was a similar offshoot. Across Europe at this time, kings were opting to introduce prerogative courts to replace the customary tribunals which diversified the laws of their kingdoms, prerogative courts with inquisitorial procedures based on the practice of the ecclesiastical tribunals. These were the courts which would shape the law and procedure of much of the continent in the modern age, but in England, with the exception of Chancery, they would fall victim to the seventeenth-century reaction against royal absolutism. Nevertheless, in the Council of the Principality and the Marches, Wales felt the impact of prerogative jurisdiction and it was to confer benefits in terms of restoring law and order.

The civilian ethos of the Council may explain why, in the coming generation, many Welshmen following a career in the law chose to practise before the courts of civilian and canonical jurisdiction rather than before the common law courts. The Council was of great assistance to the Welsh gentry, particularly after it was revived by Henry VIII in 1525. Membership or even attendance upon the Council allowed them to complete their education in practical affairs and administration, and this was particularly true of those with some legal background.[95] It may have seemed to the first generation to be born and grow to manhood in Tudor Wales that the civil not the common law was the coming system and that therefore that was the path to choose in forging a legal career.

Henry VII also continued Edward IV's practice of requiring likely wrong-doers to enter into recognizances for their good behaviour.[96] He also encouraged and rewarded the virtuous conduct of his fellow countrymen. The Welsh began to be invited to court, where Welshness was itself encouraged. Welshmen were appointed to major offices in Wales as well as being used as deputies when the principal officers were absentees. Moreover, while Henry VII – perhaps surprisingly – did not repeal the penal statutes passed during the Glyn Dŵr revolt, he perhaps more sensibly, certainly more shrewdly, continued the practice of granting denizen rights to those who kept faith with his government. These were now not only given to individuals but to whole areas or lordships, again in the manner in which Roman and Latin status had been extended more widely in the years of the Roman principate.[97] Charters of denizenship were sometimes issued for a consideration, not only ending the application of the penal statutes, but often abolishing ancient dues and partible inheritance, which must clearly have been seen as disadvantageous by the native population. The Principality of north Wales received charters accomplishing this in 1504 and 1507. Servile dues and bond status were abolished by charter in Bromfield and Yale in 1505, in Chirk and Denbigh in 1506, in Ceri and Cydewain in 1507 and in Ruthin, Dyffryn Clwyd, in 1508.[98] Under these charters, not only was the distinction between free and bond status – which had in any event become almost imperceptible – abolished, but those with denizen status could acquire lands, hold office and become burgesses in England and in the English boroughs, with primogeniture replacing partibility as their native law of inheritance.[99] All of this indicated a growing oneness between the king's subjects in Wales and his subjects in England. The eventual union of the two lands under his son was foreshadowed. The Statutes of Livery and Maintenance which ended the abuses of the keeping of retainers for private war and the undermining of justice were extended to Wales, where they attacked the similar problems of *arddel* in the March. Litigants were encouraged to take their suits from Wales to the royal courts of common law, Chancery and Star Chamber. The profile of the Welsh and of their culture was visibly raised. Distinctions between the law in Wales and that in England were mentioned at readings in the Inns of Court by eminent lawyers.[100]

Under Henry VIII, the practice of redeeming the sessions in Wales came under attack. A decree was issued by Star Chamber in 1521 regulating the practice and perhaps supplying a compromise solution to alleviate the stresses which made the native population ready to pay the *donum* for redemption. In future, the sessions were to meet twice a year, but for no longer than eight days at a time, and were not to be held between March and September.[101] These restrictions prevented them from interfering unduly with the interests of an agricultural population. In 1526, Cardinal Wolsey re-established the Council of Wales and the Marches, this time with a membership of 340 people. Indentures were imposed upon the Marcher lordships, indentures which were to be reimposed after Wolsey's fall in 1531.[102] In the same year, Dr James Denton, the chancellor to the Council, produced a plan to shire the Marches, and in 1534 legislation was introduced to prevent the suborning and perjury of jurors, to regulate the ferries operating on the Severn to prevent the escape of thieves by night, to enforce suit of court, to provide compensation for unlawful imprisonment, to abolish *commorthas* and *arddel*, and to prohibit the carrying of arms to courts and assemblies.[103] The following year, 1535, justices of the peace were created for the existing shires of Wales, that is the counties of the northern and southern Principality, together with Pembroke and Glamorgan, and the justices were to have all the powers enjoyed by their counterparts in England, including powers to extradite criminals. In 1536, statute emphasized that only the king had power to pardon certain offences, only the king could appoint justices and only the king could issue legal and judicial instructions.[104] The sun was clearly setting on the quasi-regalian authority of the Marcher lords. At the same time, the Council had a vigorous and resourceful president, dedicated to enforcing law and order throughout Wales. Bishop Rowland Lee held office from 1534 until 1542, the years which saw the Tudor policy of union carried into final effect. It marked the end of a period of transition, extending from the Edwardian annexation to the reign of Henry VIII, a period during which the Welsh, while looking back nostalgically to the golden age of their native law, had nevertheless once more embraced and accommodated a new legal tradition and gained from its adoption, while managing to maintain an independent and at times fiercely separate national identity. That independence and identity were to face further challenges in the united kingdom of England and Wales.

The Tudors and the Union with England

THE UNION OF WALES AND ENGLAND

The union of Wales and England was effected by two statutes passed during the reign of Henry VIII. These were the Act for Law and Justice to be Ministered in Wales in like Form as it is in this Realm of 1535/6 and the Act for Certain Ordinances in the King's Dominion and Principality of Wales of 1542/3. They are frequently referred to as the Acts of Union.

The 1530s was a decade which saw revolutionary change in the government of England and of English society, the most obvious features of which were the changes in religion which saw the jurisdiction of the Pope ended in England and replaced with that of the king in matters sacred as well as secular. The dissolution of the monasteries followed. Henry VIII and his advisers saw the kingdom, as the statutes state, as an empire[1] with the king as the sovereign ruler. No part of the realm could therefore be beyond his jurisdiction, be it an institutional part, such as the Church, or a peripheral territory, such as Wales. The Acts of Union accomplished the necessary incorporation of Wales into the Tudor empire.

On the eve of the union, the king's attorney, Thomas Holte, painted a gloomy picture of the condition of Wales. Juries there he found corrupt; the giving of livery to followers and supporters and their subsequent maintenance was practised to the detriment of good order and sound justice; the forced exactions called *cymortha* were still being taken, and the stealing of cattle was rife. Holte's proposed solution was to impose English law upon Wales, to abolish the partible inheritance of land and replace it with the English principle of primogeniture, and to ensure that in future homicides would no longer be settled by the payment of a fine, but if fines were paid they should go to the king, thus effectively ending the regalian right of Marcher lords to assist in or even insist upon the compounding of liability for killing in a financially favourable way. The land of Wales should be divided into shires, and justices of the peace should be appointed in them, officers who had been used very successfully to maintain order in England since the mid-fourteenth century.[2]

Nor was Holte the only proponent for such a solution to the difficulties of Wales. Dr John Price petitioned the king, asking that he 'unify' Wales and England, abolishing Welsh law in the process.[3] He wanted the same laws and privileges for the Welsh that the king's other subjects enjoyed. Those who supported Price's views, although not as wealthy as their counterparts in England, were men of influence and sometimes legal training, with practical experience of involvement in the affairs of monastic houses.[4] Welshmen would have been free to perform such functions, as the disabilities which they suffered under English law would not have prevented them from practising canon law, which may provide a clue as to why there was such a prevalence of Welshmen amongst the canon and civil lawyers of Tudor England.

The inhabitants of the Marches requested the introduction of primogeniture in 1534, and also asked for the introduction of a court of Chancery in Wales. This is an interesting, if superficially odd, dual request, for the Court of Chancery in England, a court based ultimately not upon common law but upon the royal prerogative to provide justice where the common law could not do so or could not so adequately, had been active since the late fourteenth century and had done much to circumvent the rule of primogeniture in England. This it had done by enforcing the institution called the use, the medieval forerunner of the modern trust, a device by which the legal owner of property is obligated to manage it in the interests of another, the beneficiary. By giving the legal owner-ship of property to others, feoffees, while retaining the benefit for himself, that is, remaining the beneficial owner, and instructing the feoffees as to who should enjoy the benefit after his death, a person could provide land for younger sons and daughters despite the rule of primogeniture. The use had become very popular in England during the fifteenth century because it allowed for freehold land to be unofficially devised despite the common law principle of primo-geniture, and it also enabled landowners to avoid some of the expensive feudal incidents which could arise upon succession, although legislation in the reign of Henry VII had sought to prevent such avoidance and protect the royal income arising from the incidents. The dual request for primogeniture and a court of Chancery therefore suggests that the inhabitants of the March were fully aware that in England, although primogeniture was nominally the rule, the activities of Chancery allowed for freedom of alienation upon death, which would enable them to dispose of their land more freely than either *cyfran* or primo-geniture contemplated. Ironically, in the same years as the dual request was being made, Henry VIII was seeking a means whereby he could control the bad effects of uses upon his feudal income, and the legislative outcome would be the Statute of Uses of 1536 which enacted that passive uses of freehold land, where the feoffees performed no active duties but merely acted as repositories for the legal ownership, were to be executed making the beneficiaries legal owners. The effect would be to make unofficial wills which defeated primo-geniture unworkable.[5]

Thomas Cromwell, a brother-in-law to John Price, was opposed to allowing Welshmen hold office in their native land. Rowland Lee shared his views, observing that there were few Welshmen with the necessary income to qualify as justices of the peace, even fewer with requisite judgement of men and affairs.[6] Granting Welshmen whose loyalty and ability was assured denizen status was thought to be sufficient.[7] Nevertheless, legislation was enacted in 1535, in accordance with Holte's recommendations, to permit the appointment of justices of the peace in the six shires of the Principality and in the two counties palatinate of Pembroke and Glamorgan, although the provisions never took effect, being overtaken by the provisions of the union legislation which shired the whole of Wales. Holte's views on homicide jurisdiction also bore fruit in that from 1 July 1536, it was enacted that only the king should grant pardons for murder and felony, that only he was to appoint judges, and that all writs and indictments were to issue in his name. Only one sovereign was to exercise regal powers in Henry's empire; the quasi-regalian jurisdiction of the Marcher lords was being forced into terminal decline.[8]

The 1536 Act divided the Marches of Wales into shires, in a manner similar to that in which the Edwardian annexation had shired the Principality. The new shires of Denbighshire, Montgomeryshire, Radnorshire, Brecknock and Monmouthshire thus came into being.[9] The territorial boundaries of each shire were defined, with border communities being allocated either to one of the new Welsh shires or to one of the bordering English shires. Wales therefore obtained for the very first time a legal definition of its political geography. This definition did not correspond to the ethnic division between the Welsh and the English, nor to the linguistic boundary between the two nations' respective languages. Predominantly Welsh-speaking areas found themselves in English shires, and some English-speaking areas found themselves in Wales. Parishes which were for ecclesiastical purposes situated in one of the Welsh dioceses now found that for civil purposes they were part of an English shire. The political boundary, albeit legally defined, was but one boundary between the two countries.[10]

The incorporation of the whole of Wales, both the Principality and the March, into England meant that for the first time the shires and the boroughs of Wales were to be entitled to send representatives to the Westminster parliament. Each Welsh shire was to elect one member and each county borough was to do the same. Meirioneth, however, was not allocated a county borough member, and Monmouthshire was given two shire members, making an overall total of 26 Welsh MPs. This was markedly different to the position in England where each shire and each borough was allowed two representatives; the difference was justified by the relative poverty of Wales which would have made it burdensome for the electors to have to support two members. Every freeholder owning land worth more than forty shillings a year was entitled to vote for the county representative, while in the boroughs every free burgess had a vote.[11] The first members were elected in 1542, so that they were actually members of the parliament which passed the second piece of union legislation in 1543.[12] Technically therefore it could be claimed that the union had not been imposed upon Wales in the manner of its Edwardian precedent, but had been agreed to by the representatives of the Welsh people. The first Welsh members were not distinguished by their contributions to debate at Westminster, however, for a long while being silent in the main, when indeed they were actually present at all. Their absence can partly be accounted for on the basis that membership was often seen as an honour at home rather than an office abroad, and partly because there was very little business that was specifically Welsh in the first half-century after the Union, only 16 out of 770 bills in the years 1559–81 relating particularly to Wales, albeit such an attitude betrays their view that English business did not concern them.[13]

The second Act slightly amended the structure of Welsh representation at Westminster, giving Wales an extra MP in the shape of a member for the borough of Haverfordwest.[14] The 1543 Act also introduced the system of contributory boroughs, whereby the MP for the county borough did not represent and was not elected by that borough only, but was chosen by and represented the boroughs of the county as a collectivity or at least those which were able to contribute to the costs of a member. Thus, the member for Carmarthen was elected by that borough and also Kidwelly, Llanelli, Newton and Dryslwyn. In Glamorgan, the member for Cardiff was chosen by the burgesses there and by those of Cowbridge, Llantrisant, Neath, Aberafan, Kenfig, Swansea and Loughor. The member for Montgomery was supported by the electors of Llanidloes, Llan-fyllin and Welshpool, but those of Caersws, Machynlleth and Newtown were not able to afford the privilege.[15] Many of the first members for Wales were lawyers by profession, among them the famous civilian, William Aubrey, and the common lawyer, David Williams.[16]

The 1543 Act also created officers in each of the shires, thus extending to the new shires the administrative and judicial structures of the former Principality of north Wales, albeit a reformed structure. In July 1540, it was provided that all offices which had been granted for life or for lives became void on 1 September of that year, and in November fresh appointments were made to the office of sheriff which were to endure for one year only. The 1543 Act legislated for the creation of sheriffs, coroners, escheators and high and petty constables in each of the thirteen shires. The new shires were to be served by new Chanceries and Exchequers at Brecon, for Brecknock, Radnor and Glamorgan, and at Denbigh, for Denbighshire, Flint and Montgomeryshire, mirroring those created by Edward I at Caernarfon and Carmarthen which were to continue serving the counties of Anglesey, Caernarvonshire and Meirionethshire, and Cardiganshire, Pembrokeshire and Carmarthenshire respectively. The Lord Chancellor, or if the office was in abeyance the Lord Keeper of the Great Seal, was to make arrangements for the shires to be divided into hundreds.[17] The demise of the native *cwmwd* was foreshadowed.

The sheriffs were appointed to their annual offices by the Privy Council on the nomination of the Council of Wales and the Marches.[18] They were charged

with the serving of writs, originating legal processes, the publication of proclam-
ations, the delivery of royal letters and the collection of taxes. In a judicial capacity,
they were responsible for holding the shire courts and those of the hundred, a
task which they could delegate to deputies. Although these courts would in
future have little criminal jurisdiction, as this was to pass to the justices of the
peace in Quarter Sessions, the fact that the justices had no jurisdiction in debt
meant that the shire and the hundred would continue to be important in
the settling of relatively small civil claims. The sheriffs would now also act as
returning officers at parliamentary elections for the county, which was to give
them great influence as they rarely had to account for or justify their declaration
of the election result.[19]

Albeit that Wales was now represented in the Westminster legislature, one
should not read into this any notion that the Welsh people shared in the legal
or political sovereignty of the nation. The 1536 Act had given the king power
to modify its provisions for any time up to three years, a period which had
subsequently been extended to six.[20] Its successor in 1543 gave the king power to
make whatever modification or addition to its terms he thought necessary.[21]
The Romanist principle of *quod principi placuit, legis habet vigorem* would appear
to have applied as much in the Tudor Wales of Henry VIII as in the Valois
France of Francis I or the Habsburg Spain of Philip II.

The principal institutions for the administration of justice according to the
English common law within Wales were to be the Courts of Great Session. These
were modelled on the Sessions which had been held by the justiciars within
the principality since the Edwardian annexation, Sessions which had been
imitated by the Marcher lords within their own territories but which had become
subject to the abuse of frequent redemption. The Great Sessions were to be
staffed by royal justices, the first of whom were appointed on 28 June 1541.[22]
They were four in number, each one exercising jurisdiction in a circuit consisting
of three counties: the justice of north Wales in the former Principality, now the
shires of Anglesey, Caernarvon and Meirioneth; the justice of Chester in Flintshire, Denbighshire and Montgomeryshire; the justice of Brecon in Radnorshire,
Brecknock and Glamorgan, and the justice of Carmarthen in that shire and the
neighbouring Cardigan and Pembroke. In order to maintain the balance of each
circuit containing three counties, Monmouthshire, being the nearest county to
Westminster, was not included within the jurisdiction of the Great Sessions.
Instead, notwithstanding its being predominantly, indeed overwhelmingly,
Welsh in culture and language, it was required to send its litigation to the
royal courts at Westminster or to have its criminal cases heard and its *nisi
prius* verdicts in civil causes taken on the Oxford assize circuit. Given that
England and Wales were now one unit for legal purposes, the arrangement
should never have been taken as a reflection upon the question of whether
Monmouthshire was a part of Wales or of England, but its exclusion from Great
Sessions jurisdiction as well as its double county membership in Parliament

gave it a distinctly cross-border complexion. The fact that Flint had come under the jurisdiction of the justice of Chester since the Edwardian settlement provided a precedent[23] but hardly one which was likely to be widely appreciated. The position of Monmouthshire was the prime example of how the legal and political boundary failed to reflect the social, linguistic and cultural divide.[24]

The Sessions were established by the 1543 Act,[25] their procedure was modelled on that of the Sessions in the Principality of north Wales under the Edwardian dispensation and they were to be held twice a year in each county, each session lasting for six days.[26] Each of the four circuits was to have a proto-notary, who was to act as the court's recorder, together with a marshal and a crier to attend the justice. There would also be an attorney-general, a chamberlain and a chancellor on each circuit, the last two officers serving the circuit's exchequer and chancery.[27] The Great Sessions had a very wide jurisdiction, which embraced elements which were separate in the royal courts at Westminster. Like the Court of King's Bench, the principal court of common law which since the fifteenth century only sat at Westminster, the Sessions had jurisdiction over all pleas of the Crown, that is, serious criminal charges. They also had jurisdiction over pleas of assize, that is, the assizes of novel disseisin, mort d'ancestor and so on, together with all other pleas and actions whether real, personal or mixed in the same manner as the Court of Common Pleas, which had become fixed at Westminster under the terms of Magna Carta.[28] They were also to acquire a jurisdiction in equity as enjoyed by the Court of Chancery which in England sat only at Westminster. Given that during the later sixteenth century, keen competition was to develop between King's Bench and Common Pleas concerning the latter's monopoly of hearing certain pleas, particularly as proceedings in King's Bench were often cheaper and more efficient, one wonders whether lawyers' experience of the Sessions played any part in breaking down the medieval jurisdictional barriers that separated the Westminster courts. While, initially, most allegations of serious crime and equity matters went to the Council of Wales and the Marches sitting at Ludlow, the Sessions took all actions of debt in excess of forty shillings, actions of trespass and actions on the case seeking redress for civil wrongs, minor land disputes and criminal causes relating to, for instance, the theft of livestock, wool, clothing and household goods. The debt jurisdiction alone amounted to roughly half of the Sessions' workload. On the criminal side, minor offences were punished with floggings and the pillory, while conviction for more serious offences, including grand larceny, that is, stealing goods of more than one shilling in value, led to the gallows. Hangings were a frequent occurrence in the aftermath of the Sessions.[29] The Sessions, unlike their predecessors of the same name, could not be redeemed, which made them popular.[30] However, as time went on, complaints began to surface with regard to the justices employed. They were, it was asserted, often not the best-qualified of lawyers, and they were permitted to continue practising at the bar in England while holding judicial office in Wales. It was complained that this led to them arranging the dates of their sittings to suit the demands of their practices rather than the needs of the litigants, that some were corrupt and that juries were sometimes pressured into giving verdicts. Attendance at the courts was poor and the execution of judgements at times haphazard. Many cases, it has been said, were accordingly settled out of court, although it is a common misconception that out-of-court settlement reflects badly upon the judicial process. Often it illustrates the success of the process in getting the parties to reach a settlement rather than having one imposed on them. Likewise, the criticism of the Sessions that stolen goods were often undervalued in them misunderstands the popular mechanism by which one guilty of stealing an item worth more than a shilling could be spared the gallows by undervaluing the property and thereby classifying the offence as the non-capital petty larceny rather than the capital grand larceny, a means of mercy rather than a corrupt practice or a sign of inefficiency.[31] The success of the courts is more clearly illustrated by the petition in the 1560s which asked that the number of the judges be doubled, a step which was finally taken in 1576.[32] From that date, each circuit had two judges, a chief justice and one other, called a puisne judge.

Justices of the peace were introduced into Wales as a whole by the 1536 Act.[33] The office had existed in England since the middle of the fourteenth century, but, like the Court of Chancery, it was not part of the Welsh legal scene because it had not been a feature of the English legal system at the time of the Edwardian settlement. They were first appointed in 1542, and under the terms of the 1543 Act they were to be appointed by the Lord Chancellor on the advice of the Privy Council, the Council of Wales and the Marches and the justices of the Great Sessions. There were to be eight of them in each county, together with a *custos rotulorum*, who was to preside over the county JPs, assisted by a legally qualified clerk to the justices. The twenty pounds property qualification which operated in England was not to apply in Wales, out of deference to the comparative poverty of even its governing classes. Despite the limits set by the 1543 Act to the number of justices in each county, by 1575, there were 99 in the seven counties of the former Principality and palatinates alone, and therein there was far from an even distribution. The numerical excess was in part the result of the extra duties placed upon the justices by legislation, but it was also partly due to the ambition of landowners and professional men to serve on the peace commission even if they were not really able to fulfil its obligations. There were complaints that unfit persons were appointed, and certainly there were a large number of non-residents on the commission.[34]

The main function of the justices of the peace was to hold the county Quarter Sessions, which, as their name indicated, were held four times a year.[35] These courts dealt with minor offences: disorderly conduct, often in church or in the churchyard; petty stealing; the playing of illegal games and the like. They also had a constantly increasing administrative jurisdiction given them by statute, in particular in matters relating to the Poor Law, where they had to determine issues of affiliation, provide for apprenticeships, control vagrancy and provide poor relief. They were also charged with licensing and controlling taverns, determining wage levels, and policing abuses of rights of common.[36]

The shire court was to be held by the sheriff on a monthly basis, with the hundred courts meeting under him or his deputy every two to three weeks. The sheriff was to visit each hundred twice a year to conduct his tourn. The shire court was primarily intended for freeholders and dealt in the main with small debts and minor trespasses.[37] Marcher lords, who had once had plenary jurisdiction within their territories where the king's writ did not run before the union, were now no longer permitted to try Pleas of the Crown, but in relation to civil as opposed to criminal matters, they were still permitted to hold their manorial courts, the court being the hundred court for the manor where the two units were coterminous and the court for free tenants. The Marcher lords retained some of their quasi-regalian privileges, such as their rights to treasure trove and wreck, but these were now becoming seen as property rights rather than rights of jurisdiction.[38] Parishes also emerged as important units for administration, being charged with keeping a record of baptisms, marriages and burials, as well as having responsibility to take care of roads and bridges and to administer the detail of the Poor Law.[39]

What were now the boroughs of Wales, and no longer constitutionally at any rate the English boroughs within Wales, had their distinct legal and administrative arrangements. Each had its charter, together with a mayor, or sometimes a portreeve or bailiff, aldermen and a council of burgesses. The mayor was elected annually and carried out within the borough the functions of the deputy lord-lieutenant, the sheriff, the coroner, the escheator and those of a JP. He was assisted by a borough recorder and common attorneys. The borough could make by-laws, local laws which related in the main to trade, the conduct of markets and fairs, manufacturing, public health, vagrancy and poor relief. Where the borough was situated in what had been a Marcher lordship, the oversight of the Marcher lord was exercised by his steward, but this oversight was now aimed at protecting his property rather than his jurisdiction.[40]

Within the towns and boroughs of Wales, there were guilds of traders and artisans which regulated the practice of their respective trades and crafts. Frequently, these guilds imposed restrictions upon their members, while membership was of course essential to transact business within the community concerned. The result was that some craftsmen found their opportunities so severely hampered that they emigrated to rural areas away from the towns and their guild restrictions to pursue their callings. Thus it was for example that the weavers of Wales were to be found in the countryside rather than in the towns.[41]

The mayors' role as deputy lord lieutenants in the boroughs mirrored the role of the deputy lord lieutenant in each county. The lord lieutenant was in charge of the county militia, but in Wales, the President of the Council of Wales and the Marches was *ex officio* the lord lieutenant of every county. During the reign of Elizabeth, the presidents were men of a very different stamp from Rowland Lee who prided himself on being no respecter of persons or their status and openly encouraged his own reputation for brutality in suppressing crime.[42] Sir Henry Sidney held the office from 1559 to 1586, and was succeeded by Henry Herbert, the second earl of Pembroke, who remained in office until 1601. The Council, which had emerged as a prerogative court before the union, was put on a statutory footing by the 1543 Act.[43] From then until the crisis of Stuart government under Charles I in the 1630s, it was a major institution in both the government and the administration of justice within Wales, enjoying a substantial amount of judicial business, averaging 1,200 cases every year, in the main civil litigation. Its success made it a magnet for aspiring lawyers, who enjoyed high incomes from the fees derived from litigants, although it was suspected that the lawyers and Council officials encouraged numerous trivial and sometimes malicious cases in order to sustain their profits. In fairness, however, this criticism hardly distinguishes the Council from most other judicial bodies of the time.[44]

The Council was responsible for executing the orders of the Privy Council within Wales and the March, but during the second half of Elizabeth's reign, criticism of its inefficiency in this regard mounted and this was coupled with complaints from the common law courts at Westminster, particularly the Court of Exchequer which dealt with litigation in which the sovereign had a financial interest, that the Council was trespassing on the jurisdiction of local courts and thereby causing losses to the royal revenues.[45] It must however be recalled that this was the period when jurisdictional competition between prerogative courts and those of common law, not to mention among the common law courts themselves, was increasing in intensity and these criticisms of the Council may merely reflect the prevailing mood. Opposition from amongst the common lawyers certainly developed during the 1590s,[46] a decade of intense jurisdictional competition at Westminster. What cannot be gainsaid is that the Council provided a forum in which an increasing number of gentry from Wales, some with a legal background, were able to obtain experience of practical administration and of political business.[47] It was staffed in the main by lawyers and gentry, the lawyers making a sterling contribution to the Council's work, although the gentry element eventually became numerically more significant.[48] As a prerogative court, it took in some measure a civilian approach to its work rather than a common law perspective, and its influence in drawing Welshmen to the practice of civil and canon law before the tribunals of the Church and the Admiral in London should not be discounted.

The judicial functions of the Council were defined by the Privy Council in Instructions in 1553, 1574 and 1586. It was particularly charged with the hearing of the suits of poor persons, like the prerogative Court of Requests in England.

Like the prerogative court of Star Chamber, it had jurisdiction over mis-demeanours and breaches of the peace, particularly with regard to persons of influence who might escape the justice of the common law tribunals through the power they wielded. Unlike Star Chamber, it also held a commission of oyer and terminer, which gave it a jurisdiction coterminous with the Great Sessions over treason, murder and felony. Again, it was able to exercise its jurisdiction in cases where the Sessions might be less confident in dealing with a powerful miscreant, and very significantly in dealing with such cases it was able, as a prerogative court, to extract evidence by torture, thus combining in a way unknown in England, the methods of Star Chamber with the juris-diction of the common law. Again with a view to ensuring good order even in respect of the most influential of persons, it had jurisdiction over matters such as piracy, wrecking, crimes likely to disturb the peace, the misgovernment of officials, false verdicts of juries, and livery and maintenance. Some of these clearly indicate fears that former Marcher lords might be loath to surrender some of their former jurisdictional prerogatives, while the Council's powers to punish rumour-mongers and adulterers reflect the transfer that was occurring within England of jurisdiction in relation to defamation and matrimonial offences from the Church courts to those of the Crown. The Council dealt with disputes concerning the enclosure of land, villein service and other manorial concerns. It could also try cases under the Elizabethan penal statutes, for instance in relation to defence, commerce, industry, the supply of food, the control of prices, employment issues and very importantly questions concerning the Elizabethan religious settlement, where its work mirrored that of the prerog-ative court of High Commission in England.[49]

The Council could also review the decisions of the courts of common law within Wales. This jurisdiction was again highly significant when compared to developments in England. The Court of King's Bench at Westminster had successfully asserted a jurisdiction to review the decisions of the Court of Common Pleas some centuries earlier, but the Court of Exchequer had resisted a similar claim by the King's Bench. Accordingly, a special court to review Exchequer decisions had been established by statute in 1358, called the Court of Exchequer Chamber.[50] The King's Bench, however, was itself only review-able by Parliament, and as Parliament did not necessarily meet regularly this meant that there was no guarantee of an early review of alleged errors of law by the King's Bench. During the reign of Elizabeth, when Parliament only met on six occasions in all, matters came to a head with a further review court, confusingly also called the Court of Exchequer Chamber, being set up by statute in 1585 to act as a review body for King's Bench.[51] Against this background of competition, acrimony and confusion, the Council's review jurisdiction in Wales appears satisfyingly simple and straightforward.[52]

Moreover, the Council enjoyed a jurisdiction to fill gaps in the common law as administered within Wales. This has rightly been described as an 'ample

Equity jurisdiction',[53] which made the Council in effect by the start of the seventeenth century Wales's answer to the Court of Chancery in England. This development was notwithstanding the substantial number of cases finding their way from Wales to the Court of Chancery at Westminster. The Council also carried out various police functions, supervised the work of lesser courts and officials and had a hand in the apprehension of criminals and pirates. Its was a very broad jurisdiction, which coupled with the swiftness and cheapness of its procedures made it a very popular tribunal.[54]

CONSEQUENCES OF THE UNION

One unpopular feature of the union legislation was its insistence upon English as the official language of government, administration and the law within Wales. A knowledge of English was an essential qualification to hold public office, and it was to be the language used in the courts. This meant that persons who gave evidence in Welsh had to have their evidence interpreted, although there are strong indications that Welsh was sometimes accepted informally to allow business to proceed more efficiently. In 1576, Sir William Gerard, the Justice of South Wales, criticized the giving of evidence through an interpreter as a practice likely to lead to miscarriages of justice through misunderstandings and recommended, under the new dispensation which required two justices on each circuit, one justice should always be Welsh-speaking, much as Archbishop Pecham had recommended with regard to the government of the border diocese of Lichfield three centuries previously. Subsequent generations have seen in the linguistic attitude of the union legislation an attempt to suppress the Welsh language, particularly when one remembers that it was the English delegates at the fifteenth-century Council of Constance who believed 'difference of language . . . by divine and human law the greatest and most authentic mark of a nation and the essence of it'.[55]

In 1549, during the reign of Henry VIII's son, Edward VI, the Act of Uniformity effectively made English the language of worship within the reformed Church.[56] Services in Latin were abolished and a Prayer Book in English was introduced. Although a French version was hastily prepared for the king's subjects in Calais and the Channel Islands, no such provision was made for the people of Wales, nor for the king's subjects in Cornwall, Ireland and the Isle of Man.[57] For the majority in those lands, a less familiar language which they did not know was substituted for a more familiar one. Whereas under Henry VIII, much in the life of the Church remained the same despite the king having supplanted the Pope as the head within the kingdom, apart that is from the dissolution of the monasteries, under Edward VI the Church turned in a distinctly Protestant direction. The 1549 legislation allowed clerics to marry, which meant that in Wales, where the rule of clerical celibacy had never firmly taken root, many clergy unions were regularized.[58] This was to cause problems when, on Edward's death in 1553, his Catholic sister Mary ascended the throne and sought to return the kingdom to the papal fold. A statute in 1553 prohibited married clergy from saying Mass after 20 December of that year, and this led to a substantial number of deprivations in Wales, particularly in the dioceses of Bangor and St David's.[59] On Mary's death in 1558, her sister Elizabeth and her ministers sought to establish a religious settlement which would win the hearts and minds of her subjects as well as secure the salvation of their souls, and also ensure the nation's security. While bishops such as Thomas Davies of St Asaph worked hard to establish canon law and sound administration in their dioceses,[60] Bishop Richard Davies of St David's, working with the Renaissance scholar William Salesbury, promoted a bill in 1563 to have both the Bible and the Prayer Book produced in Welsh, although the Lords amended the bill to ensure that where in Wales a Welsh Bible was used, *both* Welsh and English versions of the Bible should be available side by side to encourage the learning of English.[61] The Welsh Bible was completed by 1588 and was to be a bulwark in securing the future of the language.[62]

The absence of a Bible in the native tongue may have contributed to the problem of recusancy, that is, retention of the Catholic faith, within Wales. During the 1580s, the number of recusants being prosecuted in Wales increased significantly, particularly in the south-east, where for instance the number of prosecutions in Glamorgan rose from four in 1584 to twenty-seven in 1587, and in the north-east, where the chief justice of the Chester circuit, Sir George Bromley, was a committed Protestant reformer.[63] Fears of invasion from Catholic Spain probably account for the increased vigilance, and the 1590s witnessed a vigorous campaign by the Privy Council against recusancy, during which the Council at Ludlow was warned to guard against English recusants taking flight into Wales where it was perceived the Council was lacking in energy in dealing with the issue. In 1593, commissions of inquiry were set up in single shires to address the problem and the Council was required to take steps to stop worship at former Catholic shrines. Wales was seen to be too dilatory in adopting the reformed faith,[64] particularly perhaps following the publication of the Welsh Bible.

The introduction of the English common law into Wales coincided with the great increase in land available for secular occupation following the dissolution of the monasteries. The monasteries themselves had leased substantial tracts of land to lay tenants, which may have encouraged the granting of leaseholds in Wales before the dissolution and set a pattern for the granting of their former estates after they were confiscated.[65] Much monastic land was leased to lay tenants after the dissolution, the tenants being permitted to buy the freeholds from the Crown subsequently. A busy market for former monastic land existed in Elizabeth's reign when freeholds were sold to leading families, anxious to build up their estates. Lawyers were among the most keen purchasers, often buying subject to the claims of existing leaseholders, taking initially a lease of the profits for twenty-one years in return for a purchase price of four to six years rent, and thereafter buying the freehold.[66] The monasteries had also begun the practice of leasing their rights to mills, fisheries, timber and minerals, rather than exploiting those resources for themselves, and this also continued when their estates fell into the hands of laymen, with a steady growth in the number of mineral leases in particular.[67] This established the pattern whereby mineral rights were usually exploited by contractors rather than the landowners themselves.[68]

It was not only the land of former monasteries which found itself on the market. Other church lands were also sold and leased. Bishop Anthony Kitchen of Llandaff (1545–63) sold farms belonging to his see and leased others in moves which were primarily designed to increase his popularity within his diocese, given his somewhat precarious position as a former abbot who had been consecrated bishop.[69] Difficulties were however experienced when Mary Tudor deprived married clergy of their livings to discover that rights to the tithe and glebe which had been owned by monasteries and leased to lay impropriators, as the purchasers of such rights were called, were not easily recoverable to support her reinstated Catholic clergy.[70] The disposal of monastic and other ecclesiastical land had occurred so swiftly that very little ecclesiastical land remained in the Crown's own hands by Elizabeth's reign,[71] in effect ensuring that the Henrician and Edwardian religious changes could not readily be reversed.

Leaseholds were also used to bring to an end customary tenures, allowing landlords greater freedom to increase rents in line with profits and tenants greater freedom to alienate and manage their interests. Often, landowners would charge an entry fine for granting a new lease, a technique which allowed them in effect to auction the new lease to the highest bidder.[72] Such economic advantages played a potent role in ending native customs.

The introduction of English land law by the union legislation brought freedom of alienation and the possibility of entailing and mortgaging land into Wales.[73] The greatest change was without doubt the introduction of primogeniture, ending the Welsh custom of partible inheritance amongst the sons. The 1536 Act had provided for the retention of the Welsh customs of inheritance,[74] but this concession to the native law was rescinded in the 1543 Act.[75] The *volte face* may not however be as studiedly opposed to native custom as might at first blush appear. In 1536, freehold land was not devisable according to the English common law, that is, one could not make a will leaving one's land to whom one chose on whatever terms one chose. Freehold land had to pass to one's heir, usually one's eldest son. The circumvention of this rule by granting the land during one's lifetime to feoffees to hold to one's use, with instructions as to whose use they were to hold it or to whom they were to transfer it after one's death, had itself been prevented in effect by the Statute of Uses of 1536. Therefore, if the Welsh in 1536 were to have any freedom to adopt the customs of their choice, those customs had to be preserved by the legislation, which they were. The reaction in England however to the loss of the power to devise land unofficially by means of feoffments to uses resulted in such an outcry, indeed rebellion as it was one of the causes of the Pilgrimage of Grace, that for the first time freehold land became devisable by statute in 1540. The Statute of Wills of that year allowed two-thirds of freehold land held by chivalric tenures to be freely devised, and all freehold land held by socage tenure. There was therefore no further need to specifically preserve the native customs of Wales after 1540, as those who wished to follow native practice could do so by incorporating their wishes in a will. Thus, no express saving of native customs was required in the 1543 Act.

Primogeniture was readily adopted by many Welsh landowners eager to build up their individual family estates. A lively market for land developed in Wales, not only with gentry consolidating their holdings, but with ambitious yeomen able to do likewise and rise to the ranks of the gentry, not to mention professional and business men who chose to invest their gains in land and acquire the social status that went with being a landowner.[76] Lawyers were prominent among those who prospered and bought land, men such as William Jones of Castellmarch in Anglesey, who became Chief Justice of Ireland, David Williams of Breconshire and John Vaughan in Cardiganshire.[77] Amongst all classes, there was a growth in the use of marriage settlements[78] to establish individual choice as to how property was to be enjoyed, devices which could have been used to preserve native traditions if the families so wished, and there were some who, in the 1570s, complained of the effects of primogeniture upon the social fabric of Wales.[79] By and large, however, the gentry and the aspiring middle classes would appear to have embraced these changes enthusiastically.

The most attractive feature of the English common law in this regard was the possibility it afforded of keeping intact a family estate in the hands of one person, while retaining the freedom to create settlements to provide for other members of the family and indeed to buy from and sell land to strangers like any other property. The composition entered into in 1574 by the earl of Leicester with the free tenants of Arwystli and Cyfeiliog in Montgomeryshire illustrates this freedom very well; he was able, four years later, with Crown permission, to grant the lands to four feoffees to hold to the use of the freeholders on terms agreed with them.[80] The new freedoms made for greater flexibility in the terms of tenure.

Nothing perhaps indicated more clearly the individual as opposed to family ownership of land following the union than the encroachment upon former waste and the enclosure of land to bring it into cultivation. Much activity of this sort occurred, other than in those few areas, such as Ceredigion and Cyfeiliog, where *cyfran* survived. Enclosing what had been open ground was a common cause of disputes, some of which ran for a century, but on the whole the contentions were fewer and less bitter in Wales than in England because the enclosing had as its goal the bringing of land into arable cultivation rather than to create pasture, and thus did not result in depopulation of the country-side.[81] The greater prosperity which the new system of landholding brought in its wake may have been one reason for the increase in charitable giving, mainly for the relief of poverty and the provision of almshouses, but also for the maintenance of schools, roads, bridges, sermons and the availability of Bibles.[82] This was the age which led to the passing of the Statute of Charitable Uses, 1601, upon which the modern law of charity in England and Wales is founded. Greater wealth also resulted in ventures such as the creation of joint-stock partnerships. This development was interestingly connected with the Crown's insistence upon its exclusive regalian right, called Mines Royal, to mine for gold, silver, quicksilver, copper and tin. German experts were brought into the country to assist in the exploitation of these metals, and as a result joint-stock partnerships on the German model came to be established. The German legal heritage included a strong tradition of corporate personality absent from the civilian tradition of Roman law, but destined to influence commercial development in future generations. The joint-stock enterprises were one of the first harbingers of such development in England and Wales. A Royal Mint was established in Aberystwyth in 1638.[83]

If primogeniture led to the consolidation of family estates in the hands of eldest sons, it was not good news for their younger brothers who would no longer share in the family land by automatic right of inheritance. The need for younger sons to make their own way in the world and establish their own fortunes and families led to an increase in the number of Welshmen who were attracted to the royal court to serve in the sovereign's personal bodyguard, or to serve the court in administrative and governmental roles. Many Welshmen also entered business and the professions at Westminster and in London, and gradually within Wales itself, the senior clergy became resident Welshmen, often being the younger sons of gentry, sometimes substantial freeholders in their own right and with the benefit of a good education.[84]

The century following the union saw a considerable increase in the number of Welshmen attending the universities and the Inns of Court, especially from Elizabeth's reign onwards. Over 2,000 attended the universities at this time compared with less than 500 recorded enrolments during earlier times. The vast majority, 1,762, went to Oxford where in 1571 Dr Huw Price, a doctor of canon law, had founded Jesus College. The remainder, 242, went to Cambridge, where there were connections between north Wales and Queens', Magdalene and St John's colleges, at the last-mentioned of which Sir John Wynn of Gwydir had endowed both fellowships and scholarships. At the Inns of Court, almost 700 Welshmen entered during this period, over 200 of them graduates, and Welshmen accounted for a substantial number of those practising civil and canon law before the courts of the Admiral and the Church respectively.[85] These civil lawyers, including such illustrious names as William Aubrey, David

Lewis, Thomas Yale, John Herbert and Edward Carne, practised from Doctors' Commons in London.[86] Referring to these civilians, George Owen of Henllys in Pembrokeshire commented of his fellow countrymen that 'many of them have proved excellent in the Civil Laws', while William Camden remarked that Wales produced 'judicious civilians' and 'skilful common lawyers'.[87]

As with the clergy, many of the lawyers from post-union Wales were the younger sons of gentry, who by dint of their education and earnings became members of that class in every county in the land.[88] Law was the profession perceived to be particularly favoured by Welshmen, Robert Wynn in 1611 regarding it as the only route to worldly honour.[89] With some hyperbole, Humphrey Llwyd was to claim that the majority of common lawyers were Welsh,[90] and there is no doubting that Lincoln's Inn and Gray's Inn were especially regarded as Welsh enclaves,[91] as was Doctors' Commons.[92] At Oxford, the fellowship at All Souls was thought inordinately Welsh in composition; when in 1566, the queen visited Oxford, three out of the four civilians who greeted her were Welsh, including her 'little doctor', William Aubrey.[93] The eloquence of the Welsh had frequently been remarked upon in earlier times,[94] and this may well have led them into professions such as the law and the Church where a command of language was an asset.

Not all of the Welshmen who attended the Inns intended to be lawyers. Many were drawn by the knowledge of law and of manners that could be obtained there, knowledge which would assist in the running of their estates and enable them to serve on the quorum of the Quarter Sessions in their native shires. Education, particularly in the law and in administration, had become an essential qualification for public office, alongside loyalty and ability. Such a background helped advance a career as a justice of the peace or as a Member of Parliament; between a quarter and a third of those who held the offices of JP or sheriff in the counties of the Carmarthen circuit in the first century following the union had been educated at either Oxford, Cambridge or the Inns of Court.[95] In addition, those who had been to the universities and the Inns brought the values of the Renaissance and of humanism home to Wales.[96] Dr Geoffrey Glyn of Doctors' Commons founded the Friars School in Bangor, and many Welsh youths were attracted to England's finest schools for their education, such as Westminster in the shadow of the Abbey where for sixty years the deans were Welshmen.[97] At home, building landed estates in the aftermath of the dissolution of the monasteries made legal practice both popular and lucrative.[98]

Wales was a good country in which to be a lawyer in the century after the union, for there was a considerable increase in litigation, and therefore in the profits arising therefrom. William Harrison was to comment that the Welsh were addicted to going to law,[99] but in truth England experienced much the same phenomenon at this time, remarkably causing the royal courts to strive to find ways of discouraging over-popular actions such as suits for defamation.[100]

In Wales, litigation had replaced violent self-help as the regular means of redress, and this indicates a substantial success on the part of the new legal order. If some suits were trivial and others malicious, and if lawyers profited from both and were increasingly distrusted as a result, it is nevertheless true that trivial disputes and malicious quarrels now took the parties before the courts whereas a century earlier they might have led to bloodshed. Even if they profited in consequence, lawyers are hardly to be castigated for encouraging such an outcome.[101]

The shift from lawlessness to litigation was however neither instant nor total. Although the exaction of *cymortha* had been banned in 1534, it was still occasionally raised, and as late as 1576, the eminent civilian, Dr David Lewis, the first principal of Jesus College, Oxford, complained to Walsingham that the former Marches still had their lawless elements, with both *arddel* and *cymortha* still being practised. Influential offenders were still able to escape justice in his view, and the Council of Wales and the Marches needed to put its house in order if it was to deal effectively with them.[102]

The growth of lay participation in government and the increase in legal knowledge which resulted from it was partly responsible for bringing lawlessness to an end, but the process, as Lewis's opinions illustrate, was slower on the March than in the older shires. Glamorgan, which had been a very violent county prior to the union was as orderly as the rest of Wales by the seventeenth century.[103] However, the records of the Great Sessions, the Quarter Sessions and the lesser courts indicate a deal of violence still in Welsh society, with homicides, assaults, threats of violence and thefts remaining prevalent, as well as other problems such as vagrancy and absence from church. Professor Sir Glanmor Williams has remarked that the homicides were 'not coldly premeditated crimes but usually arose from acts committed in the heat of the moment'.[104] However, the sixteenth-century common law relating to homicide had come to distinguish murder from the lesser crime of manslaughter or chance medley, specifically according to whether the killing was premeditated or upon a sudden occasion in hot blood, often in the course of a fight or *chance melée*. Whereas a person convicted of murder could not escape the death penalty for a first offence by claiming benefit of clergy, the person convicted of manslaughter could, and what the records may therefore be indicating is one of two things: either the homicide was deliberately reduced to manslaughter in order to enable the convict to escape the gallows, in the same manner that goods were valued at less than a shilling to effect the same result, or, as is known to have been happening in England, those experienced in the habits of violence wishing to kill another would deliberately provoke a fight which appeared to be upon a sudden occasion in order to create the impression that they were only guilty of the lesser offence. The legislature responded by making the killing of an unarmed man by stabbing subject to an irrebuttable presumption of malice aforethought, but the problem was not completely resolved until the judges redefined murder in the early eighteenth century.[105]

Piracy also remained a problem in post-union Wales. Both the Tudor and Stuart monarchs appointed vice-admirals to protect the coasts and to prevent piracy. Early in the reign of Elizabeth, the harbours of Wales were grouped under three head ports: those of the south-west under Milford, those of the south-east under Cardiff and those of the north under Chester. Each of these ports acquired customs officers in the shape of a controller, a customer, a searcher and a surveyor.[106] As well as dealing with piracy, the customs officers were charged with the prevention of smuggling as there was considerable local resistance to the payment of customs dues.[107]

Despite the jurisdiction of the Great Sessions within Wales and the Council of Wales and the Marches at Ludlow, a great deal of litigation from Wales came before the royal courts at Westminster. In particular, resort was frequent to the Court of Chancery, the Exchequer, the Court of Requests and the Star Chamber, courts which were able to entertain cases which, while outside the jurisdiction of the Great Sessions, were within that of the Council. This was in part the result of Westminster being seen as the ultimate seat of authority and government, where Welshmen now played a key role as MPs and as ministers of the Crown; Sir John Herbert, a member of Doctors' Commons, became second secretary of state. The fact that Welshmen frequented the court and parliament meant that it was sometimes more convenient for them to litigate at Westminster than at Ludlow, and this was to lead to the common law courts of King's Bench and Common Pleas beginning to invade the civil jurisdiction of both the Council and the Great Sessions during the closing years of the sixteenth century.[108] This can again in part be explained by convenience to those at court of suing there rather in Wales, and also in part by the general jurisdictional competition of the age. However, two other factors cannot be discounted. First, the Great Sessions only sat in a county twice a year for six days on each occasion, while the courts at Westminster were in daily session during the four legal terms, and there were complaints that the Sessions in Wales were sometimes held at times which were inconvenient to litigants merely to suit the demands of the Westminster practices of the judges. Secondly, and this applies more to the tendency to litigate in Star Chamber in preference to the Council at Ludlow, a tendency which increased greatly during Elizabeth's reign,[109] suing at Westminster avoided problems that might arise due to the influence of one's opponents at Ludlow. Lawlessness among the gentry was regularly proceeded against in Star Chamber rather than at Ludlow, albeit that some such suits were malicious.[110]

The increased invasion of the Council's jurisdiction in the last decade of Elizabeth's reign may point to misgivings at Westminster with regard to the Council's efficiency, particularly in dealing with recusancy. Part of the Council's problem was that it had jurisdiction not only over those parts of Wales which had been within the March, but also over the border districts which were now in English counties. These border counties made dedicated efforts to free themselves from the Council's jurisdiction. Bristol managed to extract itself in 1562 and Cheshire in 1569, but Worcester's efforts in 1576 proved futile. This opposition to the Council from the border shires of England increased during the seventeenth century, when attempts at reform shipwrecked on the obstacles created by the lawyers who practised at Ludlow, whose influence was considerable and who resisted attempts to curb their numbers.[111] Under the Stuarts, the Council increasingly became a court of law rather than an executive body, and as a prerogative court it was tarnished by association with Stuart views of monarchy and the prerogative. By the 1630s, when Charles I was governing without calling Parliament, the Council was extending its jurisdiction to civil matters, which excited criticism not least because it led to neglect of its criminal work, posing a threat to good order and the rule of law. However, civil work paid better for lawyers and the large number of officials serving the body.[112] Despite the fact that the Welsh gentry, particularly those who had been MPs and had had to be at Westminster when Parliament was sitting, had looked more and more away from Ludlow and to the royal courts at Westminster, especially the King's Bench, to adjudicate their quarrels, the Council remained the centre of a distinctly Welsh political life, which preserved the institution's value in the eyes of many Welshmen.[113] In some measure, it became a focus for Welsh unity away from the royal court, as Stuart government began to diverge from the style of the Tudors. Some may even have mourned the passing of the Tudor period, with the traditional nostalgia for a golden age now past, but one which on this occasion the Welsh had recognized while it persisted and had embraced with enthusiasm.

This may account for the attempts, such as those of the attorney-general for north Wales, Richard Lloyd of Esclus, to save the Council or at least delay its abolition, when Stuart government broke down amidst civil war in the 1640s. It was suggested that it should be retained as a court for both common law and equity matters where the Welsh justices could sit when not on circuit around the counties taking the Great Sessions. This proposal would have created at Ludlow a court as permanent as those in Westminster Hall, have ended the conflict of interest for justices between their legal practices and their judicial duties, and have converted the Council from being a prerogative court to one of unobjectionable jurisdiction. As a prerogative court, however, the Council was irredeemable. Its criminal jurisdiction was abolished along with that of Star Chamber in 1641, and the following year saw the demise of its jurisdiction in both civil and administrative matters.[114] Welsh lawyers, by and large, supported the king rather than Parliament in the conflict which ensued, and Welsh lawyers were prominent among those captured by the parliamentary forces at Hereford in December 1645, including the Chief Justice of Brecon, Marmaduke Lloyd, his puisne colleague Walter Rumsey, and David Jenkins, the puisne justice on the Carmarthen circuit.[115]

Lawyers such as these, and landowners generally, were supporters of the union. It had, as George Owen of Henllys observed, emancipated the Welsh, given them opportunities to acquire learning and civility, together with the freedom to trade and traffic through England.[116] By and large, it was to learning rather than commerce that Welshmen remained primarily attracted. The professional men and the gentry supported the Elizabethan religious settlement for reasons which also applied to their support for the union: it gave them a Church in which they had influence, and, in the sacred sphere as in the secular, it connected with their dual loyalty to the Tudors, the Welsh dynasty which had given them a role in government, and their very Welshness, which they associated with the use of their native tongue. The union was perceived to have given the people of Wales a measure of self-government, in that they had acquired representation at the Westminster parliament and had their own justices of the peace. The Welsh Bible and Prayer Book were presented and perceived as a return to the native British tradition in Christianity which pre-dated the Roman mission to the English and the papal pretensions of the high Middle Ages.[117] Writers such as Bishop Richard Davies traced the Welsh pedigree back to the sons of Noah and that of the native British to Brutus who had fled from Troy.[118]

It should not however be forgotten that the union of Wales and England was but one example of a process of amalgamation within the realms of Christian kings which was typical of late fifteenth- and sixteenth-century kingship. In 1495, the emperor had brought a measure of unity to his German dominions by incorporating Roman law wholesale as the law of the Imperial State Court, the *Reichskammergericht*, making one system of law common to all his dominions.[119] The kings of France ordered the compilation of definitive editions of the diverse legal customs of their realm, and encouraged the scholarly search for common rules and principles which could be presented as being French, rather than just local, law.[120] The marriage of Anne of Brittany in 1525 to the king of France led to the union of the duchy and the kingdom by edict in 1532, a remarkably similar step to the union of Wales and England. In Spain, republication of the *Siete Partidas* as the *Recopilación* began to unify the laws of the various kingdoms which had been jealously retained in earlier centuries.[121] In many of these lands, kingship was also moving into an absolutist mode, a mode which the Tudors' use of prerogative powers and courts, and Henry VIII's retention of the right to legislate for Wales by his mere *fiat*,[122] by implication to some extent favoured.

Wales was not however simply absorbed into the English kingdom. It retained a separate legal, if not a political, identity. In the Courts of Great Sessions and in the Council of Wales and the Marches it had institutions which were unique to itself, and which therefore recognized a measure of constitutional autonomy. It was also given the means whereby to preserve some of its own native customs, and even *cyfran*, which had not been universally popular among the landed classes for some centuries, was to survive in various places including Builth, Cyfeiliog, Gower, Dinmael and Abergavenny. If the irregularities created along the border, and in particular the anomalous position of Monmouth-shire, marred the new territorial arrangements, it is nevertheless the case that the new counties were to continue in existence until 1974, and that loyalty to those counties survived that reorganization to play a role in the creation of the unitary authorities in Wales in 1996.[123]

With one exception, the refusal to accept the Welsh language as an equal partner in secular affairs even though it had won its place in the reformed Church and thereby assured its future, the union was viewed in a positive light by the Welsh. It gave them status and opportunity. It was a view shared by their rulers in England, James I presenting the union between Wales and England as both a precedent and an exemplar of the benefits of unity when dealing with Anglo-Scottish relations.[124] For once, the Welsh appeared to be enjoying the age in which they lived, not harking back to better times which they hoped would return.

The Age of the Great Sessions

THE JURISDICTION OF THE GREAT SESSIONS

The introduction of the Great Sessions gave Wales, with the exception of Monmouthshire, a legal identity which was for the first time uniform while remaining distinct from England.[1] The law administered was however English law and the language of its administration was officially English. That English was to be the language of the law was a requirement of the 1536 statute,[2] yet there is evidence that Welsh was not only the language used mainly in the local courts, but that it was also widely employed at both the Quarter Sessions and the Great Sessions. It is known for instance that Lewis Morris had interrogatories translated into Welsh for witnesses in Cardiganshire, and Welsh was seen as an important qualification for public offices within Wales and also for employment as an officer, such as a steward or a bailiff, on the private estates of the gentry. When the survival of Great Sessions came under threat in the early nineteenth century, the Member of Parliament for Cardigan, Thomas Wood, argued that the Sessions must be retained for as long as the Welsh language remained in existence.[3] Lawyers, such as Sir Peer Mytton and Judge David Jenkins of Hensol,[4] were often in the vanguard of those who were careful to maintain their mother tongue and encourage its literature, while among the Welsh the law was seen as a profession which while lucrative was nevertheless respectable, with legal practices often being family businesses, handed on from generation to generation. Local lawyers would be educated at the grammar schools and then apprenticed to an attorney, while for those with higher ambitions, an education at a public school was advisable for entry to the London Inns of Court and thereby to the upper echelons of the profession. Such a practice, particularly if it led to the holding of a recordership, was a known route to a seat in Parliament.[5] For Welshmen generally, and the gentry in particular, the union with England was seen as a success.[6]

The Great Sessions themselves were in advance of the central royal courts at Westminster in terms of the organization of their jurisdiction. A litigant from Monmouthshire, commencing a civil action before the king's courts, would initially have to choose whether to sue in either the King's Bench, the Common Pleas or the Exchequer. Originally, the jurisdictional divides between these courts were real: the Exchequer was concerned with matters of financial interest to the king; the King's Bench with other pleas, most notably violent wrongs and breaches of his peace, which particularly concerned him, while the Common Pleas was the court for litigation between subjects lacking any royal interest. Matters were however more complicated because, while the Common Pleas had been stationary at Westminster since Magna Carta, the King's Bench had continued to move around the realm periodically, having jurisdiction over all pleas in the county in which it happened to be sitting. Moreover, whereas a formal writ was required to commence litigation in the Common Pleas and before the King's Bench when it was not sitting in the relevant county, when it was sitting in the county concerned, litigation before it could be commenced much less formally, and therefore more speedily and more cheaply, by bill, a simple written statement of the cause of action or plaint.

During the fifteenth century, the King's Bench ceased to travel the country, so that other than for the county of Middlesex in which Westminster Hall was situated, litigation before it had to be commenced by writ. It was still however cheaper to have one's case tried by the King's Bench, in that one could be represented before that court by an apprentice, as barristers were then called, rather than having to employ a serjeant at law, the lawyers who stood at the pinnacle of the profession, treated as equals by the justices and from whose ranks the justices were exclusively recruited. However, the Common Pleas had exclusive jurisdiction over certain actions, most notably pleas concerning land, so that the extra expense of a serjeant could not be avoided. During the sixteenth century, however, it began to be argued that remedies, in the main actions of trespass and actions of trespass on the case, which had originally been devised to supplement the older remedies, should be usable in appropriate circumstances in their stead. In other words, litigants should be allowed to choose between suing under an older form of action in the Common Pleas and having to pay for a serjeant to represent them, and being able to employ an action of trespass before the King's Bench at the lesser expense of an apprentice's fee. Not surprisingly, the King's Bench favoured such a development while the Common Pleas did not. Eventually, at the start of the seventeenth century, in a series of decisions relating to a variety of causes of action, the right to choose was upheld.[7]

From a Welsh perspective, this development in the first century of the Great Sessions is interesting, because in Wales there was only one court doing the work of both the Common Pleas and the King's Bench, so that this conflict of jurisdiction had from the outset been avoided. Whereas Monmouthshire litigants had to face this problem, those from the other twelve counties did not, and it is worth remembering that the lawyers, including the justices, who served the Great Sessions, also practised in England. It is therefore distinctly possible that the situation in Wales may have shaped the ultimate destiny of the jurisdictional divides at Westminster.

Technically, the King's Bench should not have been entertaining actions without a royal interest unless they arose in the county in which it was sitting. However, once the King's Bench settled at Westminster, a fiction was developed to overcome this handicap to its business, the bill of Middlesex. This device operated through the assertion that the place where the litigation arose, regardless of its true location, was within Middlesex. This claim would not be challenged, as both parties would wish to be before the King's Bench rather than the Common Pleas, and thereby the court got jurisdiction. Once the defendant was within the court's jurisdiction, the main issue between the parties could be tried. From a Welsh perspective, this is again interesting, in that the Great Sessions enjoyed the advantage of being permitted to hear causes from the county in which they were sitting by either writ or bill. The speedier, cheaper process by bill was always available to Welsh litigants. Jurisdiction was however limited to the county in which the court was sitting, which caused problems if one of the parties, usually the defendant, took themselves into another county to defeat the court's authority.

To complete the picture, it should be added that during the seventeenth century, the Exchequer also devised a fiction to extend its jurisdiction. This fiction was the allegation of *quo minus*. A plaintiff owed money by a defendant would claim that the latter's failure to pay rendered him to that extent less, *quo minus*, able to pay his dues to the king. Thereby, a royal financial interest was established, giving the Exchequer jurisdiction. Most monetary claims, that is, most claims, could be accommodated within this fiction, so that litigants ended up with a choice of which royal court of common law should hear their action. While the Great Sessions never had a concomitant jurisdiction with the Exchequer, they were from the first courts in which the jurisdictional divides, which had to be overcome in England by devious means, never posed a problem because they were never present.[8]

The other royal court which sat at Westminster Hall was the Court of Chancery, a court which granted remedies which were not available at common law or remedies in situations where the common law's redress was not adequate. Most typically, the common law remedy for breach of contract was damages to cover the disappointed party's loss, whereas Chancery could prevent a breach arising by issuing an injunction or order that the contract be carried out, through a decree of specific performance. Until the nineteenth century, these equitable remedies, so-called from the system of rules, equity, which the Court of Chancery administered, could not be had from the common law courts, nor could Chancery award damages, so that if both kinds of remedy were required, as where a past breach had caused loss and the plaintiff required compensation for this as well as an order preventing future breaches of an ongoing contract, actions before both a common law court and Chancery would have to be commenced.

In Wales, again, the situation was simpler. Although the Henrician legislation did not specifically give the Great Sessions a jurisdiction in equity, they came to exercise one. How this occurred has vexed historians. Some argue that the creation of chanceries at Caernarfon and Carmarthen by Edward I of itself was sufficient to have created the possibility of an equitable jurisdiction within the medieval Principality, a jurisdiction which was then extended to the rest of Wales through the extension of the Sessions. This, however, relies upon a preparedness to see in the secretarial chancery of the thirteenth century the potential of the later court, a view which is somewhat anachronistic. Others argue that the equitable jurisdiction did not arise until after 1689, when Wales's prime equitable tribunal, the Council at Ludlow, was finally abolished, its jurisdiction being inherited by the Great Sessions. This is a neat explanation, but the facts are less tidy, there being evidence of the Great Sessions having exercised an equitable role from their inception.

Regardless of when and how the Great Sessions acquired their equitable jurisdiction, they were exercising one by the year 1700, which meant that again in twelve counties of Wales litigants faced a simpler, more straightforward procedure than their counterparts in England and Monmouthshire, who again would not enjoy the benefits of such an unified process until the reforms of the nineteenth century.

The Council of Wales and the Marches was finally abolished in 1689, but this was following its reinstatement with the restoration of the monarchy in 1660, it having been abolished along with other prerogative courts in 1641.[9] Many Welsh lawyers, such as Judge David Jenkins, were staunch royalists, and although loyalties as between king and Parliament were often shaped by self-interest, Welshmen were by and large horrified at the trial and execution of Charles I. Only two Welsh members of Parliament were involved in the trial and signed the death warrant, Thomas Wogan, the member for Cardigan boroughs, and John Jones of Maesygarnedd, who was Oliver Cromwell's brother -in-law. March 1649 saw the end of the monarchy and the House of Lords, with a republic being proclaimed on 19 May. These events did not find a welcome among the ranks of the Welsh gentry, who had prospered under the Tudor and Stuart dynasties, and who would withdraw from the public arena until the Restoration in 1660.[10]

WALES UNDER THE COMMONWEALTH

Under the Cromwellian regime, Wales's representation in Parliament was altered. Each county, other than Merionethshire, was given two members, with borough seats being allotted to Cardiff and Haverfordwest. The franchise was conferred not on forty shilling freeholders, but on those with property to the value of £200. Welshmen generally were not appointed to positions of authority in Wales, reflecting their lack of enthusiasm for the Protector's government. Nevertheless, Serjeant John Glynne was appointed chief justice of north Wales in 1655, and Evan Seys became attorney-general of Glamorgan.[11] Lawyers, like clergy, were in the main vilified, the 'thieves and pick-purses' of Vavasor Powell's gibe.[12] Wales was to be ruled by committees, staffed mainly by the lower orders with but limited gentry participation.[13] Justices of the peace were expected to shoulder a deal of new work, much of which was anathema to them. They were expected to inquire into conspiracies and the secret meetings of dissidents, to police the keeping of the Puritan Sabbath, punish drunkenness, swearing and lewd behaviour, publish banns as a preliminary to civil marriages and settle matrimonial disputes, tasks which had previously fallen to the clergy and the ecclesiastical jurisdiction. While fast days were to be rigorously enforced, virtually all forms of traditional merry-making were enjoined. The whole package was massively unpopular with Welsh justices who did not support the Commonwealth's cause. Those who did tended to qualify for appointment as commissioners under the 1650 Act for the Better Propagation and Preaching of the Gospel in Wales, a statute similar to others passed for Ireland, the north of England and New England.[14]

The 1650 Act established a commission of 71, under the leadership of Thomas Harrison. Of these 71 commissioners, 43 of whom were based in the south and 28 in the north, only two were Welsh-speaking and a quarter of them were English, in the main from the border counties. The Welsh commissioners were mainly upwardly mobile yeomen and lesser squires, lawyers and officials, with few members of the established gentry class. Many had duties elsewhere, leaving it to a more dedicated core of fifteen in both the north and the south to do the work, who in turn delegated much of their responsibilities to inner circles of six members. These small groups exercised substantial powers to eject clergy from their livings, end the holding of livings in plurality and even to hear and determine charges of misconduct against clerics, condemning on the evidence of two witnesses, the full proof of both biblical and romano-canon law.[15] The verdict of five commissioners was sufficient to remove a cleric from his living, and twelve commissioners could dispose of any appeal. In the space of three years, 278 clergy lost their benefices under this procedure, two-thirds of them in south Wales.[16]

The ejections left a lot of parishes without an incumbent. Vacancies had to be filled from among the ranks of ministers approved by the regime. A Commission for the Approbation of Publique Preachers was established in 1654 both to approve and to appoint ministers to vacant livings. There were 25 commissioners for Wales, mostly drawn from the English border counties, who found it appallingly difficult to find suitably qualified candidates. Only 38 appointments were made, and of these only two were Welsh, causing extreme dismay among a population used to services and sermons in their own tongue. Itinerant ministers were appointed to preach on circuit in areas which had once enjoyed resident ministers. The outcome further distanced the ordinary people from the republic and its government, adding to the disaffection caused by the introduction of civil marriage, strict sabbatarianism, the abolition of holy days – including Christmas – together with the festivals and ceremonies that went with them, as well as prohibiting the secular pleasures of the alehouse, the revels, maypoles, cockfights and bear-baiting. The punishment of drunkenness and of swearing was also unpopular.[17]

Along with the resentment felt at the enforcement of these moral laws, there was also much disquiet concerning the elevation of low-born and uneducated persons to positions of authority as justices of the peace and officers. The unwillingness of educated persons of social standing to serve the regime was a major contributory factor in this. In August 1655, Major-General James Berry was given authority throughout Wales to eliminate conspiracies, stop rioting, horseracing, bear-baiting, dramatic productions and the keeping of unlawful alehouses, as well as to collect taxes and administer the Poor Law. He was also charged with supervising the duties of the justices of the peace,[18] who clearly were no longer trusted to fulfil their role. A high-water mark in middle-class dissatisfaction was reached when the justices of north Wales found themselves being preached to at a service in Beaumaris by Benjamin the blacksmith, and by 1659 even a Puritan like Morgan Llwyd was advocating liberty of conscience.[19] Not that the regime conferred no benefits; it did establish sixty-three schools in the towns and markets of Wales, marking the first attempt to introduce a system of primary education into the country, but even here it had difficulties. None of the schools was Welsh.

RESTORATION WALES

The Restoration of the monarchy in 1660 was welcomed by most Welshmen. Although it was a condition of the king's return that the hated prerogative courts of Star Chamber and High Commission should not be resurrected, the Council of Wales and the Marches was reinstated, probably in acknowledgement, as in the case of Chancery which was hardly thought of as belonging to the same family of courts as Star Chamber, that it was a useful and valuable jurisdiction.[20] The Restoration saw families once more encourage their sons to follow a career in the law as a route to obtaining a position in society. Successful lawyers again found their way into Parliament, although Welsh members were not distinguished for actually being present at Westminster. Numerous Welsh lawyers did however achieve distinction under Charles II. In the civilian branch of the profession, Sir Leoline Jenkins became one of the most learned and renowned Admiralty lawyers in the history of the court, serving as its president from 1680 to 1684. George Jeffreys, in spite of his 'bloody' reputation, carved out a route to the top of his profession which was as rapid as it was controversial; Chief Justice of Chester in 1680, he became Chief Justice of the King's Bench in 1683. Sir John Vaughan of Trawscoed was Chief Justice of the Common Pleas from 1668 to 1684, a post he held without fear of expressing strong personal views against the suppression of freedom of conscience in matters of religion and in favour of the Great Sessions. He famously defended the right of a jury to bring in a verdict manifestly contrary to the judge's summing up.[21] His son, Edward, was with William Williams of Llanforda, later Speaker of the House of Commons and Solicitor-General, one of the drafters of the first Exclusion Bill in 1679, but the father's pamphlet *Process into Wales*, defending the Sessions, played a significant part in calling Welsh members to their defence.[22]

Charles II's reign saw a number of legislative measures which sought to buttress the authority of the Church of England, yet at times sought also to acknowledge some measure of dissent, while the fear of what the dissenters had practised during the Commonwealth period continued to make the notion of complete religious freedom utopian. The Corporation Act of 1661 required all those holding public office to subscribe to allegiance to the king and to the Church of England. The first Conventicle Act of 1664 effectively outlawed public worship among dissenting groups, by prohibiting worship other than according to the rites of the Church in non-family groups exceeding five in number. The Welsh bishops were in the main stringent in countering dissent.[23]

A decade after the Restoration, however, the king clearly felt his position to be sufficiently secure to allow a larger measure of toleration in matters of faith. In 1672, he issued a Declaration of Indulgence which permitted public worship in contravention of the Conventicle Act provided the places of worship concerned were licensed. The move proved very popular in Wales, where 185 licenses were issued for places of worship, 136 of which were in the south. The pendulum was destined to swing back against such freedom, and in 1679 the first Exclusion Act was passed, commanding a slight majority among the Welsh members voting, allowing for the removal of dissenters from public office. Twenty-seven justices of the peace lost their positions in Montgomeryshire and south-east Wales, and the borough charters of Brecon, Carmarthen and Cardiff underwent amendment so as to increase royal influence and control over civic government in those places. Five Roman Catholic recusants were executed for treason in 1679, all of whom have since been canonized.[24]

As Charles's reign drew to a close, fear of Catholicism spread, the king's heir being his brother James, a known Catholic sympathizer. The rebellion of Charles's illegitimate son, the duke of Monmouth, was defeated and it was George Jeffreys CJKB who presided over the Bloody Assize which wrought judicial vengeance upon the perpetrators. Jeffreys had his reward; he became the youngest lord chancellor in the history of the realm. Nor was he alone in being a Welsh holder of high legal office under James II: Sir John Trevor, who presided over James's one and only parliament, became Master of the Rolls; William Williams, a former Speaker of the Commons, was appointed Solicitor-General. In total, seven of the principal law officers during James II's four-year reign were Welsh, symptomatic of the return to the law and public office by Welshmen which occurred after the Restoration and also of the fact that within Wales fortunes made in professional life, such as in the law, by families such as the Trevors, the Jeffreys, the Williamses and later the Kenyons, were regarded as acceptable. Lawyers and professional men generally were respected and given social standing.[25]

The king's Catholic leanings were not popular in Wales. In April 1687, he followed his late brother's example in issuing his first Declaration of Indulgence. In effect, he was dispensing with a law made by Parliament by a prerogative act in a manner reminiscent of the preferred style of government of his father, Charles I. The judges were instructed to obtain votes of thanks for this measure from the Grand Juries within the counties, but in Wales only Merionethshire made such a return. The President of the Council of Wales and the Marches, the duke of Beaufort, himself a Roman Catholic, ordered the deputy lieutenants of each county[26] and all of the justices of the peace to appear before him at Ludlow, but only half of the 320 expected to attend turned up. The unpopularity of the king's policies increased when he placed five dissenters onto the peace commission in both north and south Wales, and had the borough charter of Swansea recast to permit officials to be removed more readily by Order in Council.[27]

The unpopularity of the king's actions did not stay his hand. In May 1688, he issued a second Declaration of Indulgence, which led to a protest from the archbishop of Canterbury and seven other bishops including Bishop William Lloyd of St Asaph. For their trouble, they found themselves arraigned on a charge of sedition, the prosecution being conducted by William Williams of Llanforda. Seditious libel had been a charge that would have been heard by Star Chamber until its abolition in 1641. At the Restoration, the erstwhile jurisdiction of Star Chamber had passed to the King's Bench, but whereas Star Chamber had been an inquisitorial court, sitting without a jury, King's Bench employed adversarial common law procedures which left issues of fact to be determined by a jury. Two questions fell for determination: were the words used seditious and had the defendants uttered or published them. The courts were to hold that the first of these questions was a matter of law, for the judge to determine, leaving the jury with the bare question of whether the defendants had spoken or written them. This in effect meant that the judges, who were royal or at least government appointees, were the sole judges of what was and what was not legitimate criticism of the government.

The Seven Bishops' case[28] was to be a turning point in the reign. Sir John Powell of Carmarthen delivered a key judgement against the king. The bishops were acquitted, but Powell was dismissed by James for what was seen as his disloyalty. In effect, the king was undermining the independence of his own justices and placing himself above the law in the same manner as his father had attempted.[29] Amid fears of civil war, James fled the country and Parliament invited his son-in-law, William of Orange, to assume the throne alongside

James's daughter Mary. The 'Glorious Revolution' brought to the throne a king and queen in effect chosen by Parliament, and the Convention Parliament laid the foundations of the new, constitutional monarchy, with many of the features of constitutionalism, including judicial independence, established by the Bill of Rights of 1689. The Revolution brought to an end the career of Judge Jeffreys who died in the Tower of London, after having attempted to flee the country disguised as a sailor.[30]

The chief institutional casualty of the Revolution in Wales was the Ludlow Council. It was abolished by the Convention Parliament. It had, for over a century, been an object of criticism among the common lawyers of Westminster Hall who were eager to profit from taking over its jurisdiction in the same manner as King's Bench had benefited from the demise of Star Chamber. It was attacked as a prerogative court, and had only managed to survive because successive kings, like James I, had recognized its value in upholding law and order in the shires and also enabling commerce to develop under its tutelage. It had shown its capacity to discipline even the most powerful of subjects, men like Sir John Wynn who had been humbled before the Council by the Great Sessions justice, Sir Richard Lewkenor, who took exception to the manner in which Sir John mistreated his tenants.[31] The prestige of the Council had however diminished after the Restoration, in part because it was no longer served by presidents of the calibre of the Herberts and the Sidneys. In particular, the presidency of the marquis of Worcester, later duke of Beaufort, had damaged the Council by association with James II's extreme policies in matters of religion and of state. Even at the close of Charles II's reign, this tendency was evident, for John Arnold and Sir Trevor Williams found themselves summoned to appear before the King's Bench in November 1683 on a charge of *scandalum magnatum* for daring to be critical of Worcester.[32] *Scandalum magnatum* was the crime of putting between the king and his magnates, or between members of the nobility themselves, by circulating slanderous rumours. Such conduct was forbidden in England by chapter 1 of the Statute of Westminster I of 1275, passed to protect Edward I from some of the political problems from which his father, Henry III, had suffered. Fewer than half a dozen prosecutions had been brought under its provisions throughout the Middle Ages.[33] The demise of the Council has however been seen as the beginning of the end of Wales's claim to be a separate jurisdiction from England, in that the Council had been the tribunal of review above the Great Sessions and it had been suggested that it might sit as a permanent court in the manner of the courts at Westminster when the Sessions justices were not on circuit. Its demise, however, served to make the Sessions themselves a focus of unity and national pride within Wales, in some ways in succession to the Ludlow Council.[34]

The demise of James II marked in many ways the beginning of the end of Wales's special loyalty to the monarchy, which had begun under the Tudors, continued under the early Stuarts, who were viewed as the successors of the

Welsh dynasty, and had been very evident during the Civil War, the Commonwealth and at the Restoration. With the reigns of William and Mary, and later
Queen Anne, the special relationship of Wales and the monarchy drew to a
close, and by the time the Hanoverians came to the throne in 1714, it had well
and truly ended. Deference to royal rights ceased almost immediately upon
William and Mary's accession, as evidenced by Sir Carbery Pryse's challenge,
before the Court of Exchequer in 1690, to the regalian right of Mines Royal,
which had been reasserted at the Restoration. Sir Carbery's successful test
case on the issue was motivated by the discovery of a rich mineral deposit on his
land at Esgair-hir in Cardiganshire. Following his victory before the courts, an
Act of Parliament in 1693 allowed landowners to exploit minerals upon their
lands provided precious metals were available to the Crown. The monopoly
of the Mines Royal Society over all mineral deposits was therefore effectively
at an end. Landowners were now free to mine for copper, tin, lead and iron
upon their land provided they permitted the Crown or its agents to purchase
the ore extracted within thirty days of its being mined and at a fixed statutory
rate. The compromise solution is remarkably similar to those to be found
regarding seigniorial and regalian rights in the early native laws of Wales,
where for instance fish caught in rivers had to be shared between the captor
and the landowner, where there were rights to purchase honey at fixed rates,
and where by the charter of liberties given to the burgesses of Swansea royal
fish taken on the beach could be claimed by the lord in return for a fixed
payment.[35] Indeed, similar provisions were to continue to apply in parts of
Wales until the union with regard to whatever the sea washed up on land,
including dead fish and wreck. Sir Carbery Pryse's victory began the process
by which landowners were enriched by mineral exploitation of their lands.
Initially, he himself set up a joint-stock company to exploit his reserves, and it
was in this context of mineral exploitation that such ventures took off for
the first time. Sir Carbery's venture was taken over on his death in 1694 by
Humphrey Mackworth, who founded the Mine Adventurers in 1700. Although
Mackworth's activities were eventually tainted with fraud according to a House
of Commons inquiry in 1708, the Mine Adventurers marked a key stage in the
development of companies within the kingdom, having amongst other
features a welfare scheme, albeit of doubtful efficacy, for its employees. The
joint-stock endeavours often brought English capitalists into mining on the
estates of Welsh landowners, so that a norm was established by which the landowners leased their mineral rights to the mining companies for a royalty of
one-tenth or sometimes even one-seventh of the profits. The presence of deposits
of silver in the Cardiganshire lead mines ensured however that tensions concerning mineral rights between the Crown and the local landowners were to
surface again from the 1730s onwards.[36]

The gap opening up between the monarchy and the people of Wales was also
evidenced by the changed nature of the episcopal bench after the Revolution.

Until 1690, the Welsh bench was composed of able bishops, men like the ecclesiastical lawyer Humphrey Lloyd who was bishop of St Asaph, and the majority of the bishops were Welsh-speaking. They were as a group determined that the established Church should not be undermined by religious dissent within Wales, and were critical of what they judged to be light-handedness on the part of the justices of the peace and of the Great Sessions in dealing with dissent. At the start of the eighteenth-century, Welsh was widely used as the language of ecclesiastical administration, but this use declined sharply as English bishops began to be appointed to Welsh sees. This in turn led to their appointing English clergy to Welsh parishes, often in areas where very few of the population spoke any English at all. Not surprisingly, this process gradually alienated the native population who were accustomed to worshipping God in their own language and to hearing the scriptures read and expounded in their mother tongue. In 1766, matters came to a head when a cleric who was unable to speak Welsh was appointed to the livings of Trefdraeth and Llangwyfan in Anglesey, parishes where 95 per cent of the faithful were monoglot Welsh-speakers. In *Dr Bowles case*,[37] the propriety of the appointment was challenged on the grounds that a non-Welsh-speaker was not fit to be appointed to the livings. The Court of Arches, the principal ecclesiastical court of the province of Canterbury ruled that the ability to speak Welsh was an essential qualification for such a post, but also held that as Dr Bowles had already been inducted into the livings, he could not be removed as he had the freehold in them. The main thrust of the decision was as a consequence ignored, high-handed English bishops remaining ready to appoint non-Welsh-speakers to benefices in predominantly Welsh-speaking areas, safe in the knowledge that once inducted they were secure in their benefices.[38]

THE EIGHTEENTH CENTURY

Royalism in Wales declined after the Revolution, and the loyalty attracted by the Tudors and Stuarts was never enjoyed by the Hanoverians. In 1688, Wales initially supported James II, leading Catholics such as the duke of Beaufort and the Carnes of Glamorgan rallying people to the Stuart cause, but the change was eventually accepted. When in 1715, Scotland rose in support of a Stuart claimant against George I, Wales lay largely dormant, despite some rioting in Wrexham and some support for the Pretender in Cardiff. The 1745 rebellion, however, produced greater interest among the Welsh. David Morgan, a barrister from Penygraig-Taf, became the Pretender's 'counsellor', a position for which he paid with his life, being executed on 30 July 1746. Considerable sections of the Welsh gentry, evincing something akin to nationalist sympathies, amounted to a Jacobite party within Wales, the leading figure being Sir Watkin Williams Wynne. However, the failure of the rebellion quickly quenched the ardour of such high Toryism, and the gentry were not long in reaccommodating themselves to Hanoverian rule. There were Tories back on the Peace Commission throughout Wales by 1760, and were back by 1748 in Cardiganshire.[39]

Wales was not alone in feeling that its distinct identity was being lost if not deliberately overlooked during the eighteenth century. In 1707 the Act of Union with Scotland had ended the life of the Scottish parliament at Edinburgh. The London government's reaction to the Scottish rebellions was to place its faith in even greater centralization. The office of Secretary of State for Scotland was abolished in 1746, immediately after the second rising.[40] Although the Westminster parliament was now the legislature for the whole of Britain, Scotland still had its own legal system and its own courts, the Act of Union having made no provision for the review of decisions of the Scottish Court of Session by either the Westminster courts or Parliament. The House of Lords, however, despite there being no statutory basis for the claim, asserted its right to a review jurisdiction over the Court of Session, and this claim was successfully maintained in the half-century following the union. At much the same time, and for much the same reasons, the Court of King's Bench began to assert that it had a concurrent jurisdiction with the Great Sessions in Wales. While it was accepted that the Court of Exchequer had jurisdiction over Welsh litigation, in that the Sessions had never been granted jurisdiction over Exchequer business, and that the Court of Chancery had concurrent jurisdiction with the Great Sessions, so that Welsh cases could be heard there during term from counties where the Great Sessions were not sitting, it had been generally believed in Wales that King's Bench and Common Pleas matters could only be heard in Wales before the Great Sessions for the king's writ did not run in Wales. During the eighteenth century, the King's Bench began to claim that litigants were free to approach it directly for remedies at Westminster so that they were not inconvenienced by the fact that the Sessions only sat for six days twice a year in their county. The King's Bench jurisdiction would also overcome the problems encountered by plaintiffs who found that the defendants to their action had removed themselves out of the county and therefore beyond the reach of the Sessions there.

In 1723, the King's Bench successfully asserted its concurrent jurisdiction in criminal matters in the case of *R* v *Athoe*,[41] when it successfully moved a murder trial by writ of *certiorari* from Wales to Hereford Assizes. The judges who upheld the move commented unfavourably on the chances of justice being done in such cases in Wales, where they asserted local knowledge and family relationships thwarted fair trials. It was also said that the Welsh had no more respect for the law of murder than the Scots did for that of high treason, a valuable indicator of the factors mobilizing contemporaneous legal developments. Attention would then appear to have been turned to civil matters, where a concurrent jurisdiction was claimed but refuted in *Lampley* v *Thomas* in 1747.[42] Despite the clear refutation of the King's Bench case in *Lampley* v *Thomas*, the issue was raised once again in 1769 in *Lloyd* v *Jones*,[43] when Yates J accepted that a King's Bench writ of *latitat* could issue into Wales to bring a defendant before the court, thus ruling that the king's writ did indeed run into Wales in civil matters. Ten years later, Buller J in *Penry* v *Jones*[44] finally sealed the issue by ruling that the matter had been authoritatively disposed of by Yates J's decision in 1769. Henceforth, Welsh litigants had a choice of forum within which to commence their litigation. Not only could King's Bench review the decisions of the Great Sessions on a writ of *certiorari*, it, and the Common Pleas, could actually deal with litigation from Wales from start to finish in exactly the same manner as litigation from England and Monmouthshire was adjudicated.

The one concession, and that controversial, which was made to the jurisdiction of the Great Sessions was given by statute in 1773. It was enacted that for claims of less value than £10, and not concerning freehold land, the Great Sessions alone should be competent. In effect, this made the Great Sessions into a sort of small claims court for Wales, and also meant, as was quickly pointed out by critics of the legislation, that while such small claims from England and Monmouthshire were cognizable by the courts at Westminster, such claims from Wales were excluded. The 1773 Act and the decision in *Penry* v *Jones* together relegated the Great Sessions to a position of inferior jurisdiction. It is therefore perhaps not surprising that, within a year, Edmund Burke was arguing in the House of Commons that the separate Welsh jurisdiction was unnecessary and, in that it was also uneconomical, ought to be abolished.[45] This was not an age in which the rights of distinct communities to self-determination were making much of an impact upon the British government. Indeed, as events in the American colonies were illustrating, insensitivity to the needs of such communities had led to open rebellion.

If the central authorities at Westminster were critical of the Great Sessions as maintainers of law and order in Wales, great faith would appear to have been placed in the justices of the peace. Many members of the gentry class saw sitting as JPs at the Quarter Sessions infinitely preferable and indeed of greater importance than sitting as MPs at Westminster.[46] They remained well-educated men. During the second half of the eighteenth century, roughly half had attended the universities, the vast majority going to Oxford, and many gentry families sent their sons, or at least their eldest sons, to a public school, the most popular being Westminster and Eton. Fewer, however, were attending the Inns of Court, although it should not be forgotten that the Inns themselves were at this time in serious decline as educational institutions. The younger sons of gentry families and the sons of lesser families tended to be educated at grammar schools in Wales.[47]

Justices of the peace were responsible for a broad and ever-increasing range of legal and administrative tasks. They fixed wages in relation to prices and held annual 'sessions of labourers', convened by the constables, in order to deal with the paying of excessive wages, to resolve employment disputes between masters and their servants, and to settle terms of hire for labour in the coming year. In deciding issues under the Statute of Artificers, 1563, they were assisted by juries composed of twenty-four freeholders, this maintaining the native south Wales tradition of the landed classes acting as judges in the local courts.[48]

Justices could issue warrants for arrest or search and seizure sitting alone in their residences, but in pairs they constituted petty sessions with wider powers. In this guise, they administered the Poor Law,[49] licensed alehouses, governed weights and measures, saw to the removal of paupers to their native parishes under the Settlement Act 1662, and gave orders to the constables in relation to the maintenance of roads and bridges. Population shifts from country to town and the increase of trade and traffic during the eighteenth century made these very important functions. The number of justices increased markedly during the century, and this despite a raising of the property qualification for office from £20 a year to £100 a year in 1731, which increase was meant to prevent unsuitable persons from being appointed. Clergy, widely regarded for their efficiency as magistrates, served on the bench, inevitably giving further cause for dissatisfaction and dissent from the established Church, which became ever more associated with secular, English authority. Justices were also recruited from the lesser squirearchy, the ranks of stewards, merchants and lawyers, although many justices regarded their position as a sort of honour, rarely actually attending sessions or performing any duties of office.[50]

The stature of the Quarter Sessions, as well as initially of the Great Sessions, increased following the abolition of the Council at Ludlow. The demise of the Council also meant that the office of lord lieutenant, and not merely deputy, was now open to the county families. Service as a justice was an avenue which might lead young gentlemen to election as members of Parliament. Under the Property Qualification Act, 1711, candidates were required to have realty to the value of £600 per annum to stand for a county seat or £300 per annum to stand for a borough. Forty-shilling freeholders enjoyed the franchise in the county elections, while in the boroughs, the freemen enjoyed the vote as one of the privileges of their status, along with a monopoly of trade within the borough, the rights to pasture their animals on the common land and to serve as officials within the borough and to sit as members of the council. The status of freeman could be acquired by birth, apprenticeship within the borough or even by election at the court leet, the borough court to which all freemen owed suit. Electoral contests were however rare in eighteenth-century Wales, and those who had a vote might never have had an opportunity of exercising it. In the elections of 1734, contests only took place in four county and five borough seats within Wales, while in 1747 two county seats only were contested.[51]

The sixteenth century had seen Wales alter from a land where violent self-help was a regular mode of redress to one in which there was much resort to litigation. This change marked the success of the new legal procedures and indeed of the new law and legal system which union provided. The numerous actions for the stealing of cattle and to resolve disputes over rights of pasture in particular testify to the manner in which legal action had overtaken violent reaction. By the eighteenth century, Wales was becoming renowned for the low incidence of crime within its borders. From the white gloves regularly presented to the Great Sessions justices when there was no serious crime for them to try in the county, Wales became known as *gwlad y menyg gwynion*. The reliability of this evidence for the lawful condition of the country has met with some scepticism. It has been pointed out that prosecutions for serious crimes declined as the number of offences attracting capital punishment increased, that number almost doubling during the course of the eighteenth century to reach over 200 by 1820. The death penalty was deemed appropriate for servants who stole from their masters and for any stealing of sheep. Unsurprisingly perhaps, stolen goods were regularly undervalued, so that the theft became petty larceny which did not attract the death penalty rather than grand larceny which did. Likewise, many homicides were deemed to be unpremeditated, so that the offence was one of manslaughter and not murder. Manslaughter was a clergyable offence, that is, one for which a first offender could claim benefit of clergy and escape punishment. Originally intended to prevent clerics being condemned by secular tribunals, by the end of the medieval period it was available to any man who could read or make a show of being able to do so, was extended to some women in 1624, to all women in 1692 and to everyone without recourse to a test of literacy in 1707.[52] To prevent convicts claiming the privilege on a second occasion, those who had received the benefit, other than members of the nobility, were branded on the hand with the letter H for homicide or T for theft as was appropriate. Therein lies the substance of the much recounted tale of the woman from Llangaffo in Anglesey who was burnt in the hand for stealing forty shillings. This was not her punishment, for grand larceny attracted the death penalty but was clergyable. As women had but recently been admitted to the privilege, the branding of women was a new phenomenon.[53] Most petty thieves found themselves stripped and whipped as a punishment, for example, Elizabeth Lewis of Merthyr who was whipped for stealing a petticoat valued, perhaps mercifully, at 11*d*. Mercy was widespread, with only a small number of those convicted for capital offences, in the main premeditated murderers, ending up on the gallows. Only 9 per cent of those sentenced to death on the Brecon circuit between 1753 and 1819 were actually put to death. The rest had their sentences commuted to transportation, Australia taking over from the American colonies as the principal destination after the latter's successful rebellion. However one interprets what was occurring with regard to mercy, it remains probable that crime was itself on the decrease in Wales.[54]

The strength of religious belief and conviction was widely regarded as a contributory factor. The spread of Nonconformity is credited with making Wales a moral and law-abiding nation. There is evidence also that there was much informal dispute settlement taking place, some of this in Methodist meeting places in obedience to the biblical teaching.[55] Welsh men of evangelical persuasion, such as John Vaughan and John Phillips, were in the vanguard of those advocating reforms to the prison system; Thomas Pryce wanted to see libraries established there, while Robert Powell wanted to see regular religious services held in prisons. The idea of punishment as a form of rehabilitation was taking hold.[56]

The Toleration Act of 1689 allowed dissenters to worship freely provided their places of worship were licensed, but they nevertheless suffered many social disabilities for their beliefs. For instance, dissenters were to remain barred from holding local office and from attendance at the universities until 1828.[57] There were also times when they suffered persecution for their beliefs, often by legal means. They were sometimes refused burial of their dead in churchyards and burial grounds belonging to the Church of England, and Methodist preachers suffered occasional disruption of their services, sometimes even being offered violence.[58] It was not unknown for the gentry to seek to have them prosecuted for their activities: the leading figures of Howel Harris, Daniel Rowland, Howel Davies and William Williams Pantycelyn all appeared in court between 1741 and 1744. Griffith Jones, an Anglican clergyman and the founder of the celebrated circulating schools which did so much to promote literacy among the laity, was hauled before the court of the bishop of St David's for preaching outside of his parish, which he vehemently denied ever having done other than lawfully by invitation.[59] Even after his death, Jones's work provoked controversy. On his death in 1761, his supporter Madam Bevan continued the work of the circulating schools, and when she died in 1779, she bequeathed £10,000 to continue the work. In 1786, two of her trustees challenged the will. Judgement was eventually given in favour of the bequest, but not until 1804, by which time the hiatus caused by the unresolved litigation had led to the schools dying out.[60] The payment of tithes to support the ministry of the established Church was another frequent cause of litigation before the Sessions, the diocesan consistory courts and even the provincial Court of Arches in London. Resentment was particularly keen at the taking of tithes by lay impropriators, that is laymen who had acquired what had once been ecclesiastical property and with it the right to the tithes originally meant to support the parish priest. Such impropriators were expected to provide a clergyman to care for the parish and pay him a stipend out of their income, in all probability still leaving them with a profit, but some took the profits without making adequate provision for the spiritualities of the place.[61] Such practices fuelled resentment, occasional disobedience to the request to pay, and more generally advanced the cause of religious Nonconformity. Resort to violence was rare, and when it occurred it had less to do with a longing for dramatic social or political change and more to do with specific grievances of the moment, such as profiteering by farmers and traders when food was in short supply or over the issue of enclosures.

There was rioting in 1740 and 1757–8 arising from the perceived injustice of prices, and again in Swansea in 1794 and Aberystwyth and Haverfordwest in the following year. The expensive nature of food was the cause of these outbreaks as of those which occurred in Denbigh, Bala, Wrexham and Oswestry.[62]

Enclosure of land was achieved amicably in many parts of Wales, and discontent tended to be confined to those places where arable land was enclosed in order to provide pasture and when interference occurred with rights of common on the lord's waste. The increase in pastoralism at the expense of arable farming followed from the introduction of primogeniture into Wales, as the land was as a consequence being less intensively farmed for crops.[63] Younger sons, with no land necessarily to inherit, tended to abandon the country in favour of the towns, and patterns of landholding in the rural areas changed as a result. Much land owned by the gentry was entailed so as to prevent spendthrift heirs being able to sell or mortgage their interests and deprive future generations of the family of their inheritance.[64] Land was leased to tenants, and improvements in agricultural practice led to a reluctance from the 1760s onwards to grant the traditional leases for three lives, landlords preferring to lease for twenty-one years only or even at will, so that rents could be raised periodically and improvements in agricultural practice by the tenantry encouraged upon pain of non-renewal.[65] The larger estates which resulted from non-partible inheritance by primogeniture led to landowners employing stewards to manage their property, and many of these were feared, indeed hated, figures, one of the most notorious being the duke of Beaufort's steward in his lordship of Gower, Gabriel Powell, 'the Dark Angel'. Powell was particularly disliked, as were other stewards, for encroaching upon common land and the lord's waste where tenants were traditionally allowed to intercommon, in order to exploit minerals, a practice which the eminent jurist William Jones who practised at the bar in Wales castigated in his response to Edmund Burke's criticisms of the Great Sessions.[66] The beginnings of the coal industry and trade in coal led to many landowners asserting mineral rights over both common land and as against their copyhold tenants, some of whom found themselves being evicted from encroachments made by them or their families in earlier years upon the common land, a practice which was much resented.[67] Those who found themselves evicted from encroachments or with leases unrenewed sometimes fell back on the Welsh custom of building a makeshift dwelling overnight, *tŷ un nos*, entitling them to the land on which it was built and from three to ten acres surrounding it as a freehold.[68]

The main cause of enclosures in Wales however was the need for more arable land during the Napoleonic wars. The first enclosure by Act of Parliament had not occurred until 1733 and from then until 1775 only thirteen such Acts were passed, enclosing only 28,596 acres. In the first fifteen years of the nineteenth century, 76 Acts were passed, enclosing 200,000 acres. The legislation required the consent of two-thirds or even four-fifths of the landowners affected for such enclosure, but in Wales the owner of the local estate together with the tithe impropriator usually sufficed to achieve the necessary majority. Commissioners were appointed to survey the lands in question. The infamous stewards were often appointed to fulfil this role, for which they were paid £3 a day. As a consequence, they tended to proceed with their work at a leisurely pace, but in this regard there is little evidence of injustice, the Quarter Sessions being charged with the hearing of any objections.[69]

Towns grew during the eighteenth century at the expense of the country-side, primogeniture being part of the cause of this shift in population. Trade and transport improved as towns prospered. Restrictions upon Welsh involvement in trade were gradually eased. Although trade in Welsh cloth had been exempted from statutory regulation prior to the union, in that the cloth was thought too coarse to merit attention, the system of supervision and inspection of cloth known as alnage was introduced in 1542, the justices of the peace becoming responsible for its implementation. It was once again exempted from statutory regulation in 1557 and in 1624, the year in which the penal statutes passed as a result of the Glyn Dŵr revolt were finally expunged from the statute book, the monopoly rights of the Shrewsbury Drapers with regard to Welsh cloth also ended. Aberystwyth acquired a mint in 1638 to mint coins from the silver mined locally by Thomas Bushell.[70]

Whereas in due course joint-stock companies were formed to exploit mineral rights, trade in the towns, markets and ports relied more upon partnerships than companies, in which the middle classes, yeomen and gentry mainly, combined to raise the capital to trade by sea. Lawyers were to be found participating in such endeavours, John Wood for instance founding the first Cardiff bank.[71] Banks were often run by cattle drovers, and bore appropriate names as a consequence – *Banc yr Eidion Du*, the Black Ox Bank, at Aberystwyth being an example. Demand for Welsh meat had increased dramatically in the wake of the Irish Cattle Act, 1666, which had prohibited the import of Irish livestock. Welsh cattle drovers prospered as a result, playing an important role as local bankers and investors, although they were greatly feared to be disreputable, some known to have absconded to Ireland with the funds of others. Cattle dealers had to be licensed by the Quarter Sessions, and licences would only be given to married men.[72] Trade such as that in cattle required good communications by road. Under the 1555 Act, roads were to be maintained by the parish, with the parish vestry being accountable to the Quarter Sessions for their upkeep. Every able-bodied man in the parish was expected to provide six days labour a year to maintain the roads, although the personal labour service was often commuted for a money payment. Parishes could be presented by the justices of the peace to the Quarter Sessions for failing in their duty. The maintenance of bridges was a different matter, responsibility resting with a special county committee. From 1691, counties were allowed to levy a rate in order to maintain roads and bridges, but the Welsh counties were slow to act upon this power, Glamorgan being the first to do so in 1764.[73] Such measures indicated that the effectiveness of the statutory scheme introduced by the 1555 Act was past, and the second half of the eighteenth century saw the coming of turnpike roads to Wales, turnpike Acts being passed to allow the development of such roads. By and large, these were welcomed in that they were beneficial to trade and travel, bringing artists into the country whose work would eventually spawn a tourist trade as the Romantic movement inspired people to seek the picturesque and sublime. Among the turnpike roads which improved transport in Wales at this time were those from Hereford to Brecon in 1757, extended to Haverfordwest in 1787, that from Newtown to Aberystwyth in 1769, and that from Cardiff through Neath to Carmarthen.[74]

The shift of population from rural to urban areas also resulted in a sharp increase in the number of poor persons in the towns. As with the levying of rates for roads, Wales had been slow to implement the provisions of the Elizabethan Poor Law. Monmouthshire was virtually alone under the Stuarts in having implemented the system, which is significant given that it was grouped administratively and legally with English rather than other Welsh counties. Thomas Pennant, writing of the early eighteenth century, attributed this to the greater respect for family and neighbourliness existing in Wales at that time: 'filial piety had at that time full possession of the breasts of children, or great affection on the part of more distant relations, and the pangs of poverty were as much as possible alleviated'.[75] The Poor Rate began to be levied in the second half of the eighteenth century and the cost of maintaining poor persons increased alarmingly. As a result, parishes began to implement with some severity the settlement provisions of the 1662 Poor Law Act, returning paupers to other parishes if they had no settlement where they were seeking relief. Such returns could be appealed to the Quarter Sessions, usually by the receiving parish also seeking to avoid any obligation. Under the 1697 Act, paupers might be required to wear badges indicating their status, a humiliation which was employed to discourage application for aid. Workhouses were introduced by the Knatchbull Act of 1723.[76] By the end of the eighteenth century, the social stigma and fear attached to having to apply for Poor Law relief had led to a surge in popularity for the establishment of Friendly Societies and Savings Societies as a private insurance against future hardship.[77]

Emigration also promised an escape from religious discrimination, poverty and general lack of opportunity at home, although many left Britain for the colonies for positive rather than negative reasons. The growth of large estates as a consequence of primogeniture led to Anglicans as well as dissenters leaving Wales to get land in the colonies, and sometimes distinctly Welsh communities were established in the new country; the inhabitants of Merion, Pennsylvania, sought the right to use their own language for their civic purposes. Lawyers were again among those who emigrated and showed enterprise in their new homes. Among the most distinguished was John Rice Jones, reputedly the first lawyer to practise west of the Ohio, and who became the first attorney-general of Indiana, where he drafted that state's first code of law before moving on to Missouri where he was one of the commissioners who drafted that state's constitution and was to serve as a justice of its supreme court.[78]

America could seem to some a promised land, where 'natural' rights and customs would be respected and protected, rather than vilified and suppressed. Criticism of rapacious stewards, lawyers and their like were generally motivated by defence of native ways rather than in pursuit of revolutionary social change. There is widespread evidence of the desire of the Welsh people to retain their traditional customs despite the demands of English law. It was noted that Welsh women continued to enjoy greater independence than their counterparts in neighbouring England, largely because of the survival of a traditional native perspective upon their status, and traditional practices, such as the right of the builder of a *tŷ un nos* to the freehold of the land he occupied, continued to be respected. It was recorded in Landimore in Gower in 1639 that tenants there had time out of mind burnt lime so as to compost their lands, an echo not only of Welsh custom but also of the ancient Roman servitude of *calcis coquendi*.[79] Sometimes this harking back to older practices flew full in the face of contemporary legal expectations: it was a major bone of contention along the coasts, including Gower, that locals continued to behave as though they had a right to wreck. For them it was neither illegal not immoral to take such goods, and a customs official was told in 1745 that what the sea threw up on land was as much the property of the locals who took it as his.[80] It was a taking 'hallowed by custom and tradition', 'manna bestowed from heaven by the bounteous Almighty'.[81]

Such insistence by the ordinary people, the *gwerin*, upon what they perceived to be their natural rights was to be found also among Welsh men of education and intellect who were drawn to support the cause of liberty and the revolution in the American colonies. Faced with an established Church and an indifferent governing class, the ordinary people of Wales had encountered in the Methodist Sunday schools institutions which confirmed their native sentiments. There, the congregations chose the teachers, leading them to be called 'cradles of democracy'. By encouraging literacy and learning among even the humblest social classes, the Sunday schools, which were Welsh in speech, gave ordinary people confidence and a sense of the importance of their own conscience and judgement, coupled with a belief that it was ability not birth that allowed the acquisition of learning.[82] The products of these academies saw the refusal of officials to register meeting houses for worship at the request of dissenting ministers and to allow the dead to be buried in Anglican churchyards as evidence of the need for reform at home in the same manner that the treatment of the American colonies had caused rebellion abroad. The dissenting academies produced intelligent and articulate intellectual leaders, who gave their support to constitutional reform and to the American colonists.[83]

The *doyen* of those supporting political liberty and human rights was Dr Richard Price (1723–91), a native of Llangeinor in Glamorgan, who acquired greater fame in Europe and America than in his native Wales, largely because he wrote in English and, while his works were translated into Dutch, French and German, they were not rendered into Welsh. Price became a very influential figure in America, where Thomas Jefferson was one of sixteen of the signatories of the Declaration of Independence who were of Welsh descent. Price was made an honorary American citizen, and Yale University, itself named after a Welshman, gave Price a doctorate on the very same day as one was conferred on George Washington. In 1776, the year of the Declaration of Independence, Price published his *Observation on the Nature of Civil Liberty*, a work which was deemed to have made readers more prepared to accept the arguments of Thomas Paine's *Rights of Man*. Following the ideas of John Locke on popular sovereignty, Price argued that self-determination was a necessary ingredient for liberty. In his later work, *On Love of Country*, he pressed the case for the repeal of the penal laws and other religious inequalities, giving as his reason the need for individuals to exercise their consciences in making choices if there was to be moral and civic progress. In this work, he also advocated the need for parliamentary reform, and it elicited a reply from Edmund Burke in the form of his *Reflections on the Revolution in France*. Price also laid the foundations of modern insurance.[84]

Roughly contemporary with Price was David Williams (1738–1816) of Waenwaelod on Caerphilly mountain, a republican who established a Deist club in company with Benjamin Franklin. His *Letters on Political Liberty* advocated universal manhood suffrage, smaller parliamentary constituencies, voting by ballot, annual parliaments and stipends for MPs. He also published *Lessons to a Young Prince by an Old Statesman* and, in 1790, his *Observations on the Constitution*.[85]

One of the most influential jurists of the age was William Jones (1746–94), the son of a distinguished father of the same name, who had moved from Anglesey to London where the younger William was raised. A prodigious linguist, indeed polymath, he practised at the bar before the Great Sessions before being appointed to a judgeship in India where he laid the foundations of the study of Islamic and Hindu law, both by his translations and systematic presentations. Shortly before he set sail for India, his political work provoked a celebrated trial. Jones was married to the daughter of Dr Jonathan Shipley, the bishop of St Asaph, whose son William Davies Shipley was dean of the cathedral. In an essay entitled *Principles of Government in a Dialogue between a Scholar and a Peasant*, published in 1782, Jones advocated not only universal male suffrage but also the people's right to armed resistance in the face of authoritarian government. The tract was published by his brother-in-law, the dean, who was prosecuted for seditious libel for his trouble. Tried at Shrewsbury Assizes in August 1784, the dean was acquitted and Jones's pamphlet translated into

Welsh and even staged as a play across north Wales, gaining a far greater public as a result of the trial that it would otherwise have enjoyed.[86]

Barristers in Wales, such as Robert Morris of Swansea and Sir Watkin Lewes, were supporters of John Wilkes's Bill of Rights Society, and the Revd Christopher Wyvill's Yorkshire Association campaigning for constitutional reform found emulators in Wales where reform societies were established in Flintshire and Breconshire to organize petitions for reform. The London Corresponding Society also attracted individual members from Wales. Wyvill espoused specific ideas for reform in Wales, including increasing the number of county members of Parliament by four, the extra members being given to Carmarthenshire, Denbighshire, Glamorgan and Monmouthshire.[87]

Not all proposals for reform were however so welcome in Wales. In 1780, Edmund Burke had attacked the courts of Great Sessions, initially wanting to see a reduction in the number of Welsh circuits to two, North Wales and Chester and South Wales, but eventually advocating total abolition. The rationale of his views was that Wales and England needed to be better united. While there had been much criticism of the Sessions within Wales on the basis that the judges were second-rate lawyers, often ignorant of the law and lacking in common sense, that the lawyers who served the courts were greedy and the interpreters poor,[88] the threat of abolition excited support, the Sessions coming to be seen in some quarters as an emblem of Wales's distinct identity. One of the chief complaints about the Sessions had been eradicated by the courts themselves. This concerned the rule that judgement for a debt could proceed to execution against a defendant even if he had not received notice of the action in order to defend himself. The reason for this affront to natural justice lay in the fact that, as the courts only sat for six days at a time, there was often insufficient time after settling the plaintiff's pleadings to summon the defendant and ensure his attendance. Mounting dissatisfaction with this procedure led to the adoption by the courts of what they termed the New Rule, allowing at least a fortnight's notice to be given of the impending action while the courts were not sitting so as to ensure that there was time to summon the defendant and allow him to be heard in his own defence. The Chester circuit adopted the New Rule in 1709, Carmarthen in 1730, Brecon by 1748 and North Wales in 1757. The New Rule did not however preclude the older procedure which was not finally abolished until 1790 on the Carmarthen circuit, 1794 in north Wales, 1816 in Chester and by the following year in Brecon.

The campaign for reform or abolition continued nevertheless. In 1817, a House of Commons Select Committee was established to inquire into the administration of justice in Wales and, whereas it began by advocating reform, it ended by apparently favouring abolition. One of the Select Committee's principal recommendations was that the Great Sessions should be allowed exclusive jurisdiction in claims of up to £50 rather than the £10 decreed in 1773, and this reform was made by statute in 1824. Pleadings could also now be delivered in vacations, witnesses could be examined by commission, and justices could make rules which should apply not only in the county in which they were sitting but throughout their circuit. They were also empowered to hear motions and petitions during vacations, a reform which was bound to be stillborn given most of the judges were not be found in Wales when the courts were not sitting. The only recommendation of the 1817 Select Committee not enacted was the reduction in the length of sessions from six days.

Despite the 1824 reforms, the fate of the Great Sessions was sealed when in 1828 a tumultuous attack upon the administration of justice in both England and Wales was made by Henry Brougham in the House of Commons. Brougham's speech, which lasted for six hours, heralded the root and branch reform of the English legal system. In the brave new rational world foreseen by the Royal Commission on the Supreme Courts of Common Law which was established the following year, there would be no place for historical curiosities such as distinct courts for the land of Wales. Economy was also advanced as a reason for the abolition; three extra judges at Westminster were thought sufficient to cover the extra work which would accrue there as a consequence of disposing of the eight Great Sessions justices in Wales. It was a relatively simple reform to accomplish; the Great Sessions were abolished in 1830.[89]

The Nineteenth and Twentieth Centuries

REFORM OF LAW AND GOVERNMENT

With the abolition of the Great Sessions in 1830, the administration of justice in Wales became fully integrated with that of England. Civil litigation had now to be commenced at Westminster before one of the royal courts: King's Bench, Exchequer or Common Pleas for common law litigation, and Chancery for equity matters. Criminal causes were now to be taken, as had previously been the case in Monmouthshire, by assize judges, who would visit each county to try the most serious criminal cases during the legal vacations. While in the county, the assize judges also had jurisdiction to take the verdicts of juries in civil cases which had been started at Westminster, the so-called *nisi prius* jurisdiction. Final judgement in such causes would then be given at Westminster. At common law, there was no appeal on the merits of the case from the decisions of the three courts, all of which, at Westminster, sat *en banc*, that is, a bench of several judges. Difficult points of law were therefore discussed by more than one judge before judgement was given. Although there was no appeal allowed on the merits of the case, there was a possibility of review for an error of law. Jurisdiction in error lay from the Exchequer to the Court of Exchequer chamber set up for that purpose in 1358, from Common Pleas to the King's Bench, and from King's Bench to the Exchequer Chamber set up in 1585. From either Exchequer Chamber, there was a possibility of final review by the High Court of Parliament, this function being discharged by the House of Lords. This was the origin of the House of Lords as a court of ultimate decision on points of law.

In the Court of Chancery, there had originally been only one judge, the Chancellor himself. To ease his workload, the Master of the Rolls had acquired a jurisdiction over equity cases at first instance, but always subject to a right of appeal, which usually amounted to a rehearing, before the Chancellor. Delays in Chancery had become infamous, as witness the length of the litigation concerning Madam Bevan's will at the end of the previous century. In 1841, the first ever appeal jurisdiction in the royal courts was established with the Lords Justices of Appeal in Chancery in an attempt to remedy this state of affairs. The development was to prove influential.

Litigation in Chancery was commenced by bill, but before the common law courts a writ was generally needed to get a case started. The writ was based upon the plaintiff's cause of action and, if the plaintiff chose the wrong writ, he could be non-suited and forced to start all over again with the correct writ. Often, the question of whether the right writ had been used involved very nice points of law. Critics of the common law fulminated against the injustice of requiring litigants to have to choose between competing forms of action at the risk of being non-suited after much trouble and expense when even the judges sometimes had difficulty in deciding upon the correct basis for making the distinction.[1]

It was not only the Great Sessions which were to be abolished by the nineteenth-century reformers. Only three years after the Sessions went, the Real Property Limitation Act of 1833 greatly simplified the commencement of litigation concerning land by abolishing the older actions for real property, that is, freehold land. The *breve de recto*, the *praecipe in capite*, and the assizes of novel disseisin, mort d'ancestor and the writs of entry all went, leaving virtually all litigation concerning land to be tried by the writ of trespass *de ejectione firmae*. This was originally a writ devised in the thirteenth century to protect leaseholders, but had been used almost to the exclusion of the older actions since the seventeenth century. For freeholders to employ the writ, they had to utilize an elaborate fiction, sanctioned by the courts, to the effect that they had leased the land for a term of years to a totally fictitious person usually called John Doe, who had entered upon the land and been ejected by a servant of the defendant, Richard Roe. Thus was satisfied the procedural requirement that the writ of ejectment existed for leaseholders; actions for the freehold were tried on the demise, that is the lease, of the freeholder to John Doe. From 1833, the need for these fictions was ended.

The abolition of the older real actions posed a problem for the termination of entails, that is, those interests in land which passed from one generation to the next in unbroken succession as long as the entail endured. From before the sixteenth-century union, entails could be barred, that is ended, by a number of methods, leaving the land freely alienable by the owners. The most common methods were by the fine or the common recovery. The fine worked by compromising litigation in which the would-be purchaser sued the vendor, claiming he, the purchaser, had better title to the land. The vendor would agree to make an end, *finem facere*, of the dispute admitting the purchaser's superior title in return for a financial payment, in effect the purchase price. The agreement would then be recorded by the court. The common recovery also involved a manufactured law suit, but in this instance the suit proceeded to judgement, so that the court record again showed that the plaintiff took free of the entail. Both methods were usually started by a real action of the kind now abolished. Accordingly, some other method had to be found to allow entails to be barred. Statute provided one immediately; henceforth entails would be barrable by a simple deed, recognizing what had been true for centuries, namely that tenants in tail could bring the entail to an end and obtain or convey the fee simple in the land.[2]

The abolition of the real actions, and the simplification of litigation concerning land which followed thereupon, was but the beginning of a process of reform to the legal system and the land law which was to continue in the former case until the 1870s and in the latter to 1925. In the 1850s, steps were taken to abolish the forms of action altogether. The Common Law Procedure Acts provided that henceforth plaintiffs should not have to choose between an array of writs, each one suitable to a particular injury or cause of action, but that there should be instead only one original writ to commence litigation at common law, namely a writ of summons ordering the defendant to attend the court to answer the plaintiff's claim. The claim itself would now be set out in the plaintiff's written pleadings, beginning with his statement of claim. While a defendant could respond by asserting that the statement of claim did not disclose a cause of action, he could no longer non-suit the plaintiff for having chosen the wrong cause of action. Provided the pleadings manifested a cause, the case was triable.

Alongside this truly revolutionary change, the common law courts were also given the jurisdiction to grant equitable remedies, such as the specific performance of contracts and the injunction of unlawful acts.[3] No longer would litigants wishing to obtain such remedies in addition to damages have to frequent both the common law courts and the Chancery. Similarly, the Court of Chancery was given power under the Chancery Amendment Act 1858,[4] to grant damages instead of or as well as its equitable remedies, thus reciprocating the change. The eventual amalgamation of the common law and equitable jurisdictions in the 1870s was prefigured by this development.

The 1850s also witnessed a profound change in the administration of the jurisdictions of the Admiralty Court and the ecclesiastical courts which had been the preserve of the civil and canon lawyers who had trained at the universities rather than at the Inns of Court. After a long period of deliberation, in which two notable Welsh civilians, Sir John and Dr John Nichol of Merthyr Mawr in Glamorgan, had played key roles,[5] the state formally took over the jurisdiction of the Church with regard to succession and matrimonial causes. Statutes passed in 1857 transferred these jurisdictions to two new state courts, the Probate Court and the Divorce Court, both of which began to function in 1858. The former had jurisdiction over the inheritance of personalty and of estates which contained both land and personalty, while the latter as its name suggests coincided with the introduction into England and Wales of the possibility of a marriage being terminated by a decree of divorce *a vinculo matrimonio*. Previously, the Church courts had only pronounced decrees of nullity or decrees of divorce *a mensa et thoro* that is in effect a decree of what henceforth would be called judicial separation, entitling the parties to live apart but not ending their status as married persons. Henceforth, a judicial divorce would render the parties single, with the possibility of remarrying, something which previously had only been possible by a private Act of Parliament. The Church courts remained in existence, but now with only a limited jurisdiction over clergy discipline, matters of faith and doctrine, and Church property. In effect they had become the tribunals of one Christian denomination among many, albeit the one established by law in both England and Wales.

The centralization of civil jurisdiction in the royal courts at Westminster meant that all litigation, for however small the amount or relatively trivial the cause, had to be started and finished there and tried by the royal justices in the counties at *nisi prius*. Prior to 1830 in Wales, litigants had been able to choose where to sue in civil matters, but had had to sue for matters under £50 in value before the Great Sessions.[6] In 1846, new county courts were established throughout England and Wales, each with a competence limited not only to the county in which it sat, but also with regard to the maximum value of the subject-matter with which it could deal. The county courts were to be staffed by judges of inferior status to those sitting at what now became the central courts at Westminster, and who would sit alone and not *en banc*, in the same way as the justices of the superior courts sat alone when taking the assizes and the *nisi prius* trials while on circuit. In reality, Wales had only been without courts with competence in smaller claims for sixteen years from 1830 to 1846, although it had lost courts with the competence to try more serious civil cases. Nevertheless, 1846 marked the restoration of a measure of local jurisdiction within Wales, and almost immediately the question of the linguistic competence of county court judges in the Welsh language became a cause for concern and a bone of contention.[7]

The greatest changes to the legal system itself however came in the 1870s, with the passing of the Judicature Acts of 1873–5. These statutes in effect abolished the ancient courts of common law and the Court of Chancery, together with the Admiralty Court, and the recently created Probate Court and Divorce Court. These were all replaced by one court, the Supreme Court of Judicature, which was to occupy brand-new, purpose-built accommodation in London's Strand. Westminster Hall would henceforth be a purely ceremonial location. The Supreme Court was to be composed of a court of first instance, the High Court, and a Court of Appeal. The High Court was to be divided into divisions, corresponding to the older courts which were replaced, and more or less discharging the same business as those courts had entertained. There was however some rationalization. One division, the Probate, Divorce and Admiralty Division, combined the work which had once been done by the civilian courts, the Chancery Division continued the equitable work of Chancery, and the Queen's Bench Division[8] eventually from 1881 amalgamated the once disparate common law jurisdictions of the King's Bench, Exchequer and Common Pleas, the amalgamation in this case being postponed until the chief justices of the erstwhile separate courts had retired, there being separate Exchequer and Common Pleas Divisions until that time. Each division had its head: the Lord Chief Justice in the case of the Queen's Bench Division, the President of the Probate, Divorce and Admiralty Division, and the Lord Chancellor in the case of the Chancery Division, although in the last mentioned a Vice-Chancellor actually fulfilled the role, the Lord Chancellor's function being now to appoint all the judges, sit in Cabinet and be speaker of the House of Lords.

A major change in each of the divisions was that the judges who heard cases at first instance sat alone rather than *en banc*, possibly building on the experience of the county courts. It was obviously hoped that this would lead to a swifter dispatch of business. However, monocratic tribunals do not afford their judges the opportunity to consider difficult points of law with their brethren, hence the institution of monocratic courts more or less necessitated the inauguration of a Court of Appeal modelled on the Lords Justices of Appeal in Chancery. The Court of Appeal was to sit in divisions each consisting of three appeal judges, termed Lords Justices of Appeal. The head of the court was to be the Master of the Rolls, who would preside in the senior division. It was originally intended that the second instance Court of Appeal should be the ultimate appellate court, the appellate jurisdiction of the House of Lords ending. However, a change of government brought Disraeli's Conservatives back into power and in 1876 the House of Lords (Appellate Jurisdiction) Act prevented the removal of the House of Lords' judicial function and it was restored as the ultimate court of appeal to hear appeals on points of law only from the Court of Appeal. Such appeals were to be heard by Law Lords of Appeal in Ordinary, who would also continue to act as the ultimate appeal forum in civil causes from the Court of Session in Scotland, so that some law lords had always to be recruited from the ranks of the Scottish judiciary.

Within the different courts which the Supreme Court replaced, there had been different legal professions. The common law courts and the Chancery were served by advocates called serjeants and barristers, but technically advocates were the civil lawyers who pleaded before the Admiralty and the Church courts and had their base at Doctors' Commons. The rank of serjeant and the role of civilian advocates went; henceforth there were to be only barristers. Likewise, litigants were represented in the several courts by different kinds of lawyer: attorneys at common law, solicitors in Chancery and proctors or procurators before the civilian jurisdictions. These were all combined into a new profession, that of Solicitor of the Supreme Court, controlled by the Law Society.

The Supreme Court was constituted to dispose of civil litigation. Its judges continued to exercise criminal jurisdiction at the county assizes under separate commissions of oyer and terminer and general gaol delivery as previously, also continuing to take the verdicts of juries in civil matters at *nisi prius* while visiting the counties on circuit. While juries continued to be employed for serious criminal cases at the assizes, they had never been used at either the Quarter Sessions or at petty sessions, nor had they been part of the scenario in either the Court of Chancery or in the civilian jurisdictions of the Admiral and the Church. In 1933, juries would cease to be used in the vast majority of civil cases before the King's Bench Division, leaving the single judge to try both questions of law and fact, but still insisting upon that distinction in that appeals were not allowed on questions of fact. A jury of presentment was still used to find that there was a case to answer, a true bill, before a trial took place at the assizes, but such grand juries, which retain their place along with civil juries in the United States, were also abolished in England and Wales in 1933.[9]

A potent case can be made for saying that the manifold changes to both the law, through the abolition of the original writs, and the legal system in the Victorian period brought to an end the true common law of England, substituting therefore a legal system based truly on legislation with the judiciary confined to its application and interpretation. The truth is not that simple; the capacity of the judges to make law had not been ended, but it was now definitely inferior to that of Parliament. English law was not codified in the manner of civil law on the European mainland, where concise codes of national law had been promulgated for France by Napoleon, starting with the *Code civil* of 1804. However, vast tracts of the legal landscape were reduced to statutory form during the nineteenth century, dealing with such disparate topics as Wills (1837), Offences against the Person (1861), Settled Land (1882), Sale of Goods (1893), and virtually the whole of the law relating to property in land would be enacted in a reformed manner in Lord Birkenhead's corpus of property legislation in 1925.[10] Theorists, such as Jeremy Bentham, and active lawyers, such as Sir James Fitzjames Stephen, supported the cause of codification.

The retention of the House of Lords as a third and final court to dispose of appeals on points of law only also mirrored the kinds of competence being created in the civil law countries of Europe. There, too, first instance decisions were appealable to a court of appeal, with a final appeal possible on points of law to what was there generally termed the Supreme Court. However, other than in Germany, the ultimate courts of appeal on the continent did not decide the cases before them. Instead, they resolved the point of law only before either confirming the decision of the lower court or referring the case back to the appeal court from which it came for final decision, having quashed its previous decision. From this 'quashing' function, these courts are known as Supreme Courts of *Cassation*.[11]

Another major difference between the continental European jurisdictions emerging in the nineteenth century and that of England and Wales was the fact that the tribunals of first instance in the countries on the European mainland were all local courts, situated in the towns and provincial capitals. Even the appeal courts were decentralized, one being situated in every city of any importance. In England and Wales, on the other hand, the administration of civil justice was markedly centralized, with both the High Court and the Court of Appeal sitting only in the imperial capital. Criminal cases could be begun, heard and ended in the counties, but here too there was another marked difference between the continental and English approaches. In England and Wales, no appeal was allowed in criminal cases. Until 1907, the most that could occur was that difficult points of law might be reserved to a special court sitting *en banc*, the Court of Crown Cases Reserved. Only in 1907 was a Court of Criminal Appeal introduced, on the model of the civil appeal court, but with only a limited right of appeal open to the accused. The merits of a criminal conviction were not open to immediate question.[12] Judges of the Queen's Bench Division still sat *en banc* to review cases from inferior courts, including Quarter Sessions, petty sessions and the growing number of administrative tribunals, essentially reviewing points of law through use of the prerogative writs of *certiorari*, prohibition and *mandamus*.[13] A wealth of administrative law would be created through judicial activity in the Divisional Court, which remained a forum for judicial law-making. The administrative law created by the Divisional Court would also continue the tradition by which judges curtailed the zeal of the executive in the interests of the rights of the subject. Such powers would be particularly important where the executive enjoyed a large majority in the legislature.

It was not only the administration of justice that underwent root and branch reform during the nineteenth century. The character of the legislature also underwent change. The 1832 Reform Act increased the representation from Wales in the House of Commons from 27 seats to 32.[14] The counties of Glamorgan, Carmarthenshire and Denbighshire were given second members, and within Glamorgan both Swansea and Merthyr Tydfil obtained borough representatives, with 18 new contributory boroughs being added.[15] The franchise however still turned upon property ownership, the county vote being confined to free-holders, certain leaseholders and tenants of property worth more than £50 a year. In the boroughs, the franchise was given to those with premises worth more than £10 a year, and such ratepayers were disqualified from voting if they had not paid their rates in the last year. Such disqualifications were to be a feature of the franchise into the twentieth century, as was the possibility of having more than one vote. In local elections within the boroughs, for example, ratepayers who had been resident for more than three years and who had paid their rates were allowed one vote for every £50 worth of property they owned in the borough up to a maximum of six.[16]

Few elections for Parliament were contested in the middle years of the century, although the political independence shown by tenants in their voting in the 1859 elections led to irate landlords evicting some, particularly in Carmarthenshire, Cardiganshire and Caernarfonshire. The evictions by Anglican, English-speaking landlords of their Nonconformist, Welsh-speaking tenants were to have their effect in radicalizing many sections of the population. They also played a significant part in the introduction of voting by secret ballot in 1872.[17] The number of parliamentary seats in Wales was increased to thirty-three by the 1867 Reform Act, which gave Merthyr Tydfil, the largest town in Wales, a second member, and this Act also increased the numbers who enjoyed the franchise, the Welsh county electors increasing by a half, while the borough electorate went up by 250 per cent. Industrial workers living within boroughs got the vote, but those living outside of boroughs did not, and nor did agricultural labourers and women generally.[18]

The massive change to both the electorate and the parliamentary representation of Wales came with the 1884 Reform Act and the Redistribution Act of the following year. The former more than doubled the size of the electorate in Wales, making an even greater difference to its composition than in England. Householders generally obtained the vote, virtually trebling the number of voters in the Welsh counties at a stroke. Women, some classes of lodger and those in receipt of Poor Law contributions remained excluded, but nevertheless the effect was considerable. The 1885 Redistribution Act created thirty-four constituencies of more equal size throughout Wales, depriving some of the smaller boroughs of their members and dividing populous counties such as Glamorgan into parliamentary divisions. For the first time, workers could form the majority of the electors in industrial areas, most notably the Rhondda division of Glamorgan.[19]

The closing decades of the nineteenth century also saw revolutionary change to the nature of local government in Wales.[20] By and large, justices of the peace, drawn in the main from the ranks of the gentry and clergy, continued to dominate local government during the nineteenth century, with often one-fifth of the justices being clergy of the Church of England, men upon whose literacy, residence and availability in terms of time confidence could be placed.[21] However, changes in the population patterns of Wales, in particular in those areas where industrialization was being experienced, meant that the county justices were often far from conveniently distributed within the country. In Merthyr Tydfil, for instance, a town of 30,000 inhabitants by 1827, there were only two justices of the peace. The creation of the new county councils in 1888–9, followed by the introduction of the new urban and rural district councils in 1894, changed the face of local government, with elected councillors replacing the justices in governing the localities at every level from the parish to the county. The counties were still those created by the sixteenth-century Acts of Union, and thus they were to remain until 1974 when the number of Welsh counties was reduced to eight, the new counties only surviving for two decades until the Local Government Act 1994 divided Wales into twenty-two unitary authorities, a change which took effect in April 1996.[22] Coupled with the changes to the franchise and parliamentary representation, this period marked the termination of the landed gentry's control of local government in Wales, a period ushered in by the Tudor Union.[23]

LAW AND THE NATIONAL IDENTITY OF WALES

That this was the end of an era is also apparent from the extensive changes which followed with regard to the ownership of land in the first two decades of the twentieth century.[24] Wales had developed since the union into a country of large landed estates, where 60 per cent of all the land was owned by just 1 per cent of the population, a vastly different situation from that which had existed under the native laws. The replacement of partibility with primogeniture had played a substantial part in this, creating the landowning class which with the lesser gentry dominated Welsh society and local government.[25] During the eighteenth century, however, a failure of male issue in the direct line of many of these families had resulted in the estates passing to the aristocratic English husbands of Welsh heiresses, creating a situation in which Welsh estates were run by the stewards and agents of largely absentee English landlords, men who were not only divided from their tenants in language and religion, but also now largely unknown to them as well. The enclosing of land, particularly where it involved the reclaiming of property encroachments deemed legitimate by the Welsh custom of *tŷ un nos*, and the introduction of harsh game laws which were also foreign to Welsh traditions, exacerbated matters. The Ground Game Act 1831 was particularly hated in that it prevented tenants from shooting the rabbits and hares which damaged their crops and their livelihoods.[26] The introduction of shorter leaseholds had allowed landlords to review rents at each renewal, so that when in the middle years of the nineteenth century, agriculture began to prosper as a consequence of the increased demand for food from the developing industrial areas, substantial rent rises of between 5 and 30 per cent occurred in the rural areas between 1850 and 1880. From the 1870s onwards, tenants began to seek to buy the freehold of their land from their landlords, often having to borrow between a quarter and a third of the purchase price to do so.[27] For those who could not do so, the rent rises posed a real threat to their livelihood, such that the veteran Nonconformist campaigner Thomas Gee formed a Welsh Land League to campaign for rent reductions, security of tenure and a land court to adjudicate fair rents. The upshot was the appointment by Gladstone of a Royal Commission on Land in Wales and Monmouthshire which reported in 1896.[28] Following the Land Commission's report, the Liberal government introduced a Land Tenure Bill in 1897, the main provision of which was that a Land Court should be created with a judge appointed by the Board of Agriculture to fix fair rents and terms of tenure. The bill however did not pass into legislation, and government policy switched to the encouragement of the purchase of small freeholds by the agricultural population, much in the manner that was at the time being essayed in many parts of mainland Europe.[29]

The attitude of the landowners themselves changed as the century turned. The introduction of progressive rates of estate duty in the 1894 Finance Act

began to make land a less attractive form of investment, and when the maximum rate rose from 8 per cent in 1894 to 40 per cent by 1919, many landowners
were more than ready to divest themselves of their estates. The years 1910–14
saw the beginning of large-scale land sales in Wales, with Welsh tenants proving
much keener to purchase the freeholds of their lands than their opposite
numbers in England, where the tradition of tenant farming was centuries older.
The great exception to the willingness of landowners to sell their freeholds
was in the industrial areas of the South Wales Coalfield where the large
landowners made substantial incomes from leasing their mineral rights to
capitalists for a percentage return on the profits.[30] This was an example of the
general truth that other forms of investment were now much more profitable
than land ownership. Where such considerations did not apply, there was a
readiness on the part of landowners to sell and thereby create a new rural
society of small freeholders, the owner/occupiers of their land. This process
which had begun after 1910, continued during the Great War and accelerated
after 1918. The years 1918–22 saw land sales reach their zenith, with a quarter
of all freehold land in Wales changing ownership as a consequence of rents
having fallen during the war years while agricultural prices had risen, causing
income from land to decline while the value of the land itself increased at a
time when estate duty was also increasing. It was therefore in the interest of
the large landowners to sell, and this they did, altering substantially the whole
spectrum of social relationships in rural Wales in the wake of the changes
already wrought in local government. Tenants were prepared to borrow as
much as 80 per cent of the purchase price in order to buy their freeholds in the
years up to 1918, and a further spate of land sales occurred in the years 1924–5.[31]
The pattern of land ownership in Wales was speedily returned to that which
had existed before primogeniture had operated to assist in the creation of the
large estates, and the reversal interestingly occurred as the 1925 property legislation abolished primogeniture of land, as part of the recognition that land
was now but one kind of investment, and no longer that which above all had
to be preserved in the interests of providing for succeeding generations and
maintaining a position and influence in society.

The Welsh desire to own the family home and hearth, a wish that can be
traced back to the native traditions of the people, was to manifest itself again
in the later years of the twentieth century. The great landowners of south Wales,
who had been affected less than their counterparts in the rural areas of north,
mid and west Wales, had leased much of their property to developers in order
to provide housing for the industrial workers. The builders had in the main
sold the leasehold to the house purchasers for the full term, usually ninety-
nine years. By the middle years of the twentieth century, these leaseholds
were nearing expiry and the descendants of the original house-buyers, who
had largely been immigrants from rural Wales,[32] expressed a strong desire to
buy the freeholds of their houses which had often been the family home for

two or three generations. Welsh members of Parliament were instrumental in the passing of the Leasehold Enfranchisement Act 1967, which allowed the occupiers of leasehold dwellings with a rateable value of more than £40 a year to buy the freehold as of right.[33] In the 1980s, the Thatcher government's policy of offering council houses for sale to their occupiers was also to prove popular in Wales.[34]

Connected with the question of land ownership was the vexed issue of the payment of tithes. Tithes had originally been paid in kind to support the parish priest, but with the passing of ecclesiastical lands to secular owners at the Reformation, the tithe in many cases had become payable to a lay impropriator. Added to the secularization of the payment was the factor that in Wales most of the tenants paying tithes were Nonconformists who were forced thereby to support the Church of England or an Anglican landlord, sometimes a permanent absentee from the estate. Matters were exacerbated when in 1836 the Tithe Commutation Act converted tithes from payment in kind to payment in money, the amount being calculated on the basis of the average price of wheat, barley and oats over the preceding seven years. Such a calculation tended to preserve tithe income for the impropriator, often the same person as the landlord who got the rent and possibly local taxes, while the tenant had to face the consequences of reduced income in a year when the harvest was poor.[35]

Viewed as a payment to an alien Church or an absent landlord, tithes became a source of agitation and sometimes of disturbances in the 1880s.[36] Protests in north-east Wales were accompanied by the formation at Ruthin in 1886 of the Anti-Tithe League, with Thomas Gee once again to the fore. Protests began to spread, the cause now being connected directly with the cause of the disestablishment of the Church of England within Wales. One consequence was the passing of the Tithe Rent Charge Act of 1891, which made landowners rather than their tenants responsible for the payment of the tithe. While this seemingly imposed the burden on landowners who were in the main Anglicans, the reality was that the burden was passed on in the form of increased rents. Nevertheless, the measure quelled the rising tide of discontent and the Land League moved on to press its claims for disestablishment.[37]

The cause of disestablishment was bedevilled by the question of whether it was possible for law in Wales to be different from law in England, given that the two countries had been united for legal purposes by the Tudor Acts of Union. The separate legal identity which had existed until 1830 as a consequence of Wales being served by separate courts with different procedures had gone with the Great Sessions, partly explaining why they had come to be seen as an emblem of Welsh national identity. The creation of the county courts had refuelled the debate concerning the use of the Welsh language in the courts, and radical MPs such as the barrister George Osborne Morgan were scathing in their criticisms of the appointment of monoglot English-speaking judges to serve in predominantly Welsh-speaking areas.[38] In addition, Wales still preserved customs that were at variance to the rules of English law, but to which its people clung with devotion. Locals were outraged when land-owners reclaimed encroachments made by *tŷ un nos*; popular retributions such as parading a wrongdoer or his likeness on the back of a wooden horse, the *ceffyl pren*, were still preferred to conviction before the courts for some offences, and, despite the growth of Nonconformity, little stigma attached to an illegitimate child in many parts of Wales, provided the grandmother was prepared to rear the child as though it were her own. The last example possibly testifies to the perseverance of the native Welsh attitudes towards legitimacy. Whether Parliament however could legislate separately for a country which had no distinct legal system, law or judicature of its own was a difficult question, but one germane to a whole host of Welsh issues, including disestablishment, reform of land tenure, education at all levels from school to university, reform of the magistracy and, crucially as was to prove the case, temperance.[39]

The issue which was to break this deadlock and confirm the possibility of legislation which was particular to Wales was that of the Sunday opening of public houses. There is a double irony in this fact, for not only was the Sunday Closing (Wales) Act 1881 the first piece of distinctive Welsh legislation since the Commonwealth, it was also the case that the Sabbatarianism of the Common-wealth legislation had been greatly unpopular in Wales. The Act inaugurated a period in which, while it was possible to buy alcoholic beverages in England on a Sunday, or in clubs in Wales, the Welsh Sunday was protected as far as public houses were concerned. The Act however did not apply in Monmouth-shire, an odd consequence of the fact that that county had been outside of the jurisdiction of the half-century-defunct Great Sessions, but this bone of contention was removed by the extension of the Act's provisions there in 1921. The 1920s also saw resort to violence in an attempt to preserve the Sabbath. The playing of golf at the links in Aberdovey in Merionethshire provoked local people into violent protest, causing Atkin LJ, one of the most distinguished lawyers of the period and later a Law Lord of Appeal as Lord Atkin of Aberdovey, to write to the press. The sanctity of the Welsh Sunday was effectively preserved until after the Second World War when it was gradually eroded. In 1950, the county borough of Swansea held a referendum on whether cinemas should be allowed to open in the town on Sundays which resulted in a positive response. Similar referenda followed producing similar results in Cardiff and other urban areas. The idea of local referenda on sabbatarian issues was taken up by the legis-lature in the Licensing Act 1960, which provided for county by county votes to be taken every seven years on the question of the Sunday opening of public houses. The first such referendum was held throughout Wales in 1961, leading to some counties becoming 'wet', while seven years later in 1968 the second such referendum left only the counties which had once formed the medieval Principality voting against Sunday opening. Thereafter, referenda were only held in areas where a specified number of electors called for one, and gradually the whole of Wales succumbed to the alcoholic tide of modernism. Referenda ceased in the 1990s.[40]

The use of local referenda was however an interesting experiment in local democracy, an application of the principle of subsidiarity in government which in the post-war years played a key role in the political and governmental development of Europe. Some countries, most notably Italy, made considerable use of single-issue referenda to emphasize the sovereignty of the people within law-making rather than that of the legislature. Elements of local democracy can be found in nineteenth-century British law-making, for instance in the introduction of public health legislation. During the period 1848–75, the Public Health Acts of 1848 and 1858, which created a General Board of Health, together with the Sanitary Act 1866, allowed localities to establish local boards by democratic procedures. The system of inspection provided for by the Acts would be instituted locally provided one-tenth of the property owners and ratepayers petitioned for its adoption. The voluntary nature of this procedure was thought to have delayed much needed reforms in the area of public health, for the statutory system would only be imposed on a locality if its death rate rose to over 23 per 1,000 of the population. A local inquiry was also needed in advance of a private bill to enclose common land under the provisions of the General Inclosure Act, 1845.[41]

The cause célèbre of the Liberal Nonconformist majority in Wales was undoubtedly the disestablishment of the Church of England within the Welsh counties. Having closed the taverns on Sundays, they sought to extinguish the privileges of the parish churches. Two barristers elected to Parliament in 1868 were in the vanguard of the assault. While George Osborne Morgan campaigned for reform of the law relating to burial,[42] his Liberal colleague Watkin Williams proposed the first motion for disestablishment, albeit unsuccessful, in that Parliament.[43] Thereafter, the baton was to pass to David Lloyd George, himself a north Wales solicitor, who through his growing influence and astute political manipulation, succeeded in getting Lord Rosebery to introduce the first Welsh Disestablishment Bill in 1894. That bill was lost, and a further bill in the following year fell with the government when it had reached its committee stage. The Liberals were then out of power until 1906.[44]

When they returned to power, the Prime Minister, Campbell-Bannerman, set up a Royal Commission to examine the position of the Church of England and other religious bodies in Wales under the chairmanship of Lord Justice Vaughan-Williams. The Commission sat from 1906 until 1910, but the somewhat abrasive style of the chairman caused consternation among the Welsh members, leading to resignations, including that of the eminent Welsh barrister, Samuel T. Evans. A disestablishment bill was introduced by Asquith in 1909, but his government then became embroiled in a major confrontation with the House of Lords over Lloyd George's 1909 Budget. The upshot of this confrontation was the passing of the Parliament Act of 1911, which removed from the House of Lords any powers over financial legislation and also provided that any bill which had been passed on three occasions by the House of Commons could proceed immediately to receive the royal assent notwithstanding that it had been rejected on the first two occasions by the House of Lords. Legislative sovereignty thereby passed most definitely to the elected representatives of the people.

The first bill to meet with such opposition and to become law despite the Lords' refusal to cooperate in its passage was the Welsh Church Act 1914. Introduced into the Commons in April 1912, it was twice passed in the lower house and twice rejected by the Lords. Accordingly, when it was passed for the third time by the Commons on 19 May 1914, it marked not only the triumph of Nonconformity in Wales but also that of popular sovereignty at Westminster.[45] The Act disestablished the Church of England within Wales and Monmouthshire, although it allowed border parishes to choose between becoming part of an English diocese or a Welsh one, thus introducing a further boundary between Wales and England, this time for ecclesiastical purposes. The ecclesiastical law of the Church of England was no longer to apply in Wales, and the ecclesiastical courts lost their jurisdiction in those parts. Moreover, the property of the Church of England within Wales was confiscated, leading to the disendowment of the Church, the property being transferred to Welsh Church Commissioners, who were responsible for its allocation. Church buildings and parsonages were returned for the Church's use, a special trustee body being incorporated by royal charter at the request of the disestablished Church as provided by the Act to hold and manage its property for the future. This was the Representative Body of the Church in Wales. The Welsh Commissioners were to pass other property to the county councils, the university and its colleges, and national institutions such as the National Library.

The coming into force and effect of the 1914 Act was delayed by the Great War, and the Welsh Church was not finally disestablished until 31 March 1920. In the interim, although there had been campaigns among Welsh Anglicans to have the measure repealed, preparations for the future had also been made. Three leading Welsh lawyers, all Anglicans, drafted a constitution for the disestablished Church. These were John Sankey, later to be the first Labour lord chancellor, Lord Justice Bankes and Lord Justice Atkin. Their constitution, which was adopted by the Church at a Convention in Cardiff, was to be binding upon all Church members as a private contract into which they entered by accepting office or having their names entered on the electoral roll of a Welsh parish. An elaborate structure of private ecclesiastical courts was also set up for the Church and it was also provided that the ecclesiastical law of the Church of England as it was on the day of disestablishment, with certain exceptions, should remain contractually binding upon the Welsh Church and its members, subject to such changes as they might in the future make thereto. Finally, it was decided that the four Welsh dioceses should form a distinct province with an archbishop, who, like the other bishops of the Church in Wales, should in future be elected by representatives of the clergy and people of the province. The bishop of St Asaph, the Right Revd A. G. Edwards, was duly elected first archbishop of Wales.

Before the 1914 Act took effect, the desperate financial straits which the Church in Wales faced as a consequence of disendowment caused the Liberal government, with Lloyd George now Prime Minister, to repent somewhat. In 1919, the Welsh Church Temporalities Act provided the Church with some compensation for its losses, funds which thereafter the Representative Body would invest most wisely on its behalf. The 1919 Act also preserved for Wales the institution of ecclesiastical marriage, whereby marriages could be solemnized by clerics of the Church in Wales following the publication of banns in the same manner as in England without the need of civil formalities nor the presence of a civil registrar. The 1914 Act had intended that the Welsh Church should be left in the same position as the other Christian denominations in this regard, that is requiring civil formalities and the presence of a civil registrar or authorized person. The retention of ecclesiastical marriage was to be a source of some confusion in the years ahead, as in England the ecclesiastical law, now abolished in Wales, gave parishioners the right to be married in the parish churches, upon which right the state had engrafted its legislation with regard to marriage since 1753. The 1914 Act also confiscated from the churches their churchyards, giving them into the care of the local authorities, preserving to the Church members rights of way over what was now local authority land to get to their place of worship.[46] This was to prove so manifestly inconvenient that in 1945, the Welsh Church (Burial Grounds) Act gave churches the right to call for a regrant of their churchyards and burial grounds from the local authorities, a right which some, but not all, churches have exercised. This particular confiscation illustrates very clearly the strength of feeling against the established Church which had arisen as a result of its insensitive treatment of Nonconformists at moments of great vulnerability in their lives.[47]

The 1919 Act and the change of heart on marriage and burial all indicate that by the time disestablishment occurred much of the venom that had fuelled the debate in earlier decades had already disappeared. Indeed, although many Anglicans of that generation would always view disestablishment bitterly as a disaster visited upon the Church by its opponents, there were those even at the time who saw it as an opportunity. The Anglo-Catholic barrister, J. Arthur Price, saw disestablishment as restoring to Wales a Church independent of the state as it had known in the Middle Ages. It was indeed the case that the Church in Wales was now governed by its own canon law rather than the ecclesiastical law of the state. Moreover, the Church was liberated to develop as it, not the state, wished, freed from the dead hand of requiring parliamentary approval for its schemes, a need which had hampered its response to the provision of churches in the new industrial communities, where Nonconformist denominations had enjoyed much greater flexibility in responding to the needs of the new communities by providing places of worship. Gradually, the disestablished Church in Wales would become with other national institutions such as the university, the National Library and the National Museum, a new emblem of Wales's distinct national identity, in the same manner in which the Great Sessions had come to be perceived since their demise almost a century earlier.[48]

The confidence to proceed with disestablishment flowed not only from the separate legislation which had closed Welsh public houses on Sundays but also from the introduction of a distinct form of statutory education into Wales. Since the spread of voluntary education from the Sunday schools of the eighteenth century, including the circulating schools of Griffith Jones of Llanddowror, the achievement of education had become a badge of pride among the Welsh people. Alongside these initiatives and the grammar schools that had been founded since the sixteenth century, some landowners and industrial employers had also responded to the educational needs of their communities; Humphrey Mackworth had set up a charity school in Neath as early as 1705, and J. T. Price followed his example there in 1816.[49] The infamous report of the commissioners who inspected the state of education in Wales during the 1840s, maligning not only educational standards, but also the language and morality of the people, provoked a national outrage. Their work became known as the treachery of the Blue Books, *Brad y Llyfrau Gleision*.

Compulsory primary education was only achieved gradually. Building on the exclusion of children under 10 from working in the mines, the Collieries Act 1861 extended this rule to cover 10- to 12-year-olds who had not achieved basic standards of literacy. From July 1870, the Factory Extension Act 1867 made half-time attendance at school compulsory for all 8- to 13-year-olds, with a prohibition upon their working nights, which would have obviously undermined their schooling during the day. This reform came into force in the same year as the Education Act 1870 was passed dividing the country into school districts, each to be served by a school board. From 1876, parents were obligated to see that their children obtained instruction in reading, writing and arithmetic and 10- to 14-year-olds were only to be employable if they had achieved a sufficient standard in these subjects. By 1880, when those who were 10 at the time of the 1876 Act had reached the age of 14, compulsory education up to that level had been achieved.[50]

In Wales, the 1870s also saw the birth of higher education with the opening of the University College of Wales at Aberystwyth in 1872. For the first time, non-Anglicans could attend an institution of higher education at home in Wales, St David's College Lampeter having been open only to Anglicans training for the sacred ministry of the Church of England. University colleges at Cardiff and Bangor followed in 1883 and 1884 respectively, although there remained great resentment at the fact that Lampeter had powers given it by royal charter to confer its own degrees while the colleges at Aberystwyth, Cardiff and Bangor had to have their degrees validated from the University of London. This was finally remedied in 1893 with the establishment of the University of Wales, a national federal university, of which the three colleges became constituent institutions, with the power to confer its own degrees.[51]

The Welsh colleges were however faced with a serious problem of recruitment, for although elementary education was established on a firm footing in Wales, there was no system of intermediate education bridging the years between elementary school and the university. Only the grammar schools and private education existed to progress scholars from the one to the other. In 1889, the second major piece of distinctly Welsh legislation was passed by Parliament, namely the Welsh Intermediate Education Act. The Act, which was passed in the wake of the legislation setting up county councils throughout England and Wales, gave the country a new system of county secondary schools based on the local authorities created by the earlier statute. The system of county schools established by the 1889 Act are generally agreed to have given Wales a much better system of secondary education than England. When in 1902, the Balfour Education Act created a further tier of higher grade secondary schools throughout the country, Wales ended up with two tiers of secondary education, one of which, the county schools, prided itself on providing education to high academic standards leading to the universities. The Balfour Act, however, proved very unpopular within Wales, because it placed all schools under the control of local authorities, so that virtually all of the Welsh county councils refused to participate in its implementation. The Balfour scheme savoured of the centralist system of education preferred in France, whereas the Welsh authorities were proud of the diversity which their two-tier system promoted. While the county councils threatened to revolt against the dictates of the Conservative government, Lloyd George in opposition campaigned for devolution of education matters to a Welsh education body rather than rebellion as a way out of the terms of the 1902 Act. When the Liberals came back into government in 1906, an Education Bill proposed that a National Council for Wales be established to deal with education within the country, although all schools would remain under local authority control. The bill was so badly mauled during its passage through the House of Lords that it was abandoned by the government, which instead contented itself with setting up in the following year a Welsh department of the Board of Education. This Welsh department, which often found itself at odds with the Central Welsh Board which validated examinations and standards, was very ably served by both its first secretary, the Flintshire solicitor A. T. Davies, and its first schools' inspector, Owen M. Edwards, who brought to his task not only considerable intellect but also a cultural sensibility fashioned by his native land and the values of thinkers such as Ruskin and Rousseau.[52] The 1907 solution was however a compromise; there was no true devolution regarding education to the people of Wales despite the achievements of their education system. When public education was further reformed in 1918 by the Fisher Education Act, a Welsh Education Council was still not forthcoming. Nor did any devolution occur under the terms of the 1944 Butler Education Act, which ended Wales's distinctive two-tier system of secondary education. When the Welsh Joint Education Committee replaced the Central Welsh Board in 1948–9, the last vestige of a distinctive Welsh identity in matters of education ended, and a distinguished as well as a distinct chapter in the legislative history of Wales also came to an end.[53]

The insensitivity of both Conservative and Liberal governments to the Welsh dimension in education was but one manifestation of a more general failure to see Wales as having a distinct and separate identity. Justices of the peace as well as Nonconformist leaders had been openly critical of the Poor Law Amendment Act 1834 which banned the giving of outdoor relief to paupers, and dictated that parishes should be grouped into Poor Law Unions with boards of guardians, workhouses being built for the provision of indoor relief which should be unattractive so as to deter applicants.[54] The Poor Law in mid Wales came to be administered from Staffordshire and the precepts of central authority regarding the giving of relief so angered some Welsh guardians that they were deliberately exceeded. In 1927, the Bedwellty Board of Guardians was superseded for such conduct and within two years the government minister with responsibility for the Poor Law's administration, Neville Chamberlain, had replaced the Poor Law authorities with public assistance committees run by local authorities, a move vigorously condemned by Aneurin Bevan. Lord Rhondda's attempts to abolish the Poor Law altogether were largely ignored.[55]

The problems encountered with regard to the Poor Law in the late 1920s reflected the depressed state of many Welsh communities, particularly the industrial valleys of south Wales, at that time. Government policy initially focused on attempts to transfer the younger element in the workforce to more prosperous areas in England, totally disregarding the closeness of Welsh family units and any cultural or linguistic dimension to the problem. An Industrial Transference Board was established in 1928, and transference was seen as the preferred answer until, in 1934, the Special Areas Act shifted the focus to encouraging industries to locate in areas such as south Wales where there was a workforce seeking employment. The one success of this policy in Wales was the creation and development of the Treforest Industrial Estate between Cardiff and Pontypridd.[56] Meanwhile, in September 1932, the Board of Education's circular 1421, combined with circular 170 in Wales, called for a decrease in the number of free places being provided in secondary schools and the imposition of a new means test to determine the level of fees to be paid. Welsh local authorities had always done their utmost to maximize the number of free places and were outraged at this directive, several, including Merthyr Tydfil, Swansea and Newport, openly resisting the policy.[57] The inter-war years also saw the national arrangements made for Wales by the Ministry of Pensions brought to an end, the removal of the probate registry for north Wales from Bangor to Chester, and the institutionalization of the perceived division between north and south by placing north Wales under the factory inspectorate based in Liverpool and south Wales under that located in Bristol.[58]

The same insensitivity to Wales's national identity appeared again with the Labour government's policy of nationalization after the Second World War when, although Wales was given its own Gas Board, with regard to electricity it was divided between the South Wales Electricity Board and the Merseyside and North Wales Electricity Board, despite strenuous protests from James Griffiths. On the nationalized railways, Wales was part of the western region, and likewise part of the western division of the British Transport Authority.[59] These were the years when the distinctly Welsh character of secondary education ended. Not surprisingly, some saw all of these as indicating a total lack of appreciation of Wales's identity, in the same manner as the appointment of English-speaking judges to Welsh-speaking areas had inflamed opinion in the nineteenth century and the failure to achieve consistency in the application of legislation on Sunday closing, intermediate education and the disestablishment of the Church had suggested a lack of care with regard to the detail of dealing with Wales and its concerns.[60] Finally, Welsh public opinion became white with anger when in 1957 Parliament voted to allow the drowning of Cwm Tryweryn in Merionethshire to provide a reservoir for Liverpool despite the protests of the inhabitants of the threatened village of Capel Celyn, the outrage of a substantial section of Welsh public opinion and the fact that every single Labour MP from Wales in the House of Commons voted against the measure.[61]

Tryweryn was to become a by-word for government contempt for Wales, in much the same way as a generation earlier, Pen-y-berth had been. The Pen-y-berth prosecutions resulted from the blatantly criminal acts of three eminent Welshmen – Saunders Lewis, Lewis Valentine and D. J. Williams. Together they had set fire to an RAF bombing school on the Llŷn peninsula as a protest against the use of Welsh soil for training in the arts of war. Immediately after their arson attack on the bombing school, they notified the authorities of what they had done and gave themselves up. When at their trial at Caernarfonshire Assizes, the jury failed to reach a verdict, the prosecution was moved from Wales to the Central Criminal Court, the Old Bailey, in London, where all three were convicted and sentenced to terms of imprisonment, having refused to give evidence before the court in English. The reason given for moving the trial to London was the same as that given by the King's Bench when claiming jurisdiction over the Great Sessions in the eighteenth century, Welsh juries could not necessarily be trusted to reach unbiased verdicts.[62]

The crime at Pen-y-berth was instigated as a consequence of its perpetrators feeling that the siting of the bombing school in Wales was totally contrary to Welsh interests and opinion. Much crime and disorder in nineteenth-century Wales can be connected with such perceptions of injustice. Early nineteenth-century Wales exhibited very little in the way of violent crime, with theft of farm animals and barley being the commonest crimes and a deal of poaching. The end of the Napoleonic wars saw the crash of many banks and the 1820s witnessed a fall in the price of cattle with no concomitant reduction in rents, resulting in hardship. Ill-feeling generated by this situation led to rioting in the south-west, at Maenclochog in Pembrokeshire in 1820 and at Mynydd Bach in Cardiganshire two years later. The activities of agents and stewards of the landed estates of the Crown, the Church of England and absentee land-owners also caused discontent, particularly their reclamation of land which had been encroached upon as a *tŷ un nos* according to Welsh custom. Attempts to reclaim such lands were also a cause of rioting. In the growing industrial areas of the south, tensions emerged over the practice of paying workers not in money but with vouchers which could only be redeemed for goods at shops owned by the employers, so-called truck shops. Statutory intervention in the shape of the Anti-Truck Act 1831 proved ineffectual in that its provisions proved easy to evade, and in the eastern valleys of south Wales violent disorder broke out in the disturbances known as the Scotch cattle. In 1835, prosecutions of the ringleaders led to three death sentences being imposed although two were commuted to transportation. The only convict hanged, Edward Morgan, had been found guilty of the murder of the wife of one of the movement's targets. Nevertheless, he came to be regarded as something of a martyr, in the same way as Dic Penderyn became a figure of legend following his execution for his part in the Merthyr riots of 1831.[63]

Powers to arrest suspects, prohibit meetings and impose curfews to maintain order were vested at this time in the JPs. Police forces were however beginning to be established, for instance at Abergavenny in 1832 and in Glamorgan, Brecknock and Monmouthshire in 1834. Glamorgan got a full-time police force in 1841.[64] Some of the most serious rioting at this time took place in the rural south-west, where the toll-gates on the turnpike roads became the target of disaffection. The Rebecca riots, so-called because the rioters dressed as women in fulfilment of the Old Testament prophecy that the seed of Rebecca would possess the gates of her enemies,[65] broke out intermittently from 1839 until 1843. In December of the latter year, forty-one rioters were tried at Carmarthenshire Assizes, where two of the ringleaders, John Jones and David Davies, better known as *Sioni Sgubor Fawr* and *Dai'r Cantwr* respectively, were sentenced to be transported to Australia. The Report of the Commission of Enquiry into the riots suggested various reforms to the turnpike trusts, whose roads had been the object of much praise in Wales. It was recommended that the trusts should be consolidated and regulated by county road boards in every shire. It was also suggested that the toll they imposed on the carrying of lime should be halved.[66]

Chartism also produced disturbances in both south and mid Wales. The Newport rising of 1839 resulted in loss of life when troops opened fire on the marchers, while disturbances in Llanidloes led to thirty-two chartists being arraigned before Montgomeryshire Assizes in July 1839. Harsh sentences were handed down on the accused, who had been defended by Hugh Williams, a Carmarthen solicitor, who faced the massed ranks of the attorney-general and four other Queen's Counsel for the prosecution.[67]

While such disruptions of the famed peace of *gwlad y menyg gwynion* were rooted in social and economic unrest, the law itself was at times seen as oppressive and weighted against the common man. During the 1830s, farmers in the west of Glamorgan took legal action against the owners of copper-smelting works in the Swansea area over the effects of pollution upon the well-being of their animals. Their claims met with no success. On the other hand, Lord Penrhyn's action for libel against W. J. Parry, for saying that the conditions of work in his lordship's quarries were responsible for the high death rate among the workforce, met with success in the courts, although the moral victory in the country was perceived to lie with the defendant.[68]

Combinations of workmen began to be set up in Wales early in the nine-teenth century, and south Wales was to be the scene for important events in the development of the law relating to trade unions.[69] The *Taff Vale case* in 1900 saw the unions assert their right to strike without financial penalty, only for this to be questioned by the judiciary and the union left to face a bill for damages of £23,000.[70] Within a decade, however, the Trade Disputes Act had been passed to vindicate their position.[71] The South Wales Miners' Federation was instrumental in causing the government to retreat on the means test in 1935, the year before its leader James Griffiths entered Parliament. Strike action had been the context of the Tonypandy riots in 1910, and some lawyers, such as Judge Bryn Roberts, were infamous for decisions they pronounced against the miners in the courts.[72]

Welsh lawyers, however, were also prominent in campaigns for reforms in Wales and more generally. A career in the law remained a stepping stone to the world of politics, and the Liberal MPs of the later nineteenth century were often lawyers rather than landowners or gentry. The Tory and Whig grandees of an earlier generation were ousted by barristers such as Watkin Williams and Osborne Morgan. Barristers were numerous in the ranks of Welsh liberal-ism, including Ellis Griffith, David Brynmor Jones, Llewelyn Williams and Samuel Evans. The last-named rose to be both solicitor-general (1908–10) and President of the Probate, Divorce and Admiralty Division (1910–18), having been notable when a Glamorgan Member of Parliament for being the mouth-piece of the Welsh Nonconformists.[73] Thomas Artemus Jones, the plaintiff in the famous libel action of *Hulton* v *Jones*,[74] was a county court judge in north

Wales who was vociferous on the need for Welsh-speaking judges.[75] The number and influence of solicitors in Wales both increased; A. T. Davies for instance became the first secretary of the Welsh department of the Board of Education.[76]

With the disestablishment of the Church in Wales, the 'three wise men' who drafted a constitution for the new province were all eminent lawyers. John Sankey would rise through the judiciary to become lord chancellor in the first Labour government, having become a socialist as a result of chairing a review of miners' conditions of work. Lord Justice Bankes and Lord Atkin both made substantial contributions to the development of reasoned jurisprudence in the Court of Appeal, still within a generation of its creation. Atkin would go on to be a law lord and in that capacity would lay the foundations of the modern law of negligence in his speech in *Donoghue* v *Stevenson*,[77] one of the most famous decisions in the history of the common law. It did not pass notice that the decision in *Donoghue* v *Stevenson* was given by a majority of three-to-two, the two law lords who supported Lord Atkin both being Scottish, while the dissenting minority were both Englishmen. The law of England, it was said, had been laid down by two Scotsmen and a Welshman. Lord Atkin is also renowned for his dissenting speech in *Liversidge* v *Anderson*,[78] where he famously defended the liberty of the subject from unreasonable arrest even in time of war. He also clashed with the Welsh bishops in 1938 over the issue of the remarriage of divorcees in church.[79]

Other Welshmen who reached high judicial office in this period included Lord Morris of Borth-y-Gest and Lord Edmund Davies, both law lords of appeal, and Lord Elwyn-Jones who became lord chancellor after having served as attorney-general and after having been a prosecutor of the Nazi war criminals at the Nuremberg trials which followed the Second World War.[80] Both Sir John Morris and Lord Williams of Mostyn served as Labour attorney-generals, while Sir Arwyn Ungoed-Thomas, later a high court judge, and Sir Geoffrey Howe followed Sir Samuel Evans as solicitors-general.[81]

The foundation of the University of Wales meant that for the first time in the modern period legal education became available to aspiring lawyers within the country. The foundation of a Welsh law school at Aberystwyth was undertaken by T. A. Levi and the work brought to fruition under the aegis of Professor Llewelfryn Davies. In the last quarter of the twentieth century, university law schools were also established at Cardiff and Swansea, as well as at the Polytechnic of Wales, later the University of Glamorgan, at Pontypridd, while a law school for north Wales was to be established at Bangor early in the twenty-first century. As well as teaching for undergraduate law degrees, some also provide courses for subsequent professional qualification as a solicitor or barrister, so that it is now possible for every stage of legal education to be completed within Wales. Among the distinguished academic lawyers produced by Wales was Sir David Hughes-Parry, whose report on the Welsh language in the 1960s led to the passing of the Welsh Language Act 1967.[82]

Welshmen who were not lawyers have also been instrumental in promoting and shaping legal developments over the last two centuries. The Coal Mines Regulation Act 1887 had reduced the hours boys could work in the collieries, and in the following year William Abraham, the MP for the Rhondda, succeeding in getting the first Monday of every month declared a holiday for the miners, a rest day which became known as Mabon's day after the parliamentarian's bardic name. During the twentieth century, following David Lloyd George's people's budget in 1909, Aneurin Bevan was instrumental in securing the establishment of the National Health Service and James Griffiths the passing of the National Insurance Act 1946. During the 1960s, a wealth of social reforms passed into legislation while Roy Jenkins was Home Secretary, and Welsh MPs such as solicitor Leo Abse campaigned for reform on a variety of social issues.[83]

William Abraham was also famous for having dared to use the Welsh language in the House of Commons, where it is said his utterances were greeted with a laughter that swiftly turned to shame when he revealed that what had been mocked were the words of the Lord's Prayer.[84] During the nineteenth century, the state had begun to publish abstracts of certain items of legislation, such as the Mines Regulations Acts, the Factory and Workshop Acts, in order to make them more accessible to non-lawyers involved in those industries. The Home Office took the further step of having Welsh translations of these abstracts prepared and published for those who would find them more accessible in that tongue. Likewise, in the year of the Wills Act 1837, the General Register Office, together with other government departments, had some of its documents translated and made available in Welsh. The possibility was canvassed of statutes or epitomes of statutes being made available in Welsh, a suggestion which was resisted in some official quarters. Nevertheless, the Board of Agriculture commenced publication of Welsh versions of some of its pamphlets in 1893, and from 1907 began to issue the forms for its official June agricultural returns bilingually.[85]

The inferior status of the language in the eyes of government and of the courts was brought home by the circumstances of the Pen-y-berth trial in 1937. Perhaps because the aftermath of the case was feared to be having a detrimental effect upon the war effort in Wales, the Home Secretary, Herbert Morrison, had the Welsh Courts Act passed in 1942 making Welsh a valid language in all legal proceedings. After the war, the language issue remained dormant until the flooding of Cwm Tryweryn again raised the spectre of government indifference to the language amid clear signs in census returns of a gradual decline. Saunders Lewis, the celebrated veteran of the Pen-y-berth arson attack and a leading Welsh intellectual on the international stage, provoked the foundation of the Welsh Language Society, *Cymdeithas yr Iaith Cymraeg*, in 1962 with his lecture on the fate of the language, *Tynged yr Iaith*. The goal of the society was to obtain official status for Welsh and ensure its use by public bodies within Wales. The campaigns of direct action launched by *Cymdeithas* brought results. Sir Keith Joseph, as Minister for Welsh Affairs, set up a committee under Sir David Hughes-Parry, a professor of law in the University of London, to examine the status of the language in law and government. The Hughes-Parry Report recommended that the language should enjoy a special status in appointment to posts both in central and local government, with priority being given to appointing Welsh-speakers. These recommendations fell on deaf ears, but the Welsh Language Act 1967 which followed gave the language equal validity though not official status.[86]

The campaigns of direct action by *Cymdeithas* continued, although the movement suffered a split along lines very familiar in Welsh history. A splinter group, to be called *Adfer*, believed that efforts should be concentrated in maintaining Welsh language and culture in the heartlands of Wales, rather than trying to insist upon the introduction of Welsh in all areas of the country so as to make Wales a bilingual nation. The traditional tension between those seeking to preserve a separate identity and those seeking to carry that identity outwards into a wider world was once again manifested. *Adfer* was to campaign for statutory restrictions upon the purchase of houses in predominantly Welsh-speaking areas by monoglot English-speakers; *Cymdeithas* on the other hand sought provision for Welsh-language education in all parts of Wales so that Welsh parents everywhere could reclaim their linguistic heritage for their children. A Welsh Language Board was eventually established as an advisory body in 1988, but it was to graduate to become a statutory body in 1994 with powers to oversee the implementation of the Welsh Language Act 1993, a landmark enactment which had finally given the language equal status with English in public life within Wales.[87]

THE ROAD TO DEVOLUTION

Alongside the campaign for equality of status for the language, there had run a lengthy debate over the government of Wales and how Welsh interests were to be represented within the government of the United Kingdom.[88] Some issues had been devolved to Welsh bodies quite early in the twentieth century. Thus, the Welsh department of the Board of Education, albeit not a Welsh National Council, had been created in 1907. Welsh Insurance Commissioners, with very wide powers, had been established in 1912, and in 1919, by the Ministry of Health Act, the powers of the Commissioners were transferred to a new Welsh Board of Health, which commenced its work in 1921. The powers of this board were further enhanced in 1931 and 1940.[89] A Welsh department of the Ministry of Agriculture and Fisheries was also set up in 1919, but the separate arrangements existing with regard to the Ministry of Pensions were abolished at that time. Yet, despite some advances, there was no personage in government for Wales to correspond to the secretary of state for Scotland, an office revived in 1885 after having been abolished in 1746 following the 1745 rebellion. A Scottish Office was brought into being as a government department in 1934.[90]

These developments almost inevitably gave rise to questions about whether similar arrangements should be made for Wales. Questions were asked in the Commons in 1928 and 1930 about the possibility of Wales having a secretary of state, and a bill to provide for such an office was introduced to no avail in 1937.[91] The following year, the prime minister, Neville Chamberlain, refused to create such a role, giving as his reason that Wales lacked the separate legal system which made such an arrangement feasible for Scotland. This echoed the nineteenth-century argument as to why Wales could not be the subject of separate legislation. The same argument was advanced ten years later by Herbert Morrison when Clement Attlee turned down a similar request, Attlee adding that the creation of a separate Welsh Office would lead to an 'unnecessary duplication' of administration.[92]

Although Winston Churchill had also refused such requests when prime minister in 1943, when he returned to power in 1951, his government created a Ministry for Welsh Affairs, possibly in fulfilment of a suggestion by R. A. Butler while in opposition that the Conservatives would appoint an 'ambassador' for Wales. The incumbents from 1951–64 were a somewhat motley crew, beginning with the future lord chancellor, Sir David Maxwell-Fyfe (1951–4), followed by the rather more diplomatic if somewhat cynical appointment of Gwilym Lloyd George (1954–7), the son of the only Welsh prime minister. From 1957 to 1961, the post was held by Henry Brooke, and it was under his tenure that the inflammatory decision to drown Tryweryn was taken, which totally discredited him in Welsh eyes. His successor, Sir Keith Joseph (1961–4), instigated the Hughes-Parry Report which gave Welsh equal validity but not official status.[93]

In much the same manner as Attlee's refusal to create a Welsh Office may have led to the creation of the Ministry for Welsh Affairs by the incoming Conservative government, so Harold Macmillan's refusal to appoint a secretary of state for Wales in 1957 may have led to the creation of such a post becoming official Labour Party policy. On the election of a Labour government in 1964, Harold Wilson appointed the veteran campaigner for Wales, James Griffiths, to be the first secretary of state, and a Welsh Office was established with powers over housing, local government, road transport and local planning matters. To this remit would later be added in 1969 health and agriculture, with education being added later. In 1971, the Welsh Office moved its base to Cardiff, which had been granted city status in 1905 and had become the official capital of Wales in 1955.[94]

The creation of the Welsh Office in 1964 brought a measure of administrative devolution to Wales. However, the policies and the laws which the administration were to apply were still shaped at Westminster. The idea that legislative as well as administrative government might be exercised from within Wales had manifested itself during the nineteenth century, a time when national consciousness had been growing across Europe, leading to the unification of Germany and Italy, and the campaign for home rule in Ireland. Towards the end of the nineteenth century, a similar movement began to develop in Wales; *Cymru Fydd* attracted the support of eminent Welshmen, including the future prime minister David Lloyd George. He had used the spectre of self-government to coerce Lord Rosebery into proposing the first disestablishment bill in 1894.

The first legislative proposals for Welsh self-government came as part of a movement advocating devolution across the British empire. E. T. John, a retired iron manufacturer from Middlesbrough, who had returned to his native Wales and been elected to Parliament for Denbigh East in 1910, introduced a Welsh Home Rule Bill into the House of Commons in March 1914 along with Beriah Gwynfe Evans. The bill proposed a single chamber legislature of ninety members for Wales to govern the nation's domestic affairs. Its progress beyond the first reading however fell victim to the outbreak of the world war.[95]

As the war drew to a close, and the prospect of disestablishment drew near, E. T. John joined forces with the industrialist David Davies of Llandinam, to call a conference to discuss devolution in June 1918 at Llandrindod Wells. The event however attracted little interest or support. In the following year, on the other hand, a Speaker's conference on the government of Wales and Scotland discussed possible devolution of both legislative and administrative powers, but failed to agree on how a Welsh legislature should be composed and how it should be elected, although the Welsh Board of Health and the Welsh department of the Ministry of Agriculture and Fisheries were set up in its wake. Spurred on perhaps by these successes, the member for Wrexham, Sir Robert Thomas, introduced a Government of Wales Bill into the Commons on 28 April 1922, only to have it talked out at the first reading. The idea of devolution never quite disappeared from the Liberal agenda, finding support from Clement Davies and Lady Megan Lloyd George during the 1930s and 1940s.[96]

At the end of the Second World War, Wales was recognized as a distinct unit in planning for post-war reconstruction, and James Griffiths was once more in the vanguard of those calling for government recognition of Welsh identity, this time in the form of a Welsh Planning Authority. An advisory Council for Wales and Monmouthshire was set up in 1948, which remained in existence until 1966, when it was replaced by a Welsh Economic Council. The body, being only advisory, lacked power, and it is worth noting that similar bodies established in other European countries at this time, such as the Italian National Labour and Economic Council, while fundamentally advisory, were given powers to introduce legislative proposals on their own initiative.[97]

Liberal advocacy of devolution continued during the 1950s, when the Labour
MP, S. O. Davies, introduced a private member's bill promoting home rule in
1955, a year before Goronwy Roberts petitioned in the same vein with equal
lack of success.[98] By this time, some encouragement had been obtained from
the creation of the Ministry for Welsh Affairs with powers to coordinate the
making of policy for Wales across various government departments, including
agriculture, health, employment and transport.[99]

The creation of the Welsh Office with a secretary of state in 1964 gave a
further fillip to the devolutionists. Cledwyn Hughes, who succeeded James
Griffiths as secretary of state in 1966, pressed for the creation of a Welsh
regional council with legislative powers. By this time, the devolution of such
powers to regional bodies was becoming a Europe-wide phenomenon, as witnessed by the German *Länder* but also by the emergence of regional tiers of
government in France and Italy. On St David's Day 1967, Emlyn Hooson, QC
in the Commons and Lord Ogmore in the Lords both introduced a Government of Wales Bill. Disturbing by-election results for the Labour government
in Wales suggested the mood of the people was changing, and in 1969 a Royal
Commission on the Constitution was established, first under the chairmanship of Lord Crowther and, following his death, under Lord Kilbrandon.[100]

By the time the Kilbrandon Report was published in October 1973, a Conservative government was in power which had enlarged the powers of the
Welsh Office to include secondary, further and higher education in Wales, and
had also successfully negotiated British entry into the European Economic
Community, or Common Market. The latter step brought the United Kingdom
into closer contact with countries where devolution, legislative and administrative, was already taking place. The concept of subsidiarity, ensuring that
decisions were made at a level as close as possible to those affected by them,
was a driving principle of the new Europe into which the United Kingdom
now entered. Much that followed illustrated the manner in which Wales once
more began to accommodate itself to a changing legal and governmental
order of which it was a part.

The Kilbrandon Commission was divided in many ways in its findings. The
majority however came down in favour of an elected assembly for Wales, and
some – including both of the Welsh members on the Commission[101] – wanted
the assembly to have full legislative and tax-raising powers. In December
1976, a Labour government under James Callaghan, an MP for Cardiff, moved
a Devolution Bill to cover Wales and Scotland. With but a small majority in
the House of Commons which gradually disappeared altogether, the government found it necessary to promise referenda in the two countries in order to
get the proposals into law. In 1977, separate bills for Wales and Scotland were
introduced, with the proviso that a Yes vote of at least 40 per cent in the
referendum should be obtained for the scheme to proceed. The bill was
passed in 1978 and referenda held in Wales and Scotland on St David's Day

1979. All of the eight Welsh counties created by the local government reforms of 1974 voted against devolution.[102]

Later that year, a Conservative government was elected under Margaret Thatcher. Devolution vanished from the legislative agenda. However, in the absence of elected bodies to deal with the policy areas controlled in Wales by the secretary of state, unelected bodies representative of government rather than popular opinion, commonly called *Quangos*, were set up to advise and indeed sometimes decide upon policy. By the time that a Labour government was next elected in 1997, attitudes in Wales and Scotland to devolved government had changed. A referendum on devolution was held in Wales in September 1997 within months of Labour coming into office, which, by the narrowest of margins, accepted the principle of devolution. The Government of Wales Act was passed in 1998 and elections to the Welsh Assembly, *Cynulliad Cenedlaethol Cymru*, were held in May 1999. By the end of that month, Wales had for the first time ever a democratically elected government of its own.

By the end of the twentieth century, therefore, Wales had achieved a degree of devolved legislative, executive and administrative government. Changes had also taken place with regard to the administration of justice, albeit the legal system remained that of England and Wales. The structures established by the Judicature Acts 1873–5 had not remained unaltered, and the highly centralized courts system which emerged from the nineteenth-century legislation had yielded in part to the decentralist tendencies of post-war Europe.

The main changes were wrought by the Administration of Justice Act 1970 and the Courts Act 1971. The former converted the Probate, Divorce and Admiralty Division of the High Court into a new Family Division, with jurisdiction over matrimonial causes and uncontested probate matters. Contested probate matters passed to the Chancery Division and the Admiralty jurisdiction went to a special Admiralty court which, like the specialist commercial court, forms part of the Queen's Bench Division. The great change, however, was that the High Court could now sit outside of London, and does now so sit permanently in many centres including Cardiff. This meant that civil cases no longer had to be commenced in London, heard at *nisi prius* in the county and then passed back to London for judgement; the whole action was now triable locally, in the same manner as first instance tribunals sit in every major town in countries such as France, Germany and Italy. The 1971 Act abolished the assizes, with their criminal jurisdiction reaching back to the twelfth century. In their place was established a new Crown Court to deal with serious criminal cases, in which the most serious crimes would still be taken by a High Court judge with a jury, but in which other less serious offences would be tried by judges of the same status as county court judges, called circuit judges. These would also sit with a jury. The Quarter Sessions were also abolished, their competence in effect passing to the circuit judges in the Crown Court. At London, the Court of Criminal Appeal established in 1907 was replaced in

1966 by a new division of the Court of Appeal, that court now having two divisions, the Civil and the Criminal. Final appeal to the House of Lords remained, although it was now to be possible in cases where the Court of Appeal was bound by a decision of the House of Lords or by one of its own previous decisions to appeal directly from a judgement at first instance on a point of law to the Lords, 'leapfrogging' the Court of Appeal.[103]

Much of the administrative work of the Quarter Sessions had already passed to local authorities created by legislation at the end of the nineteenth century. The same was true of the non-judicial functions of the petty sessions. Lay justices in the magistrates courts continue to dispose of minor criminal charges and to deal with matrimonial causes and licensing matters, but specialist tribunals now deal with litigation arising from the increased administrative activities of government. Thus, tribunals with appeals tribunals deal with matters such as employment, social security, immigration and a range of other matters. The work of these bodies is reviewable for error of law by the Divisional Court of the Queen's Bench Division, since 2000 known as the Administrative Court when dealing with such matters, but making continued use of what are now, since 1938, the prerogative orders of *certiorari*, prohibition and *mandamus*, or more properly since 2000 quashing orders, prohibiting orders and mandating orders respectively.[104] Already in the nineteenth century, professional justices had been appointed to sit alone at the petty sessions in some areas of large population created by the industrial revolution. Wales had its share of these stipendiary magistrates, many of whom made wise and substantial contri-butions to the maintenance of order, for instance D. L. Thomas in the Rhondda at the time of the Tonypandy riots in 1910. These local professional judges have now been replaced by district judges.

Finally, the Court of Appeal could also now sit outside of London. Although such sittings remained an exception, the Criminal Division chaired by the Lord Chief Justice soon sat at Cardiff, and the Lord Bingham of Cornhill, on his appointment as Lord Chief Justice, declared that in future the office should be designated Lord Chief Justice of England and Wales.[105] Wales had therefore recovered a fair measure of legal identity by the close of the second Christian millennium.

10

Devolution and Legal Identity

The defeat of the Callaghan government's devolution proposals in 1979 brought the campaign for some measure of self-government for Wales to an abrupt end. The Conservative government which came to power in 1979 under Margaret Thatcher, and which was to remain in office until 1997 held no brief for devolution, but greatly expanded the number of functions performed in Wales by non-elected bodies, the so-called quasi-autonomous national government organizations or *Quangos*. Widespread disaffection with the consequences of government policies upon Wales during these years led to the Conservative Party losing all of its seats in Wales at the 1997 general election which brought the Labour Party back to power.

The Blair government which was elected in May 1997 was committed to devolution for Wales and Scotland, and referenda were held in both countries within months of Labour coming to power. By the narrowest of margins, devolution was approved by the Welsh electorate.[1] The reversal of the people's rejection of devolution in 1979 led to the passing of the Government of Wales Act 1998 and the inauguration of the National Assembly for Wales in 1999. Wales entered the third Christian millennium with a measure of self-government of a kind which the country had not known for centuries, and arguably of a kind which it had never previously experienced. Remarkably, within virtually the first decade of that millennium, Wales was to progress through three distinct phases of devolution.[2]

Under the 1998 Act, the Assembly received powers to legislate on matters which had previously been within the competence of government ministers, primarily the Secretary of State for Wales. Powers were given it to deal with a list of issues set out in a schedule to the Act, namely agriculture, forestry, fisheries and food; ancient monuments and historic buildings; culture (including museums, galleries and libraries); economic development; education and training; the environment; health and health services; highways; housing; industry; local government; social services; sport and recreation; tourism; town and country planning; transport; water and flood defence; and the Welsh language.[3] The Assembly's powers with regard to these areas replaced the previously existing powers of United Kingdom ministers to issue subordinate rather than primary legislation, in effect dealing with how the policies of the Westminster government were to be carried into effect within Wales, but without the power to initiate major policy changes by enacting primary legislation in the form of statutes. Likewise, the Assembly was not given powers to raise revenue by taxation, only the power to determine how revenue received from London was to be spent. From the outset, the Assembly for Wales appeared to many to be the poor relation of the Scottish Parliament which had powers to enact primary legislation and to impose taxation, albeit subject to limitations imposed by Westminster. The Scottish devolution settlement also created in Scotland a legislature, the Scottish Parliament, which was separate from the executive arm of government. The National Assembly for Wales on the other hand was created as a body corporate, embracing both the legislative and executive functions of government, with consequences for both the structure and regulation of its governance.

The Assembly was to consist of sixty Assembly Members – AMs – 40 of whom elected according to the first-past-the-post simple majority system of election employed for electing members to the House of Commons, and elected to sit as AMs for 40 constituencies which were originally the same as those for representation at Westminster.[4] However, in addition, there were to be a further 20 members elected to represent five electoral regions, each of which was originally coterminous with the constituencies for elections to the European Parliament prior to 1999. Four members are elected for each of these 5 regions, and they are elected not by simple majority but by the additional member system of proportional representation. At elections, each elector has two votes, one for the local constituency member and one for a party or for an independent candidate on the regional list. When the results of the constituency elections within the region are known, it is then possible to allocate the regional votes so as to elect the additional members. This is done by dividing the votes for each party by the number of constituency seats it has won in that region plus one, and allocating the first regional seat to the party with the highest quotient, called the electoral region figure. The number of seats for that party is then increased by one, a fresh division of its votes made, and the second seat allocated to the party which then has the highest electoral region figure. This process is repeated until all four seats have been allocated.[5]

The purpose of the additional member system is to ensure that parties with substantial support in the constituencies, but which win few seats by the simple majority system, are not entirely without representation, or perhaps more accurately to ensure that the opinions of those electors who voted for those parties are not left unrepresented, in the manner for instance that Welsh Conservative voters for the Westminster parliament found themselves totally unrepresented in the wake of the 1997 general election. The system also militates against one party completely dominating the Assembly in the manner that Labour had once dominated local government bodies in many parts of Wales in the middle years of the twentieth century. The new system certainly delivered the required adjustment at the polls in the first ordinary election for the Assembly in 1999. No party managed to achieve an overall majority of seats, and Labour had to form a minority government, later entering into a coalition with the Liberal Democrats. It is fair to say that such a result could scarcely have been dreamt of twenty or thirty years earlier and was quite a shock even at the end of the century. Ordinary elections, called ordinary general elections from 2007, are held at four-yearly intervals, normally on the first Thursday in May. The second, third and fourth such elections, held in 2003, 2007 and 2011 respectively, all equally failed to provide any party with an overall majority of seats within the Assembly.[6]

After an election, the Assembly Members must elect from among their number a Presiding Officer and a Deputy Presiding Officer to chair Assembly sessions.[7] Under the 1998 Act, the members were also to elect a First Secretary to head the Assembly executive, who then went on to appoint the other members of the executive, each with responsibility for a particular remit, such as health, education or the economy.[8] These were, in effect, the executive or cabinet, but the corporate nature of the Assembly meant that they acted for the Assembly more in the fashion of a local government executive rather than that of a national government. The fact that the executive and legislative arms of government were not separate under the 1998 Act also meant that the manner in which the Assembly was to control its executive had also to be imposed from outside by statute, with the 1998 Act providing that a plethora of Assembly subject committees had to be created, one committee corresponding to each of the appointments made by the First Secretary to the executive and overseeing the work of that executive member. This was in addition to the Audit Committee and Subordinate Legislation Committee that the Act required to be established and the regional committees for north Wales and the other parts of the nation established to safeguard local interests.[9]

From the outset, there was considerable dissatisfaction with the corporate nature of the Assembly created by the 1998 Act and the consequences it entailed, leading to the executive formally, if unofficially, referring to itself as the Assembly Government, the First Secretary as the First Minister, and the rest of the executive as ministers. Indeed, the initial dissatisfaction was such that, in July 2002, before even the Assembly's first 4-year term had expired, a Commission on the Powers and Electoral Arrangements of the National Assembly for Wales was established, under the chairmanship of Lord Richard of Ammanford QC. The Richard Commission reported on 31 March 2004, 84 years to the day that the Church in Wales had been disestablished. The Richard Report recommended that the Assembly should be given powers to enact primary legislation in those areas for which it was responsible, that its membership should be increased to allow for the increased workload, and that the method of election should be changed to the single transferable vote system of proportional representation. On tax-varying powers, it limited its recommendation to saying that while these would be desirable, they were not essential to the Assembly's proposed work. It also called for a reconstitution of the Assembly with a separate legislature and executive.[10]

The Secretary of State for Wales responded by publishing a white paper, *Better Governance for Wales*,[11] which put forward an alternative approach. The white paper proposed to institutionalize the division which had already developed in practice between the Assembly as a legislative body and the Assembly Government as an executive body, and to end the somewhat elaborate statutory requirements that the Assembly must have certain committees, allowing the Assembly instead to decide in its standing orders what committees it should have. It proposed that in future the Welsh First Minister and executive should be appointed by the Crown and that subordinate legislation should be made by those ministers and not by the Assembly, in the same manner as by United Kingdom and Scottish ministers. The role of the Assembly would then be to scrutinize the subordinate legislation so made rather than make it itself as under the 1998 Act. However, the white paper did not envisage the Assembly achieving substantial primary legislative powers in the foreseeable future; instead, it proposed that the Secretary of State for Wales should be enabled to obtain by Order in Council, from time to time, powers for the Assembly to make primary legislation relating to Wales on matters currently within the Assembly's limited competence. If and when, eventually, greater primary legislative powers were to be contemplated, the white paper envisaged the need for a further referendum, and only foresaw such powers being given on matters currently devolved to the Assembly. Thus, no increase in the membership nor change to the method of election was proposed, other than preventing candidates from standing in a local constituency *and* on a regional party list, a highly controversial proposal which almost caused the entire package to fail. The white paper wished to allow plenary elections to be held between ordinary elections, but these would not replace the next ordinary election unless held within 6 months of the expected ordinary election date. A two-thirds majority of members would have to agree to such an early election, and also any request for a referendum on primary legislative powers. The latter request would also have to be agreed by the Secretary of State who would, if agreeable, put the matter before the Westminster parliament for its approval before a referendum was held. It is interesting to note that in other European countries, such as Italy, a two-thirds majority in the legislature when a constitutional change is proposed obviates the need for a referendum.

The recommendations of the white paper formed the basis of the Government of Wales Act 2006, the provisions of which came into force and effect following the ordinary general election in May 2007. That election saw Labour emerge as the largest party within the Assembly, but again without sufficient seats to form a majority government. After a month in power as a minority government, the Labour Party formed a coalition government with Plaid

Cymru under the title of the One Wales Coalition. The coalition survived until the May 2011 ordinary general election, with important consequences for the future legal development of Wales.

The Welsh government formed in May 2007 was now formally separate as an executive from the National Assembly, the legislature. The Assembly no longer elected its First Secretary, but instead nominated a member to the Queen for appointment as First Minister. The First Minister then nominated the other members of the executive to the Queen for formal appointment as Welsh Ministers. The First Minister may also appoint Deputy Ministers, but the total number of Welsh Ministers and Deputy Ministers must not exceed twelve. The First Minister also nominates to the Queen a legally-qualified person, who may or may not be an Assembly Member, for appointment as Counsel General, the Welsh Government's principal legal adviser.[12] Although not one of the Welsh Ministers, the Counsel General enjoys greater security of tenure than the Welsh Ministers as he may not be removed from office by the First Minister without the agreement of the Assembly. Even if not an AM, the Counsel General may participate and speak in Assembly meetings, and may even introduce legislative proposals, but may not vote unless an AM. The Counsel General under the 2006 Act is a political appointee, whereas under the 1998 settlement, the post was that of an Assembly official within the Senior Civil Service.

Many of the powers and duties placed upon the Assembly as a body corporate by the 1998 Act, but which would of course have been carried out by its executive, were formally transferred to the Welsh Ministers under the 2006 Act. The Assembly for instance had been charged with ensuring as far as was appropriate that obligations under European Community legislation relating to Wales were met.[13] The 1998 Act specifically provided that the Assembly had to conform to the requirements of Community law in framing its subordinate legislation,[14] and that it could be designated and thereby empowered as the appropriate authority to make regulations under section 2(2) of the European Communities Act 1972.[15] The 2006 Act places the duty of ensuring that Community obligations are met upon the Welsh Ministers and provides that their powers are limited by European law.[16] The same is true with regard to the United Kingdom's obligations under the European Convention on Human Rights, obligations which have become part of domestic law by statute.[17] Westminster government ministers are empowered to intervene to prevent any breaches of the United Kingdom's international obligations by the Welsh Ministers and to ensure their compliance with such obligations.[18]

The Welsh Ministers have also inherited the duty to make appropriate arrangements to achieve equality of opportunity,[19] and schemes with regard to sustainable development.[20] They are required to sustain and promote local government in Wales by setting out how they propose to do this in a local government scheme and by setting up a Partnership Council to assist them in so doing.[21] They must also provide a scheme relating how they intend to promote the work of voluntary organizations,[22] and one setting out how they intend to take business interests into account.[23] The 2006 Act further requires the Welsh Ministers to adopt a Welsh language strategy and a Welsh language scheme.[24]

The formal separation of the Assembly as a legislature from the Welsh Assembly Government brought to an end its existence as a body corporate. It was accordingly necessary for some other body with legal personality to be created to own property, enter into contracts, employ and pay officials and when necessary undertake litigation on behalf of the Assembly. For such purposes, the 2006 Act created a body called the Assembly Commission with powers to carry out these functions. Assembly officials, working for the Assembly Commission, now form a corps of public servants in Wales akin to the parliamentary service at Westminster and distinct as a body from the officials of the government who remain within the employ of the Home Civil Service. Wales was acquiring the apparatus of a functioning parliamentary democracy.[25]

One major change which flowed from the separation of the legislative and executive arms of government in Wales was that the powers to make subordinate legislation which the Assembly had inherited from the Secretary of State in 1999 and exercised on its own account during the first two assemblies from 1999 until 2007 now passed on once more into the hands of the Welsh Ministers.[26] Whereas for the previous eight years, such subordinate legislation, made in the main by statutory instrument, had been debated in and made by the Assembly itself, henceforth the greater part of such subordinate legislation would be made by the Welsh Ministers. For the Assembly, this meant a major change of focus and practice. As at Westminster and Holyrood, only occasionally would subordinate legislation now require the approval of the Assembly to be made. The more usual practice would be for the Welsh Ministers to make such subordinate legislation which would become law at once, the Assembly only having an opportunity to annul the legislation according to what is termed the negative procedure. Only when the so-called affirmative procedure was prescribed would the formal approval of the Assembly be needed for the law to be made. Not surprisingly, given that the Assembly had been used to debating and approving every such piece of legislation during the previous 8 years of its existence, the change was met with some suspicion and resentment.

The Assembly however had its compensations for, as proposed by the Westminster government in its white paper, the Government of Wales Act 2006 provided the Assembly with the possibility of enacting primary legislation. The Act indeed set out two models by which primary law-making powers could be devolved to Wales, one a gradual process which the Act itself inaugurated without requiring a referendum, and the other a more comprehensive devolution of primary law-making powers in the devolved areas, but which would require the approval of the Welsh electorate in a referendum for its implementation.[27] Many thought – opponents of devolution in particular – that the significant step of conferring primary as opposed to secondary law-making powers upon the Assembly was being taken without consulting the people of Wales, while continuing to insist that they should be consulted at a later date regarding the extent of such power.

Both of the models for devolving primary law-making powers were constructed on the basis of the subordinate law-making powers which had already been devolved from the Secretary of State to the Assembly and thence to the Welsh Ministers. Where the 1998 Act had identified eighteen areas in which specific functions had been devolved, the 2006 Act grouped them into twenty fields or headings; namely agriculture, fisheries, forestry, and rural development; ancient monuments and historic buildings; culture; economic development; education and training; environment; fire and rescue services and promotion of fire safety; food; health and health services; highways and transport; housing; local government; the National Assembly for Wales; public administration; social welfare; sport and recreation; tourism; town and country planning; water and flood defence; and the Welsh language. In Schedule 7 to the Act, there were listed under these twenty headings the one hundred or so subjects over which the Assembly could achieve the competence to legislate, each subject corresponding to executive functions which had since 1964 been devolved from Whitehall to Wales. The Assembly would acquire competence to legislate in relation to all of these, subject to certain exceptions and general restrictions which were also listed in the Schedule,[28] following a positive result on the question of whether this model of legislative devolution should be introduced. Were a referendum to produce a positive response, the Assembly would be able to pass Acts making law for Wales in relation to the devolved subjects, which Acts could alter or even repeal statutory provisions made for Wales in Acts of the Westminster parliament.[29] They would not require ratification, neither by the United Kingdom government nor by Parliament, but would become law following the formality of royal assent.

That model of devolution, contained in Part 4 and Schedule 7 to the 2006 Act, required a referendum of the electorate in Wales to take effect. The other model however came into force automatically following the holding of the 2007 ordinary general election. It too was based on the executive functions which had been devolved piecemeal since 1964 and in effect continued that approach by providing a mechanism by which the competence to make primary legislation would be conferred piece by piece upon the Assembly by Parliament. The same twenty headings to be found in Part 1 of Schedule 7 were listed as fields in Part 1 of Schedule 5 to the 2006 Act, but unlike the corresponding headings in Schedule 7, these fields – with the exception of Field 13 relating to the National Assembly itself – were barren, no legislative competence having been granted to the Assembly under them by the 2006 Act itself.

Instead, it was intended that the competence of the Assembly should accrue gradually by the insertion of matters into these fields, matters in relation to which the Assembly would be empowered to legislate for Wales by means of Measures, subject once more to certain general restrictions set out in the Schedule.[30] Matters could be placed into the fields in one of two ways: either Parliament could place matters there in an enactment, or the Assembly could apply to Parliament for a matter or matters to be inserted by means of an Order in Council, orders which became known as legislative competence orders or LCOs.

The parliamentary route had the advantage that, provided the Westminster government had a parliamentary majority, the success of an application for powers was assured once the UK government was persuaded to support it. The disadvantage was that, for the route to be used, there would have to be a bill within the UK government's legislative programme suitable to act as a vehicle for delivery of the matters. The route was also open to criticism in that the insertion of a matter by a UK Act would be the result of an agreement between the governments in Wales and Westminster. The National Assembly did not need to be consulted regarding, let alone have an opportunity to approve, such an accretion to its powers.

The LCO route, on the other hand, was much more respectful of the Assembly's interest. Such orders could be promoted not only by the Welsh government but also by individual Assembly Members, Assembly committees or the Assembly Commission. The Assembly was required to approve the draft order, before it was forwarded to the Secretary of State, who had either, within 60 days, to lay it before the two Houses of Parliament for approval or else give reasons for refusing to do so. The Lords and Commons, like the Assembly, could debate the draft order but not amend it, and, if approved, the order would then be presented to the Queen in Council for final approval. On being made by the Queen in Council, the matters contained in the order would be inserted into Schedule 5 and the Assembly would be competent thereafter to legislate as often as it wished in relation to the matter, for the competence granted – whether by Act of Parliament or by Order in Council – was enduring.[31]

To be certain of success along the LCO route, however, required assurance that the majority, if any, commanded by the UK government in Parliament would be deployed to approve the draft order when presented, and also of course assurance that the Secretary of State would be agreeable to laying the draft order for approval. To avoid the costly disaster of an LCO failing after Assembly approval, it was necessary therefore for the Welsh government to have reached an understanding with the UK government regarding the matter's content. It soon became apparent as applications for competence were commenced that this was not necessarily going to be an easy or straight-forward process. Several such applications took years to progress, and even relatively simple non-controversial applications were not dealt with swiftly.[32] In addition, every proposed LCO was subjected to scrutiny by committees of both the Assembly and Parliament before even being introduced in draft to either body for approval. The upshot was that delays in obtaining legislative competence threatened to undermine the ability of the Welsh government to deliver on some of its manifesto commitments, because the time available to introduce, progress and pass Assembly Measures based on the competence sought was seriously eroded as a consequence of delays over which the Welsh government had no control. There were inevitably fears that if such delays were occurring when the political party in power at Westminster was also the senior partner in the coalition government in Wales, what would occur if after the 2010 parliamentary election, a party of a different political complexion came to power at Westminster, or if, as seemed possible and did in fact occur, no party had an overall majority in the House of Commons, so that a government majority for insertion of a matter by enactment or for approval of a draft order could no longer be guaranteed. Given the need for Parliament to be in session to approve draft orders, pass bills and to scrutinize proposed orders in committee, the spectre of a hung parliament requiring a second general election within a calendar year also brought home the danger that events at Westminster could undermine delivery of legislation in Cardiff Bay.

One of the commitments made in the Welsh coalition government's One Wales Agreement was to hold a referendum on moving to the more comprehensive model of devolution provided by Part 4 of the 2006 Act within the lifetime of the Third Assembly. The catastrophic defeat suffered by the devolutionists in the 1979 referendum and the hair's breadth victory enjoyed by them in 1998 raised concerns as to whether such a referendum on greater legislative powers was winnable. Moreover, there was widespread concern regarding the extent to which all but a few people closely involved in the government of Wales understood the complexities of the choice that would be on offer. Partly to raise awareness of the nature of the choice and partly to discover whether a referendum was winnable, the Welsh government established an All Wales Convention under the chairmanship of the former United Kingdom Ambassador to the United Nations, Sir Emyr Jones-Parry, to take evidence on the working of the settlement and the appetite for moving on. While raising concerns about the level of understanding and even the interest of the general population in the question, the Convention duly reported that it was possible for an affirmative result to be achieved.[33] Winning the referendum had however become for many proponents of devolution no longer simply an ambition to achieve greater legislative power for the Assembly and autonomy for the nation, but an absolute imperative to get Wales out of the mire into which the existing settlement had plunged the legislative process.

The referendum on moving to the more comprehensive model of primary law-making powers for the Assembly was held on 3 March 2011, just two months before the end of the Third Assembly's term. The vote in favour was convincing. With 35·6% of the electorate voting, 63·5% voted in favour of enhanced powers with 36·5% voting against, a resounding majority for those in favour. Monmouthshire alone of the 22 Welsh local authority areas returned a negative result and that by the narrowest of margins.[34] A great deal had clearly changed since 1979.

The AMs who were elected therefore in the ordinary general election of May 2011 returned to a legislative body with vastly increased legislative powers. The Assembly was now free to legislate in relation to any of the subjects listed under the twenty headings in the 2006 Act and the regular difficulties of obtaining competence to do so were a thing of the past. Within the space of twelve years, the Assembly had moved from being the inheritor of the Secretary of State's powers to make subordinate legislation to being a legislature with primary law-making powers on a host of subjects important to the nation.

The office of Secretary of State for Wales continues in existence, although the necessity for its continuance has not escaped question. He or she continues to be required to consult with the Assembly concerning the Westminster govern-ment's legislative programme where appropriate, that is in so far as it affects Wales,[35] and is also entitled by statute to attend and participate in Assembly sessions, but not to vote therein.[36] While it is a common feature of the work of legislative bodies on mainland Europe that some office-holders who are not members of the legislature can take part in debates in the chambers but not vote, this is something of a novel departure in the United Kingdom, as is the right of the Assembly and, from 2007, the Welsh Ministers to exercise a limited legislative initiative within the Westminster parliament.[37] This again mirrors the rights of regional parliaments in many European countries to exercise the legislative initiative.[38]

The Government of Wales Acts are laws which have been enacted specific-ally for Wales and which enable the country to frame specific laws for its own governance. They are the most important statutory enactments relating to Wales since the sixteenth-century Acts of Union, which interestingly were also two statutes passed within a decade of each other. It is sometimes suggested that the Government of Wales Acts amount to a constitution for Wales, and they undoubtedly define in part the nation's constitutional position within the UK.

The legislatures and executives of countries with written constitutions frequently allow for challenges to both primary and secondary legislation on the grounds that such legislation has transgressed the constitution. In the same manner both the 1998 and 2006 Acts make provision for challenges to Assembly legislation and that of the Welsh Ministers on the grounds that the terms of the devolution settlement have been breached, by for example trespassing upon the areas encompassed by the exceptions or general restrictions contained in the statute or by being incompatible with either European Union law or the UK's obligations under the European Convention on Human Rights.

Schedule 9 to the Government of Wales Act 2006, which replaced Schedule 8 to the 1998 Act, provides what is to happen if the Assembly is believed to have abused or exceeded its powers. It is open for any person to raise such a devolution issue before the courts, or for the Attorney-General or the Counsel General to do so. A court may dismiss such an issue as frivolous or vexatious, but if it is not held to be so, then such an issue raised in a Magistrates Court can be referred to the High Court, and such an issue raised in any other court can be passed for determination to the Court of Appeal. If a devolution issue is first raised in the Court of Appeal, under the 1998 Act it could be passed for determination to the Judicial Committee of the Privy Council. If a devolution issue was first raised before the House of Lords sitting as the supreme appellate tribunal, the Lords were either to dispose of it themselves or refer it to the Judicial Committee.

The Attorney-General, the Counsel General or the Assembly could refer any devolution issue to the Judicial Committee for determination, and it was the Judicial Committee also which had appellate jurisdiction over devolution issues which had been determined in either the High Court, on the reference of a Magistrates Court, or by the Court of Appeal.

However, during the years in which Wales' devolution settlement was developing, the Constitutional Reform Act 2005 replaced the appellate jurisdiction of the House of Lords and of the Judicial Committee of the Privy Council with a new final instance tribunal for the whole of the United Kingdom, which also took over the responsibilities of the Judicial Committee with regard to devolution issues. The new final appellate court, called the Supreme Court of the United Kingdom,[39] sits in London. Once again, the reform brings the legal systems of the United Kingdom into closer conformity with those of its partners in the European Union. The new Supreme Court will continue to combine the functions discharged in most continental countries by the Supreme Court of Cassation and the Constitutional Court, but the new court does not have powers to question the validity of primary legislation passed by the United Kingdom parliament, although it will continue to be able to declare such legislation to be contrary to the European Convention on Human Rights under the Human Rights Act 1998. It does however have power to review the validity of primary legislation passed by the devolved legislatures.

The reform raises afresh questions such as whether the Court of Appeal should sit permanently in more than one location, as do appeal courts on mainland Europe. Given that Wales will now have an increasing number of laws which are peculiarly its own, and that the number of such laws is destined to increase, it would seem sensible that appeals relating to such laws should be heard within Wales rather than in London. The question has also been canvassed as to whether the new final instance court need always sit in London, or whether it might not be preferable for it to perambulate occasionally to at least Belfast, Edinburgh and Cardiff to deal with devolution issues, an arrangement which parties and their lawyers are likely to find more convenient. For the present, that suggestion appears to have been met with a negative response. However, there is growing support for the concept of Wales once again having its own distinct judicial organization, as it did under the Great Sessions, subject to final appeal or to review by the United Kingdom Supreme Court.[40]

Several factors combine to fuel the debate as to the exact legal status of Wales as a law district or jurisdiction. Wales now has its own legislature and its own government, albeit that the competence of both is limited and subject to the overriding sovereignty of the United Kingdom parliament and government. The laws made by the National Assembly extend to England and Wales, even though they can apply only in relation to Wales. This technical distinction between extent and applicability reinforces the jurisdictional integrity of the two nations, although the reality is that there are now some laws of England and Wales that only apply in England and some that only apply in Wales, although some – the majority – continue to apply in both countries.[41] What the common extent of the three kinds entails is that they can all be enforced and interpreted by courts in either country. To that extent, it is denied that Wales is a separate jurisdiction.

There are however some tribunals which exist solely to administer justice with regard to laws which apply in Wales. The jurisdiction of such tribunals is therefore undeniably Welsh. Wales also has its own dedicated courts, albeit embraced within the one jurisdiction of England and Wales, to deal with Administrative, Chancery, Commercial, and Technology and Construction matters respectively.[42] It has its own branch of the Courts' Service, and the former Wales and Chester circuit has shed its connection with Cheshire to become the Wales region. Many therefore see it as anomalous that laws made in Wales by a Welsh legislature and which apply solely in relation to Wales can be adjudicated upon and interpreted throughout the length and breadth of England. There is certainly a case to answer to the effect that the first-instance adjudication of laws in the devolved areas and second-instance appeals concerning them should be heard only by courts sitting in Wales, notwithstanding that a final review at third instance might still lie on points of law to the Supreme Court of the United Kingdom. There are good reasons also, as will be seen, why even in non-devolved areas a distinct court structure should exist in Wales to deal with litigation at least at first and second instance.

The sixteenth-century Acts of Union required that English be the official language of the annexed territories, whereas the Government of Wales Acts provide that the Assembly must treat Welsh and English on equal terms,[43] and that legislation produced by the Assembly and by the Welsh Ministers must ordinarily be in both languages.[44] The combined effect of these enactments is to apply to the Assembly and the Welsh Government the principle of language equality enshrined in the Welsh Language Act 1993, section 3(2)(b) of which requires such equality in the conduct of public business and in the administration of justice in Wales. Section 22 of that Act provides that Welsh may be spoken in any legal proceedings in Wales.

The primary and secondary legislation made for Wales by its distinct legislature and executive are therefore distinct in that they form of corpus of law unique within the United Kingdom in that they are made bilingually. It is important to stress that these laws are made in the two languages, not made in one and then translated into the other. Assembly bills, for instance, are drafted in both languages prior to introduction, introduced in both languages, scrutinized and debated upon in both committee and plenary sessions in both languages and passed into law in both languages. The laws made by the Assembly and the Welsh Ministers are not made in English, nor in Welsh, but in both languages. With Parliament having decreed that the two language versions are to be treated as of equal validity for all purposes,[45] it cannot therefore be safe to interpret the meaning of one text without having due regard to the meaning of the other. This has far-reaching implications for the education, qualifications and composition of the legal professions, affecting practitioners, as they expound the law to their clients, and the judiciary, who will be called upon to adjudicate upon and interpret these laws in court. The consequences of this development must either apply to lawyers throughout England and Wales, or else a distinguishing feature of the context within which justice is now administered in Wales must be recognized, for it must also be remembered that the right to use the Welsh language in legal proceedings and for legal purposes within Wales is not confined to the law relating to devolved subjects. Questions have therefore been asked regarding the desirability of empanelling bilingual juries for trials in which both languages are to be employed.[46] At the end of the day, it must not be forgotten that it is a statute of the UK parliament, the Welsh Language Act 1993, which demands that the two languages be treated equally in the administration of justice.[47]

The 1993 Act made the Welsh Language Board, consisting of fifteen members, the guardian of this principle of equality in Welsh public life, requiring it to promote and facilitate the use of Welsh.[48] This was to be achieved by the Board giving notice to public bodies within Wales, and those outside of Wales which exercise their powers within Wales, to prepare Welsh language schemes.[49] Failure to provide such a scheme or to implement one which the Board had approved could be investigated by the Board, which could recommend to the Secretary of State, if its report were not heeded, that he should give directions to the delinquent body with regard to implementing its policy. The Secretary of State was able to enforce such directions if necessary by a prerogative order of *mandamus*.[50] The granting of such an order would be a matter for the Administrative Court, formerly the Divisional Court of the Queen's Bench Division of the High Court.

Although the work of the Board in promoting the use of Welsh won great praise, there was dissatisfaction with its lack of power when it came to the compliance of public bodies. The One Wales Coalition therefore obtained competence for the Assembly to legislate in relation to the Welsh language,[51] and, although the competence granted was severely restrictive, the Welsh Language Measure 2011 was enacted confirming the official status of the Welsh language within Wales, creating a new post of Welsh Language Commissioner to take over elements of the work of the Board, and to provide for a more effective regime of enforcement with regard to standards of bilingualism which public bodies were expected to achieve. In addition, as a consequence of the limitations placed upon the competence granted, the Measure established a tribunal to deal with appeals from determinations made by the Commissioner. The Commissioner was also given powers to investigate alleged interferences with the freedom of people to use the Welsh language with one another.

The Welsh Language Measure was one of 22 measures passed by the Assembly during its third term.[52] In addition, the Assembly, between 1999 and 2007, and the Welsh Ministers thereafter have made between them well over two thousand statutory instruments of general application. These, together with the small number of statutes applicable to Wales only passed by the UK parliament at the request of the Assembly, have served to bring into existence a substantial body of law applicable only to Wales, and some of those developments have been very significant. Wales, for instance, established the UK's first Children's Commissioner and followed this with a similar post with regard to the interests of older persons.[53] Both the education system and the health service in Wales have developed a distinct ethos from those in existence in its eastern neighbour. Differences of policy, and not just regarding the implementation of policy, have clearly emerged. Wales has developed and is developing a distinct legal identity, in much the same way as across Europe, smaller nations have either emerged from larger state entities or achieved their own legal identity within those larger state structures.

At several points in this discussion, it has been noted how developments during the last half-century appear to be moving the legal arrangements of England and Wales towards some degree of convergence with those of the other member states of the European Union. The European dimension to the current law of Wales is another chapter which has opened relatively recently. Upon the United Kingdom's accession to the European Community in 1972, the law of the European Community became binding upon the United Kingdom and its citizens. The courts of England and Wales, like those of Scotland and Northern Ireland, became responsible for ensuring that domestic law and practice was not at variance with European Community law. If it were, then the courts would so declare, but leave it to Parliament to remedy the situation if a change in enacted law were needed. In addition, it was open to any subject to appeal a decision of the domestic courts regarding Community law to the European Court of Justice which sits in Luxembourg. On issues of Community law, the European Court of Justice is the court of final instance. Wales is therefore locked into several legal systems at the present time. It has some laws which are peculiarly its own, made for it by the Assembly under its current limited powers; it remains part of the law district which is England and Wales for most legal purposes, but it is also part of the law district which is the European Union for a very large number of important areas, from commerce to the environment, the number of which is increasing as indeed the Union itself expands through the accession of other states. Many of the states of the European Union have experienced devolution of various kinds in the years since the Second World War. Germany is a federal state, Italy has fifteen ordinary and five special regions, Spain is composed of autonomous communities. Italy's special regions are special because of their distinctive cultural, sometimes linguistic, identity. In the special region of Trentino-Alto Adige, for instance, even the province of Bolzano has power to frame legislation, in deference to its peculiarly German character. In Spain, the autonomous communities have powers to depart from the general civil law of the country in favour of their own particular customs, their local foral laws.[54] These usually relate to the law of family property and succession, but in Catalonia, the local law extends to the form and regulation of contractual obligations as well. One especial feature of the local laws of the Spanish autonomous communities is that in those communities which possess them, there is a local final court of appeal, the *Tribunal Superior de Justicia*, which ousts the jurisdiction of the Supreme Court of Cassation in Madrid with regard to the local laws. Models for judicial as well as legislative and administrative devolution, already exist within the new Europe.[55]

Wales entered the twenty-first century as part of the United Kingdom but also as part of the new, expanding Europe of the European Union. There are many who see this new dimension for Wales as opportune, giving the nation the chance to assert its individuality within a family of nations some of which are of like size or even smaller. Moreover, the European ideal of subsidiarity, of facilitating decision making at a level as close as is feasible to those who are affected by the consequences, accords well with the devolution Wales is currently experiencing. Wales' approach to the new Europe is more enthusiastic than that of neighbouring England, and that precisely because Wales has extensive experience of having been a smaller partner, often not even a partner, within a greater political whole and knows that it can maintain, because it has maintained, a separate identity within such a context. For Wales, the experience of European unification merely presents a fresh challenge of the kind it has faced many times previously in its history: as part of the Roman empire, as the neighbour of the centralized monarchy of medieval England, and as part of the developing union of nations in the modern era which would become the United Kingdom at the heart of a world empire. In each phase, Wales has assimilated much of what such associations have had to offer, but also preserved what it values of its own customs and culture, most obviously the Welsh language.

Not everyone would subscribe to such an optimistic perspective upon the place of Wales in the modern world. Some would see the development of a global culture, with English as one of the main languages if not the dominant language, as a threat to the future identity of Wales and its language. Over the last two centuries, there have been repeated attempts to create a peculiarly Welsh community within some safe haven away from powerful external influences. At one time, such hopes centred upon the establishment of Welsh communities by emigrants in what were then distant corners of the world, with Pennsylvania and Patagonia being the most famous examples. More recently, the pressure has been to demarcate an area of the Welsh heartland, where Welsh is the language of everyday life and Welsh concepts of family and community remain relatively unspoilt, as a *Bro Gymraeg*, where the Welsh way of life could be jealously protected and preserved.

What is perhaps most remarkable about this division of opinion is not that it exists but that it continues to exist in a manner which is typical of virtually the whole of Welsh history. A glance at a modern map of political divisions in Wales, such as that showing the distribution of seats among the parties after the 1997 general election to the Westminster parliament, reveals divisions familiar certainly from the later Middle Ages and arguably from Roman times. Support for the two major British political parties is drawn most consistently from the coastal areas of north and south, where Norman lords established their palatine control and where earlier the Romans had had most influence. Along the borders, where the Marcher lords had established mixed jurisdictions in the medieval period, there remains strong support for the Liberal Democrats, a legacy of the Liberal loyalties which gave way to Labour support in the areas where industry invaded. Finally, in the fastnesses of Gwynedd and in the counties of Ceredigion and Carmarthen, what was the Principality of post-Edwardian Wales, Plaid Cymru has its greatest strength, the lands which saw the least Roman, Anglo-Saxon and Anglo-Norman influence. Just as in earlier generations, border accommodations were resented in the strongholds of the west, and in like manner as Bede complained that the English had had to be converted by a Roman missionary because the neighbouring Welsh were too pre-occupied maintaining their Christian culture in the face of the threat of Anglo-Saxon paganism to export it, so today there are some who would put up the barricades against the infiltration of modern, global English culture.

In each age, however, there have been Welsh people prepared and willing to take their talents and culture out into a wider world. In the post-Roman world, these were the Celtic saints who, contrary to Bede's strictures, did carry their Christian faith to new territories. There were Welshmen who played a full part in the life of Christendom during the high Middle Ages, and most particularly perhaps Welshmen who seized the opportunities afforded by the Tudor conquest of England to advance their careers and the standing of their families by playing full roles in the life of the Tudor court, the professions which served it and in the political and social life of modern Wales. In each age, there has been a tension between those who have feared for the future and those who have embraced the opportunities which change has brought.

The future of post-devolution Wales within the new Europe produces similar tensions, which the past suggests are predictable. The past also suggests that despite those fears, or perhaps because of their sobering influence, Wales has a tradition of being able to assimilate what is valuable in the new while retaining as its own what it most values from the past. In terms of its legal history, under the Romans, the native princes, the Normans, the Plantagenets, the Tudors and their successors, it has consistently managed to hold to the idea of a national identity despite fragmented government and often the existence of more than one legal system governing its people. Such is the Wales of the twenty-first century, with its laws being made in Cardiff, Westminster and Brussels, and adjudicated by a variety of courts. In that, there is nothing new for Wales, and therefore no reason for doubting that Wales will continue to develop in a manner true to its rich legal heritage while contributing fully to the larger world of which it is not an adjunct but an integral part.

Notes

Chapter 1

1   See E. Guest, 'On the boundaries which separated England and Wales', *Archaeologica Cambrensis* (3rd ser.), 7 (1861), 269–92.
2   See N. Chadwick, *The Celts* (London, 1971), pp. 31, 33–5; M. Green and R. Howell, *Celtic Wales* (Cardiff, 2000), pp. 118–19.
3   See, for instance, P. Vinogradoff, *Roman Law in Medieval Europe* (Oxford, 1929; reprinted with an introduction by P. G. Stein, Cambridge, 1968).
4   It has been said that writing and education was one of the greatest gifts which the Romans brought to Britain and northern Europe generally, and that the native poetry of the Christian, post-Roman centuries may have imbedded within it Christianized elements of the pre-Christian traditions: see Chadwick, *Celts*, p. 52; Green and Howell, *Celtic Wales*, pp. 118–19.
5   Thus, the law texts record three kinds of homage, three dangerous wounds, three kinds of purchase of land, three persons not to be buried in consecrated ground, three privy things, three precious things of a kindred, three unclaimable things, and so on, and three is also used as a unit of legal measurement, as in three ancestors' lifetimes, three ebb tides and three flows, three moons, three nights and three days, and so on. Groups of three were also used in the art of the native British people, where for instance their depiction of the pre-Christian deities often involved their presentation in groups of three which may have been thought to increase their power and their efficacy in the same manner as grouping information in triads increased its power to be transmitted efficiently. See G. Webster, *The British Celts and their Gods under Rome* (London, 1986), pp. 66, 70. For a detailed study of the Welsh legal triads, see S. E. Roberts, *The Legal Triads of Medieval Wales* (Cardiff, 2007; repr. 2011), hereafter *Triads*.
6   See Webster, *British Celts*, p. 22.
7   M. Richter, *Medieval Ireland: The Enduring Tradition* (London, 1988), p. 20.
8   Tacitus, *Annales*, 14.
9   J. Rhys and D. Brynmor-Jones, *The Welsh People*, 4th edn (London, 1906), pp. 254–5.
10 A similar situation developed in Athens, where the roles of the three magistrates, the eponymous *archon*, the polemarch and the king *archon*, may have emerged from the jurisdiction of an earlier single ruler.
11 See T. G. Watkin, *An Historical Introduction to Modern Civil Law* (London, 1999), pp. 27–8.
12 See T. P. Ellis, *Welsh Tribal Law and Custom in the Middle Ages* (Oxford, 1926; Aalen, 1982), p. 379; W. Linnard, *Trees in the Law of Hywel* (Aberystwyth, 1979). The oak

was valued at 120*d*, while a yew which was not dedicated to a saint, that is not growing on consecrated ground, was valued at only 16*d* or 20*d*.

[13] Pliny, *Nat. Hist.*, 16, 10, 28–9, cited in Webster, *British Celts*, p. 22.

[14] On *defixiones*, see Webster, *British Celts*, pp. 135–6.

[15] See W. Davies, *Wales in the Early Middle Ages* (Leicester, 1982), p. 177, citing Giraldus Cambrensis, *The Journey through Wales*, 189.

[16] See Chadwick, *Celts*, p. 134, Green and Howell, *Celtic Wales*, pp. 33–5 and 64–5. For the Roman law, see Justinian, *Institutes*, 1. 3. 4; Digest, 49. 15. 5, 2, preserving the classical law.

[17] See, for instance, E. Owen, 'Holy wells, or water veneration', *Archaeologica Cambrensis* (5th ser.), 8 (1891), 8–16.

[18] See Justinian, *Institutes*, 2. 1. 16, 17; Digest, 41. 1. 51, preserving the classical law.

[19] Chadwick, *Celts*, p. 228; Webster, *British Celts*, pp. 120–1.

[20] 1 Samuel 15.

[21] See, for instance, H. S. Green et al., 'The Caergwrle Bowl: its composition, geological source and archaeological significance', *Reports of the Institute of Geological Sciences*, 80(i) (1981), 171–89.

[22] D. Jenkins (trans. and ed.), *Hywel Dda: The Law* (Llandysul, 1986), pp. 39 and 45. The *brycan* was a speckled cloth used as a bed covering at night, a garment by day and as a shroud in death; *Bleg.*, 60–7; *Ior.*, 44; *Col.*, 2; *Cyfn.*, 89–96 (236–40); *Latin A*, 142–6; *Latin B*, 225–6; *Latin D*, 344–5; *Latin E*, 474.

[23] Jenkins, *The Law*, p. 99; *Bleg.*, 108/32.

[24] For a discussion of such content, see P. Mac Canna, 'Elfennau cyn-Gristnogol yn y Cyfreithiau', *BBCS*, 23(4) (1970), 309–16.

[25] Webster, *British Celts*, p. 110.

[26] Gildas, *De excidio Britanniae*, ch. 4; Davies, *Wales*, p. 169.

[27] *Bleg.*, 47/1–6; *Ior.*, 43; *Col.*, 616; *Cyfn.*, 64–7 (213–14); *Latin A*, 135; *Latin B*, 205; *Latin D*, 377; Jenkins, *The Law*, p. 40.

[28] This is similar to the linguistic development in Latin, whereby *hostis*, which originally meant any foreigner, eventually came to mean enemy, whereas non-hostile foreigners became known as *peregrini*, those wandering through the fields of the land, *per agros*. The Welsh laws actually describe such foreigners as walking the king's lands: 'echenawc estronawl yn kerdet tir y brenhin' (*Llyfr Blegywryd*, 47. 1).

[29] The other packhorses were a deceased person's best beast, his *ebidew*; the payment made to a ruler usually upon marriage for the loss of a maiden's virginity, the *amobr*; and two fines for respectively serious and less serious wrongdoing, the *dirwy* and the *camlwrw*. All might legitimately be seen as payments that might once have been made by way of sacrifice to the gods, the ruler in later ages standing in as the human representative of the divine power.

[30] Green and Howell, *Celtic Wales*, pp. 35–6.

[31] Chadwick, *Celts*, p. 126.

[32] Gaius, *Institutes*, 4.

[33] Genesis 30.

[34] See P. Cramer, *Baptism and Change in the Early Middle Ages (c.200–1150)* (Cambridge, 1993).

[35] Green and Howell, *Celtic Wales*, pp. 58–60.

[36] Ibid., p. 55.

[37] Ibid., p. 23.

[38] See J. Fenton, 'On the ancient modes of burial of the Cymry or Celtic Britons', *Archaeologica Cambrensis* (3rd ser.), 6 (1860), 25–33; G. H. Jones, 'Some parallels between Celtic and Indian institutions', *Archaeologica Cambrensis* (6th ser.), 1 (1900), 109–25; G. R. J. Jones, 'Early settlement in Arfon: the setting of Tre'r Ceiri', *CHST*, 24 (1963), 1–20; E. Laws, 'Pembrokeshire raths', *Archaeologica Cambrensis* (5th ser.), 3 (1886), 97–9; W. Llewellin, 'The Raths of Pembrokeshire', *Archaeologica Cambrensis* (3rd ser.), 10 (1864), 1–13; R. Moore-Colyer, 'Agriculture in Wales before and during the second millennium BC', *Archaeologica Cambrensis*, 146 (1996), 15–33; C. A. Smith, 'Late prehistoric and Romano-British enclosed homesteads in northwest Wales', *Archaeologica Cambrensis*, 126 (1977), 38–52.

Chapter 2

[1] On the Roman frontiers in Wales and relations with the native population, see M. G. Jarrett (ed.), *The Roman Frontier in Wales*, 2nd edn, ed. V. E. Nash Williams (Cardiff, 1969); M. G. Jarrett and J. C. Mann, 'The tribes of Wales', *WHR*, 4(2) (1968–9), 161–74; R. E. Wheeler, 'Roman and native in Wales: an imperial frontier problem', *THSC* (1920–1), 40–96.

[2] J. Rhys and D. Brynmor-Jones, *The Welsh People*, 4th edn (London, 1906), pp. 95–6.

[3] Gildas, *De excidio Britanniae*, ch. 25.

[4] G. Webster, *The British Celts and their Gods under Rome* (London, 1986), pp. 138–9.

[5] On the roots of British Christianity in the Roman period, see G. C. Boon, 'A trace of Romano-British Christianity at Caerwent', *Monmouthshire Antiquary*, 1(1) (1961), 8–9; R. W. Morgan, *St. Paul in Britain: or the origin of British as opposed to Papal Christianity*, 2nd edn (Oxford and London, 1880); C. Thomas, *Christianity in Roman Britain to AD 500* (London, 1981); Webster, *British Celts*.

[6] Julian the Apostate (361–3) had pagan temples built, for instance at Lydney in Gloucestershire. M. Green and R. Howell, *Celtic Wales* (Cardiff, 2000), p. 79: Zosimus reports the British rebelled in the early fifth century against Roman rule and Roman law.

[7] Thomas, *Christianity*, p. 58; Green and Howell, *Celtic Wales*, pp. 82–3.

[8] Thomas, *Christianity*, p. 53; Green and Howell, *Celtic Wales*, p. 82.

[9] Webster, *British Celts*, p. 136. The word means a solemn admonition.

[10] Thomas, *Christianity*, p. 197; Green and Howell, *Celtic Wales*, pp. 80–2.

[11] This had not been Diocletian's intention; his plan had been that both should have coterminous jurisdiction throughout the Roman world.

[12] The names indicated that one, *Superior*, was nearer to Rome and the other, *Inferior*, further from the capital. The names reflect an ancient application of the principle which still features in modern discourse: trains go up to London and down to the provinces.

[13] This is strictly accurate. One class of persons, *dediticii*, being foreigners or freed slaves of bad character who were not allowed within fifty miles of Rome upon pain of enslavement, were excluded from the grant.

[14] See, generally, A. N. Sherwin White, *The Roman Citizenship*, 2nd edn (Oxford, 1973).

[15] Latinity usually conferred the right to trade with Roman citizens using contractual forms accepted and enforced under Roman civil law (*commercium*). Exceptionally in the later republic and earlier empire, it might also include the capacity to contract a full Roman law marriage (*conubium*).

[16] Formal manumission originally involved a state element, through the presence of a magistrate or the need for the consent of a popular assembly. When later such checks were not required, legislation in the form of the *lex Aelia Sentia* and the *lex Fufia Caninia*, both from Augustus' time, limited the powers of owners to manumit indiscriminately.

[17] The definition can be found in Justinian, *Institutes* 1. 1. 1.

[18] Justinian, *Institutes* 1. 1. pr.; Digest, 1. 1. 10.

[19] Papinian, one of the most famous jurists, was praetorian prefect and was actually at York with the emperor Septimius Severus, and it is claimed Ulpian travelled with him as one of his assessors, another being an equally famous jurist, Paul.

[20] The text of the *edictum perpetuum* has been reconstructed from the extracts to be found in the Digest by Otto Lenel; O. Lenel, *Das Edictum Perpetuum* (Leipzig, 1927; repr. Aalen, 1985).

[21] A judge who acted improperly was said to have made the cause his own, *iudex qui litem suam fecit*.

[22] A system of appeals at common law in England and Wales was only introduced in the 1870s, but an appeal from the High Court is permitted to the Court of Appeal and thence to the Supreme Court of the United Kingdom, the final and highest appeal court.

[23] This manner of dealing with juristic opinion had been enacted by Hadrian. The later Law of Citations of Theodosius II and Valentinian III was promulgated in 426, after the Romans had left Britain.

[24] The two principal English edns of Gaius are F. de Zulueta, *The Institutes of Gaius*, 2 vols (Oxford, 1946) and W. M. Gordon and O. F. Robinson, *The Institutes of Gaius* (London, 1988). There are several good edns of Justinian's *Institutes* in English, including J. B. Moyle, *The Institutes of Justinian* (Oxford, 1883; 5th edn, 1912); T. C. Sandars, *The Institutes of Justinian* (new impression, London, 1962); J. A. C. Thomas, *The Institutes of Justinian* (Amsterdam, 1975); P. Birks and G. McLeod, *Justinian's Institutes* (London, 1987). R. W. Lee's *Elements of Roman Law*, 4th edn (London, 1956) contains the text in English trans. only. The leading English edn of the Digest is Alan Watson's, with an English trans. of the text as edited by T. Mommsen and P. Krueger, published in Philadelphia, 1985 (4 vols). The leading English textbooks on Roman law are W. W. Buckland, *A Textbook of Roman Law from Augustus to Justinian*, 3rd edn, by P. G. Stein (Cambridge, 1963); J. A. C. Thomas, *Textbook of Roman Law* (Amsterdam, 1976).

[25] Four children were required if the woman had been freed from slavery.

[26] Twenty years was the required period if the parties were not in the same province; a thirty-year period would operate to prescribe title even if the parties were not in good faith. See Justinian, *Codex repetitae praelectionis*, 7. 33. 12; 7. 39. 8.

[27] In effect, in Justinian's law, *usucapio* only applied to moveables, and *longi temporis praescriptio* applied to land.

[28] Gaius, *Institutes*, 4. 4.

[29] Three hundred asses were payable for a freeman's broken bone; 150 for that of a slave. Twenty-five asses were payable for lesser injuries and insults. The text of the XII Tables can be found in E. H. Warmington (ed. and trans.), *Remains of Old Latin*, 3 (Loeb Classical Library, London, 1938), pp. 424–515; the leading modern edn is M. H. Crawford (ed.), *Roman Statutes* vol. 2 (London, 1996) , pp. 555–721.

[30] The medieval jurists were to divide *locatio conductio* into these three categories: *locatio conductio rei, operis faciendi* and *operum*.

[31] H. E. M. Cool, 'A Romano-British gold workshop of the second century', *Britannia* 17 (1986), 231–7.

Chapter 3

[1] See P. Llewellyn, *Rome in the Dark Ages* (London, 1971).

[2] See T. G. Watkin, *An Historical Introduction to Modern Civil Law* (London, 1999), ch. 4.

[3] The Edict of Theodoric was formerly attributed to Theodoric the Ostrogoth who ruled at Ravenna (490–526), but recent scholarship attributes it to an earlier Visigothic leader of the same name.

[4] Justinian was emperor in the east at Byzantium from 527 until 565. Under his direction was produced the great compendium of Roman law which was to be known in later ages as the *Corpus iuris civilis*. This consisted of three parts: a Code of extant imperial legislation; the Digest, which contained excerpts from the writings of the jurists, itself a vast work exceeding the length of the Bible by half; and the *Institutes*, a textbook for students of the law modelled on the similarly entitled work of Gaius.

[5] See C. Thomas, *Christianity in Roman Britain to AD 500* (London, 1981) pp. 351–2; J. K. Knight, 'Glamorgan AD 400–110: archaeology and history', in H. N. Savory (ed.), *Glamorgan County History, Volume II: Early Glamorgan Pre-History and Early History* (Cardiff, 1984), p. 318; M. Richter, *Medieval Ireland: The Enduring Tradition* (London, 1988), p. 29. On the history of Christian continuity in Wales in this period, see S. Baring Gould, 'The Celtic monasteries', *Archaeologica Cambrensis* (5th ser.), 17 (1900), 249–76; E. G. Bowen, 'The Celtic saints in Cardiganshire', *Ceredigion*, 1 (1950–1), 3–17; E. G. Bowen, *Saints, Seaways and Settlements* (Cardiff, 1977); E. G. Bowen, *The Settlements of Celtic Wales* (Cardiff, 1956); J. D. Bullock, 'Early Christian memorial formulae', *Archaeologica Cambrensis*, 105 (1956), 133–41; D. S. Evans (ed.), *The Lives of the Welsh Saints by G. H. Doble* (Cardiff, 1971); J. D. Evans and M. J. Francis, 'Cynog: spiritual father of Brycheiniog', *Brycheiniog*, 27 (1994–5), 15–24; J. K. Knight, '*In tempore Iustini consulis*: contacts between the British and Gaulish churches before Augustine', in A. Detsicas (ed.), *Collectanea Historica: Essays in Memory of Stuart Rigold* (Maidstone, 1981); H. Williams, 'Some aspects of the Christian church in Wales during the fifth and sixth centuries', *THSC* (1893–4) 55–132; J. W. Willis-Bund, 'The early Welsh monasteries', *Archaeologica Cambrensis* (5th ser.), 8 (1891), 262–76; J. W. Willis-Bund, 'The Teilo churches', *Archaeologica Cambrensis* (5th ser.), 10 (1893), 193–217; P. A. Wilson, 'Romano-British and Welsh Christianity', *WHR*, 3 (1 and 2) (1966–7), 5–21, 103–20.

[6] This is the story recounted by Bishop Richard Davies of St David's, writing in the sixteenth century. See A. D. Carr, *Medieval Wales* (London, 1995), pp. 7–8.

[7] E. G. Bowen, *The Settlements of Celtic Wales* (Cardiff, 1956), pp. 14–16.

[8] For this change of heart, see Bowen, *Saints, Seaways*, pp. ix–xii.

[9] The importance of the Cynog tradition has recently been most interestingly explored by G. A. Elias in '*Llyfr Cynog* of *Cyfraith Hywel* and St Cynog of Brycheiniog', *WHR*, 23(1) (2006), 27–47.

[10] Bowen, *Settlements*, p. 44.
[11] The English form of the name is probably derived from the Goidelic *Illtuaith*; see G. O. Pierce, *Place Names in Glamorgan* (Cardiff, 2002), pp. 107–8.
[12] Knight, 'Glamorgan AD 400–110', p. 375.
[13] Bowen, *Settlements*, p. 64.
[14] Ibid., pp. 67–8.
[15] Ibid., pp. 70–1.
[16] Ibid., pp. 79–84.
[17] Ibid., p. 2.
[18] Knight, 'Glamorgan AD 400–110', p. 368.
[19] W. Davies, *Wales in the Early Middle Ages* (Leicester, 1982), p. 181.
[20] R. W. D. Fenn, 'The age of the saints', in D. Walker (ed.), *A History of the Church in Wales* (Penarth, 1976), p. 20; Knight, 'Glamorgan AD 400–110', p. 327.
[21] J. C. M. Toynbee, 'Christianity in Roman Britain', *Journal of the British Archaeological Association* (3rd ser.), 16 (1963), 1–124 at 24; Thomas, *Christianity*, pp. 274, 355.
[22] Bowen, *Settlements*, pp. 24–5; Bowen, *Saints, Seaways*, pp. 93–5, 67–8.
[23] Bowen, *Settlements*, pp. 106–7; Bowen, *Saints, Seaways*, p. 58.
[24] Bowen, *Settlements*, pp. 112 and 114.
[25] Bowen, *Saints, Seaways*, p. 201.
[26] Knight, 'Glamorgan AD 400–110', pp. 377–8.
[27] Davies, *Wales*, p. 39. See also W. E. Griffiths, 'The excavation of a Romano-British hut-group at Cors-y-gedol in Merionethshire', *BBCS*, 18(1) (1958), 119–30; G. R. J. Jones, 'Society and settlement in Wales and the marches, 500 BC to AD 1100 [review article]', *CHST*, 47 (1986), 7–24.
[28] Fenn, 'Age of saints', pp. 17–18.
[29] Bowen, *Settlements*, p. 44; Bowen, *Saints, Seaways*, pp. 136–7.
[30] Bowen, *Settlements*, p. 26.
[31] D. Walker, *Medieval Wales* (Cambridge, 1990), pp. 11–12.
[32] On Macsen, see G. Thomas, 'O Maximus i Macsen', *THSC* (1983), 7–21; J. F. Matthews, 'Macsen, Maximus and Constantine', *WHR*, 11(4) (1982–3), 431–48; M. G. Jarrett, 'Magnus Maximus and the end of Roman Britain', *THSC* (1983), 22–35.
[33] The form *Llanelen* reflects this dedication.
[34] This claim persisted into later centuries: see R. R. Davies, *Conquest, Coexistence, and Change: Wales 1063–1415* (Oxford, 1987), also published as *The Age of Conquest: Wales 1063–1415* (Oxford, 1991), p. 78.
[35] J. Rhys and D. Brynmor-Jones, *The Welsh People*, 4th edn (London, 1906), pp. 131–2.
[36] A. W. Wade-Evans, *Welsh Medieval Law* (Oxford, 1909; Aalen, 1979), p. xxxi.
[37] See N. Chadwick, 'Bretwalda – Gwledig – Vortigern', *BBCS*, 19(3) (1961), 225–30.
[38] See K. L. Maund, *The Welsh Kings* (Stroud, 2000), p. 19.
[39] Cunedda is said to have been the son of Eternus, the son of Paternus (called *Peisrudd*), the son of Tacitus.
[40] Wade-Evans, *Welsh Medieval Law*, pp. xxxv–xxxvii.
[41] Vortigern, the son of Vitalis, the son of Vitalinus.
[42] On Vortigern, see D. P. Kirby, 'Vortigern', *BBCS*, 23(1) (1968), 37–59; J. H. Ward, 'Vortigern and the end of Roman Britain', *Britannia*, 3 (1972), 277–89.
[43] Carr, *Medieval Wales*, p. 4.
[44] See Thomas, *Christianity*, p. 242; G. O. Pierce, 'The evidence of place names', in H. N. Savory (ed.), *Glamorgan County History, Volume II: Early Glamorgan Pre-History*

and Early History (Cardiff, 1984), p. 482; P. V. Webster, The Roman period', in H. N. Savory (ed.), *Glamorgan County History, Volume II: Early Glamorgan Pre-History and Early History* (Cardiff, 1984), pp. 308–9.

45 Bowen, *Settlements*, p. 20; Bowen, *Saints, Seaways*, pp. 51–3. See also M. Miller, 'Consular years in the *Historia Brittonum*', *BBCS*, 29(1) (1980), 17–34.

46 Fenn, 'Age of the saints', p. 10.

47 Ibid., p. 15.

48 Walker, *Medieval Wales*, p. 1; Davies, *Conquest*, p. 20.

49 See further Rhys and Brynmor-Jones, *Welsh People*, pp. 35, 106–7; Davies, *Wales*, p. 102; Maund, *Welsh Kings*, pp. 24–32.

50 See further Rhys and Brynmor-Jones, *Welsh People*, pp. 130, 24–5.

51 Maund, *Welsh Kings*, pp. 20–2. On the Irish influence at this time, see M. Dillon, 'The Irish settlement in Wales', *Celtica*, 12 (1977), 1–11; E. MacNeill, 'Ireland and Wales in the history of jurisprudence', in D. Jenkins (ed.), *Celtic Law Papers Introductory to Welsh Medieval Law and Government* (Brussels, 1973), pp. 171–92; J. Rhys, 'The Goidels in Wales', *Archaeologica Cambrensis* (5th ser.), 12 (1895), 18–39; K. Meyer, 'Early relations between Gael and Brython', *THSC* (1895–6), 55–86. On Vortepor and like inscriptions, see J. Rhys, 'Notes on the inscriptions on the tombstone of Vortipore', *Archaeologica Cambrensis* (5th ser.), 12 (1895), 307–313; E. Lewis, 'The discovery of the tombstone of Vortipore . . .', *Archaeologica Cambrensis* (5th ser.), 12 (1895), 303–313; P. Mac Cana, 'Votepori', *BBCS*, 19(2) (1961), 116–17; J. Romilly Allen, 'Early Christian art in Wales', *Archaeologica Cambrensis* (5th ser), 16 (1899), 1–69.

52 Bowen, *Settlements*, pp. 99–101.

53 Richter, *Medieval Ireland*, p. 29; Wade-Evans, *Welsh Medieval Law*, p. xlii.

54 Thomas, *Christianity*, p. 274; N. Chadwick, *The Celts* (London, 1971), p. 73.

55 Davies, *Conquest*, pp. 4, 16. See also I. Williams, 'When did the British become Welsh?', *AAST* (1939), 27–38.

56 Knight, 'Glamorgan AD 400–110', p. 317. See also R. W. Banks, 'On the early history of the land of Gwent', *Archaeologica Cambrensis* (5th ser.), 2 (1885), 241–56. On *Venta*, see E. McClure, 'Note on the meaning of *Venta* in British place names', *Archaeologica Cambrensis* (6th ser.), 9 (1909), 239–40.

57 Davies, *Wales*, p. 181; Pierce, 'The evidence of place names', pp. 463, 485.

58 Bowen, *Saints, Seaways*, p. 97.

59 Ibid., pp. 67–70.

60 Ibid., pp. 14, 79; Webster, 'The Roman period', p. 303.

61 M. Green and R. Howell, *Celtic Wales* (Cardiff, 2000), pp. 69, 71, 72.

62 Davies, *Conquest*, pp. 18–19.

63 Contra: D. Jenkins (trans. and ed.) *Hywel Dda: The Law* (Llandysul, 1986), p. xxxiv.

64 A. R. Wiliam (ed.), *Llyfr Iorwerth* (Cardiff, 1960), p. xxxv; H. D. Emanuel, *The Latin Texts of the Welsh Laws* (Cardiff, 1967), p. 92; Jenkins, *The Law*, p. xxxiv.

65 Gildas, *Historia Brittonum*, ch. 63; *De Excidio Britanniae*, ch. 35.

66 Davies, *Conquest*, pp. 125–6, for the later evidence.

67 Jenkins, *The Law*, p. 184 (quoting from *Llyfr Cyfnerth*); *Cyfn.*, 141–2 (283). The quote is from the latter.

68 Rhys and Brynmor-Jones, *Welsh People*, p. 245. On the possible significance of the absence of the ordeal in the Welsh laws, see T. G. Watkin, 'Saints, seaways and dispute settlements', in W. M. Gordon and T. D. Fergus (eds), *Legal History in the Making* (London and Rio Grande, 1991), pp. 1–9.

[69] Fenn, 'Age of the saints', pp. 17–18; *Bleg.*, 49/20–50/11; *Ior.*, 94, 115; *Cyfn.*, 99–100 (244); *Latin A*, 146–7.

[70] Davies, *Wales*, pp. 52, 184; *Canu Aneurin*, B40.

[71] Bowen, *Saints, Seaways*, p. 201; Green and Howell, *Celtic Wales*, pp. 59–60; Knight, 'Glamorgan AD 400–110', p. 345.

[72] Bowen, *Saints, Seaways*, pp. 204–5. See G. R. J. Jones, 'The tribal system in Wales: a re-assessment in the light of settlement studies', *WHR*, 1(2) (1960–3), 111–32, at 130; L. Alcock, 'Settlement patterns in Celtic Britain', *Antiquity* (1962), 51–4; G. R. J. Jones, [a response] *Antiquity* (1962), 54–5; L. Alcock, *Dinas Powys* (Cardiff, 1964), appendix 3, p. 196.

[73] See G. R. L. Jones, 'Early territorial organization in Gwynedd . . . and Elmet', *Northern History*, 10 (1975), 3–27.

[74] Green and Howell, *Celtic Wales*, pp. 87–90.

[75] Ibid., p. 2.

[76] Ibid., pp. 100–1.

[77] Ibid., pp. 118–19.

[78] Davies, *Wales*, p. 169.

[79] Ibid., pp. 171, 174.

[80] Richter, *Medieval Ireland*, p. 48.

[81] Davies, *Conquest*, p. 11.

[82] See Green and Howell, *Celtic Wales*, pp. 98–9; Maund, *Welsh Kings*, pp. 23, 24; Bowen, *Settlements*, p. 20; Bowen, *Saints, Seaways*, p. 56.

[83] Richter, *Medieval Ireland*, p. 62.

[84] Rhys and Brynmor-Jones, *Welsh People*, pp. 24–5.

[85] Richter, *Medieval Ireland*, p. 61.

[86] T. P. Ellis, *Welsh Tribal Law and Custom in the Middle Ages* (Oxford, 1926; Aalen, 1982), p. 2.

[87] Thomas, *Christianity*, p. 274.

[88] Richter, *Medieval Ireland*, p. 29.

[89] Davies, *Wales*, p. 181.

[90] Bowen, *Settlements*, p. 20; Bowen, *Saints, Seaways*, pp. 51–3.

[91] Bowen, *Saints, Seaways*, p. 53.

[92] Knight, 'Glamorgan AD 400–110', p. 335.

[93] Ibid., p. 337.

[94] Bowen, *Saints, Seaways*, pp. 161, 183.

[95] J. Black, *A New History of Wales* (Stroud, 2000), p. 41.

[96] Bowen, *Saints, Seaways*, pp. 76–7.

[97] Bowen, *Settlements*, p. 16 and n.1.

[98] See C. M. Radding, *The Origins of Medieval Jurisprudence: Pavia and Bologna 850–1150* (New Haven and London, 1988).

[99] Chadwick, *Celts*, p. 87. On coinage and settlement, see also J. L. Davies, 'Coinage and settlement in Roman Wales and the Marches: some observations', *Archaeologica Cambrensis*, 132 (1983), 78–94.

[100] Fenn, 'Age of the saints', p. 22.

[101] Knight, 'Glamorgan AD 400–110', p. 339.

[102] *Book of Aicill*, 3.83, 85; *Senchas Mór*, 1.73. Thus, Mephibosheth of all Saul's descendants is permitted to survive and live in David's court, he being no threat to the king as he was lame in both feet as a result of a mishap in infancy. See 2 Samuel 4 and 9.

[103] Bowen, *Settlements*, pp. 70–1. On the history of Israel, see P. Kyle McCarter, Jr., 'The patriarchal age', in H. Shanks (ed.), *Ancient Israel* (Washington, DC, 1989), pp. 1–30.

[104] On linguistic influence, see J. Hines, 'Welsh and English: mutual origins in post-Roman Britain', *Studia Celtica*, 34 (2000), 81–104; for important discoveries regarding the use of Roman law by the native population, see L. J. Korporowicz, 'Roman law in Roman Britain: an introductory survey', *Journal of Legal History* 33 (2012), 133–51; and on the Biblical influence, see T. G. Watkin, 'Cyfraith Cymru', in T. Roberts, *Yr Angen am Furiau* (Llanrwst, 2009), pp. 64–80.

[105] See Bede, *Historia Ecclesiastica Gentis Anglorum*, 1. 22.

Chapter 4

[1] For the reasoning behind the conclusion that Merfyn was more the nephew of Cynan and Hywel, see below. For the history of the early rulers, see K. Maund, *The Welsh Kings* (Stroud, 2000); K. L. Maund, *Handlist of the Acts of the Welsh Native Rulers 1132–1283* (Cardiff, 1996); K. D. Pringle, 'The kings of Demetia', *THSC* (1970), 70–6; (1971), 140–4; G. T. O. Bridgeman, 'The princes of upper Powys', *Montgomeryshire Collections*, 1 (1868), 1–194.

[2] This is contradicted by Giraldus Cambrensis writing in the twelfth century.

[3] Until 920, he shared his inheritance with his brother Clynog, but became sole ruler on the latter's death in that year.

[4] N. Chadwick, *The Celts* (London, 1971), pp. 89–90.

[5] Ibid.

[6] Gwynedd had connections under Rhodri with the court of Charles the Bald: see previous chapter.

[7] A. W. Wade-Evans, *Welsh Medieval Law* (Oxford, 1909; Aalen, 1979), p. liii; *Bleg.*, 2/5–8; *Cyfn.*, 1–2 (146); *Latin B*, 192; *Latin C*, 276; *Latin E*, 435.

[8] Chadwick, *Celts*, pp. 110–11; *Bleg.*, 2/12–13; *Latin E*, 435.

[9] T. P. Ellis, *Welsh Tribal Law and Custom in the Middle Ages* (Oxford, 1926; Aalen, 1982), I, 6; D. Jenkins (trans. and ed.), *Hywel Dda: The Law* (Llandysul, 1986), p. 1; *Ior.*, 1.

[10] J. Rhys and D. Brynmor-Jones, *The Welsh People*, 4th edn (London, 1906), pp. 176–7. The principal texts are now available in modern scholarly edns. These are H. D. Emanuel, *The Latin Texts of the Welsh Laws* (Cardiff, 1967); I. F. Fletcher, *Latin Redaction A* (Aberystwyth, 1986); D. Jenkins (ed.), *Llyfr Colan* (Cardiff, 1963); D. Jenkins, *Damweiniau Colan* (Aberystwyth, 1973); A. R. Wiliam (ed.), *Llyfr Iorwerth* (Cardiff, 1960); S. J. Williams and J. E. Powell (eds), *Llyfr Blegywryd* (Cardiff, 1961); and Wade-Evans, *Welsh Law*, which is based primarily on *Llyfr Cyfnerth*. The most famous English trans. of the native laws is A. Owen, *The Laws and Institutions of Wales* (London, 1841), while the best modern trans. is D. Jenkins (trans. and ed.), *Hywel Dda: The Law*. There are also excellent introductions to the content of the native laws: T. M. Charles-Edwards, *The Welsh Laws* (Cardiff, 1989) in English and in Welsh; D. Jenkins, *Cyfraith Hywel* (Llandysul, 1976). A very full, but now dated account, is T. P. Ellis, *Welsh Tribal Law and Custom in the Middle Ages*. The twentieth century saw the growth of a considerable body of scholarly literature on the native laws: see T. M. Charles-Edwards, 'Naw Kynywedi Teithiauc', in D. Jenkins and M. E.

Owen (eds), *The Welsh Law of Women* (Cardiff, 1980), pp. 23–39; T. M. Charles-Edwards, 'The seven bishop-houses of Dyfed', *BBCS*, 24 (1970–2), 247–62; T. M. Charles-Edwards, M. E. Owen and D. B. Walters, *Lawyers and Laymen* (Cardiff, 1986); G. Edwards, 'Studies in the Welsh Laws since 1928', *WHR, Special Number, 1963:* 1–18; J. G. Edwards, 'Hywel Dda and the Welsh law-books', in D. Jenkins (ed.), *Celtic Law Papers Introductory to Welsh Medieval Law and Government* (Brussels, 1973), pp. 135–60; T. P. Ellis, 'Legal references, terms and conceptions in the "Mabinogion"', *Y Cymmrodor*, 39 (1928), 86–148; H. Emanuel, 'The Latin texts of the Welsh laws', *WHR, Special Number, 1963:* 25–32; D. Jenkins (ed.), *Celtic Law Papers Introductory to Welsh Medieval Law and Government* (Brussels, 1973); D. Jenkins and M. E. Owen, *The Welsh Law of Women* (Cardiff, 1980); D. Jenkins and M. E. Owen, 'Welsh law in Carmarthenshire', *Carmarthenshire Antiquary*, 18 (1982), 17–28; D. Jenkins, 'Legal and comparative aspects of the Welsh Laws', *WHR, Special Number, 1963:* 51–60; D. Jenkins, 'The significance of the Law of Hywel', *THSC* (1977), 54–76; D. P. Kirby, 'Hywel Dda: anglophile?', *WHR*, 8(1) (1976), 1–13; W. Linnard, *Trees in the Law of Hywel* (Aberystwyth, 1979); H. Loyn, 'Wales and England in the tenth century: the context of the Athelstan charters', *WHR*, 10(3) (1980–1), 283–301; M. E. Owen, 'Y Trioedd Arbennig', *BBCS*, 24(4) (1972), 434–50; T. Jones Pierce, 'Social and historical aspects of the Welsh Laws', *WHR, Special Number, 1963:* 33–50; H. Pryce, 'The prologues to the Welsh lawbooks', *BBCS*, 33 (1986), 151–87; W. Samuel, 'The ancient laws of Dyfed', *Pembrokeshire Historian*, 3 (1971), 42–52; D. Stephenson, *Thirteenth-Century Welsh Law Courts* (Aberystwyth, 1980); R. Thurneysen, 'Das keltische Recht', *Zeitschrift der Savigny-Stiftung für Rechtsgeschichte (Germanistische Abteilung)*, 55 (1935), 81–104, trans. as 'Celtic law', in D. Jenkins (ed.), *Celtic Law Papers Introductory to Welsh Medieval Law and Government* (Brussels, 1973), pp. 49–70; D. B. Walters, *The Comparative Legal Method: Marriage, Divorce and the Spouses' Property Rights in Early Medieval European Law* (Aberystwyth, 1983); *WHR, Special Number, 1963: The Welsh Laws*; A. R. Wiliam, 'Y Deddfynnay Cymraeg', *NLWJ*, 8 (1953/4), 97–103; A. R. Wiliam, 'Restoration of the Book of Cynog [Peniarth MS 35]', *NLWJ*, 25(3) (1987/8), 245–56; A. R. Wiliam, 'The Welsh texts of the laws', *WHR, Special Number, 1963:* 19–24.

[11] Chadwick, *Celts*, pp. 110–11.

[12] *Bleg.*, xv, 1/19; *Cyfn.*, 1–2 (146); *Latin D*, 316. For the importance of Hywel in the production of the law texts, and of the jurists after whom they are named, see J. G. Edwards, 'The royal household and the Welsh lawbooks', *Transactions of the Royal Historical Society* (5th ser.), 13 (1963), 163–76; T. P. Ellis, 'Hywel Dda: Codifier', *THSC* (1926–7), 1–69; H. Emanuel, 'Llyfr Blegywryd a Llawysgrif Rawlinson 821', *BBCS*, 19(1) (1960), 23–8; H. D. Emanuel, 'Blegywryd and the Welsh laws', *BBCS*, 20(3) (1963), 256–60; H. D. Emanuel, 'The Book of Blegywryd and Ms. Rawlinson 821', in D. Jenkins (ed.), *Celtic Law Papers Introductory to Welsh Medieval Law and Government* (Brussels, 1973), pp. 161–70; D. Jenkins 'A family of medieval Welsh lawyers', in D. Jenkins (ed.), *Celtic Law Papers Introductory to Welsh Medieval Law and Government* (Brussels, 1973), pp. 121–34; D. Jenkins, 'Iorwerth ap Madog', *NLWJ*, 8 (1953/4), 164–70; R. Stacey, 'The archaic core of Llyfr Iorwerth', in T. M. Charles-Edwards, M. E. Owen and D. B. Walters (eds), *Lawyers and Laymen* (Cardiff, 1986), pp. 15–46.

[13] Ellis, I, 4.

[14] Sir W. H. Holdsworth, *A History of English Law*, 16 vols (London, 1922–66), II, 21–5; H. D. Emanuel, *The Latin Texts of the Welsh Laws* (Cardiff, 1967), p. 91.

[15] Emanuel, *Latin Texts*, pp. 31–4; Ellis, I, 33; Wade-Evans, *Welsh Medieval Law*, p. xxiii.

[16] Rhys and Brynmor-Jones, *Welsh People*, pp. 186–7.

[17] W. Davies, *Wales in the Early Middle Ages* (Leicester, 1982), p. 116.

[18] Wade-Evans, *Welsh Medieval Law*, p. xxiii.

[19] D. Jenkins (trans. and ed.), *Hywel Dda: The Law* (Llandysul, 1986), p. 154; *Ior.*, 110/1–15; Ellis, I, 22.

[20] Emanuel, *Latin Texts*, pp. 84–5.

[21] A. D. Carr, *Medieval Wales* (London, 1995), pp. 67–8; R. R. Davies, *Conquest, Coexistence, and Change: Wales 1063–1415* (Oxford, 1991), p. 18.

[22] Emanuel, *Latin Texts*, p. 83.

[23] Ibid, pp. 93–4.

[24] Rhys is known for example to have made changes to the law with regard to the value of animals. Whereas until his time, beasts the value of which were not given in the law books could be valued by sworn approvers, he extended such valuations to all animals whether the texts gave them a value or not.

[25] Emanuel, *Latin Texts*, pp. 6–7, 27–9.

[26] Ibid., p. 29.

[27] Jenkins, *The Law*, p. 94; *Col.*, 528–31.

[28] Maund, *Welsh Kings*, p. 74; Davies, *Wales*, p. 127.

[29] Jenkins, *The Law*, pp. 89–90, 92; *Ior.*, 77, 78.

[30] Chadwick, *Celts*, pp. 110–11. For the extent of Irish influence, see, for instance, D. Brynmor-Jones, 'Foreign elements in Welsh mediaeval law', *THSC* (1916–17), 1–51; D. Brynmor-Jones, 'The Brehon Laws and the relation to the ancient Welsh institutes', *THSC* (1904–5), 7–36.

[31] Davies, *Wales*, p. 127.

[32] Wade-Evans, *Welsh Medieval Law*, p. 300.

[33] Jenkins, *The Law*, pp. xi, xxiii.

[34] This law introduced a method of head-counting the opinions of certain principal jurists to prevent confusion developing in litigation through a surfeit of juristic opinion. See T. G. Watkin, *An Historical Introduction to Modern Civil Law* (London, 1999), pp. 59–60.

[35] Ellis, I, 7; *Bleg.*, 107.

[36] Ellis, I, 26.

[37] Ellis, I, 31; *Bleg.*, 4/1–5; *Cyfn.*, 3 (147–8); *Triads*, Q3.

[38] Emanuel, *Latin Texts*, p. 89.

[39] Ibid., and Rhys and Brynmor-Jones, *Welsh People*, p. 203; *Ior.*, 4; *Cyfn.*, 3–4 (148); *Latin A*, 110; *Latin B*, 194; *Latin C*, 277; *Latin D*, 318; *Latin E*, 437.

[40] Davies, *Conquest*, pp. 58–9; Davies, *Wales*, pp. 123–5.

[41] Ellis, I, 32; *Ior.*, 4.

[42] Jenkins, *The Law*, p. 12; *Bleg.*, 13/15–20; *Latin D*, 323; *Triads*, Q5, Q250.

[43] There is a considerable literature on the laws of court. See D. Stephenson, 'The laws of court: past reality or present ideal', in T. M. Charles-Edwards, M. E. Owen and P. Russell (eds), *The Welsh King and his Court* (Cardiff, 2000), pp. 400–14; P. C. Bartrum, 'Achau brenhinoedd a tywysogion Cymru', *BBCS*, 19(3) (1960–2), 201–25; D. Jenkins, '*Bardd Teulu* and *Pencerdd*', in T. M. Charles-Edwards, M. E. Owen and P. Russell (eds), *The Welsh King and his Court* (Cardiff, 2000), pp. 142–66; D. Jenkins, '*Cynghellor* and Chancellor', *BBCS*, 27(1) (1976), 115–18; D. Jenkins, 'Hawk and

hound: hunting in the laws of court', in T. M. Charles-Edwards, M. E. Owen and P. Russell (eds), *The Welsh King and his Court* (Cardiff, 2000), pp. 255–80; D. Jenkins, 'Kings, lords and princes: the nomenclature of authority in thirteenth-century Wales', *BBCS*, 26(4) (1976), 451–62; D. Jenkins, 'Prolegomena to the Welsh laws of court', in T. M. Charles-Edwards, M. E. Owen and P. Russell (eds), *The Welsh King and his Court* (Cardiff, 2000), pp. 15–28; M. E. Owen, 'The laws of court from Cyfnerth', in T. M. Charles-Edwards, M. E. Owen and P. Russell (eds), *The Welsh King and his Court* (Cardiff, 2000), pp. 425–77; M. E. Owen, 'Medics and medicine', in T. M. Charles-Edwards, M. E. Owen and P. Russell (eds), *The Welsh King and his Court* (Cardiff, 2000), pp. 116–41; M. E. Owen, 'Royal propaganda: stories from the law-texts', in T. M. Charles-Edwards, M. E. Owen and P. Russell (eds), *The Welsh King and his Court* (Cardiff, 2000), pp. 224–54; M. E. Owen, 'Bwrlwm Llys Dinefwr: brenin, bardd a meddyg', *Carmarthenshire Antiquary*, 32 (1996), 5–14; H. Pryce, 'The household priest (Offeiriad Teulu)', in T. M. Charles-Edwards, M. E. Owen and P. Russell (eds), *The Welsh King and his Court* (Cardiff, 2000), pp. 82–93; P. Russell, 'Swydd, swyddog, swyddwr: office, officer and official', in T. M. Charles-Edwards, M. E. Owen and P. Russell (eds), *The Welsh King and his Court* (Cardiff, 2000), pp. 281–95; P. Russell, 'The laws of court from Latin B', in T. M. Charles-Edwards, M. E. Owen and P. Russell (eds), *The Welsh King and his Court* (Cardiff, 2000), pp. 478–526; J. B. Smith, '*Ynad Llys, Brawdwr Llys, Iudex Curie*', in T. M. Charles-Edwards, M. E. Owen and P. Russell (eds), *The Welsh King and his Court* (Cardiff, 2000), pp. 94–115; R. C. Stacey, 'King, queen and *edling* in the laws of court', in T. M. Charles-Edwards, M. E. Owen and P. Russell (eds), *The Welsh King and his Court* (Cardiff, 2000), pp. 29–62; D. B. Walters, 'Comparative aspects of the tractates of the laws of court', in T. M. Charles-Edwards, M. E. Owen and P. Russell (eds), *The Welsh King and his Court* (Cardiff, 2000), pp. 382–99.

[44]   On the native Welsh administrative and territorial divisions, see W. Davies, 'Land and power in early medieval Wales', *Past and Present*, 81 (1978), 3–23; B. Howells, 'The distribution of customary acres in south Wales', *NLWJ*, 15(2) (1967–8), 226–33; P. Jenkins, 'Regions and cantrefs in early medieval Glamorgan', *Cambridge Medieval Celtic Studies*, 15 (1988), 31–50; G. R. J. Jones, '"Tir Telych", the Gwestfau of Cynwyl Gaeo and Cwmwd Caeo', *Studia Celtica*, 28 (1994), 81–96; G. R. J. Jones, '*Llys* and *maerdref*', in T. M. Charles-Edwards, M. E. Owen and P. Russell (eds), *The Welsh King and his Court* (Cardiff, 2000), pp. 296–318; G. R. J. Jones, 'The distribution of bond settlements in north-west Wales', *WHR*, 2(1) (1964), 19–36; T. Jones Pierce, 'The *gafael* in Bangor manuscript 1939', *THSC* (1942), 158–88; M. Richards, *Welsh Administrative and Territorial Units* (Cardiff, 1969); E. Rowlands, 'Mesur tir: land measurement', *Studia Celtica*, 14/15 (1979/80), 270–84.

[45]   *Maenor* in the south, possibly reflecting the influence of the English *manor*.

[46]   Rhys and Brynmor-Jones, *Welsh People*, pp. 218–19; Jenkins, *The Law*, pp. 120–1. The mention of summer pasture suggests the practice of transhumance, which is borne out by the names *hendre* and *hafod*, which refer respectively to winter and summer residences: Davies, *Wales*, p. 40. On *hendre* and *hafod*, see also E. Davies, 'Hafod, hafoty and lluest: their distribution, features and purpose', *Ceredigion*, 9(1) (1980), 1–41; E. Davies, 'Hendre and hafod in Caernarvonshire', *CHST*, 40 (1979), 17–46; E. Davies, 'Hendre and hafod in Denbighshire', *DHST*, 26 (1977), 49–72; E. Davies, '*Hendre* and *hafod* in Merioneth', *JMHRS*, 7(1) (1973), 13–27; J. E. Lloyd, '*Hendre* and *hafod*', *BBCS*, 4(3) (1928), 224–5; M. Richards, '*Hafod* and *hafoty* in

Welsh place-names, a semantic study', *Montgomeryshire Collections*, 56 (1959–60), 13–20.

[47] *Cyfn.*, 53–4 (204), gives the acre as being 18 rods (yards) by 2 rods (yards), each rod being 18 feet. This would make the *erw* roughly the equivalent of a quarter of an English acre, making the *tyddyn* roughly the equivalent of an acre. On the Welsh land measurements, see also A. N. Palmer, 'Notes on the ancient Welsh measures of land', *Archaeologica Cambrensis* (5th ser.), 13 (1896), 1–19; A. N. Palmer, *A History of Ancient Tenures of Land in the Marches of North Wales* (Wrexham, 1885; 2nd edn, with E. Owen, 1910); T. Jones Pierce, 'A note on ancient Welsh measurements of land', *Archaeologica Cambrensis*, 97 (1942/3), 195–204.

[48] J. K. Knight, 'Sources for the early history of Morgannwg', in *Glamorgan County History*, vol. 2, pp. 401–2.

[49] Davies, *Wales*, pp. 43–4. See also G. R. J. Jones, 'Post-Roman Wales', in H. P. R. Finberg (ed.), *The Agrarian History of England and Wales*, vol. 1/2 (London, 1972), pp. 283–382; G. R. J. Jones, 'Multiple estates and early settlement', in P. H. Sawyer (ed.), *Medieval Settlement* (London, 1976), pp. 15–40.

[50] Chadwick, *Celts*, p. 110. On the native Welsh tribal and family divisions, see L. Alcock, 'Some reflections on early Welsh society and economy', *WHR*, 2(1) (1964–5), 1–7; A. D. Carr, '*Teulu* and *penteulu*', in T. M. Charles-Edwards, M. E. Owen and P. Russell (eds), *The Welsh King and his Court* (Cardiff, 2000), pp. 63–81; T. M. Charles-Edwards, 'Some Celtic kinship terms', *BBCS*, 24 (1970–2), 105–22; S. Davies, 'The *Teulu*, *c.*633–1283', *WHR*, 21(3) (2003), 413–54; D. Jenkins, 'Y Genedl Alanas yng Nghyfraith Hywel', *BBCS*, 22(3) (1967), 228–36; M. G. Jenkins, 'Rhifo carennydd yng nghyfraith Rhufain, yr Eglwys, a Chymru', *BBCS*, 20(4) (1964), 348–72; G. R. J. Jones, 'The ornaments of a kindred in medieval Gwynedd', *Studia Celtica*, 18/19 (1983/4), 135–46; G. R. J. Jones, 'The tribal system in Wales: a re-assessment in the light of settlement studies', *WHR*, 1(2) (1960–3), 111–32; G. R. L. Jones, 'Medieval Welsh society (review article)', *CHST*, 34 (1973), 30–43; C. McAll, 'The normal paradigms of a woman's life in the Irish and Welsh texts', in D. Jenkins and M. E. Owen (eds), *The Welsh Law of Women* (Cardiff, 1980), pp. 7–22; M. E. Owen, 'Shame and reparation; women's place in the kin', in D. Jenkins and M. E. Owen, *The Welsh Law of Women* (Cardiff, 1980), pp. 40–68; F. Seebohm, 'The historical importance of the Cymric tribal system', *THSC* (1895–6), 1–22.

[51] There are various sources of evidence for this change which will be discussed as they are encountered below.

[52] The sounds *P* and *C* in many languages occur in words with a common root. In Latin, for instance, both *Quintus* and *Pontius* indicated a fifth son.

[53] Ellis, I, 16; *Bleg.*, 79/30.

[54] Ellis, I, 176; *Bleg.*, 108. *Triads*, Q146. It is interesting to note that these occupations are all connected with the ancient tasks of the Druids, but had since separated into several professions and arts. The inclusion of smiths would appear to stem from the ritual, almost religious, significance attached to the making of weapons and possibly also of metal vessels such as cauldrons.

[55] Ellis, I, 163, 190; *Bleg.*, 112/16–20; *Cyfn.*, 127–9 (271–2); *Triads*, X38, Q75.

[56] *Bleg.*, 112/20–3; *Ior.*, 5; *Cyfn.*, 127–9 (271–2); *Triads*, X38, Q75.

[57] Ellis, I, 159.

[58] Rhys and Brynmor-Jones, *Welsh People*, p. 61. This was the rule attributed by the Roman jurists to the *ius gentium*; see Gaius, *Institutes*, 1. 78; Justinian, *Institutes*, 1. 4, pr.

[59] Carr, *Medieval Wales*, p. 94; Ellis, I, 190.

[60] See the famous words of the Roman captain, Claudius Lysias, to St Paul concerning his having bought the privilege: Acts 22:28.

[61] Davies, *Conquest*, pp. 119–20; Ellis, I, 172–3; *Ior.*, 112.

[62] Ellis, I, 165, 168.

[63] Ellis, I, 69–70, 171–2; *Bleg.*, 81/17–30, 111/7–8; *Ior.*, 53, 86; *Col.*, 32.

[64] Ellis, I, 187; *Bleg.*, 87/17–30, 111/7–8; *Ior.*, 53, 86; *Col.*, 32, 601; *Cyfn.*, 62 (211); *Latin E*, 474; *Triads*, Q169.

[65] Chadwick, *Celts*, p. 110. The third was *galanas*, the composition payment for homicide which is discussed below.

[66] Davies, *Conquest*, pp. 116–17.

[67] See *Cyfn.*, 117–18 (259); Ellis, II, 81–2, 85; Ellis, I, 360; *Ior.*, 110. On compensation in the native laws and their relation to other systems, see M. E. Harris, 'Compensation for injury: a point of contact between early Welsh and Germanic law?', in T. G. Watkin (ed.), *The Trial of Dic Penderyn and Other Essays* (Cardiff, 2003), pp. 39–76.

[68] Ellis, I, 363; *Ior.*, 97; *Cyfn.*, 128–9 (272); *Latin A*, 142; *Latin B*, 223.

[69] Rhys and Brynmor-Jones, *Welsh People*, pp. 210–11; Carr, *Medieval Wales*, p. 95; *Bleg.*, 60; *Ior.*, 44; *Col.*, 2, 46; *Cyfn.*, 93–4 (239); *Latin A*, 142–6; *Latin B*, 225–6; *Latin D*, 344; *Latin E*, 474; *Triads*, X9–10, Q119, Q232.

[70] Davies, *Wales*, pp. 156–7. There were famous ecclesiastical dynasties such as that of Sulien of Llanbadarn Fawr and his famous sons, Ieuan and Rhigyfarch, the biographer of St David.

[71] Carr, *Medieval Wales*, p. 95; Davies, *Wales*, p. 72; *Latin A*, 141–2; *Latin B*, 220–5; *Latin D*, 341–4; *Latin E*, 469–74.

[72] Ellis, I, 436–7; *Col.*, 32; *Latin A*, 141–2.

[73] Rhys and Brynmor-Jones, *Welsh People*, pp. 210–11; *Ior.*, 8; *Col.*, 7–19, 45; *Cyfn.*, 132–5 (277); *Latin A*, 146; *Latin C*, 288; *Triads*, Q154, Q183.

[74] See Watkin, *Historical Introduction*, ch. 9.

[75] Ellis, I, 426; *Bleg.*, 79/10.

[76] See further Ellis, I, 430–1, who discusses Giraldus Cambrensis's view of the Welsh laws.

[77] Rhys and Brynmor-Jones, *Welsh People*, pp. 212–14; *Cyfn*, 89–90 (236, 319); Ellis, I, 414, 418–19; *Bleg.*, 60–7; *Ior.*, 45.

[78] Jenkins, *The Law*, p. 132; *Ior.*, 99; *Col.*, 54.

[79] Rhys and Brynmor-Jones, *Welsh People*, pp. 195, 205–6; *Ior.*, 97–8.

[80] Davies, *Wales*, pp. 70–1.

[81] Wade-Evans, *Welsh Medieval Law*, p. 293; Jenkins, *The Law*, pp. 130–1.

[82] Ellis, I, 336, 382–6; *Ior.*, 98/2–9.

[83] *Mancipatio* was a formal ceremony by which property was transferred from one person to another. It is described by Gaius: *Institutes*, 1. 119.

[84] *Cyfn.*, 128–30 (272–3); Ellis, I, 445–51; *Ior.*, 100–3; *Triads*, X40, Q76, Q185–6; Jenkins, *The Law*, pp. 132–7.

[85] Rhys and Brynmor-Jones, *Welsh People*, pp. 193, 396–7. On the native Welsh law relating to land and other property, see R. W. Banks, 'On the ancient tenures and services of the land of the bishop of St David's', *Archaeologica Cambrensis* (5th ser.) 2 (1885), 65–71; C. A. Gresham, 'Gavelkind and the unit system', *Archaeological Journal*, 128 (1971), 174–5; G. R. J. Jones, 'The *gwely* as a tenurial institution', *BBCS*, 30 (1996); D. Jenkins, 'A lawyer looks at Welsh land law', *THSC* (1967), 220–48; 'A second look at Welsh land law', *THSC*, NS 8 (2002), 13–93; 'Property interests in the classical Welsh law of women', in D. Jenkins and M. E. Owen (eds), *The Welsh*

Law of Women (Cardiff, 1980), pp. 69–92; A. N. Palmer, *A History of Ancient Tenures of Land in the Marches of North Wales* (Wrexham, n.d.); A. N. Palmer, *The History of the Ancient Tenures in the Marches of North Wales*, 2nd edn, with E. Owen (1910); D. B. Walters, 'The European legal context of the Welsh law of matrimonial property', in D. Jenkins and M. E. Owen (eds), *The Welsh Law of Women* (Cardiff, 1980), pp. 115–31.

[86] Ellis, I, 61–2; *Bleg.*, 74–8; *Ior.*, 82; *Col.*, 583–9; *Cyfn.*, 49–51 (199–200); *Latin A*, 132–4; *Latin B*, 227–9; *Latin E*, 478–80; *Triads*, X5.

[87] M. Green and R. Howell, *Celtic Wales* (Cardiff, 2000), p. 23.

[88] E. G. Bowen, *Saints, Seaways and Settlements* (Cardiff, 1977), pp. 43–4.

[89] Davies, *Wales*, p. 77.

[90] Rhys and Brynmor-Jones, *Welsh People*, p. 400.

[91] Davies, *Wales*, pp. 41, 74; *Ior.*, 97–8.

[92] For treatment of this issue in a novel, see Bruce Chatwin, *On the Black Hill* (London, 1982).

[93] Carr, *Medieval Wales*, p. 97. *Llan* eventually came to mean a church within an enclosure, that is, a church within a churchyard, but originally meant any enclosure, a usage which survives in composite terms to this day, for example, *perllan* 'an orchard', *corlan* 'a sheepfold', *gwinllan* 'a vineyard'. The Latin redactions translate *llan* as 'church', suggesting that the translator had lost the sense of what he was translating, although one version preserves 'orchard'; *Ior.*, 88; *Col.*, 617; *Latin B*, 231; *Latin C*, 289; *Latin E*, 482; *Triads*, Q188, Q194.

[94] Ellis, I, 330; *Ior.*, 88; *Latin E*, 482.

[95] *Gofyn* means 'to ask' or 'to demand', and the name reflects a connection with the *demandant*, as the plaintiff or claimant was called in the English writ of right, from the French *demander*.

[96] Ellis, I, 253–4.

[97] Ellis, II, 110–11; *Ior.*, 875–11; *Latin B*, 229; *Latin E*, 480–1; *Triads*, X23; Jenkins, *The Law*, pp. 110–11.

[98] Rhys and Brynmor-Jones, *Welsh People*, p. 222.

[99] The oldest rules of inheritance in Roman law gave property to the *gens*, also a wider kinship or tribal group, in the absence of family heirs.

[100] Davies, *Wales*, pp. 128–9; *Ior.*, 89.

[101] It is possible that this rule reflects thirteenth-century concerns regarding alienations to churches and other mortmain corporations similar to those experienced at that time in neighbouring England and elsewhere.

[102] Ellis, I, 208; Jenkins, *The Law*, p. 82; *Ior.*, 71/1–11. This would prevent any dispute thereafter as to whether the land could revert to private ownership.

[103] In the way that in Roman law, property dedicated to the gods was *extra commercium*, but now as property without an earthly owner, under the feudal overlord's protection.

[104] Ellis, I, 194–5; *Ior.*, 71/1–11; *Damweiniau Colan*, 199–201. On the relationship between the Church and the native secular rulers in Wales, see T. P. Ellis, 'The Catholic Church in the Welsh laws', *Y Cymmrodor*, 42 (1931), 1–68.

[105] Ellis, I, 196.

[106] Ellis, II, 261; *Bleg.*, 82/8–16; *Cyfn.*, 55–6 (206).

[107] Ellis, I, 268–9; *Ior.*, 83; *Col.*, 590–2.

[108] Ellis, I, 279; *Bleg.*, 49/20–50/11; *Ior.*, 94, 115; *Cyfn.*, 99–100 (244); *Latin A*, 146–7.

[109] Ellis, I, 390.

[110] Rhys and Brynmor-Jones, *Welsh People*, pp. 208–9; Ellis, I, 389.

[111] Ellis, I, 249–50; cf. *Bleg.*, 32/27–33/3.

[112] Ellis, I, 253; *Ior.*, 64.

[113] Jenkins, *The Law*, pp. 46–7; *Ior.*, 45.

[114] Ellis, II, 34–5; *Ior.*, 45.

[115] Ellis, II, 36.

[116] *Cyfn.*, 140–1 (282), 417–8 (197); *Triads*, U38.

[117] Ellis, I, 215–22.

[118] Ten years if the previous owner were in the same province; twenty years if not. See Justinian, *Codex repetitae praelectionis*, 7. 33. 12. 1; 7. 39. 8, pr; *Novels*, 119. 8.

[119] Jenkins, *The Law*, pp. 111–12. It is also said that a person who abandoned land did not lose title until the ninth generation. This may reflect the time needed for the right to a share in *cyfran* to have passed, the fifth generation, and then three lifetimes. *Cyfn.*, 50–1 (200–1).

[120] Ellis, II, 273.

[121] Davies, *Wales*, pp. 33–4.

[122] Carr, *Medieval Wales*, p. 98; *Cyfn.*, 107–8 (251); Ellis, II, 54–5; Jenkins, *The Law*, pp. 186–7; *Damweiniau Colan*, 233.

[123] See T. G. Watkin, 'Legal cultures in mediaeval Wales', in T. G. Watkin (ed.), *Legal Wales: Its Past; Its Future* (Cardiff, 2001), pp. 21–40; Ellis, II, 53–4. *Cyfn.*, 81 (226), 107–8 (251).

[124] Ellis, II, 52; Jenkins, *The Law*, p. 188; *Bleg.*, 51–2; *Latin A*, 127; *Latin B*, 201–2; *Latin C*, 286–7; *Latin E*, 466–7; *Cyfn.*, 131 (275).

[125] Carr, *Medieval Wales*, p. 98; Davies, *Wales*, pp. 34, 41. The use of honey in making mead features in the Roman jurists' discussion of *specificatio*. See Justinian, *Institutes*, 2. 1. 25.

[126] Ellis, II, 55–6; *Bleg.*, 55/4; *Ior.*, 42; *Cyfn.*, 81 (226); *Latin A*, 149–50; *Latin B*, 242; *Latin E*, 483; *Triads*, Q61, Q205; *Damweiniau Colan*, 22–4; Jenkins, *The Law*, p. 186.

[127] See Justinian, *Institutes*, 2. 1. 39.

[128] Ellis, II, 50; Jenkins, *The Law*, pp. 40–1; *Ior.*, 43.

[129] Ellis, I, 339; *Cyfn.* 114–15 (258); Jenkins, *The Law*, pp. 40–1; *Ior.*, 43.

[130] Ellis, II, 50; *Cyfn.* 113–14 (257); Jenkins, *The Law*, p. 112; *Damweiniau Colan*, 357.

[131] See ch. 1; *Bleg.*, 47/1–6; *Ior.*, 43; *Col.*, 616; *Cyfn.*, 66–7 (213–14); *Latin A*, 135; *Latin B*, 205; *Latin D*, 377.

[132] Ellis, II, 51; *Ior.*, 43.

[133] Ellis, I, 342; Jenkins, *The Law*, pp. 188–90; *Ior.*, 138; *Triads*, Q85.

[134] *Cyfn.*, 61 (210).

[135] Ellis, II, 27–32.; *Latin A*, 124–5; *Latin B*, 258; *Latin D*, 376–7.

[136] Ellis, I, 254; *Ior.*, 113, 124.

[137] *Ior.*, 124; *Col.*, 229; *Cyfn.*, 68–9 (215–16).

[138] Jenkins, *The Law*, p. 174; *Ior.*, 124; *Col.*, 229.

[139] Davies, *Wales*, p. 54.

[140] Ellis, I, 376–7; *Bleg.*, 87–90; *Ior.*, 121–30; *Cyfn.*, 68–82 (215–27); *Latin A*, 152–7; *Latin B*, 232–6; *Latin D*, 358–62; *Latin E*, 484–8.

[141] Rhys and Brynmor-Jones, *Welsh People*, p. 226; Jenkins, *The Law*, p. 64; *Ior.*, 68. See H. Pryce, 'Duw yn lle Mach: Briduw yng Nghyfraith Hywel', in T. M. Charles-Edwards, M. E. Owen and D. B. Walters (eds), *Lawyers and Laymen* (Cardiff, 1986), pp. 47–71.

[142] Rhys and Brynmor-Jones, *Welsh People*, p. 225; Ellis, II, 248; *Ior.*, 69.

[143] See Exodus 22: 26; Deuteronomy 24: 10–17.

[144] Ellis, II, 15; *Ior.*, 64.

[145] Ellis, II, 6.

[145a]T. M. Charles-Edwards and P. Russell, *Tair Colofn y Gyfraith: the Three Columns of Law in Medieval Wales: Homicide, Theft and Fire* (Bangor, 2007).

[146] Rhys and Brynmor-Jones, *Welsh People*, p. 232; Ellis, II, 70–1. The author has elsewhere described this approach to wrongdoing as victim-based in that its point of departure is an undeserved wrong to the victim rather than wrongful conduct on the part of the defendant, the latter approach being a defendant-based analysis of liability.

[147] Ellis, II, 72; *Ior.*, 104–10.

[148] Ellis, II, 93; *Ior.*, 104–10.

[149] Ellis, II, 94–5. There are similarities to English law, where murder, the most heinous form of homicide, was originally a secret killing, and the late fourteenth- century statutory rule that killing by ambush (*agait*), assault or with malice aforethought (*prepense*) was unpardonable. Likewise, in the sixteenth century, killing by the use of poison was deemed unclergyable by statute.

[150] Jenkins, *The Law*, p. 24; *Ior.*, 17.

[151] Ellis, II, 97; *Col.*, 278, 279; *Bleg.*, 33/27–9; *Cyfn.*, 46 (195).

[152] Ellis, II, 94; *Bleg.*, 32/27–33/3.

[153] *Cyfn.*, 114–17 (258), 125–6 (268).

[154] Jenkins, *The Law*, p. 146; *Bleg.*, 30–3; *Ior.*, 104; *Col.*, 242–333, 397; *Cyfn.*, 35–9 (184–7), 253; *Latin A*, 121–2; *Latin B*, 209–11; *Latin D*, 332–3; *Latin E*, 448–51.

[155] See for Roman law, Justinian, *Institutes*, 4. 12. 1; for the Bible, Jeremiah 31: 29–30.

[156] Wade-Evans, *Welsh Medieval Law*, pp. 185–7. In reality, payments were garnered from and distributed amongst four generations of a family as it was very unlikely that a family with great-grandparents living would extend to fifth cousins, or that one with fifth cousins would have surviving great-grandparents. A group of four generations, however constructed, would appear to be the most likely to exist.

[157] Ellis, I, 65; *Bleg.*, 34–6; *Ior.*, 111; *Col.*, 334–411; Jenkins, *The Law*, pp. 156–69.

[158] Ellis, II, 153; *Ior.*, 112; Jenkins, *The Law*, p. 159.

[159] Ellis, II, 154.

[160] Ellis, II, 381.

[161] Jenkins, *The Law*, p. 165; *Ior.*, 115; *Col.*, 395; *Cyfn.*, 104 (248); *Damweiniau Colan*, 443, 444.

[162] Ellis, II, 156.

[163] Ellis, II, 148; Jenkins, *The Law*, p. 166; *Ior.*, 113, 115.

[164] Rhys and Brynmor-Jones, *Welsh People*, pp. 234–6; *Ior.*, 97, 115.

[165] Ibid; *Ior.*, 113, 114; *Col.*, 381–6.

[166] Ellis, II, 148–51; *Ior.*, 112; *Cyfn.*, 40 (189).

[167] Ibid; *Bleg.*, 35/14; *Ior.*, 111; *Col.*, 383, 387–93; *Triads*, Q35.

[168] *Ior.*, 111. No trial was necessary for *lladrad cynharchawl* as guilt was manifest. No death penalty arose where there had been a trial as a conviction based upon evidence was never regarded as being as sure as one based upon capture in the act.

[169] Davies, *Wales*, p. 64.

[170] Ellis, I, 172–3; *Ior.*, 112; *Damweiniau Colan*, 276–8; Jenkins, *The Law*, pp. 166–7.

[171] Jenkins, *The Law*, p. 165; *Ior.*, 115; *Col.*, 388, 392.

[172] Gaius 3. 193: 'res tota ridicula est'.

[173] Ellis, II, 245–6; *Bleg.*, 124; *Latin A*, 145; *Latin B*, 223; *Latin E*, 472.

[174] Ellis, II, 187.

[175] Ellis, II, 173; Jenkins, *The Law*, pp. 143, 156–7, 169; *Ior.*, 104, 111, 116; *Cyfn.*, 111–12 (255).

[176] Ellis, II, 176; Jenkins, *The Law*, pp. 143, 156–7, 169; *Ior.*, 104, 111, 116.

[177] Jenkins, *The Law*, p. 206; *Damweinau Colan*, 173–6.

[178] Jenkins, *The Law*, p. 208; *Ior.*, 158.

[179] Ellis, II, 45; Jenkins, *The Law*, p. 182; Wade-Evans, *Welsh Medieval Law*, 79/19–24; *Bleg.*, 53–4/22; *Cyfn.*, 82–3 (227–8); *Latin A*, 147–8; *Latin E*, 465–6.

[180] Jenkins, *The Law*, p. 187; *Latin A*, 157; *Damweiniau Colan*, 217.

[181] Ellis, I, 367; Jenkins, *The Law*, p. 196; *Bleg.*, 56/10–13; *Ior.*, 146; *Cyfn.*, 41–2 (190); *Latin A*, 137; *Latin B*, 218; *Latin D*, 338; *Latin E*, 462; *Triads*, X75, Q113, Q256.

[182] *Bleg.*, 56/1–18; *Ior.*, 146; *Cyfn.*, 41–2 (190); *Latin A*, 137; *Latin B*, 218–19; *Latin D*, 338; *Latin E*, 461–2.

[183] Jenkins, *The Law*, p. 198; Wade-Evans, *Welsh Medieval Law*, 42/21–5; *Bleg.*, 56/14–18; *Cyfn.*, 42–3 (191); *Latin B*, 218; *Latin E*, 462.

[184] Ellis, I, 369; Jenkins, *The Law*, p. 197; *Bleg.*, 56/19–57/14; *Ior.*, 147; *Cyfn.*, 24–5 (170), 42–3 (191); *Latin A*, 137–8; *Latin B*, 219; *Latin D*, 338–9; *Latin E*, 462–3; *Triads*, U3, K15.

[185] Ellis, II, 185; *Bleg.*, 80–1.

[186] Ellis, II, 184–5.

[187] See Ellis, II, 187.

[188] Ellis, II, 182; *Bleg.*, 78/11–12; *Col.*, 283–4; *Cyfn.*, 52–3 (202); *Triads*, X23.

[189] Ellis, II, 225–7; *Bleg.*, 15–18; 102–5; *Cyfn.*, 15 (159); *Latin A*, 115; *Latin B*, 198–9; *Latin C*, 283; *Latin D*, 324–5; *Triads*, X13, Q8, Q213.

[190] Rhys and Brynmor-Jones, *Welsh People*, pp. 239–40; Jenkins, *The Law*, p. xxxi; *Cyfn.*, 15 (159); Ellis, II, 230, 411.

[191] Ellis, II, 81; Jenkins, *The Law*, p. 17; *Ior.*, 10.

[192] Ellis, II, 229; Jenkins, *The Law*, pp. 141–2; *Damweiniau Colan*, 420; *Bleg.*, 16–17; *Ior.*, 104.

[193] Ellis, II, 210; *Bleg.*, 101.

[194] The Law of Citations was almost certainly meant to be of only temporary effect. It was promulgated in 426, and in 429 a project was undertaken to excerpt both imperial enactments and juristic opinions which were worth preserving. The former only was realized, with the promulgation in 438 of the Theodosian Code. The failure of the latter part of the project left the Law of Citations in force for over a century. See Watkin, *Historical Introduction*, pp. 58–60, and 66, n.9.

[195] In other parts of Europe, the revived Roman law found its way into native systems by supplementing local customs when they proved inadequate.

[196] Ellis, II, 409. It will be recalled that the king's chaplain acted as a scribe to record the decisions of the royal court; *Bleg.*, 101.

[197] Ellis, II, 196; Davies, *Wales*, p. 63.

[198] Davies, *Wales*, p. 138.

[199] *Llyfr Iorwerth*, xxxv.

[200] Jenkins, *The Law*, pp. xi, xv and xxiii.

[201] Ibid., p. xxiv.

[202] Rhys and Brynmor-Jones, *Welsh People*, p. 242. On pleading before the native courts, see T. M. Charles-Edwards, 'Cynghawsedd: counting and pleading in medieval Welsh law', *BBCS*, 33 (1986), 188–98.

[203] Ellis, II, 234; Emanuel, *Latin Texts*, p. 11.

[204] Wade-Evans, *Welsh Medieval Law*, pp. 298–9; Ellis, II, 279–80; *Bleg.*, 73–4; *Col.*, 441–2; *Cyfn.*, 47–8 (197); *Latin D*, 394; *Latin E*, 477.

[205] Ellis, I, 195; II, 198–200. Clerks were not to stand trial in both the secular and the ecclesiastical tribunals for the same wrong: Jenkins, *The Law*, p. 168; *Damweiniau Colan*, 372.

[206] See Ellis, II, 207; *Bleg.*, 98–105.

[207] See Ellis, II, 342–3; *Bleg.*, 98–105; *Cyfn.*, 117–19 (259–60).

[208] See Ellis, II, 411; *Bleg.*, 98–105.

[209] See Ellis, II, 223; *Bleg.*, 98–105.

[210] Rhys and Brynmor-Jones, *Welsh People*, p. 245; T. G. Watkin, 'Saints, Seaways and Dispute Settlements', in W. M. Gordon and T. D. Fergus, *Legal History in the Making* (London and Rio Grande, 1991), pp. 1–9; *Bleg.*, 36–9; *Latin A*, 124; *Latin D*, 348; *Triads*, X76

[211] See Ellis, II, 408.

[212] Ellis, II, 305; Jenkins, *The Law*, p. 68; *Col.*, 89; *Damweiniau Colan*, 325.

[213] It is possible therefore that knowledge of the Welsh customs may throw some light on the origins of the Roman practice by analogy.

[214] Ellis, II, 31; Jenkins, *The Law*, p. 161; *Ior.*, 113; *Col.*, 452–63.

[215] Ellis, II, 382; Jenkins, *The Law*, pp. 161–2; *Ior.*, 113; *Col.*, 378–96.

[216] Ellis, II, 397–400; see Jenkins, *The Law*, pp. 156–69; *Ior.*, 110–15; *Triads*, Q129.

[217] Ellis, II, 289–90; Jenkins, *The Law*, p. 159; *Ior.*, 113; *Bleg.*, 35/15–22; *Cyfn.*, 100–1 (245).

[218] Jenkins, *The Law*, pp. 95–6; *Ior.*, 81; Ellis, II, 317–18, 321, 334–5. *Bleg.*, 37/26–8 attributes the rule to Roman law, but this may be a twelfth-century rationalization. It is more likely to have come into Welsh law as a result of the Church's influence and possibly in the sub-Roman period.

[219] Ellis, II, 361, 383; Jenkins, *The Law*, p. 162; *Ior.*, 98, 114.

[220] *Cyfn.*, 124–5 (267).

[221] Jenkins, *The Law*, p. 164; *Bleg.*, 93, 154.

Chapter 5

[1] For the general history of Wales at this time, see R. R. Davies, *The Age of Conquest: Wales 1063–1415* (Oxford, 1987); R. R. Davies, *The First English Empire: Power and Identities in the British Isles 1093–1343* (Oxford, 2000); R. Turvey, *The Welsh Princes, 1063–1283* (London, 2002); D. Walker, *Medieval Wales* (Cambridge, 1990); J. E. Morris, *The Welsh Wars of Edward I* (Oxford, 1901). For published documents of the period, see the excellent collection in H. Pryce (ed.), *The Acts of Welsh Rulers 1120–1283* (Cardiff, 2005).

[2] For the impact of the Norman invasion, see H. R. Loyn, *The Governance of Anglo-Saxon England 500–1087* (London, 1984); W. L. Warren, *The Governance of Norman and Angevin England 1086–1272* (London, 1987). For a complete overview of the legal development of England at this time, see Sir J. H. Baker, *An Introduction to English Legal History*, 4th edn, (London, 2002).

[3] The Norman *manor*, the English vill or hundred and the ecclesiastical parish were often the same unit looked at from three different perspectives. The manor court and the hundred court often merged and in its merged form became known as the court leet.

[4] See T. G. Watkin, 'Feudal theory, social needs and the rise of the heritable fee', *Cambrian Law Review*, 10 (1979), 39–62.

[5] If the deceased tenant had no sons, the land was partitioned amongst his daughters, but the husband of the eldest became responsible for ensuring the performance of the services.

[6] As tenants became free to provide soldiers to perform the services in their place, the use of champions also becomes sensible.

[7] The word *eyre* is derived from the Latin *iter* meaning 'a journey'.

[8] The Orthodox churches had fallen out of communion with Rome in 1054 ostensibly as a result of the inclusion within the papal liturgy of the *filioque* clause in the Nicene creed which asserts that God the Holy Spirit proceeds from God the Son as well as from God the Father: *qui patre filioque procedit*.

[9] On the history of the March at this time, see G. T. Clarke, 'The Earls, Earldom and Castle of Pembroke', *Archaeologica Cambrensis* (3rd ser.), 5 (1859), 1, 81–91, 188–201, 241–5; 6 (1860), 1, 81–97, 189–95, 254–72; 7 (1861), 185–204; 'The signory of Gower', *Archaeologica Cambrensis* (5th ser.), 10 (1893), 1, 292–308; 11 (1893), 122–30; M. Griffiths, 'Native society on the Anglo-Norman frontier: the evidence of the Margam charters', *WHR*, 14(2) (1988–9), 179–216; M. Howell, 'Regalian right in Wales and the March: the relation of theory to practice', *WHR*, 7(3) (1975), 269–88; J. E. Lloyd, 'Wales and the coming of the Normans, 1039–1093', *THSC* (1899–1900), 122–79; J. Y. W. Lloyd, *The History of the Princes, the Lords Marcher, and the Ancient Nobility of Powys Fadog, and the Ancient Lords of Arwystli, Cedewen and Meirionydd*, 3 vols (London, 1881–2); K. Mann, 'The March of Wales: a question of terminology', *WHR*, 18(1) (1996–7), 1–13; C. O. S. Morgan, 'Some account of the history and descent of the lordship marcher or county of Wentllwch', *Archaeologica Cambrensis* (5th ser.), 2 (1885), 257–70; A. Morris, 'Chepstow Castle and the barony of Striguil', *Archaeologica Cambrensis* (6th ser.), 9 (1909), 407–32; D. H. Owen, 'Tenurial and economic developments in north Wales in the twelfth and thirteenth centuries', *WHR*, 6(2) (1972–3), 117–42; H. Owen, 'The Flemings in Pembrokeshire', *Archaeologica Cambrensis* (5th ser.), 12 (1895), 96–106; D. Crouch, 'The slow death of kingship in Glamorgan, 1067–1159', *Morgannwg*, 29 (1985), 20–41; J. B. Smith, 'The lordship of Glamorgan', *Morgannwg*, 2 (1958), 9–37; D. Walker, 'The lordship of Builth', *Brycheiniog*, 20 (1982/3), 23–33.

[10] Davies, *Conquest*, pp. 39–40; H. D. Emanuel, *The Latin Texts of the Welsh Laws* (Cardiff, 1967), p. 70; J. G. Edwards, 'The Normans and the Welsh March', *Proceedings of the British Academy*, 42 (1956), 155–77; J. G. Edwards, 'The historical study of the Welsh law books', *Transactions of the Royal Historical Society* (5th ser.) 12 (1962), 141–55.

[11] Davies, *Conquest*, pp. 37–9.

[12] Walker, *Medieval Wales*, p. 35.

[13] T. P. Ellis, *Welsh Tribal Law and Custom in the Middle Ages* (Oxford, 1926; Aalen, 1982), I, 339–41.

[14] Ellis, I, 346.

[15] Ellis, I, 338.

[16] Ellis, I, 348.

[17] Ellis, I, 147–9.

[18] D. Jenkins, *Hywel Dda: The Law* (Llandysul, 1986), p. 110; D. Jenkins, *Damweiniau Colan* (Aberystwyth, 1973), 410.

[19] Ellis, II, 309–10.

[20] Davies, *Conquest*, p. 282.

21 Jenkins, *The Law*, p. 52; *Bleg.*, 63/31–2.
22 See T. G. Watkin, 'Legal cultures in mediaeval Wales', in T. G. Watkin (ed.), *Legal Wales: Its Past; Its Future* (Cardiff, 2001), pp. 21–40.
23 Ellis, II, 53–6.
24 Since the Reformation, Gloucester Cathedral.
25 Davies, *Conquest*, pp. 141–2.
26 For instance Swansea. See further Watkin, 'Legal cultures in mediaeval Wales', pp. 21–40; R. W. Banks, 'On the early charters to towns in Wales', *Archaeologica Cambrensis* (4th ser.), 9 (1878), 81–100; C. A. Seyler, 'The early charters of Swansea and Gower', *Archaeologica Cambrensis* (7th ser.), 4 (1924), 59–79, 299–325; 5 (1925), 157–256.
27 W. Davies, *Wales in the Early Middle Ages* (Leicester, 1982), p. 33; *Vita Iltuti*, cc. 8–10.
28 Ellis, I, 401.
29 Ellis, II, 13–14.
30 On the position of the Welsh Church at this time, see J. E. Lloyd, 'Bishop Sulien and his family', *NLWJ*, 2(1) (1941/2), 1–6; J. A. Price, 'The ecclesiastical constitution of Wales on the eve of the Edwardian conquest', *Y Cymmrodor*, 26 (1916), 191–214; H. Pryce, *Native Law and the Church in Medieval Wales* (Oxford, 1993); R. Richards, 'The Cistercian abbeys of Wales', *DHST*, 1 (1952), 1–19; G. Williams, *The Welsh Church from Conquest to Reformation* (Cardiff, 1963).
31 Davies, *Wales*, pp. 126–7.
32 Davies, *Conquest*, p. 325.
33 A. D. Carr, *Medieval Wales* (London, 1995), p. 51; Davies, *Conquest*, pp. 182–3, 185; Ellis, I, 11–12.
34 Davies, *Conquest*, p. 129.
35 Ibid., pp. 264–5.
36 Carr, *Medieval Wales*, p. 51; Walker, *Medieval Wales*, p. 69.
37 Walker, *Medieval Wales*, pp. 14, 71.
38 Ibid., pp. 87–8.
39 Davies, *Conquest*, pp. 127–8.
40 On Giraldus, his career and aspirations for St David's, see J. C. Davies, 'Giraldus Cambrensis 1146–1946', *Archaeologica Cambrensis*, 99 (1946/7), 85–108, 256–80; H. J. Randall, 'Giraldus Cambrensis as a lawyer', *BBCS*, 11(1) (1941), 74; M. Richter, 'Giraldus Cambrensis: the growth of the Welsh nation', *NLWJ*, 16 (1969–70), 193–252; 17 (1971–2), 1–50; M. Richter, 'Professions of obedience and the metropolitan claims of St David's', *NLWJ*, 15(2) (1967–8), 197–214; D. Walker, 'Gerald of Wales: a review of recent work', *JHSCW*, 24 (1974), 13–26; C. H. Williams, 'Giraldus Cambrensis and Wales', *JHSCW*, 1 (1947), 6–14; G. Williams, 'An old man remembers: Gerald the Welshman', *Morgannwg*, 22 (1988), 7–20.
41 Walker, *Medieval Wales*, pp. 72–3. The cause of Winchester in England was in part the result of the disappointment of Bishop Henry of Blois at being passed over for the see of Canterbury in favour of Theobald of Bec. Henry was a grandson of William the Conqueror and the brother of King Stephen, as well as being the papal legate in England. He attempted to gain his archbishopric by having Winchester promoted to metropolitical status, but failed.
42 Walker, *Medieval Wales*, pp. 76–8; Davies, *Conquest*, pp. 190–1.
43 See H. Hughes, 'Giraldus de Barri: an early ambassador for Wales', *Brycheiniog*, 38 (2006), 35–48. Ecclesiastics across Europe had often been connected with royal houses, for instance Henry of Blois in England, but the Norman prelates were more usually independent of the kings they served.

[44] Davies, *Conquest*, p. 145.

[45] Ibid., p. 193.

[46] See F. de Zulueta and P. G. Stein, *The Teaching of Roman Law in England around 1200* (Selden Society supplementary ser., 8; London, 1990).

[47] See T. G. Watkin, *An Historical Introduction to Modern Civil Law* (London, 1999), p. 89.

[48] Davies, *Conquest*, p. 192.

[49] See above, p. 56; *Triads*, Q217.

[50] Davies, *Conquest*, p. 185.

[51] Ibid., p. 194.

[52] Ibid., p. 203.

[53] Ellis, II, 199–200; *Bleg.*, 103–5.

[54] Jenkins, *The Law*, p. 168, *Damweiniau Colan*, 503, 504.

[55] Ellis, I, 196.

[56] Ellis, I, 249.

[57] Emanuel, *Latin Texts*, pp. 67–8.

[58] Ibid., p. 18, commenting on Iorwerth.

[59] Ibid., p. 40.

[60] Ibid., pp. 30–1.

[61] *Ior.*, 1/1.

[62] See *Llyfr Colan*, pp. xxxii–xxxiii.

[63] Emanuel, *Latin Texts*, pp. 92–3; *Domesday Book* (London, 1992, 2002), pp. 493–4.

[64] J. Rhys and D. Brynmor-Jones, *The Welsh People*, 4th edn (London, 1906), p. 30.

[65] Davies, *Conquest*, p. 273.

[66] Ibid., p. 96.

[67] Ibid., pp. 282–7.

[68] For the modern edns, see ch. 4, n.10.

[69] See above, p. 46.

[70] See Davies, *Conquest*, p. 423.

[71] When Richard died in 1199, he was succeeded by his younger brother, John, but some felt that the throne should have gone to Richard's nephew, Arthur, the son of a deceased brother who had been older than John. John was succeeded by his son, Henry III, even though the heir was still an infant, a sure sign that the rules of succession had become accepted and respected. There was no further upset to the rules of primogeniture until the deposition of Richard II in 1399.

[72] See T. G. Watkin, 'The political philosophy of the *Lord King*', in C. W. Brooks and M. Lobban (eds), *Communities and Courts in Britain: 1150–1900* (London and Rio Grande, 1997), pp. 1–12.

[73] K. L. Maund, *The Welsh Kings* (Stroud, 2000), pp. 68, 79, 81; Davies, *Conquest*, p. 27.

[74] Davies, *Conquest*, p. 42.

[75] On the Lord Rhys, see R. Turvey, *The Lord Rhys: Prince of Deheubarth* (Llandysul, 1997); R. K. Turvey, 'King, prince or lord? Rhys ap Gruffydd and the nomenclature of authority in twelfth-century Wales', *Carmarthenshire Antiquary*, 30 (1994), 5–18; P. Bartrum, 'Plant yr Arglwydd Rhys', *NLWJ*, 14(1) (1965–6), 97–104.

[76] Maund, *Welsh Kings*, p. 102; Davies, *Conquest*, p. 51. On Owain Gwynedd, see J. B. Smith, 'Owain Gwynedd', *CHST*, 32 (1971), 8–17.

[77] Davies, *Conquest*, p. 52; Maund, *Welsh Kings*, pp. 102–3, 106; Walker, *Medieval Wales*, p. 47.

[78] Carr, *Medieval Wales*, pp. 45–6; Maund, *Welsh Kings*, pp. 106–7; Davies, *Conquest*, pp. 53–4. *Contra*: Turvey, *The Lord Rhys*.

[79] Carr, *Medieval Wales*, pp. 45–6; Walker, *Medieval Wales*, p. 47.

[80] Maund, *Welsh Kings*, p. 108; Ellis, I, 375; Jenkins, *The Law*, p. 164. The mark is first mentioned in *Llyfr Cyfnerth* at this time: Jenkins, *The Law*, p. 173.

[81] Emanuel, *Latin Texts*, pp. 11–12.

[82] Ibid., pp. 62–4.

[83] *Llyfr Colan*, p. xxv; and see T. Jones-Pierce, *University of Birmingham Historical Journal*, 3 (1950–1), 119, 125.

[84] Emanuel, *Latin Texts*, pp. 62, 72.

[85] Ibid., pp. 11–12; Davies, *Conquest*, p. 221.

[86] Maund, *Welsh Kings*, p. 115; Davies, *Conquest*, p. 291.

[87] By the writs of *aiel*, *besaiel* and *cosinage*, dealing respectively with inheritance from a grandparent, great-grandparent or a collateral relative. These were introduced in 1237.

[88] *Cyfn.*, 53–4 (203–4).

[89] Ellis, I, 259–60; II, 358–61; *Bleg.*, 71/24–73/7; *Ior.*, 84; *Col.*, 566–72; *Cyfn.*, 48–50 (198–9); *Latin A*, 130–1; *Latin B*, 226, 229; *Latin C*, 288–9; *Latin D*, 384–5; *Latin E*, 477; *Triads*, X4, Q222, Q227; Jenkins, *The Law*, pp. 102–3.

[90] Davies, *Conquest*, p. 127.

[91] Cf. Carr, *Medieval Wales*, p. 67.

[92] The Grand Assize was probably introduced by the Assize of Windsor in 1179.

[93] Davies, *Conquest*, p. 95.

[94] See A. D. Carr, 'The last days of Gwynedd', *CHST*, 43 (1982), 7–22.

[95] Maund, *Welsh Kings*, p. 117; Davies, *Conquest*, p. 239; Pryce, *Acts*, 221, pp. 371–4.

[96] Davies, *Conquest*, p. 294; Pryce, *Acts*, 221, pp. 371–4.

[97] On such matrimonial alliances, see E. Byam, 'Matrimonial alliances of the royal family of England with the princes and magnates of Wales', *Archaeologica Cambrensis* (3rd ser.), 14 (1868), 147–51; A. J. Roderick, 'Marriage and politics in Wales, 1066–1282', *WHR*, 4(1) (1968), 1–20. But see also Pryce, *Acts*, 253, pp. 414–16.

[98] See J. E. Lloyd, 'The mother of Gruffydd ap Llywelyn', *BBCS*, 1(4) (1923), 335.

[99] Maund, *Welsh Kings*, pp. 117, 123, 126; Walker, *Medieval Wales*, p. 103; Davies, *Conquest*, p. 239

[100] Davies, *Conquest*, pp. 294–5; Pryce, *Acts*, 233, pp. 386–8.

[101] Davies, *Conquest*, p. 297.

[102] Carr, *Medieval Wales*, p. 57; Maund, *Welsh Kings*, p. 121; Davies, *Conquest*, p. 244.

[103] Maund, *Welsh Kings*, p. 121; Davies, *Conquest*, p. 242–3, 299; Pryce, *Acts*, 241, pp. 398–9.

[104] Emanuel, *Latin Texts*, p. 50.

[105] See 1352 Statute of Treasons in England; also Pryce, *Acts*, 261 and 262, pp. 428–30.

[106] Davies, *Conquest*, pp. 245, 299; Maund, *Welsh Kings*, p. 126.

[107] Davies, *Conquest*, p. 246.

[108] Walker, *Medieval Wales*, pp. 106–7.

[109] *Ior.*, 110; Emanuel, *Latin Texts*, pp. 42–4.

[110] On Dafydd, see R. Maud, 'David, the last prince of Wales: the ten "lost" months of Welsh history', *THSC* (1968), 43–62; M. Richter, 'David ap Llywelyn, the first prince of Wales', *WHR*, 5(3) (1971), 205–19. On the history of Gwynedd generally at this time and the use of the title prince of Wales, see G. A. Williams, 'The succession to Gwynedd, 1238–47', *BBCS*, 20(4) (1964), 393–413; R. Williams, 'Dolforwyn Castle and its lords', *Archaeologica Cambrensis* (6th ser.), 1 (1900), 299–317; J. B. Smith, 'Offra Principis Wallie domino Regi', *BBCS*, 21(4) (1966), 362–7; D. Stephenson, *The Governance of Gwynedd* (Cardiff, 1984).

[111] Maund, *Welsh Kings*, p. 127; Pryce, *Acts*, 291, pp. 457–60.

[112] It illustrates Professor S. F. C. Milsom's view that Henry II was not seeking to interfere with the customs of his lords' courts but to ensure that they were operating properly according to their own customs and principles: see S. F. C. Milsom, *The Legal Framework of English Feudalism* (Cambridge, 1972).

[113] Maund, *Welsh Kings*, pp. 127–8; Davies, *Conquest*, pp. 300–1; Pryce, *Acts*, 300–6, pp. 466–78. The terms of the regrant illustrate the principle that, on doing homage and paying a relief, the tenant is always regranted the land by his lord and a new tenancy created: see T. G. Watkin, '*Quia emptores* and the entail: subinfeudation and the family settlement in thirteenth-century England', *Tijdschrift voor Rechtsgeschiedenis*, 59 (1991), 353–74.

[114] Davies, *Conquest*, pp. 226–7.

[115] Walker, *Medieval Wales*, pp. 106–7; Davies, *Conquest*, p. 253.

[116] Ellis, II, 90; Davies, *Conquest*, p. 127.

[117] Gruffydd was being held hostage in the Tower of London and tried to escape by letting a sheet out of the window and climbing down it. The sheet tore and he fell to his death. On Gruffydd ap Llywelyn, see J. W. James, 'Fresh light on the death of Gruffydd ap Llywelyn', *BBCS*, 22(2) (1967), 168–9; 30 (1 and 2) (1982), 147.

[118] Davies, *Conquest*, pp. 118, 257–8, 325–6; Maund, *Welsh Kings*, pp. 137–8; Maud, 'David, the last prince', 43–62.

[119] Davies, *Conquest*, pp. 257–8.

[120] For the English monarchy's ultimately unsuccessful attempts to insist upon their right as feudal overlord to permit their tenants to alienate, see J. M. W. Bean, *The Decline of English Feudalism* (Manchester, 1968), ch. 2.

[121] Maund, *Welsh Kings*, p. 136; Davies, *Conquest*, pp. 259–60.

[122] Davies, *Conquest*, pp. 259–60.

[123] Ibid., p. 262.

[124] Ibid., p. 263.

[125] Carr, *Medieval Wales*, p. 62; Pryce, *Acts*, 312, pp. 483–5. See also C. W. Lewis, 'The treaty of Woodstock, 1247', *WHR*, 2(1) (1964–5), 37–65.

[126] Maund, *Welsh Kings*, p. 129; Davies, *Conquest*, pp. 303–5.

[127] Davies, *Conquest*, pp. 306–7.

[128] Ibid., pp. 308–9.

[129] Walker, *Medieval Wales*, pp. 113–15.

[130] Ibid., p. 113; Maund, *Welsh Kings*, pp. 130–1.

[131] Maund, *Welsh Kings*, pp. 130–1; Pryce, *Acts*, 331–42, pp. 503–12.

[132] Emanuel, *Latin Texts*, pp. 51–2.

[133] Maund, *Welsh Kings*, p. 132; Walker, *Medieval Wales*, p. 119; Davies, *Conquest*, p. 314; Pryce, *Acts*, 361, pp. 533–6.

[134] Walker, *Medieval Wales*, pp. 120–1; Davies, *Conquest*, pp. 314–5; Maund, *Welsh Kings*, pp. 132–3; Pryce, *Acts*, 363, pp. 536–42.

[135] Walker, *Medieval Wales*, p. 124; Davies, *Conquest*, p. 327.

[136] Davies, *Conquest*, pp. 329–30.

[137] Ibid., pp. 319–20.

[138] Maund, *Welsh Kings*, p. 136.

[139] In 1290, the statute *Quia emptores* was to abolish grants by subinfeudation and require all transfers of the full estate in fee simple to be by substitution for the existing tenant. No new feudal lordships could therefore be created; the feudal ladder could only shrink from then on.

[140] Pryce, *Acts*, 402–5, pp. 589–96; C. A. Gresham, 'The Aberconway Charter: further consideration', *BBCS*, 30 (3 and 4) (1983), 311–47.

[141] Carr, *Medieval Wales*, p. 77; Walker, *Medieval Wales*, pp. 125–7; Maund, *Welsh Kings*, pp. 139–40; Davies, *Conquest*, pp. 335–6.

[142] Maund, *Welsh Kings*, p. 141.

[143] Davies, *Conquest*, p. 340–1.

[144] Maund, *Welsh Kings*, pp. 141, 148; see also D. Stephenson, 'The politics of Powys Wenwynwyn', *Cambridge Medieval Celtic Studies*, 7 (1984), 39–61.

[145] Davies, *Conquest*, pp. 230–9. Powys had become divided as a result of these partitions into Powys Fadog in the north-east and Powys Wenwynwyn in the south-west, each taking its name from a ruler of the area, Madog and Gwenwynwyn respectively.

[146] See A. J. Roderick, 'The dispute between Llywelyn ap Gruffydd and Gruffydd ap Gwenwynwyn (1278–82)', *BBCS*, 8(3) (1936), 248–54.

[147] Carr, *Medieval Wales*, p. 77; Davies, *Conquest*, pp. 344–6, 348; Maund, *Welsh Kings*, pp. 142–3. See also J. E. Lloyd, 'Edward the First's commission of enquiry of 1280–1: an examination of its origin and purpose', *Y Cymmrodor*, 25 (1915), 1–20; 26 (1916), 252. D. Stephenson, 'The Arwystli Case', *Montgomeryshire Collections*, 94 (2006), 1–13.

[148] Emanuel, *Latin Texts*, pp. 78–80. This is also found in the *Cyfnerth* tradition, where the justification of valuing a man's blood at only 24*d* is given as being that the blood of Christ who was true God as well as true man was valued at 30 silver pennies.

[149] J. Black, *A New History of Wales* (Stroud, 2000), p. 61.

[150] On Llywelyn ap Gruffydd, the leading biographical account is the masterpiece, J. B. Smith, *Llywelyn ap Gruffudd Prince of Wales* (Cardiff, 1998). On the prince's reign and death, see also J. E. Lloyd, 'Llywelyn ap Gruffydd and the lordship of Glamorgan', *Archaeologica Cambrensis* (6th ser.), 13 (1913), 56–64; R. R. Davies, 'Llywelyn ap Gruffydd, prince of Wales', *JMHRS*, 9(3) (1981–4), 264–77; J. E. Lloyd, 'The death of Llywelyn ap Gruffydd', *BBCS*, 5(4) (1931), 349–353; Ll. B. Smith, 'Llywelyn ap Gruffydd and the Welsh historical consciousness', *WHR*, 12(1) (1984), 1–28; 'The *gravamina* of the community of Gwynedd against Llywelyn ap Gruffydd', *BBCS*, 31 (1984), 158–76; J. B. Smith, 'Llywelyn ap Gruffydd and the March of Wales', *Brycheiniog*, 20 (1982/3), 9–22; 'Llywelyn ap Gruffydd, Prince of Wales and Lord of Snowdon', *CHST*, 45 (1984), 7–36; D. Stephenson, 'Llywelyn ap Gruffydd and the struggle for the Principality of Wales, 1258–1282', *THSC* (1983), 36–47; A. J. Taylor, 'The death of Llywelyn ap Gruffydd', *BBCS*, 15(3) (1953), 207–9; J. D. H. Thomas, 'Llywelyn y Llyw Olaf', *Brycheiniog*, 2 (1956), 143–52.

Chapter 6

[1] See Ellis, I, 338; *Ior.*, 92.

[2] On the boroughs following the Edwardian Conquest, there is an extensive literature: see B. Evans, 'Grant of privileges to Wrexham, 1380', *BBCS*, 19(1) (1960), 42–6; R. T. Jenkins, 'The Borough of Bala *c*.1350', *BBCS*, 11 (3 and 4) (1944), 167; A. Jones, 'Petitions to King Edward by the burgesses of Flint 1295–1300', *FHSJ*, 9 (1922), 39–43; F. Jones, 'Welsh bonds for keeping the peace, 1283 and 1295', *BBCS*, 13(3)

(1949), 142–4; W. G. Jones, 'The charter of the borough of Criccieth', *BBCS*, 4(3) (1928), 229–31; W. G. Jones, 'The court rolls of the borough of Criccieth', *BBCS*, 2(2) (1923), 149–60; W. G. Jones, 'Documents illustrative of the history of the north Wales boroughs', *BBCS*, 3(2) (1926), 149–52; 4 (3) (1928), 225–8; J. E. Lloyd, 'Edward I and the county of Flint', *FHSJ*, 6 (1916–17), 15–26; D. H. Owen, 'The Englishry of Denbigh: an English colony in medieval Wales', *THSC* (1974 and 1975), 57–76; D. J. M. Peregrine, 'Cardigan's ancient borough', *Ceredigion*, 2 (1952), 117–18; T. Jones-Pierce and J. Griffiths, 'Documents relating to the early history of the borough of Caernarfon', *BBCS*, 9(3) (1938), 236–46; D. Pratt, 'The medieval borough of Holt', *DHST*, 14 (1965), 9–74; W. Rees, 'The charters of the boroughs of Brecon and Llandovery', *BBCS*, 2(3) (1924), 243–61; W. Rees, 'The mediaeval Lordship of Brecon', *THSC* (1915–16), 165–224; W. Rees, *South Wales and the March 1284–1415: A Social and Agrarian Study* (Oxford, 1924); I. J. Saunders, 'The boroughs of Aberystwyth and Cardigan in the early fourteenth century', *BBCS*, 15(4) (1954), 282–92; I. J. Saunders, 'Trade and industry in some Cardiganshire towns in the Middle Ages', *Ceredigion*, 3(4) (1959), 319–36; I. J. Saunders, 'The borough of Lampeter in the early fourteenth century', *Ceredigion*, 4(2) (1961), 136–145; A. J. Taylor, 'The earliest burgesses of Flint and Rhuddlan', *FHSJ*, 27 (1975–6), 152–9; H. Taylor, 'The first Welsh municipal charters', *Archaeologica Cambrensis* (5th ser.), 9 (1892), 102–19; H. Taylor, 'The lords of Mold', *FHSJ*, 6 (1916–17), 37–62; G. Usher, 'The foundation of an Edwardian borough: the Beaumaris charter, 1296', *AAST* (1967), 1–16.

3   On the genesis of the statute, see Ll. B. Smith, 'The Statute of Wales, 1284', *WHR*, 10(2) (1980–1), 127–54; W. H. Waters, 'The first draft of the Statute of Rhuddlan', *BBCS*, 4(4) (1929), 345–8; P. A. Brand, 'An English legal historian looks at the Statute of Wales', in T. G. Watkin (ed.), *Y Cyfraniad Cymreig* (Bangor, 2005), pp. 20–56.

4   Statute of Rhuddlan, c. 1; I. Bowen, *The Statutes of Wales* (London and Leipzig, 1908), pp. 2–3. Justinian's directions to the Digest commissioners are recorded in his *constitutio Deo auctore*, which is published with the Digest.

5   Statute of Wales, cc. 12 and 13, I. Bowen, *Statutes*, pp. 24–6. See D. Walker, *Medieval Wales* (Cambridge, 1990), p. 143; R. R. Davies, *The Age of Conquest: Wales 1063–1415* (Oxford, 1987), pp. 367–70; T. P. Ellis, *Welsh Tribal Law and Custom in the Middle Ages* (Oxford, 1926; Aalen, 1982) I, 390–1, 452.

6   Statute of Wales, c. 14, Bowen, *Statutes*, pp. 26–7. See Davies, *Conquest*, pp. 367–8.

7   On the government of the Principality during this period, see R. A. Griffiths, *The Principality of Wales in the Later Middle Ages: The Structure and Personnel of Government, vol. 1, South Wales 1277–1536* (Cardiff, 1972).

8   On the shiring of the south, see J. Goronwy Edwards, 'The early history of the counties of Carmarthen and Cardigan', *English Historical Review*, 31 (1916), 90–8.

9   Davies, *Conquest*, pp. 364–5.

10 Statute of Rhuddlan, cc. 2–5; Bowen, *Statutes*, pp. 3–9. See A. D. Carr, *Medieval Wales* (London, 1995), pp. 83–4; Davies, *Conquest*, pp. 364–5; G. Williams, *Recovery, Reorientation and Reformation: Wales c.1415–1642* (Oxford, 1987), republished as *Renewal and Reformation: Wales c.1415–1642* (Oxford, 1993), pp. 32–3.

11 Williams, *Renewal*, pp. 32–3.

12 Ibid., pp. 32–3.

13 See Ellis, II, 136.

14 Statute of Rhuddlan, c. 6; Bowen, *Statutes*, pp. 9–15; Walker, *Medieval Wales*, p. 142.

[15] See below, ch 7.
[16] Statute of Rhuddlan, c. 6.
[17] Davies, *Conquest*, pp. 369–70.
[18] Statute of Rhuddlan, c. 11, Bowen, *Statutes*, p. 23.
[19] Statute of Rhuddlan, c. 14, Bowen, *Statutes*, pp. 26–7.
[20] On the legal position in the March, see R. R. Davies, 'The law of the March', *WHR*, 5(1) (1970), 1–30; C. Hopkinson and M. Speight, *The Mortimers: Lords of the March* (Logaston, 2002); H. Owen, 'English law in Wales and the Marches', *Y Cymmrodor*, 14 (1901), 1–41; D. Pratt, 'A local border dispute, 1277–1447', *FHSP*, 21 (1964), 46–55; W. R. B. Robinson, 'The Marcher lords of Wales 1525–31', *BBCS*, 26 (3)(1975), 342–52.
[21] Davies, *Conquest*, pp. 369–70.
[22] Williams, *Renewal*, pp. 36–8.
[23] A *vifgage*, a live gage, is one where money is borrowed on the security of land, the legal title to the land being transferred to the lender by the borrower. The money must be repaid before the land is redeemed, and while the repayment is outstanding, the lender keeps the profits of the land as his interest on the loan. A dead gage, a *mortgage*, on the other hand, requires the payment of interest in addition to the lender keeping the profits.
[24] See Ellis, I, 196.
[25] Williams, *Renewal*, pp. 36–8.
[26] Ellis, I, 400–1.
[27] Ibid.
[28] Davies, *Conquest*, p. 37.
[29] Ibid., p. 392.
[30] Ellis, I, 207.
[31] Davies, *Conquest*, pp. 379–80.
[32] Carr, *Medieval Wales*, p. 97.
[33] According to *Annales Monastici*, 3, 338; 4, 310; see J. B. Smith, 'The Origins of the Revolt of Rhys ap Maredudd', *BBCS*, 21 (1964–6), 151–63 at 163; Davies, *Conquest*, pp. 380–1.
[34] Davies, *Conquest*, p. 385.
[35] Ibid., p. 392.
[36] Ibid., p. 376.
[37] J. Black, *A New History of Wales* (Stroud, 2000), p. 89.
[38] Williams, *Renewal*, p. 145.
[39] Davies, *Conquest*, pp. 424, 448; Williams, *Renewal*, p. 145. On the education of the Welsh generally at this time, see L. S. Knight, 'Welsh cathedral schools to 1600 A.D.', *Y Cymmrodor*, 29 (1919), 76–109; L. S. Knight, 'Welsh schools from AD 1000 to AD 1610', *Archaeologica Cambrensis* (6th ser.), 19 (1919), 1–18, 276–91, 515–25; R. W. Hays, 'Welsh students at Oxford and Cambridge universities in the Middle Ages', *WHR*, 4(4) (1969), 325–65; G. Usher, 'Welsh students at Oxford in the Middle Ages', *BBCS*, 16(3) (1955), 193–8.
[40] Carr, *Medieval Wales*, pp. 83–4.
[41] The use of *cwyn*, complaint, is particularly interesting as it mirrors the opening words of the writ *Questus est nobis* . . . 'It has been complained to us . . .'.
[42] Davies, *Conquest*, pp. 422–4.
[43] Walker, *Medieval Wales*, pp. 160–1.
[44] Ibid., p. 149. On the *prid*, see also Ll. B. Smith, '*Tir Prid*: deeds of gage of land in late medieval Wales', *BBCS*, 27(2) (1977), 263–77.

45 Davies, *Conquest*, pp. 400–1.
46 Ibid., pp. 432–3. On the changes to family landholding in Wales at this time, see M. H. Brown, 'Kinship, land and law in fourteenth-century Wales: the kindred of Iorwerth ap Cadwgan', *WHR*, 17(4) (1994–5), 493–519; E. A. Lewis, 'The decay of tribalism in north Wales', *THSC* (1902–3) 1–75.
47 Davies, *Conquest*, pp. 427–8.
48 Walker, *Medieval Wales*, p. 168.
49 Davies, *Conquest*, p. 146.
50 Ibid., p. 427; Williams, *Renewal*, p. 80.
51 Davies, *Conquest*, pp. 431–2.
52 Carr, *Medieval Wales*, p. 97; Davies, *Conquest*, pp. 428–9, 431–2.
53 Two ordinances were issued: one for the south and west, the other for the north. Bowen, *Statutes*, pp. 27–9.
54 28 Ed. 3, c. 2; Bowen, *Statutes*, pp. 30–1.
55 Williams, *Renewal*, pp. 41–3; Davies, *Conquest*, p. 402. On the legal position of Wales and the March generally in the period between the Edwardian Conquest and the Tudor union, see R. R. Davies, 'The survival of the blood-feud in medieval Wales', *History*, 54 (1969), 338–57; R. R. Davies, 'The twilight of Welsh law', *History*, 51 (1966), 143– 64; R. R. Davies, 'Buchedd a moes y Cymry', *WHR*, 12 (1984), 155–74; R. R. Davies, 'The administration of law in medieval Wales: the role of the Ynad Cwmwd', in T. M. Charles-Edwards, M. E. Owen and D. B. Walters (eds), *Lawyers and Laymen* (Cardiff, 1986), pp. 258–73; R. R. Davies, 'The status of women and the practice of marriage in late-medieval Wales', in D. Jenkins and M. E. Owen (eds), *The Welsh Law of Women* (Cardiff, 1980), pp. 93–114; C. James, 'Tradition and innovation in some later medieval Welsh lawbooks', *BBCS*, 40 (1993), 148–56; D. Jenkins, 'Law and government in Wales before the Act of Union', in D. Jenkins (ed.), *Celtic Law Papers Introductory to Welsh Medieval Law and Government* (Brussels, 1973), pp. 23–48; T. A. Jones, 'Owen Tudor's marriage', *BBCS*, 11(2) (1943), 102–9; C. McNall, 'The commote and county courts of Wales, 1277–1350', in T. G. Watkin (ed.), *Legal Wales: Its Past; its Future* (Cardiff, 2001), pp. 1–20; T. Jones-Pierce, 'The law of Wales – the last phase', *THSC* (1963), 7–32; A. C. Reeves, 'The great sessions in the lordship of Newport in 1503', *BBCS*, 26(3) (1975), 323–41; Ll. B. Smith, '"Cannwyll disbwyll a dosbarth": gwŷr cyfraith Ceredigion yn yr oesoedd canol diweddar', *Ceredigion*, 10(3) (1986), 229–53
56 Carr, *Medieval Wales*, p. 113.
57 Walker, *Medieval Wales*, p. 175.
58 Carr, *Medieval Wales*, pp. 114–15.
59 The legal scholars of this age, the Commentators, are often said to have taken the learned laws out of the classroom and into the courtroom.
60 Walker, *Medieval Wales*, pp. 114–15; Davies, *Conquest*, p. 464. On Wales and the Schism, see J. R. Gabriel, 'Wales and the Avignon papacy', *Archaeologica Cambrensis* (7th ser.), 3 (1923), 70–86; A. O. H. Jarman, 'Wales and the Council of Constance', *BBCS*, 14 (1951), 220–2.
61 2 Hen. 4, cc. 12 and 20; Bowen, *Statutes*, pp. 31, 33–4; Davies, *Conquest*, pp. 443, 458–9; Walker, *Medieval Wales*, p. 170.
62 2 Hen. 4, c. 12; Bowen, *Statutes*, p. 31; Davies, *Conquest*, pp. 443, 458–9; Walker, *Medieval Wales*, p. 170.
63 2 Hen. 4, c. 19; Bowen, *Statutes*, p. 33; Davies, *Conquest*, pp. 458–9.
64 2 Hen. 4, c. 27, 28, 29; Bowen, *Statutes*, pp. 34–5; Davies, *Conquest*, pp. 458–9.

[65] 2 Hen. 4, c. 31, 33; Bowen, *Statutes*, pp. 35–6; Davies, *Conquest*, pp. 458–9.

[66] 2 Hen. 4, c. 32; Bowen, *Statutes*, p. 36.

[67] 2 Hen. 4, c. 34; Bowen, *Statutes*, p. 36; Davies, *Conquest*, pp. 458–9. See also H. Thomas, *A History of Wales*, 1485–1660 (Cardiff, 1972), pp. 9–10; Williams, *Renewal*, pp. 10–11.

[68] 2 Hen. 4, c. 16; Bowen, *Statutes*, pp. 31–2.

[69] Williams, *Renewal*, p. 11.

[70] Ibid., pp. 13–14.

[71] G. Owen, *Description of Pembrokeshire*, 3 vols (London, 1906), pp. 35–6, cited in Williams, *Renewal*, pp. 13–14. On the Glyn Dŵr rebellion and its effects, see generally R. R. Davies, 'Race relations in post-conquest Wales: confrontation and compromise', *THSC* (1974 and 1975), 32–56; R. R. Davies, *The Revolt of Owain Glyn Dŵr* (Oxford, 1995); R. R. Davies, 'Owain Glyn Dŵr and the Welsh squirearchy', *THSC* (1968), 150; J. E. Lloyd, 'Trouble in Wales about 1410', *BBCS*, 5(2) (1930), 155–6; J. E. Lloyd, 'Owain Glyn Dŵr: his family and early history', *THSC* (1918–19), 128–45; J. Cule, 'A note on Hugo Glyn and the statute banning Welshmen from Gonville and Caius College', *NLWJ*, 16(2) (1969–70), 185–91.

[72] Davies, *Conquest*, p. 457; Williams, *Renewal*, p. 30.

[73] Williams, *Renewal*, p. 81.

[74] Davies, *Conquest*, p. 456; Williams, *Renewal*, p. 165.

[75] By virtue of the Statute of Uses and Mortmain 1391, by which Richard II extended the provisions of Edward I's 1279 Statute of Mortmain to gifts to the use of mortmain corporations as well as directly to the corporations themselves.

[76] Williams, *Renewal*, p. 66.

[77] Ibid., p. 74. On the Cistercians in Wales, see E. G. Bowen, 'The monastic economy of the Cistercians at Strata Florida', *Ceredigion*, 1 (1950–1), 34–7; D. H. Williams, 'The Cistercians in Wales: some aspects of their economy', *Archaeologica Cambrensis*, 114 (1965), 2–47; D. H. Williams, *The Welsh Cistercians: Aspects of their Economic Activity* (Pontypool, 1969).

[78] Williams, *Renewal*, pp. 11, 167 and 171.

[79] Ibid., p. 94.

[80] Ibid., p. 44.

[81] Ibid., p. 193.

[82] Carr, *Medieval Wales*, pp. 119–20.

[83] Davies, *Conquest*, pp. 457–8.

[84] Carr, *Medieval Wales*, pp. 119–20; Walker, *Medieval Wales*, p. 181.

[85] Thomas, *History*, p. 11.

[86] Williams, *Renewal*, p. 47.

[87] Thomas, *History*, p. 11; Williams, *Renewal*, p. 175.

[88] On the Council, see D. Lewis, 'The court of the President and Council of Wales and the Marches from 1478 to 1575', *Y Cymmrodor*, 12 (1897), 1–64; D. E. Lowe, 'The council of the prince of Wales and the decline of the Herbert family during the second reign of Edward IV (1471–1483)', *BBCS*, 27(2) (1977), 278–97.

[89] Carr, *Medieval Wales*, p. 128; Williams, *Renewal*, p. 52.

[90] J. Rhys and D. Brynmor-Jones, *The Welsh People*, 4th edn (London, 1906), p. 363.

[91] Williams, *Renewal*, p. 52.

[92] Ibid., pp. 54–5.

[93] Rhys and Brynmor-Jones, *Welsh People*, p. 363; Thomas, *History*, pp. 25–6; Williams, *Renewal*, pp. 53–4.

[94] Rhys and Brynmor-Jones, *Welsh People*, p. 363. Sir Edward Coke, *Institutes of the Laws of England* (London, 1817; repr. 1985), iv, c. 48; Lewis, 'The Court of the President of the Council of Wales and the Marches', 1–64; D. Lleufer Thomas, 'Further notes on the Court of the Marches', *Y Cymmrodor*, 13 (1899), 97–163.

[95] J. G. Jones, *Early Modern Wales: c. 1525–1640* (London, 1994), pp. 50, 180.

[96] Williams, *Renewal*, pp. 54–5.

[97] Ibid., pp. 235, 239, 241, 242–3.

[98] Carr, *Medieval Wales*, p. 129.

[99] Thomas, *History*, p. 27; Williams, *Renewal*, pp. 242–3.

[100] See Thomas Frowyk, 'Reading on *Prerogativa Regis* c. 13', in J. H. Baker, *Spelman's Reading on Quo Warranto* (Selden Society, 113; London, 1997), pp. 36–40 at 38, discussed in T. G. Watkin, 'Legal cultures in mediaeval Wales', in T. G. Watkin (ed.), *Legal Wales: Its Past; Its Future* (Cardiff, 2001), pp. 21–40. On the Tudor policy towards Wales before the union, see R. Robinson, 'Early Tudor policy towards Wales', *BBCS*, 20(4) (1964), 421–38; 21(1) (1964), 43–72; 21(4) (1966), 334–61; J. B. Smith, 'Crown and community in the principality of north Wales in the reign of Henry Tudor', *WHR*, 3(2) (1966–7), 145–71.

[101] Thomas, *History*, pp. 34–35.

[102] Williams, *Renewal*, pp. 253–4.

[103] Many of these practices were anathema to the Welsh themselves, for instance the civilian William Aubrey savagely criticized the custom of demanding *commortha*.

[104] Williams, *Renewal*, pp. 259–60; Thomas, *History*, pp. 42–3.

Chapter 7

[1] 'This realm of England is an Empire' state the opening words of the preamble to the Statute of Appeals, 1533.

[2] J. G. Jones, *Early Modern Wales: c. 1525–1640* (London, 1994), p. 54.

[3] Ibid., p. 76. One tradition has a similar petition coming from Sir Richard Herbert.

[4] H. Thomas, *A History of Wales, 1485–1660* (Cardiff, 1972), p. 46.

[5] See Sir John Baker, *The Oxford History of the Laws of England, Volume VI: 1483–1558* (Oxford, 2003), pp. 653–86.

[6] Jones, *Early Modern Wales*, p. 54; Thomas, *History*, pp. 41–2.

[7] Thomas, *History*, p. 27.

[8] An Act for Re-continuing Liberties in the Crown, 27 Henry 8, c. 24, ss. 1, 2, 3, 18; I. Bowen, *The Statutes of Wales* (London and Leipzig, 1908), pp. 73–5. See G. Williams, *Renewal and Reformation: Wales c.1415–1642* (Oxford, 1987), pp. 263–4. On the union and its effects, see generally: D. Jenkins, 'The date of the "Act of Union"', *BBCS*, 23(4) (1970), 345–6; E. A. Lewis, 'Three legal tracts concerning the court leet in Wales after the Act of Union', *BBCS*, 9(4) (1939), 345–56; J. E. Lloyd, 'The date of the Act of Union of England and Wales', *BBCS*, 7(2) (1934), 192; T. O. Morgan, 'Wales and its Marches, and the counties formed out of or augmented thereby', *Archaeologica Cambrensis* (3rd ser.), 3 (1857), 81–95; W. Rees, 'The union of England and Wales', *THSC* (1937), 27–100; P. R. Roberts, 'The "Act of Union" in Welsh history', *THSC* (1972–3), 49–72; P. R. Roberts, 'The "Henry VIII Clause": delegated legislation and the Tudor Principality of Wales', in T. G. Watkin (ed.), *Legal Record*

and Historical Reality (London and Ronceverte, 1989), pp. 37–50; P. R. Roberts, 'Tudor legislation and the political status of "the British Tongue"', in G. H. Jenkins (ed.), *The Welsh Language before the Industrial Revolution* (Cardiff, 1997), pp. 123–52; W. R. B. Robinson, 'The establishment of royal customs in Glamorgan and Monmouthshire under Elizabeth', *BBCS*, 23(4) (1970), 347–96; T. F. Tout, 'The Welsh shires: a study in constitutional history', *Y Cymmrodor*, 9 (1888), 201–26; P. Williams, 'The Welsh borderland under Queen Elizabeth', *WHR*, 1(1) (1960), 19–36; W. Williams, 'The Union of England and Wales', *THSC* (1907–8), 47–117; W. O. Williams, 'The social order in Tudor Wales', *THSC* (1967), 167–78.

9 Jones, *Early Modern Wales*, pp. 81–2.
10 Williams, *Renewal*, p. 273.
11 Jones, *Early Modern Wales*, p. 176.
12 Williams, *Renewal*, p. 270.
13 Ibid., p. 335. On the parliamentary representation of Wales at Westminster in the century and a half following the union, see A. H. Dodd, 'Wales's parliamentary apprenticeship (1536–1625)', *THSC* (1942), 8–72; P. S. Edwards, 'The parliamentary representation of the Welsh boroughs in the mid-sixteenth century', *BBCS*, 27(3) (1977), 425–39; E. G. Jones, 'County politics and electioneering 1558–1625', *CHST*, 1 (1939), 37–46.
14 Jones, *Early Modern Wales*, p. 176.
15 Thomas, *History*, p. 75.
16 Ibid., p. 78.
17 Williams, *Renewal*, p. 269.
18 Ibid., p. 271.
19 Ibid., p. 344.
20 Thomas, *History*, p. 50.
21 Ibid., p. 51; Williams, *Renewal*, p. 271.
22 Thomas, *History*, p. 50.
23 Jones, *Early Modern Wales*, pp. 81–2.
24 Williams, *Renewal*, p. 273.
25 Jones, *Early Modern Wales*, pp. 81–2.
26 Thomas, *History*, p. 51.
27 Ibid., p. 62.
28 Williams, *Renewal*, pp. 339–40; Thomas, *History*, p. 62.
29 Williams, *Renewal*, pp. 339–40.
30 Ibid., p. 275.
31 Thomas, *History*, p. 63; Williams, *Renewal*, p. 340.
32 Thomas, *History*, p. 63
33 Jones, *Early Modern Wales*, p. 77.
34 In 1573–4, out of 24 JPs in Pembrokeshire, only 9 were resident, with only 17 out of 29 and 8 out of 23 being resident in Carmarthenshire and Cardiganshire respectively. Jones, *Early Modern Wales*, p. 113; Thomas, *History*, p. 50; Williams, *Renewal*, pp. 270–1, 345–6. On the Welsh magistracy generally after the union, see G. E. Jones, 'Local administration and justice in sixteenth century Glamorgan', *Morgannwg*, 9 (1965), 11–37; J. G. Jones, 'Reflections on concepts of nobility in Glamorgan, *ca.*1540–1640', *Morgannwg*, 25 (1981), 11–42; J. G. Jones, 'The Welsh language in local government: justices of the peace and the courts of quarter sessions *c.*1536–1800', in G. H. Jenkins (ed.), *The Welsh Language before the Industrial Revolution* (Cardiff, 1997), pp. 181–206.

[35] Thomas, *History*, pp. 63–4; Williams, *Renewal*, pp. 270–1, 341.

[36] Williams, *Renewal*, p. 341.

[37] Thomas, *History*, pp. 51, 63–4; Williams, *Renewal*, p. 341.

[38] Williams, *Renewal*, pp. 268–9, 341.

[39] Ibid., p. 341.

[40] Ibid., pp. 341–2.

[41] Ibid., p. 396.

[42] Thomas, *History*, pp. 41–2.

[43] Jones, *Early Modern Wales*, pp. 81–2; Thomas, *History*, p. 51; Williams, *Renewal*, pp. 270–1, 336.

[44] Jones, *Early Modern Wales*, pp. 125–6; Williams, *Renewal*, pp. 338–9.

[45] Thomas, *History*, pp. 59–60.

[46] Williams, *Renewal*, pp. 336–7.

[47] Jones, *Early Modern Wales*, p. 180.

[48] Williams, *Renewal*, pp. 336–7. This may perhaps reflect the south Wales tradition of landowners acting as judges in the native Welsh courts.

[49] Thomas, *History*, p. 59; Williams, *Renewal*, pp. 336–7. The principal text on the legal history of England at this time is now Sir John Baker, *The Oxford History of the Laws of England, vol. 6, 1483–1558* (Oxford, 2003). On the role of the Council and of Star Chamber in Wales, see C. S. L. Davies, 'Wales and Star Chamber: a note', *WHR*, 5(1) (1970), 71; H. A. Lloyd, 'Wales and Star Chamber: a rejoinder', *WHR*, 5(3) (1971), 257–60; C. A. J. Skeel, *The Council in the Marches of Wales: A Study in Local Government during the Sixteenth and Seventeenth Centuries* (London, 1904); D. Ll. Thomas, 'Further notes on the Court of the Marches', *Y Cymmrodor*, 13 (1899), 97–163; P. Williams, *The Council in the Marches of Wales under Elizabeth I* (Cardiff, 1958); P. H. Williams, 'The Star Chamber and the Council of the Marches in Wales 1558–1603', *BBCS*, 16(4) (1956), 287–97.

[50] Statute 31 Edward III, c. 12.

[51] Statute 27 Eliz. I, c. 8.

[52] Thomas, *History*, p. 59.

[53] Williams, *Renewal*, p. 337.

[54] Thomas, *History*, p. 59; Williams, *Renewal*, pp. 336–7.

[55] Williams, *Renewal*, p. 445. Generally, Jones, *Early Modern Wales*, pp. 81–2; Thomas, *History*, p. 63; Williams, *Renewal*, pp. 334, 457. On the effects of the union upon the Welsh language and the change wrought by the Elizabethan policy, see W. O. Williams, 'The survival of the Welsh language after the Union of England and Wales', *WHR*, 2(1) (1964), 67–93.

[56] Williams, *Renewal*, p. 457.

[57] Ibid., pp. 297, 457.

[58] Thomas, *History*, pp. 95–6, 139–40; Williams, *Renewal*, p. 297.

[59] Thomas, *History*, pp. 95–6.

[60] Jones, *Early Modern Wales*, p. 151; J. G. Jones, 'Thomas Davies and William Hughes: two reformation bishops of St Asaph', *BBCS*, 39 (1980–2), 320–5.

[61] Williams, *Renewal*, p. 314. On Salesbury, see also G. Williams, 'The achievement of William Salesbury', *DHST*, 14 (1965), 75–96.

[62] On William Morgan's difficulties with his parishioners, see I. ap O. Edwards, 'William Morgan's quarrell with his parishioners at Llanrhaeadr ym Mochnant', *BBCS*, 3 (1927), 298–339; N. M. W. Powell, 'Dr William Morgan and his parishioners at Llanrhaeadr ym Mochnant', *CHST*, 49 (1988), 87–116.

[63] Williams, *Renewal*, p. 320.

[64] Ibid., pp. 327–8, 330.

[65] Jones, *Early Modern Wales*, p. 131–2.

[66] Thomas, *History*, pp. 90–1. It is interesting to note that such land was acquired by an initial lease followed by a later release of the freehold reversion. The technique of transferring the freehold in two stages, by lease and release, was to become an important conveyancing device during the second half of the sixteenth century as a means of avoiding the publicity required for transfers of freehold land. See A. W. B. Simpson, *A History of the Land Law*, 2nd edn (Oxford, 1986), pp. 188–90; Sir J. H. Baker, *Introduction to English Legal History*, 4th edn (London, 2002), pp. 305–6.

[67] Williams, *Renewal*, p. 392.

[68] On the disposal of the monastic lands, see A. Jones, 'The estates of the Welsh abbeys at the dissolution', *Archaeologica Cambrensis*, 92 (1937), 269–86; A. Jones, 'The property of the Welsh friars at the dissolution', *Archaeologica Cambrensis*, 91 (1936), 30–50; G. Williams, 'The dissolution of the monasteries in Glamorgan', *WHR*, 3(1) (1966), 23–43; G. Williams, 'The Elizabethan settlement of religion in Wales and the Marches 1559–60', *JHSCW*, 2 (1950), 61–71.

[69] Jones, *Early Modern Wales*, p. 135.

[70] Ibid., pp. 139–40; Williams, *Renewal*, p. 392.

[71] Jones, *Early Modern Wales*, p. 146.

[72] Williams, *Renewal*, p. 390.

[73] Ibid., p. 388.

[74] 27 Henry 8, c. 26, s. 35; Bowen, *Statutes*, p. 92.

[75] 34 and 35 Henry 8, c. 26 s. 91; Bowen, *Statutes*, p. 122.

[76] Thomas, *History*, p. 54.

[77] Williams, *Renewal*, p. 388.

[78] Ibid., p. 384.

[79] Jones, *Early Modern Wales*, p. 102.

[80] Rhys and Brynmor-Jones, *Welsh People*, pp. 409–11. See also S. L. Adams, 'The composition of 1564 and the Earl of Leicester's tenurial reformation in the lordship of Denbigh', *BBCS*, 26 (1974–6), 479–511.

[81] Williams, *Renewal*, pp. 384, 386–7.

[82] Thomas, *History*, pp. 72–3.

[83] Williams, *Renewal*, p. 399.

[84] Thomas, *History*, pp. 23–4, 108. On the education of Welshmen at this time, see 'Montgomeryshire men who matriculated at Oxford University, 1571–1622', *Montgomeryshire Collections*, 25 (1891), 81–4; Croesor (R. Owen), 'Admission of Anglesey natives to Gray's Inn 1521–1889', *AAST* (1933), 123–5; 'Montgomeryshire extracts from the register of admissions to Gray's Inn, 1521–1889', *Montgomeryshire Collections*, 61 (1969–70), 164–6; W. Griffith, 'Jesus College, Oxford and Wales: the first half-century', *THSC* (1996), 21–44; R. B. Jones, '"All the Welshmen abiding and studying in Oxford"', *THSC* (1986), 157–72; L. S. Knight, 'The origin of the Welsh grammar school', *Y Cymmrodor*, 31 (1921), 81–111.

[85] Jones, *Early Modern Wales*, pp. 27–8; Williams, *Renewal*, p. 434. On the Welsh civilians, see B. P. Levack, *The Civil Lawyers in England 1603–1641: A Political Study* (Oxford, 1973); G. D. Squibb, *Doctors' Commons: A History of the College of Advocates and Doctors of Law* (Oxford, 1977); T. G. Watkin, 'Cyfreithwyr Cymru Oes y Dadeni', in T. G. Watkin (ed.), *Y Cyfraniad Cymreig* (Bangor, 2005), pp. 57–72; T. G. Watkin, 'The Welsh civilians', in T. G. Watkin (ed.), *Y Cyfraniad Cymreig* (Bangor, 2005), pp. 73–9.

[86] Entries for all of whom will be found in the *New Oxford Dictionary of National Biography* (Oxford, 2004).

[87] Williams, *Renewal*, p. 462.

[88] Ibid., p. 412.

[89] Ibid., p. 431.

[90] Jones, *Early Modern Wales*, pp. 108–9.

[91] Thomas, *History*, p. 112.

[92] During the second half of the sixteenth century, almost a quarter, 14 out of 58, of the advocates admitted to Doctors' Commons were Welsh: see Squibb, *Doctors' Commons: A History of the College of Advocates and Doctors of Law.*

[93] Williams, *Renewal*, p. 467.

[94] Ibid., p. 470.

[95] Jones, *Early Modern Wales*, pp. 108–9.

[96] Jones, *Early Modern Wales*, pp. 27–8; Williams, *Renewal*, p. 430.

[97] Williams, *Renewal*, pp. 464, 466.

[98] Jones, *Early Modern Wales*, pp. 108–9.

[99] Williams, *Renewal*, pp. 350–1, 356; Jones, *Early Modern Wales*, p. 39.

[100] One of the most remarkable explosions of litigation before the English courts of common law involved the action on the case for words, a remedy for spoken defamation. The courts sought eventually to stem the tide of such actions by always construing the offending words in the gentler sense, *mitiori sensu*, with some remarkable results: see Baker, *Introduction to English Legal History*, pp. 436–47.

[101] On law and order in Wales and the Marches after the union, see E. J. L. Cole, 'Some Radnorshire criminal records of the sixteenth century', *Radnorshire Society Transactions*, 29 (1959), 20–3; E. J. L. Cole, 'Thieves, robbers, and gaol-breakers', *Radnorshire Society Transactions*, 35 (1965), 30–2; T. W. Hancock, 'Montgomeryshire causes heard and determined before the Court of Marches, sitting at Ludlow, in Trinity Term, 1617', *Montgomeryshire Collections*, 19 (1886), 251–6; J. G. Jones, 'Governance, order and stability in Caernarvonshire, *ca*.1540–1640', *CHST*, 44 (1983), 7–52; J. G. Jones, 'Law and order in Merioneth after the Acts of Union 1536–43', *JMHRS*, 10(2) (1986), 119–41; N. M. W. Powell, 'Crime and community in Denbighshire during the 1590s: the evidence of the records of the Court of Great Sessions', in J. G. Jones (ed.), *Class, Community and Culture in Tudor Wales* (Cardiff, 1989), p. 261; W. R. B. Robinson, 'The litigation of Edward, earl of Worcester, concerning Gower, 1590–1596', *BBCS*, 22(4) (1968), 357–88; 23(1) (1968), 60–99.

[102] Jones, *Early Modern Wales*, pp. 41, 91–2.

[103] Ibid., p. 210; Williams, *Renewal*, p. 356.

[104] Williams, *Renewal*, p. 421.

[105] In *R v Mawgridge* (1707) Kel. 119. See further Sir J. F. Stephen, *A History of the Criminal Law of England*, 3 vols (London, 1883; repr. New York, 1973), vol. 3, pp. 1–107; T. G. Watkin, 'Hamlet and the law of homicide', *Law Quarterly Review*, 100 (1984), 282–310.

[106] Milford in 1565, Cardiff in 1573 and Chester, located at Beaumaris, in 1577. On Beaumaris, see C. M. and K. Evans, 'The Beaumaris charter of incorporation, 1562', *AAST* (1950), 1–50.

[107] Williams, *Renewal*, pp. 376–7, 401, 402–403.

[108] Jones, *Early Modern Wales*, pp. 199–202; Williams, *Renewal*, p. 335.

[109] Williams, *Renewal*, p. 335.

[110] Jones, *Early Modern Wales*, pp. 105–6.

[111] Ibid., pp. 190–1.
[112] Ibid., pp. 199–202.
[113] Ibid., p. 193.
[114] Ibid., pp. 199–202.
[115] Thomas, *History*, pp. 187–8.
[116] Williams, *Renewal*, p. 462.
[117] Ibid., pp. 331, 459–60.
[118] The latter tradition having been popularized during the Middle Ages by works such as those of Geoffrey of Monmouth.
[119] This was only partly successful as too many exceptions were allowed. See T. G. Watkin, *An Historical Introduction to Modern Civil Law* (London, 1999), pp. 98–9.
[120] Ibid., p. 122.
[121] Ibid., pp. 126–7.
[122] Williams, *Renewal*, pp. 270–1.
[123] Ibid., p. 274.
[124] Ibid., p. 474.

Chapter 8

[1] On the history of the Great Sessions generally and the source material for their work, see W. R. Williams, *The History of the Great Sessions in Wales 1542–1830* (Brecknock, 1899); G. Parry, *A Guide to the Records of the Great Sessions in Wales* (Aberystwyth, 1995); E. J. L. Cole, 'Early records of the Great Sessions', *Radnorshire Society Transactions*, 32 (1962), 54–7; K. O. Fox, 'An edited calendar of the first Brecknockshire plea roll of the Courts of the King's Great Sessions in Wales, July 1542', *NLWJ*, 14(4) (1965–6), 469–84; E. J. Sherrington, 'The plea rolls of the courts of Great Sessions, 1541–75', *NLWJ*, 13(4) (1963–4), 363–73; W. Ll. Williams, 'The King's Court of Great Sessions in Wales', *Y Cymmrodor*, 26 (1916), 1–87.
[2] 27 Henry 8, c. 26, s. 20; I. Bowen, *The Statutes of Wales* (London and Leipzig, 1908), p. 87.
[3] H. Thomas, *A History of Wales, 1485–1660* (Cardiff, 1972), p. 171; E. D. Evans, *A History of Wales, 1660–1815* (Cardiff, 1976), p. 232; R. Suggett, 'The Welsh language and the Court of Great Sessions', in G. H. Jenkins (ed.), *The Welsh Language before the Industrial Revolution* (Cardiff, 1997), pp. 153–80.
[4] On Jenkins, see J. D. H. Thomas, 'Judge David Jenkins, 1582–1663', *Morgannwg*, 8 (1964), 14–34.
[5] Thomas, *History*, pp. 172–3; Evans, *History*, p. 185.
[6] G. H. Jenkins, *The Foundations of Modern Wales: Wales 1642–1780* (Oxford, 1989), pp. 300–1.
[7] In relation to contractual actions, the question was whether the action on the case in *assumpsit* could be used in place of debt; it was resolved that it could in *Slade's case* (1602) B.& M. 420. A similar question as to whether the action on the case for nuisance could be used instead of the older remedy of the assize was also resolved in favour of case in *Cantrell v Churche* (1601) B. and M. 588; Cro. Eliz. 845; Noy 37. By the time of the Commonwealth, the action of trespass for ejectment, originally devised for leaseholders, had, by the use of fictions, come to replace the older remedies by which freeholders could recover their lands.

8 On Exchequer proceedings concerning Wales at this time, see T. I. Jeffreys Jones, *Exchequer Proceedings concerning Wales in tempore James I* (Cardiff, 1955).

9 On the Council in the early seventeenth century and the campaign regarding its jurisdiction, see P. Williams, 'The activity of the Council of the Marches under the early Stuarts', *WHR*, 1(2) (1960–3), 133–54; P. Williams, 'The attack on the Council in the Marches, 1603–1642', *THSC*, 1 (1961), 1–22.

10 Thomas, *History*, pp. 215–16; Jenkins, *Wales 1642–1780*, pp. 31, 24.

11 Jenkins, *Wales 1642–1780*, p. 33.

12 Ibid., pp. 58–9.

13 Ibid., p. 35.

14 Thomas, *History*, pp. 233–4.

15 On the requirement of two witnesses for full proof according to canon law, see T. G. Watkin, *An Historical Introduction to Modern Civil Law* (London, 1999), pp. 336, 382, 388. The rule, originally introduced by Constantine, was derived from the Mosaic law: Deuteronomy, 19, 15.

16 Jenkins, *Wales 1642–1780*, pp. 49–52; Thomas, *History*, pp. 218–20.

17 Thomas, *History*, p. 226; Jenkins, *Wales 1642–1780*, p. 81.

18 Jenkins, *Wales 1642–1780*, p. 34.

19 Thomas, *History*, pp. 238–9; Jenkins, *Wales 1642–1780*, pp. 57–8, 80.

20 On another popular prerogative jurisdiction, see E. A. Lewis and J. C. Davies, *Records of the Court of Augmentations relating to Wales and Monmouthshire* (Cardiff, 1954).

21 *R v Bushell*, 6 State Trials 999; *Bushell's case* (1670) Vaugh 135, Freem KB 1, 1 Mod Rep 119, T Jo 13.

22 Evans, *History*, pp. 12, 16, 18–19, 20, 32–3; Jenkins, *Wales 1642–1780*, p. 153. On the distinguished Welsh lawyers of the Stuart period, see G. W. Keeton, 'George Jeffreys: his family and friends', *THSC* (1967), 39–56; D. Mathew, 'The Welsh influence among the legal advisers of James II', *THSC* (1938), 119–24; A. D. Powell, 'Miscellaneous early Chancery proceedings about Radnorshire and the Marches, *c.*1538–1639', *Radnorshire Society Transactions*, 36 (1966), 25–41; G. W. Keeton, 'Judge Jeffreys: towards a re-appraisal', *WHR*, 1(3) (1960–3), 265–78; A. H. Dodd, '"Tuning" the Welsh Bench 1680', *NLWJ*, 6 (1949/50), 249–59; H. J. Owen, 'Chief Baron Richards of the Exchequer', *JMHRS*, 4(1) (1961), 37–46.

23 Jenkins, *Wales 1642–1780*, p. 184.

24 Evans, *History*, pp. 18–19, 32–33; Jenkins, *Wales 1642–1780*, p. 189. On the prosecution of Nonconformist dissenters, see W. T. Morgan, 'The prosecution of nonconformists in the consistory courts of St David's, 1661–1668', *JHSCW*, 12 (1962), 28–54.

25 Evans, *History*, pp. 20, 183.

26 The Lord President was *ex officio* the Lord Lieutenant of every county in Wales.

27 Evans, *History*, p. 21.

28 12 State Trials 183–521. See the discussion in Sir J. F. Stephen, *A History of the Criminal Law of England*, vol. 1 (London, 1883; repr. New York , 1973), p. 414.

29 Evans, *History*, pp. 21–2; Jenkins, *Wales 1642–1780*, p. 147.

30 See his entry in the *Dictionary of National Biography*; also A. W. B. Simpson (ed.) *Biographical Dictionary of the Common Law* (London, 1984).

31 G. Williams, *Renewal*, pp. 474–5.

32 Jenkins, *Wales 1642–1780*, p. 144.

33 The provision did however spawn an action on the case whereby nobles who felt they had been so maligned could seek damages, an action which proved popular during the later fifteenth century. Prosecutions for libel, *libella famosa*, for daring to

criticize magistrates, that is any public officer, were frequent before Star Chamber under the early Stuarts. Worcester may have felt that *scandalum magnatum* before the King's Bench was his natural remedy given the demise of the prerogative court.

[34] Jones, *Early Modern Wales*, pp. 193–4; Thomas, *History*, pp. 192–3; Evans, *History*, p. 22.

[35] See ch. 4 above.

[36] Evans, *History*, pp. 137, 139, 141, 149–50; Jenkins, *Wales 1642–1780*, pp. 120, 122.

[37] See E. M. White, 'The established Church, dissent and the Welsh language *c.*1660–1811', in G. H. Jenkins (ed.), *The Welsh Language before the Industrial Revolution* (Cardiff, 1997), pp. 235–88 at 243; G. H. Jenkins, '"Horrid unintelligible jargon": the case of Dr Thomas Bowles', *WHR*, 15(4) (1991), 494–523. A very full account of the case was published by the Society of Cymmrodorion: *The depositions, arguments and judgement in the cause of the churchwardens of Trefdraeth in the county of Anglesey against Dr Bowles* (London, 1773). The pamphlet can be viewed on the website of the National Library of Wales: *www.llgc.org.uk.*

[38] Evans, *History*, pp. 27, 28, 72; Jenkins, *Wales 1642–1780*, pp. 232, 346.

[39] Evans, *History*, pp. 22, 60, 61, 63; Jenkins, *Wales 1642–1780*, pp. 150, 310. On Jacobitism in Wales, see J. P. Jenkins, 'Jacobites and freemasons in eighteenth-century Wales', *WHR*, 9(4) (1978–9), 391–406; D. Nicholas, 'The Welsh Jacobites', *THSC* (1948), 467–74; J. A. Price, 'A note on Welsh "Jacobitism"', *THSC* (1920–1), 36; H. M. Vaughan, 'Welsh Jacobitism', *THSC* (1920–1), 11–39; P. D. G. Thomas, 'Jacobitism in Wales', *WHR*, 1(3) (1960–3), 279–300.

[40] J. Black, *A New History of Wales* (Stroud, 2000), p. 199.

[41] (1723) 1 Strange 553.

[42] (1747) 1 Wils. 193.

[43] (1769) 1 Dougl. 213, n.10.

[44] (1779) 1 Dougl. 213.

[45] See Glyn Parry, *A Guide to the Records of the Great Sessions in Wales* (Aberystwyth, 1995), pp. xxxv–xl.

[46] Concerning the gentry, JPs and MPs, see P. Jenkins, *The Making of a Ruling Class: The Glamorgan Gentry 1640–1790* (Cambridge, 1983); 'The creation of an "ancient gentry": Glamorgan, 1760–1840', *WHR*, 12(1) (1984–5), 29–49; T. H. Lewis, 'Attendances of justices and grand jurors at the Courts of Quarter Sessions in Wales, 16th–18th century', *THSC* (1942), 108; T. H. Lewis, 'The administration of justice in the Welsh county in relation to other organs of justice, higher and lower', *THSC* (1945), 151–66; T. H. Lewis, 'The justice of the peace in Wales', *THSC* (1943–4), 120–32; R. L. Lloyd, 'Welsh masters of the bench of the Inner Temple from early times until the end of the 18th century', *THSC* (1937), 145–200; (1938) 155–246; P. R. Roberts, 'The Merioneth gentry and local government *circa* 1650–1838', *JMHRS*, 5(1) (1965), 21–38; M. C. J, 'Montgomeryshire magistracy, 1687: their replies to James II's questions, touching the repeal of the Penal Laws and Test Act', *Montgomeryshire Collections*, 13 (1880), 163–8; J. G. Jones, 'Caernarvonshire administration: the activities of the Justices of the Peace, 1603–1660', *WHR*, 5(2) (1970), 103–63; R. A. Roberts, 'Caernarvonshire and the Middle Temple', *CHST*, 17 (1956), 41–4.

[47] Evans, *History*, p. 14.

[48] Thomas, *History*, p. 162.

[49] On the administration of the Poor Law, see A. E. Davies, 'Some aspects of the operation of the old Poor Law in Cardiganshire 1750–1834', *Ceredigion*, 6 (1968–71), 1–44; A. H. Dodd, 'The Old Poor Law in north Wales 1750–1850', *Archaeologica*

Cambrensis (7th ser.), 6 (1926), 111–32; C. Flynn-Hughes, 'Aspects of the old poor law administration and policy in Amlwch parish, 1770–1837', *AAST* (1950), 71–9; T. I. J. Jones, 'The parish vestries and the problem of poverty 1783–1833', *BBCS*, 14(3) (1951), 222–35; G. D. Owen, 'The Poor Law system in Carmarthenshire during the eighteenth and early nineteenth centuries', *THSC* (1941), 71–86; H. H. C. Summers, 'The poor, 1685–1734', *Montgomeryshire Collections*, 38 (1918), 147; B. B. Thomas, 'The old Poor Law in Ardudwy Uwch-Artro', *BBCS*, 7(2) (1934), 153–91.

50 Jenkins, *Wales 1642–1780*, pp. 167, 273, 324.
51 Thomas, *History*, pp. 166–7; Evans, *History*, p. 186; Jenkins, *Wales 1642–1780*, pp. 155, 302–3. On elections in Wales at this time, see A. H. Dodd, 'Caernarvonshire elections to the Long Parliament', *BBCS*, 12 (1946), 44–8; A. H. Dodd, 'Flintshire politics in the seventeenth century', *FHSJ*, 14 (1953–4), 22–46; A. H. Dodd, 'The pattern of politics in Stuart Wales', *THSC* (1948), 8–91; A. H. Dodd, 'Wales in the parliaments of Charles I', *THSC* (1945), 16–49; (1946–7), 59–96; A. H. Dodd, 'Welsh opposition lawyers in the Short Parliament', *BBCS*, 12 (1948), 106–7; A. H. Dodd, 'The Caernarvonshire election dispute of 1640–41 and its sequel', *BBCS*, 14 (1950), 42–4; K. Evans, 'Caernarvon Borough and its contributory boroughs', *CHST*, 9 (1948), 41–5; T. Richards, 'The Anglesey Election of 1708', *AAST* (1943), 23–34; G. Roberts, 'Parliamentary representation of the Welsh boroughs', *BBCS*, 4(4) (1929), 352–60; 'The county representation of Anglesey in the eighteenth century', *AAST*, (1930), 60–78; P. D. G. Thomas, 'County elections in eighteenth-century Carmarthenshire', *Carmarthenshire Antiquary*, 4 (1962–3), 32–8, 124–30; P. D. G. Thomas, 'Eighteenth-century elections in the Cardigan borough constituency', *Ceredigion*, 5(4) (1967), 402–23; P. D. G. Thomas, 'Sir George Wynne and the Flint borough election of 1727–1741', *FHSPJ*, 20 (1962), 39–57; P. D. G. Thomas, 'The parliamentary representation of Caernarvonshire, 1749–84', *CHST*, 20 (1959), 72–86; P. D. G. Thomas, 'The parliamentary representation of Merioneth during the eighteenth century', *JMHRS*, 3(2) (1958), 128–36; P. D. G. Thomas, 'The Montgomery borough constituency', *BBCS*, 20(3) (1963), 293–304; P. D. G. Thomas, 'Parliamentary elections in Brecknockshire, 1689–1832', *Brycheiniog*, 6 (1960), 99–114; P. D. G. Thomas, 'Anglesey politics, 1689–1727', *AAST* (1962); P. D. G. Thomas, 'The Cardigan boroughs election of 1741', *Ceredigion*, 6(1) (1968), 128–36; P. D. G. Thomas, 'The Montgomeryshire election of 1774', *Montgomeryshire Collections*, 59 (1965–6), 116–29; R. D. Rees, 'Electioneering ideals current in south Wales, 1790–1832', *WHR*, 2(3) (1964–5), 233–50; D. Williams, 'The Pembrokeshire elections of 1831', *WHR*, 1(1) (1960), 37–64; G. Roberts, 'Parliamentary history of Beaumaris 1555–1832', *AAST* (1933), 97–109; P. D. G. Thomas, 'Glamorgan politics 1700–1750', *Morgannwg*, 6 (1962), 52–77; M. Bevan-Evans, 'Local Government in Treuddyn, 1752–1821', *FHSP*, 22 (1965–6), 25–39.
52 By 21 Jac. 1, c. 6; 3 Will. and Mar., c. 9; 6 Anne, c. 9. See generally T. F. T. Plucknett, *A Concise History of the Common Law*, 5th edn (London, 1956), pp. 439–41.
53 See Jenkins, *Wales 1642–1780*, p. 337.
54 Thomas, *History*, pp. 125, 152; Jenkins, *Wales 1642–1780*, pp. 118, 171–2, 334–5. On one aspect of transportation, see D. Beddoe, 'Carmarthenshire women and criminal transportation to Australia, 1787–1852', *Carmarthenshire Antiquary*, 13 (1977), 65–71.
55 Evans, *History*, pp. 90–1. Following the teaching of St Paul: 'Dare any of you, having a matter against another, go to law before the unjust, and not before the saints?' (1 Cor. 4:1).

[56] Evans, *History*, pp. 31–2.

[57] Jenkins, *Wales 1642–1780*, pp. 194–5.

[58] Evans, *History*, p. 39; Jenkins, *Wales 1642–1780*, pp. 357–9.

[59] Evans, *History*, p. 99.

[60] Ibid., p. 107; Jenkins, *Wales 1642–1780*, p. 377.

[61] Jenkins, *Wales 1642–1780*, p. 272.

[62] Evans, *History*, pp. 195, 224–5; Jenkins, *Wales 1642–1780*, pp. 328–9. On disorder in Wales at this time, see W. L. Davies, 'The riot at Denbigh in 1795', *BBCS*, 4 (1927), 61–73; D. J. V. Jones, 'Life and death in eighteenth-century Wales: a note [punishment and pardon]', *WHR*, 10(4) (1980–1), 536–48; K. L. Gruffydd, 'The vale of Clwyd corn riots of 1740', *FHSPJ*, 27 (1975–76), 36–42; D. J. V. Jones, *Before Rebecca: Popular Protests in Wales, 1793–1835* (Harmondsworth, 1973); D. J. V. Jones, 'The corn riots in Wales, 1793–1801', *WHR*, 2(4) (1964–5), 323–50; D. J. V. Jones, 'The Merthyr Riots of 1800', *BBCS*, 23(2) (1969), 166–79; D. J. V. Jones, 'The strike of 1816', *Morgannwg*, 11 (1967), 27–45; D. J. V. Jones, 'The Amlwch riots of 1817', *AAST* (1966), 93–102; G. Parry, 'Erlynwyr a throseddwyr yn sir Gaernarfon (1730–1830)', *CHST*, 57 (1996), 47–64.

[63] Thomas, *History*, pp. 145–6; 149–50.

[64] Evans, *History*, p. 182; Jenkins, *Wales 1642–1780*, p. 94.

[65] Jenkins, *Wales 1642–1780*, p. 268. On enclosures in Wales and other contemporary changes in landholding practices, see A. H. Dodd, 'The enclosure movement in north Wales', *BBCS*, 3 (1926), 210–15; J. Chapman, 'Parliamentary Enclosure in Wales: Comparisons and Contrasts', *WHR*, 21(4) (2003), 761–9; M. C. J, 'Enclosure of common lands in Montgomeryshire', *Montgomeryshire Collections*, 12 (1879), 267–98; 15 (1882), 191–6; E. T. Jones, 'The enclosure movement in Anglesey', *AAST* (1925), 21–58; J. L. Jones, 'A seventeenth-century land dispute', *NLWJ*, 13(3) (1963–4), 278–88; W. H. Morris, 'Eighteenth-century leases', *Carmarthenshire Antiquary*, 5 (1964–9), 21–24; J. Mostyn, 'The enclosure movement in Radnorshire', *Radnorshire Society Transactions*, 18 (1948), 70–1; P. R. Roberts, 'The gentry and land in eighteenth century Merioneth', *JMHRS*, 4(4) (1961–4), 324–39; R. U. Sayce, 'Popular enclosures and the one night house', *Montgomeryshire Collections*, 47 (1942), 109–20; R. U. Sayce, 'The old summer pastures', *Montgomeryshire Collections*, 54 (1955–6), 117–45; 55 (1957–8), 37–86; K. W. Swett, 'Widowhood, custom and property in early modern north Wales', *WHR*, 18(2) (1996–7), 189–227; C. Thomas, 'Colonization, enclosure and the rural landscape', *NLWJ*, 19(2) (1975–6), 132–46.

[66] Jenkins, *Wales 1642–1780*, pp. 97, 330–2. On the reputation of stewards, see J. Martin, 'Private enterprise versus manorial rights: mineral property disputes in eighteenth-century Glamorgan', *WHR*, 9(2) (1978–9), 155–75; J. Martin, 'Estate stewards and their work in Glamorgan, 1660–1760', *Morgannwg*, 23 (1979), 9–28; T. Ridd, 'Gabriel Powell: the uncrowned king of Swansea', *Glamorgan Historian*, 5 (1968), 152–60; P. Morgan, 'The Glais Boundary Dispute, 1756', *Glamorgan Historian*, 9 (1972), 203–10.

[67] Jenkins, *Wales 1642–1780*, pp. 294, 276–7.

[68] Ibid., p. 278.

[69] Evans, *History*, pp. 128–30.

[70] Thomas, *History*, pp. 128, 138, 145–6; Williams, *Renewal*, p. 478.

[71] Thomas, *History*, p. 141; Evans, *History*, p. 178.

[72] Jenkins, *Wales 1642–1780*, pp. 112–13; Evans, *History*, p. 125.

[73] Evans, *History*, p. 169.

[74] Jenkins, *Wales 1642–1780*, p. 297; Black, *New History*, p. 135. On roads, trade and transport generally, see A. H. Dodd, 'The roads of north Wales', *Archaeologica Cambrensis* (7th ser.), 5 (1925), 121–48; J. S. Gardner, 'The justices of the peace and the repair and maintenance of bridges and highways in Denbighshire in the seventeenth century', *Cambrian Law Review*, 16 (1985), 52–76; A. H. T. Lewis, 'The early effects of Carmarthenshire's Turnpike Trusts, 1760–1800', *Carmarthenshire Historian*, 4 (1967), 41–54; R. T. Pritchard, 'Montgomeryshire turnpike trusts', *Montgomeryshire Collections*, 57 (1961–2), 2–16; R. T. Pritchard, 'Caernarvonshire turnpike trust', *CHST*, 17 (1956), 62–74; R. T. Jenkins, 'A drover's account book', *CHST*, 6 (1945), 46–57; O. Parry, 'The financing of the Welsh cattle trade in the eighteenth century', *BBCS*, 8(1) (1935), 46–61.

[75] Jenkins, *Wales 1642–1780*, p. 169.

[76] Evans, *History*, p. 194; Jenkins, *Wales 1642–1780*, pp. 338–9.

[77] Evans, *History*, pp. 194–5.

[78] Ibid., pp. 252, 254, 257. On John Rice Jones and other Welshmen in America, see A. H. Dodd, 'A Merioneth pioneer of the American mid-west: John Rice Jones', *JMHRS*, 2 (1953–6), 249–59; D. Williams, 'The contribution of Wales to the development of the United States', *NLWJ*, 2 (1941/2), 97–108; E. A. Jones, 'Welshmen in the American War of Independence', *Y Cymmrodor*, 27 (1917), 230–63.

[79] Jenkins, *Wales 1642–1780*, p. 341; Thomas, *History*, p. 158; Jenkins, *Wales 1642–1780*, p. 278; Thomas, *History*, p. 123.

[80] The words and even more so the sentiments echo those of Gruffydd ab Owen at Oxwich in 1558: 'Frenchman's goods it is, and our own, for such as took it ought to have it'. On the significance of such remarks, see T. G. Watkin, 'Oxwich revisited: an examinaton of the background to *Herbert's case* 1557–58', *THSC*, NS 8 (2001), 94–118 at 101, 111–12.

[81] Jenkins, *Wales 1642–1780*, p. 333. The ancient Celts had thought of divine gifts being conveyed by water, a concept present in the Arthurian legend and also perhaps in the Welsh laws treating the sea as the king's packhorse, bringing him divine gifts which accrued for the people's benefit if not gathered within a limited period.

[82] Evans, *History*, p. 113.

[83] Jenkins, *Wales 1642–1780*, pp. 316–17.

[84] Evans, *History*, pp. 208, 212–13, 215, 242; Jenkins, *Wales 1642–1780*, pp. 317–18. On Price, see I. M. Fothergill and D. Williams, 'French opinion concerning Dr Richard Price', *BBCS*, 5 (1929), 72–4; D. O. Thomas, 'Richard Price, 1723–91', *THSC* (1971), 45–64; P. Frame, 'The Apostle of Liberty: the political thinking of Richard Price', *Planet: the Welsh Internationalist*, 163, 70–86.

[85] Evans, *History*, pp. 216–17; Jenkins, *Wales 1642–1780*, pp. 318–19. See also E. A. Jones, 'Two Welsh correspondents of John Wilkes', *Y Cymmrodor*, 29 (1919), 110–50.

[86] *R v Shipley* (1783) 21 *State Trials* 953; Sir J. F. Stephen, *A History of the Criminal Law*, vol. 2, (London, 1883; repr. New York, 1973) pp. 330–43. Jenkins, *Wales 1642–1780*, p. 319. On Jones, see M. J. Franklin, *Sir William Jones* (Cardiff, 1995); M. J. Franklin (ed.), *Sir William Jones: Selected Poetical and Prose Works* (Cardiff, 1995); A. Murray (ed.), *Sir William Jones 1746–94: A Commemoration* (Oxford, 1998); J. Davies, 'Sir William Jones as linguist and author', *Y Cymmrodor*, 8 (1887), 62–82; 9 (1888), 304–24; D. J. Ibbetson, 'Sir William Jones', in T. G. Watkin (ed.), *Legal Wales: Its Past; Its Future* (Cardiff, 2001), pp. 41–62; G. Cannon and M. J. Franklin, 'A Cymmrodor claims kin in Calcutta: an assessment of Sir William Jones as philologer, polymath, and pluralist', *THSC* (NS), 11 (2005), 50–69; Caryl Davies, '"Romantic Jones":

the picturesque and politics on the South Wales circuit 1775–81', *NLWJ*, 28 (3) (1993–4), 255–78; D. J. Ibbetson (ed.), *An Essay on the Law of Bailments by Sir William Jones* (Bangor, 2007); E. W. C. Jones, 'Sir William Jones', *AAST* (1930), 79–85. R. E. Jenkins, 'Thomas Pennant and the *Dean of St Asaph's case*', *THSC* (1984), 77–94. On the Welsh contribution in India generally, see W. R. Owain-Jones, 'The contribution of Welshmen to the administration of India', *THSC* (1970), 250–62.

87 Jenkins, *Wales 1642–1780*, pp. 32, 313; D. G. Evans, *A History of Wales, 1815–1906* (Cardiff, 1989), p. 158.

88 Jenkins, *Wales 1642–1780*, pp. 336–7.

89 1 Will. 4, c. 70. See also M. H. Jones, 'Montgomeryshire and the abolition of the Court of Great Sessions 1817–1830', *Montgomeryshire Collections*, 60 (1967–8), 85–103. M. Escott, 'How Wales lost its judicature: the making of the 1830 Act for the abolition of the Courts of Great Sessions', *THSC* (NS), 13 (2007), 134–59; M. E. Jones, '"An invidious attempt to accelerate the extinction of our language": the abolition of the Court of Great Sessions and the Welsh language', *WHR*, 19 (1998–9), 226–64.

Chapter 9

1 The classic example of this is *Scott* v *Shepherd* (1773) Wm Blackstone, 892. The plaintiff, an infant, had lost the sight in one eye after the defendant, also a minor, had thrown a firework into a crowded area. The plaintiff sued, using the action of trespass, but it was countered that he should have used the action of trespass on the case, because the firework had not struck him immediately, but had been thrown onwards by two other people acting to defend themselves and their property against possible injury. Had the defence succeeded, the plaintiff would have had to restart the action despite the fact that there was no doubt that the defendant was liable under one form of action or the other.

2 Fines and Recoveries Act 1834.

3 By virtue of the Common Law Procedure Act 1854.

4 Also known as Lord Cairns' Act.

5 B. Hutton, 'Sir John Nicholl of Merthyr Mawr: the reform of the testamentary jurisdiction of the ecclesiastical courts', in T. G. Watkin (ed.), *Legal Wales: Its Past; Its Future* (Cardiff, 2001), pp. 89–100; B. Hutton, 'Dr John Nicholl of Merthyr Mawr: the reform of the testamentary jurisdiction of the ecclesiastical courts', in T. G. Watkin (ed.), *The Trial of Dic Penderyn and Other Essays* (Cardiff, 2003), pp. 128–50.

6 The amount had been under £10 from 1773 until 1824.

7 On the use of Welsh in the courts, and on the language issue generally at this time, see D. Jenkins, 'Y Gymraeg mewn Llys a Llan', in T. G. Watkin (ed.), *The Trial of Dic Penderyn and Other Essays* (Cardiff, 2003), pp. 1–38; J. G. Jones, 'The national petition on the legal status of the Welsh language', *WHR*, 18(1) (1996–7), 92–124; D. W. Powell, 'Y llysoedd, yr awdurdodau a'r Gymraeg: y Ddeddf Uno a Deddf yr Iaith Gymraeg', in T. M. Charles-Edwards, M. E. Owen and D. B. Walters (eds), *Lawyers and Laymen* (Cardiff, 1986), pp. 287–315; B. L. Davies, 'The right to a bilingual education in nineteenth-century Wales', *THSC* (1988), 133–52; B. Thomas, 'A cauldron of rebirth: population and the Welsh language in the nineteenth century', *WHR*, 13(4) (1986–7), 418–37; M. E. Jones, '"Wales for the Welsh": the Welsh County Court Judgeships *c.*1868–1900', *WHR*, 19 (1998–9), 642–78.

[8]   Only in the reign of Queen Victoria did the title *King's Bench* mutate to *Queen's Bench* in deference to the sex of the sovereign.

[9]   By virtue of the Administration of Justice (Miscellaneous Provisions) Act 1933. The use of jury trials in civil cases had been declining steadily since the Judicature Acts of the previous century.

[10] The Birkenhead legislation, called after F. E. Smith, consists of the Law of Property Act 1925, the Settled Land Act 1925, the Trustee Act 1925, the Administration of Estates Act 1925 and the Land Registration Act 1925. A code of criminal law virtually emerged in 1861, including the Larceny Act, the Forgery Act, the Malicious Mischief Act, the Coinage Act and the Offences against the Person Act, all of that year.

[11] As in modern France, Italy and Spain. The courts are so-called because they do not themselves dispose of cases by decision. They merely decide whether the court below has correctly interpreted and applied the law, upholding its decision if that is so, but quashing its decision and remitting the case for rehearing in the lower court if there was in Cassation's view an error. The name *Cassation* derives from this quashing function.

[12] An appeal on the merits required the leave of either the court or the trial judge. Otherwise, appeals were only permissible on points of law or, with the leave of the court, against sentence.

[13] They were to become prerogative orders by virtue of the Administration of Justice (Miscellaneous Provisions) Act 1938.

[14] On the place of Wales and Welshmen in the movement for parliamentary reform, see D. Wager, 'Welsh politics and parliamentary reform, 1780–1832', *WHR*, 7(4) (1974–5), 427–49; R. Wallace, 'Wales and the parliamentary reform movement', *WHR*, 11(4) (1982–3), 469–87.

[15] D. G. Evans, *A History of Wales, 1815–1906* (Cardiff, 1989), pp. 165–6 . The Act was the third attempt to get reform onto the statute book. Two earlier bills had failed in the previous two years. For their details, see ibid., pp. 160, 165.

[16] Ibid., pp. 273, 278.

[17] Ibid., pp. 202, 292; K. O. Morgan, *Rebirth of a Nation: A History of Modern Wales* (Oxford and Cardiff, 1981), p. 11.

[18] Evans, *Wales, 1815–1906*, p. 287. On elections in Wales during this period, see K. O. Fox, 'The Merthyr election of 1906', *NLWJ*, 14(2) (1965–6), 237–41; E. G. Jones, 'Borough politics and electioneering (1826–1882)', *CHST*, 17 (1956), 75; B. Jones, *Etholiadau'r Ganrif/Welsh Elections 1885–1997* (Talybont, 1999); E. G. Jones, 'Sir Charles Paget and the Caernarvonshire Boroughs, 1830–32', *CHST*, 21 (1960), 81–128; I. G. Jones, 'Dr Thomas Price and the election of 1868 in Merthyr Tydfil', *WHR*, 2(2) (1964–5), 147–72; 2(3) (1964–5), 251–70; 'The elections of 1865 and 1868 in Wales', *THSC* (1964), 41–68; D. G. Lloyd Hughes, 'David Williams, Castell Deudraeth, and the Merioneth elections of 1859, 1865 and 1868', *JMHRS*, 5(4) (1965–8), 335–51; J. Morgan, 'Denbighshire's *annus mirabilis*: the borough and county elections of 1868', *WHR*, 7(1) (1974), 63–87; K. O. Morgan, 'Cardiganshire politics: the Liberal ascendancy, 1885–1923', *Ceredigion*, 5 (4) (1967), 313–46; K. O. Morgan, 'Democratic politics in Glamorgan, 1884–1914', *Morgannwg*, 4 (1960), 5–27; L. J. Williams, 'The Rhondda election of 1885', *Morgannwg*, 6 (1962), 78–94.

[19] Evans, *Wales, 1815–1906*, p. 302; Morgan, *Rebirth*, pp. 27–8. Beaumaris, Cardigan, Haverfordwest, Radnor and Brecon all lost their borough members. Glamorgan was divided into five divisions; Caernarfonshire into two. For details of the changes and the election results for this period, see Jones, *Etholiadau'r Ganrif/Welsh Elections*.

20 See I. Bowen, 'Grand juries, justices of the peace and Quarter Sessions in Wales', *THSC* (1933–5), 51–104.
21 Evans, *Wales, 1815–1906*, pp. 136, 235.
22 D. G. Evans, *A History of Wales, 1906–2000* (Cardiff, 2000), pp. 5, 240; Morgan, *Rebirth*, p. 86. See also I. B. Rees, 'The restoration of local democracy in Wales', *THSC* (1993), 139–82.
23 Evans, *Wales, 1906–2000*, p. 5.
24 Morgan, *Rebirth*, pp. 177–8.
25 Ibid., p. 9.
26 Evans, *Wales, 1815–1906*, p. 213.
27 Ibid., pp. 196, 200.
28 Ibid., p. 304; Morgan, *Rebirth*, p. 83; J. Graham Jones, 'Select committee or royal commission? Wales and the "land question"', *WHR*, 17 (2) (1994–5), 205–29.
29 Morgan, *Rebirth*, pp. 84–5; on the similar developments in mainland Europe, see T. G. Watkin, *The Italian Legal Tradition* (London, 1997), p. 207; T. G. Watkin, *An Historical Introduction to Modern Civil Law* (London, 1999), p. 254.
30 On the practice of leasing the mineral rights to speculators rather than the landowners mining themselves, see J. Davies, 'The Dowlais lease, 1748–1900', *Morgannwg*, 12 (1968), 37–66.
31 Evans, *Wales, 1815–1906*, pp. 210, 32; Morgan, *Rebirth*, p. 171; Evans, *Wales, 1906–2000*, p. 15. On the great changes in land ownership at this time, see J. Davies, 'The end of the great estates and the rise of freehold farming in Wales', *WHR*, 7(2) (1974), 18–212; Jones, 'Select committee or royal commission? Wales and the "land question"', 205–29; P. Jones-Evans, 'Evan Pan Jones: land reformer', *WHR*, 4(2) (1968–9), 143–59.
32 Professor Brinley Thomas has demonstrated that large-scale immigration from outside of Wales was not a feature of the industrial areas until the 1890s. See Thomas, 'A cauldron of rebirth: population and the Welsh language in the nineteenth century', 418–37.
33 Morgan, *Rebirth*, pp. 346–7. G. Ll. H. Griffiths, 'The hundred years war: the development of the movement towards leasehold enfranchisement in Wales', in T. G. Watkin (ed.), *The Trial of Dic Penderyn and Other Essays* (Cardiff, 2003), pp. 180–96.
34 Evans, *Wales, 1906–2000*, p. 198.
35 Evans, *Wales, 1815–1906*, p. 141.
36 On the tithe war, see F. P. Jones, 'Rhyfel y Degwm 1886–91', *DHST*, 2 (1953), 71–106.
37 Evans, *Wales, 1815–1906*, pp. 207–8, 307. See W. B. George, 'Welsh disestablishment and Welsh nationalism', *JHSCW*, 20 (1970), 77–91; R. T. Jones, 'The origins of the nonconformist disestablishment campaign', *JHSCW*, 20 (1970), 39–76.
38 Evans, *Wales, 1815–1906*, p. 293.
39 Ibid., pp. 293, 140; Morgan, *Rebirth*, p. 351. See W. R. Lambert, 'The Welsh Sunday Closing Act, 1881', *WHR*, 6(2) (1972–3), 161–89; W. R. Lambert, *Drink and Sobriety in Victorian Wales c.1820–c.1895* (Cardiff, 1983).
40 J. Black, *A New History of Wales* (Stroud, 2000), p. 173; Evans, *Wales, 1906–2000*, pp. 178, 181–2; Morgan, *Rebirth*, pp. 201, 353–4.
41 Evans, *Wales, 1815–1906*, pp. 43, 275; 144.
42 J. B. Edwards, 'Sir George Osborne Morgan MP (1826–97): nineteenth-century mould breaker', *DHST*, 46 (1997), 69–86. On the burial controversy, see C. Stevens, 'The "burial question": controversy and conflict c.1860–1890', *WHR*, 21(2) (2002), 328–56.

[43] Morgan, *Rebirth*, pp. 12, 27.

[44] Evans, *Wales, 1815–1906*, pp. 304–5; Morgan, *Rebirth*, p. 115. The standard biography of Lloyd George is K. O. Morgan, *David Lloyd George: Welsh Radical as World Statesman* (Cardiff, 1963).

[45] Evans, *Wales, 1815–1906*, pp. 304–5; Morgan, *Rebirth*, pp. 141–2.

[46] The churchyards would only pass to the local authority when the incumbent moved, retired or died, as existing incumbents had the freehold in the churchyards which was not to be disturbed. Incoming incumbents after disestablishment no longer enjoyed the parson's freehold.

[47] Morgan, *Rebirth*, p. 184.

[48] Ibid., p. 114; Evans, *Wales, 1815–1906*, p. 78; Evans, *Wales, 1906–2000*, p. 5. The National Library of Wales and the National Museum of Wales were set up by statute in 1907. The Church in Wales was not the creature of statute; the Welsh Church Act merely excluded the Welsh dioceses from the Church of England. The Church in Wales was then set up autochthonously.

[49] Evans, *Wales, 1815–1906*, p. 111.

[50] Ibid., p. 263. On the development of the legal framework for education in Wales, see D. Evans, 'The Welsh Intermediate Education Act, 1889', *THSC* (1939), 101–32; L. W. Evans, 'School boards and the works school system after the Education Act of 1870', *NLWJ*, 15(1) (1967–8), 89–100; L. W. Evans, 'Sir John and Lady Charlotte Guest's education scheme at Dowlais in the mid-nineteenth century', *NLWJ*, 9 (1955–6), 265–86; L. W. Evans, 'The Welsh National Council for Education, 1903–6', *WHR*, 6(1) (1972), 49–88; L. Hargest, 'The Welsh Educational Alliance and the 1870 Elementary Education Act', *WHR*, 10(2) (1980–1), 172–206; P. J. Randall, 'The origins and establishment of the Welsh Department of Education', *WHR*, 7(4) (1975), 450–71; D. Salmon, 'The story of a Welsh Education Commission (1846–7)', *Y Cymmrodor*, 24 (1913), 189; B. B. Thomas, 'The establishment of the "Aberdare" Departmental Committee, 1880: some letters and notes', *BBCS*, 19(4) (1962), 318–34; A. L. Trott, 'The implementation of the 1870 Elementary Education Act in Cardiganshire', *Ceredigion*, 3(3) (1958), 207–30; J. R. Webster, 'The first reports of Owen M. Edwards on Welsh intermediate schools', *NLWJ*, 10(3) (1958), 390–4; O. Wheeler, 'The Welsh Intermediate Education Act, 1889', *THSC* (1939), 101–32; W. P. Wheldon, 'The Welsh Department, Ministry of Education, 1907–1957', *THSC* (1957), 18–36; H. G. Williams, 'The Forster Education Act and Welsh Politics, 1870–74', *WHR*, 14(2) (1988–9), 242–68; W. M. Williams, 'The Welsh Intermediate Education Act, 1889', *THSC* (1939), 101–32.

[51] Evans, *Wales, 1815–1906*, pp. 268–9.

[52] Evans, *Wales, 1906–2000*, pp. 68, 114; Morgan, *Rebirth*, pp. 37–8, 101, 105, 111–12. The last reverberations of the Balfour revolt occurred with the litigation in 1909 concerning the Oxford St School in Swansea: see *Board of Education* v *T. J. Rice and others* (1911) AC 179.

[53] Evans, *Wales, 1906–2000*, p. 114; Morgan, *Rebirth*, pp. 168, 298, 356–7.

[54] On the administration of the later Poor Law in Wales at this period, see E. A. Benjamin, 'Of paupers and workhouses [Aberystwyth Union]', *Ceredigion*, 10 (1985), 147–54; A. C. Davies, 'The old poor law in an industrializing parish, Aberdare, 1818–36', *WHR*, 8(3) (1977), 285–311; A. E. Davies, 'Sir Hugh Owen and the new poor law', *BBCS*, 21(2) (1964–6), 166–70; A. E. Davies, 'The new poor law in a rural area', *Ceredigion*, 8(3) (1978), 245–90; I. Dewar, 'George Clive and the establishment of the new poor law in south Glamorgan', *Morgannwg*, 11 (1967), 46–70; C. Flynn-Hughes,

'Aspects of poor law administration and policy in Amlwch Parish, 1834–1848', *AAST* (1945), 48–60; C. Flynn-Hughes, 'The Bangor workhouse', *CHST*, 4 (1942), 88; C. Flynn-Hughes, 'The workhouses of Caernarvonshire 1760–1914', *CHST*, 7 (1946), 88–100; D. Jones, 'Pauperism in the Aberystwyth Poor Law Union, 1870–1914', *Ceredigion*, 9(1) (1980), 78–101; D. J. V. Jones, '"A dead loss to the community": the criminal vagrant in mid-nineteenth-century Wales', *WHR*, 8(3) (1976–7), 312–43; T. Davies Jones, 'Poor law administration in Merthyr Tydfil Union, 1834–94', *Morgannwg*, 8 (1964), 35–62; J. E. Thomas, 'The poor law in West Glamorgan, 1834 to 1930', *Morgannwg*, 18 (1974), 45–69; D. E. Williams, 'The poor law in operation in the parish of Rumney, 1825–30', *THSC* (1966), 341–71.

55 Evans, *Wales, 1815–1906*, pp. 140–2; Morgan, *Rebirth*, pp. 205, 236, 169.
56 Evans, *Wales, 1906–2000*, pp. 28–30.
57 Morgan, *Rebirth*, p. 293.
58 Evans, *Wales, 1906–2000*, p. 104; Morgan, *Rebirth*, p. 205.
59 Morgan, *Rebirth*, p. 310.
60 Evans, *Wales, 1815–1906*, p. 293; Morgan, *Rebirth*, p. 140.
61 Evans, *Wales, 1906–2000*, p. 222. On Tryweryn, see W. L. Jones, *Cofio Tryweryn* (Llandysul, 1988). Liverpool City Council apologized for its actions in 2005.
62 Morgan, *Rebirth*, pp. 254–5. See also D. Jenkins, *Tân yn Llŷn* (1937), trans. by A. Corkett, as *A Nation on Trial: Penyberth 1936* (Cardiff, 1998).
63 Evans, *Wales, 1815–1906*, pp. 11, 130–6. On crime and disorder in Wales generally at this time, see M. Bevan-Evans, 'The Mold riot of 1831', *FHSJ*, 13 (1952–3), 72–6; D. Hopkin, 'The Llanelli riots, 1911', *WHR*, 11(4) (1982–3), 488–515; R. W. Ireland, 'Putting oneself on whose county? Carmarthenshire juries in the mid-nineteenth-century', in T. G. Watkin (ed.), *Legal Wales: Its Past; Its Future* (Cardiff, 2001), pp. 63–88; D. J. V. Jones, 'The Carmarthen riots of 1831', *WHR*, 4(2) (1968–9), 129–42; D. J. V. Jones, 'The Scotch cattle and their black domain', *WHR*, 5(3) (1971), 220–49; A. M. O'Brien, 'Churchill and the Tonypandy riots', *WHR*, 17(1) (1994–5), 67–99; R. G. Parry, 'Trosedd a chosb ym Meirionydd yn chwedegau cynnar a bedwaredd ganrif ar bymtheg: tystiolaeth cofnodion y llys chwarter', in T. G. Watkin (ed.), *The Trial of Dic Penderyn and Other Essays* (Cardiff, 2003), pp. 78–109; G. Parry, *Launched to Eternity: Crime and Punishment 1700–1900* (Aberystwyth, 2001). On the anti-Jewish disturbances of the early twentieth century, see specifically G. Alderman, 'The anti-Jewish riots of August 1911 in south Wales', *WHR*, 6(2) (1972–3), 190–200; U. Henriques, 'The Jews and crime in south Wales before World War I', *Morgannwg*, 29 (1985), 59–73; C. Holmes, 'The Tredegar riots of 1911: anti-Jewish disturbances in south Wales', *WHR*, 11(2) (1982–3), 214–25; W. D. Rubinstein, 'The anti-Jewish riots of 1911 in south Wales: a re-examination', *WHR*, 18(1997) 667–99; G. Alderman, 'The anti-Jewish riots of August 1911 in south Wales: a response', *WHR*, 20 (2000–1), 565–71. On the Merthyr riots and the trial of Dic Penderyn, see N. Cooke, '*The King* v *Richard Lewis & Lewis Lewis* (Cardiff, 13 July 1831): the Trial of Dic Penderyn', in T. G. Watkin (ed.), *The Trial of Dic Penderyn and Other Essays* (Cardiff, 2003), pp. 110–27; S. Jones, 'Richard Lewis and Dic Penderyn: the man and the martyr', *Transactions of the Port Talbot Historical Society*, 3(1) (1977); D. J. V. Jones, 'The Merthyr riots of 1831', *WHR*, 3(2) (1966–7), 173–205; G. A. Williams, 'The insurrection of Merthyr Tydfil in 1831', *THSC* (1965), 222–43; G. A. Williams, 'The making of radical Merthyr', *WHR*, 1(2) (1960–3), 161–92; G. A. Williams, 'The Merthyr riots: settling the account', *NLWJ*, 11(1) (1959–60), 124–41. The article by Nicholas Cooke provides a substantial reassessment of the status of Dic Penderyn

as an innocent working-class martyr through examining transcripts of the trial from the viewpoint of a forensic advocate.

64 Evans, *Wales, 1815–1906*, pp. 136, 138. On the development of police in Wales, see J. F. Jones, 'Carmarthenshire rural police force', *Carmarthenshire Antiquary*, 4 (1962), 45–8; J. F. Jones, 'Kidwelly borough police force', *Carmarthenshire Antiquary*, 4 (1963), 152–9; G. G. Lerry, 'The policemen of Denbighshire', *DHST*, 2 (1953), 107–52; H. Owen, *History of the Anglesey Constabulary* (Bangor, 1952); D. Richter, 'The Welsh police, the Home Office and the Welsh tithe war of 1886–91', *WHR*, 12(1) (1984–5), 50–75. On gaols in Wales at this time, see T. H. Lewis, 'Documents illustrating the county gaol and house of correction in Wales', *THSC* (1946–7), 232–49; H. J. Owen, 'The common gaols of Merioneth during the eighteenth and nineteenth centuries', *JMHRS*, 3 (1957–60), 1–30. On transportation, see D. Beddoe, 'Carmarthenshire women and criminal transportation to Australia, 1787–1852', *Carmarthenshire Antiquary*, 13 (1977), 65–71.

65 Genesis 24: 60.

66 Evans, *Wales, 1815–1906*, pp. 143–4; 33–4. On the Rebecca riots, see 'A "Rebecca" item', *Carmarthenshire Antiquary*, 3 (1959), 37; E. Davies, 'Who was Rebecca?', *Montgomeryshire Collections*, 28 (1894), 142–4; W. L. Davies, 'Notes on Hugh Williams and the Rebecca Riots', *BBCS*, 11 (1941), 160–7; W. H. Howse, 'Knighton and Rebecca', *Radnorshire Society Transactions*, 13 (1943), 54–5; D. J. V. Jones, 'Distress and discontent in Cardiganshire, 1814–1819', *Ceredigion*, 5(3) (1966), 280–9; E. D. Jones, 'A file of "Rebecca" papers', *Carmarthenshire Antiquary*, 1 (3–4) (1943–4), 21–63; T. H. Lewis, 'The Rebecca movement in Carmarthenshire', *Carmarthenshire Antiquary*, 1 (3–4) (1943–4), 6–15; J. D. Owen, 'Y Beca', *Carmarthenshire Antiquary*, 1 (3–4) (1943–44), 16–20; D. Rees, 'Rebecca in Gower', *Gower*, 27 (1976), 26–32; D. Williams, 'A report on the turnpike trusts', *NLWJ*, 8 (1953/4), 171–5; D. Williams, 'Rebecca in Caernarvonshire', *CHST*, 10 (1949), 115–18; D. Williams, *The Rebecca Riots: A Study in Agrarian Discontent* (Cardiff, 1955); D. E. Williams, 'Documents relating to rural discontent in west Wales', *NLWJ*, 11(2) (1959–60), 177–80.

67 Evans, *Wales, 1815–1906*, p. 148. On Chartism in Wales, see O. R. Ashton, 'Chartism in mid-Wales', *Montgomeryshire Collections*, 62 (1971), 10–57; D. J. V. Jones, 'Chartism at Merthyr: a commentary on the Meetings of 1842', *BBCS*, 24(2) (1971), 230–45; D. J. V. Jones, 'Chartism in Welsh communities', *WHR*, 6(3) (1972–3), 243–61; E. R. Morris, 'Who were the Montgomeryshire Chartists?', *Montgomeryshire Collections*, 58 (1963–4), 27–49; D. Williams, *John Frost: A Study in Chartism* (Cardiff, 1939). On Hugh Williams, see W. H. Morris, 'Hugh Williams and Kidwelly', *Carmarthenshire Antiquary*, 3(3) (1961), 161–78.

68 Evans, *Wales, 1815–1906*, p. 46; Morgan, *Rebirth*, pp. 76–7.

69 See L. J. Williams, 'The new unionism in south Wales, 1889–92', *WHR*, 1(4) (1963), 413–29.

70 *Taff Vale Ry v Amalgamated Society of Railway Servants*, [1901] AC 426.

71 Trade Disputes Act 1906 (6 Edward 7, c. 47).

72 Evans, *History*, p. 153; Evans, *Wales, 1815–1906*, p. 312; Morgan, *Rebirth*, p. 144. See also J. Eaton, 'The judgeship of John Bryn Roberts in Glamorgan, 1906–18', *WHR*, 13(1) (1986), 44–71.

73 See G. Eaton, 'Sir Samuel Thomas Evans, judge and politician', *Neath Antiquarian Society Transactions* (1980–1), 15–30.

74 [1910] AC 20. The case concerned an article in the *Sunday Chronicle* in which a fictitious character, bearing the name of Artemus Jones, was reported to be behaving

disreputably in Dieppe. The real Artemus Jones sued the newspaper successfully for the libel.

[75] See R. M. Morris, 'Syr Thomas Artemus Jones (1870–1943)', *DHST*, 35 (1986), 23–38; R. J. L. Thomas, 'Legal Wales: its modern origins and its role after devolution: national identity, the Welsh language and parochialism', in T. G. Watkin (ed.), *Legal Wales: Its Past; Its Future* (Cardiff, 2001), pp. 113–66.

[76] Morgan, *Rebirth*, p. 13; Evans, *Wales, 1815–1906*, p. 290–1; Morgan, *Rebirth*, pp. 12, 34, 129, 144.

[77] [1932] AC 562. The pronouncements of judges in the House of Lords are traditionally referred to as speeches rather than judgements, in that technically they speak either for or against a motion that the appeal before them be allowed.

[78] [1942] AC 206. See also Lord Bingham, 'Lord Atkin of Aberdovey', in T. G. Watkin (ed.), *Y Cyfraniad Cymreig* (Bangor, 2005), pp. 90–101.

[79] On the controversy, see A. Crockett, '"Un o'r barnwyr doethaf erioed": Lord Atkin of Aberdovey v The Archbishop of Wales et al.', in T. G. Watkin (ed.), *Legal Wales: Its Past; Its Future* (Cardiff, 2001), pp. 101–12. On Lord Atkin generally, see G. Lewis, *Lord Atkin* (London, 1983).

[80] See C. I. J. McNall. 'Lord Elwyn-Jones', in T. G. Watkin (ed.), *Y Cyfraniad Cymreig* (Bangor, 2005), pp. 160–81.

[81] Sir John Morris was attorney-general 1997–9; Lord Williams of Mostyn 1999–2001. Sir Arwyn Ungoed-Thomas was solicitor-general during 1951; Sir Geoffrey Howe 1970–2. Sir Geoffrey Howe also played a significant part in public inquiries, leading him to influence the manner in which they are conducted: see The Right Hon. Lord Howe, 'The Aberfan Disaster', in T. G. Watkin (ed.), *The Garthbeibio Murders and Other Essays* (Bangor, 2011), pp. 97–128. Sir John Morris has published an autobiography in which he reflects, amongst other things, on his time as attorney-general: see The Right Hon. Lord Morris, *Fifty Years in Politics and the Law* (Cardiff, 2011).

[82] On the development of legal education in Wales, see L. A. Sheridan, 'University legal education in Cardiff', *Cambrian Law Review*, 4 (1973), 94–102, and J. A. Andrews, 'A century of legal education', *Cambrian Law Review*, 34 (2003), 3–26. On the career of Hughes Parry, see R. Gwynedd Parry, *David Hughes Parry: A Jurist in Society* (Cardiff, 2010). See R. Gwynedd Parry, '"A master of practical law": Sir David Hughes-Parry (1893–1973)', in T. G. Watkin (ed.), *Y Cyfraniad Cymreig* (Bangor, 2005), pp. 102–59.

[83] Evans, *Wales, 1815–1906*, pp. 190, 212. These measures included the Sexual Offences Act 1967, which decriminalized acts of gross indecency committed in private by consenting adults, the Abortion Act 1967 and the Divorce Reform Act 1969.

[84] See E. W. Evans, *Mabon* (Cardiff, 1959), p. 40; Mabon was speaking in the debate on the failure to appoint Welsh-speaking judges to the county courts.

[85] J. Rhys and D. Brynmor-Jones, *The Welsh People*, 4th edn (London, 1906), pp. 540–1; Evans, *Wales, 1815–1906*, p. 199.

[86] Evans, *Wales, 1906–2000*, p. 219; Morgan, *Rebirth*, pp. 270, 380, 383–4, 389. On the struggle regarding the language, see also C. H. Williams, 'Non-violence and the development of the Welsh Language Society, 1962–ca.1974', *WHR*, 8(4) (1977), 426–55; G. O. Williams, 'Brwydr yr Iaith', *THSC* (1971), 7–15.

[87] Morgan, *Rebirth*, p. 374; Black, *New History*, p. 215; Evans, *Wales, 1906–2000*, p. 240.

[88] On the lengthy and difficult campaign for independence or some measure of devolved government for Wales, see G. Daniel, 'The government in Wales', *THSC*,

(1969), 99; J. G. Jones, 'Government, order and the "perishing souls of Wales"', *THSC* (1993), 47–82; J. G. Jones, 'Lloyd George, Cymru Fydd and the Newport meeting of January 1896', *NLWJ*, 29(4) (1996), 435–53; K. O. Morgan, 'Gladstone and Wales', *WHR*, 1(1) (1960), 65–82; K. O. Morgan, 'Nationalists and Mr Gladstone', *THSC* (1960), 36–52; R. A. Roberts, 'Cymru Fu: some contemporary comments', *THSC* (1895–6), 87–103.

[89] Evans, *Wales, 1906–2000*, p. 104; Morgan, *Rebirth*, p. 205.

[90] For the gradual increase in the powers of the Scottish Office and its transfer from London to Edinburgh, see Michael Lynch, *Scotland: A New History* (London, revised edn, 1992), pp. 435–42.

[91] On attempts to create an office of secretary of state for Wales, see J. G. Jones, 'Early campaigns to secure a Secretary of State for Wales', *THSC* (1988), 153–76; J. R. R. McConnel, '"Sympathy without relief is rather like mustard without beef": devolution, Plaid Cymru and the campaign for a Secretary of State for Wales, 1937–1938', *WHR*, 22 (2004–5), 535–57.

[92] Black, *New History*, p. 199; Evans, *Wales, 1906–2000*, pp. 104, 213, 222; Morgan, *Rebirth*, p. 298, 377–8.

[93] Morgan, *Rebirth*, pp. 298, 379.

[94] Ibid., pp. 57, 388. See also E. W. Edwards, 'Cardiff becomes a city', *Morgannwg*, 9 (1965), 80–7.

[95] Evans, *Wales, 1906–2000*, p. 70; Morgan, *Rebirth*, p. 119.

[96] Morgan, *Rebirth*, p. 178; Evans, *Wales, 1906–2000*, p. 104; Morgan, *Rebirth*, pp. 204–5; Evans, *Wales, 1906–2000*, p. 216.

[97] Morgan, *Rebirth*, pp. 271, 299, 332; Evans, *Wales, 1906–2000*, p. 222; on Italy, see Watkin, *The Italian Legal Tradition*, pp. 69–70.

[98] Evans, *Wales, 1906–2000*, pp. 216, 218; Morgan, *Rebirth*, p. 380.

[99] Morgan, *Rebirth*, p. 332.

[100] Ibid., p. 388; Evans, *Wales, 1906–2000*, p. 217; Morgan, *Rebirth*, p. 392; D. Tanner, 'Richard Crossman, Harold Wilson and devolution 1966–70: the making of government policy', *Twentieth-Century British History*, 17 (2006), 545–78.

[101] Sir Ben Bowen Thomas and Sir Alun Talfan Davies, QC.

[102] Morgan, *Rebirth*, pp. 395, 399.

[103] On the nature of these changes, and the potential for judicial devolution in the future, see F. Jones, 'Ave atque vale: a brief review of the history of the quarter sessions in Carmarthenshire', *Carmarthenshire Historian*, 9 (1972), 5–30; H. Moseley, 'Gweinyddiad y gyfraith yng Nghymru', *THSC* (1972–3), 16–36; Thomas, 'Legal Wales', pp. 113–66.

[104] Administration of Justice (Miscellaneous Provisions) Act 1938; Practice Direction (Administrative Court : Establishment) [2000] 1 WLR 1654.

[105] The change of title was made in 1998; see Thomas, 'Legal Wales', pp. 113–66, at 165, n.197.

Chapter 10

[1] Of those voting, 50.3% were in favour; 49.7% were against. Only 50.1% of the electorate participated. Nevertheless, the result was a major *volte-face* from that of the 1979 referendum, when with 58.8% of the electorate voting, only 20.3% of those voting were in favour, with 79.7% opposed.

2   For an analysis of the first devolution settlement within Wales and its workings, see R. Rawlings, *Delineating Wales: Constitutional, Legal and Administrative Aspects of National Devolution* (Cardiff, 2003).

3   Government of Wales Act 1998 (cited hereafter as GoWA 1998), s. 2.

4   The proposed reduction in the number of MPs from Wales elected to Westminster from forty to thirty from 2015 onwards will bring this correspondence to an end.

5   GoWA 1998, ss. 4, 6 and 7; GoWA 2006, ss. 1–9.

6   GoWA 1998, s. 3. GoWA 2006, ss. 3–5, which also now permits extraordinary general elections to be held. As elections to the House of Commons at Westminster are in future also to be held at fixed intervals with the next being in 2015, the next Assembly elections are postponed to 2016 to avoid both elections being held at the same time. Although this avoids the problem for 2015, it is unclear what is to happen in 2020 when both the fixed four-year Assembly term and the fixed five-year parliamentary term will once more expire in the same year.

7   GoWA 1998, s. 52; GoWA 2006, s. 25.

8   GoWA 1998, s. 53.

9   GoWA 1998, ss. 57–61.

10 See *Report of the Richard Commission on the Powers and Electoral Arrangements of the National Assembly for Wales* (Cardiff, 2004).

11 Cm 6582 (London, 2005).

12 GoWA 2006, ss. 45–51.

13 GoWA 1998, s. 106; GWA 2006, s. 80.

14 GoWA 1998, s. 106; GoWA 2006 s. 94(6)(c).

15 GoWA 1998, s. 29; GoWA 2006, s. 59.

16 GoWA 2006, s. 80.

17 GoWA 1998, s. 107; Human Rights Act 1998; GoWA 2006, s. 81.

18 GoWA 1998, s. 108; GoWA 2006, s. 82.

19 GoWA 2006, s. 77. Previously a duty of the Assembly, GoWA 1998, s. 120, which has still obligations in this regard: GoWA 2006, s. 35(2).

20 GoWA 1998, s. 121; GoWA 2006, s. 79.

21 GoWA 2006, s. 72 and 73. Previously a duty of the Assembly, GoWA 1998, s. 113.

22 GoWA 2006, s. 74. Previously a duty of the Assembly, GoWA 1998, s. 114.

23 GoWA 2006, s. 75.

24 GoWA 2006, s. 78.

25 GoWA 2006, s. 27; Schedule 2, and see Lord Dafydd Elis-Thomas, 'O gorff corfforaethol i wasanaeth seneddol/From body corporate to parliamentary service', *Wales Journal of Law and Policy*, 4 (2005–6), 7–16.

26 For the transfer of functions from the Secretary of State to the Assembly, see GoWA 1998, ss. 57–8, and Schedule 3; for the transfer of functions from the Assembly to the Welsh Ministers, see GoWA 2006, s. 22, and Schedules 2 and 3. For a convenient summary of Transfer of Functions Orders by which the powers of the Secretary of State had been acquired from 1964 until 1999, see S. Beasley, 'The National Assembly – "A Voice for Wales"?', *Statute Law Review*, 24 (2003), 211–36.

27 The two models of devolution are set out in Parts 3 and 4 respectively of the 2006 Act, together with Schedules 5 and 7 respectively.

28 The exceptions, like the subjects, are listed under the headings in Part 1 of the Schedule, but apply to all of the subjects regardless of whether they appear under the same heading. The general restrictions are listed in Part 2, with exceptions to

the restrictions in Part 3. The headings and the subjects under them were subsequently amended prior to the referendum in 2011 which signalled popular consent for the Assembly Act provisions to become operable.

29 GoWA 2006, ss. 107–8. This was also true of the Assembly Measures which could be made under Part 3 and Schedule 5: GoWa 2006, ss. 93–4.

30 As with Schedule 7, the general restrictions are listed in Part 2 of the Schedule, with exceptions to the restrictions to be found in Part 3.

31 GoWA 2006, s. 95.

32 The most serious delays were experienced with the Environment LCO and the Welsh Language LCO (National Assembly for Wales (Legislative Competence) (Environment) Order 2009 and the National Assembly for Wales (Legislative Competence) (Welsh Language) Order 2009), both of which took years to progress. Even the, by comparison, straightforward Red Meat LCO (National Assembly for Wales (Legislative Competence) (Agriculture and Rural Development) Order 2009) took the best part of a year. The Affordable Housing LCO (National Assembly for Wales (Legislative Competence) (Housing and Local Government) Order 2010), had superseded an earlier draft (National Assembly for Wales (Legislative Competence) (Housing) Order 2009), which had been approved by the National Assembly but had to be replaced after it encountered political opposition at Westminster.

33 *All Wales Convention Report* (November 2009).

34 Of those voting, 50·64% voted 'No' as against 49·36% voting 'Yes', a difference of only 360 votes on a turnout of 35·83%. On the referendum generally, see R. W. Jones and R. Scully, *Wales says Yes: Devolution and the 2011 Welsh Referendum* (Cardiff, 2012).

35 GoWA 1998, s. 31; GoWA 2006, s. 33.

36 GoWA 1998, s. 76; GoWA 2006, s. 32.

37 GoWA 1998, s. 37; GoWA 2006, s. 65. The Assembly may only promote private bills or oppose the same if the action is mandated by a two-thirds majority of its members voting on the motion.

38 The Counsel General, if not an AM, as has been seen, also has the right to participate and speak, but not vote, in Assembly proceedings, and may also exercise a legislative initiative within the Assembly, even if not a member.

39 The former Supreme Court of Judicature, consisting of the High Court and the Court of Appeal, has been renamed 'the Senior Courts of England and Wales', a somewhat lacklustre title which may betray the fact that the official title of the existing Supreme Court of Judicature had initially been overlooked by those proposing the change.

The Constitutional Reform Act also brought to an end the role of the Lord Chancellor as an active member of the judiciary and as the person responsible for appointing other judges, both of which roles conflicted with the doctrine of the separation of powers, whereby legislative, judicial and executive powers should not be exercised by the same individuals or bodies. The presence of the Law Lords within the legislature had also offended against this doctrine. Thus, once more, the United Kingdom appears to have moved closer to the models of government espoused by its European partners. The same is true of the Judicial Appointments Commission established by the 2005 Act to take over the Lord Chancellor's role in making judicial appointments. Similar bodies are common on mainland Europe, for instance the *Consiglio Superiore della Magistratura* in Italy.

[40] For discussion of this issue, see for instance Sir Roderick Evans, *Cymru'r Gyfraith: Camu 'Mlaen* (Cardiff, 2006); Carwyn Jones, *Y Gyfraith yng Nghymru: Y Deng Mlynedd Nesa* (Cardiff, 2008); Sir David Lloyd Jones, 'The machinery of justice in a changing Wales', *THSC* (NS), 14 (2010), 123–38; T. H. Jones and J. M. Williams, 'Wales as a jurisdiction', *Public Law* (2004), 78–101; R. G. Parry, *Cymru'r Gyfraith* (Caerdydd, 2012).

[41] The two former categories are set to increase in number, while the last mentioned, though now the largest, is likely to decrease.

[42] See N. Cooke and M. Jarman, 'The administrative court in Wales', *Wales Journal of Law and Policy*, 4 (2005–6), 102–5.

[43] GoWA 1998, s. 47; GoWA 2006, s. 35(1).

[44] GoWA 1998, s. 66; GoWA 2006, s. 11(5), which replicates for Assembly Acts the previous provisions regarding Assembly Measures in s. 98(5).

[45] GoWa 2006, s. 156, previously GoWA 1998, s. 122.

[46] See R. Gwynedd Parry, 'Random selection, linguistic rights and the jury trial in Wales', *Criminal Law Review* (2002), 805–16; '"An important obligation of citizenship": language, citizenship and jury service', *Legal Studies*, 27 (2007), 188–215.

[47] See Gwion Lewis, *Hawl i'r Gymraeg* (Talybont, 2008); T. St J. N Bates, 'Bilingualism in legislation', *Statute Law Review*, 20 (1999), 105–6; Keith Bush, 'Approaches to UK legislative drafting: the Welsh perspective', *Statute Law Review*, 25 (2004), 144–50.

[48] Welsh Language Act 1993, ss. 2 and 3 (cited hereafter as WLA).

[49] WLA, s. 7.

[50] WLA, s. 20. Now properly called a mandating order.

[51] The Welsh Language LCO (National Assembly for Wales (Legislative Competence) (Welsh Language) Order 2009).

[52] Of these, seventeen were proposed by the government, with three having been proposed by back-bench Assembly Members, and one each by an Assembly Committee and the Assembly Commission.

[53] For a discussion of such developments, see O. D. Rees, 'Devolution and the Children's Commissioner for Wales: challenges and opportunities', *Contemporary Wales*, 23 (2010), 52–70; O. D. Rees, 'Family and child law in Wales: recent developments', *Family Law* [2010], 186–9; O. D. Rees, 'Devolution and the development of family law in Wales', *Child and Family Law Quarterly* [2008], 45–63; and O. D. Rees, 'The Children's Commissioner for Wales: the first five years', *childRIGHT*, 226 (2006), 16–19. The creation of a Public Service Ombudsman for Wales is discussed in M. Seneviratne, 'A new Ombudsman for Wales', *Public Law* (2006), 6–14, and the eventual incorporation of parts of the United Nations Convention on the Rights of the Child into the law applicable in Wales is anticipated in Jane Williams, 'Incorporating children's rights: the divergence in law and policy', *Legal Studies*, 27 (2007), 261–87.

[54] *Leyes civiles forales*, often continuing the local *fueros* which date from the medieval period before complete reconquest from the Moors had been achieved.

[55] On devolution in Spain, see E. M. Blanco, *The Spanish Legal System* (London, 1996); C. Villiers, *The Spanish Legal Tradition* (London, 1999). On Italy, see T. G. Watkin, *The Italian Legal Tradition* (London, 1997); on Germany, see N. G. Foster and S. Sule, *German Legal System and Laws*, 3rd edn (Oxford, 2002).

Glossary

abetments *(Native Welsh Law)*. The nine means of abetting the commission of a wrong.

actio familiae erciscundae *(Roman Law)*. Action taken by heirs to divide the inheritance.

action on the case *(English Law)*. A legal proceeding in which a civil remedy was sought for a wrong, the facts of which were set out within the body of the writ; later such a proceeding where the harm had been suffered as the indirect or consequential result of the defendant's actions.

Admiralty *(English Law)*. The court of the Lord High Admiral, exercising a jurisdiction over mercantile cases with a foreign element and therefore proceeding according to the international customs of merchants based on continental civil law rather the common law.

Admiralty Court *(English Law)*. State court established in 1857 replacing that of the ADMIRAL with jurisdiction over mercantile cases involving a foreign element.

adneu *(Native Welsh Law)*. Loan for safe keeping.

Aedilician edict. The edict of the CURULE AEDILE.

aestimatum *(Roman Law)*. The INNOMINATE CONTRACT of sale or return.

affiliation. Procedure to determine the paternity of a child.

agweddi *(Native Welsh Law)*. Property given to a wife by her husband on the occasion of their marriage which she would keep if the marriage terminated without blame on her part.

aiel *(English Law)*. Writ extending the ASSIZE OF MORT D'ANCESTOR to cover inheritance from grandparents.

aillt *(Native Welsh Law)*. A lowly-born yet originally free person, dependent on a person of noble birth or a gentleman.

alieni iuris *(Roman Law)*. The condition of those who were in the power of another, usually the PATERFAMILIAS, and thereby unable to own property or enter into contracts without his consent or ratification.

alltud *(Native Welsh Law)*. A foreigner.

alltud cenedlauc *(Native Welsh Law)*. A foreigner who has established a native kinship group.

alnage. A system of supervising and inspecting cloth.

amobr *(Native Welsh Law)*. Payment due to the lord (originally to the PENCENEDL?) when a maiden was married or otherwise lost her maidenhood.

amod *(Native Welsh Law)*. Agreement.

amod deddfol *(Native Welsh Law)*. Obligation entered into by hand clasp before witnesses.

anghyfarch *(Native Welsh Law)*. Secret taking of another's property, subsequently admitted.

angynharchawl *(Native Welsh Law)*. Category of theft where the thief was not caught in the act, or red-handed, but had to have the theft proved against him.

anoddeu *(Native Welsh Law)*. Taking of another's property by mistake.

appeal of felony *(English Law)*. An accusation of serious wrongdoing brought by the victim or the victim's family to secure punishment and compensation.

apprentice *(English Law)*. Barrister who had not yet become a SERJEANT AT LAW.

arddel. Payment to come within the protection of a lord, particularly a Marcher lord.

arddelw *(Native Welsh Law)*. Claim that moveable property belonged to one.

arglwydd *(Native Welsh Law)*. Lord, including the feudal sense.

argyfreu *(Native Welsh Law)*. Paraphernalia. The chattels a woman brings with her for her personal use upon marriage.

assarts. Land brought into cultivation and thereby into ownership, often by clearing forests or wastes.

Assembly Acts. Primary legislation enacted since 2011 by the National Assembly for Wales, and equivalent in status to Acts passed by the United Kingdom parliament.

Assembly Measures. Primary legislation enacted between 2007 and 2011 by the National Assembly for Wales, and equivalent in status to Acts passed by the United Kingdom parliament.

assize *(English Law)*. (1) A meeting of the king with his nobility; (2) the decisions taken at such meetings; (3) remedies given by such assemblies; (4) later, the law courts which met in accordance with the decisions of such meetings.

assize of mort d'ancestor *(English Law)*. Remedy to allow the heir of a deceased tenant to enter upon his inheritance if someone had taken the land unjustly before he could do so.

assize of novel disseisin *(English Law)*. Remedy to allow a person unjustly deprived of the possession of freehold land without a judgement to recover it speedily before the royal courts.

assizes *(English Law)*. The courts of commissioners who toured the country several times each year to take criminal trials under the provisions of the Assize of Clarendon, 1166, and the Assize of Northampton, 1176.

attorney. Representative of the litigant before the courts of common law.

banns. Invitations to the public to raise legal objections most commonly to forthcoming marriages.

benefit of clergy *(English Law)*. The right of those in ecclesiastical orders, both holy orders and minor orders, not to be punished other than before an ecclesiastical tribunal, leading to convicts who could establish their literacy avoiding punishment for a first offence.

benffyc *(Native Welsh Law)*. Loan.

benffyg *(Native Welsh Law)*. Loan for use.

bequest. Gift of personal property by will.

besaiel *(English Law)*. Writ extending the ASSIZE OF MORT D'ANCESTOR to cover inheritance from great-grandparents.

bill *(English Law)*. Procedure whereby an action could be commenced before a court by simple written plaint without need of a formal writ issued by the CHANCERY.

bill of Middlesex *(English Law)*. A device used before the KING'S BENCH to commence litigation, which strictly belonged before another court, by fictitiously claiming that the cause had arisen in the county of Middlesex where the court of KING'S BENCH, being at Westminster, was located.

bloodwyte *(Anglo-Saxon Law)*. Fine for the shedding of blood.

bona vacantia. Goods without an owner, such as the property of a deceased person with no heirs.

bond *(English Law)*. Written promise, usually to pay money.

borough recorder. The judge of the borough court.

brad. Treason

brawdwyr *(Native Welsh Law)*. Judges, those performing a judicial function.

Bretwalda *(Anglo-Saxon)*. Title of respect given to an overking, recognized as *primus inter pares* by fellow rulers.

breve de recto *(English Law)*. Remedy allowing a demandant to assert his right to freehold land against the tenant in possession (*seisin*), the WRIT OF RIGHT.

briduw *(Native Welsh Law)*. Obligation undertaken by formal oath, calling upon God to witness the transaction.

brithemin *(Native Irish Law)*. Legal scholars.

caeth *(Native Welsh Law)*. A slave.

calcis coquendi. PRAEDIAL SERVITUDE allowing one to burn lime on another's land.

camlwrw *(Native Welsh Law)*. A penalty payment.

canghellor *(Native Welsh Law)*. The chancellor, or secretary, of the king.

canllaw *(Native Welsh Law)*. Guide; ATTORNEY.

canon law. The law made by the Church for the Church; the internal law of the Church.

cantref *(Native Welsh Law)*. A territorial division consisting of one hundred TREFI.

Cassation, Supreme Court of. In civil law countries, the tribunal of final competence which reviews the decisions of lower courts for error of law.

castle guard *(English Law)*. Freehold land tenure, requiring the tenant to serve as a watchman at a castle, usually in border country or on the coast, for a fixed number of days every year.

ceidwad *(Native Welsh Law)*. Witness as to ownership of property.

cenedl *(Native Welsh Law)*. The group to which one belonged by birth; nation, cf. the Roman GENS.

certiorari *(English Law)*. Prerogative writ, later prerogative order, requiring the record of a tribunal of inferior competence to be examined before the King's court to ensure no error of law has occurred.

chamberlain. A royal official, in charge of the ruler's chamber.

chance medley *(English Law)*. An unpremeditated killing on a sudden occasion in hot blood; a killing less serious than murder; manslaughter.

chance melée *(English Law)*. An unpremeditated killing on a sudden occasion in hot blood; a killing less serious than murder; manslaughter.

charter *(English Law)*. Written document, for instance granting rights to a borough or corporation.

chivalric tenure *(English Law)*. The holding of freehold land by military service.

codex Gregorianus *(Roman Law)*. Late third century AD collection of extant legislation, LEGES.

codex Hermogenianus *(Roman Law)*. A second collection of extant legislation from the late third century AD.

codex Theodosianus *(Roman Law)*. A fifth-century collection of extant legislation, ordered by the emperor Theodosius II, which enjoyed considerable influence in Western Europe thereafter.

cognitio *(Roman Law)*. The system of dealing with litigation in imperial times.

comitia *(Roman Law)*. Assembly of the citizens for legislative purposes and for the election of magistrates.

commodatum *(Roman Law)*. A REAL CONTRACT, a loan to use the thing lent and to return it.

commercium *(Roman Law)*. The capacity to enter into contracts under the IUS CIVILE.

commissioners *(English Law)*. The technically proper term for the judges of ASSIZE.

Common Pleas *(English Law)*. One of the three royal courts of common law.

common recovery *(English Law)*. Action for the recovery of land by which an ENTAIL could be barred, allowing the land to be alienated contrary to the terms of the original grant.

commorthas. Payments of money to assist a lord or his retinue; gatherings to raise such money.

compurgator. An OATH-HELPER; one who swears in support of another's oath that that other is not a perjuror.

Concordia discordantium canonum. Systematic treatment of canon law produced by Gratian *c.*1140–2.

consensual contract. An agreement which becomes legally binding by virtue of a meeting of minds between the parties, *consensus ad idem*, on certain key elements of it.

consideration *(English Law)*. The essential ingredient for making an unwritten agreement a legally binding contract, originally the reason (consideration) for so doing.

consistory court. The bishop's diocesan tribunal.

consortium *(Roman Law)*. The joint inheritance by heirs of the deceased's estate.

constitutio Antoniniana *(Roman Law)*. Law issued by the emperor Caracalla in AD 212 by which all free persons within the empire, other than DEDITICII, became Roman citizens.

contract. A legally binding agreement creating obligations.

conubium *(Roman Law)*. The capacity to contract a Roman marriage.

coparcenary *(English Law)*. A sharing of lands between two or more heirs, particularly daughters.

copyhold *(English Law)*. The customary TENURE of land within a MANOR whereby the tenant's title was witnessed by his copy of the roll of the manorial court; a later name for villein tenure.

coroner *(English Law)*. A Crown official employed within every shire to look after the royal revenues, one of which being the fine for an unexplained death which led to the institution of the coroner's inquest in such cases.

corpori corpore *(Roman Law)*. 'By the body to the body'; the harm had to be caused directly.

cosinage *(English Law)*. Writ extending the ASSIZE OF MORT D'ANCESTOR to cover inheritance from collateral relatives.

county assizes. The tribunals which dealt with the most serious criminal cases prior to 1972 and took the verdict in civil causes at NISI PRIUS.

County Court. Tribunal established by statute in 1846 with limited competence to try civil causes in each county in England and Wales.

Court Leet *(English Law)*. A MANORIAL court having the right to view the frankpledge, that is carry out the function of the HUNDRED court in ensuring that every adult male was placed within a TITHING.

Court of Appeal. Tribunal with full competence to hear appeals in civil causes, and since 1971, criminal cases.

Court of Arches *(English Law)*. The highest ecclesiastical tribunal within the province of Canterbury, sitting at the church of St Mary-le-Bow (hence, Arches) in London.

Court of Chancery *(English Law)*. Court presided over by the chancellor as keeper of the king's conscience which exercised the royal prerogative to do justice where the common law failed to provide a remedy or its remedy was inadequate.

Court of Criminal Appeal. Tribunal established in 1907 to hear appeals in limited circumstances from first instance criminal convictions.

Court of Requests *(English Law)*. A prerogative court dealing with small claims and the suits of poor persons.

Court of Session. The supreme court of justice in Scotland.

Courts of Great Sessions. The tribunals provided to administer justice within twelve counties of Wales following the union with England and having competence to hear the most serious criminal and civil litigation.

covenant *(English Law)*. Literally an agreement, but from the thirteenth century, a written agreement under seal.

cowyll *(Native Welsh Law)*. Morning gift, given by the husband to the wife as a sign of his recognition that she had been a virgin when they married.

Crown Cases Reserved. Court which dealt with questions of law left undecided at criminal trials on the ASSIZE circuits, there being no appeals at that time from criminal convictions.

curator *(Roman Law)*. Guardian appointed to safeguard the property of a PATERFAMILIAS who had become mad or spendthrift. Later, also, of young people who were SUI IURIS, but who were vulnerable to being taken advantage of by their more experienced elders.

curtesy *(English Law)*. Right of a husband to a life interest in one half of his deceased wife's lands provided there was a child of the marriage.

curule aedile *(Roman Law)*. Magistrate responsible for the forum and the market, and thereby for the development in his edict of the law of sale.

custos rotulorum. Keeper of the rolls of the court; custodian of the court records; president of the JUSTICES OF THE PEACE in a county.

cwmwd *(Native Welsh Law)*. A territorial division consisting of fifty TREFI.

cwyn newydd difeddiant. Complaint of recent dispossession; the Welsh for ASSIZE OF NOVEL DISSEISIN.

cydfodau. Treaties, particularly those concerned with the extradition of criminals from one Marcher lordship to another.

cyfnewid *(Native Welsh Law)*. Exchange (including sale).

cyfran *(Native Welsh Law)*. Sharing of land among male descendants.

cyfrif *(Native Welsh Law)*. Land of a TAEOG in an unfree TREF.

cymyn *(Native Welsh Law)*. Testamentary gift.

cynghaws *(Native Welsh Law)*. Pleader; ADVOCATE.

cynharchawl *(Native Welsh Law)*. Category of theft where the thief was caught in the act, or red-handed.

cynllwyn. Ambush, premeditated plot.

cynnwys. Permission, hence (1) share of an illegitimate son in the family inheritance, because by permission of his legitimate brothers; (2) monetary payment to be readmitted to property by permission of the lord.

da *(Native Welsh Law)*. Goods; moveable property.

dadanhudd *(Native Welsh Law)*. Remedy allowing an heir to recover land he should have inherited from a deceased ancestor.

daered *(Native Welsh Law)*. Mortuary payment to the Church from the deceased's property.

damdwng *(Native Welsh Law)*. Oath, sworn on relics, that one was the owner of property.

damnum iniuria datum *(Roman Law)*. Wrongful damage, compensatable under the provisions of the Lex Aquilia.

damweiniau. Recorded cases, instances, of a legal principle or rule.

dawnbwyd *(Native Welsh Law)*. A food render.

De donis conditionalibus *(English Law)*. Chapter 1 of the Statute of Westminster II, 1285, giving remedies to heirs in tail, and others expecting to obtain land in accordance with the terms of an entailed grant, when they failed to do so because the tenant had alienated the land during his lifetime contrary to the terms of the grant.

de similibus simile iudicium dandum est. Principle that like cases should be decided alike.

De viris religiosis *(English Law)*. Statute of Mortmain of 1279 banning alienations of land to the Church and other corporations which would place the land in their hand in perpetuity.

debt *(English Law)*. Writ for the recovery of a fixed sum of money owed.

decreta *(Roman Law)*. Decisions of the emperor as the final judge in individual cases, making law.

Decretum. The commonly used name for Gratian's *Concordia discordantium canonum*, the fundamental text of medieval canon law.

dediticii *(Roman Law)*. Hostile foreigners, suffered to remain free within the empire upon pain of being enslaved if they came too near Rome.

delict *(Roman Law)*. A wrongful act giving rise to an obligation to make recompense.

demise *(English Law)*. The granting of a Lease of land.

denizen status. Grant of rights equal to those of burgesses or native-born Englishmen to those who were neither so as to improve their legal and social position.

depositum *(Roman Law)*. A Real Contract, whereby a thing is lent for safe keeping.

dial *(Native Welsh Law)*. Revenge.

difeddiant. Dispossession.

dirwy *(Native Welsh Law)*. A penalty payment.

distain *(Native Welsh Law)*. A Steward.

district judge. A local judge of inferior competence replacing the Stipendiary Magistrate.

Divisional Court. A collegiate tribunal consisting of two or three judges of the Queen's Bench Division.

divorce a mensa et thoro. Decree terminating the obligation of spouses to cohabit while leaving the bond of marriage undissolved.

divorce a vinculo matrimonio. Decree terminating a valid marriage, giving the parties the capacity to contract marriage with others.

Divorce Court. State court established in 1857 replacing the jurisdiction of the ecclesiastical courts over matrimonial causes and having the power, for the first time in English law, to terminate existing marriages by judicial decree of divorce.

divortium *(Roman Law)*. The termination of a marriage by the consent of both spouses.

Doctors' Commons. The premises in the City of London from which ADVOCATES practising before the ADMIRALTY and the ecclesiastical courts exercised their profession.

doethion *(Native Welsh Law)*. Those learned in the law.

dognfanag *(Native Welsh Law)*. Private accusation of theft for fear of the rank or wealth of the culprit.

dolus. Deceit; deliberate or reckless conduct.

dower *(English Law)*. Property, usually land, promised by a husband to his wife at the church door on the occasion of their wedding to support her in widowhood.

dowry. Payment by the bride's father to the husband on the occasion of the couple's marriage.

ebidew *(Native Welsh Law)*. The payment to the lord of the deceased's best beast upon the latter's death.

ecclesiastical law. The law made by the state to govern its relations with the Church; the external law governing the Church alone.

echwyn *(Native Welsh Law)*. Loan for consumption.

edicta *(Roman Law)*. Written statements by the elected republican magistrates of the policies they would follow during their year of office. Later, issued by emperors, having the force of law.

edictum perpetuum *(Roman Law)*. The codified version of the edict of the URBAN PRAETOR composed for the emperor Hadrian in AD 120 by the jurist Salvius Julianus.

edling *(Native Welsh Law)*. The heir to the throne, a term borrowed from England.

emancipation *(Roman Law)*. Means by which a child in PATRIAPOTESTAS could be freed from the *pater*'s power while the *pater* was yet living, and thus become SUI IURIS.

emptio/venditio *(Roman Law)*. The CONSENSUAL CONTRACT of sale.

entail *(English Law)*. Freehold estate whereby the land is inheritable by lineal descendants of the grantee only.

epistolae *(Roman Law)*. Letters containing legal opinions written by the emperor in response to questions.

equity *(English Law)*. System of rules employed by the COURT OF CHANCERY to provide justice where the common law failed to do so or failed to do so adequately.

erw *(Native Welsh Law)*. A territorial division, an acre.

escheat *(English Law)*. Return of freehold land to the lord if held by a convicted felon or upon failure of heirs.

estate *(English Law)*. The length of time that a grant of freehold land would last – for life or until the grantee's descendants died out, or until his wider family died out.

Exchequer *(English Law)*. One of the three royal courts of common law.

exchequer *(English Law)*. Department of state dealing with the royal finances.

Exchequer Chamber *(English Law)*. (1) A tribunal established in 1358 to hear complaints concerning error of law in the Court of EXCHEQUER; (2) a tribunal established in 1585 to hear complaints of error of law in the court of KING'S BENCH; (3) a room in which the judges and SERJEANTS met occasionally to discuss difficult questions of law.

eyre *(English Law)*. Tour of the country or a shire undertaken by royal commissioners; a judicial circuit.

familia *(Roman Law)*. The family or household, including domestic slaves and capable of meaning the family property as well.

fealty *(English Law)*. Oath of faithfulness taken by a freehold tenant to his lord.

fee simple *(English Law)*. Freehold estate by which land was given to the tenant and his heirs. A fully heritable estate.

feoffees *(English Law)*. Those who were the legal owners of property held to the USE of others.

feudal incidents *(English Law)*. Payments or sources of income to which the king or a lord were entitled upon certain occurrences.

ffyrnygrwydd dywuynau *(Native Welsh Law)*. Wilful destruction of another's property rendering it useless.

final concord *(English Law)*. Agreement, usually in writing, by which litigating parties were reconciled; the document recording that agreement.

foot of the fine *(English Law)*. The bottom part of the document recording a FINAL CONCORD, the part retained by the royal court.

formula *(Roman Law)*. Instructions sent by the PRAETOR to a judge, informing him of the issues to be decided in a particular case, together with the possible solutions open to him.

franchise *(English Law)*. The grant of a freedom or right by the Crown to a subject or subjects; sometimes used to describe the right to vote at elections.

freehold *(English Law)*. Land tenure the terms of which were agreed by lord and tenant and not by the custom of the locality.

furtum *(Roman Law)*. Theft, a DELICT requiring compensation

furtum usus *(Roman Law)*. Theft of the use of a thing, as where it is lent for one purpose and used for another by the borrower.

gafael *(Native Welsh Law)*. A territorial division.

galanas *(Native Welsh Law)*. Homicide, and more generally the compensation payment therefor.

general eyre *(English Law)*. Judicial circuit of the whole country, regularly undertaken from the twelfth to the fourteenth centuries.

geni a meithrin *(Native Welsh Law)*. Plea of having owned an animal from birth and having reared it.

gens *(Roman Law)*. Those who formed a descent group sharing the same name, cf. the Scottish *clan*.

Glossa ordinaria. The comprehensive gloss of the entire text of Justinian's Digest completed by Accursius *c*. 1265.

glossators. The school of jurists who flourished in Bologna in the eleventh to thirteenth centuries.

gobr estyn. Payment to the lord when an heir entered upon his inheritance.

gofyniad *(Native Welsh Law)*. Action for recovering land by disappointed heirs following a wrongful alienation.

gowyn *(Native Welsh Law)*. Payment to a wife in compensation for her husband's adultery.

grand assize *(English Law)*. Method of trying claims to title of freehold land by jury.

grand jury *(English Law)*. The JURY OF PRESENTMENT, which vouched that an accused person should be tried for the wrong.

grand larceny *(English Law)*. Stealing of property valued at one shilling or more, which carried a capital penalty.

grand serjeanty *(English Law)*. Freehold land tenure by honourable personal service to the king.

gwaddol *(Native Welsh Law)*. Property given to a wife by her family on the occasion of her marriage; cf. DOWRY.

gwaradwydd *(Native Welsh Law)*. Hurt to a person's honour; shame.

gwarchadw *(Native Welsh Law)*. Lawful possession which could mature into ownership.

gweli dafod *(Native Welsh Law)*. Insulting language.

gwely *(Native Welsh Law)*. Family land.

gwestfa *(Native Welsh Law)*. The duty to entertain the king on his itinerary around his kingdom; eventually the duty to render that amount in food or later money.

Gwledig *(Native Welsh Law)*. Title of respect given to an overking, recognized as *primus inter pares* by fellow rulers.

gwr dyfod *(Native Welsh Law)*. A person who acquires land by taking possession rather than by inheritance.

gwrthrychiad *(Native Welsh Law)*. Heir-apparent.

gwybyddiad *(Native Welsh Law)*. One bearing testimony to words, acts or deeds witnessed in person.

gwyr bonheddig *(Native Welsh Law)*. Gentlemen; the gentry.

gwystl *(Native Welsh Law)*. Pledge of moveables; security.

heriot *(English Law)*. Mortuary payment to the lord of a dead villein's best beast; cf. Welsh EBIDEW.

High Commission *(English Law)*. Prerogative court charged with enforcing the Reformation settlement.

High Court. Tribunal with full competence to hear civil causes at first instance.

homage *(English Law)*. Oath taken by a military tenant of freehold land to defend his lord and fight for him.

hundred *(English Law)*. A territorial division of the shire.

immoveable property. Land, or anything built upon or planted in land, or any right pertaining to land.

imperitia culpae adnumeratur. 'Skill is reckoned as fault'; a maxim requiring higher standards of care from skilled persons in the exercise of their work.

in consimili casu *(English Law)*. Principle contained in chapter 24 of the Statute of Westminster II, 1285, that where a writ existed in one case but was not available in another very similar situation, a writ should be given to remedy that very similar case.

inaedificatio *(Roman Law)*. Acquisition of ownership by building upon one's land.

indentures *(English Law)*. Deeds executed on a single piece of parchment by more than one person and then divided along a jagged edge resembling teeth to provide copies for each person.

iniuria *(Roman Law)*. An unjust harm; an injury.

injunction *(English Law)*. Remedy in EQUITY ordering a person to abstain from conduct which was harming or could or would harm the plaintiff's interests on pain of imprisonment for contempt; occasionally ordering the defendant to perform some act to prevent a harm arising (a mandatory injunction).

innominate contracts *(Roman Law)*. CONTRACTS which did not fit into any of the four main contractual categories (REAL, VERBAL, LITERAL, CONSENSUAL) but were enforceable once one of the parties had performed his side of the bargain.

Instructions. Method by which the procedure and work of the Council of Wales and the Marches was regulated by the English government through the PRIVY COUNCIL.

intercommon *(English Law)*. The mutual enjoyment of common rights by local inhabitants.

interdicts *(Roman Law)*. PRAETORIAN remedies by which the possession of property was protected.

iudex pedaneus *(Roman Law)*. A deputy judge appointed to assist the governor of a Roman province in imperial times.

iudex qui litem suam fecit *(Roman Law)*. 'A judge who made the case his own', that is gave wrong judgement. Such a judge had committed a QUASI-DELICT known by this name and was liable to the wronged party.

ius civile *(Roman Law)*. The civil law of Rome, that is the law applicable between citizens.

ius gentium *(Roman Law)*. Law common to all mankind; law applied by the PEREGRINE PRAETOR in situations where one or more of the parties were not Roman citizens.

ius honorarium *(Roman Law)*. Law contained in the edict of the URBAN PRAETOR, governing the administration of justice between citizens.

ius honorum *(Roman Law)*. The right to stand for public office, particularly the chief magistracies.

ius naturale *(Roman Law)*. The law of nature; the law which nature appears to teach all animals, identifiable by proper use of the human faculty of reason.

ius vitae necisque *(Roman Law)*. 'The right of life and death', by which a PATERFAMILIAS could put to death his slaves and in strict law his children, although the recorded instances of the latter are very rare.

iustae nuptiae *(Roman Law)*. A marriage between citizens in accordance with the IUS CIVILE.

iustum matrimonium *(Roman Law)*. A marriage between citizens in accordance with the IUS CIVILE.

judicial separation. Decree terminating the obligation of spouses to cohabit while leaving the bond of marriage undissolved.

Junian Latins *(Roman Law)*. Slaves freed informally, who therefore had not become Roman citizens but who could attain the higher status by service to the state. So-called from the LEX JUNIA.

jurisdiction in error *(English Law)*. Power of a tribunal to oversee the correctness of a lower tribunal's decisions in matters of law.

jury of presentment. Body of people from the county who confirmed to the ASSIZE judges that there was a criminal case for the accused to answer.

justices in eyre *(English Law)*. The commissioners who undertook the judicial circuit called an EYRE.

justiciar *(English Law)*. Chief minister of the king in the twelfth and early thirteenth centuries.

Justicies *(English Law)*. Writ to commence litigation before the SHERIFF in the shire court when the parties so preferred.

King's Bench *(English Law)*. One of the three royal courts of common law.

King's peace *(English Law)*. The royal protection of persons, places, occasions.

lance licioque *(Roman Law)*. Ritual search for stolen goods.

Latin status *(Roman Law)*. An intermediate status between being a PEREGRINE and a Roman citizen, with some but not all the rights of a citizen.

latitat *(English Law)*. 'He lies hidden'; an allegation that a fugitive defendant is to be found in a certain county.

Law Lords of Appeal in Ordinary. The most senior appeal judges within the United Kingdom, sitting in the House of Lords, with competence to hear appeals from England and Wales, Scotland and Northern Ireland.

Law of Citations *(Roman Law)*. Fifth-century solution to the problem of conflicting juristic opinions.

Law Society. The organization representing the interests of and regulating the profession of SOLICITOR OF THE SUPREME COURT.

lay impropriators. Those who at the Reformation purchased from the Crown estates previously held by monastic foundations comprising the rectory of a parish, thereby entitling them to the TITHES payable by the people of the parish to the rector.

LCO. See *Legislative Competence Order*.

lease *(English Law)*. Grant of land for a fixed length of time measured in years rather than in lifetimes.

leasehold *(English Law)*. Grant of land for a fixed length of time in return for a money rent.

leges *(Roman Law)*. Plural of LEX.

Legislative Competence Order. An order in council which, between 2007 and 2011, conferred upon the National Assembly for Wales an enduring power to pass primary legislation in the form of Assembly Measures in relation to a matter or matters set out in the order.

legitima portio *(Roman Law)*. Fraction of the estate which family members were entitled to inherit.

lex *(Roman Law)*. Enacted law, made by the COMITIA.

lex Aelia Sentia *(Roman Law)*. Law restricting the freedom of citizens to MANUMIT slaves.

lex Aquilia *(Roman Law)*. Law of 267 BC requiring compensation to be made for wrongful damage to the property of others.

lex Falcidia *(Roman Law)*. Law of 40 BC by which heirs were guaranteed at least a quarter of the estate inherited from the deceased.

lex Fufia Caninia *(Roman Law)*. Law restricting the freedom of citizens to MANUMIT slaves.

liege homage *(English Law)*. Form of HOMAGE sworn to one's chief lord, thereby having precedence over any other oath of HOMAGE.

literal contract. An agreement which becomes legally binding by virtue of its being made or evidenced in writing.

livery and maintenance. Practice whereby a person places himself under the protection of another more powerful than himself in return for receiving some clothing or badge to display that allegiance and the support of that other in obtaining employment or before the courts.

locatio/conductio *(Roman Law)*. The CONSENSUAL CONTRACT of hire.

longi temporis praescriptio *(Roman Law)*. Acquisition of provincial land by long possession.

Lord Justice of Appeal. A judge appointed to hear cases at second instance in the COURT OF APPEAL.

Lord Justices of Appeal in Chancery. Judges hearing appeals from decisions at first instance in the Court of Chancery.

love-days. Days upon which disputes might be reconciled.

lladrad *(Native Welsh Law)*. Wrongful taking of property in the owner's absence and subsequently denied.

llan *(Native Welsh Law)*. Enclosure; eventually the area enclosing a church, the churchyard.

lleidr cyhoeddog *(Native Welsh Law)*. TAEOG found guilty of theft on three occasions.

llog *(Native Welsh Law)*. Hire.

llw gweilydd *(Native Welsh Law)*. Ritual challenge to take an oath denying a theft.

llys *(Native Welsh Law)*. A court.

machni *(Native Welsh Law)*. SURETYSHIP.

maenol *(Native Welsh Law)*. A territorial division, corresponding to the Norman MANOR.

maer *(Native Welsh Law)*. With the CANGHELLOR, the most important royal official, being a sort of REEVE.

maerdref *(Native Welsh Law)*. The TREF in the CWMWD held by the official called the MAER or mayor.

mamwys *(Native Welsh Law)*. Custom by which the grandsons of a Welshman might inherit his land alongside his sons if their mother had been married to a foreigner by RHODD CENEDL.

mancipatio *(Roman Law)*. Formal conveyance of the most important forms of property (*res mancipi*).

mandamus *(English Law)*. Prerogative writ, now a prerogative order, by which the Court of KING'S BENCH, later the DIVISIONAL COURT of the QUEEN'S BENCH DIVISION, now the Administrative Court, of the HIGH COURT orders a public official to carry out one or more of his duties at the suit of a person aggrieved at the failure to do so.

mandata *(Roman Law)*. Orders of the emperor to imperial officials having the force of law in the instant situation and having persuasive force thereafter.

mandate *(Roman Law)*. Consensual contract whereby one person commissions another to do things on his behalf, in particular enter into legal relationships with third parties.

mandatum *(Roman Law)*. The CONSENSUAL CONTRACT of MANDATE.

manifest theft *(Roman Law)*. Theft where the thief is caught in the act or caught red-handed.

manor *(English Law)*. Norman territorial division, roughly equivalent to a village or group of villages.

manumission *(Roman Law)*. The method by which slaves were freed and became citizens.

manus *(Roman Law)*. 'Hand'. A marriage with *manus*, always the exception not the rule, led to the wife passing from her own family into that of her husband. Most Roman marriages were free marriages, *liberum matrimonium*, whereby the wife remained a member of her own family, independent of her husband.

March. The border territory between England and Wales; lordships not within the Principality.

marriage by rhodd cenedl *(Native Welsh Law)*. Marriage of a daughter with the consent of her family.

mechnïaeth *(Native Welsh Law)*. Obligation entered into with sureties taken.

mesne *(English Law)*. A tenancy situated between that of the person in possession (*seisin*) of freehold land and the king.

metus. Fear.

Mines Royal *(English Law)*. Claim of the English crown to a monopoly over mineral rights within the realm and their exploitation.

mortgage. The giving of land as security for a loan, the produce of the land not going towards the repayment of the debt.

moveable property. All forms of property which are not IMMOVEABLE.

mutual pledging *(Native Welsh Law)* challenge to the correctness of a judge's judgement.

mutuum *(Roman Law)*. A REAL CONTRACT, a loan for consumption of the thing lent with the obligation to pay back its equivalent.

nawdd *(Native Welsh Law)*. Protection, cf. 'Peace' as in 'the king's peace'; the peace of God'.

nec vi nec clam nec precario *(Roman Law)*. By neither force, stealth nor permission.

nemo respondetur sine brevi regis *(English Law)*. No one should answer for a free tenement without the king's writ. The principle by which the king, beginning with Henry II (1154–89) protected the possession *(seisin)* of freehold tenants.

nisi prius *(English Law)*. 'Unless before'. Provision introduced in 1285 allowing the Assize judges to take verdicts in civil litigation arising in the shire. It worked by having the litigation commenced at Westminster and then adjourned to a future date, unless before that date the Assize judges could take the verdict in the locality. The date set always allowed such a local verdict to be taken. The system continued until 1971.

non-manifest theft *(Roman Law)*. Theft where the wrong has to be proved from evidence because the thief is not taken in the act or caught red-handed.

nullity. Decree, in matrimonial causes, stating that parties had not been validly married.

oath helpers. Those swearing to one's veracity; Compurgators.

occupatio *(Roman Law)*. Method of acquiring ownership of property by taking possession of it.

oratio *(Roman Law)*. The speech made by the emperor or his representative in introducing a legislative proposal before the senate, sometimes itself regarded as the source of the law enacted.

ordeal. Method of trying the veracity of an oath by the judgement of God (originally pagan).

Order in Council. A form of subordinate legislation made by Her Majesty in her Privy Council.

oyer and terminer *(English Law)*. The duty given to the Assize judges to hear and determine the cases set before them.

pannage *(English Law)*. Right to allow pigs to feed off acorns in forests.

Papal Curia. The court of the Pope; the highest ecclesiastical tribunal in pre-Reformation Western Christendom.

parish vestry. The assembly of the parishioners of the parish.

parlement. A French medieval law court.

partibility *(English Law)*. Rule of inheritance allowing property to be divided among a group of heirs.

paterfamilias *(Roman Law)*. The head of the family or household; the oldest living male ancestor.

patriapotestas *(Roman Law)*. The power of the Paterfamilias over the other members of the family.

pays de droit écrit *(Medieval French Law)*. The land of the written law, being those parts of southern France where the Vulgar Roman law had retained its strongest hold.

pays des coutumes *(Medieval French Law)*. The land of the customs, being those parts of northern France where the customary law varied from area to area.

peace *(English Law)*. The protection of the king or some other lord, as in 'the king's peace'.

peculium *(Roman Law)*. A small portion of the family property given to a son in Potestas to manage and thereby gain experience in readiness for eventually becoming Sui Iuris with property of his own to manage.

pencenedl *(Native Welsh Law)*. Head of the wider birth-related grouping; clan chief.

penteulu *(Native Welsh Law)*. Head of the family.

peregrine *(Roman Law)*. A friendly foreigner within the bounds of the empire, able to trade with Roman citizens under the Ius Gentium.

peregrine praetor *(Roman Law)*. The magistrate responsible for the adminstration of justice between foreigners at Rome or between citizens and foreigners. The law in his edict formed the Ius GENTIUM.

permutatio *(Roman Law)*. The INNOMINATE CONTRACT of exchange.

personal action. Legal proceeding leading to compensation for the wrongful invasion of a right.

petty larceny *(English Law)*. Stealing of property valued at less than one shilling, which did not carry a capital penalty.

petty sessions *(English Law)*. The local courts of the JUSTICES OF THE PEACE; magistrates courts.

pignus *(Roman Law)*. A REAL CONTRACT, whereby a thing is given as security for a loan of money.

pleas of the crown *(English Law)*. Serious wrongs which were always to be tried by the king's justices.

portreeve *(English Law)*. Borough official charged with overseeing the markets and fairs; a mayor.

possessory assizes *(English Law)*. Remedies for the recovery of the possession *(seisin)* of freehold land.

possessory interdicts. Methods of ensuring protection of possession while ownership was being determined in a dispute.

praecipe *(English Law)*. Writ commanding a freehold tenant, properly a TENANT-IN-CHIEF, to give his land to another or else appear before the king's justices to explain why he had not done so.

praecipe in capite *(English Law)*. Writ of *praecipe* for land held in chief of the king.

praedial servitudes. Rights of a landowner over the land of another.

precarium *(Roman Law)*. The INNOMINATE CONTRACT of gratuitous letting.

presentment *(English Law)*. Method by which the community could put a notorious wrongdoer on trial by presenting him to the ASSIZE judges.

prid. Arrangement by which GWELY land could be extra-legally 'sold' by placing it as security for a loan which was never repaid but periodically renewed.

primogeniture *(English Law)*. Rule of inheritance to land, favouring the eldest son.

princeps *(Roman Law)*. Original title of the emperors, meaning 'first citizen'.

Principality. That part of Wales under the direct control of the English crown from the Edwardian conquest until the Acts of Union.

priodas *(Native Welsh Law)*. Marriage.

priodawr *(Native Welsh Law)*. Owner, proprietor.

priodolder *(Native Welsh Law)*. Ownership, proprietorship.

Privy Council, Judicial Committee of. Tribunal advising the sovereign as to how to dispose of legal cases on appeal from the colonies and the Commonwealth, together with the discharge of other judicial functions including some under the Government of Wales Act 1998.

Probate Court. State court established in 1857 replacing the jurisdiction of the ecclesiastical courts over the succession to the estates of deceased persons.

Probate, Divorce and Admiralty Division. One of the three divisions of the HIGH COURT, renamed the FAMILY DIVISION in 1970.

proctor. Originally one representing a client before the ADMIRALTY or the ecclesiastical courts, but not arguing the client's case.

Proculians *(Roman Law)*. One of the two principal schools of juristic opinion, the other being the SABINIANS.

procurator. One who cared for legal proceedings on behalf of another; an ATTORNEY.

prohibition *(English Law)*. Prerogative writ, now a prerogative order, by which the Court of KING'S BENCH, later the DIVISIONAL COURT of the QUEEN'S BENCH DIVISION of the HIGH COURT, now the Administrative Court, forbids tribunals of inferior jurisdiction to hear a case because they lack the competence or jurisdiction to do so.

protonotary. The keeper of the record of the COURTS OF GREAT SESSIONS.

prudentes *(Roman Law)*. Those learned in the law; the jurists.

puisne judge. (1) A judge of the royal courts other than the Chief Justice; (2) since 1875, a HIGH COURT judge.

Quarter Sessions *(English Law)*. Courts meeting every three months in each county, staffed by local JUSTICES OF THE PEACE.

quasi-contract. An obligation arising from the conferring of a benefit which was not due, and therefore requiring recompense.

quasi-delict *(Roman Law)*. An act causing harm to another requiring recompense to be made by a person who was not to blame, either because liability for the act was strict or because the person was vicariously responsible for the act of the wrongdoer.

Queen's Bench Division. One of the three divisions of the HIGH COURT.

quia dominus remisit curiam suam *(English Law)*. Writ of PRAECIPE for land held of a lord who did not hold a court for his tenants.

Quia emptores *(English Law)*. Statute of 1290 by which purchasers of freehold land in FEE SIMPLE were in future to obtain a grant by SUBSTITUTION from the previous tenant and not one by way of SUBINFEUDATION, so as to become the previous tenant's sub-tenant. It marked the beginning of the end of feudal landholding.

quo minus *(English Law)*. A device used before the EXCHEQUER to commence litigation, which strictly belonged before another court, by claiming that the plaintiff was 'to that extent less' able to meet his financial obligations to the Crown because the defendant had not paid him a debt or other finiancial obligation.

quod principi placuit legis habet vigorem *(Roman Law)*. 'What is pleasing to the prince has the force of an enacted law'. The principle of the legislative autonomy of the emperor as an absolute ruler, adopted in later times by other absolute monarchs.

rapina *(Roman Law)*. Robbery, that is stealing by force, a DELICT requiring compensation.

real action. Legal proceeding leading to the recovery of the specific item of property claimed.

real contract. An agreement which becomes legally binding by virtue of some thing, a *res*, being transferred from one party to another.

recognizances. Undertakings of SURETYSHIP, particularly for good behaviour or appearance in court.

redeeming of sessions. Practice by which a locality paid a sum of money to a Marcher lord in lieu of having judicial sessions in the lordship, or to end the sessions early.

reeve *(English Law)*. Someone placed in charge of another's concerns, affairs or business.

relief *(English Law)*. Payment by an heir to the lord to enter upon his freehold inheritance as a new tenant.

reprisal. The taking of a chattel or a person as a security or hostage for the payment of compensation for a wrong done by another of the same country or family.

repudium *(Roman Law)*. The termination of a marriage by the unilateral act of one spouse.

res extra commercium *(Roman Law)*. Things incapable of being owned by private individuals.

res in commercio *(Roman Law)*. Things capable of being owned by private individuals.

rescripta *(Roman Law)*. Replies to legal questions in the name of the emperor and having the force of law.

responsa prudentium *(Roman Law)*. The responses or opinions of those learned in the law to legal questions, regarded as a source of law.

rhaith *(Native Welsh Law)*. Proof by COMPURGATION.

rhaith of cenedl *(Native Welsh Law)*. Support by the oath of one's wider family; a form of COMPURGATION

rhaith of country *(Native Welsh Law)*. Support by the oath of one's neighbours; a form of COMPURGATION.

rhaith of kin *(Native Welsh Law)*. Support by the oath of one's family; a form of COMPURGATION.

rhandir *(Native Welsh Law)*. A territorial division.

rhath *(Native Welsh Law)*. Homestead.

rhwym dadl *(Native Welsh Law)*. Points of difference between the parties in litigation.

Sabinians *(Roman Law)*. One of the two principal schools of juristic opinion, the other being the PROCULIANS.

sanctuary *(Canon Law)*. Place of ecclesiastical refuge for a fleeing criminal.

sarhad *(Native Welsh Law)*. Injury, insult, harm, cf. Roman INIURIA; the compensation payment for such harm.

Sarum Oath *(English Law)*. Oath taken by William the Conqueror from all free men in his realm on Salisbury Plain in 1086 by which they promised him allegiance before any other lord.

scabini. Lay judges in medieval Italy.

scandalum magnatum *(English Law)*. The slander of magnates; the crime of spreading rumours which strained relations either between the King and a member or members of the nobility or between the nobles themselves, subjected to a statutory penalty by the Statute of Westminster I, 1275, chapter 34.

Schöffen. Lay judges in medieval Germany.

sedition *(English Law)*. The crime of undermining the authority of the state or its government.

seditious libel *(English Law)*. The publication in writing of words bringing state officials, magistrates, into disrepute; wrongful criticism of government.

senatusconsultum *(Roman Law)*. Advice of the senate, which under the early emperors came to have the force of an enacted law.

serjeant at law *(English Law)*. The most senior members of the English Bar, from whose ranks the royal judges were chosen.

servitudes *(Roman Law)*. Property rights over the property of others.

sheriff *(English Law)*. The king's REEVE in the shire.

shire moot *(English Law)*. Meeting of the free men in medieval shires, to transact among other things, judicial business.

shire reeve *(English Law)*. The king's reeve in the shire (before the Norman conquest, the local lord's reeve)

socage *(English Law)*. Freehold land tenure, usually for an agricultural service.

societas *(Roman Law)*. The CONSENSUAL CONTRACT of partnership.

solicitor. Originally one representing a client before the COURT OF CHANCERY, but not arguing the client's case.

Solicitor of the Supreme Court. Official title of the new profession created in the nineteenth century to replace those of ATTORNEY, SOLICITOR and PROCTOR.

specific performance *(English Law)*. Remedy in EQUITY ordering a person to perform a contractual obligation.

Star Chamber *(English Law)*. Prerogative court which met in the room of that name at Westminster, with particular reponsibility for investigating and punishing serious crimes against the state and the misdeeds of the powerful.

Statute of Mortmain *(English Law)*. Statute DE VIRIS RELIGIOSIS of 1279 banning alienations of land to the Church and other corporations which would place the land in their hand, their 'dead hand', in perpetuity.

steward *(English Law)*. One placed in charge of another's affairs.

stipendiary magistrate. A judicial officer paid to perform the functions of the unpaid JUSTICES OF THE PEACE within the magistrates courts.

stipulatio *(Roman Law)*. A VERBAL CONTRACT, requiring exact reciprocity of spoken question and answer.

subcriptiones *(Roman Law)*. Imperial answers to petitions from citizens, with the response written at the foot of the petition.

subinfeudation *(English Law)*. Grant of land by which the grantee became the grantor's tenant.

substitution *(English Law)*. Grant of land whereby the grantee replaced the grantor as the grantor's lord's tenant.

suffrage. The right to vote at elections.

suffragium *(Roman Law)*. The right to vote in the COMITIA.

sui iuris *(Roman Law)*. The condition of those who were in their own power, most typically the PATERFAMILIAS, able to own property, enter into contracts, etc.

suit *(English Law)*. Duty to follow, e.g. attend a person's court, grind corn at their mill, etc.

suit of mill *(English Law)*. Duty to have one's corn ground at the lord's mill.

Supreme Court of Judicature. Tribunal established by the Judicature Acts 1873–5 with full competence in civil causes at first instance and on appeal, consisting of the HIGH COURT and the COURT OF APPEAL.

surety. A person who pledges himself or his property as security for another's faithfulness.

surreption *(Native Welsh Law)*. Secret taking of another's property, subsequently admitted; ANGHYFARCH.

taeog *(Native Welsh Law)*. An unfree person, a bondman.

tafodiog *(Native Welsh Law)*. Sufficient testimony of one person alone.

teithi *(Native Welsh Law)*. Essential characteristics of a thing, such that if it is found to lack them, a purchaser has good cause for complaint.

tenants-in-chief *(English Law)*. Those holding lands directly of the king.

tenure *(English Law)*. The terms upon which land was held.

testamenti factio *(Roman Law)*. The capacity to make, take under and witness a will.

testamentum *(Roman Law)*. Binding statement of how property was to devolve upon the death of the owner; a will.

teulu *(Native Welsh Law)*. Family, household.

Theodosian Code *(Roman Law)*. A fifth-century collection of extant legislation, ordered by the emperor Theodosius II, which enjoyed considerable influence in western Europe thereafter.

tir cyfrif *(Native Welsh Law)*. Land in an unfree TREF held in common by the inhabitants.

tir gwelyawc *(Native Welsh Law)*. The land that was subject to family rules of inheritance.

tithes. Payment of one-tenth of the produce of land, or of other income, to the Church.

tithing *(English Law)*. Division of the HUNDRED, consisting of ten free men.

tourn *(English Law)*. The twice-yearly visit of the SHERIFF to each HUNDRED in the shire to ensure that every free man was placed within a TITHING.

trais *(Native Welsh Law)*. Open taking of another's property without consent.

transactio *(Roman Law)*. The INNOMINATE CONTRACT by which litigation was compromised before the final verdict (literally *trans-actio*).

transportation *(English Law)*. The removal of convicted criminals from the country as a punishment.

treasure trove. Precious metals found hidden, usually in the ground.

trefgefery *(Native Welsh Law)*. System of holding land in an unfree TREF.

trespass *(English Law)*. A wrong; later one caused by direct force.

trespass de ejectione firmae *(English Law)*. Wrong of ejecting a leaseholder from the land DEMISED to him; the remedy for such a wrong, later used also by freeholders.

trespass on the case *(English Law)*. A wrong suffered by the plaintiff as an indirect result or as a consequence of the defendant's actions.

treweloghe *(Native Welsh Law)*. Sharing of land amongst the inhabitants of an unfree TREF.

trial by battle. Norman method of trying the oaths of two litigants, victory being regarded as manifesting the judgement of God.

true bill. Finding by the JURY OF PRESENTMENT, or GRAND JURY, that the accused had a case to answer, thereby putting him on trial.

trustee *(English Law)*. A person holding the legal title of property for the benefit of another under a TRUST.

tutor *(Roman Law)*. Guardian of those who were SUI IURIS but not capable of managing their own affairs, for example young children whose PATERFAMILIAS had died.

Twelve Tables *(Roman Law)*. Written statement of the law issued *c*.450 BC.

tŷ un nos. The Welsh custom whereby a person who managed to build a dwelling on land during the hours of darkness and have smoke rising from its chimney by first light was entitled to the land thus occupied; perhaps originally a house with the obligation of providing for the king or lord for one night each year only.

tyddyn *(Native Welsh Law)*. A territorial division, being a smallholding, enough for one man and his family (literally *tŷ dyn*).

tystion *(Native Welsh Law)*. Those giving testimony as to what they had witnessed in court.

uchelwyr *(Native Welsh Law)*. Aristocracy; the nobility.

urban praetor *(Roman Law)*. The republican magistrate responsible for the administration of justice between citizens.

use *(English Law)*. An arrangement whereby one person or group of people, having the lawful ownership of property, was required to hold it for the benefit of others, which arrangement came to be enforced in the COURT OF CHANCERY; the medieval forerunner of the modern trust.

usucapio *(Roman Law)*. Acquisition of ownership by long possession.

usufruct *(Roman Law)*. Right to use and enjoy the property of another person; a personal servitude.

utriusque iuris. Of both laws, that is, Roman civil and canon law.

verbal contract. An agreement which becomes legally binding by virtue of the use of specific, spoken words.

vifgage. The giving of land as security for a loan, the produce of the land going towards the repayment of the debt.

villeinage *(English Law)*. Unfree land tenure, whereby the land was given to support the tenant who had to work at the lord's bidding.

visitation. Supervisory visit by a person in authority.

vox unius, vox nullus. One witness is no witness.

wadium *(Anglo-Saxon Law)*. Means by which a man was allowed to stand surety for himself.

waed tir *(Native Welsh Law)*. Family land, TIR GWELYAWC, exceptionally capable of alienation in satisfaction of a compensation payment for homicide, GALANAS.

wager of law *(English Law)*. Method of trial by which one party swore to the justice of his cause, and won the case if eleven or twelve others would support his oath with their own; COMPURGATION.

wardship *(English Law)*. Right of the lord of a military tenure to take possession of freehold land upon its inheritance by an infant (i.e. a minor) and keep the income for himself until the heir came of age.

waste *(Native Welsh Law)*. Land, or other property, which was open to exploitation by the king.

Witan *(Anglo-Saxon)*. The Anglo-Saxon assembly of the king and his nobility.

writ of ejectment *(English Law)*. The writ by which a leaseholder wrongfully ejected from the land DEMISED to him could at first obtain compensation and later the return of the land; the remedy was subsequently also used by freeholders to recover land.

writ of right *(English Law)*. Remedy allowing a demandant to assert his right to freehold land against the tenant in possession *(seisin)*.

writs of entry *(English Law)*. Remedies allowing for the recovery of the possession of freehold land where the sitting tenant's entry was defective in some particular.

wrth prid *(Native Welsh Law)*. Payment in return for a transfer of land.

wynebwerth *(Native Welsh Law)*. Loss of face.

XII Tables *(Roman Law)*. Written statement of the law issued *c.*450 BC.

Bibliography

'A magistrate's report on looting near Cefnsidan, 1833', *Carmarthenshire Antiquary*, 3 (1959), 35–6.

'A "Rebecca" item', *Carmarthenshire Antiquary*, 3 (1959), 37.

'A seventeenth-century land dispute', *NLWJ*, 13 (1963–4), 278–88.

Adams, S. L., 'The Composition of 1564 and the Earl of Leicester's tenurial reformation in the lordship of Denbigh', *BBCS*, 26 (1974–6), 479–511.

Alcock, L., 'Some reflections on early Welsh society and economy', *WHR*, 2(1) (1964–5), 1–7.

Alderman, G., 'The anti-Jewish riots of August 1911 in south Wales', *WHR*, 6(2) (1972–3), 190–200.

—— 'The anti-Jewish riots of August 1911 in south Wales: a response', *WHR*, 20 (2000–1) 565–71.

Andrews, J. A., 'A century of legal education', *Cambrian Law Review*, 34 (2003), 3–26.

Anners, E. and Jenkins, D., 'A Swedish borrowing from Welsh Medieval Law', *WHR*, 1(3) (1960–3), 325–33.

Ashton, O. R., 'Chartism in mid-Wales', *Montgomeryshire Collections*, 62 (1971), 10–57.

Bailey Williams, A., 'Courtship and marriage in the late 19th century in Montgomery-shire', *Montgomeryshire Collections*, 51 (1949–50), 116–26.

Baker, Sir J. H., *An Introduction to English Legal History*, 4th edn (London, 2002).

—— *The Oxford History of the Laws of England, Volume VI: 1483–1558* (Oxford, 2003).

Baker, R. and Birdsey, J., 'The good, the bad and the elusive – aspects of the excise service in the eighteenth century', *DHST*, 50 (2001), 58–75.

Ball, E., 'Glamorgan members during the Reform Bill period', *Morgannwg*, 10 (1966), 5–30.

Banks, R. W., 'On the early charters to towns in Wales', *Archaeologia Cambrensis* (4th ser.), 9 (1878), 81–100.

—— 'On the ancient tenures and services of the land of the bishop of St David's', *Archaeologia Cambrensis* (5th ser.) 2 (1885), 65–71.

—— 'On the early history of the land of Gwent', *Archaeologia Cambrensis* (5th ser.), 2 (1885), 241–56.

Baring Gould, S., 'The Celtic monasteries', *Archaeologia Cambrensis* (5th ser.), 17 (1900), 249–76.

Bartrum, P. C., 'Achau Brenhinoedd a Tywysogion Cymru', *BBCS*, 19 (1960–2), 201–25.

—— 'Plant yr Arglwydd Rhys', *NLWJ*, 14(1) (1965–6), 97–104.

Bates, T. St J. N., 'Bilingualism in legislation', *Statute Law Review*, 20 (1999), 105–6.

Beasley, S., 'The National Assembly – "A Voice for Wales"?', *Statute Law Review*, 24 (2003), 211–36.

Bebbington, D. W., 'The evangelical conscience', *Welsh Journal of Religious History*, 2 (2007), 27–44.

Beddoe, D., 'Carmarthenshire women and criminal transportation to Australia, 1787–1852', *Carmarthenshire Antiquary*, 13 (1977), 65–71.

Benbough-Jackson, M., '"Landlord careless"? Landlords, tenants and agriculture in four estates in west Wales, 1850–75', *Rural History: Economy, Society, Culture*, 14 (2003), 81–98.

Benjamin, E. A., 'Of paupers and workhouses [Aberystwyth Union]', *Ceredigion*, 10 (1985), 147–54.

Bevan-Evans, M., 'Local government in Treuddyn, 1752–1821', *FHSP*, 22 (1965–6), 25–39.

—— 'The Mold riot of 1831', *FHSJ*, 13 (1952–3), 72–6.

Bingham, The Right Hon. Lord, 'The Atkin Lecture – Christ College Brecon, 2003', in T. G. Watkin (ed.), *Y Cyfraniad Cymreig* (Bangor, 2005), pp. 90–101.

Bishop, J., 'Scope and limitations in the Government of Wales Act 2006 for tackling internet abuses in the form of "flame trolling"', *Statute Law Review*, 33 (2012), 207–16.

Black, J., *A New History of Wales* (Stroud, 2000).

Boon, G. C., 'A trace of Romano-British Christianity at Caerwent', *Monmouthshire Antiquary*, 1(1) (1961), 8–9.

Bowen, E. G., 'The Celtic saints in Cardiganshire', *Ceredigion*, 1 (1950–1), 3–17.

—— 'The monastic economy of the Cistercians at Strata Florida', *Ceredigion*, 1 (1950–1), 34–7.

—— *The Settlements of Celtic Wales* (Cardiff, 1956).

—— *Saints, Seaways and Settlements* (Cardiff, 1977).

Bowen, I., *The Statutes of Wales* (London and Leipzig, 1908).

—— 'Grand juries, justices of the peace and quarter sessions in Wales', *THSC* (1933–5), 51–104.

Bowen, L. (ed.), *Family and Society in Early Stuart Glamorgan: the Household Accounts of Sir Thomas Aubrey of Llantrithyd, c.1565–1641* (South Wales Record Society, vol. 19; Cardiff, 2006).

—— 'Wales and religious reform in the Long Parliament', *THSC* (NS), 12 (2006), 36–59.

Brand, P. A., 'An English legal historian looks at the Statute of Wales', in T. G. Watkin (ed.), *Y Cyfraniad Cymreig* (Bangor, 2005), pp. 20–56.

Breeze, A., 'Roman Tribunes and Early Dyfed Kings', *WHR*, 21 (2002/3), 757–61.

Bridgeman, G. T. O., 'Ancient lords of Mechain', *Montgomeryshire Collections*, 1 (1868), 195–203.

—— 'The princes of upper Powys', *Montgomeryshire Collections*, 1 (1868), 1–194.

—— 'The Welsh lords of Kerry and Arwystli', *Montgomeryshire Collections*, 1 (1868), 233–52.

Brigstocke, F. T., 'The settlement of a medieval dispute at Carmarthen', *Carmarthenshire Antiquary*, 2(4) (1957), 212–13.

Brown, M. H., 'Kinship, land and law in fourteenth-century Wales: the kindred of Iorwerth ap Cadwgan', *WHR*, 17(4) (1994–5), 493–519.

Brown, R. L., 'Clandestine marriages in Wales', *JHSCW*, 25 (1976), 66–71.

—— 'Clandestine marriages in Wales', *THSC* (1982), 74–85.

—— 'Mr. Jelf's proprietary chapel at a Welsh watering place', *JMHRS*, 12(1) (1994–7), 43–51.

—— 'Traitors and compromisers: the shadow side of the Church's fight against disestablishment', *Journal of Welsh Religious History*, 3 (2000), 35–53.

—— 'John Hughes, Attorney', *Montgomeryshire Collections*, 92 (2004), 79–88.

Brynmor-Jones, D.,'The Brehon Laws and the relation to the ancient Welsh institutes', *THSC* (1904–5), 7–36.

—— 'Foreign elements in Welsh mediaeval law', *THSC* (1916–17), 1–51.

Bullock, J. D., 'Early Christian memorial formulae', *Archaeologia Cambrensis*, 105 (1956), 133–41.

Bush, K., 'Approaches to UK legislative drafting: the Welsh perspective', *Statute Law Review*, 25 (2004), 144–50.

—— 'Assembly Measures and the new royal badge of Wales', in T. G. Watkin (ed.), *The Garthbeibio Murders and Other Essays* (Bangor, 2011), 152–7.

—— 'Getting real about Welsh devolution', in T. G. Watkin (ed.), *The Garthbeibio Murders and Other Essays* (Bangor, 2011), 137–51.

—— 'A tale of two cities – legislating for member remuneration at Cardiff Bay and at Westminster', *Statute Law Review*, 33 (2012), 141–50.

Byam, E., 'Matrimonial alliances of the royal family of England with the princes and magnates of Wales', *Archaeologia Cambrensis* (3rd ser.), 14 (1868), 147–51.

Cannon, G. and Franklin, M. J., 'A Cymmrodor claims kin in Calcutta: an assessment of Sir William Jones as philologer, polymath, and pluralist', *THSC* (NS), 11 (2005), 50–69.

Carpenter, D. A., 'Dafydd ap Llywelyn's submission to King Henry III in October 1241: a new perspective', *WHR*, 23(4) (2006–7), 1–12.

Carr, A. D., 'An Edeirnion inquisition', *JMHRS*, 6 (1969), 1–7.

—— 'The aristocracy in decline: the native Welsh lords after the Edwardian Conquest', *WHR*, 5(2) (1970), 103–29.

—— 'The last days of Gwynedd', *CHST*, 43 (1982), 7–22.

—— *Medieval Wales* (London, 1995).

—— '*Teulu* and *Penteulu*', in T. M. Charles-Edwards, M. E. Owen and P. Russell (eds), *The Welsh King and his Court* (Cardiff, 2000), pp. 63–81.

Chadwick, N., 'Bretwalda – Gwledig – Vortigern', *BBCS*, 19(3) (1961), 225–30.

—— *The Celts* (London, 1971).

Chapman, J., 'Parliamentary Enclosure in Wales', *WHR*, 21 (2002/3), 761–69.

Chapman, M. Ll., 'Disputes over presentations to the rectory of Llandrinio during the Tudor period', *Montgomeryshire Collections*, 91 (2003), 1–14.

Charles-Edwards, T. M., 'Some Celtic kinship terms', *BBCS*, 24 (1970–2), 105–22.

—— 'The seven bishop-houses of Dyfed', *BBCS*, 24 (1970–2), 247–62.

—— 'Naw Kynywedi Teithiauc', in D. Jenkins and M. E. Owen, *The Welsh Law of Women* (Cardiff, 1980), pp. 23–39.

—— '*Cynghawsedd*: counting and pleading in medieval Welsh law', *BBCS*, 33 (1986), 188–98.

——, M. E. Owen and D. B. Walters, *Lawyers and Laymen* (Cardiff, 1986).

—— *The Welsh Laws*, (Cardiff, 1989).

—— and N. A. Jones, '*Breintiau Gwŷr Powys*: the liberties of the men of Powys', in T. M. Charles-Edwards, M. E. Owen and P. Russell (eds), *The Welsh King and his Court* (Cardiff, 2000), pp. 191–223.

—— *Early Irish and Welsh Kinship* (Oxford, 1993).

—— 'Food, drink and clothing in the Laws of Court', in T. M. Charles-Edwards, M. E. Owen and P. Russell (eds), *The Welsh King and his Court* (Cardiff, 2000), pp. 319–37.

—— M. E. Owen and P. Russell (eds), *The Welsh King and His Court* (Cardiff, 2000).

—— 'Iorwerth Manuscript E (and B)', in T. M. Charles-Edwards and P. Russell, *Tair Colofn y Gyfraith: the Three Columns of Law in Medieval Wales: Homicide, Theft and Fire* (Bangor, 2007), pp. 258–307.

—— 'The galanas tractate in Iorwerth: texts and the legal development', in T. M. Charles-Edwards and P. Russell, *Tair Colofn y Gyfraith: the Three Columns of Law in Medieval Wales: Homicide, Theft and Fire* (Bangor, 2007), pp. 92–107.

—— 'The Welsh law of theft: Iorwerth *v* the rest', in T. M. Charles-Edwards and P. Russell, *Tair Colofn y Gyfraith: the Three Columns of Law in Medieval Wales: Homicide, Theft and Fire* (Bangor, 2007), pp. 108–30.

—— 'The three columns: a comparative perspective', in T. M. Charles-Edwards and P. Russell, *Tair Colofn y Gyfraith: the Three Columns of Law in Medieval Wales: Homicide, Theft and Fire* (Bangor, 2007), pp. 26–59.

—— and P. Russell, *Tair Colofn y Gyfraith: the Three Columns of Law in Medieval Wales: Homicide, Theft and Fire* (Bangor, 2007).

Charmley, G., 'Alfred Thomas and Wales in parliament', *THSC* (NS), 14 (2010), 39–60.

Clarke, G. T., 'The earls, earldom and castle of Pembroke', *Archaeologia Cambrensis* (3rd ser.), 5 (1859), 1, 81–91, 188–201, 241–5; 6 (1860), 1, 81–97, 189–95, 254–72; 7 (1861), 185–204.

—— 'The signory of Gower', *Archaeologia Cambrensis* (5th ser.), 10 (1893), 1, 292–308; 11 (1893), 122–30.

Clements, F., 'John Denman: Denbighshire's first chief constable', *DHST*, 55 (2007), 126–43.

—— 'Sergeant W. R. Breese: a policeman in rural nineteenth-century Denbighshire', *DHST*, 56 (2008), 121–32.

Cole, E. J. L., 'Abstracts from Radnorshire wills in the Prerogative Court of Canterbury', *Radnorshire Society Transactions*, 5 (1935) 54–6; 6 (1936), 9–14; 7 (1937), 11–14; 8 (1938), 51–5; 11 (1941), 37–8; 13 (1943), 35–7; 17 (1947), 42; 21 (1951), 35–7; 23 (1953), 45–9.

—— 'A fourteenth century court roll', *Radnorshire Society Transactions*, 17 (1947), 16–18.

—— 'Radnorshire wills – archdeaconry of Brecon', *Radnorshire Society Transactions*, 20 (1950), 74–7.

—— 'Court rolls of Presteigne and Norton', *Radnorshire Society Transactions*, 22 (1952), 37–48.

—— 'New Radnor town charters', *Radnorshire Society Transactions*, 23 (1953), 31–9.

—— 'A Llanyre charter of 1291–2', *Radnorshire Society Transactions*, 25 (1955), 20–1.

—— 'Some Radnorshire criminal records of the sixteenth cnetury', *Radnorshire Society Transactions*, 29 (1959), 20–3.

—— 'Early records of the Great Sessions', *Radnorshire Society Transactions*, 32 (1962), 54–7.

—— 'Thieves, robbers, and gaol-breakers', *Radnorshire Society Transactions*, 35 (1965), 30–2.

—— 'Clandestine marriages: the awful evidence from a consistory court', *Radnorshire Society Transactions*, 46 (1976), 68–72.

Cooke, N., '*The King* v *Richard Lewis & Lewis Lewis* (Cardiff, 13 July 1831): the trial of Dic Penderyn', in T. G. Watkin (ed.), *The Trial of Dic Penderyn and Other Essays* (Cardiff, 2003), pp. 110–27.

—— and M. Jarman, 'The administrative court in Wales', *Wales Journal of Law and Policy*, 4 (2005–6), 102–5.

Cool, H. E. M., 'A Romano-British gold workshop of the second century', *Britannia* 17 (1986), 231–7.

Crickhowell, The Right Hon. Lord, 'The Conservative Party and Wales', *NLWJ*, 34 (2004–5), 48–100.

Crockett, A., '"Un o'r barnwyr doethaf erioed": Lord Atkin of Aberdovey *v* The Archbishop of Wales *et al*', in T. G. Watkin (ed.), *Legal Wales: Its Past; its Future* (Cardiff, 2001), pp. 101–12.

Croesor (R. Owen), 'Admission of Anglesey natives to Gray's Inn 1521–1889', *AAST* (1933), 123–5.

Crouch, D., 'The slow death of kingship in Glamorgan, 1067–1159', *Morgannwg*, 29 (1985), 20–41.

Crump, J. J., 'Repurcussions of the execution of William de Braose', *Historical Research*, 73 (2000), 197–212.

Cule, J., 'A note on Hugo Glyn and the statute banning Welshmen from Gonville and Caius College', *NLWJ*, 16(2) (1969–70), 185–91.

Cunliffe, B., *The Extraordinary Voyage of Pytheas the Greek* (Harmondsworth, 2001, 2002).

Daniel, G., 'The government in Wales', *THSC* (1969), 99–126.

Davies, A. C., 'The old Poor Law in an industrializing parish, Aberdare, 1818–36', *WHR*, 8(3) (1977), 285–311.

Davies, A. E., 'Sir Hugh Owen and the new Poor Law', *BBCS*, 21(2) (1964–6), 166–70.

—— 'Some aspects of the operation of the old Poor Law in Cardiganshire 1750–1834', *Ceredigion*, 6 (1968–71), 1–44.

—— 'The new poor law in a rural area', *Ceredigion*, 8(3) (1978), 245–90.

Davies, B. L., 'The right to a bilingual education in nineteenth-century Wales', *THSC* (1988), 133–52.

Davies, C. S. L., 'Wales and Star Chamber: a note', *WHR*, 5(1) (1970), 71.

Davies, Caryl, '"Romantic Jones": the picturesque and politics on the south Wales circuit 1775–81', *NLWJ*, 28(3) (1993–4), 255–78.

Davies, Conrad, 'The Rebecca riots – letters from the front', *Carmarthenshire Antiquary*, 37 (2004), 88–103.

Davies, D. Seaborne, 'Welsh makers of English law', a lecture broadcast on BBC Radio Four from Wales, 13 November 1967 (London, 1967; repr. 1968), also reprinted in T. G. Watkin (ed.), *Y Cyfraniad Cymreig* (Bangor, 2005), pp. 1–19.

Davies, D. Stedman, 'Radnorshire wills', *Radnorshire Society Transactions*, 3 (1933), 5–15; 4 (1934), 3–5.

Davies, Dewi, 'The early years of the turnpike trust in Cardiganshire', *Ceredigion*, 14(3) (2001–4), 7–19.

Davies, Edmund, 'Judicial quality', *THSC* (1982), 7–24.

Davies, Edward, 'Hendre and hafod in Merioneth', *JMHRS*, 7(1) (1973), 13–27.

—— '*Hendre* and *hafod* in Denbighshire', *DHST*, 26 (1977), 49–72.

—— 'Hendre and hafod in Caernarvonshire', *CHST*, 40 (1979), 17–46.

—— 'Hafod, hafoty and lluest: their distribution, features and purpose', *Ceredigion*, 9(1) (1980), 1–41.

Davies, Elwyn, 'Who was Rebecca?', *Montgomeryshire Collections*, 28 (1894), 142–4.

Davies, G. P., 'Y Gymraeg a'r gyfraith', *Wales Law Journal*, 1 (2001–2), 29–39.

Davies, H. M., 'Loyalism in Wales 1792–1793', *WHR*, 20 (2000–1), 687–716.

Davies, John (The Rev.), 'Account of a Welsh marriage contract deed made 3 Charles I', *Montgomeryshire Collections*, 13 (1880), 355–8.

Davies, John (Norfolk), 'Sir William Jones as linguist and author', *Y Cymmrodor*, 8 (1887), 62–82; 9 (1888), 304–24.

Davies, John (Prof.), 'The Dowlais lease, 1748–1900', *Morgannwg*, 12 (1968), 37–66.

—— 'The end of the great estates and the rise of freehold farming in Wales', *WHR*, 7(2) (1974), 18–212.

—— *Hanes Cymru* (Harmonsdworth, 1990).

—— 'Caerdydd: dinas a phrifddinas', *THSC* (NS), 12 (2006), 136–46.

Davies, J. C., 'Montgomeryshire manorial records in the National Library of Wales from 1536 onwards', *Montgomeryshire Collections*, 48 (1944), 53–85.

—— 'Giraldus Cambrensis 1146–1946', *Archaeologia Cambrensis*, 99 (1946/7), 85–108, 256–80.

Davies, J. L., 'Coinage and settlement in Roman Wales and the Marches: some observations', *Archaeologia Cambrensis*, 132 (1983), 78–94.

Davies, M., 'Gruffydd ap Llywelyn: King of Wales', *WHR*, 21(2) (2002), 207–48.

Davies, R. R., 'The twilight of Welsh law', *History*, 51 (1966), 143–64.

—— 'Owain Glyn Dŵr and the Welsh squirearchy', *THSC* (1968), 150–69.

—— 'The survival of the blood-feud in medieval Wales', *History*, 54 (1969), 338–57.

—— 'The law of the March', *WHR*, 5(1) (1970), 1–30.

—— 'Race relations in post-conquest Wales: confrontation and compromise', *THSC* (1974 and 1975), 32–56.

—— 'The status of women and the practice of marriage in late-medieval Wales', in D. Jenkins and M. E. Owen (eds), *The Welsh Law of Women* (Cardiff, 1980), pp. 93–114.

—— 'Llywelyn ap Gruffydd, prince of Wales', *JMHRS*, 9(3) (1981–4), 264–77.

—— 'Buchedd a moes y Cymry', *WHR*, 12 (1984), 155–74.

—— 'The administration of law in medieval Wales: the role of the Ynad Cwmwd', in T. M. Charles-Edwards, M. E. Owen and D. B. Walters (eds), *Lawyers and Laymen* (Cardiff, 1986), pp. 258–73.

—— *The Age of Conquest: Wales 1063–1415* (Oxford, 1987).

—— *The Revolt of Owain Glyn Dŵr* (Oxford, 1995).

—— *The First English Empire: Power and Identities in the British Isles 1093–1343* (Oxford, 2000).

Davies, Sean, 'The Teulu *c*.633–1283', *WHR*, 21 (2002/3), 413–54.

Davies, T. G., 'Judging the sanity of an individual: some south Wales civil legal actions of psychiatric interest', *NLWJ*, 29(4) (1996), 455–67.

—— 'The Welsh contribution to mental health legislation in the nineteenth century', *WHR*, 18(1) (1996), 40–62.

Davies, T. P., 'Extracts from the records of some manorial courts', *Radnorshire Society Transactions*, 18 (1948), 72–5; 19 (1949), 71–7.

Davies, W., 'Land and power in early medieval Wales', *Past and Present*, 81 (1978), 3–23.

—— *Wales in the Early Middle Ages* (Leicester, 1982).

Davies, W. L., 'The riot at Denbigh in 1795', *BBCS*, 4 (1927), 61–73.

—— 'Notes on Hugh Williams and the Rebecca riots', *BBCS*, 11 (1941), 160–7.

Dewar, I., 'George Clive and the establishment of the New Poor Law in south Glamorgan', *Morgannwg*, 11 (1967), 46–70.

Dillon, M., 'The Irish settlement in Wales', *Celtica*, 12 (1977), 1–11.

Dodd, A. H., 'The roads of north Wales', *Archaeologia Cambrensis* (7th ser.), 5 (1925), 121–48.

—— 'The enclosure movement in north Wales', *BBCS*, 3 (1926), 210–15.

—— 'The old Poor Law in north Wales 1750–1850', *Archaeologia Cambrensis* (7th ser.), 6 (1926), 111–32.

—— 'Wales's parliamentary apprenticeship, (1536–1625)', *THSC* (1942), 8–72.

—— 'Wales in the parliaments of Charles I', *THSC* (1945) 16–49; (1946–7), 59–96.

—— 'Caernarvonshire elections to the Long Parliament', *BBCS*, 12 (1946), 44–8.

—— 'The pattern of politics in Stuart Wales', *THSC* (1948), 8–91.

—— 'Welsh opposition lawyers in the Short Parliament', *BBCS*, 12 (1948), 106–7.

—— '"Tuning" the Welsh Bench 1680', *NLWJ*, 6 (1949/50), 249–59.

—— 'The Caernarvonshire election dispute of 1640–41 and its sequel', *BBCS*, 14 (1950), 42–4.

—— 'Flintshire politics in the seventeenth century', *FHSJ*, 14 (1953–4), 22–46.

—— 'A Merioneth pioneer of the American mid-west: John Rice Jones', *JMHRS*, 2 (1953–6), 249–59.

Dunn, A., 'Inheritance and lordship in pre-reformation England: George Neville, Lord Bergavenny (*c.*1470–1535)', *Nottingham Medieval Studies*, 48 (2004), 116–40.

Dybikowski, J., 'David Williams (1738–1816) and Jacques-Pierre Brissot: their correspondence', *NLWJ*, 25 (1987–8), 71–97.

Eaton, G., 'Sir Samuel Thomas Evans, judge and politician', *Neath Antiquarian Society Transactions* (1980–1), 15–30.

Eaton, J., 'The judgeship of John Bryn Roberts in Glamorgan, 1906–18', *WHR*, 13(1) (1986), 44–71.

Edwards, E. W., 'Cardiff becomes a city', *Morgannwg*, 9 (1965), 80–7.

Edwards, G., 'Studies in the Welsh Laws since 1928', *WHR, Special Number, 1963: The Welsh Laws*, 1–18.

Edwards, I. ap O., 'William Morgan's quarrell with his parishioners at Llanrhaeadr ym Mochnant', *BBCS*, 3 (1927), 298–339.

Edwards, J. B., 'Sir George Osborne Morgan MP (1826–97): nineteenth-century mould breaker', *DHST*, 46 (1997), 69–86.

Edwards, J. G., 'The early history of the counties of Carmarthen and Cardigan', *English Historical Review*, 31 (1916), 90–8.

—— (ed.), *Flint Pleas, 1283–1285* (Flintshire Historical Record Society, Hawarden, 1922).

—— 'Flint pleas 1283–1285', *FHSP*, 8 (Hawarden, 1922), 1–49.

—— 'The royal household and the Welsh lawbooks', *Transactions of the Royal Historical Society*, (5th ser.), 13 (1963), 163–76.

—— *The Principality of Wales, 1267–1967: A Study in Constitutional History* (Caernarfon, 1969).

—— 'Hywel Dda and the Welsh law-books', in D. Jenkins (ed.), *Celtic Law Papers Introductory to Welsh Medieval Law and Government* (Brussels, 1973), pp. 135–60.

Edwards, N. (ed.), *Landscape and Settlement in Medieval Wales* (Oxford, 1997).

Edwards, P. S., 'The parliamentary representation of the Welsh boroughs in the mid-sixteenth century', *BBCS*, 27(3) (1977), 425–39.

Elias, G. A., 'Llyfr Cynog of Cyfraith Hywel and St Cynog of Brycheiniog', *WHR*, 23 (1) (2006–7), 27–47.

Elis-Thomas, The Right Hon. Lord, 'O gorff corfforaethol i wasanaeth seneddol/ From body corporate to parliamentary service', *Wales Journal of Law and Policy*, 4 (2005–6), 7–16.

Ellis, B., 'Denbighshire quarter sessions rolls in the eighteenth century', *DHST*, 50 (2001), 76–97.

—— 'Flintshire quarter sessions rolls, 1752–1830', *FHSJ*, 36 (2003), 96–113.

—— 'Montgomeryshire quarter sessions during the first half of the eighteenth century', *Montgomeryshire Collections*, 92 (2004), 33–55.

Ellis, T. P., 'Hywel Dda: codifier', *THSC* (1926–7), 1–69.

—— 'Legal references, terms and conceptions in the "Mabinogion"', *Y Cymmrodor*, 39 (1928), 86–148.

—— 'The Catholic Church in the Welsh laws', *Y Cymmrodor*, 42 (1931), 1–68.

—— *Welsh Tribal Law and Custom in the Middle Ages* (Oxford, 1926; Aalen, 1982).

Emanuel, H. D., 'Blegywryd and the Welsh laws', *BBCS*, 20(3) (1963), 256–60.

—— 'Notaries public and their marks recorded in the archives of the dean and chapter of Hereford', *NLWJ*, 8 (1953/4), 147–63.

—— 'The Book of Blegywryd and Ms. Rawlinson 821', in Jenkins, D. (ed.), *Celtic law papers introductory to Welsh medieval law and government* (Brussels, 1973), pp. 161–70.

—— *The Latin Texts of the Welsh Laws* (Cardiff, 1967).

—— 'Llyfr Blegywryd a Llawysgrif Rawlinson 821', *BBCS*, 19(1) (1960), 23–8.

—— 'The Latin texts of the Welsh Laws', *WHR, Special Number, 1963: The Welsh Laws*, 25–32.

Escott, M., 'How Wales lost its judicature: the making of the 1830 Act for the abolition of the Courts of Great Sessions', *THSC* (NS), 13 (2007), 134–59.

Evans, B., 'Grant of privileges to Wrexham, 1380', *BBCS*, 19(1) (1960), 42–6.

Evans, C., 'Y Faled a therfysgoedd Beca yn ne orllewin Cymru', *Journal of the Pembrokeshire Historical Society*, 9 (2000), 21–38.

Evans, C. M. and K., 'The Beaumaris charter of incorporation, 1562', *AAST* (1950), 1–50.

Evans, D., 'The Welsh Intermediate Education Act, 1889', *THSC* (1939), 101–32.

Evans, D. G., *A History of Wales, 1815–1906* (Cardiff, 1989).

—— *A History of Wales, 1906–2000* (Cardiff, 2000).

Evans, D. R., *Cymru'r Gyfraith: Camu 'Mlaen* (Cardiff, 2006).

Evans, D. S. (ed.), *The Lives of the Welsh Saints by G. H. Doble* (Cardiff, 1971).

Evans, E., 'Some Cyfeiliog manorial customs', *Montgomeryshire Collections*, 52 (1951–2), 29–37.

Evans, E. D., *A History of Wales, 1660–1815* (Cardiff, 1976).

—— 'A Cardiganshire Crown land dispute', *Ceredigion*, 14 (2001–4), 101–18.

—— 'Harlech: a forsaken borough', *JMHRS*, 14 (2004–5), 197–212.

—— 'Politics and parliamentary representation in Merioneth 1536–1644', *JMHRS*, 15 (2006–7), 4–28; 142–69.

—— 'The patriot of his native country', *NLWJ*, 32 (2000–1), 293–303.

Evans, E. W., *Mabon* (Cardiff, 1959).

Evans, J. D. and M. J. Francis, 'Cynog: spiritual father of Brycheiniog', *Brycheiniog*, 27 (1994–5), 15–24.

Evans, J. G., *Devolution in Wales: Claims and Responses, 1937–1979* (Cardiff, 2006).

Evans, K., 'Caernarvon borough and its contributory boroughs', *CHST*, 9 (1948), 41–5.

Evans, L. W., 'Sir John and Lady Charlotte Guest's education scheme at Dowlais in the mid-nineteenth century', *NLWJ*, 9 (1955–6), 265–86.

—— 'School boards and the works school system after the Education Act of 1870', *NLWJ*, 15(1) (1967–8), 89–100.

—— 'The Welsh National Council for Education, 1903–6' *WHR*, 6(1) (1972), 49–88.

Evans, N. and P. O'Leary, 'All the trappings of a great state occasion . . .: the opening of the Senedd', *Planet: the Welsh Internationalist*, 179, 30–7.

Evans, W. G., 'Meirioneth and the "Treachery of the Blue Books", 1847', *JMHRS*, 12(4) (1994–7), 348–65.

Eyre Evans, G., 'Some Radnor presentments AD 1694', *Archaeologia Cambrensis* (6th ser.), 18 (1918), 101–22.

Fenton, J., 'One of the ancient modes of burial of the Cymry or Celtic Britons', *Archaeologia Cambrensis* (3rd ser.), 6 (1860), 25–33.

Fletcher, I. F., *Latin Redaction A* (Aberystwyth, 1986).

Flynn-Hughes, C., 'The Bangor workhouse', *CHST*, 5 (1944) 88–100.

—— 'Aspects of the Old Poor Law administration and policy in Amlwch parish, 1770–1837', *AAST* (1945), 48–60.

—— 'The workhouses of Caernarvonshire 1760–1914', *CHST*, 7 (1946), 88–100.

—— 'Aspects of Poor Law administration and policy in Amlwch parish, 1834–1848', *AAST* (1950), 71–9.

Ford, P. K. and E. P. Hamp, 'Welsh *asswynaw* and Celtic legal idiom', *BBCS*, 26(2) (1975), 147–60.

Fordham, G., 'The road books of Wales', *Archaeologia Cambrensis* (7th ser.), 7 (1927), 276–91.

Foster, B., 'The Usk houses of correction and the early days of Usk county gaol', *Gwent Local History*, 94 (Spring, 2003), 3–33.

Foster, I. Ll., 'Summary and suggestions', *WHR, Special Number, 1963: The Welsh Laws*, 61–7.

Fothergill. I. M. and Williams, D., 'French opinion concerning Dr Richard Price', *BBCS*, 5 (1929), 72–4.

Fox, K. O., 'An edited calendar of the first Brecknockshire plea roll of the Courts of the King's Great Sessions in Wales, July 1542', *NLWJ*, 14(4) (1965–6), 469–84.

—— 'The Merthyr election of 1906', *NLWJ*, 14(2) (1965–6), 237–41.

Frame, P., 'The Apostle of Liberty: the political thinking of Richard Price', *Planet: the Welsh Internationalist*, 163, 70–86.

Franklin, M. J., *Sir William Jones* (Cardiff, 1995).

—— (ed.), *Sir William Jones: Selected Poetical and Prose Works* (Cardiff, 1995).

—— *Orientalist Jones: Sir William Jones, Poet, Lawyer, and Linguist, 1746–1794* (Oxford, 2012).

Gabriel, J. R., 'Wales and the Avignon papacy', *Archaeologia Cambrensis* (7th ser.), 3 (1923), 70–86.

—— 'Notes on the Exchequer tallies in the National Museum of Wales', *Archaeologia Cambrensis* (7th ser.), 4 (1924), 189–240.

Gardner, J. S., 'The justices of the peace and the repair and maintenance of bridges and highways in Denbighshire in the seventeenth century', *Cambrian Law Review*, 16 (1985), 52–76.

Garrett, M., 'Recalcitrance and acceptance: aspects of centralisation under the poor law in Cardiganshire', *Ceredigion*, 15(1) (2005–8), 73–106.

George, W. B., 'Welsh disestablishment and Welsh nationalism', *JHSCW*, 20 (1970), 77–91.

Gray, M., 'The clergy as remembrancers of the community', *Monmouthshire Antiquary*, 16 (2000), 113–20.

Green, H. S., et al., 'The Caergwrle Bowl: its composition, geological source and archaeological significance', *Reports of the Institute of Geological Sciences*, 80(i) (1980), 171–89.

Green, M. and R. Howell, *Celtic Wales* (Cardiff, 2000).

Gresham, C. A., 'Gavelkind and the unit system', *Archeological Journal*, 128 (1971), 174–5.

—— 'The Aberconway Charter: further consideration', *BBCS*, 30 (3 and 4) (1983), 311–47.

Griffith, W., 'Jesus College, Oxford and Wales: the first half-century', *THSC* (1996), 21–44.

Griffiths, A. and Aaron, C., with Manley, J., 'Measuring a measure: Much ado about £50 a week?', *Statute Law Review*, 33 (2012), 281–303.

Griffiths, G. Ll. H., 'The hundred years war: the development of the movement towards leasehold enfranchisement in Wales', in T. G. Watkin (ed.), *The Trial of Dic Penderyn and Other Essays* (Cardiff, 2003), pp. 180–96.

Griffiths, G. M., 'Glimpses of Cardiganshire in sessions records', *Ceredigion*, 5, (1966), 264–79.

Griffiths, M., 'Manor court records and the historian: Penmark, Fonmon and Barry, 1570–1622', *Morgannwg*, 25 (1981), 43–78.

—— 'Native society on the Anglo-Norman frontier: the evidence of the Margam charters', *WHR*, 14(2) (1988–9), 179–216.

Griffiths, R. A., *The Principality of Wales in the Later Middle Ages: The Structure and Personnel of Government, vol. 1, South Wales 1277–1536* (Cardiff, 1972).

—— *Conquerors and Conquered in Medieval Wales* (Stroud and New York, 1994).

Griffiths, W. E., 'The excavation of a Romano-British hut-group at Cors-y-gedol in Merionethshire', *BBCS*, 18(1) (1958), 119–30.

Gruffydd, K. Ll., 'The vale of Clwyd corn riots of 1740', *FHSPJ*, 27 (1975–6), 36–42.

—— 'Elihu Yale: an indiscreet incident', *Clwyd Historian*, 32 (Spring, 1994), 17–20.

Guest, E., 'On the boundaries which separated England and Wales', *Archaeologia Cambrensis* (3rd ser.), 7, (1861), 269–92.

Halloran, K., 'Welsh kings and the English court, 928–956', *WHR*, 25 (2011), 297–313.

Hamer, E., 'Ancient Arwystli: its earthworks and ancient remains', *Montgomeryshire Collections*, 1 (1868), 207; 2 (1869), 42–70.

—— 'Ancient Arwystli', *Archaeologia Cambrensis* (3rd ser.), 14 (1868), 1–23.

Hancock, T. W., 'Montgomeryshire causes heard and determined before the Court of Marches, sitting at Ludlow, in Trinity Term, 1617', *Montgomeryshire Collections*, 19 (1886), 251–6.

Hankins, F., 'From parish pauper to union workhouse inmate', *Brycheiniog*, 29 (1996–7), 53–85.

Hargest, L., 'The Welsh Educational Alliance and the 1870 Elementary Education Act', *WHR*, 10(2) (1980–1), 172–206.

Harris, M. E., 'Compensation for Injury: A point of contact between early Welsh and Germanic law?', in T. G. Watkin (ed.), *The Trial of Dic Penderyn and Other Essays* (Cardiff, 2003), pp. 39–76.

Harrison, J. F. C., 'Robert Owen: the quest for the new moral world', *Montgomeryshire Collections*, 62 (1971), 1–9.

Haycock, M., 'Jones y dwyrain 1746–1794', *Y Traethodydd* (Autumn, 1994), 226–34.

Hays, R. W., 'Welsh students at Oxford and Cambridge universities in the Middle Ages', *WHR*, 4(4) (1969), 325–65.

Henriques, U., 'The Jews and crime in south Wales before World War I', *Morgannwg*, 29 (1985), 59–73.

Hines, J., 'Welsh and English: mutual origins in post-Roman Britain', *Studia Celtica*, 34 (2000), 81–104.

Holden, B. W., 'The making of the middle March of Wales: 1066–1250', *WHR*, 20 (2000–1) 207–26.

Holmes, C., 'The Tredegar riots of 1911: anti-Jewish disturbances in South Wales', *WHR*, 11(2) (1982–3), 214–25.

Hopkin, D., 'The Llanelli riots, 1911', *WHR*, 11(4) (1982–3), 488–515.

Hopkinson, C. and Speight, M., *The Mortimers: Lords of the March* (Logaston, 2002).

Howard, S., 'Riotous community: crowds, politics and society in Wales *c*.1700–1840', *WHR*, 20 (2000–1), 656–86.

—— *Law and Disorder in Early Modern Wales: Crime and Authority in the Denbighshire Courts, 1660–1730* (Cardiff, 2008).

Howe, The Right Hon. Lord, 'The Aberfan Disaster', in T. G. Watkin (ed.), *The Garthbeibio Murders and Other Essays* (Bangor, 2011), pp. 97–128.

Howell, M., 'Regalian right in Wales and the March: the relation of theory to practice', *WHR*, 7(3) (1975), 269–88.

Howells, B., 'The distribution of customary acres in South Wales', *NLWJ*, 15(2) (1967–8), 226–33.

Howse, W. H., 'Knighton and Rebecca', *Radnorshire Society Transactions*, 13 (1943), 54–5.

—— 'Court rolls of the manor of Norton', *Radnorshire Society Transactions*, 14 (1944), 43–51.

—— 'Records of the Radnorshire General Sessions at the Shire Hall, Presteigne', *Radnorshire Society Transactions*, 13 (1943), 65–75; 14 (1944), 6–15.

—— 'Electioneering as it once was', *Radnorshire Society Transactions*, 15 (1945), 4–7.

—— 'The early friendly societies of Radnorshire', *Radnorshire Society Transactions*, 28 (1958), 27–30.

—— 'The Court of the Council of Wales and the Marches: an attorney's royal warrant of 1613', *Radnorshire Society Transactions*, 29 (1959), 24–7.

—— 'A high sheriff's warrant of appointment, 1579', *Radnorshire Society Transactions*, 30 (1960), 39–41.

—— 'The duties of two sheriff's officers in the seventeenth century', *Radnorshire Society Transactions*, 30 (1960), 34–8.

Hughes, C., '"A very creditable portion of Welsh history": the Rebecca riots in Radnorshire', *RHST*, 67 (1997), 101–16.

Hughes, D. and Davies, H. G., 'Accessible bilingual legislation for Wales', *Statute Law Review*, 33 (2012), 103–21.

—— 'Deddfwriaeth hygyrch a dwyieithog i Gymru', *Statute Law Review*, 33 (2012), 122–40.

Hughes, E., 'The letters of Chief Justice Spencer Cowper from the North Wales Circuit, 1717–1719', *THSC* (1955), 50–6.

Hughes, H., 'Giraldus de Barri: an early ambassador for Wales', *Brycheiniog*, 38 (2006), 35–48.

Hutton, B., 'Sir John Nicholl of Merthyr Mawr: the reform of the testamentary jurisdiction of the ecclesiastical courts', in T. G. Watkin (ed.), *Legal Wales: Its Past; Its Future* (Cardiff, 2001), pp. 89–100.

—— 'Dr John Nicholl of Merthyr Mawr: the reform of the testamentary jurisdiction of the ecclesiastical courts', in T. G. Watkin (ed.), *The Trial of Dic Penderyn and Other Essays* (Cardiff, 2003), pp. 128–50.

Huws, C. F., 'Is meaning plain and ordinary? Are you sure about that?', *Statute Law Review*, 33 (2012), 230–51.

—— 'The language of education law in England and/or Wales', *Statute Law Review*, 33 (2012), 252–80.

Huws, D., '*Leges Howelda* at Canterbury', *NLWJ*, 19(4) (1975–6), 340–4.

—— *The Medieval Codex with Reference to the Welsh Law Books* (Aberystwyth, 1980).

—— 'Descriptions of the Welsh manuscripts', in T. M. Charles-Edwards, M. E. Owen and P. Russell (eds), *The Welsh King and his Court* (Cardiff, 2000), pp. 415–24.

Huws, Daniel, 'The manuscripts', in T. M. Charles-Edwards and P. Russell, *Tair Colofn y Gyfraith: the Three Columns of Law in Medieval Wales: Homicide, Theft and Fire* (Bangor, 2007), pp. 196–212.

Ibbetson, D. J., 'Sir William Jones', in T. G. Watkin (ed.), *Legal Wales: Its Past; Its Future* (Cardiff, 2001), pp. 41–62.

—— (ed.), *An Essay on the Law of Bailments by Sir William Jones* (Bangor, 2007).

Insley, C., 'Fact and fiction in thirteenth-century Gwynedd: the Aberconway Charters', *Studia Celtica*, 33 (1999), 235–50.

Ireland, R. W., 'Putting oneself on whose county? Carmarthenshire juries in the mid-nineteenth-century', in T. G. Watkin (ed.), *Legal Wales: Its Past; Its Future* (Cardiff, 2001), pp. 63–88.

—— *'A Want of Order and Good Discipline': Rules, Discretion and the Victorian Prison*, (Cardiff, 2007).

—— 'Caught on camera: Cardiganshire criminal portraits in context', *Ceredigion*, 15(2) (2005–8), 11–26.

—— 'Reflections on a silent system', in T. G. Watkin (ed.), *The Garthbeibio Murders and Other Essays* (Bangor, 2011), pp. 65–77.

—— *The Carmarthen Gaoler's Journal*, 1845–1850, 2 vols (Bangor, 2010).

'Irregular marriages in the eighteenth century', *Montgomeryshire Collections*, 60 (1967–8), 169–70.

Ius Romanum Medii Aevi (Milan, 1961–).

Jack, R. I., *Medieval Wales* (London, 1972).

James, C., 'Tradition and innovation in some later medieval Welsh lawbooks', *BBCS*, 40 (1993), 148–56.

—— '*Ban wedy i dynny*: medieval Welsh law and early protestant propaganda', *Cambrian Medieval Celtic Studies*, 27 (1994), 61–86.

James, E. W., 'Welsh ballads and American slavery', *Welsh Journal of Religious History*, 2 (2007), 59–86.

James, H., 'Roman Carmarthenshire', *Carmarthenshire Antiquary*, 37 (2000), 23–46.

James, J. W., 'Fresh light on the death of Gruffydd ap Llywelyn', *BBCS*, 22(2) (1967), 168–9; 30 (1 and 2) (1982), 147.

James, L. S., 'Discourses of Labour: The Cases of William Abraham and Gerhard Stötzel, 1890–1914', *THSC* (NS), 12 (2006), 101–20.

Jarman, A. O. H., 'Wales and the Council of Constance', *BBCS*, 14 (1951), 220–2.

Jarrett, M. G. (ed.), *The Roman Frontier in Wales*, 2nd edn, ed. V. E. Nash Williams (Cardiff, 1969).

—— 'Magnus Maximus and the end of Roman Britain', *THSC* (1983), 22–35.

—— and Mann J. C., 'The tribes of Wales', *WHR*, 4(2) (1968–9), 161–74.

Jenkins, D., 'Iorwerth ap Madog', *NLWJ*, 8 (1953/4), 164–70.

—— 'Legal and comparative aspects of the Welsh laws', *WHR, Special Number, 1963: The Welsh Laws*, 51–60.

—— (ed.), *Llyfr Colan* (Cardiff, 1963).

—— 'A lawyer looks at Welsh land law', *THSC* (1967), 220–48.

—— 'Y Genedl Alanas yng Nghyfraith Hywel', *BBCS*, 22(3) (1967), 228–36.

—— 'The date of the "Act of Union"', *BBCS*, 23(4) (1970), 345–6.

—— 'A family of medieval Welsh lawyers', in D. Jenkins (ed.), *Celtic Law Papers Introductory to Welsh Medieval Law and Government* (Brussels, 1973), pp. 121–34.

—— (ed.), *Celtic Law Papers Introductory to Welsh Medieval Law and Government* (Brussels, 1973).

—— *Damweiniau Colan* (Aberystwyth, 1973).

—— 'Law and government in Wales before the Act of Union', in D. Jenkins (ed.), *Celtic Law Papers Introductory to Welsh Medieval Law and Government* (Brussels,1973), pp. 23–48.

—— *Cyfraith Hywel* (Llandysul, 1976).

—— '*Cynghellor* and Chancellor', *BBCS*, 27(1) (1976), 115–18.

—— 'Kings, lords and princes: the nomenclature of authority in thirteenth-century Wales', *BBCS*, 26(4) (1976), 451–62.

—— 'The significance of the Law of Hywel', *THSC* (1977), 54–76.

—— 'Property Interests in the Classical Welsh Law of Women', in D. Jenkins and M. E. Owen, *The Welsh Law of Women* (Cardiff, 1980), pp. 69–92.

—— (trans. and ed.), *Hywel Dda: The Law* (Llandysul, 1986).

—— *Tân yn Llŷn* (1937), trans. by A. Corkett as *A Nation on Trial: Penyberth 1936* (Cardiff, 1998).

—— '*Bardd Teulu* and *Pencerdd*', in T. M. Charles-Edwards, M. E. Owen and P. Russell (eds), *The Welsh King and his Court* (Cardiff, 2000), pp. 142–66.

—— 'Hawk and hound: hunting in the laws of court', in T. M. Charles-Edwards, M. E. Owen and P. Russell (eds), *The Welsh King and his Court* (Cardiff, 2000), pp. 255–80.

—— 'Prolegomena to the Welsh laws of court', in T. M. Charles-Edwards, M. E. Owen and P. Russell (eds), *The Welsh King and his Court* (Cardiff, 2000), pp. 15–28.

—— 'Y Gymraeg mewn Llys a Llan', in T. G. Watkin (ed.), *The Trial of Dic Penderyn and Other Essays* (Cardiff, 2003), pp. 1–38.

—— 'Crime and tort and the three columns of law', in T. M. Charles-Edwards and P. Russell, *Tair Colofn y Gyfraith: the Three Columns of Law in Medieval Wales: Homicide, Theft and Fire* (Bangor, 2007), pp. 1–25.

—— and Owen, M. E., 'Welsh law in Carmarthenshire', *Carmarthenshire Antiquary*, 18 (1982), 17–28.

—— and Owen, M. E., *The Welsh Law of Women* (Cardiff, 1980).

Jenkins, G. H., *The Foundations of Modern Wales: Wales 1642–1780* (Oxford, 1989).

—— '"Horrid unintelligible jargon": the case of Dr Thomas Bowles', *WHR*, 15(4) (1991), 494–523.

—— (ed.), *The Welsh Language before the Industrial Revolution* (Cardiff, 1997).

Jenkins, Gwyn, 'Huw T. Edwards a Datganoli', *THSC* (NS), 14 (2010), 96–109.

Jenkins, J. G., 'The woollen industry in Montgomeryshire', *Montgomeryshire Collections*, 58 (1963–4), 50–69.

Jenkins, J. P., 'Jacobites and freemasons in eighteenth-century Wales', *WHR*, 9(4) (1978–9), 391–406.

Jenkins, M. G., 'Rhifo carennydd yng nghyfraith Rhufain, yr Eglwys, a Chymru', *BBCS*, 20(4) (1964), 348–72.

Jenkins, P., 'The creation of an "ancient gentry": Glamorgan, 1760–1840', *WHR*, 12(1) (1984–5), 29–49.

—— 'Regions and cantrefs in early medieval Glamorgan', *Cambridge Medieval Celtic Studies*, 15 (1988), 31–50.

—— *A History of Modern Wales 1536–1990* (London, 1992).

Jenkins, R. E., 'Thomas Pennant and the dean of St Asaph's case', *THSC* (1984), 77–94.

Jenkins, R. T., 'The borough of Bala *c.*1350', *BBCS*, 11 (3–4) (1944), 167.

—— 'A drover's account book', *CHST*, 6 (1945), 46–57.

Jenkins, S., 'Devolution through London eyes', *THSC* (NS), 10 (2004), 175–84.

John, M., 'A sacking matter in Narberth: sentimental treatment of vagrants', *Journal of the Pembrokeshire Historical Society*, 13 (2004), 43–56.

Johnstone, N., 'Llys and Maerdref: the Royal Courts of the Princes of Gwynedd', *Studia Celtica*, 34 (2000), 167–210.

Jones, A., 'Petitions to King Edward by the burgesses of Flint 1295–1300', *FHSJ*, 9 (1922), 39–43.

—— 'The property of the Welsh friars at the dissolution', *Archaeologia Cambrensis*, 91 (1936), 30–50.

—— 'The estates of the Welsh abbeys at the dissolution', *Archaeologia Cambrensis*, 92 (1937), 269–86.

Jones, B., *Etholiadau'r Ganrif/Welsh Elections 1885–1997* (Talybont,1999).

Jones, C., *Y Gyfraith yng Nghymru: Y Deng Mlynedd Nesa'* (Cardiff, 2008).

Jones, D., 'Sir Rhys ap Thomas', *Archaeologia Cambrensis* (5th ser.), 9 (1892), 81–101; 192–214.

Jones, D., 'Pauperism in the Aberystwyth Poor Law Union, 1870–1914', *Ceredigion*, 9,(1) (1980), 78–101.

Jones, D. J. V., 'The corn riots in Wales, 1793–1801', *WHR*, 2(4) (1964–5), 323–50.

—— 'The Amlwch riots of 1817', *AAST* (1966), 93–102.

—— 'Distress and discontent in Cardiganshire, 1814–1819', *Ceredigion*, 5(3) (1966), 280–9.

—— 'The Merthyr riots of 1831', *WHR*, 3(2) (1966–7), 173–205.

—— 'The strike of 1816', *Morgannwg*, 11 (1967), 27–45.

—— 'The Carmarthen riots of 1831', *WHR*, 4(2) (1968–9), 129–42.

—— 'The Merthyr riots of 1800', *BBCS*, 23(2) (1969), 166–79.

—— 'Chartism at Merthyr: a commentary on the meetings of 1842', *BBCS*, 24(2) (1971), 230–45.

—— 'The Scotch cattle and their black domain', *WHR*, 5(3) (1971), 220–49.

—— 'Chartism in Welsh communities', *WHR*, 6(3) (1972–3), 243–61.

—— *Before Rebecca: Popular Protests in Wales, 1793–1835* (Harmondsworth, 1973).

—— '"A dead loss to the community": the criminal vagrant in mid-nineteenth-century Wales', *WHR*, 8(3) (1976–7), 312–43.

—— 'Life and death in eighteenth-century Wales: a note [punishment and pardon]', *WHR*, 10(4) (1980–1), 536–48.

Jones, D. L., 'William Herle and the office of rhaglaw in Elizabethan Cardiganshire', *NLWJ*, 17 (1971–2), 161–82.

Jones, D. Ll., 'The fate of paupers: life in the Bangor and Beaumaris union workhouse, 1845–71', *CHST*, 66 (2005), 94–125.

Jones, David Lloyd, 'The machinery of justice in a changing Wales', *THSC* (NS), 14 (2010), 123–38.

Jones, D. R. L., 'Lewis Thomas: a blighted career in late-Georgian Swansea', *Gower*, 51 (2000), 42–52.

Jones, E. A., 'Welshmen in the American War of Independence', *Y Cymmrodor*, 27 (1917), 230–63.

—— 'Two Welsh correspondents of John Wilkes', *Y Cymmrodor*, 29 (1919), 110–50.

Jones, E. D., 'Gleanings from Radnorshire files of Great Sessions papers, 1691–1699', *Radnorshire Society Transactions*, 13 (1943), 7–34.

—— 'A file of "Rebecca" papers', *Carmarthenshire Antiquary*, 1 (3 and 4) (1943–4), 21–63.

Jones, E. G., 'County politics and electioneering 1558–1625', *CHST*, 1 (1939), 37–46.

—— 'Borough politics and electioneering (1826–1882)', *CHST*, 17 (1956), 75–85.

—— 'Sir Charles Paget and the Caernarvonshire boroughs, 1830–32', *CHST*, 21 (1960), 81–128.

Jones, E. J., 'The enclosure movement in Anglesey 1788–1866', *AAST* (2002), 23–61; (2003) 48–100.

Jones, E. T., 'The enclosure movement in Anglesey', *AAST* (1925), 21–58.

Jones, E. V., 'A Merioneth murder of 1812', *JMHRS*, 6(1) (1969), 66–104.

Jones, E. W., 'A decade of deeds: Abel Simner and the Welsh Calvinistic Methodists: part 1: the law of Mortmain, 1861–67', *THSC* (NS), 2 (1995), 100–22.

Jones, E. W. C., 'Sir William Jones', *AAST* (1930), 79–85.

Jones, F., 'Ave atque vale: a brief review of the history of the quarter sessions in Carmarthenshire', *Carmarthenshire Historian*, 9 (1972), 5–30.

Jones, F., 'Customs of the lordship and manor of Talley, 1725', *BBCS*, 25(2) (1973), 185–8.

Jones, F., 'Welsh bonds for keeping the peace, 1283 and 1295', *BBCS*, 13(3) (1949), 142–4.

Jones, F., *The Princes and Principality of Wales* (Cardiff, 1969).

Jones, F. P., 'Rhyfel y Degwm 1886–91', *DHST*, 2 (1953), 71–106.

—— 'A Welsh court of estrays', *Gwerin*, 1 (1956–7), 81.

Jones, G. E., 'Local administration and justice in sixteenth century Glamorgan', *Morgannwg*, 9 (1965), 11–37.

—— *Modern Wales: A Concise History*, 2nd edn (Cambridge, 1994).

Jones, G. H., 'Some parallels between Celtic and Indian institutions', *Archaeologia Cambrensis* (6th ser.), 1 (1900), 109–25.

Jones, G. P., 'Cholera in Wales', *NLWJ*, 10(3) (1957–8), 281–300.

Jones, G. P. and Owen., H., *Caernarfon Court Rolls, 1361–1402* (Caernarfon, 1951).

Jones, G. R. J., '"Tir Telych", the gwestfau of Cynwyl Gaeo and Cwmwd Caeo', *Studia Celtica*, 28 (1994), 81–96.

—— 'Early settlement in Arfon: the setting of Tre'r Ceiri', *CHST*, 24 (1963), 1–20.

—— 'Early territorial organization in Gwynedd . . . and Elmet', *Northern History*, 10 (1975), 3–27.

—— 'Llys and *maerdref*', in T. M. Charles-Edwards, M. E. Owen and P. Russell (ed.), *The Welsh King and His Court* (Cardiff, 2000), pp. 296–318.

—— 'Medieval Welsh Society (review article)', *CHST*, 34 (1973), 30–43.

—— 'Society and settlement in Wales and the marches, 500 BC to AD 1100 [review article]', *CHST*, 47 (1986), 7–24.

—— 'The distribution of bond settlements in north-west Wales', *WHR*, 2(1) (1964), 19–36.

—— 'The *gwely* as a tenurial institution', *Studia Celtica*, 30 (1996), 167–88.

—— 'The ornaments of a kindred in medieval Gwynedd', *Studia Celtica*, 18/19 (1983/84), 135–46.

—— 'The tribal system in Wales: a re-assessment in the light of settlement studies', *WHR*, 1(2) (1960–1963), 111–32.

Jones, I. G., 'The elections of 1865 and 1868 in Wales', *THSC* (1964), 41–68.

—— 'Dr Thomas Price and the election of 1868 in Merthyr Tydfil', *WHR*, 2(2) (1964–5), 147–72; 2(3) (1964–5), 251–70.

Jones, J. F., 'Carmarthenshire rural police force', *Carmarthenshire Antiquary*, 4 (1962), 45–8.

—— 'Kidwelly borough police force', *Carmarthenshire Antiquary*, 4 (1963), 152–9.

Jones, J. Graham, 'Early campaigns to secure a Secretary of State for Wales', *THSC* (1988), 153–76.

—— 'Government, order and the "perishing souls of Wales"', *THSC* (1993), 47–82.

—— 'Select committee or royal commission? Wales and the "land question"', *WHR*, 17(2) (1994–5), 205–29.

—— 'The national petition on the legal status of the Welsh language', *WHR*, 18(1) (1996–7), 92–124.

—— '"Quietly I hope to push on Welsh questions substantially": Thomas Edward Ellis as second whip', *JMHRS*, 14 (2004–5), 230–9.

—— 'Dame Margaret in Cardiganshire', *Ceredigion*, 14(4) (2001–4), 105–21.

—— 'Lloyd George's Diary for 1885', *CHST*, 69 (2008), 37–60.

—— 'Michael Davitt, David Lloyd George and Thomas Edward Ellis: The Welsh Experience', *WHR*, 18 (1997), 450–82.

—— 'S. O. Davies and the Government of Wales Bill 1955', *Llafur*, 8(3) (2002), 67–77.

—— 'Sir J. Herbert Lewis and Thomas Edward Ellis: political friends', *JMHRS*, 15 (2006–7), 70–88.

—— 'The journalist as politician: W. Llewelyn Williams MP 1867–1922', *Carmarthenshire Antiquary*, 37 (2001), 79–98.

—— 'Thomas Edward Ellis and the temperance campaign', *JMHRS*, 14 (2004–5), 175–84.

—— 'Lloyd George, Cymru Fydd and the Newport meeting of January 1896', *NLWJ*, 29(4) (1996), 435–53.

Jones, J. Gwynfor, 'Caernarvonshire administration: the activities of the Justices of the Peace, 1603–1660', *WHR*, 5 (2) (1970), 103–163.

—— 'Cyfraith a threfn yn sir Gaernarfon *ca.*1600–1640: yr uchelwyr a'r byd gweinyddol', *CHST*, 47 (1986), 25–70.

—— 'Governance, order and stability in Caernarvonshire, *ca.*1540–1640', *CHST*, 44 (1983), 7–52.

—— 'Law and order in Merioneth after the Acts of Union 1536–43', *JMHRS*, 10(2) (1986), 119–41.

—— 'Reflections on concepts of nobility in Glamorgan, *ca.*1540–1640', *Morgannwg*, 25 (1981), 11–42.

—— 'The Welsh gentry and the image of the "Cambro-Briton" *c.*1603–1625', *WHR*, 20 (2000–2001), 615–55.

—— 'The Welsh language in local government: justices of the peace and the courts of quarter sessions *c.*1536–1800', in G. H. Jenkins (ed.), *The Welsh Language before the Industrial Revolution* (Cardiff, 1997), pp. 181–206.

—— 'Thomas Davies and William Hughes: two reformation bishops of St Asaph', *BBCS*, 39 (1980–2), 320–5.

—— 'Cyfieithiad Rowland Vaughan, Caer-gai o *Eikon Basilike*', *Studia Celtica*, 36 (2002), 99–138.

—— *Early Modern Wales: c.1525–1640* (London, 1994).

Jones, J. L., 'A seventeenth-century land dispute', *NLWJ*, 13(3) (1963–4), 278–88.

Jones, K. W., 'A farewell to Quarter Sessions', *CHST*, 33 (1972), 248–53.

Jones, M. A., 'Cultural Boundaries within the Tudor State: Bishop Rowland Lee and the Welsh Settlement of 1536', *WHR*, 20 (2000–1), 227–53.

Jones, M. C., 'The feudal barons of Powys', *Montgomeryshire Collections*, 1 (1868), 257–423.

—— 'The territorial divisions of Montgomeryshire', *Montgomeryshire Collections*, 2 (1869), 71–120.

Jones, M. E., '"An invidious attempt to accelerate the extinction of our language": the abolition of the Court of Great Sessions and the Welsh language', *WHR*, 19 (1998–9), 226–64.

—— '"Wales for the Welsh": The Welsh County Court Judgeships *c.*1868–1900', *WHR*, 19 (1998–9), 642–78.

Jones, M. H., 'The letters of Arthur James Johnes, 1809–71', *NLWJ*, 10(3) (1957–8), 329–64.

—— 'Judge A. J. Johnes, 1808–1871, patriot and reformer', *Montgomeryshire Collections*, 58 (1963–4), 3–20.

—— 'Montgomeryshire and the abolition of the Court of Great Sessions 1817–1830', *Montgomeryshire Collections*, 60 (1967–8), 85–103.

Jones, R., 'The formation of the *cantref* and the commote in medieval Gwynedd', *Studia Celtica*, 32 (1998), 169–77.

Jones, Rachael, 'The Garthbeibio Murders', in T. G. Watkin (ed.), *The Garthbeibio Murders and Other Essays* (Bangor, 2011), pp. 1–64.

—— 'The traction engine', in T. G. Watkin (ed.), *The Garthbeibio Murders and Other Essays* (Bangor, 2011), pp. 77–96.

Jones, R. B., '"All the Welshmen abiding and studying in Oxford"', *THSC* (1986) 157–72.

—— 'Sir Daniel Lleufer Thomas MA LLD FSA 1863–1940', *Carmarthenshire Antiquary*, 37 (2005), 61–71.

Jones, Rhys, 'Changing ideologies of medieval state formation: the growing exploitation of land in Gwynedd, *c.*1100–*c.*1400', *Journal of Historical Geography*, 26(4) (2000), 505–16.

Jones, R. T., 'The origins of the nonconformist disestablishment campaign', *JHSCW*, 20 (1970), 39–76.

Jones, R. W. and Scully, R., *Wales says Yes: Devolution and the 2011 Welsh Referendum* (Cardiff, 2012).

Jones, S., 'Richard Lewis and Dic Penderyn: the man and the martyr', *TPTHS*, 3(1) (1977).

Jones, T. A., 'Owen Tudor's Marriage', *BBCS*, 11(2) (1943), 102–9.

Jones, T. Davies, 'Poor Law administration in Merthyr Tydfil Union, 1834–94', *Morgannwg*, 8 (1964), 35–62.

Jones, T. H., 'Wales, devolution and sovereignty', *Statute Law Review*, 33 (2012), 151–62.

—— and J. M. Williams, 'Wales as a jurisdiction', *Public Law* (2004), 78–101.

Jones, T. I. Jeffreys, *Exchequer Proceedings concerning Wales in tempore James I* (Cardiff, 1955).

—— 'The court leet presentments of the town, borough and liberty of St Clears 1719–1889', *BBCS*, 13(1) (1948), 28–53.

—— 'The parish vestries and the problem of poverty 1783–1833', *BBCS*, 14(3) (1951), 222–35.

Jones, W. G., 'The court rolls of the borough of Criccieth', *BBCS*, 2(2) (1923), 149–60.

—— 'The charter of the borough of Criccieth', *BBCS*, 4(3) (1928), 229–31.

—— 'Documents illustrative of the history of the north Wales boroughs', *BBCS*, 3 (2) (1926), 149–52; 4 (3) (1928), 225–8.

Jones, W. J., 'The treatise of the Masters in Chancery', *NLWJ*, 10(3) (1957–8), 403–8.
Jones, W. L., *Cofio Tryweryn* (Llandysul, 1988).
—— *Cofio Capel Celyn* (Talybont, 2007).
Jones-Evans, P., 'Evan Pan Jones: land reformer', *WHR*, 4(2) (1968–9), 143–59.
Jukes, T., 'The Walfords – the worst fences in Newport', *Gwent Local History*, 92 (Spring, 2002), 49–66.
Keeton, G. W., 'Judge Jeffreys: towards a re-appraisal', *WHR*, 1(3) (1960–3), 265–78.
—— 'George Jeffreys: his family and friends', *THSC* (1967) 39–56.
Kirby, D. P., 'Vortigern', *BBCS*, 23(1) (1968), 37–59.
—— 'Hywel Dda: anglophile?', *WHR*, 8(1) (1976), 1–13.
Knight, J. K., '*In tempore Iustini consulis*: contacts between the British and Gaulish churches before Augustine', in A. Detsicas (ed.), *Collectanea Historica: Essays in Memory of Stuart Rigold* (Maidstone, 1981).
—— 'Glamorgan AD 400–110: archaeology and history', in H. N. Savory (ed.), *Glamorgan County History, Volume II: Early Glamorgan: Pre-History and Early History* (Cardiff, 1984), pp. 315–64.
Knight, L. S., 'Welsh cathedral schools to 1600 A. D. ', *Y Cymmrodor*, 29 (1919), 76–109.
—— 'Welsh schools from AD 1000 to AD 1610', *Archaeologia Cambrensis* (6th ser.), 19 (1919), 1–18, 276–91, 515–25.
—— 'The origin of the Welsh grammar school', *Y Cymmrodor*, 31 (1921), 81–111.
Korngiebel, D. M., 'English colonial ethnic discrimination in the lordship of Dyffryn Clwyd: segregation and integration 1282–c.1340', *WHR*, 23(2) (2006–7), 1–24.
Korporowicz, L. J., 'Roman law in Roman Britain: an introductory survey', *Journal of Legal History*, 33 (2012), 133–51.
Lambert, D., 'A voice for Wales: the National Assembly for Wales', in T. G. Watkin (ed.), *Legal Wales: Its Past; Its Future* (Cardiff, 2001), pp. 167–81.
Lambert, W. R., 'The Welsh Sunday Closing Act, 1881', *WHR*, 6(2) (1972–3), 161–89.
—— *Drink and Sobriety in Victorian Wales c.1820–c.1895* (Cardiff, 1983).
Laws, E., 'Pembrokeshire raths', *Archaeologia Cambrensis* (5th ser.), 3 (1886), 97–9.
Leighton, D., 'The Demesne Manor of Pennard in the lordship of Gower: a fourteenth-century court roll', *Studia Celtica*, 37 (2003), 183–220.
Lerry, G. G., 'The policemen of Denbighshire', *DHST*, 2 (1953), 107–52.
Levack, B. P., *The Civil Lawyers in England 1603–1641: A Political Study* (Oxford, 1973).
Levy, E., *West Roman Vulgar Law: The Law of Property* (Philadelphia, 1951).
—— *Weströmisches Vulgarrecht: Das Obligationenrecht* (Weimar, 1956).
—— 'Vulgarisation of Roman law in the early Middle Ages', in *Gesammelte Schriften*, vol. 1 (Cologne, 1963), pp. 220–47.
Lewis, A. H. T., 'The early effects of Carmarthenshire's turnpike trusts, 1760–1800', *Carmarthenshire Historian*, 4 (1967), 41–54.
Lewis, C. W., 'The treaty of Woodstock, 1247', *WHR*, 2(1) (1964–5), 37–65.
Lewis, D., 'The court of the President and Council of Wales and the Marches from 1478 to 1575', *Y Cymmrodor*, 12 (1897), 1–64.
Lewis, David, 'A great blessing to the people employed: conflicting views of the truck system in the Llynfi Valley, 1840–1870', *Morgannwg*, 48 (2004), 35–46.
Lewis, E., 'The discovery of the tombstone of Vortipore . . .', *Archaeologia Cambrensis* (5th ser.), 12 (1895), 303–13.
Lewis, E. A., 'The decay of tribalism in north Wales', *THSC* (1902–3) 1–75.
—— 'A contribution to the commercial history of medieval Wales', *Y Cymmrodor*, 24 (1913), 86–188.

—— 'The account roll of the chamberlain of the principality of north Wales from Michaelmas 1304 to Michaelmas 1305', *BBCS*, 1(3) (1922), 256–75.

—— 'The account roll of the chamberlain of the principality of west Wales from Michaelmas 1301 to Michaelmas 1302', *BBCS*, 2(1) (1923), 49–86; corrigenda, 160.

—— 'The proceedings of the small hundred court of the commote of Ardudwy in the county of Merioneth from 8 October 1325 to 18 September 1326', *BBCS*, 4 (2) (1928), 153–66.

—— 'Proceedings of the leet courts of north Radnorshire in 1688', *Radnorshire Society Transactions*, 4 (1934), 18–23; 5 (1935), 4–15.

—— 'The court leet of Llanwddyn', *Montgomeryshire Collections*, 44 (1936), 1–31.

—— 'Three legal tracts concerning the court leet in Wales after the Act of Union', *BBCS*, 9(4) (1939), 345–56.

—— 'A schedule of the quarter session records of the county of Montgomery at the National Library of Wales', *Montgomeryshire Collections*, 46 (1940), 156–82; 47 (1942), 26–63.

—— 'The court rolls of the manor of Broniarth 1429–64', *BBCS*, 11(1) (1941), 54–74.

—— 'List of early chancery proceedings concerning Radnorshire up to 1558', *Radnorshire Society Transactions*, 11 (1941), 52–64.

—— 'Radnorshire cases in the court of augmentations', *Radnorshire Society Transactions*, 13 (1943), 56–9.

—— (with an introduction by J. C. Davies), 'Leet proceedings of the manor of Arwystli Uwchcoed at the National Library of Wales: 1784–1800', *Montgomeryshire Collections*, 47 (1942), 183–207; 48 (1944), 11–29.

—— and Davies, J. C., *Records of the Court of Augmentations relating to Wales and Monmouthshire* (Cardiff, 1954).

Lewis, Gwion, *Hawl i'r Gymraeg* (Talybont, 2008).

Lewis, T. H., 'Attendances of justices and grand jurors at the courts of quarter sessions in Wales, 16th–18th century', *THSC* (1942), 108–22.

Lewis, T. H., 'The justice of the peace in Wales', *THSC* (1943–4), 120–32.

—— 'The Rebecca movement in Carmarthenshire', *Carmarthenshire Antiquary*, 1 (3–4) (1943–4), 6–15.

—— 'The administration of justice in the Welsh county in relation to other organs of justice, higher and lower', *THSC* (1945) 151–66.

—— 'Documents illustrating the county gaol and house of correction in Wales', *THSC* (1946–7), 232–49.

Linnard, W., *Trees in the Law of Hywel* (Aberystwyth, 1979).

Llewellin, W., 'The raths of Pembrokeshire', *Archaeologia Cambrensis* (3rd ser.), 10 (1864), 1–13.

Lloyd, H. A., 'Wales and Star Chamber: a rejoinder', *WHR*, 5(3) (1971), 257–60.

—— 'Corruption and Sir John Trevor', *THSC* (1974–5), 77–102.

Lloyd, J., 'Surveys of the manors of Radnorshire', *Archaeologia Cambrensis* (5th ser.), 17 (1900), 1–23, 110–28.

Lloyd, J. D. K., 'An early 19th century apprentice's indenture', *Montgomeryshire Collections*, 53 (1953–4), 81–2.

—— 'The robber's grave in Montgomeryshire churchyard', *Montgomeryshire Collections*, 56 (1959–60), 21–44.

Lloyd, J. E., 'Wales and the coming of the Normans, 1039–1093', *THSC* (1899–1900), 122–79.

—— 'Llywelyn ap Gruffydd and the lordship of Glamorgan', *Archaeologia Cambrensis* (6th ser.), 13 (1913), 56–64.

—— 'Edward the First's commission of enquiry of 1280–1: an examination of its origin and purpose', *Y Cymmrodor*, 25 (1915), 1–20; 26 (1916), 252.

—— 'Edward I and the county of Flint', *FHSJ*, 6 (1916–17), 15–26.

—— 'Owain Glyn Dŵr: his family and early history', *THSC* (1918–19), 128–45.

—— 'The mother of Gruffydd ap Llywelyn', *BBCS*, 1(4) (1923), 335.

—— 'Hendre and hafod', *BBCS*, 4(3) (1928), 224–5.

—— 'Trouble in Wales about 1410', *BBCS*, 5(2) (1930), 155–6.

—— 'The death of Llywelyn ap Gruffydd', *BBCS*, 5(4) (1931), 349–53.

—— 'The date of the Act of Union of England and Wales', *BBCS*, 7(2) (1934), 192.

—— 'Bishop Sulien and his family', *NLWJ*, 2(1) (1941/2), 1–6.

Lloyd, J. Y. W., *The History of the Princes, the Lords Marcher, and the Ancient Nobility of Powys Fadog, and the Ancient Lords of Arwystli, Cedewen and Meirionydd*, 3 vols (London, 1881–2).

Lloyd Hughes, D. G., 'David Williams, Castell Deudraeth, and the Merioneth elections of 1859, 1865 and 1868', *JMHRS*, 5(4) (1965–8), 335–51.

—— 'Ystad y Goron yng ngogledd Cymru 1282–1849', *NLWJ*, 31 (1999–2002), 283–334.

Lloyd, R. L., 'Welsh masters of the bench of the Inner Temple from early times until the end of the 18th century', *THSC* (1937), 145–200; (1938), 155–246.

Lovering, G. W. J., 'The Monmouthshire Elections of 1868', *Gwent Local History*, 90 (Spring, 2001), 17–34.

Lowe, D. E., 'The Council of the Prince of Wales and the decline of the Herbert family during the second reign of Edward IV (1471–1483)', *BBCS*, 27(2) (1977), 278–97.

Loyn, H., 'Wales and England in the tenth century: the context of the Athelstan charters', *WHR*, 10(3) (1980–1), 283–301.

—— 'Llanfyllin: the charter and the laws of Breteuil', *Montgomeryshire Collections*, 85 (1997), 13–21.

Lupoi, M., *Alle radici del mondo giuridico europeo* (1994), trans. A. Belton as *The Origins of the European Legal Order* (Cambridge, 2000).

Lynch, M., *Scotland: A New History* (London, revised edn, 1992).

Lynch, P. I., 'Court poetry, power and politics', in T. M. Charles-Edwards, M. E. Owen and P. Russell (eds), *The Welsh King and His Court* (Cardiff, 2000), pp. 167–90.

M. C. J., 'Enclosure of common lands in Montgomeryshire', *Montgomeryshire Collections*, 12 (1879), 267–98; 15 (1882), 191–6.

M. C. J., 'Montgomeryshire magistracy, 1687: their replies to James II's questions, touching the repeal of the Penal Laws and Test Act', *Montgomeryshire Collections*, 13 (1880), 163–8.

McAll, C., 'The normal paradigms of a woman's life in the Irish and Welsh texts', in D. Jenkins and M. E. Owen (eds), *The Welsh Law of Women* (Cardiff, 1980), pp. 7–22.

MacCana, P., 'Votepori', *BBCS*, 19(2) (1961), 116–17.

—— 'Elfennau cyn-Gristnogol yn y Cyfreithiau', *BBCS*, 23(4) (1970), 309–16.

McClure, E., 'Note on the meaning of *Venta* in British place names', *Archaeologia Cambrensis* (6th ser.), 9 (1909), 239–40.

McNall, C., 'The commote and county courts of Wales, 1277–1350', in T. G. Watkin (ed.), *Legal Wales: Its Past; Its Future* (Cardiff, 2001), pp. 1–20.

—— 'Elwyn Jones: A Welshman at the Nuremberg Trials', in T. G. Watkin (ed.), *Y Cyfraniad Cymreig* (Bangor, 2005), pp. 160–81.

MacNeill, E., 'Ireland and Wales in the history of jurisprudence', in D. Jenkins (ed.), *Celtic Law Papers Introductory to Welsh Medieval Law and Government* (Brussels, 1973), pp. 171–92.

McConnel, J. R. R., '"Sympathy without relief is rather like mustard without beef": devolution, Plaid Cymru and the campaign for a Secretary of State for Wales, 1937–1938', *WHR*, 22 (2004–5), 535–57.

Mann, K., 'The March of Wales: a question of terminology', *WHR*, 18(1) (1996–7), 1–13.

Martin, J., 'Private enterprise *versus* manorial rights: mineral property disputes in eighteenth-century Glamorgan', *WHR*, 9(2) (1978–9), 155–75.

—— 'Estate stewards and their work in Glamorgan, 1660–1760', *Morgannwg*, 23 (1979), 9–28.

Mathew, D., 'The Welsh influence among the legal advisers of James II', *THSC* (1938), 119–24.

Matthews, J. F., 'Macsen, Maximus and Constantine', *WHR*, 11(4) (1982–3), 431–48.

Maud, R., 'David, the last Prince of Wales: the ten "lost" months of Welsh history', *THSC* (1968), 43–62.

Maund, K. L., *Handlist of the Acts of the Welsh Native Rulers 1132–1283* (Cardiff, 1996).

—— *The Welsh Kings* (Stroud, 2000).

Melding, D., *Will Britain survive beyond 2020?* (Cardiff, 2009).

—— 'Foreword', *Statute Law Review, Special Issue on Welsh Devolution*, 33 (2012), 97–102.

Meyer, K., 'Early relations between Gael and Brython', *THSC* (1895–6), 55–86.

Miles, D., 'A unique mayoralty', *Journal of the Pembrokeshire Historical Society*, 16 (2007), 93–99.

Miller, M., 'Consular years in the *Historia Brittonum*', *BBCS*, 29(1) (1980), 17–34.

Minkes, J., 'Wales and the "Bloody Code": the Brecon circuit of great sessions in the 1750s', *WHR*, 22 (2004–5), 673–704.

'Montgomeryshire men who matriculated at Oxford University, 1571–1622', *Montgomeryshire Collections*, 25 (1891), 81–4.

'Montgomeryshire extracts from the register of admissions to Gray's Inn, 1521–1889', *Montgomeryshire Collections*, 61 (1969–70), 164–6.

Moore-Colyer, R., 'Agriculture in Wales before and during the second millennium BC', *Archaeologia Cambrensis*, 146 (1996), 15–33.

Morgan, C. O. S., 'Some account of the history and descent of the lordship marcher or county of Wentllwch', *Archaeologia Cambrensis* (5th ser.), 2 (1885), 257–70.

Morgan, G., 'Dowries for daughters in west Wales, 1500–1700', *WHR*, 17 (1994–5), 534–49.

Morgan, Gerald, 'Ewyllysiau Cymraeg y Cardis 1725–1847', *Ceredigion*, 15(3) (2005–8), 1–12.

—— 'Llunio ewyllysiau yn y Gymraeg yn sir Gaernarfon', *CHST*, 69 (2008), 26–36.

Morgan, J., 'Denbighshire's *annus mirablilis*: the borough and county elections of 1868', *WHR*, 7(1) (1974), 63–87.

Morgan, K. O., 'Democratic politics in Glamorgan, 1884–1914', *Morgannwg*, 4 (1960), 5–27.

—— 'Gladstone and Wales', *WHR*, 1(1) (1960), 65–82.

—— 'Nationalists and Mr Gladstone', *THSC* (1960), 36–52.

—— *David Lloyd George: Welsh Radical as World Statesman* (Cardiff, 1963).

—— 'Cardiganshire politics: the Liberal ascendancy, 1885–1923', *Ceredigion*, 5(4) (1967), 313–46.

—— Rebirth of a Nation: A History of Modern Wales (Oxford and Cardiff, 1981).

Morgan, R. W., St Paul in Britain: or the origin of British as opposed to Papal Christianity, 2nd edn (Oxford and London, 1880).

Morgan, T. O., 'Wales and its Marches, and the counties formed out of or augmented thereby', Archaeologia Cambrensis (3rd ser.), 3 (1857), 81–95.

Morgan, W. T., 'Disputes before the consistory court of the diocese of St David's concerning elections of churchwardens', JHSCW, 3 (1953), 90–9.

—— 'The consistory courts in the diocese of St David's, 1660–1858', JHSCW, 7 (1957), 1–24, 58–81.

—— 'Disputes concerning seats in church before the consistory courts of St David's', JHSCW, 11 (1961), 65–88.

—— 'The prosecution of nonconformists in the consistory courts of St David's, 1661–1668', JHSCW, 12 (1962), 28–54.

Morris of Aberavon, The Right Hon. Lord, 'The contribution of Welsh lawyers', THSC (NS), 13 (2007), 213–24.

—— Fifty Years in Politics and the Law (Cardiff, 2011).

Morris, A., 'Chepstow Castle and the barony of Striguil', Archaeologia Cambrensis (6th ser.), 9 (1909), 407–32.

Morris, E. R., 'Who were the Montgomeryshire Chartists?', Montgomeryshire Collections, 58 (1963–4), 27–49.

Morris, J. E., The Welsh Wars of Edward I (Oxford, 1901).

Morris, R., 'Rebecca and the Dilwyns', Gower, 54 (2003), 76–9.

Morris, R. M., 'Syr Thomas Artemus Jones (1870–1943)', DHST, 35 (1986), 23–38.

Morris, W. H., 'Hugh Williams and Kidwelly', Carmarthenshire Antiquary, 3(3) (1961), 161–78.

—— 'Eighteenth-century leases', Carmarthenshire Antiquary, 5 (1964–9), 21–4.

Moseley, H., 'Gweinyddiad y gyfraith yng Nghymru', THSC (1972–3), 16–36.

Mostyn, J., 'The enclosure movement in Radnorshire', Radnorshire Society Transactions, 18 (1948), 70–1.

Navarro, M., 'A substantial body of different Welsh law: a consideration of Welsh subordinate legislation', Statute Law Review, 33 (2012), 163–91.

Nicholas, D., 'The Welsh Jacobites', THSC (1948) 467–74.

O'Brien, A. M., 'Churchill and the Tonypandy Riots', WHR, 17(1) (1994–5), 67–99.

O'Loughlin, T., 'Giraldus Cambrensis and the sexual agenda of the twelfth-century reformers', Journal of Welsh Religious History, 8 (2000), 1–15.

Owain-Jones, W. R., 'The contribution of Welshmen to the administration of India', THSC (1970), 250–62.

Owen, D. H., 'Tenurial and economic developments in north Wales in the twelfth and thirteenth centuries', WHR, 6(2) (1972–3), 117–42.

—— 'The Englishry of Denbigh: an English colony in medieval Wales', THSC (1974–5), 57–76.

Owen, E., 'Holy wells, or water veneration', Archaeologia Cambrensis (5th ser.), 8 (1891), 8–16.

Owen, G. D., 'The Poor Law system in Carmarthenshire during the eighteenth and early nineteenth centuries', THSC (1941) 71–86.

Owen, H., 'The Flemings in Pembrokeshire', Archaeologia Cambrensis (5th ser.), 12 (1895), 96–106.

—— 'English law in Wales and the Marches', Y Cymmrodor, 14 (1901), 1–41.

—— 'A survey of the lordship of Haverford in 1577', *Archaeologia Cambrensis* (6th ser.), 3 (1903), 39–55.

Owen, H., *History of the Anglesey Constabulary* (Bangor, 1952).

Owen, H. J., 'Merioneth Quarter Sessions – Sessions Roll – Easter 1733', *JMHRS*, 2 (1953–6), 45–54.

—— 'The common gaols of Merioneth during the eighteenth and nineteenth centuries', *JMHRS*, 3 (1957–60), 1–30.

Owen, H. J., 'Chief Baron Richards of the Exchequer', *JMHRS*, 4(1) (1961), 37–46.

Owen, J. D., 'Y Beca', *Carmarthenshire Antiquary*, 1 (3–4) (1943–4), 16–20.

Owen, M. E., 'Y Trioedd Arbennig', *BBCS*, 24(4) (1972), 434–50.

—— 'Shame and reparation; women's place in the kin', in D. Jenkins and M. E. Owen (eds), *The Welsh Law of Women* (Cardiff, 1980), pp. 40–68.

—— 'Bwrlwm Llys Dinefwr: Brenin, Bardd a Meddyg', *Carmarthenshire Antiquary*, 32 (1996), 5–14.

—— 'The laws of court from Cyfnerth', in T. M. Charles-Edwards, M. E. Owen and P. Russell (eds), *The Welsh King and his Court* (Cardiff, 2000), pp. 425–77.

—— 'Medics and medicine', in T. M. Charles-Edwards, M. E. Owen and P. Russell (eds), *The Welsh King and his Court* (Cardiff, 2000), pp. 116–41.

—— 'Royal propaganda: stories from the law-texts', in T. M. Charles-Edwards, M. E. Owen and P. Russell (eds), *The Welsh King and his Court* (Cardiff, 2000), pp. 224–54.

—— 'Cyfnerth Manuscript X', in T. M. Charles-Edwards and P. Russell, *Tair Colofn y Gyfraith: the Three Columns of Law in Medieval Wales: Homicide, Theft and Fire* (Bangor, 2007), pp. 238–57.

—— 'Tân: the Welsh law of arson and negligent burning', in T. M. Charles-Edwards and P. Russell, *Tair Colofn y Gyfraith: the Three Columns of Law in Medieval Wales: Homicide, Theft and Fire* (Bangor, 2007), pp. 131–45.

—— 'The Excerpta de Libris Romanorum et Francorum and Welsh Law', in T. M. Charles-Edwards and P. Russell, *Tair Colofn y Gyfraith: the Three Columns of Law in Medieval Wales: Homicide, Theft and Fire* (Bangor, 2007), pp. 171–95.

Owen-John, F., 'The Gower union and the Penmaen workhouse: the role played by Dr. Henry Vause Ellis (1860–1890)', *Gower*, 51 (2000), 71–9.

Packer, I., 'Lloyd George and land reform', *THSC* (NS), 15 (2009), 127–45.

Painting, D., 'Swansea and the abolition of the slave trade', *Minerva: the Journal of Swansea History*, 15 (2007–8), 10–18.

Palmer, A. N., *A History of Ancient Tenures of Land in the Marches of North Wales* (Wrexham, 1885; 2nd edn, with E. Owen, 1910).

—— 'Notes on the ancient Welsh measures of land', *Archaeologia Cambrensis* (5th ser.), 13 (1896), 1–19.

Parker, K., 'Parliamentary enclosures in Radnorshire', *RHST*, 73 (2003), 127–47.

—— 'Radnorshire and the new poor law to circa 1850', *RHST*, 74 (2004), 167–98.

—— 'Radnorshire and the old poor law, *c*.1800–1836', *RHST*, 72 (2002), 139–49.

Parry, G., *A Guide to the Records of the Great Sessions in Wales* (Aberystwyth, 1995).

—— 'Erlynwyr a throseddwyr yn sir Gaernarfon (1730–1830)', *CHST*, 57 (1996), 47–64.

—— *Launched to Eternity: Crime and Punishment 1700–1900* (Aberystwyth, 2001).

Parry, O., 'The financing of the Welsh cattle trade in the eighteenth century', *BBCS*, 8(1) (1935), 46–61.

Parry, R. G., 'Trosedd a chosb ym Meirionydd yn chwedegau cynnar a bedwaredd ganrif ar bymtheg: tystiolaeth cofnodion y llys chwarter', in T. G. Watkin (ed.), *The Trial of Dic Penderyn and Other Essays* (Cardiff, 2003), pp. 78–109.

—— '"A master of practical law": Sir David Hughes Parry (1893–1973)', in T. G. Watkin (ed.), *Y Cyfraniad Cymreig* (Bangor, 2005), pp. 102–51.

—— '"An important obligation of citizenship": language, citizenship and jury service', *Legal Studies*, 27 (2007), 188–215.

—— 'Federalism and university governance: Welsh experiences in New Zealand', *WHR*, 23(1) (2006–7), 124–59.

—— 'Random selection, linguistic rights and the jury trial in Wales', *Criminal Law Review* (2002), 805–16.

—— 'Sir David Hughes Parry as lawyer and economist', *THSC* (NS), 13 (2007), 193–212.

—— *David Hughes Parry: A Jurist in Society* (Cardiff, 2010).

—— *Cymru'r Gyfraith: Sylwadau ar Hunaniaeth Gyfreithiol* (Caerdydd, 2012).

Paterson, D. R., 'The pre-Norman settlement of Glamorgan', *Archaeologia Cambrensis* (7th ser.), 2 (1922), 37–60.

Patterson, N. W., 'Honour and shame in medieval Welsh society: a study of the role of burlesque in the Welsh laws', *Studia Celtica*, 16–17 (1981–2), 73–103.

Peregrine, D. J. M., 'Cardigan's ancient borough', *Ceredigion*, 2 (1952), 117–18.

Philips, M., '*Defod a Moes y Llys*', in T. M. Charles-Edwards, M. E. Owen and P. Russell (eds), *The Welsh King and his Court* (Cardiff, 2000), pp. 347–61.

Pierce, G. O., 'The evidence of place names', in H. N. Savory, *Glamorgan County History, Volume II: Early Glamorgan: Pre-History and Early History* (Cardiff, 1984), pp. 456–92.

Pierce, T. J., 'A Caernarvonshire manorial borough', *CHST*, 3 (1941), 9–32; 4 (1942), 35–50; 5 (1944), 12–40.

—— 'The *gafael* in Bangor manuscript 1939', *THSC* (1942), 158–88.

—— 'A note on ancient Welsh measurements of land', *Archaeologia Cambrensis*, 97 (1942/3), 195–204.

—— 'An eighteenth-century borough court book [Nefyn]', *CHST*, 19 (1958), 81–101.

—— 'The law of Wales – the last phase', *THSC* (1963), 7–32.

—— 'Social and historical aspects of the Welsh laws', *WHR, Special Number, 1963: The Welsh Laws*, 33–50.

—— and Griffiths, J., 'Documents relating to the early history of the borough of Caernarfon', *BBCS*, 9(3) (1938), 236–46.

Pill, The Right Hon. Sir Malcolm, 'The Rt. Hon. Sir Tasker Watkins, VC, GBE, DL: an address at the service of thanksgiving for his life', in T. G. Watkin (ed.), *The Garthbeibio Murders and Other Essays* (Bangor, 2011), pp. 158–69.

Powell, A. D., 'Proceedings in Star Chamber in 1615 regarding connections of Richard Powell, Esq.', *Radnorshire Historical Society Transactions*, 28 (1958), 41–54.

—— 'John Probert and his lawsuits II', *Radnorshire Historical Society Transactions*, 33 (1963), 11–35.

—— 'Abstracts from miscellaneous Star Chamber cases of the Radnor–Hereford border', *Radnorshire Historical Society Transactions*, 35 (1965), 36–42.

Powell, A. D., 'Miscellaneous early Chancery proceedings about Radnorshire and the Marches, c.1538–1639', *Radnorshire Historical Society Transactions*, 36 (1966), 25–41.

Powell, D. W., 'Y llysoedd, yr awdurdodau a'r Gymraeg: y Ddeddf Uno a Deddf yr Iaith Gymraeg', in T. M. Charles-Edwards, M. E. Owen and D. B. Walters (eds), *Lawyers and Laymen* (Cardiff, 1986), pp. 287–315.

Powell, G., '"They shall no longer see as through a glass darkly": Robert Owen and the Welsh Enlightenment', *Montgomeryshire Collections*, 91 (2003), 53–69.

Powell, N. M. W., 'Dr William Morgan and his parishioners at Llanrhaeadr ym Mochnant', *CHST*, 49 (1988), 87–116.

—— 'Crime and community in Denbighshire during the 1590s: the evidence of the records of the Court of Great Sessions', in J. G. Jones (ed.), *Class, Community and Culture in Tudor Wales* (Cardiff, 1989), p. 261.

Powell, N. W., 'Do numbers count? Towns in early modern Wales', *Urban History*, 32(1) (2005), 46–67.

Pratt, D., 'A local border dispute, 1277–1447', *FHSP*, 21 (1964), 46–55.

—— 'The medieval borough of Holt', *DHST*, 14 (1965), 9–74.

—— 'Medieval Bromfield and Yale: the machinery of justice', *DHST*, 53 (2004), 19–78.

—— 'A Rhyl shipwreck, 1309–10', *DHST*, 52 (2003), 37–52.

Price, B., 'Two Tenby duels and their associations', *Journal of the Pembrokeshire Historical Society*, 14 (2005), 57–74.

Price, J. A., 'A note on Welsh "Jacobitism"', *THSC* (1920–1), 36–9.

—— 'The ecclesiastical constitution of Wales on the eve of the Edwardian conquest', *Y Cymmrodor*, 26 (1916), 191–214.

Pringle, K. D., 'The kings of Demetia', *THSC* (1970), 70–6; (1971), 140–4.

Pritchard, R. T., 'Caernarvonshire turnpike trust', *CHST*, 17 (1956), 62–74.

—— 'Montgomeryshire turnpike trusts', *Montgomeryshire Collections*, 57 (1961–2), 2–16.

Probert, R., 'Chinese whispers and Welsh weddings', *Continuity and Change*, 20 (2005), 211–28.

Pryce, A. I., 'Westminster School and its connection with north Wales prior to the Victorian era', *AAST* (1932), 91–104.

Pryce, H., 'Duw yn lle Mach: Briduw yng Nghyfraith Hywel', in T. M. Charles-Edwards, M. E. Owen and D. B. Walters (eds), *Lawyers and Laymen* (Cardiff, 1986), pp. 47–71.

—— 'The prologues to the Welsh lawbooks', *BBCS*, 33 (1986), 151–87.

—— *Native Law and the Church in Medieval Wales* (Oxford, 1993).

—— 'The Household priest (Offeiriad Teulu)', in T. M. Charles-Edwards, M. E. Owen and P. Russell (eds), *The Welsh King and his Court* (Cardiff, 2000), pp. 82–93.

—— (ed.), *The Acts of Welsh Rulers 1120–1283* (Cardiff, 2005; repr., 2010).

—— 'Law books and literacy in medieval Wales', *Speculum*, 75 (2000), 29–671.

—— 'The context and purpose of the earliest Welsh lawbooks', *Cambrian Medieval Celtic Studies*, 39 (2000), 39–63.

Pryce, W. T. R., 'Region or national territory? Regionalism and the idea of the country of Wales, c.1927–1998', *WHR*, 23(2) (2006–7), 99–152.

Randall, H. J., 'Giraldus Cambrensis as a lawyer', *BBCS*, 11(1) (1941), 74.

Randall, P. J., 'The origins and establishment of the Welsh Department of Education', *WHR*, 7(4) (1975), 450–71.

Rawlings, R., *Delineating Wales: Constitutional, Legal and Administrative Aspects of National Devolution* (Cardiff, 2003).

Rees, D., 'Rebecca in Gower', *Gower*, 27 (1976) 26–32.

Rees, D. Ben, 'Bywyd a gwaith D. O. Evans AS', *Ceredigion*, 14(3) (2001–4), 61–70.

Rees, I. B., 'The restoration of local democracy in Wales', *THSC* (1993), 139–82.

Rees, Lowri Ann, '"The wail of Miss Jane": the Rebecca riots and Jane Walters of Glanmedeni, 1843–4', *Ceredigion*, 15(3) (2005–8), 37–68.

Rees, O. D., 'Devolution and the Children's Commissioner for Wales: challenges and opportunities', *Contemporary Wales*, 23 (2010), 52–70.

—— 'Family and child law in Wales: recent developments', *Family Law* [2010], 186–9.

—— 'Devolution and the development of family law in Wales', *Child and Family Law Quarterly* [2008], 45–63.

—— 'The Children's Commissioner for Wales: the first five years', *childRIGHT*, 226 (2006), 16–19.

—— 'Devolution and family law in Wales: a potential for doing things differently?', *Statute Law Review*, 33 (2012), 192–206.

Rees, R. D., 'South Wales and Monmouthshire newspapers under the Stamp Act', *WHR*, 1(3) (1960–3), 301–24.

—— 'Electioneering ideals current in south Wales, 1790–1832', *WHR*, 2(3) (1964–5), 233–50.

Rees, W., 'The mediaeval lordship of Brecon', *THSC* (1915–16), 165–224.

—— 'The charters of the boroughs of Brecon and Llandovery', *BBCS*, 2(3) (1924), 243–61.

—— *South Wales and the March 1284–1415: A Social and Agrarian Study* (Oxford, 1924).

—— 'The union of England and Wales', *THSC* (1937), 27–100.

—— *A Survey of the Duchy of Lancaster Lordships in Wales 1609–1613* (Cardiff, 1953).

Reeves, A. C., 'The Great Sessions in the lordship of Newport in 1503', *BBCS*, 26(3) (1975), 323–41.

Report of the Richard Commission on the Powers and Electoral Arrangements of the National Assembly for Wales (Cardiff, 2004).

Rhys, E., *The Laws of the Round Table* (London, 1905).

Rhys, J., 'The Goidels in Wales', *Archaeologia Cambrensis* (5th ser.), 12 (1895), 18–39.

—— 'Notes on the inscriptions on the tombstone of Vortipore', *Archaeologia Cambrensis* (5th ser.), 12 (1895), 307–13.

—— and D. Brynmor-Jones, *The Welsh People*, 4th edn (London, 1906).

Rhys, M., *Ministers' Accounts for West Wales, 1277 to 1306* (London, 1936).

Richards, G. M., 'The sites of some medieval gallows', *Archaeologia Cambrensis*, 113 (1964), 159–65.

Richards, M., 'The marriage settlement of Ellen, daughter of Ellis Wynne of Lasynys 1724', *JMHRS*, 3 (1957–60), 296–301.

—— 'Hafod and hafoty in Welsh place-names: a semantic study', *Montgomeryshire Collections*, 56 (1959–60), 13–20.

—— 'Local government in Cardiganshire', *Ceredigion*, 4(3) (1962), 272–82.

—— 'The significance of *Is* and *Uwch* in Welsh commote and cantref names', *WHR*, 2(1) (1964), 9–18.

—— *Welsh Administrative and Territorial Units*, (Cardiff, 1969).

Richards, R., 'The Cistercian abbeys of Wales', *DHST*, 1 (1952), 1–19.

Richards, T., 'The Anglesey Election of 1708', *AAST* (1943), 23–34.

Richter, D., 'The Welsh police, the Home Office and the Welsh tithe war of 1886–91', *WHR*, 12(1) (1984–5), 50–75.

Richter, M., 'Professions of obedience and the metropolitan claims of St David's', *NLWJ*, 15(2) (1967–8), 197–214.

—— 'David ap Llywelyn, the first Prince of Wales', *WHR*, 5(3) (1971), 205–19.

—— 'Giraldus Cambrensis: the growth of the Welsh nation', *NLWJ*, 16 (1969–70), 193–252, 293–318; 17 (1971–2), 1–50.

—— *Medieval Ireland: The Enduring Tradition* (London, 1988).

Robbins, K., 'Episcopacy in Wales', *Journal of Welsh Religious History*, 4 (1996), 63–78.

Roberts, G., 'Parliamentary representation of the Welsh boroughs', *BBCS*, 4(4) (1929), 352–60.

—— 'The county representation of Anglesey in the eighteenth century', *AAST* (1930), 60–78.

—— 'Borough records at Caernarfon', *BBCS*, 6(1) (1931), 65–70.

—— 'Parliamentary history of Beaumaris 1555–1832', *AAST* (1933), 97–109.

—— *The Municipal Development of the Borough of Swansea to 1900* (Swansea, 1940).

Roberts, P. R., 'The gentry and land in eighteenth century Merioneth', *JMHRS*, 4(4) (1961–4), 324–39.

—— 'The Merioneth gentry and local government *circa* 1650–1838', *JMHRS*, 5(1) (1965), 21–38.

—— 'The "Act of Union" in Welsh history', *THSC* (1972–3), 49–72.

—— 'The "Henry VIII Clause": delegated legislation and the principality of Wales', in T. G. Watkin (ed.), *Legal Record and Historical Reality* (London and Ronceverte, 1989), pp. 37–50.

—— 'Tudor legislation and the political status of "the British Tongue"', in G. H. Jenkins (ed.), *The Welsh Language before the Industrial Revolution* (Cardiff, 1997), pp. 123–52.

Roberts, R. Arthur, 'Caernarvonshire and the Middle Temple', *CHST*, 17 (1956), 41–4.

Roberts, Richard Arthur, 'Cymru Fu: some contemporary comments', *THSC* (1895–6), 87–103.

Roberts, R. O., 'Boonland: an unusual form of tenure', *Folk Life*, 12 (1974), 104–6.

Roberts, S. E., 'Legal practice in fifteenth-century Brycheiniog', *Studia Celtica*, 35 (2001), 307–23.

—— 'Law texts and their sources in late medieval Wales: the case of *H* and tales of other legal manuscripts', *WHR*, 24(2) (2008–9), 41–59.

—— *Llawysgrif Pomffred: An Edition and Study of Peniarth MS 259B* (Leyden, 2011).

—— *The Legal Triads of Medieval Wales* (Cardiff, 2007; repr., 2011).

Roberts, S. K., 'Office-holding and allegiance in Glamorgan in the civil war and after: the case of John Bird', *Morgannwg*, 44 (2000), 11–31.

—— 'Patronage, office and family in early modern Wales: the Carnes of Nash Manor and Ewenni in the seventeenth century', *WHR*, 23(2) (2006–7), 25–49.

Roberts, Stephen, 'Propogating the gospel in Wales', *THSC* (NS), 10 (2004), 57–75.

Robinson, D. J., 'Crime, police and the provincial press: a study of Victorian Cardiff', *WHR*, 25 (2010/11), 551–75.

Robinson, R., 'Early Tudor policy towards Wales', *BBCS*, 20(4) (1964), 421–38; 21(1) (1964), 43–72; 21(4) (1966), 334–61.

Robinson, W. R. B., 'The litigation of Edward, earl of Worcester, concerning Gower, 1590–1596', *BBCS*, 22(4) (1968), 357–88; 23(1) (1968), 60–99.

—— 'The establishment of royal customs in Glamorgan and Monmouthshire under Elizabeth', *BBCS*, 23(4) (1970), 347–96.

—— 'The Marcher lords of Wales 1525–31', *BBCS*, 26(3) (1975), 342–52.

—— 'The County Court of the Englishry of Gower', *NLWJ*, 29(3) (1995–6), 357–89.

—— 'Prince Arthur in the Marches of Wales', *Studia Celtica*, 36 (2002), 89–98.

—— 'The administration of the lordship of Monmouth under Henry VII', *Monmouthshire Antiquary*, 18 (2002), 23–40.

—— 'The administration of the lordship of Monmouth under Henry VIII', *Monmouthshire Antiquary*, 19 (2003), 129–46.

—— 'The Testimony of Dame Gwenllian Norris and others concerning disputed lands in Peterston-super-Ely, 1423', *Morgannwg*, 46 (2002), 9–19.

Rocher, R., 'Sir William Jones as a satirist: an ethic epistle to the second Earl Spencer', *THSC* (NS), 11 (2005), 70–104.

Roderick, A. J., 'The dispute between Llywelyn ap Gruffydd and Gruffydd ap Gwenwynwyn (1278–82)', *BBCS*, 8(3) (1936), 248–54.

—— 'Villa Wallensica', *BBCS*, 13(2) (1949), 90–2.

—— 'Marriage and politics in Wales, 1066–1282', *WHR*, 4(1) (1968), 1–20.

Romilly Allen, J., 'Early Christian art in Wales', *Archaeologia Cambrensis* (5th ser.), 16 (1899), 1–69.

Rowlands, E., 'Mesur tir: land measurement', *Studia Celtica*, 14/15 (1979/1980), 270–84.

Rowlands, I., 'The 1201 Peace between King John and Llywelyn ap Iorwerth', *Studia Celtica*, 34 (2000), 149–66.

Rowley-Morris, E., 'An ancient jury', *Montgomeryshire Collections*, 27 (1893), 267–8.

Rubinstein, W. D., 'The anti-Jewish riots of 1911 in south Wales: a re-examination', *WHR*, 18 (1997), 667–99.

Russell, P., 'The laws of court from Latin B', in T. M. Charles-Edwards, M. E. Owen and P. Russell (eds), *The Welsh King and his Court* (Cardiff, 2000), pp. 478–526.

—— *Swydd, swyddog, swyddwr*: office, officer and official', in T. M. Charles-Edwards, M. E. Owen and P. Russell (eds), *The Welsh King and his Court* (Cardiff, 2000), pp. 281–95.

—— 'Latin D', in T. M. Charles-Edwards and P. Russell, *Tair Colofn y Gyfraith: the Three Columns of Law in Medieval Wales: Homicide, Theft and Fire* (Bangor, 2007), pp. 213–37.

—— 'The arrangement and development of the three columns tractate', in T. M. Charles-Edwards and P. Russell, *Tair Colofn y Gyfraith: the Three Columns of Law in Medieval Wales: Homicide, Theft and Fire* (Bangor, 2007), pp. 60–91.

—— 'Y naw affaith: aiding and abetting in Welsh law', in T. M. Charles-Edwards and P. Russell, *Tair Colofn y Gyfraith: the Three Columns of Law in Medieval Wales: Homicide, Theft and Fire* (Bangor, 2007), pp. 146–170.

Salmon, D., 'The story of a Welsh Education Commission (1846–7)', *Y Cymmrodor*, 24 (1913), 189–237.

Samuel, W., 'The ancient laws of Dyfed', *Pembrokeshire Historian*, 3 (1971), 42–52.

Saunders, I. J., 'The boroughs of Aberystwyth and Cardigan in the early fourteenth century', *BBCS*, 15(4) (1954), 282–92.

—— 'Trade and industry in some Cardiganshire towns in the Middle Ages', *Ceredigion*, 3(4) (1959), 319–36.

—— 'The borough of Lampeter in the early fourteenth century', *Ceredigion*, 4(2) (1961), 136–45.

Sayce, R. U., 'Popular enclosures and the one night house', *Montgomeryshire Collections*, 47 (1942), 109–20.

—— 'The old summer pastures', *Montgomeryshire Collections*, 54 (1955–6), 117–45; 55 (1957–8), 37–86.

Seaman, A., 'Conversion, Christianity and the late Roman transition', *Archaeologia Cambrensis*, 155 (2006), 135–42.

Seebohm, F., 'The historical importance of the Cymric tribal system', *THSC* (1895–6), 1–22.

Seneviratne, M., 'A new Ombudsman for Wales', *Public Law* [2006], 6–14.

Seyler, C. A., 'The early charters of Swansea and Gower', *Archaeologia Cambrensis* (7th ser.), 4 (1924), 59–79, 299–325; 5 (1925), 157–256.

Shankland, T., 'Sir John Phillips; the Society for Promoting Christian Knowledge; and the charity-school movement in Wales, 1699–1737', *THSC* (1904–5), 74–216.

Sheail, J., 'Sustaining rural communiites: the Agriculture (Improvement of Roads) Act, 1955', *WHR*, 18(2) (1996–7), 295–317.

Sheridan, L. A., 'University legal education in Cardiff', *Cambrian Law Review*, 4 (1973), 94–102.

Sherrington, E. J., 'The plea rolls of the courts of Great Sessions, 1541–75' *NLWJ*, 13(4) (1963–4), 363–73.

Skeel, C. A. J., *The Council in the Marches of Wales: A Study in Local Government during the Sixteenth and Seventeenth Centuries* (London, 1904).

Smith, C. A., 'Late prehistoric and Romano-British enclosed homesteads in north-west Wales', *Archaeologia Cambrensis*, 126 (1977), 38–52.

Smith, J. B., 'The lordship of Glamorgan', *Morgannwg*, 2 (1958), 9–37.

—— 'Offra Principis Wallie domino Regi', *BBCS*, 21(4) (1966), 362–7.

—— 'Crown and community in the principality of north Wales in the reign of Henry Tudor', *WHR*, 3(2) (1966–7), 145–71.

—— 'Owain Gwynedd', *CHST*, 32 (1971), 8–17.

—— 'Llywelyn ap Gruffydd and the March of Wales', *Brycheiniog*, 20 (1982/3), 9–22.

—— 'Dower in thirteenth-century Wales: a grant of the commote of Anhunog, 1273', *BBCS*, 30 (3–4) (1983), 348–55.

—— 'Llywelyn ap Gruffydd, prince of Wales and lord of Snowdon', *CHST*, 45 (1984), 7–36.

—— 'Land endowments of the period of Llywelyn ap Gruffydd', *BBCS*, 34(2) (1987), 150–64.

—— *Llywelyn ap Gruffudd Prince of Wales* (Cardiff, 1998).

—— 'Ynad llys, brawdwr llys, iudex curie', in T. M. Charles-Edwards, M. E. Owen and P. Russell (eds), *The Welsh King and his Court* (Cardiff, 2000), pp. 94–115.

—— 'Judgement under the law of Wales', *Studia Celtica*, 39 (2005), 63–103.

—— 'Thomas Peter Ellis (1873–1936): lawyer and historian', *JMHRS*, 15 (2006–7), 89–121.

Smith Ll. B., 'The Arundel charters to the lordship of Chirk in the fourteenth century', *BBCS*, 23(2) (1969), 153–66.

—— '*Tir Prid*: deeds of gage of land in late medieval Wales', *BBCS*, 27(2) (1977), 263–77.

—— 'The Statute of Wales, 1284', *WHR*, 10(2) (1980–1), 127–54.

—— 'The *gravamina* of the community of Gwynedd against Llywelyn ap Gruffydd', *BBCS*, 31 (1984), 158–76.

—— 'Llywelyn ap Gruffydd and the Welsh historical consciousness', *WHR*, 12(1) (1984), 1–28.

—— '"Cannwyll disbwyll a dosbarth": gwŷr cyfraith Ceredigion yn yr oesoedd canol diweddar', *Ceredigion*, 10(3) (1986), 229–53.

Squibb, G. D., *Doctors' Commons: A History of the College of Advocates and Doctors of Law* (Oxford, 1977).

Squires, H. L., 'Early Montgomeryshire wills', *Montgomeryshire Collections*, 16 (1883), 299–304; 17 (1884), 121–48.

—— and Rowley-Morris, E., 'Early Montgomeryshire wills at Hereford Registry', *Montgomeryshire Collections*, 19 (1886), 1–80.

Stacey, R. C., 'The archaic core of Llyfr Iorwerth', in T. M. Charles-Edwards, M. E. Owen and D. B. Walters (eds), *Lawyers and Laymen* (Cardiff, 1986), pp. 15–46.

—— 'Clothes talk from medieval Wales', in T. M. Charles-Edwards, M. E. Owen and P. Russell (eds), *The Welsh King and his Court* (Cardiff, 2000), pp. 338–46.

—— 'King, queen and *edling* in the laws of court', in T. M. Charles-Edwards, M. E. Owen and P. Russell (eds), *The Welsh King and his Court* (Cardiff, 2000), pp. 29–62.

—— 'Divorce, medieval Welsh style', *Speculum*, 77 (2002), 1107–1127.

—— 'Hywel in the world', *Haskins Society Journal*, 20 (2008), 175–203.

—— 'Learning to plead in medieval Welsh law', *Studia Celtica*, 38 (2004), 107–24.

Statute Law Review, Special Issue on Welsh Devolution, 33(2) (2012).

Stephen, Sir J. F., *A History of the Criminal Law of England*, 3 vols (London, 1883; repr. New York, 1973).

Stephenson, D., *Thirteenth-Century Welsh Law Courts* (Aberystwyth, 1980).

—— 'Llywelyn ap Gruffydd and the struggle for the principality of Wales, 1258–1282', *THSC* (1983), 36–47.

—— *The Governance of Gwynedd* (Cardiff, 1984).

—— 'The laws of court: past reality or present ideal', in T. M. Charles-Edwards, M. E. Owen and P. Russell (eds), *The Welsh King and his Court* (Cardiff, 2000), pp. 400–14.

—— 'The Arwystli Case', *Montgomeryshire Collections*, 94 (2006), 1–13.

Stevens, C., 'The "Burial Question": Controversy and Conflict, *c.*1860–1890', *WHR*, 21 (2002/3), 328–56.

Stewart, J. and King, S., 'Death in Llantrisant: Henry Williams and the new poor law in Wales', *Rural History: Economy, Society, Culture*, 15 (2004), 69–87.

Stone, L., 'Kinship and forced marriage in early eighteenth-century Wales', *WHR*, 17(3) (1994–5), 357–64.

Suggett, R., 'The Welsh language and the Court of Great Sessions', in G. H. Jenkins (ed.), *The Welsh Language before the Industrial Revolution* (Cardiff, 1997), pp. 153–80.

Summers, H. H. C., 'The poor, 1685–1734', *Montgomeryshire Collections*, 38 (1918), 147.

Summers, Veronica, 'Criminals or scapegoats? The Irish and crime in nineteenth-century Cardiff', *Llafur*, 8(2) (2001), 63–73.

Swett, K. W., 'Widowhood, custom and property in early modern north Wales', *WHR*, 18(2) (1996–7), 189–227.

Tanner, D., 'Richard Crossman, Harold Wilson and devolution 1966–70: the making of government policy', *Twentieth-Century British History*, 17 (2006), 545–78.

Taylor, A. J., 'The death of Llywelyn ap Gruffydd', *BBCS*, 15(3) (1953), 207–9.

—— 'The earliest burgesses of Flint and Rhuddlan', *FHSPJ*, 27 (1975–6), 152–9.

Taylor, H., 'The first Welsh municipal charters', *Archaeologia Cambrensis* (5th ser.), 9 (1892), 102–19.

—— 'The lords of Mold', *FHSJ*, 6 (1916–17), 37–62.

Thomas, Ben Bowen, 'The establishment of the "Aberdare" departmental committee, 1880: some letters and notes', *BBCS*, 19(4) (1962), 318–34.

—— 'The old poor law in Ardudwy Uwch-Artro', *BBCS*, 7(2) (1934), 153–91.

Thomas, Brinley, 'A cauldron of rebirth: population and the Welsh language in the nineteenth century', *WHR*, 13(4) (1986–1987), 418–37.

Thomas, Charles, *Christianity in Roman Britian to AD 500* (London, 1981).

Thomas, Colin, 'Colonization, enclosure and the rural landscape', *NLWJ*, 19(2) (1975–1976), 132–46.

—— 'Enclosure and the rural landscape of Merioneth in the sixteenth century', *JMHRS*, 15 (2006–7), 129–41.

Thomas, D. Ll., 'Further notes on the Court of the Marches', *Y Cymmrodor*, 13 (1899), 97–163.

Thomas, D. O., 'Richard Price, 1723–91', *THSC* (1971), 45–64.

Thomas, G., 'O Maximus i Macsen', *THSC* (1983), 7–21.

Thomas, H., *A History of Wales, 1485–1660* (Cardiff, 1972).

Thomas, H. M., '"With this ring" – the importance of the heiress in the descent of three Glamorgan estates', *Morgannwg*, 49 (2005), 67–78.

Thomas, J. D. H., 'Llywelyn y Llyw Olaf', *Brycheiniog*, 2 (1956), 143–52.

—— 'Judge David Jenkins, 1582–1663', *Morgannwg*, 8 (1964), 14–34.

Thomas, J. E., 'The poor law in West Glamorgan, 1834 to 1930', *Morgannwg*, 18 (1974), 45–69.

Thomas, J. G., 'The distribution of the commons in part of Arwystli at the time of the enclosure', *Montgomeryshire Collections*, 54 (1955–6), 27–33.

Thomas, P. D. G., 'The parliamentary representation of Merioneth during the eighteenth century', *JMHRS*, 3(2) (1958), 128–36.

—— 'The parliamentary representation of Caernarvonshire, 1749–84', *CHST*, 20 (1959), 72–86.

—— 'Parliamentary elections in Brecknockshire, 1689–1832', *Brycheiniog*, 6 (1960), 99–114.

—— 'Jacobitism in Wales', *WHR*, 1(3) (1960–3), 279–300.

—— 'Anglesey politics, 1689–1727', *AAST* (1962), 35–54.

—— 'Glamorgan politics 1700–1750', *Morgannwg*, 6 (1962), 52–77.

—— 'Sir George Wynne and the Flint borough election of 1727–1741', *FHSPJ*, 20 (1962), 39–57.

—— 'County elections in eighteenth-century Carmarthenshire', *Carmarthenshire Antiquary*, 4 (1962–3), 32–8, 124–30.

—— 'The Montgomery borough constituency', *BBCS*, 20(3) (1963), 293–304.

—— 'The Montgomeryshire election of 1774', *Montgomeryshire Collections*, 59 (1965–6), 116–29.

—— 'Eighteenth-century elections in the Cardigan borough constituency', *Ceredigion*, 5(4) (1967), 402–23.

—— 'The Cardigan boroughs election of 1741', *Ceredigion*, 6(1) (1968), 128–36.

Thomas, R. J. L., 'Legal Wales: its modern origins and its role after devolution: national identity, the Welsh language and parochialism', in T. G. Watkin (ed.), *Legal Wales: Its Past; Its Future* (Cardiff, 2001), pp. 113–66.

—— 'The maintenance of local justice', in T. G. Watkin (ed.), *Y Cyfraniad Cymreig* (Bangor, 2005), pp. 182–231.

Thornton, D. E., 'The death of Hywel Dda: a note', *WHR*, 20 (2000–1), 743–9.

Thornton, T., 'Dynasty and territory in the early modern period: the Princes of Wales and their western British inheritance', *WHR*, 20 (2000–1), 1–33.

Thurneysen, R., 'Das keltische Recht', *Zeitschrift der Savigny-Stiftung für Rechtsgeschichte (Germanistische Abteilung)*, 55 (1935), 81–104, trans. as 'Celtic law', in D. Jenkins (ed.), *Celtic Law Papers Introductory to Welsh Medieval Law and Government* (Brussels, 1973), pp. 49–70.

Tout, T. F., 'The Welsh shires: a study in constitutional history', *Y Cymmrodor*, 9 (1888), 201–26.

Treharne, R. F., 'The Franco-Welsh treaty of alliance in 1212', *BBCS*, 18(1) (1958), 60–75.

Trott, A. L., 'The implementation of the 1870 Elementary Education Act in Cardiganshire', *Ceredigion*, 3(3) (1958), 207–30.

Turvey, R. K., 'King, prince or lord? Rhys ap Gruffydd and the nomenclature of authority in twelfth-century Wales', *Carmarthenshire Antiquary*, 30 (1994), 5–18.
—— *The Lord Rhys: Prince of Deheubarth* (Llandysul, 1997).
—— *The Welsh Princes, 1063–1283* (London, 2002).
—— 'Pembrokeshire probates – a provisional list', *Journal of the Pembrokeshire Historical Society*, 9 (2000), 90–4.
Usher, G., 'A survey of the honour of Denbigh in 1334', *DHST*, 3 (1954), 5–40.
—— 'Welsh students at Oxford in the Middle Ages', *BBCS*, 16(3) (1955), 193–8.
—— 'The foundation of an Edwardian borough: the Beaumaris Charter, 1296', *AAST* (1967), 1–16.
Vaughan, H. F. J., 'Chief of the noble tribes of Gwynedd', *Archaeologia Cambrensis* (5th ser.), 8 (1891), 241–61.
Vaughan, H. M., 'Welsh Jacobitism', *THSC* (1920–1), 11–39.
Wade-Evans, A. W., *Welsh Medieval Law* (Oxford, 1909; Aalen, 1979).
—— 'The Llancarfan charters', *Archaeologia Cambrensis*, 87, (1932), 151–65.
Wager, D., 'Welsh politics and parliamentary reform, 1780–1832', *WHR*, 7(4) (1974–5), 427–49.
Walker, D., 'A note on Gruffydd ap Llywelyn, 1039–63', *WHR*, 1(1) (1960), 83–94.
—— 'Gerald of Wales: a review of recent work', *JHSCW*, 24 (1974), 13–26.
—— (ed.), *History of the Church in Wales* (Penarth, 1976).
—— 'The lordship of Builth', *Brycheiniog*, 20 (1982/3), 23–33.
—— *Medieval Wales* (Cambridge, 1990).
Walker, R. F., 'The Manorbier court rolls, 1686–98 and the Trefloyne rentals, 1711–36', *NLWJ*, 29(1) (1995–6), 39–62.
Wallace, R., 'Wales and the parliamentary reform movement', *WHR*, 11(4) (1982–3), 469–87.
Walters, D. B., 'The European legal context of the Welsh law of matrimonial property' in D. Jenkins and M. E. Owen (eds), *The Welsh Law of Women* (Cardiff, 1980), pp. 115–31.
—— *The Comparative Legal Method: Marriage, Divorce and the Spouses' Property Rights in Early Medieval European Law* (Aberystwyth, 1983).
—— 'Roman and romano-canonical law and procedure in medieval Wales', *Recueil de mémoires et travaux publié par la Société d'Histoire du Droit et des Institutions des Anciens Pays de Droit Écrit*, 15 (1991), 67–102.
—— 'Comparative aspects of the tractates of the laws of court', in T. M. Charles-Edwards, M. E. Owen and P. Russell (eds), *The Welsh King and his Court* (Cardiff, 2000), pp. 382–99.
Ward, J. H., 'Vortigern and the end of Roman Britain', *Britannia*, 3 (1972), 277–89.
Waters, W. H., 'The first draft of the Statute of Rhuddlan', *BBCS*, 4(4) (1929), 345–8.
—— 'Roll of the county court of Anglesey', *BBCS*, 4(4) (1929), 350–2.
—— 'A north Wales coroner's account', *BBCS*, 4(4) (1929), 348–50.
—— 'Documents relating to the office of escheator for north Wales, 1209–1210', *BBCS*, 6(4) (1933), 360–8.
—— 'Documents relating to the sheriff's tourn in north Wales', *BBCS*, 6(4) (1933), 354–60.
Watkin, T. G., *The Italian Legal Tradition* (London, 1997).
—— *An Historical Introduction to Modern Civil Law* (London, 1999).
—— 'Legal cultures in mediaeval Wales', in T. G. Watkin (ed.), *Legal Wales: Its Past; Its Future* (Cardiff, 2001), pp. 21–40.

—— 'Oxwich revisited: an examination of the background to *Herbert's case 1557–58'*, *THSC*, NS 8 (2001), 94–118.

—— (ed.), *Legal Wales: Its Past; Its Future* (Cardiff, 2001).

—— (ed.), *The Trial of Dic Penderyn and Other Essays* (Cardiff, 2003).

—— 'Cyfreithwyr Cymru Oes y Dadeni', in T. G. Watkin (ed.), *Y Cyfraniad Cymreig* (Bangor, 2005), pp. 57–72.

—— 'The Welsh civilians', in T. G. Watkin (ed.), *Y Cyfraniad Cymreig* (Bangor, 2005), pp. 73–89.

—— (ed.), *Y Cyfraniad Cymreig* (Bangor, 2005).

—— 'Cyfraith Cymru', in T. Roberts, *Yr Angen am Furiau* (Llanrwst, 2009), pp. 64–80.

Webster, G., *The British Celts and their Gods under Rome* (London, 1986).

Webster, J. R., 'The first reports of Owen M. Edwards on Welsh intermediate schools', *NLWJ*, 10(3) (1958), 390–4.

Webster, P. V., 'The Roman period', in H. N. Savory, *Glamorgan County History, Volume II: Early Glamorgan: Pre-History and Early History* (Cardiff, 1984), pp. 277–314.

Welsh History Review (WHR), Special Number, 1963: The Welsh Laws.

Wheeler, O., 'The Welsh Intermediate Education Act, 1889', *THSC* (1939), 101–32.

Wheeler, R. E., 'Roman and native in Wales: an imperial frontier problem', *THSC*, (1920–1921) 40–96.

Wheldon, W. P., 'The Welsh Department, Ministry of Education, 1907–1957', *THSC* (1957), 18–36.

'Whippinge-posts', *Montgomeryshire Collections*, 24 (1880), 88.

White, R. and S., 'Digwyddiad wrth dyrpeg Nant 1824', *AAST* (1969–70), 223–33.

White, S. R. G., 'A burial ahead of its time? The *Crookenden Burial Case* and the sanctioning of cremation in England and Wales', in T. G. Watkin (ed.), *The Trial of Dic Penderyn and Other Essays* (Cardiff, 2003), pp. 151–79.

Wiliam, A. R., 'Y Deddfynnay Cymraeg', *NLWJ*, 8 (1953/4), 97–103.

—— *Llyfr Iorwerth* (Cardiff, 1960).

—— 'The Welsh texts of the laws', *WHR, Special Number, 1963: The Welsh Laws*, 19–24.

—— 'Restoration of the Book of Cynog [Peniarth MS 35]', *NLWJ*, 25(3) (1987/8), 245–56.

Williams, Charles H., 'Giraldus Cambrensis and Wales', *JHSCW*, 1 (1947), 6–14.

Williams, Colin H., 'Non-violence and the development of the Welsh Language Society, 1962–*ca*.1974', *WHR*, 8(4) (1977), 426–55.

Williams, D., *John Frost: A Study in Chartism* (Cardiff, 1939).

—— 'The contribution of Wales to the development of the United States', *NLWJ*, 2 (1941/2), 97–108.

—— 'Rebecca in Caernarvonshire', *CHST*, 10 (1949), 115–18.

—— 'A report on the turnpike trusts', *NLWJ*, 8(1953/4), 171–5.

—— 'The borough of Kidwelly in the nineteenth century', *BBCS*, 16(3) (1955), 199–207.

—— *The Rebecca Riots: A Study in Agrarian Discontent* (Cardiff, 1955).

—— 'The Pembrokeshire elections of 1831', *WHR*, 1(1) (1960), 37–64.

Williams, D. Elwyn, 'The poor law in operation in the parish of Rumney, 1825–30', *THSC* (1966), 341–71.

Williams, D. Emrys, 'Documents relating to rural discontent in west Wales', *NLWJ*, 11(2)(1959–60), 177–80.

Williams, D. G. T., 'Devolution: the past and future', *Wales Journal of Law and Policy*, 4 (2005–6), 17–23.

—— 'The law of England and Wales: the Welsh contribution', *THSC* (NS), 12 (2006), 161–176.

Williams, D. H., 'The Cistercians in Wales: some aspects of their economy', *Archaeologia Cambrensis*, 114 (1965), 2–47.

—— *The Welsh Cistercians: Aspects of their Economic Activity*, (Pontypool, 1969).

Williams, D. J., 'Bodfel, Barbados and Slavery', *CHST*, 68 (2007), 51–5.

Williams, G., 'The Elizabethan settlement of religion in Wales and the Marches 1559–60', *JHSCW*, 2 (1950), 61–71.

—— *The Welsh Church from Conquest to Reformation* (Cardiff, 1963).

—— 'The achievement of William Salesbury', *DHST*, 14 (1965), 75–96.

—— 'The dissolution of the monasteries in Glamorgan', *WHR*, 3(1) (1966), 23–43.

—— *Renewal and Reformation: Wales c.1415–1642* (Oxford, 1987).

—— 'An old man remembers: Gerald the Welshman', *Morgannwg*, 22, (1988), 7–20.

Williams, G. A., 'The Merthyr riots: settling the account', *NLWJ*, 11(1) (1959–60), 124–41.

—— 'The making of radical Merthyr', *WHR*, 1(2) (1960–3), 161–92.

—— 'The succession to Gwynedd, 1238–47', *BBCS*, 20(4) (1964), 393–413.

—— 'The insurrection of Merthyr Tydfil in 1831', *THSC* (1965) 222–43.

Williams, G. O., 'Brwydr yr Iaith', *THSC* (1971), 7–15.

Williams, H., 'Some aspects of the Christian church in Wales during the fifth and sixth centuries', *THSC* (1893–4), 55–132.

Williams, H. G., 'The Forster Education Act and Welsh Politics, 1870–74', *WHR*, 14(2) (1988–9), 242–68.

Williams, I., 'When did the British become Welsh?', *AAST* (1939), 27–38.

Williams, Jane, 'Incorporating children's rights: the divergence in law and policy', *Legal Studies*, 27 (2007), 261–87.

Williams, John, 'A new law of adult social care: a challenge for law reform in Wales', *Statute Law Review*, 33 (2012), 304–22.

Williams, L. J., 'The Rhondda election of 1885', *Morgannwg*, 6 (1962), 78–94.

—— 'The new unionism in south Wales, 1889–92', *WHR*, 1(4) (1963), 413–29.

Williams, P., *The Council in the Marches of Wales under Elizabeth I* (Cardiff, 1958).

—— 'The Welsh borderland under Queen Elizabeth', *WHR*, 1(1) (1960), 19–36.

—— 'The activity of the Council of the Marches under the early Stuarts', *WHR*, 1(2) (1960–3), 133–54.

—— 'The attack on the Council in the Marches, 1603–1642', *THSC*, 1 (1961), 1–22.

Williams, P. H., 'The Star Chamber and the Council of the Marches in Wales 1558–1603', *BBCS*, 16(4) (1956), 287–97.

Williams, R., 'Dolforwyn Castle and its lords', *Archaeologia Cambrensis* (6th ser.), 1 (1900), 299–317.

Williams, S. J. and Powell, J. E., *Llyfr Blegywryd* (Cardiff, 1961).

Williams, W. Ll., 'The King's Court of Great Sessions in Wales', *Y Cymmrodor*, 26 (1916), 1–87.

—— 'The Union of England and Wales', *THSC* (1907–1908), 47–117.

—— *The Making of Modern Wales* (London, 1919).

Williams, W. M., 'The friends of Griffith Jones: a study in educational philanthropy', *Y Cymmrodor*, 46 (1939), 1–106.

—— 'The Welsh Intermediate Education Act, 1889', *THSC*, (1939), 101–32.

Williams, W. O., *Calendar of the Caernarvonshire Quarter Sessions Records (1541–1588)* (Caernarfon, 1956).

—— 'The survival of the Welsh language after the Union of England and Wales', *WHR*, 2 (1) (1964), 67–93.

—— 'The social order in Tudor Wales', *THSC*, (1967), 167–78.

Williams, W. R., *The History of the Great Sessions in Wales 1542–1830* (Brecknock, 1899).

Williams-Jones, K., 'Llywelyn's charter to Cymmer Abbey in 1209', *JMHRS*, 3 (1957–60), 45–78.

—— 'A Mawddwy court roll', *BBCS*, 23(4) (1970), 329–44.

Willis-Bund, J. W., 'The early Welsh monasteries', *Archaeologia Cambrensis* (5th ser.), 8, (1891), 262–76.

—— 'The Teilo churches', *Archaeologia Cambrensis* (5th ser.), 10 (1893), 193–217.

Wilson, P. A., 'Romano-British and Welsh Christianity', *WHR*, 3 (1–2) (1966–7), 5–21, 103–20.

Winder, W. H. D., 'A law report of a Great Sessions judgement', *BBCS*, 12 (1941), 48–51.

Woodward, N., 'Burglary in Wales, 1730–1830: evidence from the Great Sessions', *WHR*, 24(2) (2008–9), 60–91.

—— 'Infanticide in Wales, 1730–1830', *WHR*, 23(3) (2006–7), 94–125.

Zulueta, F. de, *The Legacy of Rome* (Oxford, 1925).

Index